Additional praise for Environmental Anthropology

"This Reader provides a glimpse of the wide variety of ways that anthropologists have thought about the human environment and an equally appropriate view of the diversity of those environments: ranging from the Arctic tundra and Nilotic plains of Sudan to the rainforests of Indonesia and highlands of New Guinea. This is a must-read book for students and scholars alike."

James J. Fox, The Australian National University

"Anthropology has, throughout its history, had much to say about the natural environment and the complex relations between society and nature. *Environmental Anthropology* draws together the very best that Anthropology has to offer including the now classic contributions by Roy Rappaport, Gregory Bateson, Robert Carneiro and Julian Steward. An indispensable text for any student grappling with the knotty problems of the shifting meanings of environment and the dynamics practices by which societies transform, and are in turned transformed by, the earth."

Michael Watts, University of California, Berkeley

Cover image: This is a photograph of a Nuer youth imitating the bent horns (called *ma gut*) of his favorite ox while he sings to it. Nuer train the horns of their favorite oxen into aesthetically pleasing shapes. The bent horns (and their representation) symbolize the intersection of nature and culture that is the subject of this book. The photograph was taken by E. E. Evans-Pritchard in October or November 1936 among the Nuer Leek Karlual in the Southern Sudan. It is reproduced, with permission, from the collection of the University of Oxford's Pitt-Rivers Museum.

Blackwell Anthologies in Social & Cultural Anthropology (ASCA)

Environmental Anthropology

A Historical Reader

Edited by

Michael R. Dove and Carol Carpenter

Blackwell
Publishing

BLACKWELL PUBLISHING
350 Main Street, Malden, MA 02148-5020, USA
9600 Garsington Road, Oxford OX4 2DQ, UK
550 Swanston Street, Carlton, Victoria 3053, Australia

First published 2008 by Blackwell Publishing Ltd

5   2012

Library of Congress Cataloging-in-Publication Data

Environmental anthropology : a historical reader / Michael R. Dove and Carol Carpenter, editors.
     p. cm.—(Blackwell anthologies in social & cultural anthropology ; 10)
   Includes bibliographical references and index.
   ISBN 978-1-4051-1125-6 (hardcover : alk. paper)—ISBN 978-1-4051-1137-9 (pbk. : alk. paper)   1. Human ecology—Cross-cultural studies.   I. Dove, Michael R. II. Carpenter, Carol.

   GF41.E415 2007
   304.2—dc22

                                                                2007012825

A catalogue record for this title is available from the British Library.

Set in 9 on 11 pt Sabon
by SNP Best-set Typesetter Ltd., Hong Kong
Printed and bound in Singapore
by C.O.S. Printers Pte Ltd

For further information on
Blackwell Publishing, visit our website at
www.blackwellpublishing.com

To our daughter and daily inspiration, Margaret Rose.

Contents

**The limits of knowledge and its implications for
understanding environmental relations: Bateson and Ingold**

Figures and Tables

Figures

Tables

Editors' Biographical Notes

Michael R. Dove earned his Ph.D. in anthropology at Stanford University. He is the Margaret K. Musser Professor of Social Ecology, Professor of Anthropology, Curator of Anthropology at the Peabody Museum, and Coordinator of the joint doctoral degree program between the School of Forestry and Environmental Studies and the Anthropology Department at Yale University. His research focuses on the environmental relations of local communities in less-developed countries, especially in South and Southeast Asia. His most recent book is *Conserving Nature in Culture: Case Studies from Southeast Asia* (co-edited with P. Sajise and A. Doolittle), and he is currently completing books on Southeast Asian grasslands, the historic participation of remote Bornean tribes in global commodity production, and rethinking conservation in Southeast Asia.

Carol Carpenter earned her Ph.D. in anthropology at Cornell University. She is Senior Lecturer in Natural Resource Social Science at the School of Forestry and Environmental Studies and Adjunct Lecturer in Anthropology at Yale University. Her teaching and research interests focus on theories of social ecology, social aspects of sustainable development and conservation, and gender in agrarian and ecological systems. Her current interests involve exploring the environmental implications of relatively invisible economic and political sectors.

Preface

Genesis of the Project

There has been a marked revival of interest in environmental anthropology in recent years, following a decade or two in which this subdiscipline attracted relatively little attention. This efflorescence of interest reflects public preoccupation with the environment and perceived threats to it, and the increasing prominence of environmental issues, politics, and movements. The developments in anthropology share some of both the strengths and weaknesses of this preoccupation. Thus, much of the recent work in environmental anthropology is crisis-driven and focused on the here and now. Often missing from this work is a wider and deeper perspective, including a perspective on the historical, political as well as theoretical context in which this work is being carried out.

Current work in environmental anthropology cannot be appreciated without understanding the fact that this represents only the most recent surge on a rather long curve. There have, in fact, been at least three (if not more) distinct periods of intense interest in environmental anthropology: one immediately prior to and following World War II, one during the rise of environmentalism in the 1960s, and the latest pacing the rise of postmodern theory in the 1990s. The cyclic dynamics of interest in this field can offer us a unique insight into the evolution of both anthropology and environmental studies during the 20th century. Our purpose in this collection is to analyze these dynamics and try to define both where the field has come from and where it is heading.

Our personal interest in editing this volume has to do with our own past and future trajectories. We have been involved in the study of people and environment in South and Southeast Asia since the mid-1970s and have personally witnessed and been involved in some of the major developments in the field of environmental anthropology. In addition, we both hold appointments in Yale's School of Forestry and Environmental Studies, the oldest such school in the U.S., as well as in Yale's Anthropology Department. We represent anthropology within the Forestry School, and we represent environmental anthropology to the rest of the university. These roles have led us to ponder at length what environmental anthropology represents, both today and in the past, and to gather together for our courses readings that best illustrate this. We have felt in the past the lack of an existing reader for this purpose.

Selection of Materials

The history of anthropological work on the environment encompasses much of the history of anthropology. It is impossible to do complete justice to it in a single reader, so we have of necessity had to be very selective in thinking about materials to include here, striving for a sort of archaeology of key, persisting themes in the field. Our criteria for selecting papers to include were as follows.

We have tried to select works that reflect, and played a role in, major discussions and developments within environmental anthropology. We have tried to select works that are still not only readable but interesting and relevant. We have tried to select memorable works, which deliver an argument in such a way that a reader will still recall it five or ten years hence. We have with one exception (Mauss) selected works that could be reprinted in their entirety, to avoid the loss of authoritativeness that accompanies excerpted papers. We have selected works that are neither strictly theoretical essays nor derivative critiques of the works of others, in favor of original, ethnographic, case studies. We believe that this grounding is responsible, in part, for the timeless relevance of some of the best writing in environmental anthropology. We have selected works that have a strong underlying thematic focus, which reflects our decision to organize this volume not around so-called "schools" of environmental anthropology, neatly distinguished by approach and era, but around a number of persistent, cross-cutting, and interlinked themes.

We have selected papers that can be thematically linked to multiple other papers in the volume, thereby constituting a sort of intra-volume "dialogue" that reflects the larger one that has characterized the development of the field of environmental anthropology itself. We have designed the volume so that this dialogue takes place both within and between its subsections. By revealing these links, we hope that a strength of the volume will be the way that it investigates the intellectual history of the field. Our final selections were guided by the desire to organize the volume into a series of paired papers which "speak" to each other in a stimulating way. (It is interesting and doubtless explicable in the same terms that a number of the papers we selected are themselves either explicitly or implicitly comparative, whether in space – Barth, Geertz, Hawkes, Hill and O'Connell, Li, Waddell, or time – Ellen, Firth, Mauss.) Because of our interest in the cross-fertilizations that have stimulated and been stimulated by the best work in environmental anthropology, we have grouped together readings that will prod the reader to make linkages that he or she might not customarily make. This is consistent with a theme in some of the best research in this field, which is that it can be productive to rethink orthodox categories of knowledge.

We selected works insofar as possible to mix (1) canonical and more recent pieces, (2) different traditions of study within environmental anthropology, (3) the geographic locations of the study sites, and (4) the nationalities and genders of the authors. Where space constraints have obliged us to exclude important topics, authors, and writings, as well as relevant writing from outside anthropology, we have tried to cover these lacunae in our Introduction.

Michael R. Dove and Carol Carpenter
Yale University
June 24, 2006

Acknowledgments

We are indebted to many people and institutions for their support during the long gestation of this reader, foremost amongst whom must be the extremely patient and supportive series editor, Parker Shipton, and our editors at Blackwell Publishing, Jane Huber and Rosalie Robertson. We developed much of the structure and content of this reader in an advanced seminar that we taught at Yale in the Spring of 2002, "Society and Environment," and we are grateful to the wonderful students in this class for critiquing and expanding our ideas. We are grateful to the Yale School of Forestry and Environmental Studies for putting a variety of resources at our disposal, without which this reader would not have been possible. A series of indomitable student research interns have been of invaluable assistance, as has our stalwart secretary, Ann Prokop. None of the afore-mentioned people or institutions is responsible for the content of this volume however, whose shortcomings are ours alone.

Text Credits

Chapter 24: Ingold, Tim, 1993. Globes and Spheres: The Topology of Environmentalism. *From* Environmentalism: The View from Anthropology. Kay Milton, ed. Pp. 31–42. ASA Monograph 33. London: Routledge. © 1993 Routledge. Reproduced by permission of Taylor & Francis Books UK. Reprinted by permission of the Association of Social Anthropologists.

Introduction: Major Historical Currents in Environmental Anthropology

Michael R. Dove and Carol Carpenter

Background

The cross-cultural study of society and environment has ancient antecedents, the earliest of which were prompted by the observation that different types of environments are often inhabited by different types of people, which led to the invoking of the former to explain the latter. Such explanation was driven by one of the most fundamental questions of the human condition: why are people different? Hippocrates, perhaps the most important classical scholar of society–environment relations, whose scholarship laid the foundation for millennia of theorizing about the relationship between latitude and degree of social advancement, said that his scholarship was driven by the desire to account for differences among people. Glacken (1967:85) has written that "If Hippocrates had shown an interest in accounting for similarities rather than differences, the history of environmental theories would have been entirely different."

Historic works on society and environment

Thucydides, in his *The Peloponnesian War* (1959, Book I:2), presented one of the most sophisticated explanations of how environmental differences create social differences. He observed that highly productive lands led to covetousness, foreign invasion and frequent comings-and-goings of populations. In contrast, he said, the sterile soils of Attica freed it from the threat of such violence, as a result of which it was long inhabited by the same people, which allowed it to prosper, grow, and colonize other regions. Far more common in classical times, however, was the theory that environment affected human society not through its political economy but through its physiology. The key work was Hippocrates' treatise *Airs, Waters, Places* (1923), in which he distinguishes the three basic environments of the world, extreme heat, extreme cold, and environments intermediate between these two, and argues that these differences account for the major differences in cultural types. Aristotle, in his *Politics* (1908–56), applies this thesis to the political arena to explain why the politically most advanced nations of the world are located in temperate climates. Hippocrates' thesis is further applied by Pliny in his *Natural History* (1938–63, vol. II:80) to account for the origin of racial differences. Ancient Greek and Roman scholarship on the environment represents, of course, just one of many intellectual traditions around the world. Even more ancient Vedic teachings in the Indian sub-continent sounded some similar themes, with Aryan culture being seen as a product of the dry savanna-like *jangala* and that of the barbarians being linked to the moist forest *anupa* (Dove 1992; Zimmermann 1987).

This causal association of climate and human nature surfaces in the medieval writings of the Arab scholar ibn Khaldûn (1967), who derived passionate human personalities from hot climates and stolid personalities from cold ones, and more generally argued that the further from temperate regions a people lived, the more intemperate and animal-like their behavior became. This thesis was most influentially developed during the Enlightenment by Montesquieu in his *The Spirit of the Laws* (1989), in which he discusses how legislators should adjust their laws to the conditions of climate and soil that, he suggests, determine culture. Similar causal arguments are promulgated today, although the effects of geography and climate are now typically separated. Thus, some scholars try to account for the current geopolitical map in terms of geography (Diamond 1997), whereas others interpret human history in terms of climatic perturbation (Grove and Chappell 2000).

Throughout this history, the extent to which nature determines culture has been a heatedly contested question. The approach exemplified by Aristotle's theories was non-evolutionary: natural and cultural diversity was thought to unfold over space, not time. As diversity began to be studied through time, however, simple associations of culture and geography fell prey to the complexities of the historical record. Thus, d'Holbach (1774, III:6) wrote, "Can it be claimed that the sun which once shone on the freedom loving Greeks or Romans is today shedding different rays upon their degenerate descendants?" And Hegel famously wrote, "Where the Greeks once lived, the Turks now live, and there's an end on it" (Geertz 1963:6), meaning that if two such different societies can sequentially occupy the same environment, then environment must be irrelevant to social development. Observation of the historical record also increasingly led to the asking of the reverse question, not how does the environment affect society but how, over time, does human activity affect, and especially degrade, the environment?[1]

The Nature–Culture Dichotomy

Questioning the nature–culture dichotomy: From Posey's indigenous knowledge to Fairhead and Leach's politics of knowledge

Environmental anthropology sits astride the dichotomy between nature and culture, a conceptual separation between categories of nature, like wilderness and parks, and those of culture, like farms and cities.[2] This dichotomy makes it seem like common sense that parks must be set aside from people, and that real nature is not found in cities. The underlying narrative in fact tells us that people degrade nature, and thus that nature must be saved from culture. Environmental anthropologists have historically questioned this dichotomy, and continue to do so. The authors in this section, Darrell Posey[3] (on Brazil) and James Fairhead and Melissa Leach[4] (on Guinea, West Africa), represent this questioning stance: both of their studies question the assumption that culture necessarily degrades nature.[5] Both studies argue that what were assumed to be remnants of natural forest surrounded by degraded savanna were in fact created by people; they argue that the savanna is relatively natural and the forest islands cultural or anthropogenic.

In environmental anthropology questioning the nature–culture dichotomy has often been concerned with the damaging political consequences of this dichotomy for people, especially research subjects, in the real world. The nature–culture dichotomy underlies much conservation and sustainable development policy, for example. This means that the research of environmental anthropologists often has serious implications for policy. In short, in the hands of policy makers, the conceptual dichotomy between nature and culture, in particular the belief that people necessarily threaten and degrade nature, has negative political consequences. Both Posey and Fairhead and Leach were involved with the development and conservation world, and wrote in large part for policy audiences.[6]

Though the two studies are remarkably similar, there seem to be no significant links between the authors: Fairhead and Leach, whose work followed Posey by over a decade, merely cite him in their 1996 book. The two studies are based on different continents, but perhaps significantly examine similar ecological zones, forest-savanna edges[7], and similar human livelihoods, swidden farming. This may be due to the fact that forest is readily viewed as natural, in contrast to both savanna and swidden, which tend to be seen as nature degraded by culture.

Anthropogenic forest islands confuse the nature–culture dichotomy not only because they look natural but are cultural, but also because they are cultural in a subtle way: "managed" (Posey) or "enriched" (Fairhead and Leach) rather than strictly cultivated. This raises the interesting question of how conscious and deliberate this "management" is. Both Posey and Fairhead and Leach have written a great deal about such non-agricultural indigenous influences on the land. Fairhead and Leach view this land enrichment as a "constellation" of everyday and short-term practices with verifiable long-term effects. They write: "While villagers do intentionally precipitate these vegetational changes, their agency in this is not always so overt. Short-term agricultural and everyday activities can sometimes in themselves lead unintentionally to these long-term and beneficial vegetational results; villagers know the results and appreciate them, but do not necessarily work for them" (Fairhead and Leach 1996:207). Posey exaggerates the cultivation-like aspects of Kayapó practices, calling them "management," "semi-domestication," and "nomadic agriculture," in order (as he suggests in his 1998 chapter) to counter developers who base land claims on cultivation. He argues (1998) that it was only his immersion in the emic knowledge and the myths of the Kayapó that allowed him to see this management, which is otherwise invisible to Western eyes.[8] But he is also aware of the everyday, unconscious character of these practices, as is clear in his description of Kayapó planting tubers, seeds, or nuts that they have collected during the day while squatting to defecate (96).

Both Posey and Fairhead and Leach explore indigenous perceptions of nature and culture, and in doing so contribute to another major trend in the questioning of the nature–culture dichotomy. For other works that emphasize this approach, see the section "Social identity and perception of the landscape" in this Introduction.

Both studies also stress indigenous awareness of ecosystem communities versus individual species of plants. Posey (97) gives a nice example of the Kayapó "companions of the banana," a group of "two dozen varieties of edible tubers and numerous medicinal plants" that flourish in the shade and soil conditions found under banana trees. Fairhead and Leach explore this in depth in their 1996 book.[9]

Posey's research was carried out in the early 1980s (begun in 1977) and Fairhead and Leach's research was carried out in 1992–94. During this decade the paradigm in environmental anthropology shifted, producing two very different approaches to a very similar problem: Posey emphasizes indigenous (ecological) knowledge, and Fairhead and Leach emphasize the politics of (policy) knowledge.[10] In essence, both studies are correcting the mistaken idea that forest islands are remnants of natural forest, with Posey emphasizing the correction, the indigenous knowledge that produced the islands, and Fairhead and Leach emphasizing the mistake (though their 1996 book covers both aspects).

Indigenous knowledge

Indigenous knowledge, an approach of which Posey was an early and important promoter, had the strength of arguing that indigenous peoples had important environmental knowledge which could contribute to conservation; when linked to indigenous management, as in Posey's work, it was even more importantly part of an argument for indigenous land rights.[11] However, it had weaknesses too. One, already mentioned above, was the tendency to exaggerate indigenous management in order to strengthen its political weight. Another was that in order to argue that indigenous knowledge was in fact knowledge it had to be "translated" into Western terms: thus the collection of plant specimens and their "scientific" identification, evident in Posey's Table 1.1.

In an important sense the politics of indigenous knowledge undermines the science, and science was Posey's Achilles heel. His research on forest islands was criticized by the geographer Eugene Parker[12], who argued quite convincingly that, far from being created by the Kayapó, they were natural, the result of forest advance or retreat at the edge of forest and savanna. Parker (1993:721) essentially accuses Posey of poor science, saying that his research is characterized by "apparent misstatement, unsupported assertions, and a remarkably careless approach to the presentation of data and facts."

The importance of Darrell Posey, and of the indigenous knowledge and management approach more generally, lies not in scientific rigor but in the political uses of science. As Parker (1993:715) says, meaning to be derisive: "Posey's work is among the most widely noted, cited, and publicized research in lowland Amazonia both within and, in particular, beyond anthropology." Posey championed indigenous land rights and intellectual property rights, and received wide recognition as an activist and environmentalist.

The politics of knowledge

Fairhead and Leach argue that what they call "a vision of degradation" was so strong that French colonial policy makers and contemporary Guineans "read history backwards," interpreting forest islands in Guinea as relics of an original forest destroyed by local land use, when in fact local land use created the islands out of savanna.[13] Their work in general serves as one of the very finest case studies illustrating, in wonderful detail, that mistaken ideas, particularly ideas about nature and culture, can cause misinterpretations of landscape and history with very significant policy ramifications. This particular article stresses the complicity of social scientists in this misreading, and adds a social science twist to the degradation narrative: that the social order of pre-colonial peoples kept land use in balance with nature, but its breakdown (along with overpopulation) under colonialism inevitably led to deforestation.

The work of these two authors is most notable for going far beyond the fact that a discourse exists and warps policy. In their 1996 book (see especially chapter 8), they trace in great detail the history of the interaction between government policies (based on the degradation discourse) and local land use practices (based on an opposing discourse), including the varying effectiveness of government implementation and local resistance to it. They conclude that, in spite of deep misunderstanding, local practices produced the vegetation changes that policy was aiming for (Fairhead and Leach 1996:260). They also conclude (see especially chapter 9) that this history of interaction maintained the powerful degradation discourse.

Fairhead and Leach were clearly influenced by Foucault[14], and by fellow Africanists and anthropologists who based their work on Foucault, especially James Ferguson (1990). But the language they use, "narratives," "stories," "visions," and a specific "degradation discourse" (rather than discourse in general), is more accessible.[15] This approach is not limited to ethnographers of Africa, of course; another key figure is Arturo Escobar (1995), who applied Foucault to Columbia. For more on this approach, see the section "Environmental campaigns and collaborations" in this Introduction.

The main "work" of Posey's writings, appropriate to his time, was to establish the fact that what looked natural might be cultural, and thus that indigenous people should be seen as models for conservation, rather than as opposed to it and thus denied land rights. His ideas did influence environmental policy: donors now often view traditional societies as supporting conservation, and policy interventions often promote the strengthening or re-establishment of traditional societies to support conservation efforts. Fairhead and Leach must take on the more subtle errors that followed this partial correction. As they state in the final sentence of this reading: "Environmental policy can call on no moral high ground in recreating the natural (or the social that went with it). It becomes very clearly a question of social or political choice about what vegetation forms are desirable at any given time in social history, and about ensuring that conflicting perspectives on this . . . are adequately articulated and addressed" (115–116). The work of Posey and of Fairhead and Leach helps us see something that is conceptually confusing and thus difficult to see, but has been there all along all around us: the overlapping of nature and culture for which we have no term. Even more importantly, they demonstrate the importance to local peoples of our conceptual difficulties.

How cattle problematize the nature–culture divide: From Evans-Pritchard's "cattle complex" to Harris' "sacred cows" and beyond

Anthropological study of the nature–culture boundary in cattle-rearing societies has focused on the concept of the so-called "cattle complex," seminal writings on which came from E. E. Evans-Pritchard (1902–73) and Marvin Harris (1927–2001). Evans-Pritchard was professor of social anthropology at Oxford from 1946 to 1970. His most influential work concerned the non-Muslim peoples of the Southern Sudan, including the Nuer, about whom he wrote not only *The Nuer* (1940) from which the essay reprinted here is taken but also *Kinship and Marriage Among the Nuer* (1951) and *Nuer Religion* (1956), and the Azande, whose witchcraft beliefs he analyzed in the magisterial 1937 *Witchcraft, Oracles and Magic Among the Azande*. Marvin Harris taught at Columbia until 1980 and then at the University of Florida up to the time of his death. He is best known for his history of anthropological theory (1968) and his development and application of a cultural materialist approach to a variety of so-called "riddles of culture," including dietary taboos, warfare, and cannibalism, which he published in a series of both academic and popular books (e.g., 1974, 1979, 1985).

The cattle complex

The debate over the cattle complex dates to the 1926 publication by Melville Herskovits of "The Cattle Complex in East Africa," which describes the central role of cattle in the culture of African pastoral societies. Related concepts include Evans-Pritchard's use in 1940 of the term *cattle idiom* for the Nuer, Richards' use of *cattle cult* in 1948 for the Southern Bantu and, more recently, Ferguson's use of *bovine mystique* in 1990 for the Basotho. The term *sacred cow*, used by Harris in the 1960s, refers to something quite similar: the drawing of a cultural boundary between secular, mundane, material life on the one hand, and on the other hand the ritual and sacred sphere of cattle rearing. Herskovits (1926:259,516) initiated this tradition of study with his dramatic examples of a boundary between the livestock and agricultural spheres in particular (a division recognized in the biblical divide between the tiller Cain and the herder Abel):[16] "To eat milk and meat on the same day is regarded as dangerous throughout this region [of the Suk] while if anyone chews raw millet he may not drink milk for seven days." The concept of the cattle complex is unusual: there are few if any analogous terms (e.g., no fish complex or crop complex), although the Asian labels of bamboo/rice/hydraulic societies perhaps qualify.

Schneider (commenting on Heston 1971:205) argues that Herskovits' presentation of the cattle complex was essentially "a claim for irrationality in human behavior." The cultural focus on cattle was in effect deemed to be not only "different" but irrational, and debate over this issue dominated the anthropological literature on cattle for the rest of the 20th century. There are possible psychological connotations to the early use of the term *cattle complex* (cf. Beidelman 1966), accompanied as it was by statements about emotional "identification" by owners with cattle. Evans-Pritchard (119) notes that among the Nuer this identification has a linguistic dimension as well: "The linguistic identification of a man with his favourite ox cannot fail to affect his attitude to the beast, and to Europeans the custom is the most striking evidence of the pastoral mentality of the Nuer."[17] Mair (1985) insisted that the concept of the cattle complex came not from Herskovits' work but from the misapplication to it of psychoanalytic ideas by colonial British who had heard of but not read Freud.[18]

The early writers on the cattle complex were intrigued by their observation of cultural norms that elevated cattle to a seemingly unusual position vis-à-vis humans. This is reflected in the references to men saying that they would rather starve than sell their cattle or committing suicide when their cattle die or are stolen or confiscated, as in Herskovits (1926:264, 269): "Similar to the story about the horror felt by the Mkamba at killing a cow even when he was starving, is that told of the Mwila who chose death at the hands of invading Barotsi rather than flee and leave his cattle." Richards (1948:97) articulates the perplexity of the Western observer in writing that "The herd is less important as a source of meat, milk, and leather, than as the object of social ambitions, rivalries and emotions."

The evidence gathered by many of the same ethnographers who argue for the strength of the cattle complex shows that these arguments were over-drawn. Their emphasis was on dramatic instances of the inflexibility of the ritual boundaries between the sacred livestock sphere and the mundane agricultural sphere (e.g., killing oneself rather than parting with a cow), not on why the boundaries had to exist in the first place. Ritual regulation of the boundary around cattle was only necessary because, even in "cattle complex" societies, much more was going on besides cattle rearing, often including agriculture.[19] As Evans-Pritchard (118) writes of the Nuer: "They are pre-eminently pastoral, though *they grow more millet and maize than is commonly supposed* [emphasis added]." Richards (1948:97) similarly writes of the Southern Bantu, "The people are therefore more passionately attached to cattle, than to any other possession, *even though they are more dependent on their fields for support* [emphasis added]."[20] These are composite economies containing multiple sectors, one of which is culturally valorized over the others, regardless of its actual economic importance.[21] This valorization led ethnographers to give less attention to less culturally marked activities of equal or greater economic importance.

Harris' analysis of the sacred cow focused on demonstrating that the boundaries separating sacred and profane uses of the cow are, here too, permeable. He cites Gandhi's famous 1954 comment on the mistreatment of the Indian cow as evidence of, in effect, boundary violation:

> How we bleed her to take the last drop of milk from her, how we starve her to emaciation, how we ill-treat the calves, how we deprive them of their portion of milk, how cruelly we treat the oxen, how we castrate them, how we beat them, how we overload them . . . I do not know that the condition of the cattle in any other part of the world, is as bad as in unhappy India. (144)

Gandhi was essentially saying that the Hindu doctrine of *ahimsa* (which affirms the unity of life as symbolized in the veneration and protection of cattle) actually constitutes less of a boundary around the cow than is found in societies without cow-worship. The periodic enactment of anti-slaughter legislation in India also attests to the fact that *ahimsa* alone does not constitute an impenetrable barrier.[22]

Transfers and transformations

Although unique cultural boundaries are drawn around cattle rearing in cattle complex societies, cattle are pre-eminent boundary-crossers. The most obvious way in which this is true involves the ability of cattle and other livestock to exploit scattered or distant resources through transhumant or nomadic patterns of movement. Less dramatic and commensurately less studied is the ubiquitous movement of livestock between agricultural communities and fodder sources in nearby forests (Blaikie and Brookfield 1987:46). The challenge of understanding these sorts of animal and resource flows is heightened by attendant physical and conceptual transformations. Most obviously, fodder resources are transformed into the milk, blood, meat, and leather of cattle, as well as waste products like urine and dung.[23] Less obvious are the further transformations involving these waste products, notably dung, which is transformed into energy when burned or into soil fertility when spread on fields as manure.

The transfer of resources between different environments via the medium of cattle is often interpreted in terms of the "subsidy" of one environment by another. Thus, Carpenter (1997, 2001) argues that fodder gathering in state forests by Pakistani women subsidizes their families' farms (and ultimately the urban markets for which those farms produce food). Subsidies, like this one between state forests and private farmlands, are inherently political in nature. Changes in proprietary relations are one of the most important and contentious of the transformations brought about by the alimentary processes of cattle, with the eating of one person's resource turning it into another's. The example of fodder in state forests being eaten by peasant cattle is globally common. Dove (2007a) describes the gathering of grasses in state forests in Central Java to stall-feed cattle in villages, the manure from which is used to sustain the productivity of their agricultural fields. The grasses/manure represent a fugitive transfer of nutrients from state lands to village lands. Cattle-driven transfers in resource control can even take place within households: Carpenter (1997, 2001) describes how women prefer to feed crop stubble to livestock to support their milk production economy, instead of ploughing the stubble under, which benefits the male-dominated crop production sector.[24] Similarly, Harris posed the novel thesis that untended cows tend to be owned by the poor and feed off the lands of the wealthy, thus in effect transferring resources to the former from the latter.[25]

Shifts in resource control carried out through the medium of cattle are often complicated by the fact that they entail a transformation of the use-sphere or transactional order (Bloch and Parry 1989:23–24). This refers to a shift in resources between the two distinct spheres of economic activity that characterize most households, distinguished by a focus on the household versus the group, an orientation toward the market versus subsistence, and an emphasis on individual short-term needs versus the needs of long-term social reproduction (Gudeman 1986). Ferguson (1990) describes a case in Lesotho, wherein livestock represent a separate transactional sphere oriented toward the long-term social and economic reproduction of the wider society, which is walled-off from the short-term monetary needs and transactions of the household. There is often a directional bias to relations between the two sectors: whereas cash can be invested in livestock in Lesotho, livestock cannot easily be converted into cash. In other cases, however, the barrier to resource flows between the cattle and non-cattle sectors is two-way (Shipton 1989). Harris argues that the perceived barrier between the sacred sphere of Indian cows and the secular sphere of Indian food and agriculture is far more permeable than imagined, and that cattle resources regularly cross this barrier in the form of traction energy, dung/manure, milk, meat, and leather. Transfers of resources across such barriers tend to be normatively laden and, thus, both culturally obfuscated and emotionally infused.

Evans-Pritchard and Harris

Evans-Pritchard's *The Nuer*, published in 1940 and based on research carried out in the 1930s, was one of the defining works of early-20th-century anthropology. It was a landmark example of long-term field research based on participant-observation (he even acquired his own cattle). It reflected the beginning of the move away from comparative, culture-area work like that of Herskovits in the 1920s toward the sort of approach pioneered by Malinowski, with whom Evans-Pritchard studied. Evans-Pritchard claims (1940:15) that conditions among the Nuer made it impossible to employ the more formal methods of interviewing that he had used previously among the Azande and so he "had to fall back on direct observation of, and participation in, the everyday life of the people." The result is a highly empathetic study of the Nuer. The Nuer world is a world of cattle and Evans-Pritchard successfully conveys some sense of this to his readers, setting the standard for generations to come of "thick description" (in Geertz's [1973] sense) of subsistence practices. His description of the ubiquitous usefulness of cattle to the Nuer, furnishing as they do everything from skins for beds to scrota for bags to dung ashes for tooth powder, is compelling, as too is his insight into the human–cattle intimacy afforded by bathing in their urine, picking ticks from their bellies, and sleeping by their sides. His paragraph on the use of thumb, fingers, hand, and thighs when milking is perhaps unequaled until Conklin's (1957:92–97) description of rice planting among the Hanunóo.[26]

The chapters in *The Nuer* on "Interest in Cattle," "Oecology," and "Time and Space" were important, early contributions to ecological anthropology. Evans-Pritchard's attention to emic views and language made his work especially important for the early development of ethnoecology and ethnoscience approaches. His in-depth analysis of the semantics of a particular sphere of life (cattle) was infrequently equaled until decades later. He elicited terminology for "several hundred color permutations" and "several thousand expressions" for referring to livestock in general (133, 134). Evans-Pritchard (132) justified his work on this "linguistic profusion" in terms of both the importance of cattle in Nuer life and the fact that a "cattle vocabulary" was used to articulate all other dimensions of Nuer life as well. As he memorably put it, "Their social idiom is a bovine idiom" (120).

Contemporary criticism of Evans-Pritchard's work focuses on his perceived inattention to social differentiation and politics within local societies as well as to the wider political systems within which they, and also their ethnography, are situated. A related critique is that Evans-Pritchard ignored perturbation and change in favor of depicting essentially ahistorical states of social equilibrium. This is the view taken in the major restudy of the Nuer carried out by Hutchinson (1996:28). Rosaldo (1986) and Geertz (1988), focusing on Evans-Pritchard's ethnographic writing, argue that he downplays the colonial political context in which his work was carried out and privileges his own authority as scientist and author.

Whereas Evans-Pritchard was very much a product of his era, his work nonetheless often escapes that era's norms. In the chapter reprinted here, for example, he acknowledges that the colonial government commissioned his study, he describes a government military force surrounding his research camp, he acknowledges the legacy of state depredations in current Nuer mistrust toward the government and the adaptiveness of their mobility and "elusiveness" in this regard, and he states that Nuer-government conflict and tensions generally impeded his research. He even transcribes a Nuer song in which there are references to "strangers" (Government forces) and to "bewilderment/perplexity" occasioned by foreign invasion (135). He is also not oblivious to historical change: he speculates about historic shifts in the Nuer balance between animal husbandry and agriculture and uses this to explain a historically elevated level of aggression among the Nuer.

In the work reprinted here, Harris revived the interest of the previous generation of scholars in the cattle complex. Whereas Evans-Pritchard showed us that other people could relate to cattle in a way that seemed completely foreign to Western scholars, Harris showed us that our preconceptions of how another society related to cattle in seemingly foreign ways might be completely wrong. Harris demonstrated the coexistence of a ritualized sphere of cattle activity and a non-ritualized sphere of everyday life and asked about the relationship between them. He must be credited not only with stimulating an enormous debate on this single subject but also with drawing the attention of anthropologists back to the material dimensions of life (which had been noticeably neglected in ethnographic work in India at that time, for example) and stimulating the wider development of cultural materialist approaches.

Harris' critics claimed that he treated rural Indian communities as homogeneous and unconflicted and, thus, took an essentially apolitical view of them. He was accused of treating these communities not only as harmonious but as unchanging. Henderson (1998) argues that the historically contingent, post-independence land dynamics of India (the opening of new agricultural land, the closure of the commons, and acquisition of farmer status by tenants) triggered the cattle boom observed by Harris, which was followed by a bust as these dynamics played themselves out. Harris' development of a functional, evolutionary paradigm of explanation of sacred cattle came in for heated criticism within anthropology (e.g., Diener, Nonini, and Robkin 1978), as did his perceived downplaying of the importance of religion. But a surprising amount of the published debate over Harris' analysis turned on fine-grained agricultural economic data, which suggested an implicit acceptance of Harris' terms of debate. An unusual number of the contributors to this debate also came from disciplines other than anthropology, many from the natural sciences, which reflected (and clearly added to) the accelerated opening of anthropology to other fields in the 1960s.

Harris' attention to detailed, quantitative economic and ecological data played an important role in the early development of ecological anthropology, although his excessively reductionist methods also cost the field some credibility. His role in leading anthropologists to think about their de facto dichotomization of material and symbolic spheres was salutary, as was his role in suggesting that environmental relations can have political dimensions, which helped to lay the intellectual groundwork for the emergence of political ecology in the 1980s. Finally, Harris' analysis represented a clear break with the anthropological tradition of community study, taking on as he did Indian society as a whole.

Writing against "irrationality"

Throughout the 20th century, Western scholars and development experts viewed the traditional livestock sector as irrational, within the context of a wider Western discourse of underdevelopment that many scholars now regard as politically biased and self-privileging (Escobar 1995). Debate over the irrationality of the cattle complex dates back to Herskovits' work in the 1920s (and this debate extends to Herskovits' own stance on the topic). The currency of such beliefs at the time that Evans-Pritchard carried out his study of the Nuer is reflected in his felt need to ask (126) "whether the Nuer, who are so reliant on their cattle and who value them so highly, are competent herdsmen." Evans-Pritchard (129) answers this question, unequivocally, in the affirmative, writing: "Nuer cattle husbandry could not in any important particular be improved in their present oecological relations; that, consequently, more knowledge than they possess would in no way assist them; and that, as will be shown, were it not for their unceasing vigilance and care the cattle would not survive the harsh conditions of their environment." This was a politically courageous statement to make, in a report commissioned by a colonial government whose "civilizing" mission would have been better supported by a negative answer.

Harris' study, several decades later, is framed even more explicitly as an attempt to answer this charge of irrationality (138): "I have written this paper because I believe the irrational, non-economic, and exotic aspects of the Indian cattle complex are greatly overemphasized at the expense of rational, economic, and mundane interpretations." The first section of his article is a detailed review of published characterizations of Indian cattle as "surplus," "useless," "uneconomic," and "superfluous" (139). The principal point of Harris' analysis is that Indian cattle management is not irrational and that Indian cattle have, notwithstanding their ritual status, secular value. He provides an apt quotation from Gandhi, again, regarding the dualistic character of Indian cattle: "Why the cow was selected for apotheosis is obvious to me. The cow was in India the best companion. She was the giver of plenty. Not only did she give milk but she made agriculture possible." Opler, in a published comment on Harris' original article (63), writes: "For Harris' central criticism of the claim that India's animal or agricultural resources have been 'mismanaged' . . . no anthropologist . . . could have reasonable objection." But Harris' counter-assertion, that India's animal resources were *not* mismanaged, got lost in the decades of subsequent debate. And, indeed, popular belief in the irrationality of the cattle complex continues. Thus, Dyson-Hudson and Dyson-Hudson (1969:76) write of herding in Uganda: "Too often, however, the absence of market rationality in traditional herding systems is taken to be the absence of rationality of any kind." And Chambers (1983:77) argued that it was Western animal husbandry experts who truly suffered from a "cattle complex":

Their attachment to exotic cattle to the exclusion of native beasts and other domestic species may have had aesthetic and emotional dimensions, but there was also a degree of irrationality . . . The "meat and milk complex" of the expatriates was based on their professional training for the conditions and needs of rich, temperate countries and was inappropriate for those which were poor and tropical.

Ecology and Social Organization

Early essays on social organization and ecology: Mauss and Steward

In this section we have paired two early essays on the relation between social organization and ecology: Marcel Mauss's *Seasonal Variations of the Eskimo: A Study in Social Morphology*[27], first published in 1904[28], and Julian H. Steward's "The Great Basin Shoshonean Indians: An Example of a Family Level of Sociocultural Integration," first published in 1938. Steward, an important figure in American anthropology, is generally recognized as the "father" of ecological anthropology.[29] Mauss is a key figure in the development of French anthropology, the most prominent scholar in the French *Année Sociologique* after his uncle, Emile Durkheim. His work presaged and directly influenced E. E. Evans-Pritchard (especially *The Nuer* [1940]) and Claude Lévi-Strauss.[30] Mauss is not usually associated with environmental anthropology, but his essay on the Eskimos (now more correctly termed *Inuit*) has been described as "the first ethnographic attempt to adopt a holistic, ecological approach to the analysis of a society," "a remarkable first attempt to develop an ecological approach within which to consider a whole range of complex social phenomena," which contributed to "a common ecological perspective within anthropology" (Fox 1979:6,12,14).

Mauss and Steward share views of the relation between social organization and ecology that are far more complex than earlier environmental determinism, as we will see. They also share evolutionary concerns; essentially they are interested in the most simple social organizations and the most demanding environments, in order to understand how environment might have shaped early societies. This interest generated these two essays on hunter-gatherers (also called foragers; see discussion of Lee in the section "Bounded and balanced community" in this Introduction) in extreme environments (the Inuit in the arctic coast, the Shoshone in the arid steppes). But their differences are significant. In somewhat comparable societies, Mauss saw simple social wholes, while Steward saw only adaptive families.

Arguments against environmental determinism

The issue central to these essays is the relation between, on the one hand, the organization ("morphology" in Mauss and "integration" in Steward) of society, and, on the other hand, ecology ("the land" in Mauss). In an important sense this relation parallels that between culture and nature so central to environmental anthropology. In the first half of the 20th century, anthropologists debated the environmental determinism of the 19th century and earlier.[31] Environmental determinism in general viewed the relation between culture and ecology as "a simplistic mechanism," a direct connection "between weather and topography and the character or ethos of a people" (Murphy 1977:21). In Mauss and Steward the relation between social organization and ecology is neither simple nor direct. But social organization clearly plays the predominant role in Mauss, while ecology plays that role in Steward.

For Mauss, the Inuit served as a privileged case study because although their social organization seemed on the surface to be environmentally determined, he found ample evidence in their winter life of a social whole. They lived in a "dispersed" fashion in the summer and "gathered together" in the winter. They were thus animal-like. Mauss (162) argues that Inuit hunting technology "forces the group to live like the animals they hunt": "the population congregates or scatters like the game." But Mauss's review of the ethnographic record reveals that the religiosity and sociability of Inuit winter culture elaborates a social whole: "at the very moment when the form of the group changes, one can observe the simultaneous transformation of religion, law and moral life" (167). Mauss thus argues, against ecological determinism, that though the configuration of the land, its mineral riches, its fauna and flora affect the organization of society, it cannot "produce effects" on its own: "For men to gather together, instead of living in a dispersed fashion, it is insufficient simply to assert that the climate or a configuration of the land draws them together; their moral, legal and religious organization must also allow a concentrated way of life" (158–159). Winter concentrations of seals allow winter concentrations of people, but they do not account for the existence of the social whole that the Inuit create and celebrate in their winter religious life.

Mauss's object in this essay is closely related to Durkheim's (1915) in *Elementary Forms*: to document the origin of society, which they understood as the idea of society as a whole or totality that supersedes individuals. For Durkheim religion and society are not separate; social institutions derive from religion, and vice versa. In particular, religion derives from clan assemblies, which "generate effervescence, a state in which clan members become aware of forces transcending the individual" (Allen 2000:77). Mauss's study of the Inuit shows a people who transcend individuality (or at least the dispersion of nomadic families) seasonally, a people whose "effervescent" winter culture creates and maintains a simple society. In fact Allen (2000:84) argues that Durkheim's ideas in *Elementary Forms* actually derive from Mauss's essay on the Eskimos.

Steward's position towards environmental determinism is best understood as a response to his professor (and Mauss's contemporary) Alfred L. Kroeber. Kroeber (1963:205) says that "culture can be understood primarily only in terms of cultural factors," but that "no culture is wholly intelligible without reference to the . . . environmental factors with which it is in relation." He says that cultures are necessarily adapted to a particular environment, and that once this adaptation has occurred they tend to change slowly (Kroeber 1963:6). Kroeber, best known for the idea of the culture area, documented correlations between cultural areas and natural areas in North America (in Kroeber 1963, originally completed in 1931). Kroeber did not theorize beyond these specific correlations, however, declaring that "the interactions of culture and environment" are "exceedingly complex," making "generalization unprofitable" (Kroeber 1963:205). His student Steward made it his life's work to generalize about these very interactions.

For Steward, as Murphy (1977:22) points out, the critical fact is not the environment nor the culture: "Rather, it is the process of work in the fullest sense: the division of labor and the organization, timing, cycling, and management of human work in pursuit of subsistence." Steward, in other words, focused on the organization of subsistence production, which he viewed as "cultural ecological adaptations."[32] Work in its fullest sense, and particularly including how labor is organized, thus stands between the environment and social organization. And work could distance culture from nature, allowing culture to rise above nature: Steward hypothesized that as subsistence problems were solved, "the effect of ecology becomes more difficult to ascertain" (Murphy 1977:24).

For Steward the Shoshone were an ideal case for clarifying the limiting effect of ecology on work and thus social organization:

> Shoshonean society was affected not only by the erratic and unpredictable occurrence of practically all principal foods [ecology] and by the limited technical skills for harvesting and storing most of them [technology], but it was also shaped by the predominant importance of wild vegetable products, which put a premium upon family separatism rather than upon co-operation [organization of labor]. (171; my notes in brackets)

Family separatism in work, in turn, resulted in the "fragmentation" of society into nuclear families. For example, the primary food of the Shoshone and the food that they relied on in winter, pine nuts, did not permit concentrated winter villages, because pine nuts were best gathered by families working alone; more importantly, they did not permit permanent villages because the location for best harvesting them changed from year to year. Mauss's Inuit, in contrast, had a primary food (seals) that permitted large, permanent winter gatherings. Murphy (1977:6) says that the foraging Shoshoneans "were the catalysts of Steward's theories," in that they represented "the struggle of man against his environment": "their very pattern of social life had to be understood as an adjustment to bleak physical reality."

Steward's focus on environmental adaptation is not environmental determinism because the economic exploitation of the environment and the organization of production is inserted between nature and culture. But the direction of influence is clearly the same. His later article with Murphy (1977:153) argues that both beaver trapping (by the Algonkians in Canada) and rubber tapping (by the Mundurucú in Brazil) are best exploited by individual families, and this determines the level of social integration (which in both cases has changed from band/village to individual families).[33] Economy and thus social organization, in other words, are adapted to the ecology of beavers and rubber.

In sum, both Mauss and Steward rejected environmental determinism, but in quite different ways. Steward focused on how work, especially the social organization of labor, was shaped by or adapted to ecology. This focus gives environmental influences an indirect but essential role. Mauss, in contrast, gives the environment a much more limited role: that of providing the opportunity for the creation of social wholes, which were actually created by culture, especially religious practices.

Both Mauss and Steward chose to examine the issue of the influence of nature on the organization of human society primarily in relation to hunting and gathering (or foraging) societies rather than cultivating ones. It is interesting to consider that foragers raise the question of nature's impact on culture, while swidden farmers (as we saw in Posey and in Fairhead and Leach) raise the opposite question, of culture's impact on nature.

Families versus social wholes

Both Mauss and Steward focus on one particular aspect of social organization: the difference between organization into separate families and organization above the family level, into a larger community. In Mauss this dynamic corresponds to the contrast between the seasons. Steward's argument in this piece, in contrast, is that the Shoshone are integrated into families with no larger community. They are, however, asking different questions. Steward asks: How does the ecology, through work, constrain social integration? Mauss asks: Given the constraints of ecology and technology on social wholes, how does the society attain them? Mauss's theory requires that he establish the existence of society above the family level; Steward's requires that he establish its absence. Embedded in these questions and theories are different views of social organization.

Mauss's interest was in social wholes. Thus he emphasizes the winter, and gives little detail about the summer, which represents the winter's opposite, the "individualized" nuclear family. The winter demonstrates social wholes in several different ways. First, there is the long-house, which holds several families (side-by-side in identical units) in contrast to the summer tent's single family. Secondly, there is the *kashim*, which is a communal house or men's house with no divisions, "always essentially *a public place* that manifests the unity of the group" (164; his emphasis). In the *kashim*, "the individuality of families . . . disappears; they all merge in the totality of the society" (164). The architecture of the communal house without family divisions represents Mauss's social whole. Finally, there is the religious life expressed in the *kashim* ceremonies, which is "pre-eminently collective," "the object and the expression of the group" (164). Seal biology and Inuit technology account for their assembling (like the seal) in winter, "But they do not explain why this concentration attains that degree of intimacy which we have . . . noted"; they do not explain the *kashim* or its ceremonies (163). Inuit could have simply placed their individualized summer tents closer together or built smaller winter houses.

The Shoshone gather in the winter also, but the ecology of the pine nuts keeps families apart even then, albeit "within easy visiting distance" (171). There is no Shoshone long-house or kashim. Of ceremonies, Steward tells us that the Shoshone have "no functional need for ceremonialism dedicated to group purposes" (175).[34] Of the circle dance, "a minor collective religious activity designed for the common good," he says that "the religious aspect was secondary and incidental to the recreational purpose" (176). Mauss would surely have viewed it differently. Steward's interest is in adaptive subsistence activities, and thus in whether or not subsistence work requires groups, and in the Shoshone case it does not. He writes: "I classify the Shoshoneans as an exemplification of a family level of sociocultural integration because in the few forms of collective activity the same group of families did not cooperate with one another or accept the same leader on successive occasions" (173). Steward is looking for permanency in leaders, villages, and social groups, and he does not find it among the Shoshone. Mauss, in contrast, does not explicitly address the question of permanency, saying only that winter housemates are kin (siblings and their children). We are thus left to conclude that Steward may very well have viewed the Inuit as being at the family level of integration, and that Mauss may very well have viewed the Shoshone as having social wholes.

Both Mauss and Steward question the nature–culture dichotomy by viewing the relation between nature and culture as a complex concrete reality in which nature and culture cannot be extricated from each other. We agree with Steward that nature, especially through its constraints on the organization of subsistence labor, does affect social organization. But we would argue with Mauss that neither the well-adapted but isolated Shoshone families nor the social exaltation of the Inuit in winter are accounted for by the difference between pine nuts and seals.

Beyond Steward: "Ecosystems with human beings in them" in Barth and Geertz

Fredrik Barth and Clifford Geertz are important anthropologists not primarily associated with environmental anthropology, who have both written influential pieces on ecology. Barth is linked to the study of ethnic relations and Geertz to symbolic anthropology. In these essays they thus both examine the role that the ecology of particular societies plays vis-à-vis their own central concern: Barth is primarily interested in the role of ecology in ethnic relations, and Geertz in the role of ecology in the symbolic "passion" of a culture.

They both build upon Steward (Geertz explicitly so), particularly on his analyses of the adaptations of human labor to available natural resources. And we argue that they both go beyond Steward as well, by writing about more complex and intertwined cultural and ecological systems, which Geertz calls "ecosystems with human beings in them" (198).[35]

These two case studies involve settled agriculturalists (in Barth's case including associated herders), rather than Steward's and Mauss's foragers.

Ecological niches and ethnic relations

The article by Fredrik Barth[36] is an elegant analysis of the relations between three ethnic groups, demonstrating the importance of environmental factors. He uses the animal ecology idea of "niche," looking at resources necessary to a particular societies' subsistence and social organization and the competition for those resources. Barth's analyses often sound like Steward's best analyses of subsistence labor, except that they carry this sort of analysis beyond foragers to farming and herding groups, and even more importantly, to relations between groups.[37]

The Pathans of the Swat valley of northern Pakistan must double crop (planting twice in a year) to support their social organization, that is, to produce a surplus with which to attract political followers[38]; this limits their "niche" to areas where the growing season is long enough to allow double cropping. The Kohistanis combine a single annual crop with transhumance (raising livestock, especially water buffalo), which once allowed them to occupy the entire area, but the Pathans pushed them north out of the area where two crops were possible. They are further differentiated into the lower-altitude, eastern Kohistanis, who can maintain high livestock populations, and the higher-altitude, western Kohistanis, whose livestock populations are limited. Pathan–Kohistani relations are fairly simple: they occupy different territories, have a history of Pathan aggression, and Pathan exiles can become Kohistani but not the reverse. On top of this conceptual grid is a third group, the Gujars, who occupy small niches inside the Pathan and part of the Kohistani territories. With the Gujars, the term "niche" takes on more meaning than a simple territory defined by some natural limitation to agriculture or livestock raising. Gujars practice transhumance in symbiotic relation to the cultivating Pathans (herding Pathan animals and trading animal products for crops). The Gujar niche is both natural – since the Pathan have few livestock, they do not use their own crop residues or hillside fodders, and social – the Pathans look down on herding, but have no lower castes available to take on this job. In the Kohistani area the Gujars have no niche at all in the low-altitude east, because is it well filled with Kohistani animals. In the high-altitude west, however, a small niche exists in the summer, especially for sheep and goats.

Barth's discussion of the Pathan not being able to cross the boundary where double-cropping is impossible sounds a lot like Steward's discussion of the Shoshone social organization being limited by the irregularity of pine-nut harvests. But there is a very important difference: in Steward's case the bottom line is the necessity to eat, to survive; for Barth, in contrast, the Pathan "need" two crops per year not to survive but to support their political system. In Steward, in other words, one can say that nature (the pine-nut harvest) constrains culture (social organization). In Barth, though natural constraints remain important, they matter for cultural (political, ethnic) reasons.

Eric Waddell's work on Enga responses to frosts (see the section " 'Natural' disasters and social order" in this Introduction) can be read alongside Barth as another example of the role of ecology in ethnic relations.

"The infolding of setting and society" (199)

Clifford Geertz's[39] analysis of the ecology of Bali and Morocco is clearly colored by his interpretive, culture-as-text approach to anthropology. For him the environment is an integral part of the text that is culture, no more external to a particular society "than the storms in *Lear* are external to the play or the moors in *Wuthering Heights* are external to what passes between Cathy and Heathcliffe" (199). Geertz talks explicitly of the "whole" that is nature and culture, the "infolding of setting and society". He writes: "An established society is the end point of such a long history of adaptation to its environment that it has . . . made of that environment a dimension of itself" (199). Yet the role of ecology in Geertz's analyses of Bali and Morocco is larger than in Barth's analysis of the Swat valley of Pakistan, and in this Geertz is closer to Steward than Barth is. As Geertz says, "Environment is, therefore, and long has been, more than a passive, residual, limiting sort of factor in shaping Moroccan and Balinese life. It is and has been an active, central, and creative one" (192). In Barth the Pathan need one particular sort of niche, and the Gujars another, but he does not explore the details of these different niches nor their integration into Pathan and Gujar culture. Barth is essentially interested in the consequences of ecological niches for political and ethnic relations. Geertz's "thicker" view of culture integrates ecology and social structure much more closely.

It is this integrative aspect of Geertz's work that sets him apart from Steward as well. Steward also wrote about irrigation, and was particularly interested in Karl Wittfogel's (1957) theory on the relation between irrigation and states. In one of the last pieces he wrote in his life, Steward (1977c:95) sometimes sounds like Geertz (and even Kroeber): "The role of sociocultural institutions and hydraulic controls must have been intricately interrelated." But his aim in that piece continues to be one of generalizing the complex, so he ends up attempting to delineate cross-cultural similarities ("the factors and processes . . . are fairly limited in number and are rather similar cross-culturally" [97]) rather than differences, which contrasts his work to Geertz's. Geertz argues in this essay (190) that a cross-cultural, comparative approach is important to human ecology, because it prevents "the cultural aspects from decaying into a mere reflection of the ecological." He refers to Steward's stance against determinism in the same paragraph. However, Steward's use of cross-cultural comparison is significantly different from Geertz's. Steward is looking for general patterns of adaptation to ecology with evolutionary significance for social organization[40]; Geertz is trying to interpret the very different texts of irrigation in Balinese and Moroccan cultures.

In *Agricultural Involution* (1971), Geertz's most often cited "ecological" work, his analysis is closer to Steward. In *Involution*, he analyzes Dutch colonial policies, especially regarding sugar production, identifying very different effects in the swidden areas of outer Indonesia compared to sawah (wet rice)-based Java. In Java, agriculture became increasingly intensive within rigid boundaries, as peasants were forced to produce sugar for Dutch estates as well as rice (and other subsistence crops) for themselves, on tiny plots supporting an increasing population: "Slowly, steadily, relentlessly, they were forced into a more and more labor-stuffed sawah pattern" of "tremendous populations absorbed on minuscule rice farms," in the "ultimately self-defeating process" that Geertz calls "agricultural involution" (1971:80). In the outer islands, in contrast, tobacco, tea, rubber, etc. estates existed alongside competing smallholder production of these commercial crops (all in a sea of unchanged swidden farmers; on swiddens, see the section "Ethnoecology and the defense of swidden agriculture" in this Introduction). Rubber is particularly interesting, as it "integrates" into swidden as well as sugar does into sawah (113), but due to differences in ecology and culture, swidden farmers produced rubber for market independently, in a way that competed with plantation production, while Javanese wet-rice farmers remained essentially coolies, lending their labor and their land to Dutch enterprises.[41] In *Involution*, Java and the outer islands are more like Steward's adaptations to ecology (albeit wonderfully complex ones) than texts. Geertz's article reprinted here, written a decade later, is far more distanced from cultural ecology.

Geertz's "infolding of setting and society" builds on and goes beyond Mauss as well as Steward; Balinese and Moroccan culture are neither adaptations to their environments nor social wholes created out of ecological opportunities. Geertz's Balinese are Mauss's dream come true: they "have a passion," as Geertz (198) says, for organizing everything into corporate groups (groups with recognized identities; in Bali often complete with temples and priests). They are like Mauss's Eskimos in the winter, times seven.[42] Geertz's Moroccans invite comparison to

Mauss's Eskimos in summer (or to Steward's Shoshone even in winter), but the contrast is revealing. The Moroccans are both individualized and socially integrated: they are integrated through an individualistic trope. They have a "passion for organizing everything in terms of the head-on encounter of individuals within a general, universalistic moral-legal code" (198–199). A non-Maussian sort of society emerges in Geertz's description of the Moroccans: a society whose wholeness lies not in groups nor collective buildings (nor in Steward's leaders), but in a "moral-legal code", "a highly developed, religiously supported (i.e., by Islam) sense for the objective reality of codified personal law" (198), that is, general rules "phrased in terms of individual rights" (197).[43] The Balinese and Moroccan "passions" are applied to water just as they are to other aspects of life: "*This general order of difference within a single cultural dimension – adaptation to the setting – extends in an overall way to the two societies as a whole*" (198; his emphasis). The Balinese and Moroccan "passions" are what Geertz seeks to understand, in contrast to Mauss, who sought social wholes.

Steward believed that nature was less and less constraining as culture became more and more complex. The "simple" Shoshone were most affected by nature. Geertz (in spite of his great respect for Steward) argues just the opposite: that more complex societies are simply increasingly wrapped up with nature:

> It used to be thought that, although environment might shape human life at primitive levels, where men were, it was said, more dependent upon nature, culture-evolutionary advance, especially technical advance, consisted of a progressive freeing of man from such conditioning. But the ecological crisis has divested us all of that illusion; indeed, it may be that advanced technology ties us in even more closely with the habitat we both make and inhabit, that having more impact upon it we in turn cause it to have more impact upon us. (199)

The year after this article was published, 1973, brought an oil crisis to the United States that must have made this quote seem prescient. Now, more than 30 years later, the strength of the illusion can be seen in the politics surrounding global warming.

"Natural" disasters and social order: Response and revelation in Firth and Waddell

What are the implications for society of short-term perturbations of nature? Two works that set the pattern for the study of this questions were written by Sir Raymond Firth and Eric W. Waddell. Firth (1901–2002), was a student of Bronislaw Malinowski and proponent of his functionalism, and a founder of economic anthropology. He taught at the London School of Economics until his retirement in 1968 and published on a wide variety of subjects and peoples, but he is best known for his work on the Tikopia of the Solomon Islands (e.g., 1940), especially for his classic (1936) monograph *We the Tikopia*. Eric W. Waddell (1939–), who studied under Harold Brookfield at the Australian National University, has taught at McGill University and is now at the University of Sydney. He has been a major contributor to the study of highland New Guinea agriculture and economics, publishing (with Krinks) a study of the Orokaiva in 1968 and a well-known study of the Enga, *The Mound Builders*, in 1972.

History of the study of disaster

When in the late 1950s Firth wrote his study of the impact on Tikopia of two cyclones, he noted that "there are hardly any investigations by anthropologists of the sociology of such critical situations" (202). The exceptions included a few studies of famine in Africa (especially Richards 1939) and volcanic eruption (e.g., Belshaw 1951; Keesing 1952). The years since have seen growing and sustained anthropological interest in such topics as famine, fire, and flood, and episodic interest in topics like deforestation, desertification, global climate change, species extinction, and HIV-AIDS. Academic interest in these topics was stimulated by the shift in scientific paradigms from one that assumed equilibria in society and environment to one that assumed just the opposite. The new paradigm, also called the "new ecology" (Scoones 1999), disputes assumptions of equilibrium, takes disturbance to be important, and emphasizes dynamic, historical, and partly unknowable relations between society and environment (Botkin 1990; Fiedler, White, and Lediy 1997; Worster 1990; see also the section "The bounded and balanced community" in this Introduction). Disaster was a ready-made subject for the new paradigm, which made inroads here while other areas of environmental study were still hobbled by "balance of nature" premises (Scoones 1999).

The premises of new ecology helped to push new sorts of questions to the forefront of disaster research, especially questions regarding socioeconomic vulnerability that causes natural perturbation to have a more harmful impact on some populations and a less harmful impact on others (Blaikie et al. 1994; Hewitt 1983; Watts 1983; Watts and Bohle 1993).[44] Related questions concerned the victims' own experience of disaster, including how they adapt to it (as in these works by Firth and Waddell) and, more broadly, how they incorporate both threat and response into the fabric of their society. This represented the development of an "ethno-disaster" approach within anthropology.[45]

Moral meteorology

A perceived arbitrariness to the occurrence and impact of natural disasters has long preoccupied human society. Voltaire (1977) asked in his *Poem Upon the Lisbon Disaster*, penned in the wake of the 1755 Lisbon earthquake that claimed 60,000 lives, "Did wiped-out Lisbon's sins so much outweigh Paris and London's, who keep holiday?" As implied in Voltaire's question, there is an ancient and widespread belief that such disasters represent divine judgments on human society, and that the state of nature can thus be interpreted as a commentary on the state of society and, in particular, the state of its leaders.[46] Elvin (1998), in his analysis of perceived human responsibility for the weather in late imperial China, terms this *moral meteorology*. Throughout Southeast Asia there are long-lived beliefs that violent perturbations in the realm of nature reflect weaknesses of state rulers and portend their downfall (Adas 1979; Dove 2007b; Harwell 2000). Firth (1959:80) says that similar beliefs, which he observed on Tikopia, reflect a "socio-centric" view of nature: "Disorder in nature, untoward events, lack of prosperity, were to be related to social defects such as the religious division of the society or the feebleness of its premier chief."

Where such beliefs hold, it follows that natural perturbation is often accompanied by social perturbation. Thus, Thucydides (1959, 2:78) observed that the coming of the plague in ancient Athens was followed by a general outbreak of lawlessness. The implications of disaster for political authority were aptly articulated to Firth (1959:92) by one of his chiefly informants, who stated: "When the land is firm (food is plentiful) people pay respect to the things of the chiefs, but when there's a famine people go and make sport of them." Governments are highly sensitive to the political implications of social disorder attendant upon disaster. Waddell (224) describes the colonial New Guinean government's (unfounded) fear that the 1972 frost would lead to a "disorganized fleeing of starving victims from the disaster area," resulting in "widespread violence, starvation, and death." A leitmotif of Indian colonial history is a similar fear that deforestation and purportedly attendant climate change would lead to famine and political unrest (Grove 1995). Whereas such state fears are often baseless, natural disasters may play a role in political regime change. Drought, fires, and volcanic eruptions seemed to play a role in the toppling of Soeharto's New Order regime in Indonesia (Dove 2007b; Harwell 2000); and Wisner (1993:137 n. 11) lists the fall of eight governments worldwide during a 25-year-period due to natural disasters and their aftermaths. Due to the real as well as imagined impact of such perturbations on political stability, there is a tendency for states to tighten their discipline during disasters. Foucault's (1995 [1975]) real-life model for the panopticon, the idealized state institution of surveillance and discipline, is the "plague city," which he calls "the utopia of the perfectly governed city."[47]

Standard disaster discourse

Public representations of natural disasters tend to follow similar, discursive forms. Standard discourses have been identified, studied, and critiqued in the fields of erosion (Blaikie 1985), forest fires (Harwell 2000), Himalayan degradation (Guthman 1997; Ives and Messerli 1989; Thompson, Warburton, and Hatley 1986), and, in the pieces reprinted here, deforestation (Fairhead and Leach) and frost (Waddell). These discourses edit reality, often in ways that privilege those who are in control of the discourse (viz., policy makers) at the expense of those who are its subjects (viz., disaster victims). Central to this privileging and de-privileging is the discursive construction of incapacity to cope with disaster on the part of its victims versus a capacity to provide relief (etc.) on the part of state and non-state disaster agencies. As Waddell (223) writes, "A fundamental premise [of government relief efforts] was that the victims had no satisfactory means of their own to cope with the crisis."

Central to disaster discourses is the perceived singularity of the event. Drawing on an equilibrium-based model of nature, the standard discourse represents disaster as an aberration, which is both preceded and followed by normality or non-disaster. Hewitt (1983:12) described the discursive means by which disasters are conceptually separated from normal everyday life, becoming what he calls "an *archipelago* of isolated misfortune." Firth (203) begins his account of the hurricanes by writing that whereas his prior research in Tikopia had concentrated on the "normal workings" of Tikopia society, in 1952–53 he was concerned with its "abnormal workings." Thus, one of his central research questions during this research was: "How far did the conventions about things normally used as food continue to operate, or cease to be observed" (1959:78). Firth fails to find any serious disruption of conventions or norms: food continues to be distributed at ceremonies (even when it is in short supply), no one put out to sea on suicide voyages (for which there is apparent precedent), and no cannibalism took place (which seems to be without precedent in any case). Both Firth and Waddell find that the behavior that they observed in the wake of disaster falls within the normal range of behavior, and so they conclude that the disasters themselves were thus "normal" disasters. Critical to questioning by Firth and especially Waddell of the abnormality of their disasters was evidence that these disasters were not unique but rather *recurring* and thus "normal" and planned-for phenomena.[48] Indeed, Waddell (225) argues that for most of the highland Enga in New Guinea, "Frost is a fact of life." Other critical literature on natural disasters has similarly argued that what outsiders perceive to be disasters are often "normal" perturbations (like the annual floods in Bangladesh [Paul 1984]), which may even constitute a resource as opposed to a problem for local populations.

Firth and Waddell regard their disasters as normal but not ahistorical. Firth suggests that the disaster he witnessed in 1952–53 represented the outcome of a long-term process involving indigenous demographic and exogenous climatic perturbation, with a minor role played by exogenous government relief efforts and opportunities for labor migration. He writes (204): "Speaking generally then, one has the impression that though the famine of 1952/3 was abnormal in the short run, in the long run it represented a movement in a pendulum swing of relations between Tikopia population and food supply that has been going on for at least a century, and probably much more." Waddell believed that the Enga adaptation to frost was changing as they became more integrated into wider political and economic systems: in particular, greater access to markets undermines traditional regional trade relations, thereby weakening one of the principal resources for households struck by frost. Government relief efforts also undermine indigenous adaptive mechanisms, at the same time as the introduction of new frost-tolerant crops makes such adaptation less crucial.

Disaster and society

Disasters affect not just humans but human communities; they affect not just groups but the institutions by which groups govern themselves. As Firth (202) puts it, "When such a lowering of the food supply takes place fairly rapidly, the strains on the social system are not simply nutritional – belly-gnawing; they depend on recognition, sentiments, moral evaluations and symbols of social relations." Throughout recorded history, the impact of disasters has been measured in terms of the amount of strain they place on the social fabric. Thucydides (1959, 2:78) weighed the impact of the plague on Athens in terms of the extent to which social institutions broke down. This same measure is used by Firth in his assessment of the impact of disasters: he asks if the social conventions that held before the disaster still held afterwards; and he concludes (1959:105) that even though Tikopia society was affected by the hurricanes, it could still be talked of as an "entity."

For observers as well as community members, the impact of disaster is often measured with respect to social integration. Firth, for example, was very interested in whether the scale of social networks of mutual assistance contracted or not in response to the famine that followed in the wake of the hurricanes. He implies that this shrinkage, although obviously adaptive to the exigencies of the moment, is inimical to social integration but is counterbalanced by the fact that the "formal structure" of social obligations persisted even if the "sphere" was curtailed, allowing him to say that societal norms do not break down (1959:86). The change was "organizational" not "structural." There was a decline in the incidence and scope of ceremonies, but those that were held still adhered to traditional principles of gift-giving. Firth, like other scholars of disaster, was attentive to any indication of a shift of orientation in the stricken community from the long-term welfare of the group to the short-term needs of the individual, to a loss of "corporate" character.[49] One of the ways that such a shift in orientation manifests itself is by a replacement of traditional exchange by market-based exchange. In the case of Tikopia, Firth asserts that this did not happen. Indeed, Firth says, traditional distributions of food at ceremonies continued even when the hosts could ill afford to make them.[50]

Contemporary disaster researchers are interested not simply in society's response to disasters but in the differential response to disaster of different segments of society. The dominant thesis in this field holds not only that the economically, socially, and politically marginal segments of society are more vulnerable to natural perturbations but also that elites are consistently able to take advantage of such perturbations to further strengthen their positions at the expense of the marginal groups (Shaw 1992; Zaman 1991; Watts 1983; Watts and Bohle 1993; Wisner 1993). Firth was ahead of his time in this respect: he carried out detailed investigations of the way that the cyclones affected the different parts of Tikopia society, in particular the chiefs versus the commoners. Whereas he is mostly concerned with the ways in which the chiefs directed the mobilization of labor and other resources, he also finds that they benefitted from their wealth and status. Overall, however, he concludes that the disaster did *not* result in any significant shift of resources from poor to rich.

In the agricultural communities that Firth and Waddell studied, the greatest impact of the disaster came from famine, and this was caused by the damage done to future crop production prospects as opposed to current food supplies. Indeed, Firth (204,210) notes that food was "extremely plentiful" in the immediate wake of the first hurricane and that the period of most severe famine on Tikopia did not come until 8–11 months later. Over such an extended period of study, the magnitude of the disaster's impact and the social response wax and wane, and this proved to be of considerable theoretical importance to Firth and Waddell. Much of Firth's analysis of the disaster response in Tikopia focuses on the gradual, step-wise attenuation of social norms as the famine progressed, as the society's most basic structures of exchange were tested but not breached. Waddell takes this sort of analysis one step further and identifies multiple, distinct stages or levels of disaster response, which differ chiefly in their scale: thus, there is a local response mechanism, an intra-regional one, and an extra-regional one. The fact that the Enga have multiple mechanisms at their disposal, and can selectively draw on them according to the severity of the frost, demonstrates to Waddell (224,231) that their response is a "structured" one and not the "disorganized flight" imagined by the colonial government, and that it is adaptive in an evolutionary sense.

Firth did not set out intending to study responses to hurricanes and, given the ethnographic norms of the time, he deserves great credit for not ignoring them. He was able to see that such disasters offer a special opportunity to the researcher. He writes of the hurricanes: "Here is an empirical test of the power of integration of the social system – a test not dependent merely upon the anthropologist's personal evaluations" (202).[51] Whereas a number of writers see disasters as a test of human nature, anthropologists like Firth saw them as a "test" of society. Firth (202) writes in this regard: "The implications of famine in social terms provide an interesting, if grim, example of the strength and weakness of a social system . . . The test of social relations as a working system is the extent to which they can withstand the strain of competing demands upon their agents."

Some scholars argue that the stress that disasters place on society is revealing, that the hidden and complex workings of society can be seen better then than during "normal" times. Thus, Solway (1994) speaks of drought as a "revelatory crisis," which reveals the fault lines of society. Malkki (1997), however, questions the division between normal and abnormal that is implicit in this thesis that a disaster can reveal something about the non-disaster part of society. She argues that disasters are part of normality and she rejects any privileging of the revelatory value of the abnormal over the normal. Central to her work is the idea that social institutions have developed to cope with extreme perturbations no less than everyday events. If such institutions are not understood, then the society as a whole cannot be understood. As Waddell (225) writes: "For most Enga . . . frost is a fact of life. Indeed, it provides the key to understanding the most distinctive element of their adaptive strategy, agricultural mounding."

Firth and Waddell

Firth's chapter is an analysis of the response to hurricane-precipitated famine among the 1,750-odd inhabitants of Tikopia in the early 1950s. He provides a rare analysis of the day-to-day role of the Tikopian chiefs in assessing the dimensions of the disaster and marshaling the society's resources to cope with it. This included mobilizing labor but not food for the greater good; communal control of food actually declined at the same time as communal control of labor increased. Firth provides a detailed analysis of the strategic changes made in food production in response to the disaster, as well as the changes made in food distribution, referring here to curtailed food sharing and ceremonial distributions of food as well as food theft.[52]

Firth presents a pioneering analysis of the social dimensions of food and eating, a subject that has only really come into its own in anthropology within the past decade. While recognizing a demographic component in Tikopia's population/food supply balance, he is skeptical of simple Malthusian interpretations (e.g., of famine as a "check" on population [203–204]). He is interested in strains on the social system "that are not simply nutritional" and in the social responses that are "dictated by social rather than economic considerations" (52;1959:77). Firth breaks new ground in his analysis of intra-community differentiation and the role it plays in the response to disaster. He finds that whereas under duress the people of Tikopia did curtail the "sphere" or scope of their food exchange obligations, they did not alter the formal "structure" of these obligations; there was no shift of resources from poor commoners to wealthy chiefs, and the basic corporate structure of the society was maintained. While acknowledging that there is variation among individuals in their response to pressures on their food supply, he says that his interest lies in studying the persistence under these conditions of "characteristic Tikopia attitudes in the use of food" (1959:77). He believes that his findings allow him to examine "the reactions of Tikopia as a social system" (1959:77). This examination encompasses cultural performance; he carries out not only an analysis of the impact of famine on ceremony and song and dance but also an analysis of the ways that a response to the famine was enacted in these cultural forms (including "songs of disaster") (1959:97–98).

Waddell analyzes the mechanisms by which a highland New Guinea group traditionally coped with extreme frosts, in particular an extreme frost event in 1972. His work is a path-breaking analysis of the frost-retardant function of the mounded beds that characterize the fields of the Enga and some other highland New Guinea groups. The mounds affect the microclimate at the field's surface and thereby provide significant protection against frost. Waddell supports his interpretation of mounding as an adaptation to frost by noting that the Enga only practice mounding above certain altitudes (the frequency and intensity of frosts increase with altitude) and that the height of the mound and certain tillage practices (both of which inhibit frost damage) also increase with altitude.

Waddell distinguishes three levels of response to frosts. At the local level, people practice mounding and also divide their fields between the valley floor, where frost tends to be worst, and valley sides, which tend to be more protected from frost. At the intra-regional level, the Enga maintain usufruct rights and fields in widely dispersed areas, which further diminishes the risk that all of their fields will be struck by the same frost incident. At the inter-regional level, the highland Enga maintain trade relations with Enga in lower altitude, frost-free regions, to which they may migrate on a temporary or even permanent basis in the event of a disastrous frost. Waddell shows that there is an association in both time and space between the magnitude of frost and the magnitude of human response.

Waddell, like Firth, was a pioneer in arguing for the normalcy of disaster, in arguing that disaster is, as he puts it, "a fact of life" (225). He explicitly frames his study as an attempt to understand not socioecological equilibrium but rather "how people adapt to departures from steady-state conditions" (224). Waddell clearly shows how the mechanisms of adaptation to frost, running the gamut from mild to extreme, are built into Enga society.[53] His principal theoretical contribution to the disaster literature lies in his demonstration of the relationship between magnitude of perturbation and magnitude of response. Few scholars can muster the local, regional, and historical data needed to examine this relationship. One of the strengths of Waddell's analysis was to show the local capacity for coping with disaster, at a time when such demonstrations were few and far between. He provides an early critique of the standard premise of government post-disaster relief efforts, that the disaster is without precedent and its victims lack the capacity to cope with it.

Methodological Challenges and Debates

Ethnoecology and the defense of swidden agriculture: Conklin and Carneiro

The first set of brief but influential readings in this section of the book, by Harold C. Conklin (1926–) and Robert L. Carneiro (1927–), concerns a hoary subject of anthropological study, swidden agriculture. Conklin did his doctoral work at Yale under Floyd G. Lounsbury and taught at Columbia and then Yale University until his retirement in 1996. He is best known for his 1954 dissertation, a pioneering contribution to ethnobotany; his 1957 monograph, 1961 bibliography, and a series of papers, including the one reprinted here (1954a), on swidden agriculture; and his 1980 *Ethnographic Atlas of Ifugao*, a unique exercise in cartographic representation and use of remote sensing data.[54] Robert L. Carneiro trained at the University of Michigan under Leslie White and subsequently co-edited two volumes of White's papers, as well as a volume of Herbert Spencer's papers, reflecting his lifelong interest in the evolution of human society (Carneiro 1967; Dillingham and Carneiro 1987; Dole and Carneiro 1960). Carneiro carried out fieldwork with three different groups in the Amazon basin, the Kuikuru Indians of central Brazil, the Amahuaca of eastern Peru, and the Yanomamo of southern Venezuela, and published extensively on their ecology and subsistence. He has taught at Brown and Columbia Universities and is currently Curator for South American Ethnology at the American Museum of Natural History in New York City.

In the mid-20th century, many of the most prominent works in anthropology dealt with swidden systems (e.g., Condominas 1977; Conklin 1957; Freeman 1970; Netting 1968; Rappaport 1968); and a number of major theoretical developments came out of the studies of such systems, including the genesis of the subfields of ethnobotany and ethnoecology. These studies also made major contributions to policy debates regarding conservation and development in the tropics and subtropics, which had long been dominated by a demonization of swidden agriculture. In colonial times, the French called swidden cultivation "nomadic agriculture" (*nomadisme agricole*) while the Dutch called it "robber agriculture" (*roofbouw*). The colonial and post-colonial English terms *shifting cultivation* or *slash-and-burn agriculture* are little better. Shifting cultivation carries connotations of nomadism, anathema to centralizing states; whereas slash-and-burn carries connotations of rampant resource destruction, anathema to resource managers and conservationists. These negative connotations continue to be seen in the use of "slash-and-burn" in colloquial English. During the corporate and governmental downsizing in the U.S. in the late 1980s and 1990s, for example, "slash-and-burn" became a popular term for describing the resulting elimination of programs, closings of plants, and laying-off of workers. Anthropologists and other scholars have made numerous efforts to come up with alternate terms, the most successful of which is *swidden*, an archaic, little used variant of old-English *swithen*, meaning to singe. No contemporary term was sufficiently neutral to be used or even rehabilitated. *Swidden* was so archaic as to have no normative loading.

(Mis)understanding swidden agriculture

The most frequently cited definition of swidden agriculture is Conklin's (1957:1): "Minimally, shifting cultivation may be defined as any agricultural system in which fields are cleared by firing and are cropped discontinuously (implying periods of fallowing which always average longer than periods of cropping)." Today swidden agriculture is practiced on 30 percent of the world's arable soils and it supports as many as one billion people, or 22 percent of the population of the developing world in tropical and subtropical zones (Thrupp, Hecht, and Browder 1997:1–4). In spite of the availability of accurate information on swidden agriculture, fundamental misunderstandings have persisted (Dove 1983).

The agricultural systems with which people in industrialized countries are most familiar mine the soil, whereas swidden agriculture (especially in the wet tropics) does not. In moist tropical forests, nutrients are rapidly cycled through the thin soil and back into the biomass atop it, and it is this store of nutrients that swidden agriculture exploits. This fundamental ecological dynamic is reflected in the way that swidden peoples themselves talk about their systems. Thus, the Kantu' of West Kalimantan, Indonesia, say that they "farm the forest" (*bumai hutan*) not the soil (Dove 1985b), just as the Mnong Gar of Cambodia say that they "eat the forest" (Condominas 1977).

Every stage of the swidden cycle is popularly misunderstood. First, many swidden cultivators prefer not older but younger forest because it is easier to clear, although such a swidden will have more weeds. A swidden cut from older forest will have fewer weeds, but it will be harder to burn. The burning of swiddens, which has become an iconic, global image of human degradation of the environment, is also misunderstood. The burn, which breaks down the forest biomass into nutrient-rich ash that cultigens can easily access, is considered by many swidden peoples to be the most important and also the most problematic determinant of a good harvest.[55] Globally circulating images of burning forest notwithstanding, it is difficult to burn rain forest. The popular misbelief that fallowed and naturally afforesting swidden land is neither managed nor claimed has also been remarkably persistent. Conklin's work, here and elsewhere, represented one of the first efforts to examine the character and dynamics of the fallow.

For most international observers, swidden agriculture denotes poverty. Most policy makers simply assume that "there are no prosperous shifting cultivators" (Bandy et al. 1993:3). The equation of poverty with swidden agriculture is implied in the title of the most important current global program on the system, the Consultative Group for International Agricultural Research's "Alternatives to Slash-and-Burn Programme: Innovations to Reduce Poverty and Conserve Tropical Forests." In fact, swidden cultivation can achieve extraordinary efficiency and productivity. Conklin calculated a return to seed ratio of between 25 and 40 to 1. In terms of returns to labor, Dove (1985a) calculated a return to swidden labor in Kalimantan that is at least twice as great as that of terraced rice in Java. Only in terms of returns to unit of cultivated land does swidden fall behind more intensive systems of agriculture. But as long as land is available, farmers prefer the system of cultivation that is least onerous with respect to their own labor, intensifying only under duress (Boserup 1965). One benefit of the low labor demands of swidden cultivation is the fact that it frees up labor for other purposes. Few if any swidden peoples have no economic activity other than swidden agriculture. Many gather and trade forest products like rattan; many others engage in smallholder commodity production for global markets (Dove 1993; Pelzer 1978).

There has been a near-universal failure in policy circles to appreciate the merits of swidden technology, which Conklin's writings have done so much to reveal.[56] The fact that much of this technology is embedded in decision making has mitigated against its recognition by outsiders. For example, one of the most complex dimensions of swidden technology is the cultivation not just of multiple crops but multiple fields per household, and their articulation to the landscape so as to minimize risk, predation, and travel time and maximize use of household labor. There is also a social dimension to swidden technology: it takes a community to practice swidden agriculture, but not because swidden societies are communalistic. The common and, in developmental circles, pejorative perception of "primitive communalism" in such societies is usually based on a misreading of reciprocal work groups, which are widely used to leaven hard tasks with the pleasures of social companionship, overcome seasonal labor bottlenecks, and distribute crops from harvest-surplus households and communities to those with harvest deficits. A further reason why a single swidden household is not viable is because of the need to satiate local pest populations with the critical mass of ripening crops that can only come from many different households and even communities making swiddens at the same time.

Many 20th-century observers have noted how aesthetically challenging the timber-strewn, inter-cropped, and generally "disorderly" appearance of a swidden is to Western eyes. But this challenge is dependent upon an erasure of Western agrarian history.[57] François Sigaut (1979:685) has documented the relative recency and importance of swidden agriculture in western Europe, noting that pockets of swidden cultivation remained in Germany, Austria, and Northern Russia until the 1950s and 1960s. Otto and Anderson (1982) show that a swidden system based on a melding of Scots-Irish and Native American practices dominated the southern uplands of the U.S. through the 19th century and persisted in remnantal form well into the 20th century.

Conklin (1957:3) created one of the first, and still one of the most influential, typologies of swidden agriculture, based on a distinction between less sustainable "partial systems" and more sustainable "integral systems." Before this distinction was established, all of swidden agriculture was tarred with the same brush as its least sustainable variants. Conklin's typology created the first conceptual space for anything other than disparagement of all swidden systems. It has since become apparent that most swidden systems fall into the category of partial systems, including swidden cultivators producing commodities for global markets, and it also has become apparent that this does not necessarily imply that they are less sustainable. These systems have been slow to win external recognition because they confound the popular image of swidden peoples as backward and isolated. For similar reasons, the wider world has been slow to recognize the simultaneous practicing of swidden and irrigated agriculture, which are popularly represented as so antithetical that their joint practice by the same people is unthinkable. This dichotomization has also characterized the scholarly literature, the classic contributions to which developed the swidden–irrigated divide as an important analytical construct (e.g., Burling 1965; Geertz 1963); but it is highly misleading. Cases where increasing population/land ratios force people to intensify their agriculture by moving from swidden to irrigated agriculture are often reported. Less often reported but not uncommon are cases in which migrants leave densely populated regions for less densely populated ones and "regress" from irrigated to swidden cultivation (Utomo 1975).[58] More remarkable yet, swidden and irrigated cultivation are often practiced at the same point in time by the same group.[59] Conklin's (1980) research among the Ifugao shows that even these makers of world-famous irrigated rice terraces also make swiddens for tubers in the hills above their terraces. The swidden–irrigated field dichotomy persists in spite of facts such as this because it is part of a powerful discourse of evolution and development, in which swidden represents a prior, backward stage and irrigated agriculture represents the modern, developed stage.

Politics and ideology

Swidden and irrigated agriculture are still commonly characterized as "upland" and "lowland" systems, respectively. In fact, recent and more regionally oriented studies have shown that upland and lowland are better understood as part of a single system (Guérin 2001).[60] The very term *upland agriculture* (or *hill agriculture*) implies an environmental explanation for what is actually a political phenomenon. Most swidden agriculture is in fact today found in upland, hilly, regions, and in this sense the use of the term *upland farming* by Conklin (241) among others is empirically correct; but this association is due to political not biogeographic factors, so the descriptor *upland farming* for swidden agriculture is more a political than a geographic or ecological term.

Some scholars have argued that swidden systems are simply too unproductive to sustain state structures. Meggers (1971), whose work provoked years of rejoinders by Carneiro among others, argued that the seemingly verdant Amazon forest was a "counterfeit paradise" that would not sustain intensive swidden agriculture, that swidden agriculture was practiced there out of necessity, and that it would not support state development. In fact, modern states favor intensive agriculture because its product is susceptible to state extraction and its people are tied by capital investment to their fields; whereas they do not favor swidden agriculture because its product is less extractable (it is dispersed, heterogeneous, and staggered in time) and, in the absence of capital investment, its people are more capable of flight.[61] Indeed, the character of swidden agriculture seems to be inherently inimical to the principles of surveillance and generalization that underpin modern state-making (Scott 1998). Thus, while people who flee the state have traditionally been viewed as practicing "unproductive" swidden agriculture as the price of their freedom, in fact it is those who cannot flee who practice intensive agriculture as the price of living under the state. In general, free peoples practice swidden agriculture because it gives them better economic returns; unfree peoples practice intensive agriculture because the state forces them to do so. Thus, the contemporary concentration of swidden agriculture in upland areas, which are inherently less suited to governmentality (Scott n.d.), is due to the fact that this is the only place where people are not prevented by the state from practicing this type of agriculture.

Environment and evolution

In Geertz's (1963:16) famous comparison of swidden and irrigated rice agriculture in Indonesia (see also the section "Beyond Steward: 'Ecosystems with human beings in them'" in this Introduction), he argues that the vegetative structure of the

former "imitates" that of a tropical forest. It now seems as if Geertz underempha-
sized the unnaturalness of irrigated fields and overemphasized the naturalness of
swiddens. Conklin's study of swidden management shows more culture and less
nature than Geertz seemed to see. The tendency to see swidden cultivation as close
to nature inevitably led to views of swidden societies as determined by nature. One
of the most influential deterministic arguments was Meggers' effort to explain the
level of sociopolitical development in the Amazon in terms of the constraints of
the biophysical environment. Based on the mathematical analysis of an actual case,
however, Carneiro demonstrated that the environment in the Amazon constrains
socioeconomic development much less than Meggers thought. The analytic tool that
Carneiro used to test Meggers' assumptions, mathematic calculations of environmental carrying capacity, is essentially a way of numerically articulating environmental constraints. It was used widely by anthropologists interested in the
environment in the 1950s and 1960s (e.g., Conklin 1957; Rappaport 1968). From
the start, however, scholars cautioned about the complexity of this calculation
(Conklin 1959) and critiqued its misapplication (Street 1969). Indeed, Brush (1975)
concluded that its chief benefit was heuristic.

The belief that swidden agriculture is uniquely constrained by the environment
is associated with evolutionary assumptions about swidden societies, which are most
clearly articulated in comparisons of swidden and irrigated cultivation, the pair
representing a classic evolutionary sequence.[62] The premise that swidden is devel-
opmentally prior to irrigated agriculture has had a drastic impact on the stance
taken towards swidden versus irrigated agriculture in modern development:
whereas the development goal for irrigated agriculture has typically merely been to
improve it, the goal for swidden agriculture, perhaps without exception, has been
to replace it.

Conklin and Carneiro

Conklin's work in ethnobotany and ethnoecology suggested the possibility of an
alternative rationale to that of high modern, Western, agricultural development. He
provided some of the first quantitative documentation of the fact that the economic
returns to swidden are relatively good. Conklin was also one of the first to suggest
that the disordered heterogeneity of the swidden system – multiple crops, multiple
stories, multiple fields – was not simply a poor effort to attain the ordered homogeneity of Western mono-cropping, but was an alternate, possibly even preferable
model in its own right. A defining aspect of Conklin's research was a focus on
everyday reality. His accounts of the unimagined dimensions of felling a tree or
making a digging stick among the Hanunóo, for example, reveal the complexity of
the mundane (Kammen and Dove 1997). Conklin was committed to an exacting
representation of this everyday reality through close-grained, textual descriptions.
An example is his six-page description of rice-planting in *Hanunóo Agriculture*
(1957:92–97), which was unheard-of detail in the 1950s. It set a standard of "thick
description" for environmental anthropology like that later set for cultural anthropology by Geertz (1973).

Conklin's study of the particulars of everyday life among the Hanunóo and Ifugao
was subtly but profoundly political: only people that "matter" get six pages devoted
to their planting technology. Such description is a political statement not only about

the value of indigenous knowledge but more broadly about the relationship between the societies of the observer and the observed. As Rosaldo (1993:186) writes, his work could be interpreted as an effort "to give voice to the voiceless." Conklin amplified this voice by employing the language and conceptual paradigms of his audience in the policy and development community. As Rosaldo writes (1993:185), "Conklin has chosen a rhetoric designed to persuade an audience of ethnographers, botanists, and agronomists, who conceivably could in turn convince policy makers." One of the lessons of Conklin's work is that representation of agriculture is not a neutral matter but is itself a zone of contestation.

Conklin's essay is one of only a handful of critiques of popular conceptions of swidden agriculture published over the past 60 years. It begins with a list of ten of "the most frequent and problematic assumptions" regarding swidden agriculture, which is followed by a detailed analysis of seven separate, named stages of the Hanunóo swidden cycle. Conklin concludes the essay by "tentatively rephrasing" the ten assumptions in question. Based on field evidence as opposed to popular perceptions, he says, calculations of productivity are more complicated, the boundary between cultivated and fallow periods is more complex, there is more regional variation, and the system is less environmentally destructive than we had supposed. The overall impact of his analysis is to reverse the terms of the debate by suggesting that the problem is not the swidden cultivators' lack of knowledge of the environment but rather our lack of knowledge of the swidden cultivators. Much of Conklin's work concerned indigenous, non-Western knowledge of the environment and its exploitation. Indeed, a published glossary of Hanunóo lists *Conklin* as a word for "things having to do with knowledge" (McDermott 1997).

Carneiro's essay addresses the implications of swidden ecology for social organization, specifically whether or not environmental factors cause swidden peoples to be mobile. Mobility has long been central to popular images of swidden peoples. Up until the past generation, the glossing of swidden cultivators as "nomadic" in scientific as well as popular writings was common; and even today, the standard colloquial term for swidden cultivation in Indonesia is *peladang berpindah-pindah* (moving swiddeners). Popular misbelief in the mobility of swidden peoples derives from the fundamental fact that, as Carneiro writes, swidden cultivation exhausts land at a faster rate than it can recover. As a result, at any given time the amount of land recovering under fallow must be many times as great as that under cultivation. This obviously necessitates the rotation of fields and movement of individuals, but does it also necessitate the rotation or movement of settlements?

Carneiro's own data on the Kuikuru, a manioc swidden-making group of the Upper Xingú region of central Brazil, showed that whereas the group had moved four times in the previous 90 years, all moves involved only a relocation of a few hundred yards. The combination of relatively frequent local moves with long-term commitment to a fixed territory seems to be not atypical of swidden cultivators;[63] and the erroneous assumption that moves are between as opposed to within territories is probably integral to the popular misunderstanding of the mobility of swidden societies. Based on his study of the Kuikuru, Carneiro concludes that swidden cultivation of manioc in the South American tropical forest can support up to 500 persons in a nucleated settlement on a long-term, sustainable basis; so the resettlement of any swidden community smaller than 500 persons cannot be attributed to environmental degradation. Citing Steward's (1949) findings that most native communities in South America range in size from just 50 to 150 people, Carneiro further concludes that most movement of swidden communities in the region must be due not to environmental degradation but to other causes. His overall conclusion is that permanent settlement *is* environmentally compatible with swidden cultivation.

Natural science models of resource-use: From Rappaport's cybernetics to the optimal foraging of Hawkes, Hill, and O'Connell

Durkheim (1964) drew from natural science organic metaphors for his analysis of the division of labor in human society, and Radcliffe-Brown (1952:12) borrowed from biology the metaphor of organic structure to illustrate his concept of "social function." Conklin (1954) and Berlin et al. (1974) borrowed the tools of linguistics and systematic botany to develop the subdiscipline of ethnoscience.[64] Two of the most influential borrowings of natural science models by anthropologists within the past generation are Roy A. Rappaport's study of ritually regulated ecosystems in Highland New Guinea and the study of optimal foraging strategies among global hunter-gatherer groups by Hawkes, Hill, and O'Connell.

Rappaport (1926–97) studied anthropology with Andrew P. Vayda at Columbia University and spent his academic career at the University of Michigan with joint appointments in the Anthropology Department and the Divinity School. His principal works on ritual and ecology are *Pigs for the Ancestors: Ritual in the Ecology of a New Guinea People* (1968, revised in 1984), *Ecology, Meaning, and Religion* (1979), and the posthumously published *Ritual and Religion in the Making of Humanity* (1999). The essay (1967) reprinted here is a synopsis of *Pigs for the Ancestors*, which is one of the most influential volumes in the history of environmental anthropology.

Kristen Hawkes (1944–) and James F. O'Connell (1943–) teach at the University of Utah, and Kim Hill (1953–) teaches at the University of New Mexico. When they wrote the essay reprinted here, Hill was doing her doctorate at the University of Utah. Hawkes and O'Connell trained at the University of Washington and the University of California at Berkeley, respectively. Together they are among the pioneers in the application of optimal foraging theory in anthropology. They have published extensively on this theory, some of the most notable examples of which include Hawkes (1993), Hawkes and O'Connell (1985, 1992), Hill (1988), Hill and Hawkes (1982), Hill et al. (1984), and O'Connell and Hawkes (1981, 1984).

Rappaport

When Rappaport arrived in 1962 among the Tsembaga, a group of 200 Maring-speaking tribesmen in the Bismarck Mountains in central Papua New Guinea, they had experienced limited externally-driven change, except for the introduction of steel tools and pacification (between 1958 and 1962) by the then-Australian authorities (Rappaport 1984:12,411). During the 14 months that he lived with the Tsembaga, much of their daily life revolved around the post-warfare *kaiko* ritual cycle (Rappaport 1984:397). Rappaport (1967:17) took as the point of departure for his analysis Homans' (1941:172) statement: "Ritual actions do not produce a practical result on the external world – that is one of the reasons we call them ritual." Rappaport counters that ritual should not be assumed a priori to be "mere epiphenomena" (263), and he argued that among the Tsembaga, ritual is "neither more nor less than part of the behavioral repertoire employed by an aggregate of organisms in adjusting to its environment" (255).

Rappaport believed that in order to develop a new perspective on ritual, he needed to widen the scope of his analysis beyond humans, and to do this he needed to borrow concepts and theories from the natural sciences. Rappaport drew from authors like Margalef (1968) (and also Bateson [1936])[65] concepts of cybernetics, feedback loops, and circuits. His use of this language was novel and powerful, for example, he suggested that ritual "resembles digital computing machines" (1979:186) and may function as "homeostats and transducers" (263). He also drew heavily on nutrition science. The first edition of *Pigs for the Ancestors* contained 56 pages of quantitative appendices, seven pages of which focused on Tsembaga nutrition.[66] To help interpret Tsembaga feasting (261), he borrowed from ecology such concepts as that of "epideictic display," which communicates conflict-relevant information on population size, and "epigamic display," which communicates information on the relative merits of eligible marriage partners (Wynne-Edwards 1962). Rappaport (1994:167) observed in later years that "I had intended to study a local group of tribal horticulturalists in the same terms that animal ecologists study populations in ecosystems." To address the resulting problem of hermeneutics – how can scientific interpretations of human behavior be reconciled with their subjects' own interpretations? – Rappaport distinguished between the "cognized environment" of the Tsembaga and the "operational environment" of anthropological observation and measurement (258).

Rappaport's effort to study a human population in the same way that animal populations are studied was hailed as an innovative assault on artificial boundaries between nature and culture (Wilson 1969:659), but it also was criticized for unrealistic premises regarding the culture, history, and political dimensions of human as opposed to animal populations. His use of cybernetic language to interpret the role that Tsembaga ritual plays in regulating key environmental variables was applauded as a creative bridging of materialistic and symbolic analyses, but it was also critiqued as vulgar materialism, naive functionalism, and "the use of fashionable metaphors from electronics" (Watson 1969:529). Rappaport's effort to document the regulatory role of ritual with detailed data on Tsembaga nutrition was praised for its rigor and boldness but also attacked as being error-ridden, "nutritional reductionism" (Rappaport 1984:369–370).

Some of Rappaport's critics took issue with the very idea of interdisciplinary borrowing. Thus, Sahlins (1976:298) accuses Rappaport of "a kind of 'ecology fetishism'"; Bennett (1976:181) says that in *Pigs for the Ancestors* "ecosystemic complexities and a generalized impression of ecological causation are plausibly suggested but never worked out in detail"; and others interpreted Rappaport's conversion of data into calories and proteins as "an attempt to dress up ethnography as hard science" (Rappaport 1984:370). Rappaport (1979:82) characterizes one critique (by Bergmann 1975) as an injunction to "quit whoring after the strange gods of physics." In fact, in the 1960s the biological sciences were in the ascendancy over the social sciences, and borrowing their concepts and language made it more likely that Rappaport's arguments would be accorded greater weight by other scientists and policy makers (Dove 2006).[67] In later years Rappaport (1994:164) was candid about the risks as well as the benefits of interdisciplinary borrowing. In the face of great suspicion of such borrowing, Rappaport modestly suggests that cybernetic models are "illustrative," that his emphasis on equilibrium had "heuristic" value, and that "biological and ecological considerations were emphasized largely because they were relatively novel and social considerations were not" (1984:viii,359,393).

Rappaport identified the "ecology movement" as one of the early influences on his research (1984:402–403), ultimately leading to a career-spanning concern with the impact of Western industrialized society on the environment, which he characterized as "inappropriate, infelicitous, and maladaptive" (1979:140). Rappaport carried out his initial field research on the Tsembaga in 1962–63, which was a time of triumphant modernism (Scott 1998). One of the most important facets of this modernism was a development discourse (Escobar 1995) that problematized the rationality of indigenous societies such as the Tsembaga. Rappaport's study of the Tsembaga argued for the rationality of what appeared to be the least rational aspect of indigenous systems (viz., the ritual expenditure of resources). It focused on the self-regulating character of indigenous systems, which implicitly undercut the modern argument for external intervention. It documented the great complexity of such systems, which was not to be fathomed without lengthy study, local residence, and reliance on local knowledge. Of most importance, it effectively used key metaphors of high modernity (including cybernetic feedback cycles) to argue for the rationality of indigenous systems and against the need for an external developmental rationality.

Rappaport (1984) suggests that the "ecological felicity" of tribal society could inform the "ecological destructiveness" of Western industrialized society. Rappaport was one of the first anthropologists to argue for the "repatriation" of anthropology (Marcus and Fischer 1986:135,137) and to offer to modern industrialized society what he called a "theory of correction" (1979:170; 1984:430–431). Rappaport's own acts of repatriation consisted of extensive studies of the hazards of offshore oil drilling and nuclear waste disposal in the U.S. He called engagement with such topics the "anthropology of trouble."[68]

Hawkes, Hill, and O'Connell

The application of optimal foraging theory in anthropology builds on earlier intellectual traditions, most obviously that of game theory (Barth 1959, Hardin 1968), whose own roots are traced back to Rousseau's discussion of the benefits of group hunting of stags versus individual hunting of hares (Alvard and Nolin 2002:537). Critics of game theory challenge its conclusions of non-cooperation with widespread evidence of voluntary coordination and cooperation in the real world (Yao et al. 1997; Alvard and Nolin 2002). Another relevant tradition of study attempts to explain the evolution of society in terms of particular "limiting" resources, such as carbohydrates, calories, or protein. Thus, a number of scholars developed the thesis that hunting and gathering was more difficult than had been thought to be the case, that it did a poor job of providing protein (especially in tropical rain forests), which was therefore a scarce resource, and that variation in protein resources was a primary determinant of variation in society (Meggers 1971). Thus, Gross (1975:538–539) argued that as protein varies in availability across the Amazon, so too does the size, form, and permanence of human settlements, as well as their social complexity and warfare patterns. Rappaport's analysis of the role of Tsembaga ritual in managing scarce protein supplies is obviously another contribution to this literature. Other scholars disagreed with the protein scarcity thesis, however, including Hawkes, Hill, and O'Connell,[69] who argue that hunting in rain forests is easy and protein supplies are abundant (cf. Beckerman 1979; Hill and Hawkes 1982).

Some scholars asked, if protein is indeed scarce, whether wild yams and other tubers constituted a sufficiently robust source of wild carbohydrates to support human subsistence in the tropical rain forest. This became known as the "wild yam thesis." Headland and Bailey (1991) argued that yams were not sufficiently abundant in the tropical rain forest, that starch was therefore a "limiting factor," and that forest-bound hunter-gatherers would need ongoing relations with farmers outside the forest or use of habitats made more productive by farming activity to obtain starch, which was reflected in the lack of evidence of "pure" hunting-gathering in tropical rain forests.[70] Headland and Bailey (1991:119–120) conclude their critique of the "wild yam thesis" by saying that extant hunter-gatherers are not remnants of Pleistocene forest populations who have just emerged from isolation into the modern world system. Some scholars (Roosevelt 1998; Wilmsen 1989) further argue that hunting-gathering is in fact a recent development and a product (not casualty) of this world system (but see Solway and Lee in the next section in this volume).[71] On the other hand, some argue that foraged plants can sustain human subsistence (Lee 1968:43). McKey (1996) says that it is difficult to test whether the tropical rain forest can sustain human subsistence, but there is no proof that it is impossible, and there is historic evidence of hunter-gatherer groups living apparently autonomous lives within it.

Optimal foraging theory itself was developed in behavioral and evolutionary ecology between the mid-1960s and mid-1980s as a tool for analyzing the subsistence behavior of animals (Schoener 1971; Sih 1980). Its central postulate is that natural selection favors efficient foraging strategies (Hawkes, Hill, and O'Connell 266), meaning strategies that maximize net energy capture (Smith and Winterhalder 1985:646; Winterhalder 1981:13), and so foraging strategies should tend to maximize biological fitness (Sih and Milton 1985:396). Hawkes, Hill, and O'Connell (265–266) trace an interest in hunter-gatherer resources back to Steward (see "Early Essays on Social Organization and Ecology" in this Introduction). Early explications of the theory and its virtues for anthropology include Winterhalder (1981), Smith and Winterhalder (1985), and Hawkes and O'Connell (1985); influential collections include Winterhalder and Smith (1981), and Hames and Vickers (1982); and reviews include Smith (1983) and Martin (1983). Optimal foraging theory actually encompasses a number of different models, variously addressing diet breadth, use of heterogeneous habitat, movement in heterogeneous habitat, and group size and settlement pattern (Winterhalder 1981:13). Examples of diet breadth analysis, which is based on the work of the population biologist Schoener (1974), include Beckerman (1982), Hill and Hawkes (1982), and Hawkes and O'Connell (1992).

In their essay, Hawkes, Hill, and O'Connell use an optimal diet model to explain behavior in uniform environments and a patch choice model to explain foraging given non-random resource distributions.

The aim of optimal foraging theory is to explain resource-related decision making in terms of a fitness cost/benefit calculus. For example, anthropologists may use this calculus to explain why hunter-gatherers take the set of resources that they do from the array that is available to them (e.g., why Aché hunters break off from hunting to gather oranges, honey, and insect larvae but not palms or fish). Optimal foraging theory applies a fine-grained cost/benefit analysis to these sorts of choices, which may include attention to formerly overlooked dimensions of subsistence like food-processing costs (Hawkes and O'Connell 1985:403). Analysis of subsistence choices is theoretically important, in part, because of what it is thought to tell us about the evolution of human society (Hawkes and O'Connell 1992). Thus, Hawkes, Hill, and O'Connell argue that their analyses of contemporary huntergatherers can explain late Paleolithic diet changes related to agricultural development.

Optimal foraging theorists argue that this body of theory produces simple and generalizable models of reality (Smith and Winterhalder 1985:647; Winterhalder 1981:13), which can produce testable hypotheses (Hawkes and O'Connell 1985:401; Smith and Winterhalder 1985:645), which may yield counter-intuitive insights (Winterhalder 1981:13), such as Hawkes, Hill, and O'Connell's finding that some of the most commonly exploited foods may have low fitness rankings. Whereas optimal foraging theorists in anthropology see simplification as one of the strengths of their work, many critics see it as a weakness. For example, Sih and Milton (1985) fault a study by Hawkes and O'Connell (1981) for carrying out a cost/benefit analysis of !Kung foraging based on the simple metric of calories, as opposed to a more complex metric of nutritive value. In response to this criticism, Hawkes, Hill, and O'Connell (280 n. 3) argue for keeping the number of variables under study to a minimum, and they say that incorporation of too many complicating factors produces confusion, not clarification (cf. Alvard and Nolin 2002:554–555; Hawkes and O'Connell 1985:401,402).

Surprisingly little discussed or critiqued is the theory's reliance on quantitative measures of observed behavior as opposed to qualitative data obtained from interviews. Unlike Rappaport's work, there is no "cognized" model in most optimal foraging theory. Ingold (1996b) interprets this failing as the result of an opposition between economic man driven by thought and optimal forager driven by natural selection, the reproduction of a post-Enlightenment divide between nature and reason. Hawkes, Hill, and O'Connell, for example, present an extended discussion as to why Aché stop hunting for one plant resource to pursue and exploit some other resource, but they do not illuminate it with explanations elicited from the Aché themselves.[72] Beckerman (1982:299) writes: "It is in this ability to ask our subjects what they are doing, if nowhere else, that human ecologists have the advantage of our biological colleagues."

In his 1981 review of optimal foraging theory, Winterhalder (1981:14) urged that its use be predicated upon: (1) identification of the assumptions that lie behind application of evolutionary ecology to anthropological subjects; (2) clear statement of the analytic decisions faced by an anthropologist using this theory; (3) isolation of points where, despite the semi-deductive nature of the approach, significant data are required to apply it; (4) identification of models and hypotheses that are particularly appropriate in human ecology investigation; and (5) some indication of the analytic shortcomings and promise of these models. In practice, there has been (for example) relatively little discussion of the equation of energy efficiency with biological fitness or its measurement in terms of calorie/hour ratios. There has been even less discussion of how natural selection works in populations of hunter-gatherers. On the other hand, as Sih and Milton (1985:399) note, optimal foraging theory has shown the importance of quantifying time budgets of hunter-gatherers (and illuminated the contributions that hunting versus gathering makes to the overall diet, for example; and see the section on Lee in "The bounded and balanced community" in this Introduction), and it has shown how to generate testable hypotheses for situations where energy is scarce (Winterhalder and Goland 1993:711).[73]

Natural science models today

When indigenous peoples were perceived as a threat to the environment, Rappaport's use of an equilibrium model to rationalize their behavior was empowering for them. But after equilibrium models fell into disrepute, it became more empowering to portray indigenous peoples as having something to tell modern industrialized societies about *dis*-equilibrium. Today, environmentalists are borrowing anthropological work on indigenous environmental knowledge to use in their critiques of modern, industrial systems of resource-use. And environmental anthropology borrows some of its most powerful theory today not from the natural sciences but from such sources as neo-Marxist political ecology and the postmodern humanities, which coincides with a shift in the ethnographic object from agriculture to supra-household, supra-community, and even supra-national subjects like protected areas, and environmental movements and institutions. Some of the scholarly attention that was formerly devoted to optimal foraging studies of hunting is today spent on studies of the impact of indigenous hunting on protected areas.

The bounded and balanced community: Solway and Lee, and Netting

The two articles in this section represent re-examinations by the authors of their own previous work, in light of paradigm shifts in anthropological theory. This allows us to explore and question two related sets of ideas important in the history of anthropology in general but particularly close to environmental anthropology: ideas about isolated, time-bound, primitive hunter-gatherers (or foragers[74]), and ideas about self-sufficient, traditional farming communities. Both sets of ideas are closely related, and ecology plays a role in both. First, anthropologists studying foragers, like Richard B. Lee, tended to focus on their adaptation to their environments, rather than on their relations to neighboring peoples or colonial states, for example (in the section "Indigeneity and natural resource politics" in this Introduction, we explore similar claims made for political reasons). Second, environmental anthropologists like Robert McC. Netting (and Roy Rappaport), especially in the 1960s and 1970s, adopted the concept of an ecosystem from biology as a way to think about the integration of nature and culture. However, especially when applied to a traditional community, the idea of an ecosystem reinforced anthropology's "holistic" habit, strengthening notions of boundedness and balance or harmony.

The idea of community

The idea of community underlies both Lee's and Netting's early work. In the history of anthropology this idea is more a methodology than a theory, a methodology for carrying out long-term research on a single community that was viewed as a microcosm of a culture. Sometimes called the "holistic" perspective, this tradition in anthropology discerned social wholes, viewed as structurally logical (structuralism) or as interdependent and functionally integrated like an organism (and adapted to their environment; functionalism).[75] Such studies tended to treat communities as though they were bounded and isolated. This approach often emphasized stability, equilibrium, and balance.

The community in anthropology was paralleled by the ecosystem in biological ecology and the study of forests; in fact the term *community* was used in biology and silviculture just as the term *ecosystem* came to be used in anthropology. The ecosystem approach viewed forests, for example, as communities of plants and animals interacting in a systemic, patterned way, as an interdependent whole, growing towards a stable "climax" condition.[76]

In the history of anthropology, the study of communities or ecosystems as integrated systems gave way to the study of competition, class, hierarchy, and power; assumptions of equilibrium and stability gave way to the study of change.[77] Studies began to focus on links between communities and the outside world, and on the wider political and economic structures in which communities were embedded. In biology and silviculture the paradigm also shifted to an emphasis on the dynamics of competition and perturbation, and this was generally accepted by 1990.[78] In anthropology, belief in the sustainability of traditional livelihoods remains (though this also has been questioned[79]), but the emphasis in the field has shifted to how people think about and actually shape nature (see Fairhead and Leach in this volume). The anthropology of community has now turned to questions of how community is symbolically created (e.g., Appadurai 1996; and see Frake in this volume).

This idea of community (but certainly not the method of long-term community research) was adopted by development and conservation organizations and NGOs (non-governmental organizations). There is now a literature by anthropologists critiquing the idea of community as used in development and conservation (see for example Brosius et al. 1998 and 2005, Li 1996, and Agrawal and Gibson 2001). The links between this idea and the public image of anthropologists is strong, leading to the misperception that contemporary anthropologists limit their research and theorizing to the community level.

The following characteristics are often associated with forager cultures and agrarian villages, both in the history of anthropology and in more recent development and conservation practice.[80]

1. The community is treated as though it were spatially bounded or isolated.
2. The community is treated ahistorically; that is, drawing spatial boundaries around a social unit also stops time.[81] The bounded social unit may be seen as prehistoric or Paleolithic, frozen in the past, representing the origins of mankind, as with the concept of the hunter-gatherer. This idea is associated with the idea of evolution, evident in Steward and also in Lee (e.g., 1968). It may also be seen as traditional.

3. The community is treated as though it were in a static, stable state of equilibrium or balance, which is evident in the concept of ecosystem. We will return to this below (see also the section " 'Natural' disasters and social order" earlier in this Introduction).

4. The community is viewed as natural, living in nature, being in harmony with nature, being naturally sustainable, often in counterpoint to modernity. This idea is clearly related to the use of indigeneity to strengthen land claims (see the section "Indigeneity and natural resource politics" in this Introduction). It is also associated with the idea of adaptation. In an important sense the concept of adaptation is opposed to change and history; adaptation of culture to nature "changes" in only one direction, towards stasis; and once it reaches stasis it will not change again, like a climax forest, unless disturbed by outside forces.

5. Such communities or social units may be viewed as being pre-economic or pre-capitalist, having for example communal ownership rather than private property, subsistence economies rather than any orientation to profit.[82]

6. Such communities may be viewed as pre-political, as having social relations characterized by equality or consensus rather than class, hierarchy, or power. These ideas are related to Durkheim's (1933) mechanical solidarity.[83]

7. Other characteristics associated with these ideas include: mobility, as with foragers, herders, or swidden farmers; and having simple technology (and thus limited control over nature).

8. Finally, these communities are seen as not changing, or not changing from within, though often being vulnerable to penetration by outsiders (including anthropologists) and by capitalism.

The idea of stasis underlying this set of ideas is easy to critique in retrospect, but it allowed anthropologists to think about the systemic nature of relations in communities and between communities and local environments. These two readings represent efforts to increase the historical depth and spatial scale of the anthropology of community.

Foragers

Anthropologists studying hunter-gatherers, since Steward, have tended to focus on their adaptation to their environment, rather than on their relations to neighboring peoples or the fact that they were embedded in markets or states. The bulk of Richard B. Lee's work on the !Kung followed this tradition; indeed his research on foragers was path-breaking in its time and remains, as it should, widely respected. Lee's detailed, long-term research (in the community tradition) exploded several myths about hunter-gatherers. His research showed that gathering is far more important to !Kung diets than hunting, that women's work thus mattered more than men's, and that the foraging life was secure rather than "nasty, brutish and short" (Solway 2003).[84]

The article by Jacqueline Solway[85] and Richard B. Lee[86] reprinted here was part of what is now known as the "Kalahari debate." It was written in response to "revisionists," and particularly to "the most outspoken critic" (286), Edwin N. Wilmsen.[87] As the article begins, "One of the dominant themes of critical anthropology in the 1970s and 1980s has been the critique of ethnographic models that depict societies as isolated and timeless" (284). Solway and Lee then present two case studies, demonstrating that although some !Kung (now more generally included among the people called San) were dependent on non-San, others were, if not "isolated and timeless," at least "substantially autonomous" (284) and actively resisting incorporation into world capitalism. Solway and Lee's idea that foragers can be "engaged" with capitalism without being "incorporated" into it, and that the level of engagement and incorporation varies between groups and through time, seems to us valuable and important, and we will return to it at the end of this section.

The factors that Solway and Lee find most critical in determining San ability to resist incorporation are ecological. They trace the effects of pre-colonial tribute systems, colonialism, and capitalism on the environment and thus on the San. In the case of the western Kweneng San, the pre-colonial extraction of furs from the Kalahari (traded to Kgalagadi for tobacco, and going to the Kwena who traded them for guns) did not critically disrupt the Kalahari or enserf the San. Kgalagadi settlement and agro-pastoralism in the colonial period, on the other hand, increased desertification in the Kalahari, and began to undermine the San's "foraging base," while leaving drier "bush" as a "hedge" for some San "against complete subordination" (290). In the 1940s and 1950s the Kgalagadi intensified their involvement in capitalism, first increasing the intensity of agro-pastoralism with plows and new well-digging technology, then taking up work in South African mines. San increasingly lost access to water, and eventually became the casual labor force for the mining Kgalagadi. The Dobe San were more isolated and retained their foraging environment much longer. No Kgalagadi-like group existed in Dobe until the 1920s and 1930s, when the Herero settled, and even then the Herero engaged in subsistence not market-oriented pastoralism (because the markets were distant and thus the prices for cattle were low). In the 1960s 70 percent of the Dobe !Kung continued to live largely by foraging (mixed with *mafisa* herding, which Solway and Lee argue combined with foraging without destroying it). "By 1970, however, four decades of intensive and expanding pastoralism had begun to take their toll on the capacity of the environment to support hunting and gathering" (295). The result was that "the !Kung became dependent largely as a consequence of the inability of their land to support a foraging mode of production" (295):

> In both cases the complete incorporation, as dependents, of the San into the agro-pastoral system was delayed as long as the bush held the possibility of an alternative livelihood ... In the last analysis ... a critical factor in moving the San into a position of dependency has been environmental degradation, which has, like an unintended scorched-earth policy, deprived them of an alternative means of livelihood. (297)

Peasants

Robert McC. Netting[88] begins the 1990 article selected for this volume by critiquing his own earlier work, his study of a Swiss mountain village published in 1981. "I may well have been guilty of the ecosystemic fallacy," he says:

> This common anthropological error involves an overemphasis on functional integration, stability, and regulatory mechanisms within the community and a relative neglect of disequilibrium, changes emanating from more inclusive political-economic systems,

and instances of evolutionary maladaptation... The nature of long-term resident field research, our anthropological reverence for a holistic perspective, and the romantic mystique of the self-sufficient, autonomous, emotionally rewarding "little community" all perpetuate our proclivity to learn a lot about a very limited group. (309)

The ecosystem of Törbel, he writes, seemed to epitomize: "a well articulated, self-sustaining interdependence of physical environment, subsistence techniques, and human population" (311). In fact he selected the village for its long history, since the 14th century, of self-sufficiency and sustainability.

Netting makes the additional interesting point that both he and his Törbel friends overemphasized stability: "It seems to me now that I was led down the garden path of the independent population subsisting on its own resources in a clearly defined geographical area by the extraordinary definite and enduring congruence between the Swiss folk model of the community and the historic realities of peasant village economy in the Alps" (310). There was also, of course, an extraordinary congruence between the concept of community in anthropology and the Swiss folk model. The result of this congruence was to conceal or downplay flows across village boundaries.

Netting in this article reviews these concealed flows across the boundaries of Törbel, identifying: (1) older flows on an ancient trail, including imported metals, salt, cash, wives; and exported cattle, labor (drivers, mule skinners, guards, soldiers, farm laborers, artisans, clerics), and (2) modern flows on a road with regular bus service, including imported cash, manufactured goods, new crops (potato), foods (maize meal, wheat bread); and exported cash (taxes) and labor (miners, craftsmen, waitresses, hotel workers, construction workers, outmigrants colonizing the Argentine interior).

However, Netting sees these flows as functioning to sustain and balance the local ecosystem. He writes: "I became aware of the often concealed interdependencies that sustained the system at its points of weakness and rectified its dangerous imbalances ... [The] local community ecosystem survived by means of significant economic and demographic flows back and forth across its boundaries" (310). Exported labor, for example, functions as a "safety valve" for local ecosystems, siphoning off population over carrying capacity (313); "without these surges and trickles of energy in both directions," he says, "the local system could never have survived" (316). Netting has not actually given up the ecosystem approach, but rather enlarged the scale at which it is integrated. The ecosystem approach, even as critiqued and qualified by Netting, still focuses on a system that reproduces itself in time, that is, that does not change; things that cross boundaries are also viewed in these terms, or in other words, boundaries though permeable are permanent, and things that cross them contribute to the integration of the system rather than disrupting it.

We might also point out that Netting's understanding of Törbel's dependence on the world system goes in only one direction: the local ecosystem depends on the world system, but the world system doesn't depend on its margins. He writes, "Though the typical farming village was something of a commercial *cul de sac*, its continued existence on the alpine margins has always required active exchange with the capitalist European centers of the world system" (311). Exported labor, for example, is not viewed as contributing to the world system's labor force, or keeping down the cost of wages for capitalist firms. Netting's view of the role of smallholders in the world is more positively stated in his 1993 book, *Smallholders, Householders*: "Reports of the death of the smallholder in a modern high-tech, large-scale world have proved to be vastly exaggerated. Indeed, scarcity of rural resources and national demands for food production create just those circumstances in which agriculture intensifies and the household organization of production demonstrates its comparative advantage" (Netting 1993:26–27). In this book the economic efficiency and environmental sustainability of small farmers is lauded as essential to the modern world.

It is interesting to draw a parallel between the ecosystem insistence on internal integration and Solway and Lee's insistence that at least some foragers retained "autonomy" long after they began interacting with outsiders. Both ideas of integration and autonomy in the face of involvement with capitalism are contradicted by much political economy, which tends to see "penetration" by capitalism inevitably disrupting traditional integration and autonomy and bringing "incorporation" into the world capitalist system.[89] But Solway and Lee's article and Netting's *Smallholders, Householders* suggest what we think is a way out of this contradiction: penetration by and incorporation into capitalism are variable and perhaps always partial, disturbing some traditional systems profoundly but leaving others relatively unchanged. There is increasing research on the ability of peasants[90] and swidden farmers[91] to market cash crops without giving up subsistence production (though whether this serves farmers' interests or those of capitalism is still in question). Future environmental anthropologists could have an important role to play in understanding the real nature of incorporation and autonomy, since the environment clearly plays an important role. As Solway and Lee argue, it is the effects of capitalism (marketoriented agro-pastoralism) on the environment of the Kalahari that have gradually made San foraging an untenable livelihood.

The Politics of Natural Resources and the Environment

Indigeneity and natural resource politics: Ellen and Li

The politics of indigeneity and natural resources have become intertwined, as shown by the influential papers on this topic by Roy F. Ellen and Tania M. Li, who are furthermore both Indonesianists. Ellen's (1999) paper is a historical analysis of interlinked changes in resource management, conceptions of nature, and relations with the wider world among the Nuaulu of Seram in the Moluccas in Eastern Indonesia. Li's (2000) paper is an analysis of how and why self-representation as indigenous resource managers developed among one group in Central Sulawesi, the lake-dwelling Lindu, and not another, the interior Lauje. The Nuaulu faced the challenge of logging, migrant settlements, and a critical state; the Lindu faced the challenge of their own resettlement to make way for a hydro-electric project. Both Ellen and Li are asking how and why self-conscious articulation of indigenous environmentalism does or does not develop. Ellen (1947–), who teaches at the University of Kent in Canterbury, trained at the University of London. He has published and edited widely on environmental anthropology, ethnoscience/classification, and indigenous knowledge (e.g., 1978, 1982, Ellen, Parkes, and Bicker 2000). Li (1959–) trained at Cambridge University and now teaches and holds a Century Research Chair at the University of Toronto. She has published a series of articles on concepts of indigeneity, community, ethnicity, and identity (e.g., 1996, 2000, 2001, 2002), as well as a collection on upland Indonesia.

In the past 15–20 years, anthropological interest in local, native, autochthonous peoples has come to be framed in terms of "indigeneity." Subjects who would formerly have been represented as "peasants or tribesmen" are often now represented as "indigenous peoples." Many local movements that once would have been represented as revolving around race, ethnicity, or religion, have come to be seen, by the participants as well as by analysts, as "indigenous rights movements" (Hodgson 2002). The increasing global awareness of the importance of indigeneity (Béteille 1998) is reflected in the development of official definitions by the United Nations in 1986 and the International Labor Organization in 1989, which emphasize historic continuity, distinctiveness, marginalization, self-identity, and self-governance. When anthropologists have examined how the concept of indigeneity is actually deployed by groups in real-world settings, they have come up with a similar list of characteristics. Li reports that the Lindu (and the NGOs who supported them) articulated their indigeneity in terms of language, political–economic autonomy, unique culture, capacity for environmental management, and spiritual attachment to their local landscape.[92]

The debate over indigeneity

At the very time that the concept of indigeneity was being popularized beyond anthropology, it began to be critiqued within the discipline, as the result of world system studies that showed that even apparently isolated communities have been caught up in global historical processes; an anti-essentialist turn, that questioned drawing sharp lines of discrimination like that between indigenous and non-indigenous; and a rise in interest in hybridity, which is the antithesis of indigeneity. Along with many governments and state elites, some scholars simply dispute the empirical validity of the indigenous "slot" (e.g., Trevor-Roper 1983; Kuper 2003). Others question the validity of the idea of "indigenous knowledge" (Agrawal 1995; Ellen and Harris 2000; Dove 2000). There also is an ongoing debate as to whether indigenous resource management can conserve the environment (Krech 1999; Redford and Sanderson 2000; Schwartzman et al. 2000).

Of most relevance to this book is the debate regarding the politics of the indigenous slot. Li begins her essay by highlighting its political perils as well as benefits. Aspirations for and articulations of indigenous identity that appear to be "inauthentic" and "opportunistic" may elicit official sanction (340). The indigenous slot is also a narrow target, which is easily over- or under-shot. Thus, Li writes (353) that if people present themselves as "too primitive," they risk resettlement; whereas if they present themselves as not primitive enough, they also risk resettlement.[93] Once indigenous status has been attained, official expectations of appropriate behavior can be exacting, as Li writes (353): "Candidates for the tribal slot who are found deficient according to the environmental standards expected of them must also beware." The greatest risk of all, however, may be incurred by those who cannot claim indigenous status. Li writes (340): "One of the risks that stems from the attention given to indigenous people is that some sites and situations in the countryside are privileged while others are overlooked, thus unnecessarily limiting the field within which coalitions could be formed and local agendas identified and supported" (cf. Gupta 1998).

Much of the initial questioning of the idea of indigeneity came from the work of Wolf (1982) and his followers on "world systems." Ellen begins his analysis by noting that the Nuaulu, notwithstanding their apparent marginality, have a long history of interaction with the wider world. Historical records do not support the concept of indigeneity as something out-of-history; indeed they suggest the counter-intuitive opposite, namely that indigeneity is a product of history. A corollary point is that indigeneity is a product of political processes. Ellen suggests that a long history of interaction with outsiders, culminating in Dutch governance, made the Nuaulu sensitive to their cultural identity vis-à-vis that of others. Li (344) writes that unlike the "*National Geographic* vision" of tribal peoples, in Indonesia there is a political nature to group formation. Where clear tribal identities are found today, she says, they can be traced to histories of confrontation and engagement (cf. Benjamin 2002). Among the contemporary Lindu, for example, a history of having to contest natural resource rights with outsiders provided the stimulus to articulate their ethnic identity and resource rights. In the contrasting case of the Lauje, Li (356) says, their historic engagement only with "more diffuse forms of power" has resulted in a less clear development of their collective identity.[94]

In a controversial article, Kuper (2003:395) argued that the idea of indigeneity was constructed to serve various global political movements, and so it should be abjured by scholars. He writes: "Should we ignore history for fear of undermining myths of autochthony? Even if we could weigh up the costs and benefits of saying this or that, our business should be to deliver accurate accounts of social processes" (Kuper 2003:400). Critics argue that Kuper ignores the historic as well as contemporary political inequities that are driving much of the current articulation of indigeneity. Robbins, in one of the commentaries published with Kuper's article, argues that deconstructing essentialist ideologies should be only the first step of anthropological practice, not the end goal. As Hodgson (2002:1040,1044) has written, instead of engaging in debates over the definition, construction, and authenticity of indigeneity, we should instead ask how and why indigenous groups are deploying the concept. The papers by Ellen and Li are pioneering contributions to this effort to understand how some groups come to be able to make indigenous claims, when most cannot.

Nature and culture

One of Ellen's principal accomplishments in the essay reprinted here is his historicization of the Nuaulu concepts of nature and culture. He describes how the widening of political and ecological horizons has caused an older, local, embedded form of environmental knowledge to give way to a qualitatively different body of knowledge of higher order environmental processes. The former embodied a small-scale concept of a nature with infinite resources; whereas the latter embodies a vision of a global ecology of finite goods. The old versus new visions of nature do not map in any simple way onto popular notions of good versus bad environmental stewardship, however. The character of any environmental history depends on where it begins, and Ellen (325) begins not with tribal harmony, as might be expected, but with tribal endorsement of "forest destruction . . . by themselves and by others, for short-term gain." Ellen sets himself the task of explaining how an indigenous people could come to endorse environmental destruction like this, and how they subsequently underwent a further transformation to become the self-conscious environmentalists that they are today. The Nuaulu letter to Ellen (333–334) shows that they initially saw logging roads as useful avenues that they could travel along; but when roads were abandoned (after areas were logged out) and subsequently succeeded to thick brush, they became noxious barriers that they had to detour around. Based on their traditional ecological logic, the Nuaulu saw many benefits in logging and land settlement; but when this logic eventually failed, Ellen says, they changed their stance.

Ellen (325) says that there has long been a process of "coevolution" between society and environment on Seram, which was reflected in extensive human modification of the forests (comparable to the landscape modifications described by Posey and by Fairhead and Leach, treated in the first section of this Introduction). The phenotype and regional distribution of the sago palm (for example) owes much to humans, and indeed, sago (a member of the genus of palms, *Metroxylon*, from whose trunk a rich starch staple food can be made) was historically a key symbol for the Nuaulu of nature–culture continuity. The idea of this continuity was supported by their reliance on vegetative versus seed propagation. All of these factors contributed to a "fuzzy" distinction between gardening and forest gathering (329). This fuzziness and the daily habit of forest gathering contributed, in turn, to the Nuaulu view of the forest (*wesie*) not as a monolithic "other" but as a combination of different biotopes and patches.

Given this historic Nuaulu conception of nature in general and forests in particular, Ellen asks how the contemporary distinction between nature and culture (between forest and village) could have developed. He suggests that one of the earliest steps in this development was the adoption of New World crops and cash-cropping for external markets, both of which diminished the economic role of sago and helped to sharpen the conceptual opposition between gardens and forest. The role of sago was further undercut by increasing cultural valorization of imported rice, which was driven by contacts with the wider world. Also important was the colonial Dutch relocation of most Nuaulu settlements from the interior to the coast of Seram during the 19th century. This entailed a shift from dispersed hamlets with scattered swiddens to nucleated villages with adjacent and clustered gardens, which greatly heightened distinctions between village and garden on the one hand, and forest on the other. Finally, the Nuaulu concept of forest has been further reified by their recent experience of environmental change and the need to participate in state environmental discourses. As a result of all of these developments, Ellen (330) says, the Nuaulu concept of forest and nature has become much more oppositional, in this respect becoming more like the concepts of coastal Muslims. Paradoxically, therefore, precisely as the divide between nature and culture became more marked, Nuaulu environmentalism developed; precisely as the Nuaulu became distanced from the forest, they became its protectors.

As a result of social and environmental changes over the past three decades, the Nuaulu have had to "renegotiate" their conceptual relationship with the forest in particular and nature in general. As the Nuaulu changed from semi-autonomous tribesmen relying on sago and forest products to dependent peasant farmers relying on food and cash crops, their conceptions of nature also changed. Many of the changes that Ellen describes are relatively recent, and some are still ongoing. As a result, some contradictory elements – some belonging to the old regime and some to the new – are simultaneously present in contemporary Nuaulu society. An example is the oppositional model of nature and culture associated with external relations of exchange, and a less oppositional model associated with internal subsistence relations. Ellen (330) suggests that the contradiction between the two represent a "dialectical function of a particular transitional history."

Articulation and consciousness

Li (340) terms the deployment of claims of indigeneity by local communities *articulation*, following the work of the sociologist and cultural theorist Stuart Hall. She enumerates a number of different variables that contribute to the success or failure of a particular effort of articulation: resource competition, local political structure, capacity to articulate identity to outsiders, urban activist interest, and local–state contest. But any given effort is historically contingent. Thus, Li (350) says that in the case of Lindu indigeneity, its "closure at a highly politicized moment," was arbitrary albeit successful. One of the principal reasons why articulations of indigeneity are arbitrary is that they are subject to contestation, which affects the types of arguments deployed. As Li (356) writes: "Articulation, in Hall's formulation, is a process of simplification and boundary-making, as well as connection." Simple portrayals of indigeneity connect, complex ones do not. "Too much fuzziness, or too broad an agenda, makes it difficult to forge connections" (355). "Fuzzy" or equivocal accounts are a handicap in politicized contexts, where simple, essentialized arguments win out.

Successful articulation depends on preconfigured "welcoming places" for the story being presented. The "audibility" of a story is greater if it fits a "familiar, preestablished pattern" (344). Li cites as an example the Lauje hills, which are as "bush" as any place could be but whose people and concerns do not connect with outsiders seeking indigeneity. In contrast, the local struggle over the Lindu hydro-electric project, which resembles a number of other high-profile cases around the world, "is a story for which the conceptual frame or 'place of recognition' already exists, and for which the intended readership has been prepared" (348). The fit or lack thereof between a local story and the global slot for it affects the amount of effort that must be spent to pick it up and, thus, the likelihood that it will be picked up at all. Li (353) writes: "For people in a hurry, it is easier to seek out conjunctures at which the articulations they seek are readily forthcoming and connections easily made." And this ultimately affects the way that indigeneity is constructed.

As Li cites Hall, the theory of articulation "enables us to think how an ideology empowers people, enabling them to begin to make some sense or intelligibility of their historical situation" (341). The theory of articulation helps us to look at the ways that indigeneity opens up room for maneuver, which would otherwise be unavailable. Agency is expressed in "the selection and combination of elements that form a recognizably indigenous identity, and also in the process of making connections" (344). This is true even if some of these elements are essentialized. As Li writes (354): "Simplified images may be the result of collaborations in which 'natives' have participated for their own good reasons." —→ *Agency*

Ellen distinguishes an older, local, embedded system of Nuaulu environmental knowledge from a newer system of knowledge of higher order environmental processes, and he does so partly on the basis of self-consciousness. He likens the new concept of forest in particular and nature in general to the new concepts of religion or culture that the Nuaulu hold, in that they are all distinctly self-conscious (cf. Hirtz 2003:892). For Li, the self-conscious articulation of indigeneity is vulnerable to a charge of being strategic, opportunistic, and inauthentic. The essays of both Li and Ellen were written to address this problem, Ellen's by asking how environmental consciousness arose in the first place, and Li's by developing the alternate analytic framework of articulation.

Environmental campaigns and collaborations: Brosius and Tsing

As anthropologists have begun writing about the politics of the environment, they have also necessarily begun focusing on the unequal relation between "indigenous" groups and environmentalists who are not indigenous. These two articles represent two very different efforts to examine this relation, by two anthropologists who have co-authored and co-edited other works together.[95] Moreover, the two case studies, also located quite close to each other geographically (in Malaysian and Indonesian Borneo), are also very different.

J. Peter Brosius[96] examines a case in which Western (or Northern) environmentalists are briefly interested in an indigenous movement to stop timber felling, which results in the erasure of the indigenous movement once the environmentalists are deflected to other issues. Anna Lowenhaupt Tsing[97] examines relations between Indonesian (not Western) environmentalists and indigenous leaders, looking very closely at the agency of the disempowered to influence the powerful. Brosius is looking at a case in which an indigenous voice bursts out on the global stage but is quickly silenced, and Tsing at the continuous efforts of indigenous agents to keep being heard, to keep being interesting and attractive, to those with more power than they have. Brosius' article is thus the almost brutal story of the birth of a powerful discourse and its ability to silence opposition; Tsing's a series of tentative moments when, in spite of powerful discourses, people may be collaborating without ever realizing it.

Brosius' article represents (and discusses) a growing literature in anthropology that critiques the involvement of Western environmentalists and their organizations in social movements.[98] This literature dates from the 1990s, when Ferguson (1990) and Escobar (1995) brought Foucault's work on the power of discourse to the anthropology of development and the environment. Environmental anthropologists began to focus their research and writing upon the institutions that were carrying out development and conservation in the Third World, though they usually began, as Brosius did, by studying the ecology of a tribal or peasant community.

Tsing's work, in contrast, keeps much closer to the usual, local object of study in anthropology, but examines relations between local people and urban visitors from an Indonesian NGO. In this finely detailed and eclectically structured essay, she describes the play of power on the ground, and finds reason for hope.

We suggest that both anthropologists have gotten something very right: that global discourses do silence the powerless, and that the powerless do sometimes do something that is not a resistance nor a contestation but a quieter manipulation within the discourse of the powerful. In environmental campaigns and collaborations, in other words, there is great reason to be pessimistic, but also significant reason to be hopeful. These readings allow us to chart the power of institutions and discourses, and the contrasting agency of individuals to work within that power.

Discourse and power

This topic is presaged at the beginning of this volume by the selection of Fairhead and Leach's (1995) "False Forest History." Like Brosius and Tsing, they write of a powerful discourse. In their case a colonial "vision," of natives degrading an ancient forest and transforming it into savanna, still commands contemporary Guinean policy. Fairhead and Leach argue that the local people believe that they in fact created the islands of forest in savanna, and that there is a lot of evidence that this silenced version of natural history is in fact the truth.

This sort of argument was introduced to anthropologists of development and the environment by James Ferguson's (1990) influential study of livestock development in Lesotho. He argues that development institutions define their target societies in particular ways that have nothing to do with reality, but are linked to Western discourses of degradation and development. Lesotho's "problem" was thus seen as one of overpopulation and poverty causing resource degradation and deepening poverty. The development solution to this "problem" was to increase livestock production. This solution failed because it obscured Lesotho's reality as a long-standing labor market for the mines of South Africa. Ferguson also revealed that Lesotho's people were meeting their real problems (low wages, structural unemployment, lack of retirement or disability benefits, etc.) by investing wages in extensive cattle production (lots of cattle, little investment of labor in cattle, banked rather than sold). Finally, Ferguson argued that unintended side-effects of development gave the state of Lesotho a much stronger rural presence than before. The discourse of degradation and development, and the machine that spawned it, rendered both the real causes of degradation and the political effects of development invisible.

Arturo Escobar (1995) was also very influential in bringing the work of Foucault to anthropologists studying development and conservation. He goes beyond Ferguson, looking at the power of dominant discourses to define local realities, and in doing so to destroy long-standing cultural meanings and practices.[99]

Because Michel Foucault's work underlies this whole discursive, power-aware trend in environmental anthropology, it is important to recognize his ideas. In Foucault's work, discourse defines ways of speaking and thinking about something (i.e., knowledge), but also ways of practicing or acting (and in fact the bulk of his work, especially his later work, concerned practices).[100] Discourse is always political in Foucault, a "discursive regime." This regime governs truth (and he uses the terms "regime of truth" and "politics of truth"). That is, a particular discursive regime sets the rules for forming statements accepted as scientifically true, determining what it is possible for science to think about. Discourse is more than a paradigm or a model, because these statements sound neutral and apolitical although they are actually laden with power. The dominant discourse is the knowledge and associated practices generally accepted as truth. A very important lesson to learn from Foucault is that a particular discourse exercises power over the dominant as well as the dominated. To put this in more comfortable language, a discursive regime defines what it is possible for anyone to think and how it is possible to act; it is an idea or action that feels "right," seems to really make sense, is comfortable and familiar, seems obvious or self-evident, feels natural or true, objective, and correct; it feels like it has nothing to do with politics or beliefs.

Foucault is usually talking about the particular discursive regime of our time, the 17th- and particularly 18th-century technical take-off in state power associated with colonialism and the development of capitalism. This regime is evident at two levels, the population and the individual. At the level of the population, this discursive regime produced an explosion of new techniques and new sciences that served to administer the population and keep it in order. These sciences include statistics and modern economics. At the level of the individual, this discursive regime produced new techniques and sciences that served to obtain productive services from individuals, and eventually to ensure that individuals would govern themselves.[101] Sciences and technologies are thus not neutral and objective but produced by and for power.

The power of (ecological) discourse: J. Peter Brosius

Peter Brosius clearly draws on these ideas in this analysis of the power of an apparently well-meaning discourse, forest certification, promoted in part by well-meaning environmental NGOs, to "displace politics," in this case leading to the destruction of a forest and a people. This article can be read as an environmental version of Ferguson's (1990) *Anti-Politics Machine*. As Brosius writes, "An immense institutional/managerial apparatus is presently descending on 'the environment,' much as it once did on development" (365).[102]

But though Brosius was clearly inspired by Ferguson, the influence of Roy Rappaport, his teacher at the University of Michigan[103], sets the tone of this article.[104] "Green Dots, Pink Hearts" is not simply an academic critique; it is also, to use Rappaport's (1993:297) term, "engaged". For Brosius, following Rappaport, discourse matters: "These rhetorical shifts had real effects" (366). Rappaport writes (in *The Anthropology of Trouble*, quoted repeatedly in Brosius' article), of two related "disorders." The first is when "the contingent and instrumental" are given first place over the "fundamental" in policy making (Rappaport 1993:299), and the second is when they also dominate values (1993:300). His example concerns ecology and economics: economics is given priority over ecology in policy decisions, and economics dominates values as well, degrading values based on ecology (1993:299–300). This, he writes, both causes troubles (e.g., environmental degradation) and reduces people's capacity "to deal with such troubles as they emerge." These points are central to Brosius. The reality that timber certification obscures is logging, which "not only undermines the basis of Penan subsistence but, by transforming sites with biographical, social, and historical significance, also destroys those things that are iconic of their existence as a society" (368). For Brosius, as for Rappaport, the power of discourse is amoral. Brosius writes: "At an ITTO [International Tropical Timber Organization] meeting in which 'criteria and indicators' of sustainability are on the agenda, images of blockades and arrests are not merely irrelevant but disruptive" (381; my brackets).

This article tells the story of a campaign inspired by Penan protests in Sarawak (Malaysian Borneo), a fairly "grassroots" response to a very real threat to livelihood. The protests were supported by a Malaysian NGO, Sahabat Alam Malaysia, Friends of the Earth Malaysia. It attracted international environmental NGOs (including IUCN [International Union for the Conservation of Nature] and WWF [World Wide Fund for Nature]), and the international press, who shaped a campaign using Penan as icons in an urgent *Fern Gully* allegory, a moral, political and ecological discourse to incite the world against Malaysian logging.[105] The Malaysian government, especially Prime Minister Mahatir, responds with accusations of eco-imperialism, which results in the local NGO withdrawing their support, and the international ones refocusing on temperate (Northern) forests and, more effectively, Northern markets for tropical hardwoods. Feeling the pinch of shrinking markets, Malaysia first tries to adopt terminology from the international popularity of sustainability, then hires international public relations firms, who focus on the new timber certification process being developed by the International Tropical Timber Organization. This process finally deflects the Northern NGOs into a bureaucratic, technoscientific and economic discourse, and the campaign loses all momentum. Timber certification effectively obscures Malaysian logging and the Penan's plight. The "green dots" of timber certification obscure the "pink hearts" of *Fern Gully*-type campaigns; in other words, "indifferent bureaucratic and/or technoscientific forms of institutionally created and validated intervention" obscure "moral and political imperatives" (365). There is nothing wrong with the green dots themselves: "The issue . . . is not whether sustainable forest management or timber certification is desirable. Rather, it is the potential for such efforts to become part of an elaborate public relations scheme, designed to obscure a highly destructive system of resource extraction and to assuage consumer and government concerns, that makes them problematic" (381).[106]

Brosius specifically critiques the role that environmental institutions have played in this obscuring of the political. This process, he writes, "is too often the work of ostensibly *environmental* institutions: not the Shell Oil Corporation, but the Forest Stewardship Council and the International Union for the Conservation of Nature" (his emphasis, 383). He suggests that as environmental NGOs displace grassroots environmental movements "they might be viewed as engaged in projects of domestication, attempting to seduce or to compel" grassroots groups "to participate in statist projects of environmental governmentality" (383), projects that envelop movements "within institutions for local, national, and global environmental surveillance and governance" (364). Anthropology has a role to play in this, to critique such discourses and institutions, and to be spokesmen for those, like the Penan, whom they silence. He begins the article with a quote from Rappaport: "Ethnography is crucial in a world in which the domination of privileged discourse, amplified by increasingly concentrated mass media, threatens to make other discourses inaudible or unintelligible" (Rappaport 1993:301).

Agency on the ground: Anna Tsing

Anna Tsing does not focus on the power of a discourse, but on the agency a powerful discourse leaves to those relatively powerless within it. This makes it a stimulating counterpoint to Brosius' essay. This article also stands on its own in its creative exploration of the implications of the "fantasies," "dreams," and "stereotypes" of "the rural, the backward, and the exotic," and of "wild nature and tribal culture" (393) which are attached to powerful discourses. It is through these fantasies that a few leaders in the Meratus mountains of Indonesian Borneo promote a "tribal" village named Mangkiling as "a place that cannot be rolled over and erased easily" (398), "a focus of regional attention," standing out of the usual "invisibility" (403).

Tsing examines a series of collaborative documents in this article, which is structured very differently from the standard case study article.[107] These documents together constitute what she calls a "tribal situation" (403), in which the powerless act out the fantasies of the powerful in a way that gives them (the powerless) agency. The first document (396–398) is a land rights claim apparently authored by a "tribal elder" named Musa, which simultaneously evokes the officialese of Indonesian bureaucracy, international environmental rhetoric, and local cultural ecology. The second (399–400) is photographs of Yuni (Musa's brother) at a Kompas Borneo (a provincial environmental NGO)/Ford Foundation workshop, in which Tsing says that his "artless, off balance stance" represents him as a "tribesman," while his presence at the workshop signifies that he is "longing for change". The third (404–406) is a series of articles in a provincial newspaper based on interviews with Sumiati (Musa's sister), similarly promoting both backwardness and a longing for development. These articles produce two revealing examples, Sumiati's claiming of commodified contraceptive herbs as indigenous knowledge (406–408), and Kompas Borneo's choice of a deaf man as a source of indigenous knowledge (408). The fourth document is a tree list, evidence of urban environmentalists and tribesmen sharing the identification of flora, but ignoring local forest management (409–412). Finally Tsing (412–417) examines a series of hybrid maps, ending with one that includes both village land claims and timber company concessions overlapping on a single map.

These documents are interpreted as showing Musa, Yuni, and Sumiati working to create community identity and resource rights out of the "stigma" of being tribal: "not just technologically and economically backward but also primitive and exotic" (406). They have done this by collaborating with urban environmentalists, an opportunity only available to those with the tribal stigma. In other words, it is the conceptual links between tribe and nature that Musa, Yuni, and Sumiati know and use. This insight is not new (see the preceding section "Indigeneity and natural resource politics" in this Introduction), but Tsing adds several new ideas to it. First, Sumiati and her brothers must simultaneously present themselves as tribal and as longing to be not tribal; they must enact both the dominant discourses of development and conservation and the contradictory fantasies of "wild nature and tribal culture." This is because outsider developers and conservationists "most despise" that to which they are "most attracted" (406). This contradiction can be understood through a gender model, in which women, the subordinated party, manipulate the fantasies of men about them. The devalued other, in other words, is also attractive. As Tsing writes: "Perhaps it is helpful to think of it in relation to the skill that women in so many places have used to make themselves attractive to men, that is, to make themselves 'feminine' as men see it" (407). Similarly, Musa, Yuni, and Sumiati enact "a fantasy in which whether they play themselves or someone else's understanding of themselves is ambiguous."

This ambiguity produces a "double-sided agency, so much their own and so much not their own" (398). It is not their own because neither the dominant discourses nor the fantasies belong to those playing the role of "tribal elder." Yet, and this is a second insight, Tsing writes convincingly that Sumiati and her brothers are transforming the terrible tribal stigma into something new and important. "To transform exotic stereotypes into community designs," she says, "is a work of magic" (406): "things that did not exist before can emerge" and "metropolitan fantasies *both* fulfil themselves *and* take the dreamers they construct by surprise" (394, her italics). "To the extent that conservation and development discourses can be engaged through these fields of attraction" – "the longing, the broken promises, the erotic draw, and the magic" that link rural community to outside experts – "local initiatives . . . become possible" (398).

Beth Conklin and Laura Graham (1995) have also written, in somewhat similar terms but of the Amazon, about collaborations.[108] In Conklin and Graham's (1995) work, like Brosius', the collaboration is transnational, between international environmental NGOs and indigenous people (see also previous section "Indigeneity and natural resource politics" in this Introduction). Conklin and Graham describe such collaborations as occurring on a "shifting middle ground," and emphasize their insecurity for local peoples rather than their agency. Stereotypes of ecologically noble savages, they write, are a "precarious foundation" for indigenous rights (Conklin and Graham 1995:697).[109]

Tsing is clearly more hopeful about such collaborations. She writes that they "offer possibilities for building environmental and social justice in the countryside as exciting as any I have heard of" (395), and even more pointedly: "Fearing simplistic representations of wild nature and tribal culture, scholars dismiss what in my opinion are some of the most promising social movements of our times" (393). Like Conklin and Graham, Tsing talks about "mobile spaces", "shifting rhetorics and narratives", and "unstable realms", but not in a negative sense; it is a place "in which new things that did not exist before can emerge" (393–394). But she also mentions the vulnerable and contested nature of tribal elders' influence in their communities and the "terrible" stigma of being primitive and exotic. Conklin and Graham focus on the dangers of living out another's fantasy, but also mention hope. In truth we just don't know what the end of either story is going to be, nor do we have any reason to think that it will be the same everywhere, or be stable anywhere. As Tsing writes, these fragile collaborations are "a planner's nightmare" (393).

Knowing the Environment

Social identity and perception of the landscape: Frake and Bloch

These two readings represent anthropology's exploration of sense of place, a multidisciplinary topic also addressed by cultural geographers, sociologists, and psychologists, among others.[110] In anthropology, sense of place is not individual but cultural; it occurs at the level of discourse rather than individual thought or emotion. The anthropology of sense of place is also largely focused on links between the imagining of place and social identity (Feld and Basso 1996:4). As a recent contributor to this literature (Thomas 2002) notes, there is now an "impressive array" of anthropological research demonstrating that "places are locales of intense emotional attachment, thick with meaning and memory, shaped by both local and translocal phonomena; they possess the 'power to direct and stabilize us, to memorialize and identify us, to tell us who and what we are in terms of *where we are* (as well as where we are *not*)'" (Thomas 2002:368, quoting in part Casey 1993). The sense of place literature in anthropology is relatively new, dating from the 1980s and especially 1990s. It began with the idea of "rootedness[111]," but increasingly (and much like the community literature) came to focus on how place was created and contested, and how it is linked to state or global sources of power.[112]

Anthropologists bring their own methodologies to this area of study, which almost necessarily involves long-term fieldwork. This is very evident in these readings, which are based on, among other things: casual conversation in pubs or sharing a view; the etymology of words for place, particular places, nature, attractive places, etc.; monuments and what people say about them; maps and how people use them; and controversies and change, and what people say about them. As Geertz writes in his Afterword to the Feld and Basso volume:

> The subject demands exactness, detail, the sort of care for the assumed and the unstated, for what is only felt or only enacted, that might best be called ethnographical tact. It is a patient art, and frequently a passive one. No one lines up people and asks them to define "place" and list three examples of it . . . To study place, or more exactly, some people or other's sense of place, it is necessary to hang around with them – to attend to them as experiencing subjects. (Geertz 1996:260)

These two readings are drawn from two edited volumes that followed conferences or seminars: the Bloch piece was written for a 1989 conference bringing together British social anthropologists' explorations of landscape[113], and the Frake piece was written for a 1993 seminar on sense of place with an American and linguistic anthropology focus.[114] Charles Frake and Maurice Bloch are both cognitive anthropologists (among other things). Both articles are about how people create a sense of place, or how they create an identity out of a landscape. These two readings were also selected because they relate sense of place to local concepts of nature. In doing so, they allow us to return to the nature versus culture tension that underlies so much of environmental anthropology.

Identifying with past and future landscapes

Charles O. Frake[115] reveals the East Anglian sense of place through a series of beautifully-written, loosely interconnected little analyses. He explores place names (showing his linguistic side), maps, local knowledge (in a section very like Scott's 1998 work on *métis*), and a discourse on "improvement." He shows a fine understanding, not only for what is said and mapped, but for what is unspoken and unmappable, culminating in a discussion of "no place" versus "a nowhere place" (447). The end result is an East Anglian identity linked to limited aspects of the contemporary landscape that evoke or refer to an imagined, and lost, past ("nowhere"). East Anglian identity, in Frake's analysis, is associated not with the contemporary landscape but with a lost landscape.

Oddly, Maurice Bloch[116] argues something similar for the Zafimaniry of eastern Madagascar. Bloch reveals the Zafimaniry sense of place through their ritualized enjoyment of views, their valuing of "clarity," and the two conflicting ways in which people leave a lasting mark on the landscape: by establishing a productive marriage, and thus a house and village; and by being commemorated in stone monuments. Transforming space (or nature, or God) into a human place requires destroying the contemporary forest, and this is what the Zafimaniry are doing, by gradually creating the permanent clearings of wet-rice cultivation. In Bloch's analysis, as we will see, the Zafimaniry are trying to transform their identity by transforming their landscape.

Sense of place for both English and Zafimaniry provides identity in part because it is a transformation of nature. As Appadurai (1996:183) writes, local sense of place is often created in opposition to nature: "neighborhoods are inherently what they are because they are opposed to something else" and "this something else is often conceptualized ecologically". In other words, both Frake's East Anglians and Bloch's Zafimaniry create place out of space by conceiving of nature as something transformed by human effort. As Lowenthal wrote: "It is an English creed that all land requires human supervision. Far from knowing best, nature needs vigilant guidance . . . The prospect of unmanaged wasteland is utterly repugnant" (448). Nature on its own is "decay, spoilage, unruly growth, untidiness"; "even 'nature' needs improvement to become, or be restored to, a 'natural' place" (448).

Of course, as Frake says, "The English do not have much in the way of untamed nature in their vicinity anyway" (448). The Zafimaniry, on the other hand, have too much. As Bloch writes: "First, the countryside is both mountainous and wooded so that it is usually very difficult to see far. The forest which has to be crossed to go from one village to another . . . is often oppressively and menacingly enveloping . . . Secondly the countryside is, for much of the time, shrouded in mists, rain, and clouds which cling to the forest" (427). The Zafimaniry, in contrast to the English, see the land as unchanging and uncaring, "simply a state of affairs which affects you and which you cannot resist": "The countryside, a manifestation of God, is therefore a permanent but uncaring environment within which impermanent and weak human beings must live" (428). In a sense what decays and spoils is people, not nature. The gentle English vocabulary does not work in this world: Zafimaniry nature cannot be "improved," "supervised," "guided," or "managed," it must be cleared. "The Zafimaniry's concern with the environment is not with how not to damage it but with how to succeed with making a mark on it" (426).

The most important parallel in these two essays is that between nature for the Zafimaniry and modernity for the English. Bloch's Zafimaniry seem to value "clarity" against nature, and Frake's East Anglians seem to value "pleasantness" against the modern landscape. The pleasantness that defines East Anglian identity lies in the past; the "clarity" that defines Zafimaniry humanity lies in the future. As the British of East Anglia look back into the past, the Zafimaniry of Madagascar look forward into the future. Neither people are "rooted" in the present landscape. Sense of place, in the works of these two anthropologists, is more "against" than rooted in nature.

Agricultural transformations

This may be true because farming plays a role in the transformation of both Zafimaniry and East Anglian landscapes; in fact both cases involve an agricultural transformation that is also a transformation of the landscape.[117] In Frake's East Anglia, people who are mostly not farmers value a vaguely agricultural landscape of ancient barns and named fields, but are troubled by marks of modern farming, like concrete silos. The context for this rural nostalgia is not, as one might expect, a backward area, but an area that "led the way, not only in England but in the world, toward capitalized, commercial, mechanized agriculture" (437). The capitalization of agriculture transformed, and continues to transform, the landscape, but: "These transformations of the real landscape have seriously threatened the image of the English countryside" (437). East Anglian identity gazes backwards to an ancient agriculture, blind to the modern agricultural landscape of the present.[118]

The Zafimaniry are on the cusp of an agricultural transformation as well, but one from swidden farming to wet-rice farming rather than one increasingly capitalized. Most Zafimaniry households recently created wet-rice fields, enough of them to transform the forest in some areas to terraced valleys. The Zafimaniry clearly understand the enormity of this change, associating it with a warming of the climate and, more astonishingly, a transformation in their own ethnic identity. "For them," Bloch writes, "people who live *an patrana* – that is, in the treeless land where irrigated rice cultivation is possible – are Betsileo; and, because their own land is becoming *an patrana*, they say that they too are becoming Betsileo" (426). All these transformations they embrace, because, Bloch thinks, "The cleared rice valleys are . . . a sign of living humans having finally successfully made their mark and attached themselves to the unchanging land" (432). Zafimaniry identity looks forward to a future of wet-rice agriculture, devaluing the swidden landscape of the present.

Both Bloch and Frake note a contrast between their own ideas about nature and those of their research subjects. Bloch (French-born, but educated and teaching in England) refers to the destruction of the rain forest: "When in the field, with my post-Rousseau, post-Sibelius sensitivities, strengthened every evening by the BBC World Service's lachrymose accounts of the disappearance of the world's rain forest, I tried as hard as I could to get my co-villagers to tell me how much they deplored the change in their environment . . . I failed to get the slightest response" (426). "No search here," Frake (an American) notes, "for the American dream of 'unspoiled wilderness' – an oxymoron to the English" (448).[119] The Norfolk Broads example, of a lake revealed to have been manmade (created by peat digging), is illuminating: "To find that one's natural paradise was manmade would be a disaster in the United States . . . Not so in East Anglia" (449).

It strikes us that all of these views are discursive evasions of the here and now; the East Anglian's lost past, the Zafimaniry's clear future, the environmentalist's disappearing rain forest, the American's wilderness – all lie elsewhere. If sense of place creates identity by rooting it to something that is not here and now, it allows all of us to avoid identifying with the worlds we have wrought. We agree with Geertz (199), that we are in fact tied in ever more closely "with the habitat we both make and inhabit," and with Cronon (1996:80), that our thinking about nature "leaves precisely nowhere for human beings actually to make their living from the land."[120]

The limits of knowledge and its implications for understanding environmental relations: Bateson and Ingold

The final pair of readings, concerning the limits to knowledge of the environment, come from scholars of two separate generations, Tim Ingold (1948–) and Gregory Bateson (1904–80). Bateson carried out fieldwork in New Guinea, publishing *Naven* in 1936, and Bali, where he collaborated with his then-wife Margaret Mead on the 1942 photographic ethnography *Balinese Character*. He pursued a less orthodox path later in his career, spending 13 years as "Ethnologist" at the Veterans' Administration hospital in Palo Alto, California, directing a federal dolphin lab in the Virgin Islands, as well as working at the Oceanographic Institute and East-West Center in Hawaii. His venturing across disciplinary lines and the boundaries of accepted theory led to an underappreciation of his work within anthropology. Ingold is the Max Gluckman Professor of Social Anthropology at the University of Manchester. He has carried out fieldwork among farmers, pastoralists, and hunters in Finland, and has published extensively in these fields (e.g., 1980, 1986, 2000).

Spaceship earth

The iconic photograph of the earth taken from space has attracted great attention from the public, academics, and policy makers (e.g., Sachs 1992; Zimmerman 1994). The role that this image came to play in galvanizing public and policy concern for the environment is reflected in its focal place in the Brundtland report (World Commission on Environment and Development 1987). Zimmerman (1994:75) writes that this image quickly became caught up in the wider debate between two disparate camps of environmentalists, "New Agers" versus "deep ecologists," the former embracing the image as one of integration and the latter rejecting it as one of separation. This paradoxical notion of separation is at the heart of Ingold's critique of the idea of the globe. He writes (462), "I am suggesting that the notion of the global environment, far from marking humanity's reintegration into the world, signals the culmination of a process of separation." Ingold sees the global vision as distancing humanity from nature and, along with others ranging from deep ecologists to environmental historians like Cronon (1996) (as well as Bateson[121]), he sees this distancing or division as central to the contemporary environmental crisis.

The "spaceship earth" vision, like other totalizing, modernist visions (e.g., the panopticon, global capitalism, the ecosystem), is both powerful and self-privileging. Ingold (464) suggests that the global vision represents itself as "real and total" compared with the "illusory and incomplete" vision of the local level. It represents the local community as being confined by its limited horizons, from which those with global vision have escaped. This privileging of global versus local ontology has practical consequences for the local communities that anthropologists study, legitimating their disempowerment in the management of their environments. Ingold's critique of global vision is part of a wider anthropological critique of the de-localizing impact of modernity (Appadurai 1996) and the negative consequences of this for the environment (Hornborg 1996).

Ingold argues that this divide between local and global visions is, in part, a division between an ontology of direct engagement and one of indirect representation. He argues that whereas the local vision, or what he calls the vision of the "sphere," can be known through "sensory attunement," the globe is apprehended only through "cognitive reconstruction" (466). Ingold (1996a:220–221) has elsewhere lauded the direct engagement with nature of hunter-gatherers compared with the modern, Western, global need to formulate nature prior to engagement. In his essay, Bateson (460) argues for a similar immediacy of experience with the environment, as reflected in his calling for an "I–Thou relationship" with nature. Such a relationship is characterized less by intellect and reason and more by affect and faith. Bateson sees love and religion as important correctives to the role played by conscious purpose in our environmental relations. Other scholars, following in Bateson's wake, have noted the importance of emotional attachment in human environmental relations (Kellert and Wilson 1993).[122]

Consciousness

Bateson (457) characterizes his research focus as concerning "the role of consciousness in the ongoing process of human adaptation." He regards individual human consciousness as problematic because the individual is not the unit of evolution. He maintains that it is the "context" that evolves, not the individual. In his famous example of the evolution of the modern horse from *Eohippus*, Bateson argues that the horse did not simply evolve in adaptation to the grassy plains, the plains also evolved in adaptation to the horse (1972:155). It is, he argues, the "constancy in the relationship between animals and environment," the ecology, that survives and evolves (1972:332, 338). Since it is not the individual or even species that is the unit of evolution and survival but rather the encompassing system, the fates of the individual and its environment are intertwined. As a result, it is impossible to compete with, dominate, or "win" against one's own environment. The problem, Bateson says (1972:338), is that the logic of individual adaptation often dictates just such competition: "Trouble arises precisely because the 'logic' of adaptation is a different 'logic' from that of the survival and evolution of the ecological system."

The difference between the logic of individual adaptation and the logic of system evolution is especially problematic, Bateson says, because of the inability of the conscious mind to perceive its own context. Individual human beings cannot comprehend the entirety of the wider systemic environmental structure in which they exist.[123] As a result, Bateson (459) argues, "there . . . [is] a *systematic* (i.e., non-random) difference between the conscious views of self and the world, and the true nature of self and the world." And "lack of systemic wisdom" is "always punished" (1972:434). This is the "double bind": one is punished for doing what is wise for oneself if it is not also wise for the system. "It is an experience of being punished precisely for being right in one's own view of the context [but not the wider system]" (1972:236).

Drawing on his work with dolphins, Bateson (1972:293,368) suggests that there are several different types or levels of learning, differentiated by greater and greater choice. Surprisingly, the training of dolphins and other animals depends on the abrogation of higher-order choice. By analogy, Bateson suggests that the exercise of choice afforded by human consciousness can be problematic, and that here too the abrogation of choice may sometimes be the wiser course.[124] As he writes (1972:370), "I regard the conscious intelligence as the greatest ornament of the human mind. But many authorities, from the Zen masters to Sigmund Freud, have stressed the ingenuity of the less conscious and perhaps more archaic level." Whereas consciousness and choice favor solutions geared to one's own context; thinking that is less dominated by conscious choice favors solutions geared to the wider system. This is the challenge for the human mind: to apply conscious reason to the fact that conscious reason itself blocks understanding of systemic nature.

Purpose

Ingold (469) associates the global perspective with the triumph of modern science and increased dependence on the "technological fix." Bateson (1972:490) similarly writes that modern technology "reinforces this arrogance, or 'hubris' vis-à-vis the natural environment." Such arrogance is problematic because it manifests itself in highly linear, deterministic planning. As Bateson (459) says, "If the total mind and the outer world do not, in general, have this lineal structure, then by forcing this structure upon them, we become blind to the cybernetic circularities of the self and the external world." For Bateson, this is literally humanity's original sin. He interprets (1972:435) the story of humanity's exile from the biblical Garden of Eden in terms of specialization, planning, and an attendant loss of awareness of the systemic character of nature. In the years since Bateson wrote, this view of planning has become widely accepted, with established ecologists like C. S. Holling documenting the ill consequences of linear, monistic, deterministic approaches to environmental management (Gunderson, Holling, and Light 1995).

Planning is often driven by the best of intentions, of which both Bateson and Ingold are skeptical. As Bateson (460) writes, "Conscious man is now fully able to wreck himself and that environment – with the very best of conscious intentions." In response to those who use the global image to articulate pressing environmental problems, Ingold (468) similarly writes, "No one, of course, denies the seriousness of the problems they address; there is good reason to believe, however, that many of these problems have their source in that very alienation of humanity from the world of which the notion of global environment is a conspicuous expression." The very notions of degradation versus conservation are grounded, Ingold claims, in an underlying discourse of separation and intervention that is ultimately at the root of this degradation. Both Ingold and Bateson identify a perverse dynamic in human environmental relations: orthodox environmental thinking explicitly asserts the unity of nature and culture while implicitly separating them, and thus it explicitly strives to ameliorate environmental degradation while implicitly reproducing the conditions of this degradation.

Bateson (1972:437) sees an increase in scientific arrogance as "the most important disaster" of the industrial revolution. He urges that we respond to our imperfect understanding of the world not with anxiety and a need to control but rather with curiosity. He concludes his essay with God's reminder to Job of the limits of his understanding: "Dost thou know when the wild goats of the rock bring forth? Or canst thou tell when the hinds do calve?" (461). Ingold sees the global vision as arrogant in its implication that we can *choose* to intervene or not in the world, an option that he regards as illusory. He cites (467) as an example of this arrogance the title to an influential collection on the global environment, *Man's Role in Changing the Face of the Earth* (Thomas 1956).[125] The title to the self-proclaimed 1990 successor to this volume, *The Earth as Transformed by Human Action*, carries the same connotations (Turner et al. 1990).[126]

Representation

Both Bateson and Ingold are interested in the use of images and metaphors to represent nature. Bateson believes that metaphors can link nature and culture. He writes favorably of the metaphoric representation that is involved in both totemism and animism, the former drawing on patterns in the natural world to explain society and the latter doing the reverse (1972:484–485). He sees both as preferable to what happens with the notion of "gods," which leads to a separation of mind from nature. Ingold, however, thinks that metaphoric representation helps to reproduce the nature–culture dichotomy. He elsewhere (1996a:123) writes about the Mbuti of Central Africa regarding the forest as their parents, and he enjoins us against reflexively interpreting this usage as metaphorical. Why, he asks, should behavior that is interpreted as "practical *involvement*" in human relations be seen merely as "metaphorical *construction*" because it involves relations with the non-human environment (1996a:125–126)? To see the forest as a parent as opposed to a parental metaphor is to recognize, he argues, that "at root the constitutive quality of intimate relations with non-human and human components of the environment is one and the same" (1996a:129).

Bateson (1972:504) suggests that the ideas of ecology are part of our own ecological system: "We are not outside the ecology for which we plan – we are always and inevitably part of it. Herein lies the charm and the terror of ecology – that the ideas of this science are irreversibly becoming a part of our own ecological system." In the years since Bateson wrote this, many scholars have followed his lead. Cronon (1992:1375) has written that the stories we tell about the environment change the way that we act vis-à-vis the environment and, hence, change the environment as well. In one of his later writings, Rappaport (1990:68, his emphasis) observed that "The concept of the ecosystem *is not simply a theoretical framework* within which the world can be analyzed. It is itself an element of that world, one that is crucial in maintaining that world's integrity in the face of mounting insults to it."

Bateson and Ingold

The collection of essays from which Bateson's piece is taken, *Steps to an Ecology of Mind: A Revolutionary Approach to Man's Understanding of Himself* (1972), is introduced on the frontispiece page with these words: "Here is the book which develops a new way of thinking about the nature of order and organization in living systems, a unified body of theory so encompassing that it illuminates all particular areas of study of biology and behavior." This is followed by an epigraph from Stewart Brand, then editor of the *Whole Earth Catalog*, which reflects the wide audience to whom Bateson's work appealed. This appeal stemmed in part from the fact that Bateson worked and wrote across disciplinary boundaries. At a time when these boundaries were even more formidable than they remain today, Bateson's use of data on animal evolution and behavior to talk about humans was captivating and powerful. Another of his cross-disciplinary forays was into the then-nascent field of cybernetics and systems theory. His borrowing and use of ideas from this field was pioneering. The concepts that he deployed, like that of homeostatic, self-regulating systems, also appeared in the contemporaneous writings of Rappaport (1968, and see the section "Natural science models of resource-use" above) and, with direct attribution to Bateson, in the work of Reichel-Dolmatoff (1975).

Whereas a generation ago Bateson (and Rappaport) and others drew on cybernetics to critique modernity, today scholars like Haraway (1991) are critiquing cybernetics itself as a dimension of modernity. One scientific development since Bateson wrote that has dated his application of systems theory is the general retreat from an equilibrium-based view of the world. Bateson framed his critique of human environmental relations in terms of errant human behavior upsetting a closed homeostatic system, a premise that few scholars still adhere to. Most scholars today (if not all conservationists) argue that disturbance is integral to the "natural order"; some ask whether human behavior, including what seem to be mistakes, might also be part of this order, which is a question that Bateson did not raise.

Ingold begins his analysis of the global perspective by presenting both early European and non-Western concepts of the sphere, which he contrasts to the concept of the globe; and he then proceeds to analyze, with forays into Kant, how the idea of the sphere was replaced by that of the globe, and what the negative implications of this are for local peoples and their environments. His central point that global vision produces a problematic detachment is a powerful one, but his thesis that this is wholly a product of late-20th-century space exploration and technology is debatable. The histories of Western (and also non-Western) environmental relations amply attest to the existence of pre-20th century patterns of detachment, hubris, and environmental abuse (Glacken 1967). This means either that the image of the globe pre-dates the space photographs or that the earlier image of the sphere shared some of its problems. Ingold also essentializes the global image. Whereas "the number of possible local perspectives is potentially infinite," he writes, "there is only one global perspective, indifferent to place and context" (468). The curiously non-anthropological idea that a global vision would not vary with the culture of the viewer reflects the fact that Ingold does not approach the global image ethnographically. Whereas he devotes much of his essay to digging into the historical and cultural richness of the idea of the sphere, including the ideas of a 16th-century Venetian astronomer and of 20th-century Yup'ik Eskimos, his discussion of the idea of the globe is, by comparison, much less ethnographic, with only the views of the "Kantian traveler" being discussed in any detail.

Conclusion

Taken together, the readings in this volume illustrate a number of key developments in the history of environmental anthropology. First is a general movement over time away from fine-grained analyses of communities toward studies that question the "natural" boundedness of communities and emphasize their linkage to wider political–ecological systems. Second, history has become increasingly important to environmental anthropology. There has been a decisive move away from synchronic and toward diachronic approaches, and there has been a similarly sharp and corollary shift away from assumptions of equilibrium toward assumptions of disequilibrium. Third, and related to the foregoing shifts in spatial and temporal orientation, environmental anthropology is not only studying politics more, it has itself become increasingly political. Practice as well as the study of practice is increasingly important. Fourth, environmental anthropology has become increasingly influenced by post-structural theory. This is reflected in greater reflexivity, an interest in studying environmental discourse, and a view of the environment as both material reality and a product of discourse. Fifth and finally, environmental anthropology is today extraordinarily interdisciplinary in character, reaching out to a multitude of other disciplines and freely crossing the natural and social sciences. This has played an important role in the recent resurgence of interest in environmental anthropology.

NOTES

1. Glacken (1967:vii) says that the three environmental questions that have dominated the history of Western thought are: How does the earth influence human culture? How have humans altered the earth? And, Is the earth a purposefully made creation?
2. For more on the nature–culture dichotomy, we suggest Cronon (1996).
3. Darrell Posey died in March 2001. At the time of his death he was with the Oxford University Institute for Social and Cultural Anthropology.
4. James Fairhead is Professor of Social Anthropology and head of the Anthropology Department at the University of Sussex. Melissa Leach is Professorial Fellow at the Civil Society and Governance program, Institute of Development Studies, University of Sussex.
5. We have selected Posey's often-cited 1985 article for this volume, and Fairhead and Leach's 1995 article for *World Development* for its presentation of degradation narratives; selected other publications by these authors appear in the References following this Introduction.
6. Posey's research was funded in part by the World Wildlife Fund, and he argued that sustainable conservation should be modeled on indigenous knowledge. Fairhead and Leach's research was funded by the Overseas Development Administration.
7. Posey uses the Portuguese term *campo/cerrado*, which means savanna and scrub savanna (Parker 1992: n. 3).
8. This is in part a further defense against Parker's critique of his work, of which more below.
9. See particularly their discussion of vegetation communities and the deflection of succession in chapter 6.

10. Posey (1998) moves towards a politics of knowledge model.
11. The Latin American literature on indigenous knowledge and management, particularly in swidden livelihood systems, goes back to Carneiro (1960, in this volume) who wrote about the uses of swidden fallows, and Linares (1976), on hunting in swiddens. These anthropologists are both mentioned and cited by Posey, but not by Fairhead and Leach (even in their book). More recent works on this topic include Roosevelt (1998) and Balée (1993, 1994).
12. See Parker (1992), Posey (1992), Parker (1993), Posey (1998).
13. They take a historical approach to this vision in the 1995 *Environment and History* version, showing that the idea of degradation and the policy solutions to it evolved during the colonial period and continued through a series of national governments. Similar analyses can be found in Hoben (1995) and Guthman (1997).
14. They use the term "Foucauldian discourse" (1996:278) for the ability of the discourse of degradation to warp science.
15. For related readings on narratives, see Roe (1991), whom they cite; we also recommend Cronon (1992).
16. This sort of division even obtains *within* individual livestock, in different customary usage regimes for blood/milk on one hand (for the household) and meat (for the group) on the other, as Dyson-Hudson and Dyson-Hudson (1969:80) note for the Karimojong of Uganda: "A herd owner's family is better off taking milk and blood from an animal and keeping the animal until it dies. It is only the meat that the family need share with the neighbors."
17. Cf. Hutchinson (1996:63 n. 4) for the literature on the "pervasive intimacy" of human–cattle relations in Africa.
18. Cf. Evans-Pritchard's (1940:13) comment that "After a few weeks of associating solely with Nuer one displays . . . the most evident symptoms of 'Nuerosis.' "
19. In addition, the cattle themselves are often being used in more utilitarian ways for subsistence than is implied by the concept of the cattle complex, as Schneider (1957) noted.
20. Cf. Dyson-Hudson and Dyson-Hudson (1969:78): "The Karimojong do practice subsistence agriculture in addition to livestock husbandry; they also collect wild fruits and berries and occasionally hunt wild game."
21. Cf. Dyson-Hudson (1972) on the difference between cattle herders' self-image and behavioral reality. This is not uncommon. See the case of the rice pond fields versus swidden sweet potato gardens of the Ifugao (Conklin 1980).
22. See Robbins' (1999) analysis of a court-ordered closing of a slaughter-house in Delhi and an ensuing butchers' strike.
23. Cf. Winterhalder, Larsen, and Thomas (1974) on the way that livestock dung concentrates and reconstitutes grasses for fuel and fertilizer in a highland Peruvian community.
24. The men's agricultural sector is more visible and public, it is more engaged with state efforts of extraction and development, and it is thus more exposed to risk. The women's livestock sector balances the public and risky sector of the household economy with a private and risk-averse sector. Carpenter (1997, 2001) argues that invisibility is crucial to protecting this sector from outside influences and that this invisibility is culturally constructed through the institution of *pardah*, referring to the veiling and seclusion of women.
25. Diener, Nonini, and Robkin (1978:230) agreed with Harris that sacred cows effect a transfer of resources but argued that it goes in the opposite direction.
26. Evans-Pritchard's synthesis of his research methods in an Appendix to the 1976 abridged edition of *Witchcraft, Oracles and Magic Among the Azande* is still one of the most insightful fieldwork guides available.

27. Due to space limitations we have reprinted selections from Mauss's essay, and omitted most of the original notes and bibliography, which make up nearly half of the original essay. For the full essay, see Mauss 1979.

28. In volume 9 of *Année Sociologique* (the printing date is 1906, but the essay bears the date of 1904/1905).

29. See Steward 1977b for his most often reprinted statement of cultural ecology, which was originally published in 1968. Julian Steward (1902–72) taught at the University of Michigan, Utah, Berkeley, Columbia, and Illinois (Barfield 1997:448–450). He carried out fieldwork among the Shoshone (see for example Steward 1977a). The Great Basin is a vast arid steppe between the Wasatch and Sierra Nevada mountains in the southwestern United States.

30. Lévi-Strauss considered *Seasonal Variations* to be a "jewel" of French socioethnographic thought (see Allen 2000:7). Marcel Mauss (1872–1950) lectured at the École Practique des Hautes Études, the Institute of Ethnology, and the College de France (Barfield 1997:313–314).

31. Mauss, and Steward's professor Alfred L. Kroeber, were both directly rejecting the 19th-century environmental determinism of Ratzel (see Mauss 1979 [Introduction] and Heizer 1963:v; see also Kroeber 1963:7).

32. Marvin Harris (1968; see previous section) praised Steward's work as a form of "cultural materialism," but Murphy (1977:35–36) argues that Steward "never found Marxian thought to be personally congenial."

33. Steward and Murphy (1977) do not consider the wider markets that drove both beaver and rubber production, nor the ecologies of trappers' and tappers' other livelihood activities.

34. The contrast with Mauss is very clear here: for Mauss the "function" of ceremonies is to create and maintain social wholes.

35. This suggests that ecosystems are amenable to types of analyses more typically applied to politics or culture alone. As Geertz writes: "The kind of sociocultural analysis that applies to kinship, village politics, child raising, or ritual drama applies equally . . . to human transactions with the environment" (199).

36. Barth was born in 1928 in Norway. The article reprinted here was originally published in 1956 in *American Anthropologist*. His Swat fieldwork was carried out in 1954. He has also carried out research and published on New Guinea and North Bali (Barth 1993), among other places. He is perhaps best known for his *Ethnic Groups and Boundaries* volume, published in 1969. He is also associated with the theory of transactionalism, which concerns the emergence of social structure out of the agency of individuals (Barth 1966). He currently teaches anthropology at both Boston University and the University of Oslo.

37. Barth does not refer to Steward. Like Steward, however, he is writing against Kroeber, whom he often cites.

38. Elsewhere Barth (1969:127,132) discusses in more detail variations of the Pathan social system, differentiating the simpler northern Pathans from the more elaborated social organization of the southern Pathans, giving ecology (especially size of surplus) as one factor behind them.

39. Geertz was born in 1926 in the U.S. He studied anthropology at Harvard (1956 Ph.D.). He carried out fieldwork in the southwest U.S., Indonesia (Java as well as Bali), and Morocco. He is best known as a symbolic anthropologist, but *Agricultural Involution* (1971) is an important work in environmental anthropology. He was Professor Emeritus at the Institute for Advanced Study at Princeton University. Geertz died in 2007.

40. "Steward . . . construes cultural ecology largely as a methodology for building evolutionary theory" (Frake 1962:53).

41. See Dove (1993).
42. Referring to Geertz 1959, which delineates seven sorts of social organizations in Balinese villages. But keep in mind Geertz's caution that Balinese *subak*s are not collective farms, but "cooperatively owned public utilities" for water distribution (194) Also see James A. Boon's (1977) work on the way individual Balinese compete within their complex grid of social groups.
43. We would like to caution that Moroccan individual water rights are not the same thing as water privatization in contemporary development practice; they are not part of the "free" market but of an old, complex, and religious legal structure along with a history of complicated local practices.
44. See Oliver-Smith and Hoffman (1999) for a review of current anthropological approaches to disaster research.
45. Cf. Sillitoe's (1994) coining of the term *ethno-meteorology*.
46. The word *disaster* comes from "ill-starred," from which follows the early definition of "a mishap due to a baleful stellar aspect" (Oxford English Dictionary 1999).
47. Foucault says that a culture memory or image of the plague, of contagion more generally, underlies all disciplinary state projects. Cf. Camus' (2001) *The Plague* as a metaphor for the fascist state.
48. The efflorescence of work on the El Niño-Southern Oscillation (ENSO) over the past two decades (within anthropology see Orlove, Chaing and Cane [2000]), helped to make scholars more sensitive to the possibilities of recurring natural perturbations.
49. The shift in interest from the needs of one's neighbors to oneself is an old theme in accounts of disaster (cf. Defoe 1992).
50. From emic as well as etic perspectives, the use of food sharing is a ubiquitous proxy for social integration.
51. Firth's interest in the integration of a social system is comparable to (and in part derived from) Mauss's (see the section "Early essays on social organization and ecology" in this Introduction).
52. Cf. Richards' (1986) analysis of responses to rice harvest failure in Sierra Leone.
53. Cf. Sillitoe (1994) on local mechanisms for coping with frost among the Wola of Papua New Guinea.
54. For a fuller appraisal of Conklin's life's work, see Kuipers and McDermott (2007).
55. Hence the report to the editors by swidden peoples in Sumbawa (Eastern Indonesia) that they "eat charcoal," based on the fact that they eat crops which are nourished by the ashes of the burnt forest.
56. Cf. Richards (1985) on technological innovation in swidden agriculture.
57. There is, however, growing scholarly interest today in the history of swidden agriculture in Scandinavia (e.g., Raumolin 1987), as well as efforts to restore swidden practices in some landscapes. A Finnish website for Koli National Park in North Karelia, eastern Finland, entitled "Swidden Heritage Alive and Well," states that "The swidden practice is being reapplied in an endeavor to restore some of the heritage landscape of the past centuries in the Koli Highlands" (Lovén n.d.).
58. Javanese history is replete with examples of people fleeing from regions of irrigated agriculture under state control to practice swidden beyond the reach of the state (Dove 1985a).
59. Some Dayak groups in Borneo cultivate both swidden fields and swamp fields with rudimentary irrigation (Padoch, Harwell, and Susanto 1998).
60. Cf. Leach's (1954) classic study of upland–lowland relations in Northern Burma.
61. An early example of state antipathy toward swidden agriculture was encountered by Carl Linnaeus during fieldwork in southern Sweden in 1749, when his sponsor the High Commissioner Baron Carl Harleman took exception to his favorable reports on

the Swedish system of swiddening and forced him to replace them with "harmless notes on manure" (Weimarck 1968:40–41).

62. As Greenough and Tsing (1994:97) have written, whereas irrigated cultivators are typically seen by development agencies as merely "poor," swidden cultivators are seen as "primitive."

63. In West Kalimantan, Indonesia, Dove (1985b:19) found that one group of Kantu' swidden cultivators had moved eleven times within the same small river valley over the course of 86 years; whereas Lawrence, Peart, and Leighton (1998) found that another group of Dayak swidden cultivators had remained within the same territory for two centuries.

64. Most recently, anthropologists have borrowed methods for textual deconstruction from the humanities, in particular literary criticism, to construct postmodern critiques of science and society.

65. Rappaport (1993:167) wrote, "I met Gregory Bateson in Hawaii in 1968 and he immediately became – and has remained – the most profound of influences upon me."

66. In response to subsequent criticisms of his nutritional analyses, Rappaport added 35 more pages on this subject in the second 1984 edition.

67. In later years Rappaport (1993:300) characterized policy makers' inability to hear arguments not put in the reigning language of modern policy as "institutional deafness."

68. Rappaport's most eloquent statement on this subject is his 1993 Distinguished Lecture *The Anthropology of Trouble* for the American Anthropological Association.

69. Hawkes, Hill, and O'Connell (271) report that the Aché diet averages 3,600 cal/day/capita, 80 percent of which is derived from meat.

70. The critique of the concept of "pure" hunter-gatherers was also supported by evidence that many such peoples were engaged in part-time farming (Sponsel 1989).

71. Cf. Lee's (1968:43) argument that hunter-gatherer societies have been selected for study not for their representativeness but for their dramatic pedagogical utility.

72. See Puri (2005) as an example of current directions in studies of hunter-gatherers, with a focus on emic perspectives, knowledge (including non-verbal knowledge), learning, and culture.

73. Analyses of the time devoted to subsistence activity in societies like that of the Aché, where foraging and eating are day-long activities (Hawkes, Hill, and O'Connell 269), have also helped to problematize the boundaries of work versus non-work and eating versus non-eating.

74. Peoples once called "hunter-gatherers" are now often called "foragers," following Richard B. Lee's work on the relatively greater importance of gathered food over hunted (Solway 2003:5).

75. In this Introduction, on social wholes see the section on Mauss in "Early essays on social organization and ecology"; on functionalism see the section on Steward that accompanies Mauss, and the discussion of Firth in " 'Natural' disasters and social order."

76. See Oliver and Larson's (1996) Introduction for a brief review.

77. This "paradigm shift" is often dated to the advent of postmodernism in the early 1980s (Clifford and Marcus 1986), but we would argue that it actually began in the 1970s, among symbolic or interpretive anthropologists influenced by Derrida (1974) and Foucault (1970), and in critiques of colonialism (Said 1978). See for example Boon (1977).

78. Stevens (1990).

79. See for example Terry Rambo (1985).

80. Much of this list is drawn from Wilmsen's (1989) critique of Lee; we consider the critique to be exaggerated and often unfair, but if applied more generally the points are important.
81. Here Wilmsen is drawing on Eric Wolf (1982).
82. Netting (1993:17f.) has a nice section on this topic.
83. Mechanical solidarity is a theoretical type of society united because all the individuals in it are like each other, which Durkheim based on Australian aborigines, a foraging society. Wilmsen (1989) critiques this, but Ingold (1992) makes this connection in more positive terms.
84. This influenced Sahlins' (1972) *Stone Age Economics*.
85. Jacqueline Solway is an associate professor and chair of International Development Studies at Trent University in Canada, studying culture and development in southern Africa. She has a 1987 Ph.D. in anthropology from the University of Toronto. We will focus on Lee in this Introduction, but it is important to note that Solway's dissertation was entitled "Commercialization and social differentiation in a Kalahari village," and that she also co-authored a paper with Lee on the Kalahari fur trade.
86. Richard B. Lee was born in 1937. He first carried out research among the Ju/'hoansi or !Kung in 1963, and continued to visit them regularly, most recently in 2003. He has taught in the anthropology department of the University of Toronto since 1972, and was in 1999 made a university professor. Lee has dedicated his career primarily to understanding foragers (Solway 2003).
87. Wilmsen is now a senior lecturer in the Department of Anthropology at the University of Texas at Austin. He carried out research in the Kalahari, southern Africa, between 1973 and 1994. His critique of Lee dates back to 1983 (Wilmsen 1983). Wilmsen (1989) argues (1) that the San were integrated into modern capitalist economies in reality, as the British colonial administration strengthened the Tswana tribute system, which extracted surplus from the San; and (2) that they were also integrated discursively in a way that obfuscates their real history.
88. Robert McC. Netting, who unfortunately died of cancer in 1995, was a Regents Professor at the University of Arizona, Tucson, where he had taught since 1972. He also taught at the University of Pennsylvania. He had a Ph.D. in anthropology from the University of Chicago (1963). He carried out research on hill farmers, among the Kofyar in Nigeria (begun in 1960) as well as in the Swiss alps. His career was dedicated to understanding smallholder farmers. He is also known as a cultural ecologist (Netting 1977).
89. See for example Schmink and Wood (1987).
90. See for example Gudeman and Rivera (1990).
91. See for example Dove (1993).
92. The difficulties of demanding such an attachment are explored in the section "Social identity and perception of the landscape" in this Introduction.
93. Cf. Ellen's (136) observation that the Indonesian category *Masyarakat terasing* (indigenous peoples) is ambivalent, having connotations of both vulnerability and threat.
94. Hirtz (2003:889) suggests that it is only the modern world that could create indigeneity: "It takes modern means to become traditional, to be indigenous." As a result, Hirtz says, "Through the very process of being recognized as 'indigenous,' these groups enter the realms of modernity."
95. E.g., Brosius et al. (2005).
96. Brosius is a Professor of anthropology at the University of Georgia, where he has taught since 1992. His Ph.D. is from the University of Michigan. He has carried out research in the Philippines as well as Malaysia.

97. Anna Tsing has a 1984 Ph.D. from Stanford University and is currently Professor of Anthropology at the University of California at Santa Cruz. Her most recent work on Indonesian Borneo, published in 2005, is *Friction*.

98. For more detail on this literature see Brosius (1999b).

99. Escobar has written critiques of environmental as well as development discourses (see for example Escobar 1996, 1998). For a recent study applying this approach, see the sociologist Michael Goldman's (2005) work on the World Bank.

100. We recommend the following pieces by Foucault: Foucault 1995 (especially "Panopticism"), Foucault 1980 (especially "Truth and Power" and "Two Lectures"), Burchell et al. 1991 (especially "Governmentality"), Dreyfus and Rabinow 1982, 1983 (especially "Afterword" by Foucault).

101. Ferguson, Escobar, and Brosius are primarily using Foucault's work on the population, but anthropologists have begun to apply his work on the individual. See for example: Triantafillou and Nielsen (2001) and Brigg (2001).

102. Another anthropologist who has written about global environmentalism (as a new, and threatening, form of governmentality) is Gupta (1998).

103. Brosius describes himself as a student of Rappaport's in Brosius 1999 (300).

104. See Rappaport's selection in this volume and Rappaport (1993). Brosius (1999:278f.) says that "Roy Rappaport stands as a particularly pivotal figure" linking the ecological anthropology of the 1960s and 70s to the discursive, "environmental" anthropology of the 1990s.

105. *Fern Gully* was a 1992 movie about magical inhabitants fighting to save the last rain forest, which was threatened by logging. The original campaign might not, of course, have served the Penan in the long run even if it had continued. We should ask if the Penan were better off as icons of conservation or as the uncivilized animals of the Malaysian state view. See for example Conklin and Graham (1995).

106. Brosius (382) makes a similar point about community, drawing a parallel between timber certification and community-based natural resource management projects, which "envelop local communities . . . in a rhetoric of participation."

107. The structure of this article resembles that of Charles Frake in this volume, and he was one of Tsing's professors at Stanford, where she earned her doctoral degree.

108. Others also write about this space. An aspect of collaborations not elucidated by Tsing is the need for local representatives of states and institutions, often at the bottoms of their own hierarchies, to compromise with locals. On this, see especially Li (1999) and Vasan (2002).

109. Conklin and Graham write about Western fantasies of tribal people, while Tsing writes about urban, educated Indonesians' fantasies about tribal people in Indonesia. The two sets of fantasies are surprisingly similar, but this is not something that Tsing comments on at all.

110. For a nice review of the context of sense of place literature in anthropology, see the Introduction to Feld and Basso (1996). They also mention works on sense of place by historians, critics, and artists.

111. See for example Richardson (1984).

112. See particularly Appadurai (1996).

113. This conference produced Hirsch and O'Hanlon (1995).

114. This conference produced Feld and Basso (1996).

115. Charles Frake is Samuel P. Capen Professor of Anthropology at The State University of New York at Buffalo. He taught formerly at the Department of Anthropology at Stanford University. He is a linguistic and cognitive anthropologist as well as a cultural ecologist. His Ph.D. came from Yale University (1955).

116. Maurice Bloch is Professor of Anthropology at the London School of Economics. He was born in France, and trained at the London School of Economics and Cambridge, where he got his Ph.D. in 1968. His fieldwork was primarily carried out in Madagascar, but also in Japan. His interests have included French Marxist theory, ideology, ritual, literacy, cognitive anthropology, and the symbolism of money.

117. See also for example van Beek and Banga (1992).

118. This is to simplify Frake's argument. The discourse of improvement, he writes, has since the 17th and 18th centuries contained a contradiction or dialectic: "The notion of 'improvement' as the restoring of a past that not only was more pleasant and more sheltered but also is part of heritage, a component of identity, lives on today in opposition to the idea of 'improvement' as progress, development, modernization, and urbanization" (450). These opposed ideas support "quite antithetical agendas for action" (449). Identity seems to have created an image of place that obscured specific changes associated with the capitalization of agriculture, and divided (local) capitalized farmers from local preservationists, tourists, and commuters.

119. The essay on the American concept of wilderness by the historian William Cronon (1996) adds depth to this contrast. He argues that alienation from nature is at the heart of the American idea of wilderness: "The dream of an unworked natural landscape is very much the fantasy of people who have never themselves had to work the land to make a living – urban folk for whom food comes from a supermarket or a restaurant instead of a field" (1996:80). Cronon is one of the most well-known environmental historian in the U.S. today, with important works on New England (Cronon 1983) and Chicago (Cronon 1991).

120. DuPuis and Vandergeest (1996), an edited volume on sense of place largely by sociologists, also explores this theme of separation between people and their ideas of "countryside."

121. Bateson writes (1972:337): "If we continue to operate in terms of a Cartesian dualism of mind versus matter, we shall probably also continue to see the world in terms of God versus man; elite versus people; chosen race versus others; nation versus nation; and man versus environment."

122. Though we agree with Ingold and Bateson's critique of the distancing global vision, we must note that Frake and Bloch's work (see previous section of this Introduction) strongly suggests that "direct engagement" or "I–Thou" relations with nature must be researched, not assumed.

123. Cf. the work by Lansing (a student of Rappaport's) on the "emergent complexity" of Balinese temple irrigation systems (1991, 2006).

124. The intentional abrogation of human choice is present in such varied endeavors as World War II submarine warfare (which utilized random number tables), stock market investment strategies, hunting-and-gathering, and agricultural decision making (Dove 1996).

125. The fact that this 1956 collection was published prior to the 1966 acquisition of the first photographs of earth from space undermines Ingold's claim that these photographs were integral to the rise of the global management paradigm.

126. Ingold (465) traces the philosophical antecedents of this arrogance to Kant, specifically to Kant's analogy between understanding the topological form of the earth and understanding the universe as a whole. However, other anthropologists like Richards (1974) have read Kant's analogy quite differently, as helping us to understand the "boundaries of our ignorance."

REFERENCES

Adas, Michael
  1979 Prophets of Rebellion: Millenarian Protest against the European Colonial Order. Chapel Hill: University of North Carolina Press.
Agrawal, Arun
  1995 Dismantling the Divide between Indigenous and Scientific Knowledge. Development and Change 26:413–439.
Agrawal, Arun, and Clark C. Gibson, eds.
  2001 Communities and the Environment: Ethnicity, Gender, and the State in Community-Based Conservation. New Brunswick, NJ: Rutgers University Press.
Allen, N. J.
  2000 Categories and Classifications: Maussian Reflections on the Social. New York: Berghahn Books.
Alvard, Michael S., and David A. Nolin
  2002 Rousseau's Whale Hunt? Coordination Among Big-Game Hunters. Current Anthropology 43(4):533–559.
Appadurai, Arjun
  1996 Modernity at Large: Cultural Dimensions of Globalization. Minneapolis: University of Minnesota Press.
Aristotle
  1908–56 12 vols. Works. W. D. Ross, trans. and ed. Vol. 10: Politica. Benjamin Jowett, trans. London: Oxford University Press.
Balée, William
  1993 Indigenous Transformation of Amazonian Forests. L'Homme 126–128, XXXIII(2–4):231–254.
  1994 Footprints of the Forest: Ka'apor Ethnobotany. The Historical Ecology of Plant Utilization by an Amazonian People. New York: Columbia University Press.
Bandy, Dale E., Dennis P. Garrity, and Pedro A. Sánchez
  1993 The Worldwide Problem of Slash-and-Burn Agriculture. Agroforestry Today 5(3): 1–6.
Barfield, Thomas, ed.
  1997 The Dictionary of Anthropology. Oxford: Blackwell.
Barth, Fredrik
  1959 Segmentary Opposition and the Theory of Games: A Study of Pathan Organization. Journal of the Royal Anthropological Society 89:5–21.
  1966 Models of Social Organization. Royal Anthropological Institute of Great Britain and Ireland, Occasional Paper no. 23.
  1993 Balinese Worlds. Chicago: University of Chicago Press.
Barth, Fredrik, ed.
  1969 Ethnic Groups and Boundaries: The Social Organization of Culture Difference. Boston: Little, Brown and Company.
Bateson, Gregory
  1936 Naven, A Survey of the Problems Suggested by a Composite Picture of the Culture of a New Guinea Tribe Drawn from Three Points of View. Cambridge: Cambridge University Press.
Bateson, Gregory, and Margaret Mead
  1942 Balinese Character: A Photographic Analysis. New York: New York Academy of Sciences.

Beckerman, Steven
  1979   The Abundance of Protein in Amazonia: A Reply to Gross. American Anthropologist 81:533–560.
  1982   Carpe Diem: An Optimal Foraging Approach to Bari Fishing and Hunting. *In* Adaptive Strategies of Native Amazonians. Raymond B. Hames and William T. Vickers, eds. Pp. 269–299. New York: Academic Press.
van Beek, Walter E. A. and Pieteke M. Banga
  1992   The Dogon and their Trees. *In* Bush Base: Forest Farm: Culture, Environment and Development. Elisabeth Croll and David Parkin, eds. Pp. 57–75. London: Routledge.
Beidelman, O. T.
  1966   The Ox and Nuer Sacrifice: Some Freudian Hypotheses about Nuer Symbolism. Man (n.s.)1:453–467.
Belshaw, Cyril S.
  1951   Social Consequences of the Mount Lamington Eruption. Oceania 21(4):241–252.
Benjamin, Geoffrey
  2002   On Being Tribal in the Malay World. *In* Tribal Communities in the Malay World: Historical, Cultural, and Social Perspectives. Geoffrey Benjamin and Cynthia Chou, eds. Pp. 7–76. Leiden/Singapore: IIAS/ISAS.
Bennett, John
  1976   The Ecological Transition. New York: Pergamon Press.
Bergmann, Frithjof
  1975   On the Inadequacies of Functionalism. Michigan Discussions in Anthropology 1:2–23.
Berlin, Brent, Dennis E. Breedlove, and Peter H. Raven
  1974   Principles of Tzeltal Plant Classification: An Introduction to the Botanical Ethnography of a Mayan-Speaking People of Highland Chiapas. New York: Academic Press.
Béteille, Andre
  1998   The Idea of Indigenous People. Current Anthropology 39(2):187–191.
Blaikie, Piers M.
  1985   The Political Economy of Soil Erosion in Developing Countries. New York: Longman.
Blaikie, Piers M., and Harold Brookfield
  1987   Land Degradation and Society. London: Methuen.
Blaikie, Piers M., Terry Canon, Ian Davis, and Ben Wisner
  1994   At Risk: Natural Hazards, People's Vulnerability, and Disasters. London: Routledge.
Bloch, Maurice, and Jonathan Parry
  1989   Introduction: Money and the Morality of Exchange. *In* Money and the Morality of Exchange. Jonathan Parry and Maurice Bloch, eds. Pp. 1–32. Cambridge: Cambridge University Press.
Boon, James A.
  1977   The Anthropological Romance of Bali 1597–1972: Dynamic Perspectives in Marriage and Caste, Politics and Religion. Cambridge: Cambridge University Press.
Boserup, Ester
  1965   The Conditions of Agricultural Growth: The Economics of Agrarian Change under Population Pressure. Chicago: Aldine.
Botkin, Daniel
  1990   Discordant Harmonies: A New Ecology for the Twenty-First Century. New York: Clarendon Press.

Brigg, Morgan
2001 Empowering NGOs: The Microcredit Movement through Foucault's Notion of Dispositif. Alternatives: Global, Local, Political 26(3):233–259.
Brosius, J. Peter
1999 Analyses and Interventions: Anthropological Engagements with Environmentalism. Current Anthropology 40(3):277–309.
Brosius, J. Peter, Anna L. Tsing, and Charles Zerner
1998 Representing Communities: Histories and Politics of Community-Based Natural Resource Management. Society and Natural Resources 11:157–168.
Brosius, J. Peter, Anna L. Tsing, and Charles Zerner, eds.
2005 Communities and Conservation: Histories and Politics of Community-Based Natural Resource Management. Walnut Creek, CA: Altamira Press.
Brush, Stephen B.
1975 The Concept of Carrying Capacity for Systems of Shifting Cultivation. American Anthropologist 77(4):799–811.
Burchell, Graham, Colin Gordon, and Peter Miller, eds.
1991 The Foucault Effect: Studies in Governmentality. Chicago: University of Chicago Press.
Burling, Robbins
1965 Hill Farms and Padi Fields: Life in Mainland Southeast Asia. Englewood Cliffs, NJ: Prentice-Hall.
Camus, Albert
2001[1947] The Plague. Robin Buss, trans. London: Allen Lane.
Carneiro, Robert L., ed.
1967 The Evolution of Society: Selections from Herbert Spencer's Principles of Sociology. Chicago: University of Chicago Press.
Carpenter, Carol
1997 Women and Livestock, Fodder, and Uncultivated Land in Pakistan. In Women Working in the Environment. Carolyn E. Sachs, ed. Pp. 157–171. Washington, DC: Taylor & Francis.
2001 The Role of Economic Invisibility in Development: Veiling Women's Work in Rural Pakistan. Natural Resources Forum 25:11–19.
Casey, Edward S.
1993 Getting Back into Place: Toward a Renewed Understanding of the Place-World. Bloomington, IN: Indiana University Press.
Chambers, Robert
1983 Rural Development: Putting the Last First. London: Longman.
Clifford, James, and George E. Marcus, eds.
1986 Writing Culture: The Poetics and Politics of Ethnography. Berkeley: University of California Press.
Condominas, Georges
1977[1957] We Have Eaten the Forest: The Story of a Montagnard Village in the Central Highlands of Vietnam. Adrienne Foulke, trans. New York: Hill and Wang.
Conklin, Beth A., and Laura R. Graham
1995 The Shifting Middle Ground: Amazonian Indians and Eco-Politics. American Anthropologist 97(4):695–710.
Conklin, Harold C.
1954 The Relation of Hanunóo Culture to the Plant World. Ph.D. dissertation, Yale University.
1957 Hanunóo Agriculture: A Report on an Integral System of Shifting Cultivation in the Philippines. Rome: Food and Agriculture Organization of the United Nations.

1959   Population-Land Balance Under Systems of Tropical Forest Agriculture. Proceedings of the Ninth Pacific Science Congress 7:63.

1961   The Study of Shifting Cultivation. Current Anthropology 2(1):27–91.

1980   Ethnographic Atlas of Ifugao: A Study of Environment, Culture, and Society in Northern Luzon. New Haven: Yale University Press.

Cronon, William
1983   Changes in the Land: Indians, Colonists, and the Ecology of New England. New York: Hill and Wang.

1991   Nature's Metropolis: Chicago and the Great West. New York: W.W. Norton.

1992   A Place for Stories: Nature, History and Narrative. Journal of American History 78(4):1347–1376.

1996   The Trouble with Wilderness, or Getting Back to the Wrong Nature. In Uncommon Ground: Rethinking the Human Place In Nature. William Cronon, ed. Pp. 69–90. New York: W. W. Norton.

Defoe, Daniel
1992[1722]   A Journal of the Plague Year. Paula R. Backschneider, ed. New York: W. W. Norton.

Derrida, Jaques
1974[1967]   Of Grammatology. Gayatri C. Spivak, trans. Baltimore: The Johns Hopkins University Press.

Diamond, Jared M.
1997   Guns, Germs, and Steel: The Fates of Human Societies. New York: W. W. Norton.

Diener, Paul, Donald Nonini, and Eugene E. Robkin
1978   The Dialectics of the Sacred Cow: Ecological Adaptation versus Political Appropriation in the Origins of India's Cattle Complex. Dialectical Anthropology 3(3):221–241.

Dillingham, Beth, and Robert L. Carneiro, eds.
1987   Ethnological Essays/Leslie A. White. Albuquerque: University of New Mexico Press.

Dole, Gertrude E., and Robert L. Carneiro, eds.
1960   Essays in the Science of Culture; In Honor of Leslie A. White, in Celebration of his Sixtieth Birthday and his Thirtieth Year of Teaching at the University of Michigan. New York: Crowell.

Dove, Michael R.
1983   Theories of Swidden Agriculture and the Political Economy of Ignorance. Agroforestry Systems 1:85–99.

1985a   The Agroecological Mythology of the Javanese, and the Political-Economy of Indonesia. Indonesia 39:1–36.

1985b   Swidden Agriculture in Indonesia: The Subsistence Strategies of the Kalimantan Kantu'. Berlin: Mouton.

1992   The Dialectical History of "Jungle" in Pakistan. Journal of Anthropological Research 48(3):231–253.

1993   Smallholder Rubber and Swidden Agriculture in Borneo: A Sustainable Adaptation to the Ecology and Economy of the Tropical Forest. Economic Botany 47(2):136–147.

1996   Process versus Product in Kantu' Augury: A Traditional Knowledge System's Solution to the Problem of Knowing. In Redefining Nature: Ecology, Culture, Domestication. R. F. Ellen and K. Fukui, eds. Pp.557–596. Oxford: Berg Publishers.

2000   The Life-Cycle of Indigenous Knowledge, and the Case of Natural Rubber Production. In Indigenous Environmental Knowledge and its Transformations. Roy F. Ellen, Peter Parkes, and Alan Bicker, eds. Pp. 213–251. Amsterdam: Harwood.

2006   Equilibrium Theory and Inter-Disciplinary Borrowing: A Comparison of Old and New Ecological Anthropologies. *In* Imagining Political Ecology. Aletta Biersack and James B. Greenberg, eds. Durham, NC: Duke University Press.

2007a   Perceptions of Local Knowledge and Adaptation on Mt. Merapi, Central Java. For: Traditional Ecological Knowledge and Crisis Management in Island Southeast Asia. Roy F. Ellen and Rajindra Puri, eds. New York: Berghahn Books.

2007b   Volcanic Eruption as Metaphor of Social Integration: A Political Ecological Study of Mount Merapi, Central Java. *In* Environment, Development and Change in Rural Asia-Pacific: Between Local and Global. John Connell and E, Waddell, eds. Pp. 16–37. New York: Routledge.

Dreyfus, Hubert L., and Paul Rabinow
1982, 1983   Michel Foucault: Beyond Structuralism and Hermeneutics. 2nd ed. Chicago: University of Chicago Press.

DuPuis, E. Melanie, and Peter Vandergeest
1996   Creating the Countryside: The Politics of Rural and Environmental Discourse. Philadelphia: Temple University Press.

Durkheim, Emile
1964[1933]   The Division of Labor in Society. George Simpson, trans. New York: Free Press.

1965[1915]   The Elementary Forms of Religious Life. Joseph W. Swain, trans. New York: The Free Press.

Dyson-Hudson, Rada
1972   Pastoralism: Self-Image and Behavioral Reality. Journal of Asian and African Studies 7(1–2):30–47.

Dyson-Hudson, Rada, and Neville Dyson-Hudson
1969   Subsistence Herding in Uganda. Scientific American 220:76–89.

Ellen, Roy F.
1978   Nuaulu Settlement and Ecology: An Approach to the Environmental Relations of an Eastern Indonesian Community. Verhandelingen 83. The Hague: Martinus Nijhoff.

1982   Environment, Subsistence, and System: The Ecology of Small-Scale Social Formations. Cambridge: Cambridge University Press.

Ellen, Roy, Peter Parkes, and Alan Bicker, eds.
2000   Indigenous Environmental Knowledge and its Transformations: Critical Anthropological Perspectives. Amsterdam: Harwood.

Ellen, Roy F., and P. Harris
2000   Introduction. *In* Indigenous Environmental Knowledge and its Transformations. Roy F. Ellen, Peter Parkes, and Alan Bicker, eds. Pp. 213–251. Amsterdam: Harwood.

Elvin, Mark
1998   Who was Responsible for the Weather? Moral Meteorology in Late Imperial China. Osiris, 2nd series, 13:213–237.

Escobar, Arturo
1995   Encountering Development: The Making and Unmaking of the Third World. Princeton: Princeton University Press.

1996   Constructing Nature: Elements for a Poststructural Political Ecology. *In* Liberation Ecologies: Environment, Development, Social Movements. Richard Peet and Michael Watts, eds. Pp. 46–68. London: Routledge.

1998   Whose Knowledge, Whose Nature? Biodiversity, Conservation, and the Political Ecology of Social Movements. Journal of Political Ecology 5:53–82.

Evans-Pritchard, E. E.
  1940   The Nuer: A description of the Modes of Livelihood and Political Institutions of a Nilotic People. New York: Oxford University Press.
  1951   Kinship and Marriage Among the Nuer. Oxford: Clarendon Press.
  1956   Nuer Religion. Oxford: Clarendon Press.
  1976[1937] Witchcraft, Oracles and Magic Among the Azande. Abr. ed. Oxford: Clarendon Press.
Fairhead, James, and Melissa Leach
  1995   Reading Forest History Backwards: The Interaction of Policy and Local Land Use in Guinea's Forest-Savanna Mosaic, 1893–1993. Environment and History I:55–91.
  1996   Misreading the African Landscape: Society and Ecology in a Forest-Savanna Mosaic. Cambridge: Cambridge University Press.
Feld, Steven, and Keith H. Basso
  1996   Introduction. In Senses of Place. Steven Feld and Keith H. Basso, eds. Pp. 3–11. Santa Fe, NM: School of American Research Press.
Ferguson, James
  1990   The Anti-Politics Machine: "Development," Depoliticization and Bureaucratic Power in Lesotho. Cambridge: Cambridge University Press.
Fiedler, Peggy L., Peter S. White, and Robert A. Lediy
  1997   The Paradigm Shift in Ecology and its Implications for Conservation. In The Ecological Basis of Conservation: Heterogeneity, Ecosystems, and Biodiversity. Steward T. A. Pickett, Richard S. Ostfield, Moshe Shachak, and Gene E. Likens, eds. Pp. 83–92. New York: Chapman and Hall.
Firth, Raymond
  1936   We, the Tikopia; A Sociological Study of Kinship in Primitive Polynesia, by Raymond Firth. London: G. Allen and Unwin.
  1940   The Work of the Gods in Tikopia. London: P. Lund, Humphries for the London School of Economics and Political Science.
Foucault, Michel
  1970[1966] The Order of Things: An Archaeology of the Human Sciences. New Yorks: Vintage Books.
  1980[1972] Power/Knowledge: Selected Interviews and Other Writings 1972–1977. Colin Gordon, ed. Colin Gordon, Leo Marshall, John Mepham, Kate Soper, trans. New York: Pantheon Books.
  1991   Governmentality. In The Foucault Effect: Studies in Governmentality. Graham Burchell, Colin Gordon, and Peter Miller, eds. Pp. 87–104. Chicago: University of Chicago Press.
  1995[1975] Discipline and Punish: The Birth of the Prison. 2nd Vintage Books edition. Alan Sheridan, trans. New York: Vintage.
Fox, James J.
  1979   Foreword. In Seasonal Variations of the Eskimo: A Study in Social Morphology. Marcel Mauss. Pp. 1–17. London: Routledge and Kegan Paul.
Frake, Charles O.
  1962   Cultural Ecology and Ethnography. American Anthropologist 64:53–59.
Freeman, Derek
  1970   Report on the Iban. New York: The Athlone Press.
Geertz, Clifford
  1959   Form and Variation in Balinese Village Structure. American Anthropologist 61:991–1012.
  1963   Agricultural Involution: The Processes of Ecological Change in Indonesia. Berkeley: University of California Press, for the Association of Asian Studies.

1973 The Interpretation of Cultures; Selected Essays. New York: Basic Books.

1988 Works and Lives : The Anthropologist As Author. Stanford, CA: Stanford University Press.

1996 Afterword. *In* Senses of Place. Steven Feld and Keith H. Basso, eds. Pp. 259–262. Santa Fe, NM: School of American Research Press.

Glacken, Clarence J.

1967 Traces on the Rhodian Shore: Nature and Culture in Western Thought from Ancient Times to the End of the Eighteenth Century. Berkeley: University of California Press.

Goldman, Michael

2005 Banking on Nature: The New Politics and Science of the World Bank. New Haven, CT: Yale University Press.

Greenough, Paul, and Anna Tsing

1994 Environmental Discourses and Human Welfare in South and Southeast Asia. Items 48(4):95–99.

Gross, Daniel R.

1975 Protein Capture and Cultural Development in the Amazon Basin. American Anthropologist 77:526–549.

Grove, Richard H.

1995 Green Imperialism: Colonial Expansion, Tropical Island Edens, and the Origins of Environmentalism, 1600–1860. Cambridge: Cambridge University Press.

Grove, Richard H., and John Chappell

2000 El Niño – History and Crisis: Studies from the Asia-Pacific Region. Cambridge: White Horse Press.

Gudeman, Stephen

1986 Economics as Culture: Models and Metaphors of Livelihood. London: Routledge.

Gudeman, Stephen, and Alberto Rivera

1990 Conversations in Colombia: The Domestic Economy in Life and Text. Cambridge: Cambridge University Press.

Guérin, Mathieu

2001 Essartage et Riziculture Humide, Complémentarité des Écosystèmes Agraires à Stung Treng au Début du XXe Siècle. Aséanie, Sciences Humaines en Asie du Sud-Est n°8, Bangkok, December 2001:35–55.

Gunderson, Lance H., C. S. Holling, and Stephen S. Light, eds.

1995 Barriers and Bridges to the Renewal of Ecosystems and Institutions. New York: Columbia University Press.

Gupta, Akhil

1998 Postcolonial Developments: Agriculture in the Making of Modern India Durham: Duke University Press.

Guthman, Julie

1997 Representing Crisis: The Theory of Himalayan Environmental Degradation and the Project of Development in Post-Rana Nepal. Development and Change 28:45–69.

Hames, Raymond B., and William T. Vickers, eds.

1982 Adaptive Strategies of Native Amazonians. New York: Academic Press.

Haraway, Donna

1991 Simians, Cyborgs, and Women: The Reinvention of Nature. London: Free Association Books.

Hardin, Garrett

1968 The Tragedy of the Commons. Science 162:1243–1248.

Harris, Marvin
　1968　The Rise of Anthropological Theory: A History of Theories of Culture. New York: Crowell.
　1974　Cows, Pigs, Wars and Witches; The Riddles of Culture. New York: Random House.
　1979　Cultural Materialism: The Struggle for a Science of Culture. New York: Random House.
　1985　Good to Eat: Riddles of Food and Culture. London: Allen and Unwin.
Harwell, Emily
　2000　Remote Sensibilities: Discourses of Technology and the Making of Indonesia's Natural Disaster. Development and Change 31(1):307–340.
Hawkes, Kristen
　1993　Why Hunter-Gatherers Work: An Ancient Version of the Problem of Public Good. Current Anthropology 34:341–351.
Hawkes, Kristen, and James F. O'Connell
　1981　Affluent Hunters? Some Comments in Light of the Alyawara Case. American Anthropologist 83:622–626.
　1985　Optimal Foraging Models and the Case of the !Kung. American Anthropologist 87(2):401–405.
　1992　On Optimal Foraging Models and Subsistence Transitions. Current Anthropology 33(1):63–66.
Headland, Thomas N., and Robert C. Bailey
　1991　Introduction: Have Hunter-Gatherers ever Lived in Tropical Rain Forest Independently of Agriculture? Theme issue. Human Ecology 19(2):115–122.
Heizer, Robert F.
　1963　Foreword. In Cultural and Natural Areas of Native North America. Alfred. L. Kroeber. Pp. v–ix. Berkeley: University of California Press.
Henderson, Carol
　1998　The Great Cow Explosion in Rajasthan. In Advances in Historical Ecology. William Balée, ed. Pp. 349–375. New York: Columbia University Press.
Herskovits, Melville J.
　1926　The Cattle Complex in East Africa. American Anthropologist 28:230–272, 361–388,494–528.
Heston, Alan
　1971　An Approach to the Sacred Cow of India. Current Anthropology 12(2):191–209.
Hewitt, Kenneth
　1983　The Idea of Calamity in a Technocratic Age. In Interpretations of Calamity, From the Viewpoint of Human Ecology. Kenneth Hewitt, ed. Pp. 3–32. Boston: Allen and Unwin.
Hill, Kim
　1988　Macronutrient Modifications of Optimal Foraging Theory: An Approach Using Indifference Curves Applied to Some Modern Foragers. Human Ecology 16:157–197.
Hill, Kim, and Kristen Hawkes
　1982　Neotropical Hunting Among the Aché of Eastern Paraguay. In Adaptive Strategies of Native Amazonians. Raymond B. Hames and William T. Vickers, eds. Pp. 139–188. New York: Academic Press.
Hill, Kim, Kristen Hawkes, A. Hurtado, and H. Kaplan
　1984　Seasonal Variance in the Diet of Aché Hunter-Gatherers in Eastern Paraguay. Human Ecology 12:145–180.

Hippocrates
    1995[1923]   8 vols. Airs, Waters, Places. *In* Vol. I: Ancient Medicine. Loeb Classical Library 147. W. H. S. Jones, trans. Cambridge: Harvard University Press.
Hirsch, Eric, and Michael O'Hanlon, eds.
    1995   The Anthropology of Landscape: Perspectives of Place and Space. Oxford: Clarendon Press.
Hirtz, Frank
    2003   It takes Modern Means to be Traditional: On Recognizing Indigenous Cultural Communities in the Philippines. Development and Change 34(5):887–914.
Hoben, Allan
    1995   Paradigms and Politics: The Cultural Construction of Environmental Policy in Ethiopia. World Development 213(6):1007–1021.
Hodgson, Dorothy L.
    2002   Introduction: Comparative Perspectives on the Indigenous Rights Movement in Africa and the Americas. American Anthropologist 104(4):1037–1049.
Holbach, Baron Paul Henri d'
    1774   Système Social, ou Principes Naturelles de la Monde et de la Politique. London.
Homans, George C.
    1941   Anxiety and Ritual: The Theories of Malinowski and Radcliffe-Brown. American Anthropologist 43:164–172.
Hornborg, Alf
    1996   Ecology as Semiotics: Outlines of a Contextualist Paradigm for Human Ecology. *In* Nature and Society: Anthropological Perspectives. Philippe Descola and Gísli Pálsson, eds. Pp. 45–62. London: Routledge.
Hutchinson, Sharon E.
    1996   Nuer Dilemmas: Coping with Money, War, and the State. Berkeley: University of California Press.
Ingold, Tim
    1980   Hunters, Pastoralists, and Ranchers: Reindeer Economies and their Transformations. Cambridge: Cambridge University Press.
    1986   Appropriation of Nature: Essays on Human Ecology and Social Relations. Manchester: Manchester University Press.
    1992   Comments. Current Anthropology 33(1):208–209.
    1996a   Hunting and Gathering As Ways of Perceiving the Environment. *In* Redefining Nature: Ecology, Culture, Domestication. Roy F. Ellen and Katsuyoshi Fukui, eds. Pp. 117–155. Oxford: Berg.
    1996b   The Optimal Forager and Economic Man. *In* Nature and Society: Anthropological Perspectives. Philippe Descola and Gísli Pálsson, eds. Pp. 25–43. London: Routledge.
    2000   Perception of the Environment: Essays on Livelihood, Dwelling and Skill. London: Routledge.
Ives, Jack D., and Bruno Messerli
    1989   The Himalayan Dilemma: Reconciling Development and Conservation. London: Routledge.
Kammen, Daniel M., and Michael R. Dove
    1997   The Virtues of Mundane Science. Environment 39(6):10–15,38–41.
Keesing, Felix M.
    1952   The Papuan Orokaiva vs Mt. Lamington: Cultural Shock and its Aftermath. Human Organization 11(1):16–22.
Kellert, Stephen R., and Edward O. Wilson, eds.
    1993   The Biophilia Hypothesis. Washington, DC: Island Press.

ibn Khaldûn
    1967   An Introduction to History: The Muqaddimah. Franz Rosenthal, trans., N. J.
            Dawood, ed. London: Routledge and Kegan Paul.
Krech III, Shepard
    1999   The Ecological Indian: Myth and History. New York/London: W. W. Norton.
Kroeber, Alfred L.
    1963   Cultural and Natural Areas of Native North America. Berkeley: University of
            California Press.
Kuipers, Joel, and Ray McDermott, eds.
    2007   Fine Description: Ethnographic and Linguistic Essays by Harold C. Conklin. Mono-
            graph 56, Southeast Asia Program, Yale University.
Kuper, Adam
    2003   The Return of the Native. Current Anthropology 44:389–402.
Lansing, J. Stephen
    1991   Priests and Programmers: Technologies of Power in the Engineered Landscape of
            Bali. Princeton, N.J.: Princeton University Press.
    2006   Perfect Order: Recognizing Complexity in Bali. Princeton, N.J.: Princeton Univer-
            sity Press.
Lawrence, D., D. R. Peart, and M. Leighton
    1998   The Impact of Shifting Cultivation on a Rainforest Landscape in West Kalimantan:
            Spatial and Temporal Dynamics. Landscape Ecology 13:135–148.
Leach, Edmund R.
    1954   Political Systems of Highland Burma; A Study of Kachin Social Structure.
            Cambridge: Harvard University Press, for the London School of Economics and
            Political Science.
Lee, Richard B.
    1968   What Hunters Do for a Living: Or, How to Make Out on Scarce Resources. In
            Man the Hunter. Richard B. Lee and Irven DeVore, eds. Pp. 30–48. Chicago: Aldine.
Li, Tania Murray
    1996   Images of Community: Discourse and Strategy in Property Relations. Development
            and Change 27:501–527.
    1999   Compromising Power: Development, Culture, and Rule in Indonesia. Cultural
            Anthropology 14(3):295–322.
    2000   Articulating Indigenous Identity in Indonesia: Resource Politics and the Tribal Slot.
            Comparative Studies in Society and History 42(1):149–179.
    2001   Boundary Work: Community, Market, and State Reconsidered. In Communities
            and the Environment: Ethnicity, Gender, and the State in Community-Based Conserva-
            tion. Arun Agrawal and Clark C. Gibson, eds. Pp. 157–179. New Brunswick: Rutgers
            University Press.
    2002   Ethnic Cleansing, Recursive Knowledge, and the Dilemma of Sedentarism. Interna-
            tional Social Science Journal 173:361–371.
Linares, Olga
    1976   Garden Hunting in the American Tropics. Human Ecology 4(4):331–349.
Lovén, Lasse, n.d. Swidden Heritage Alive and Well in Koli. Electronic document. http://
            www.metla.fi/koli/kaski/yleis-en.htm, accessed May 6, 2007.
Mair, Lucy
    1985   The Cattle Complex. Man 20(4):743.
Malkki, Liisa H.
    1997   News and Culture: Transitory Phenomena and the Fieldwork Tradition. In Anthro-
            pological Locations: Boundaries and Grounds of a Field Science. Akhil Gupta and James
            Ferguson, eds. Pp. 86–101. Berkeley: University of California Press.

Marcus, George E., and Michael M. J. Fischer
  1986 Anthropology as Cultural Critique: An Experimental Moment in the Human Sciences. Chicago: University of Chicago Press.
Margalef, Ramon
  1968 Perspectives in Ecological Theory. Chicago: University of Chicago Press.
Martin, John
  1983 Optimal Foraging Theory: A Review of Some Models and Their Applications. American Anthropologist 85:612–629.
Mauss, Marcel, with Henri Beuchat
  1979 Seasonal Variations of the Eskimo: A Study in Social Morphology. James J. Fox, trans. London: Routledge and Kegan Paul.
McDermott, Raymond
  1997 Conklin, Joyce, and the Wannaknów. American Anthropologist 99(2):257–260.
McKey, Doyle B.
  1996 Wild Yam Question. In Encyclopedia of Cultural Anthropology, vol. 4. David Levinson and Melvin Embers, eds. Pp. 1363–1366. New York: Henry Holt for HRAF.
Meggers, Betty J.
  1971 Amazonia: Man and Culture in a Counterfeit Paradise. Chicago: Aldine, Atherton.
Montesquieu, Baron Charles de Secondat de
  1989[1748] The Spirit of the Laws (De l'esprit des loix). Anne M. Cohler, Basia Carolyn Miller, Harold Samuel Stone, trans. and eds. Cambridge: Cambridge University Press.
Murphy, Robert F.
  1977 Introduction: The Anthropological Theories of Julian H. Steward. In Evolution and Ecology: Essays on Social Transformation by Julian H. Steward. Jane C. Steward and Robert F. Murphy, eds. Pp. 1–39. Urbana, IL: University of Illinois Press.
Netting, Robert McC.
  1968 Hill Farmers of Nigeria: Cultural Ecology of the Kofyar of the Jos Plateau. Seattle: University of Washington Press.
  1977 Cultural Ecology. Menlo Park, CA: Cummings Pub. Co.
  1981 Balancing on an Alp: Ecological Change and Continuity in a Swiss Mountain Community. Cambridge: Cambridge University Press.
  1993 Smallholders, Householders: Farm Families and the Ecology of Intensive, Sustainable Agriculture. Stanford: Stanford University Press.
O'Connell, James F., and Kristen Hawkes
  1981 Alyawara Plant Use and Optimal Foraging Theory. In Hunter-Gatherer Foraging Strategies: Ethnographic and Archaeological Analyses. Bruce Winterhalder and Eric A. Smith, eds. Pp. 99–125. Chicago: University of Chicago Press.
  1984 Food Choice and Foraging Sites among the Alyawara. Journal of Anthropological Research 40:504–535.
Oliver, Chadwick D., and Bruce C. Larson
  1996 Forest Stand Dynamics. Update edition. New York: John Wiley.
Oliver-Smith, Anthony, and Susanna M. Hoffman, eds.
  1999 The Angry Earth: Disaster in Anthropological Perspective. New York: Routledge.
Orlove, Benjamin S., John C. H. Chaing, and Mark A. Cane
  2000 Forecasting Andean Rainfall and Crop Yield from the Influence of El Niño on Pleiades Visibility. Nature 403(6):68–71.
Otto, John S., and N. E. Anderson
  1982 Slash-and-Burn Cultivation in the Highlands South: A Problem in Comparative Agricultural History. Comparative Study of Society and History 24:131–147.

Oxford English Dictionary
   1999   CD Rom version. New York: Oxford University Press.
Padoch, Christine, Emily Harwell, and Adi Susanto
   1998   Swidden, Sawah, and In-Between: Agricultural Transformation in Borneo. Human
      Ecology 26(1):3–20.
Paul, B. K.
   1984   Perception of and Agricultural Adjustment to Floods in Jamuna Floodplain,
      Bangladesh. Human Ecology 12(1):3–19.
Parker, Eugene
   1992   Forest Islands and Kayapó Resource Management in Amazonia: A Reappraisal of
      the Apêtê. American Anthropologist 94(2):406–428.
   1993   Fact and Fiction in Amazonia: The Case of the Apêtê. American Anthropologist
      95(3):715–723.
Pelzer, Karl J.
   1978   Swidden Cultivation in Southeast Asia: Historical, Ecological, and Economic Per-
      spectives. In Farmers in the Forest: Economic Development and Marginal Agriculture
      in Northern Thailand. Peter Kunstadter, E. C. Chapman, and Sanga Sabhasri, eds.
      Pp. 271–286. Honolulu: University of Hawaii Press.
Pliny
   1938–63   Natural History, 10 vols. H. Rackham, trans. Cambridge: Harvard University
      Press.
Posey, Darrell. A.
   1992   Reply to Parker. American Anthropologist 94(2):441–443.
   1998   Diachronic Ecotones and Anthropogenic Landscapes in Amazonia: Contesting the
      Consciousness of Conservation. In Advances in Historical Ecology. William Balée, ed.
      Pp. 104–118. Columbia: Columbia University Press.
Puri, Rajindra K.
   2005   Deadly Dances in the Bornean Rainforest: Hunting Knowledge of the Penan Balui.
      Verhandelingen 222. Leiden: KITLV.
Radcliffe-Brown, A. R.
   1952   Structure and Function in Primitive Society; Essays and Addresses. Glencoe, IL:
      Free Press.
Rambo, A. Terry
   1985   Primitive Polluters: Semang Impact on the Malaysian Tropical Rain Forest System.
      Anthropological Papers 76, Museum of Anthropology. Ann Arbor: University of
      Michigan.
Rappaport, Roy A.
   1968   Pigs for the Ancestors: Ritual in the Ecology of a New Guinea People. New Haven:
      Yale University Press.
   1979   Ecology, Meaning, and Religion. Richmond, CA: North Atlantic Books.
   1984   Pigs for the Ancestors: Ritual in the Ecology of a New Guinea People. 2nd ed. New
      Haven: Yale University Press.
   1990   Ecosystems, Populations and People. In The Ecosystem Approach in Anth-
      ropology. Emilio F. Moran, ed. Pp. 41–72. Ann Arbor: University of Michigan
      Press.
   1993   Distinguished Lecture in General Anthropology: The Anthropology of Trouble.
      American Anthropologist 95(2):295–303.
   1994   Humanity's Evolution and Anthropology's Future. In Assessing Cultural Anthro-
      pology. Robert Borofsky, ed. Pp. 153–167. New York: McGraw-Hill.
   1999   Ritual and Religion in the Making of Humanity. Cambridge, UK: Cambridge Uni-
      versity Press.

Raumolin, Jussi, ed.
1987   Special Issue on Swidden Cultivation. Suomen Antropologi (Journal of the Finnish Anthropological Society) 12(4).

Redford, Kent, and Steven E. Sanderson
2000   Extracting Humans from Nature. Conservation Biology 14:1362–1364.

Richards, Audrey I.
1939   Land, Labour and Diet in Northern Rhodesia; An Economic Study of the Bemba Tribe. Pub. for the International African Institute. Oxford: Oxford University Press.
1948   Hunger and Work in a Savage Tribe: A Functional Study of Nutrition among the Southern Bantu. Glencoe, IL: Free Press.

Richards, Paul
1974   Kant's Geography and Mental Maps. Transactions of the Institute of British Geographers 61(March):1–16.
1985   Indigenous Agricultural Revolution: Ecology and Food Production in West Africa. London: Hutchinson.
1986   Coping with Hunger: Hazard and Experiment in an African Rice-Farming System. London: Allen and Unwin.

Richardson, Miles, ed.
1984   Place: Experience and Symbol. Geoscience and Man, 24. Baton Rouge: Department of Geography and Anthropology, Louisiana State University.

Robbins, Paul
1999   Meat Matters: Cultural Politics Along the Commodity Chain in India. Ecumene 6(4):399–423.

Roe, Emery M.
1991   Development Narratives, or Making the Best of Blueprint Development. World Development 19(4):287–300.

Roosevelt, Anna C.
1998   Ancient and Modern Hunter-Gatherers of Lowland South America: An Evolutionary Problem. In Advances in Historical Ecology. William Balée, ed. Pp. 190–212. New York: Columbia University Press.

Rosaldo, Renato
1986   From the Door of His Tent: The Fieldworker and the Inquisitor. In Writing Culture: The Poetics and Politics of Ethnography. James Clifford and George E. Marcus, eds. Pp. 77–97. Berkeley: University of California Press.
1993[1989]   Culture and Truth: The Remaking of Social Analysis. 2nd ed. Boston: Beacon Press.

Sachs, Wolfgang
1992   One World. In The Development Dictionary: A Guide to Knowledge as Power. Wolfgang Sachs, ed. Pp. 102–115. London: Zed Books.

Sahlins, Marshall
1976   Comment on A. H. Berger, Structural and Eclectic Revisions of Marxist Strategy: A Cultural Materialist Critique. Current Anthropology 17:298–300.
1972   Stone Age Economics. Chicago: Aldine.

Said, Edward W.
1978   Orientalism. New York: Vintage Books.

Schmink, Marianne, and Charles H. Wood
1987   The "Political Ecology" of Amazonia. In Lands at Risk in the Third World. Peter D. Little and Michael M. Horowitz, eds. Pp. 38–57. Boulder: Westview Press.

Schneider, Harold K.
   1957   The Subsistence Role of Cattle Among the Pakot and in East Africa. American Anthropologist 59:278–300.
Schoener, Thomas W.
   1971   Theory of Feeding Strategies. Annual Review of Ecology and Systematics 2:369–404.
   1974   The Compression Hypothesis and Temporal Resource Partitioning. Proceedings of the National Academy of Sciences 71:4169–4172.
Schwartzman, Stephan, Moreira, Adriana G., and Daniel C. Nepstad
   2000   Rethinking Tropical Forest Conservation Perils in Parks. Conservation Biology 14(5):1351–1357.
Scoones, Ian
   1999   New Ecology and the Social Sciences: What Prospects for a Fruitful Engagement? Annual Review of Anthropology 28:479–507.
Scott, James C.
   1998   Seeing like a State: How Certain Schemes to Improve the Human Condition have Failed. New Haven: Yale University Press.
   n.d. Uplands. New Haven: Yale University Press.
Shaw, R.
   1992   "Nature," "Culture," and Disasters: Floods and Gender in Bangladesh. *In* Bush Base: Forest Farm. Culture, Environment and Development. Elisabeth Croll and David Parkin, eds. Pp. 200–217. London: Routledge.
Shipton, Parker
   1989   Bitter Money: Cultural Economy and Some African Meanings of Forbidden Commodities. Washington, DC: American Anthropological Association.
Sigaut, François
   1979   Swidden Cultivation in Europe: A Question for Tropical Anthropologists. Social Science Information 18(4/5):679–694.
Sih, Andrew
   1980   Optimal Foraging: Can Foragers Balance Two Conflicting Demands? Science 210:1041–1043.
Sih, Andrew, and Katherine A. Milton
   1985   Optimal Diet Theory: Should the !Kung Eat Mongongos? American Anthropologist 87(2):395–401.
Sillitoe, Paul
   1994   Whether Rain or Shine: Weather Regimes from a New Guinea Perspective. Oceania 64(3):246–270.
Smith, Eric A.
   1983   Anthropological Applications of Optimal Foraging Theory: A Critical Review. Current Anthropology 24:625–651.
Smith, Eric A., and Bruce Winterhalder
   1985   On the Logic and Application of Optimal Foraging Theory: A Brief Reply to Martin. American Anthropologist 87:645–648.
Solway, Jacqueline S.
   1994   Drought as "Revelatory Crisis": An Exploration of Shifting Entitlements and Hierarchies in the Kalahari, Botswana. Development and Change 25(3):471–498.
   2003   Politics and Practice in Critical Anthropology: The Work of Richard B. Lee: Introduction. Anthropologica 45:3–9.
Sponsel, Leslie E.
   1989   Farming and Foraging: A Necessary Complementarity in Amazonia? *In* Farmers as Hunters: The Implications of Sedentism. Susan Kent, ed. Pp. 37–45. Cambridge: Cambridge University Press.

Stevens, William K.

1990   New Eye on Nature: The Real Constant is Eternal Turmoil. New York Times, July 31:B5–B6.

Steward, Julian H.

1949   Handbook of South American Indians: vol. 5: Comparative Ethnology of South American Indians. Prepared in cooperation with the U.S. Dept. of State. Washington, DC: Government Printing Office.

1955   Theory of Culture Change: The Methodology of Multilinear Evolution. Urbana, IL: University of Illinois Press.

1977a   The Foundations of Basin-Plateau Shoshonean Society. *In* Evolution and Ecology: Essays on Social Transformation by Julian H. Steward. Jane C. Steward and Robert F. Murphy, eds. Pp. 366–406. Urbana, IL: University of Illinois Press.

1977b   The Concept and Method of Cultural Ecology. *In* Evolution and Ecology: Essays on Social Transformation by Julian H. Steward. Jane C. Steward and Robert F. Murphy, eds. Pp. 43–57. Urbana, IL: University of Illinois Press.

1977c   Wittfogel's Irrigation Hypothesis. *In* Evolution and Ecology: Essays on Social Transformation by Julian H. Steward. Jane C. Steward and Robert F. Murphy, eds. Pp. 87–99. Urbana, IL: University of Illinois Press.

Steward, Julian H. and Robert F. Murphy

1977   Tappers and Trappers: Parallel Processes in Acculturation. *In* Evolution and Ecology: Essays on Social Transformation by Julian H. Steward. Jane C. Steward and Robert F. Murphy, eds. Pp. 151–179. Urbana, IL: University of Illinois Press.

Street, John M.

1969   An Evaluation of the Concept of Carrying Capacity. The Professional Geographer 21(2):104–107.

Thomas, Philip

2002   The River, the Road, and the Rural-Urban Divide: A Postcolonial Moral Geography from Southeast Madagascar. American Ethnologist 29(2):366–391.

Thomas, William L., ed.

1956   Man's Role in Changing the Face of the Earth. Chicago: University of Chicago Press, for the Wenner-Gren Foundation for Anthropological Research and the National Science Foundation.

Thompson, Michael, Michael Warburton, and Tom Hatley

1986   Uncertainty on a Himalayan Scale: An Institutional Theory of Environmental Perception and a Strategic Framework for the Sustainable Development of the Himalaya. London: Ethnographica.

Thrupp, Lori A., Susanna Hecht, and John O. Browder

1997   The Diversity and Dynamics of Shifting Cultivation: Myths, Realities, and Policy Implications. Washington, DC: World Resources Institute.

Thucydides

1959   The Peloponnesian War: The Complete Hobbes Translation. Chicago: University of Chicago Press.

Trevor-Roper, H.

1983   The Invention of Tradition. The Highland Tradition of Scotland. *In* The Invention of Tradition. Eric Hobsbawm and Terence Ranger, eds. Pp. 15–41. Cambridge: Cambridge University Press.

Triantafillou, Peter, and Mikkel R. Nielsen

2001   Policing Empowerment: The Making of Capable Subjects. History of the Human Sciences 14(2):63–86.

Tsing, Anna Lowenhaupt

2005   Friction: An Ethnography of Global Connection. Princeton: Princeton University Press.

Turner, Billie L. II, William C. Clark, Robert W. Kates, John F. Richards, Jessica T. Mathews, and William B. Meyer, eds.

1990   The Earth as Transformed by Human Action: Global and Regional Changes in the Biosphere over the past 300 years. Cambridge: Cambridge University Press with Clark University.

Utomo, Kampto

1975   Masyarakat Transmigran Spontan di Daerah Wai Sekampung, Lampung (Spontaneous transmigrant communities in Wai Sekampung, Lampung). Yogyakarta: Gadjah Mada University Press.

Vasan, Sudha

2002   Ethnography of the Forest Guard: Contrasting Discourses, Conflicting Roles and Policy Implementation. Economic and Political Weekly 37(40):4125–4133.

Voltaire

1977   Poem Upon the Lisbon Disaster. Lincoln, MA: Pemæn Press.

Waddell, Eric W.

1972   The Mound Builders: Agricultural Practices, Environment, and Society in the Central Highlands of New Guinea. Seattle: University of Washington Press.

Waddell, Eric W., and Peter A. Krinks

1968   The Organisation of Production and Distribution Among the Orokaiva; An Analysis of Work and Exchange in Two Communities Participating in Both the Subsistence and Monetary Sectors of the Economy. Canberra: New Guinea Research Unit, The Australian University.

Watson, James B.

1969   Review: Pigs for the Ancestors: Ritual in the Ecology of a New Guinea People. American Anthropologist 71:527–529.

Watts, Michael J.

1983   The Political Economy of Climatic Hazards: A Village Perspective on Drought and Peasant Economy in a Semi-Arid Region of West Africa. Cahiers d'Études Africaines 89–90,XXIII(1–2):37–72.

Watts, Michael J., and Hans-Georg Bohle

1993   Hunger, Famine, and the Space of Vulnerability. GeoJournal 30(2):117–125.

Weimarck, Gunhild

1968   Ulfshult: Investigations concerning the Use of Soil and Forest in Ulfshult, Parish of Örkened, during the last 250 Years. Lund (Sweden): C. W. K. Gleerup.

Wilmsen, Edwin N.

1983   The Ecology of Illusion: Anthropological Foraging in the Kalahari. Reviews in Anthropology 10:9–20.

1989   Land Filled with Flies: A Political Economy of the Kalahari. Chicago: University of Chicago Press.

Wilson, H. Clyde

1969   Review: Pigs for the Ancestors: Ritual in the Ecology of a New Guinea People. Journal of Asian Studies 28(3):658–659.

Winterhalder, Bruce

1981   Optimal Foraging Strategies and Hunter-Gatherer Research in Anthropology: Theory and Models. In Hunter-Gatherer Foraging Strategies: Ethnographic and Archaeological Analyses. Bruce Winterhalder and Eric A. Smith, eds. Pp. 13–35. Chicago: University of Chicago Press.

Winterhalder, Bruce, Robert Larsen, and R. Brooke Thomas

1974   Dung as an Essential Resource in a Highland Peruvian Community. Human Ecology 2(2):89–104.

Winterhalder, Bruce, and Eric A. Smith, eds.
  1981   Hunter-Gatherer Foraging Strategies: Ethnographic and Archaeological Analyses. Chicago: University of Chicago Press.
Winterhalder, Bruce, and Carol Goland
  1993   On Population, Foraging Efficiency, and Plant Domestication. Current Anthropology 34(5):710–715.
Wisner, Ben
  1993   Disaster Vulnerability: Scale, Power and Daily Life. GeoJournal 30(2):127–140.
Wittfogel, Karl A.
  1957   Oriental Despotism. New Haven: Yale University Press.
Wolf, Eric R.
  1982   Europe and the People without History. Berkeley: University of California Press.
World Commission on Environment and Development
  1987   Our Common Future. Oxford: Oxford University Press.
Worster, Donald
  1990   The Ecology of Order and Chaos. Environmental History Review 14(1/2):1–18.
Wynne-Edwards, Vero C.
  1962   Animal Dispersion in Relation to Social Behavior. Edinburgh: Oliver and Boyd.
Yao, S., Kamei, E., Matsumoto, T., Dwyer, P. D., and M. Minnegal
  1997   Sago Games: Cooperation and Change Among Sago Producers of Papua New Guinea. Evolution and Human Behavior 18(2):89–108.
Zaman, M. Q.
  1991   Social Structure and Process in Car Land Settlement in the Brahmaputra-Jamuna Floodplain. Man 26(4):673–690.
Zimmerman, Michael E.
  1994   Contesting Earth's Future: Radical Ecology and Postmodernity. Berkeley: University of California Press.
Zimmermann, Francis
  1987   The Jungle and the Aroma of Meats: An Ecological Theme in Hindu Medicine. Berkeley: University of California Press.

Part I

The Nature–Culture Dichotomy

1

Indigenous Management of Tropical Forest Ecosystems: The Case of the Kayapó Indians of the Brazilian Amazon

Darrell Addison Posey

Introduction

Indigenous societies have been living in Amazônia for unknown millennia, during which time they developed their own strategies for management of forests and campo/cerrados. Serious investigation of indigenous ethnobiological/ethnoecological knowledge is rare, but recent studies (Alcorn, 1981; Carneiro, 1983; Denevan et al., 1984; Frechione, 1981; Hames, 1979, 1980; Kerr and Posey, 1984; Parker et al., 1983; and others) show that indigenous knowledge of ecological zones, natural resources, agriculture, aquaculture, forest and game management, tends to be far more sophisticated than previously assumed. Furthermore, this knowledge offers new models for development that are both ecologically and socially sound (Posey, 1983a; Posey, et al., 1984).

This paper presents a general outline of management strategies of the Kayapó Indians of the Brazilian Amazon to illustrate how they utilize, conserve, and even create tropical forest patches (*apêtê*) in campo/cerrado. Secondary forest management is also important, employing their knowledge of conceptually similar ecological zones to concentrate transplanted (and possibly semi-domesticated) and planted (principally domesticated) species close to population centers or areas of need. It becomes clear that the Kayapó view forest management as an integrated system of plant communities rather than individual species; likewise, manipulated wildlife and even semi-domesticated bees figure into the overall management strategies. The long-term management strategies of the Kayapó, which actually increase biological diversity, offer many fundamental principles that should guide development throughout the humic tropics along a path that is both ecologically and socially sound.

Examples in this paper are taken from the Indian Post of Gorotire (7° 48′S, 54° 46′W), which is the largest of the Northern Kayapó villages (approximately 600 Indians). The author has conducted ethnobiological research in the village since 1977 and is currently coordinating an interdisciplinary team project to investigate in depth various aspects of biological and ecological knowledge by the Indians. This paper is a preliminary report on integrated forest and campo/cerrado management by the Kayapó.

I. Management and Use of Campo/Cerrado

Little is known of indigenous campo and cerrado management, although the ecological diversity of these ecological systems provides a wealth of natural resources for Indians like the Kayapó (Posey, 1984b).

The Kayapó classify campo/cerrado (kapôt) into a variety of folk ecological zones or "ecozones". The term "ecozone" is used in this paper to refer to ecological zones recognized by indigenous peoples, i.e., cognitive or emic categories. The following typology is of principal ecozones:

kapôt kêin: "clean" campo with few trees
kapôt kumrenx: open campo with many forest patches
kapôt mêtx: low, grassy and open campo
kapôt punu: closed campo with scrub (campo fechado)
kapôt jajôre: open campo with small scrub patches
kapôt imôk krê pôk re: small open areas surrounded by scrub forest near large campos
kapôt kam imô: seasonally inundated campo
kapôt imô nõi pôk: campo openings on tops of mountains
kapôt krã nhi môk: campo rupestre

The Kayapó also recognize the following transitional types of cerrado/campo:

krã nhinon ã kapôt: campo at top of mountains
krã nhi kratx ã kapôt: campo at base of mountains
kapôt nô kà: transition zones between savanna and forest
pô'ê kô: cane breaks
pô'ê te: very closed forest with cane

Of specific interest is the Kayapó classification of forest "islands" (apêtê) that occur in campo/cerrado and are frequently managed and exploited by the Indians. Typological classification is based on size, form and dominant species in the apêtê, although full criteria have not yet been fully worked out. Principal apêtê types are:

apêtê-nu: newly formed vegetative clumps
apêt: small, low vegetative patches
apêt kryre: larger forest patch, with small trees and shrubs
apêtê ngri: forest plot with some trees and large shrubs
apêtê (kumrenx): "real apêtê" with shade from tall trees
apêti: large forest islands with many tall trees (2+ HA)
apêti poire: oblong apêti
apêti rhynh: long corridors of forest (for defense)

In the vicinity of the Kayapó village of Gorotire, a notable increase in the number of apêtê forest patches/islands is apparently found in comparison to campo areas distant from the village. This is the direct effect of indigenous influence. Although cursory examination appears to show these apêtê to be natural, closer scrutiny reveals that a sizeable percentage (as much as 75%) are indeed man-made.

A preliminary study of apêtê made with Dr. Anthony Anderson (Museu Paraense Emilio Goeldi) in November 1983 shows that of the 140 different plant species collected, only two were *not* considered useful by the Kayapó.

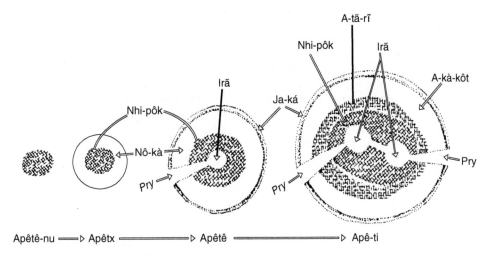

Figure 1.1 *Apêtê formation: planting zones*

Equally astonishing is that approximately 85% of the plants collected in ten samples forest "islands" were actually claimed to have been planted by the Indians (Anderson and Posey, 1985).

This amazing fact requires that we rethink what has been previously considered "natural" in campo/cerrado environments where there are indigenous populations. Even in areas where Indians have long since disappeared, the hand of human manipulation and management may still be evident.

It is impossible to know the true extent of Indian influence in forest and campo. Kayapó villages today are only remnants of ancient villages that were once linked by sizeable and extensive trails (Posey, 1983b). Old villages and campsites dot the vast area between the Araguaia and Tapajos Rivers that was the Kayapó domain. It is probable that campo/cerrado management was once widespread in other tribes throughout Brazil.

Creation of *apêtê* is in itself an interesting process. Compost heaps are prepared in existing *apêtê* from sticks, limbs, and leaves. These are allowed to rot, then are beaten with sticks to produce a mulch. This mulch is subsequently taken to a selected spot in the campo and piled onto the ground. Slight depressions in the surface are usually sought out because they are more likely to retain moisture. These depres-sions are filled with the mulch, which is mixed with soil from the mounds of a termite (*Nasutitermes*) called *rorote*, and smashed up bits of the nest of an ant called *mrum kudjà* (*Azteca* sp.). Living ants and termites are included in the mixture. The resulting mounds of earth, called *apêtê-nu*, are generally one to two meters in diameter and 50 to 60 cm. deep. The *apêtê-nu* are usually formed in August and September during the first rains of the wet season and then nurtured by the Indians as they pass along the savanna trails to their gardens (*puru-nu*). Over the years, the *apêtê-nu* "grow" into large *apê-ti* (see Figure 1.1). How long this process requires is still under study. Perhaps as much as 1HA per ten years is possible since there are *apê-ti* of 4HA in Gorotire, that has known to have been permanently inhabited for at least 40 years. This figure may be high, however, because Gorotire was an ancient campsite long before it became a permanent village.

The Kayapó create *apêtê* for a variety of reasons. Until fairly recent times, the Kayapó were still at war with other Kayapó and non-Kayapó (principally Shavante, Carajas, Tapirapé and Brazilian) groups. Their post-contact history seemed to be punctuated daily by wars, raids, and disease epidemics. The Kayapó prefer village sites in campos: *kapôt* is considered to be "healthier" than forest (*bà*) because there are fewer diseases. Campo villages, however, are hard to hide and defend. *Apêtê* are utilized as disaster shelters in cases of raids or epidemics when it is safer to temporarily abandon the village. The ideal *apêtê*, therefore, is one in which all the necessities of life are close at hand to afford self-sufficiency to families dispersed from their homes during times of emergencies. Since epidemics and periods of warfare could be prolonged, *apêtê* are a valuable resource and security to the Gorotire family. *Apêtê* have been observed being used as refuges during the threat of a measles epidemic as recently as April 1983.

Plants found in Gorotire *apêtê* are used as food (tubers, roots, fruits, nuts), medicines (for fevers, bleeding, diarrhea, body aches, dizziness, headaches, toothaches, abortives, and anti-conceptuals), materials for daily life (for baskets, cords, needles to open wounds, bow and arrow wood, insect repellents), firewood, ceremonial items (wrist bands, ear spools, lip plugs), body paint, poisons, shade, and leaves for containers and wrappings. Certain trees (e.g., *Alibertia edulis*, *Anonna crassiflora*, *Byrsonima crassifolia*, *Caryocar villosum*, and *Solanum paniculatum*) are even planted to attract game and birds. Palms (such as *Astrocaryum tucuma*, *Mauritia vinifera*, *Maximiliana regia*, *Oenocarpus bacaba*, and *Orbygnia martiana*) figure prominently in the inventory because of the variety of uses they afford. Shade trees are also highly valued, and even vines that produce drinkable water are transplanted to and replanted in *apêtê*.

Apêtê also serve as barriers, parapets, and lines of defense for the village. Warriors could hide in the bush, await their enemies, and then surprise them from their verdant palisades. *Apêti-poire* and *apêti-rhynh* are specifically used for these purposes. *Apêti-poire* are man-made forest corridors formed by uniting a chain of *apêtê*.

In peace time, *apêtê* are used as places of rest, to pass the hottest time of the day, to paint bodies of relatives with urucú (*Bixa orellana*) or genipapo (*Genipa americana*), or for supervised play for children. They are also a favored spot for sexual intercourse. Perhaps because of the latter reason, combined with the concentration of valuable resources in the *apêtê*, children are discouraged from entering

alone into these forest patches. They are told that ghosts (*karon*) hide there and that balls of light of powerful shamans (*wayanga karon*) appear there in the night. These stories serve to protect the *apêtê* and are enhanced and perpetuated by the shamans, who frequently have their medicinal gardens hidden in large *apê-ti*.

Fire is important in the management of *apêtê*, but contrary to existing theory, fire for the Kayapó is used to protect and encourage the forest patches rather than create larger campos. Campos (*kapôt*) in range of Gorotire are burned annually. The Indians say the fires produce beautiful effects in the night skies (*kaiwka metx, metire*) and have practical effects: they decrease the population of snakes and scorpions and prevent the excessive growth of grasses and thorny vines that make walking and hunting in *kapôt* difficult. Burning is not random. The time for burning is decided by the old people (*mebengêt*) and announced by the chiefs (*benadjwỳrà*). Burning occurs before the "birth" of the August moon (*muturwa katôrô nu*) and before the buds of the piquí tree (*Caryocar villosum*) are too developed. If burning occurs after this time, the highly prized fruit of the piquí (*prĩ*) will not be abundant. Not all *kapôt* are burned on the same day, nor even during the same week. When selected *kapôt* are designated to be burned, the "owners" of the *apêtê* come out to cut dried grasses and shrubs around their *apêtê* to produce a fire barrier. They then set the fires and await with branches of palms and banana brava (*Ravenala guyanensis*) to beat out any flames that come too close.

Not all *apêtê*, however, are protected from fire in this manner. The Indians recognize a group of plants that are actually stimulated by burning. These are plants that are said to "like" fire (*xêt okin*) and produce more fruit as a result. These include *Alibertia edulis*, *Byrsonima crassifolia*, *Astrocaryum tucuma*, and *Alibertia sp2*. Only *apêtê* that have an abundance of these trees are allowed to be burned.

Azteca sp. ants (*mrum kudjà*) are not only used to create soil for the *apêtè-nu* but are also highly prized for their abilities to repel saúva leaf-cutting ants (*Atta spp., mrum-krã-ti*). The *Azteca* has a pungent smell that distinguishes it to the Kayapó and is apparently the same smell responsible for repelling the saúva. Colonies of the *mrum kudjà* are broken into small pieces and carried to bits of forests where no colony exists. This transplanted colony will then begin to replicate and spread their natural protection against leaf-cutter ants.

Management of campo/cerrado is more complicated than we yet understand. A study of planting sequences and the process of maturation of *apêtê* is forthcoming. But with available data, it is obvious that our ideas of "natural" campo/cerrado and forest must be re-evaluated with an eye toward the possibility of widespread aboriginal management and manipulation of these ecosystems. Perhaps the most exciting aspect of these new data is the implication for reforestation. The Indian example not only provides new ideas about how to build forests "from scratch", but also how to successfully manage what has been considered to be infertile campo/cerrado.

II. Management and Use of Secondary Forest

(1) "Anything-but-abandoned fields"

Contrary to persistent beliefs about indigenous slash/burn agriculture, fields are not abandoned after a few years from initial clearing and planting. Recent studies show that, on the contrary, old fields offer an important concentration of highly diverse natural resources long after primary cultivars have disappeared (Carneiro, 1961; Alcorn, 1981; Denevan, et al., 1984).

Kayapó "new fields" (*puru nu*) peak in production of principal domesticated crops in two or three years but continue to bear produce for many years; e.g., sweet potatoes for four to five years, yams and taro for five to six years, manioc for four to six years, and papaya for five or more years. Some banana varieties continue to bear fruit for 15 to 20 years, urucú (*Bixa orellana*) for 25 years, and cupá (*Cissus gongyloides*) for 40 years. The Kayapó consistently revisit old fields seeking these lingering riches.

Fields take on new life as plants in the natural reforestation sequence begin to appear in maturing fields (*puru tum*). These plants soon constitute a type of forest called *ibê* (mature old fields) and provide a wide range of useful products, including: food and medicine, fish and bird baits, thatch, packaging, paints, oils, insect repellents, construction materials, fibers for ropes and cords, body cleansers, and products for craft production – to name but a few.

Old fields are perhaps most important for their concentrations of medicinal plants. In a recent survey of plants found in *puru tum* and *ibê* 94% of the 368 plants collected were of medicinal significance.

Old fields also attract wildlife to their abundant, low, leafy plants (Linares, 1976; Hames, 1979). High forests, in contrast, are sparse in game. Intentional dispersal of old fields by Indians and management of these by systematic hunting extends the human influence over the forest by providing, in effect, large "game farms" near human population concentrations. A delicate balance is necessary to manage these old fields. Game populations that are too dense can cause severe damage to crops; thus hunting provides meat for food while protecting new fields from excessive destruction. In the Kayapó division of labor, the women work in the fields while their husbands hunt in the surrounding forests.

Game animals are particularly attracted to fruit trees planted by the Kayapó in new and old fields, as well as along trails (see Table 1.1). Tree plantings illustrate long-term planning and forest management since many of the trees require many years to bear fruit; castanha do Pará (Brazil nut), for example, does not produce its first nuts for 12–20 years. In addition to attracting game, fruit and nut-producing trees are also planted to attract birds and even fish during high water river and igarapé cycles. Most of these trees also provide food important in human subsistence. Thus old fields should perhaps be called "game-farm orchards" to emphasize their diverse resources (Smith, 1977; Posey et al., 1984).

(2) Semi-domesticates in old fields

Old fields serve as important repositories of "semi-domesticated" or manipulated plants. The term "semi-domesticate" is used to indicate

Table 1.1 A partial list of tree species planted by the Kayapó indians

Scientific name	Portuguese name	Kayapó name	Planted for			Attract	
			Food	Misc.	Use	Game	Fish
Allagoptera cf. pseudocalyx	piaçaba	ngra djàre	X				
Alibertia edulis A. Rich	marmelada (lisa)	motu	X			X	
Alibertia sp.	marmelada do campo	roi-krãti	X			X	
Anonna crassiflora Mart.	Araticum	ongrê	X				
Atrocarpus integrifolia L.f.	jacá	jacá	X				
Astrocaryum tucuma Mart.	tucum (2 varieties)	roi-ti (mrà)	X	salt			
Astrocaryum vulgare Mart.	tucumã	woti	X	oil			
Bertholletia excelsa Humb. & Bonpl.	castanha do Pará	pi'ỳ	X				
Bixa orellana L.	urucú (4 varieties)	pỳ kumrenx pỳ pot ti pỳ krã re pỳ jabiê		body	paint		
Byrsonima crassifolia H.B.K.	muruci	kutenk	X				
Caryocar villosum (Aubl.) Pers.	piqui (3 varieties)	prĩ kà ti prĩ krã ti prĩ kumrenx	X X X			X	
Citrus aurantifolia (Christm.) Swingle	lima	pidgô ngrã ngrã	X				
Citrus aurantium L.	laranja	pidgô ti	X				
Citrus limonia Osbeck.	limão	pidgô poi re	X				
Coffea arabica	café	kapê					
Cordia sp.	cereja Kayapó	kudjà redjô	X			X	
Endopleura uchi	uxi	kremp	X				
Eugenia jambos L.	jambo	pidgô nore	X			X	
Euterpe oleracea Mart.	açai (2 varieties)	kamere kàk (kamere kàk ti)	X			X	
Genipa americana L.	genipapo (2 varieties)	mroti, mrotire	X	body	paint		
Hancornia speciosa Gomez	mangaba	pi-ô-tire	X				
Hymenaea courbaril L.	jatobá	moi (motx)	X			X	
Inga sp.	inga	kohnjô-kô tire, nagrãngrã, tyk	X			X	
Lecythis usitata Ledoux	sapucaia	kromu	X				
Lecythis usitata Miers, var. parensis (Ducke) Knuth	sapucaia	pi'ỳ tê krê ti	X				
Mangifera indica L.	manga	kuben poi re	X				
Manilkara huberi (Ducke) Stand.	massaranduba	krwya no kamrek				X	X
Mauritia martiana Spruce	buritirana	ngrwa ràre	X				
Mauritia vinifera Mart.	buruti	ngrwa	X				
Maximiliana maripa	inajá	rikre	X	salt			

Table 1.1 *Continued*

Scientific name	Portuguese name	Kayapó name	Planted for			Attract	
			Food	Misc.	Use	Game	Fish
Oenocarpus bacaba Mart.	bacabá	kamere	X			X	
Orgygnia martiana	babassú	rõ	X	oil	salt		
Parinari montana Aubl.	parirí	kamô	X			X	
Persea americana Mill.	abacate	kaprã	X				
Platonia insignis Mart.	bacurí	pĩ pannê ka tire	X			X	
Pourouma cecropiaefolia Mart.	imbaúbarana	atwỳrà krã krê	X			X	
Pouteria macrophylla (Lam.) Eyma	tuturubã	kamokô	X			X	
Psidium grayava L.	goiaba	pidgô kamrek	X				
Ravenata guyanensis	banana brava	tytyti djô	X				
Rollinia mucosa Baill.	biribá	biri	X				
Solanum paniculatum L.	jurubeba	miêchet ti	X			X	X
Spondias lutea L.	Cajá		X				
Spondias lutea L. (S. mombim L.)	taperabá	bàrere-krã-kryre	X				
Theobroma cacao L.	cacau	kuben krã ti	X			X	
Theobroma grandiflorum K. Schum.	cupaçú	bàri-djô	X				

plants that are intentionally manipulated by the Indians, who knowingly modify the plant's habitat to stimulate growth. The genetic consequences of this process are still unknown but merit serious study (Kerr and Posey, 1984).

Relatively open forests are given special names (*bà-ràràrà* and *bà-epti*) and are known refuges for light-loving plants that also grow well in old fields. Gathering trips to primary and secondary forests are frequently made to collect appropriate plants for transplanting into old fields.

The Kayapó also see forest areas disturbed by either natural or man-made events as habitats that approximate field clearings. Forest openings (*bà-krê-ti*) caused by trees that have fallen through natural processes (old age and storms) or that have been felled by Indians to raid bee hives create micro-environmental conditions similar to those of field clearings (Posey, 1984a). Likewise, openings due to abandoned camp and village sites, or wide swaths left by trails, are also reserves for plants that thrive in old fields. These areas are visited on gathering trips with the goal of transplanting forest plants to old fields or *apêtê*, thereby

making needed forest products more readily available.

(3) "Forest-fields"

The Kayapó custom of transplanting is only part of a much broader system that has been described (Posey, 1982, 1983a) as "nomadic agriculture" and was undoubtedly once widespread in Amazonian tribes. Until recently, Kayapó groups travelled extensively in the vast areas between the east-west boundaries of the Tocantins and Araguaya Rivers and the north-south limits of the Planalto and the Amazon River. Today the Kayapó still carry out several month-long treks per year, although much of the old network of trails and campsites is now abandoned.

Food and utensils, because of their bulk and weight, are not carried out by the Indians on treks. Food gathering for 150 to 200 people cannot, however, be left solely to chance. Thus gathered plants are transplanted into concentrated spots near trails and campsites to produce "forest-fields" that make readily available to future passersby the necessities of life, including: food, cleansing agents, hair and body oils, insect repellents, leaves for cooking, vines that supply drinkable water, house construction materials, and especially medicinals.

Forest-fields intentionally replicate naturally occurring "resource islands" (kô), which are areas where specific concentrations of useful plants are found. These resource islands include: Brazil nut groves, fruit tree stands, palmito and nut sources, cane breaks, etc.

Dependency on naturally occurring "resource islands" and their man-made "forest-field" counterparts allow Kayapó groups to travel months at a time and great distances without need of domesticated garden produce. Today only remnants of this once vast system remain.

(4)   Trailside plantings

In addition to the "forest-fields" near campsites and trails, the sides of trails (pry kôt) themselves are planting zones for the Kayapó. It is not uncommon to find trails composed of four-meter-wide cleared strips of forest. It is hard to estimate the extensiveness of aboriginal trails that interconnected distant Kayapó villages; a conservative estimate of existing trials associated with Gorotire (one of 11 modern Kayapó villages) yields 500 km of trails that average 2.5 m wide. Trailsides are planted with numerous varieties of yams, sweet potatoes, Marantaceae, *Cissus*, Zingiberaceae, Araceae, and other as yet unidentified edible tubers. Hundreds of medicinal plants and fruit trees also increase the diversity of the planted flora.

In a survey of a three-kilometer trail leading from Gorotire to a nearby garden, the following were observed: (1) 185 planted trees representing at least 15 different species; (2) approximately 1,500 medicinal plants of an undetermined number of species; and (3) approximately 5,500 food-producing plants of an undetermined number of species.

The immediate one- to four-meter wide swath provided by trail clearing is *not* the entire effective distance of human activity. An additional factor is the distance away from the trail that the Kayapó choose for defection/urination; I have measured the average distance,

a rather culturally fixed proxemic unit, at five meters (or 14 m in width, considering both sides of the trail and the trail itself).

While squatting to defecate, the Kayapó often plant tubers, seeds, or nuts they have collected during the day and stored in a fiber pouch or bag. This activity, combined with the natural process of seed transportation through fecal material, makes the overall distance near trails under human influence even more extensive and significant. The effect is further accentuated by the age of the trails: some are uncounted centuries old.

(5)   Plantations in forest openings

For the Kayapó, openings in the primary forest are called bà-krê-ti and are seen as natural prototypes for gardens. As mentioned, there are two types of bà-krê-ti: (1) openings caused by trees or limbs that fall due to old age or storms; and (2) openings that are man-made by felling large trees to take honey from bees (Posey, 1983c). Both types of forest openings create new micro-habitats and planting zones due to light reaching the forest floor and creating conditions similar to those of garden plots. The idea for planting gardens may have come from the Indian's study and use of bà-krê-ti or may be a logical extension of their management of such forest openings.

Bà-krê-ti are used to transplant domesticates and semi-domesticates like varieties of manioc, taro, cupá, yams, sweet potatoes, beans, and arrowroot. These thrive in such habitats and according to Kayapó agriculturalists, their productivity is significantly increased as the result of this transplantation.

(6)   Hill gardens

Another form of agriculture that is related to bà-krê-ti plantations is the krãi kam puru or "hill garden". Tuberous plants, like zingiberaceae, Araceae, and Marantaceae varieties, are planted in these well-drained, hillside plots. These fields are principally reserved as food sources in case of floods or of crop disasters and are considered as very valuable plant "banks" or reserves. Hill gardens are exclusively kept by old women (*mē-begnet*) under the direction of the Kayapo female chief (*menire-nhõ-benadjwỳrà*), the highest ranking female authority. To form the plantations, old fields of eight to ten years of fallow are cleared of underbrush. Pieces of tuber stock are then planted in shallow holes in fertile pockets of soil when the new rains have soaked the soils in September. Little care, other than cutting back of competing vegetation, is required to maintain these fields. Harvest occurs at the onset of the dry season (June), although representative plants are always left behind to preserve the tuber "bank" (reserve).

(7) Plant communities and microzonal planting

Another interesting aspect of Kayapó agriculture is based upon management of plant communities associated with bananas. As banana trees grow in maturing fields, they produce shading and modify soil conditions that produce a specialized microenvironment. The Kayapó know approximately two dozen varieties of edible tubers and numerous medicinal plants that thrive under these conditions and are planted in the banana plantation (*tytyti-kô*). These plants are called "companions of the banana" (*tytyti-kotam*) and continue to grow together with the banana until the height of the secondary forest is no longer conducive to the growth of the plant community. When this occurs, shoots of old bananas are transferred to new fields, while the "companions" are transplanted to already established plantations of bananas in other maturing fields.

This illustrates not only how Indians exploit the properties of fields in transition between new and old (*puru* to *ibê*) but also how microenvironmental planting zones are created to modify effects of secondary forest growth. Equally significant is the indigenous conceptualization of plant communities, rather than individual species, as the basis for ecological management. Other plant companions are under investigation for payaya, genipapo, and urucú, all of which are viewed as foci of other managed plant communities and produce their own unique microzones for planting.

(8) "Quintal" management

"Quintal" is a Portuguese word that describes areas adjacent to homes that are generally planted with useful or decorative plants. The idea is more ancient than the European introduction, since the Kayapó too rely on areas near their homes (*ki-krê-bum*) to grow useful plants. A partial *ki-krê-bum* survey has produced 86 species (estimate based on tentative identification) of food plants and dozens of additional medicinal plants.

The practice of medicine is highly elaborated for the Kayapó. Almost every household has its complement of common medicinal plants, many of which are domesticates or semi-domesticates. Shamans (*wayanga*) specialize in different disease treatments, each of which requires specific plants. Dozens of "medicine knowers" (*pidjà mari*) also effect minor cures with their own array of medicinals. Medicinal plants are often kept in secret forest plantations since their use forms part of the private knowledge of the curer; others are overtly grown in the quintal and only their use is secret. Thus each quintal reflects the medicinal knowledge and specialization (or lack thereof) of its owner.

A major result of quintal management is the formation of topsoil. Some of the richest and most productive soils in Amazônia are those called "terra preta dos índios" produced by Indian manipulation of generally poor Amazonian soils (Smith, 1980).

(9) Ken-po-ti ("Rock Gardens")

One of the most unusual ecozones manipulated by the Kayapó is the *ken-po-ti*, which is a basaltic outcropping transformed into a special "rock garden". These outcroppings frequently occur in the middle of forests. The area of exposed rock creates open spaces within the forest that become hot and dry when heated by the tropical sun. Environmental conditions in parts of *ken-po-ti* resemble those of campo/cerrrado (*kapôt*), yet their margins are shaded by the encompassing forest and water seepage is common from aquafer cracks. Thus a variety of microclimates are available for exploitation by the Indians, who concentrate plant resources in *ken-po-ti* through plantings and transplantings from a variety of other ecozones. Frequently forest mulch and rich soils are carried to the outcroppings and placed in existing cracks in the rocks or piled high between stones arranged to form planting containers. Piles of the planting medium provide productive plots for the raising of plants requiring special care and growth conditions. A managed *ken-po-ti*, in sharp contrast to its barren unmanaged counterpart, looks like a lush Japanese garden. For the Kayapó, stone outcroppings have special significance because they have special cosmic energies and are associated with powerful spiritual forces. Only shamans do not fear these forces. Thus *ken-po-ti* are mostly used by shamans, who plant some of their most powerful and important medicinals there.

An Indigenous Model of Cognitive Integration

In studies of the Kayapó Indian classification, overlapping sets have been described as being in contiguous "sequences" that form "continua" between polar types (Posey, 1983a). That is, members of classification units frequently share diagnostic characteristics with members of other contiguous units. Each unit has a "focal" or "ideal" type, which is the member that is most characteristic of the set. The greater any set member differs in characteristics from the ideal type, the more likely that member will co-occur in other sets. Extremes or poles of the continuum represent the maximal divergence possible within the domain and thereby define the parameters of the higher taxonomic grouping.

One of the most salient of the taxonomic continua in the Kayapó system is that between forest (*bà*) and campo/cerrado (*kapôt*). The ideal or "focal" type of forest is *bà-kumrenx* ("true forest"), which is the most productive of the forest types. Trees of at least eight meters in height provide many edible fruits, nuts and seeds, as well as useful woods and fibers. A herbaceous understory is rich in medicinal plants.

The "focal" *kapôt* type is *kapôt-kumrenx* ("true campo"), which is open land with knee-high grasses. The landscape is also dotted with patches of forest-like vegetation called *apêtê*.

Apêtê are the link between the poles of the *bà-kapôt* continuum (see Figure 1.2). They are composed of many sun-tolerant, heat-resistant species that survive in the demanding climate of the campo/cerrado, yet also have many forest species. Thus they unite diagnostic elements of both poles of the continuum.

Different planting zones are found within *apêtê* as represented in Figure 1.1. *Apêtê-nu*

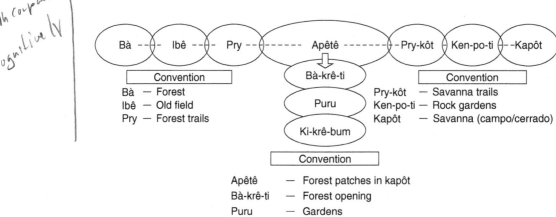

Figure 1.2 *Ethno ecological units on the bà-kapôt continuum*

consist of only one planting zone. *Apêtx* (an intermediary form between *apêtê-nu* and *apêtê*) have a relatively shady center (*nhi-pôk*), with a sunnier edge (*nô-kà*). True *apêtê* have a shady center area (*nhi-pôk*), an outer edge (*nô-kà*), and an additional shadow zone (*ja-kà*) formed by higher vegetation that shields the zone from morning or evening sun. Note that in the center of the *apêtê* is an opening where light penetrates. This is called the *irã* and functions to preserve the "patchiness" of the *apêtê* to maximize microenvironmental variation. Patchiness helps preserve the biological heterogeneity of larger *apêtê*. *Irã* are usually connected to the open *kapôt* by trails (*pry-kôt*).

Large *apêtê*, or *apê-ti*, have all the planting zones found in an *apêtê*, plus a darker, middle zone where less light can penetrate (*a-tã-rĩ*). *Irã* may be numerous to maintain patchiness and light penetration. Large *irã* are ringed by a bright zone called the *irã-nô-kà* which is good all-purpose planting zone. Trails (*pry*) connect *irã* and the *kapôt* and are frequently wide enough to provide a light margin (*pry-kôt*) that also serves as a planting strip.

Variations in planting zones, therefore, seem to be based principally upon variations of shade and light, plus associated variations in temperature and moisture. Planting zones in *apêtê* are matched with ecological types recognized by the Indians in the forest (see Table 1.2). Plants that grow well in certain forest environments can be predicted to do well in *apêtê* zonal counterparts.|For example, plants found in the dark, damp forest (*bà-tyk*) are likely to do well in the *a-tã-rĩ* or the *nhi-pôk* of an *apê-ti*. Plants that thrive in the light-penetrating forest (*bà-ràràrà*) would be planted *nô-kà* or *a-kà-kôt*. Species found at the margins of the forest or the edges of other *apêtê* would be transferred to the *ja-kà* or *a-kà-kôt*. |

Plant species are said by the Indians to have been brought for planting or transplanting in Gorotire *apêtê* from very distant areas. Most species encountered in *apêtê* are common campo species, but the Kayapó say that certain varieties have specific desired qualities (taste for food, texture for wood or fiber, medicinal properties, etc.) and were acquired from Indian groups such as the Tapirape, Karaja, Mun-

Table 1.2 *Apêtê* planting zones in relation to corresponding ecological units

Apêtê *planting zones*[1]	Corresponding ecological units[2]
nhi-pôk	bà-ràràrà, bà-kamrek, bà-krê-ti
nô-kà	bà-kôt, bà-ràràrà, bà-krê-ti
ja-kà	kapôt, bà-kôt
irã-nô-kà	bà-ràràrà, bà-kamrek, bà-krê-ti
a-tã-rĩ	bà-tyk, bà-kamrek
a-kà-kôt	bà-ràràrà, bà-kumrenx

[1] *Apêtê zones: nhi-pôk*, shady center; *nô-kà*, sunny edge; *ja-kà*, shadow zone; *irã-nô-kà*, edge of open center; *a-tã-rĩ*, darker middle zone; *a-kà-kôt*, light-penetrating margin.
[2] *Forest units: bà-kamrek*, gallery or riverine forest; *bà-ràràrà*, forest in which light penetrates to the forest floor; *bà-krê-ti*, forest openings; *bà-kôt*, forest edge; *kapôt*, campo/cerrado; *bà-tyk*, high dark forest; *bà-kumrenx*, forest with large trees and a herbaceous lower level.

drucu, Assurini, Shavante, Canela, Gavião and Sororo. Thus if stated origins of plant varieties are accepted, Gorotire *apêtê* are composed of a concentration of plant varieties brought from an area the size of Europe. Origins and processes of planting and transplanting are now under study.

Conceptually *apêtê* are related to other human-made ecological zones described in this paper, such as trail sides (*pry-kôt*) and field gardens (*puru*), since all are planted with many of the same varieties of useful herbs and fruit trees. Furthermore, old fields are managed in much the same way as *apêtê*, since long-term management of plant and animal communities is fundamental to the exploitation strategies of both. Old fields (*ibê*) for the Kayapó are like *apêtê* surrounded by forest rather than campo.

Other zones that are conceptually linked with *apêtê* are: (1) *bà-krê-ti*[1] (forest openings); (2) *ken-po-ti* (rock gardens); and (3) *ki-krê-bum* (quintal or yard).

Given the various ecological zones recognized by the Kayapó, it is possible to construct a more generalized pattern of cognitive relatedness on the *bà-kapôt* continuum. Figure 1.2

represents the overlapping sets of *bà*, *ibê*, *puru tum*, *apêtê* (and related cognates), *pry*, *ken-po-ti*, and *kapôt*. Sets with more savanna elements are placed closer to the *kapôt* pole; sets with more forest elements are placed closer to *bà*.

In this scheme, *apêtê* are intermediary between poles. Cognitive variants of *apêtê*, *puru* and *bà-krê-ti*, occupy the same classification space. That is, *puru* (fields) are considered as types of *bá-krê-ti*, which in turn are inverse models of *apêtê*. *Ki-krê-bum* (quintals) are likewise related since they unite elements of all ecological zones.

For the Kayapó the most productive ecological systems are those in secondary forest created through human activity. Whether *apêtê* forest patches in the campo, or *ibê* forest resulting from management of old fields, the Kayapó system is built upon the maintenance – or actual increase – in biological diversity. Forest "patchiness" is the principal mechanism for the preservation of diversity, both in the creation of *irã* in *apêtê* and *bà-krê-ti* in the forest. Kayapó resource management, therefore, focuses upon the intermediary forms (*apêtê*, *bà-krê-ti*, *quintal*, *pry*, etc.) between the polar forest and campo/cerrado types because it is in these zones that maximal biological diversity occurs. To put such a statement in more ecological terms, the Indians not only recognize the richness of "ecotones", they create them.

Concluding Remarks

Recognition of diagnostic similarities within a contrast continuum of forest (*bà*) and campo/cerrado (*kapôt*) allows the Kayapó Indians to manipulate a variety of ecological zones and microclimates through the exchange of botanical materials between units perceived as similar. Fundamental to indigenous management is the reliance upon a wide range of plant and animal resources integrated into long-term

exploitation of secondary forest areas and specially created concentrations of resources near areas of need (forest fields, forest openings, rock outcroppings, old fields, trailsides, agricultural plots, and hill gardens). Forest patches (*apêtê*) created by the Indians in cerrado/campo also provide dense concentrations of useful species. Maintenance, or more usually increase, in biological diversity is the key to successful indigenous conservation and exploitation.

The Kayapó example teaches us that sophisticated management must be based upon recognition of likeness between ecological units: contrast should never obscure similarity in ecological typologies. Furthermore, that secondary forest can, indeed, be maximally productive without endangering the long-term survival of native species nor ecological systems.

Creation of *apêtê* is likewise of great potential in understanding more about campo/cerrado utilization. Indigenous management of *apêtê* has far-reaching implications for the study of forestation in savanna areas and reforestation in area denuded by deforestation.

Presence of areas extensively managed by indigenous peoples emphasizes the necessity for the re-evaluation of concepts about the natural landscape. "Naturalness" of ecological communities can never be assumed without investigating the human history of the area.

This paper has merely attempted to outline some of the major principles of Kayapó forest management in an effort to show how indigenous knowledge can help generate alternative philosophies for a more rational system of resource management in the humid tropics. The Kayapó are only one of many small enclaves of native peoples located in remote parts of the world, but the lessons they have learned through millennia of accumulated experience and survival are invaluable to a modern world in much need of rediscovering its ecological and humanistic roots.

NOTE

1. It is interesting to speculate that *bà-krê-ti* and *puru* are cognitive inverses of *apêtê*.

They form relatively open, sun-penetrating patches of forest, whereas *apêtê* are relatively shady areas in the campo. The result is the same: areas of concentrated plant diversity in ecologically similar conditions. Gardens clearly show zonation (Kerr and Posey, 1984), albeit an inside-out version of *apêtê* planting zones.

REFERENCES

Alcorn, J. (1981). Huastic noncrop resource management: Implications for prehistoric rain forest management. *Human Ecology* 9 (4): 395–417.

Anthony, A. and Posey, D.A. (1985). Manejo do Campo e Cerrado pelos índios Kayapó. Boletim do Museu Goeldi (Botânica).

Carneiro, R.L. (1961). Slash-and-burn cultivation among the Kuikuru and its implications for cultural development in the Amazon Basin. In: The Evolution of Horticultural Systems in Native South America: Causes and Consequences, A Symposium. J. Wilbert, ed., pp. 47–67. Caracas: Antropologica Supplement No 2.

——. (1983). The cultivation of manioc among the Kuikuru of the Upper Xingú. In: Adaptive Responses of Native Amazonians. R. Hames and W. Vickers, eds. Academic Press.

Denevan, W., Treacy, J. and Alcorn, J. (1984). Indigenous agroforestry in the Peruvian Amazon: The example of Bora utilization of swidden fallows. In: Change in the Amazon Basin. J. Hemming, ed. Manchester, England, University of Manchester.

Frechione, J. (1981). Economic self-development by Yekuana Amerinds in southern Venezuela. PhD dissertation (Department of Anthropology), University of Pittsburgh, Pittsburgh, Pennsylvania.

Hames, R.B. (1979). Game depletion and hunting zone rotation among the Ye'Kuana and Yanomamo of Amazônias, Venezuela. Paper presented at the XLIII International Congress of Americanists, Vancouver, B.C.

——. (1980). Monoculture, polyculture, and polyvariety in tropical forest swidden cultivation. Paper read at the 79th Annual Meeting of the American Anthropological Association, Washington, DC.

Kerr, W.E. and Posey, D.A. (1984). Notas sobre a agricultura dos índios Kayapó. Interciência 9 (6): 392–400.

Linares, O. (1976). Garden hunting in the American tropics. *Human Ecology* 4 (4): 331–49.

Parker, E., Posey, D.A., Frechione, J. and da Silva, L.F. (1993). Resource exploitation in Amazônia: Ethnoecological examples from four populations. Annals of Carnegie Museum, Vol. 52, Article 8: 163–203.

Posey, D.A. (1982). Keepers of the forest. *New York Botanical Garden Magazine* 6 (1): 18–24.

——. (1983a). Indigenous ecological knowledge and development of the Amazon. In: The dilemma of Amazonian development. E. Moran, ed. Boulder, Colorado, Westview Press.

——. (1983b). Indigenous knowledge and development: An ideological bridge to the future. *Ciência e Cultura* 35 (7): 877–94.

——. (1983c). Keeping of stingless bees by the Kayapó Indians of Brazil. *Journal of Ethnobiology* 3 (1): 63–73.

——. (1984a). A preliminary report on diversified management of tropical forest by the Kayapó Indians of the Brazilian Amazon. *Advances in Economic Botany* 1: 112–26.

——. (1984b). Keepers of the campo. *New York Botanical Garden Magazine* 8 (6): 8 ff.

Posey, D.A., Frechione, J., Eddins, J. and da Silva, L.F. (1984). Ethnoecology as applied anthropology in Amazonian development. *Human Organization* 43 (2): 95–107.

Smith, N. (1977). Human exploitation of terra firma fauna in Amazônia. *Ciência e eultura* 30 (1): 17–23.

——. (1980). Anthrosols and human carrying capacity in Amazônia. *Annals of the Association of American Geographers* 70 (4): 553–66.

2

False Forest History, Complicit Social Analysis: Rethinking Some West African Environmental Narratives

James Fairhead and Melissa Leach

1. Introduction

analyses are wrong

This paper examines social science analyses that are being used to explain environmental degradation and inform policy responses to it. We focus on two cases pertinent for exploring the production of applied social science knowledge about people-environment relations. They exemplify the type of social analysis often brought to bear to explain environmental degradation in Africa, yet it can be demonstrated that what they explain so successfully has not actually taken place.

Social scene inadequate

Our examples clearly expose a spectrum of assumptions on which social science analyses – whether or not carried out by social scientists as such – tend to draw. These assumptions have strength and credibility in large part because they are linked together, diffused and stabilized within "narratives" (Roe, 1991), that is, stories of apparently incontrovertible logic which provide scripts and justifications for development action. But once dissected from the reality they seek to construct, these explanations reveal instead how the applied social sciences can be used to lend weight to popular Western perceptions about African society and environment – a mythical reality which development interventions are acting to recreate in vain. By stripping away the explained from explanations of it, our cases pave the way for rethinking people–environment relationships in this region. We do this by forwarding alternative sets of assumptions stabilized within narratives which better fit the facts.

The specific cases considered here concern Guinea's forest margin zone. They articulate, in different ways, the position that local community institutions were once better capable of controlling environmental resources than they are today, and thus of maintaining a forested environment and resisting pressure toward its degradation. This articulation enables supposed forest loss to be explained in terms of "institutional breakdown." An armory of purported factors is called to account for such social rupture whose results seem so evident in a degraded landscape. These include socioeconomic change and commercialization, increasing mobility, the weakening of traditional authority, more individuated farming, the new economic and cultural aspirations of the young, new social cleavages, the alienation of local resource control to state structures, and the emergence of "anarchic" charcoal, fuelwood and timber businesses to supply the urban market. The impact of migration is added to these arguments: Eco-ethnic integration once associated with "forest people" with supposedly forest-benign lifestyles has been disrupted by the immigration or influence of "savanna peoples." Overlaying all is the specter of population growth, as viewed through a Malthusian lens. Foreign observers today tend to date such socioenvironmental disruption to the notorious regime of Guinea's first republic (1958–84) under Sékou Touré, imaging the colonial period as environmentally friendly, while nationals tend to look to the precolonial period to find "good" society and environment. As if to make the point, one scholar forced the social-environmental Eden back to that period documented by the 13th century Arab geographers, i.e. a period where his personal moral sympathies lay (Zerouki, 1993).

Social sciences have no monopoly over these social-environmental visions in which a forest past has become a moral past. They are shared by many local administrators and school teachers, as much as external consultants and university academics. The production of history serves many ends. What will become clear is that social scientists have been complicit in producing a view of history as one of increasing tension from a harmonious past.

Treating this past as a model and set of objectives for the resolution of today's tensions, they have been forging links between social and environmental conditions in a way that assists in relieving those subjected to their study of what little resource control they have.

2. Case 1: Forest Islands of Kissidougou

(a) The deforestation narrative

Kissidougou looks degraded. The landscape is largely savanna, especially open in the dry season when fires burn off the grasses and defoliate the few savanna trees. Nonetheless, rising out of the savanna and surrounding and hiding each of the prefecture's villages, are patches of immense semi-deciduous humid forest. Scientists and policy makers consider these forest "islands" and the strips of streamside gallery forest to be relics of an original, formerly much more extensive, dense humid forest cover. Inhabitants have, they suppose, progressively converted forest into "derived" savanna by their shifting cultivation and fire-setting practices, preserving only the belt of forest around their villages to protect their settlements from fire and wind, to give necessary shade to tree crops, to assist fortifications and hiding, and to provide seclusion for secret ritual activities. They argue that today's climate would support general forest cover, and infer from the presence of "relic" forest islands that it once did:

At origin, the forest between Kissidougou and Kankan was . . . a dense, humid, semideciduous forest. The trigger of degradation is . . . the farming system and the fragility of climate and soils in tropical regions. Some primary formations still exist, however, in the form of peri-village forest islands and gallery forests on the banks of water courses. These forest islands show the existence of a dense forest, which is today replaced in large part by degraded secondary forest. All the stages of degradation are represented: wooded savanna, bush savanna and grass savanna (Kan II, *Plan d'Operation*, 1992, pp. 6–7).[1]

Deforestation is considered to provoke problems at several levels, rendering it an urgent policy concern. At the local level it leads to soil degradation and renders farming less productive and sustainable. At the regional level – the upper watershed of the Niger river – deforestation is thought to have caused irregularities in downstream river flow and in rainfall. In addition, it is contributing to global warming. Something must be done.

Social analysis has always been instrumental in explaining this problem and its recent acceleration. In the early part of this century, the celebrated French colonial botanist, Auguste Chevalier, considered greater movement and trade during the postoccupation period to be responsible for an increase in fire-setting from a previous, less forest-harmful level (Chevalier, 1909). He considered that inhabitants conserved the forest islands for cultural reasons, presumably in a sea of otherwise degraded profanity (Chevalier, 1933). In 1948, Adam published the view prevalent in earlier archives that the Mandinka were a "savanna" people who had migrated southward into the forest zone, and created savanna there (Adam, 1948). In doing so, they reportedly forced the original "forest people," more benign to that resource, south and further into the forest zone.

More recently, professional social scientists have focused on environmental issues in Kissidougou, usually in the pay of international or bilaterally funded environmental programs. One team, responsible for structuring the European Community-funded Niger river protection program, illustrate this focus thus:

Our questions sought to explain the deterioration of the environment, viz: erosion and soil impoverishment, the drying up of water sources, the origin and nature of forest destruction, the origin of perverse use of bush fire ... Parallel to the physical causes of soil erosion, there are others of a social, political and religious nature. We can suppose a strong relationship between soil erosion, environmental degradation and the break-up and impoverishment of socioeconomic structures and relations. Environmental management is strongly linked to the state of socio-cultural structures ... The more a community is in equilibrium at the level of social organisation, the healthier is the nature of its relations with the environment. There is a dialectical relationship between social, political and religious institutions and ecological equilibrium ... In these communities, ... the existence of the living is above all justified by a more or less good management of what the ancestors have left to them. This management is inscribed in the collection of laws, concrete and abstract, rational and irrational, which, once disturbed from the exterior, can be the cause of a deterioration which manifests itself as much at the level of social, religious, political and economic institutions, as at the level of the environment (Programme d'Amenagement des Hautes Bassins du Fleuve Niger, n.d., pp. 4–7).

In a second study, devoted to local fire-setting, the author aimed to give an inventory of cultural traits which function around the practice of fire. "We have tried to retrace the transition from a traditional practice to 'modern' practice. Our hypothesis was that the 'fire social system' instituted itself as such, in destroying its host 'system', the traditional one" (Zerouki, 1993, p. 1). In short, the author argues that "modernity" is responsible for disrupting the once successful integration of fire control within diffuse sets of intra and intervillage village social, cultural and political relationships. He finds that "Degradation seems to be recent" and that "it accelerates with the development of an urban network ... and population growth." The study proposed "solutions to social dysfunctioning" (Zerouki, 1993). A coresearcher on this same study expands on the causes of such "dysfunctioning":

According to inquiry on the one hand from elders . . . and on the other by IFAN in 1968, the whole region was covered with forest about 99 years ago, corresponding to the Samorian period. War chiefs used fire for better visibility and for encampments. The introduction of the locomotive during the colonial period had a serious impact on the vegetation. Since independence, there has been demystification of sacred forests and of islands considered once as cult places, the installation of wood mills, and brick-making. Nomadic farming and herding, uncontrolled bush fire, forest fire, and runaway demography, aggravate the process of vegetation degradation already begun (Fofana *et al.*, 1993. p. 49).

Other recent expert views have drawn on conventional social analysis to assert once again that the Kuranko people (who speak a Mandinka dialect) are a savanna people and brought bush fire practices with them when they pushed the Kissi further south. "As forest people, the Kissi are not as careless as savanna people with regard to fire" (Green, 1991, p. 20). In a typically racialist way, agency for degradation is diffused into the ambiguity between culture and origin.

A study of an area just over the eastern border of Kissidougou, while somewhat cynical of the crisis mold of environmental analysis, nevertheless claims that:

The degradation of forests – always qualified as "explosive" – has continued in an accelerating fashion . . . Peasant exploitation is correctly identified as the principal factor of destruction, but in general, the measures taken [since colonial times] have only treated the symptoms. The social reasons for fire setting in hunting are . . . closely linked to growing tendencies of commercialisation and monetarization in the rural milieu. This underlines the loss in importance of traditional organisations of hunters which, to date, are marked by an anti-commercial character. [Pasture will be threatened by] growing immigration of herders into the region, a consequence of the degradation of pastures in the traditional herding regions (e.g., Fouta Djallon). Traditional structures which regulate the exploitation of natural resources, most often of pre-Islamic

origin, incorporate a series of conservation aspects. Some still operate . . . but a change is beginning to show itself: a process of social change which implies a dissolution of traditional regulative structures which are not easily reconcilable with the commercialisation trends which are more and more marked in the region (Stieglitz, 1990, pp. 54, 70, 77).

The author, who considers Islam to have disrupted this "pre-Islamic" tradition, incorporates more agrodemographic explanations into her explanatory mix:

The period of cultivation being too prolonged or the fallow period too short, there is too great a loss in the nutritive materials leading finally to an irrevocable degradation of the soils. The fallow period is limited to 5–10 years. A tendency for land shortage can be seen (Stieglitz, 1990, p. 71).

This is the position on demographic change held by most analysts. Ponsart-Dureau, for example, an agronomy student advising a nearby project, considers that:

around 1945, the forest, according to the elders, reached a limit 30 km north of Kissidougou town. Today, its northern limit is found at the level of Gueckedou-Macenta, thus having retreated about 100 km . . . Demographic growth forces the villagers to exploit their land completely, and to practice deforestation which disequilibrates the natural milieu (Ponsart-Dureau, 1986, pp. 9–10 and 60).

Thus in different ways, each of these analyses contributes to a narrative now as prominent in Kissidougou's education and administrative circles as it is in social science analyses. Once Kissidougou had an extensive forest cover, maintained under low population densities and by a functional social order whose regulations controlled and limited people's inherently degrading land and vegetation use. The breakdown of such organized resource management under internal and external pressures, combined with population growth, has led to the deforestation apparently so evident in the landscape today. Observers invariably consider degradation as a recent, ongoing and aggravating problem. The social and economic changes are, like "runaway demography," always seen to be accelerating out from a "zero point" (the archetype "tradition" so dear to Malinowskian social anthropologists and the object of description in old ethnographies). A host of indicators is drawn upon to support ideas concerning recent and ongoing degradation, such as rainfall decline since the mid-1950s, the drying-up of certain water sources, and more.

Policy implications have followed logically from the assumptions contained and stabilized within this narrative, and have changed little since its first elaboration in the early colonial period. The first policy emphasis is on the reduction of upland farming – seen as inherently forest and soil degrading and becoming more so under greater individualization and population growth – in favor of swamp farming. What upland use must remain needs to be rationalized and intensified (e.g., through "model" agroforestry systems, reorganization of tenure and fallow systems). Second, policies have focused on bush-fire control through externally imposed prohibitions, regulations and practices (e.g., early-burning). Third, policies have attempted to control deforestation both through prohibitions on the felling of a list of protected tree species (largely those forest species commercially valuable for timber and most representative of the "original" forest cover) and through the reservation of certain forest patches. Fourth, there are attempts at forest reconstitution through tree planting in village territories. Uniting these policies is their recourse to technology "packages" well established in the region such as inland valley swamp development and tree planting from nurseries. Uniting them, too, is their attempt to establish or reestablish control and organization in resource management; although with changes in development philosophy, there have been changes in the levels deemed appropriate. Thus in Guinea's colonial and first republic periods, the degradation narrative justified removing the villagers' (dysfunctional, incapable) "control" over resources in favor of the state. In bush fire, upland use, timber-felling and forest reservation policies, government administrations took over resource

tenure and regulated local use through permits, fines and at times military repression. More recently, emphasis has shifted somewhat toward patching-up, reconstituting or replacing broken community control over resources: "*gestion de terroir villageois*" approaches provide a context for village-level planning of bush fire, upland and forest use, "participatory" tree planting, and reservation of forest islands in favor of "the community."

(b) The counternarrative

Examining how vegetation has actually changed in Kissidougou is a necessary first step in evaluating these social science analyses. Fortunately, a number of historical data sources make this possible – sources ignored or deemed unnecessary by social analysts convinced of the degradation they were explaining.[2] Aerial photographs exist for Kissidougou which clearly show the state of the vegetation in 1952–3. These provide incontrovertible evidence that during this recent, supposedly most degrading period, the vegetation pattern and area of forest and savanna have in fact remained relatively stable. Changes which have occurred do not involve forest loss; rather there are large areas where forest cover has increased, and where savannas have become more, not less, woody. Forest islands have formed and enlarged, and in many areas, savannas evident in the 1950s have ceded to secondary forest vegetation.

To examine vegetation change further back, we reviewed descriptions and maps of Kissidougou's landscape made during the early French military occupation (roughly the 1890s to 1910), as well as indicators of past vegetation that emerge from oral history and accounts of everyday life in the youth of today's elderly people. These sources make clear that what was true for 1952–94 is equally true for 1893–1952. Moreover, villagers suggest, quite contrary to policy interpretations, that they established forest islands around their settlements, and that it is their work which encourages the formation of secondary forest thicket in savanna. In 27 of the 38 villages we investigated, elders recounted how their ancestors had founded settlements in savanna and gradually encouraged the growth of forest around them.

Earlier documentary sources from the 1780s to the 1860s do not suggest extensive forest cover; indeed they suggest the opposite. Both Harrison, traveling to Kissi areas (c. 1780, see Hair, 1962), and, as we shall see in the next case, Seymour (1859/60) in Toma country south-east of Kissi, describe short grass savannas and an absolute scarcity of trees in places which now support extensive dense humid forest. Sims (1859/60), speaking of the area just to the southeast (between Beyla and Kerouane) writes that: "There are no trees; the whole country is prairie; for firewood the people have to substitute cow dung, and a kind of moss which grows abundantly in that country." This picture of less, not more, forest cover in the 19th century is supported by several sets of early oral history data. All the above villages claiming foundation in savanna were established during or before the 19th century. Several village foundation stories in the south refer to conflicts triggered by the scarcity of construction wood, seemingly bizarre given the present forest and thicket vegetation, and in certain areas savanna grasses are said to have changed from those associated with drier climates to those associated with wetter ones.

It appears, therefore, that social science analyses in Kissidougou have been providing explanations for forest loss which has not actually been taking place. In doing so, they have supported a vegetation-change narrative quite at odds with – even the reverse of – more demonstrable environmental "facts." This casts into question the relationships between society, demography and environment valorized in these analyses. As we suggest now, there are other ways of conceiving of these relationships – counternarratives, if you will – which better fit and explain vegetation history as demonstrated.[3]

The first reconception involves recognizing that local land use can be vegetation-enriching as well as degrading. It can (and often does) serve to increase the proportion of useful vegetation forms and species in the landscape according to prevailing local values and productivity criteria. This has often meant increas-

ing the prevalence of forest forms in a once more savanna landscape. Thus, for example, villagers have encouraged the formation of forest islands around their villages for protection, convenient shelter for tree crops and sources of gathering products, and the concealment of ritual activities. They have achieved this both through everyday use of village margin land (for instance, in the thatch and fence-grass collection and cattle-tethering which reduce flammable grasses, and in the household waste deposition which fertilizes the forest successions beginning to develop), as well as through deliberately applied techniques (such as planting forest-initiating trees and cultivating the margins to create soil conditions suitable for tree establishment). In addition, on the slopes and plateaux between forest islands, local farming and fire use practices tend to maintain existing woody cover, and upgrade soils and vegetation from savanna to forest conditions. Much farming is concentrated on land that farmers have improved, whether by long-term alterations to edaphic quality through habitation, gardening and gardening-like cultivation; or by shorter-term fallow improvement through intensive cattle-grazing, seed-source protection, the multiplication of savanna trees from suckers, or distributing forest-initiating creepers. These forms of knowledge and practice are found among all of Kissidougou's ethno-linguistic groups. There seems little basis for distinguishing between "forest" and "savanna" people.

A related reconception concerns the character of natural resource management "organization." Environmental management in this region seems to depend – and always depended – less on community-level authorities and sociocultural organizations (which might be "threatened" by social change), than on the sum of a much more diffuse set of relations; a constellation more than a structure. Indeed, the maintenance of long-term productivity is in many cases built into short-term production patterns; whether carried out for oneself, one's household or one's compound, these improvements frequently interact with others – spatially or temporally – so that the combined effect on resource enrichment is greater than the sum of their parts. Thus, the fires set in the early and mid-dry season by hunters to clear small hunting grounds, and by others to protect property and fallows, create barriers to more devastating later fires; and the small tree crop plantations which people make and protect behind their kitchen gardens add to the creation of the village forest island. For much "resource management" there is no need for village or higher level management structures to "regulate degrading pressures." Nevertheless, village authorities do intervene in certain vegetation-influencing activities – e.g., in managing early-burning around the village, in protecting palm trees, in imposing cattle-tethering dates, and in coordinating the fallow rotations of farmers' contiguous plots in some Kissi areas. Village and higher level organizations also exert control over external factors which influence the agricultural environment, such as in negotiating with prospective Fula (Peuhl) pastoralist settlers or representatives of the forest service.

In this context, socioeconomic change has been articulated in shifts in landscape enrichment priorities and in the composition of a continued resource management constellation. Villagers have, for example, adapted forest island quality to suit changing socioeconomic conditions and commercial signals – managing them as fortresses during precolonial warfare, extending them for coffee planting when this became profitable, and abandoning coffee in favor of fruit tree and gathering-product enrichment as prices fell again. Urban employment opportunities, youth emigration and more individual economic opportunities have contributed to changes in farming organization, but today's smaller farm-households use and improve fallows as large compound ones did earlier, and modern women's individualized, commercial food cropping is concentrated in the forms of upland gardening that upgrade soils and vegetation (Leach and Fairhead, 1995). Village-level authorities have played a continuing, though shifting role within this historically flexible and diverse management constellation. There have been many social and economic changes, and there are many new social and economic problems, but these changes are rendered visible in the landscape largely through changing land use and management priorities, not through organizational "breakdown" and vegetation degradation.

Explaining demonstrable vegetation change also suggests relationships between demographic and environmental change very different from the "rapid population growth-deforestation" relationship upheld by the policy narrative. Despite the problems of reconstructing precolonial populations, evidence certainly does not support the idea of dramatic population growth or even steady one-way increase. Comparing census data suggests that Kissidougou's rural population has increased by only 70% since 1917. Growth pockets have been concentrated around Kissidougou town and major road axes, and in many areas population has remained almost stagnant. Precolonial evidence suggests that certain areas had early 19th century rural populations significantly higher than today, and suffered radical depopulation during late 19th century wars. Indeed oral accounts, explorers' reports, early 16th–18th century documents which mention the region, and broader regional history and archaeology combine to suggest that Kissidougou had relatively high farming populations from the 16th century and long before. There is clearly as little evidence for dramatic population increase in the present [20th] century from a low precolonial baseline as there is for dramatic forest loss.

In this context, Kissidougou's forest increase trends might be supposed to relate to population stagnation or decline. This reversed argument, however, still depends on the assumption that local land use tends to convert forest and forest fallows to savanna, and thus that more people means more forest loss. A counternarrative better fits evidence of local land-use practices and vegetation history: from an earlier situation of greater savanna extent, there has been a broadly positive relationship between the peopling of this region and its forest cover. First, as settlements are associated with the formation of forest islands, more villages mean more forest islands. This relationship has been modified by changes in population distribution and settlement patterns, with greater multiplication of settlements and forest islands during the 19th century when dispersed settlement was a survival strategy, than in the 20th when much population growth has been accommodated through the expansion of existing settlements, and indeed some consolidation linked to depopulation. Still, new settlements and forest formation have more recently been associated with the movement of village sites. Second, greater population density assists the control of fire, both by providing the necessary labor and by creating the demand, filling the landscape with more places (upgraded fallows, plantations, settlement sites) which people need to protect. In certain cases, the density of such protected sites of denser vegetation easily enables the entire exclusion of fire from the territory. The districts where upland savannas have recently ceded to dense forest fallow vegetation correlate broadly with the areas where population has grown. By contrast, low population densities make fire prevention impossible, and are a major factor in the persistence of running fire in the north and of the particular "living with fire" management strategies used there.

Viewing people-environment relations in terms of landscape enrichment-through-use by a diverse resource management constellation responding to changing incentives thus better explains (provides a counternarrative which better fits) demonstrable vegetation and population history. Policies conceived within the degradation narrative have sometimes undermined these relations, as well as created more general problems for villagers. In removing local control over resources, they have sometimes interfered with local management of them. In the north, for example, external fire control and prohibition prevented villagers operating their sequenced management-through-use strategies,[4] forcing clandestine coping strategies and rendering village and plantation protection more difficult. Removal of local resource tenure has reduced villagers' abilities to profit from past enrichment activities (e.g., in selling their forest island trees for timber) and their incentives for further landscape enrichment. The implementation of repressive environmental policies has in effect taxed rural populations for supposedly harmful activities which were, in fact, benign or beneficial. More recent approaches, which focus on decentraliz-

ing resource control by establishing village-level organization and management plans, actually risk undermining the existing flexible, diverse constellation of resource management relations. When initiated by state agencies with considerable foreign support and presence and predefined ideas about environmental dynamics, real decentralization can be undermined. Finally, but by no means least, the investment in "redressing" Kissidougou's supposed environmental degradation, an investment reaching unprecedented levels amid current aid donor concerns, carries heavy opportunity costs in terms of other more pressing rural development problems left unaddressed.

Vegetation history and its counternarrative of landscape enrichment entail different policy implications, emphasizing support to proven local practices and determinants of change. There are clearly many techniques and land uses that serve to increase forest cover, and which could provide an effective basis for external support. In working with the local ecology of fire, soils, vegetation successions and animal dynamics, these "integrated vegetation management" practices are more locally appropriate, integrated with the social matrix and thus more cost-effective in terms of labor than are the forestry "packages" generally proposed by outside agencies. Given that farming in the region is not inevitably degrading, environmental policy may look to support as well as to "rationalize and regulate" agriculture, specifically to support those upland farming practices which improve soils and fallow vegetation rather than concentrate technical effort exclusively on swamps. Fundamentally, rather than increase external intervention in the organization of resource management within villages, the more important priority is to create the enabling policy and socioeconomic conditions in which local resource management constellations can act effectively. This implies a shift on the part of environmental agencies away from direction (through repression or organizational restructuring as in assisted "community control") toward recognizing and supporting the diverse institutions which are actually engaged in resource management, and toward a more responsive role in providing requested services at the village level.

3. Case 2: The Ziama Forest Reserve

(a) The deforestation narrative

Traveling south from Kissidougou, one enters the Upper Guinean forest region. Within Guinea this region is populous, and there are only two significant intact forest blocks, the northern-most of which is Ziama.[5] Covering an area of about 120,000 hectares, Ziama was designated a colonial forest reserve in 1932, made an international biosphere reserve within the "Man and the Biosphere" program in 1980, and is now the subject of a major World Bank financed conservation project. Policy narratives concerning Ziama reproduce those of Kissidougou to a significant extent, with one major scale exception: changes in the status of a major forest block are at stake, and the conservation concern is partly global.

The Ziama forest is considered to be under considerable threat as an important relic of a once much greater forest cover. As Table 2.1, drawn from an IUCN report on Ziama, indicates, forest cover in this part of Guinea is now only 20% of what it was "at origin," and the report emphasizes that the forest is regressing rapidly. Apart from the loss of biodiversity (of considerable international concern) this reduction is said to be causing a drying-out of the local and regional climate, evident in drier water sources and courses, thereby increasing forest loss in a vicious cycle that threatens regional agriculture.

Regional studies and administrative perceptions are based on social analysis of this deforestation and encroachment on the remaining Ziama reserve. The most detailed and explicit

version of the "analysis" is found in a socio-economic study commissioned by a conservation project (Baum and Weimer, 1992). The assumptions it forwards are stabilized within a narrative not dissimilar to Kissidougou's, involving growing populations of immigrant and indigenous farmers who have lost "traditional" values and organizational forms, and who are seeking and de-wooding forested land.

As in Kissidougou, a strong contrast is drawn between a forest people, the indigenous Toma (Loma), and a savanna people, in this case the Konianke (Mandinka), whose immigration and savanna ways threaten the forest. Thus we read of the Toma that they are "largely fixed in their customary conceptions and habitual mode of life" (Baum and Weimer, 1992). The authors explain that the Toma "historical and social evolution as a people in a forest environment . . . favours a tendency to contemplation and sobriety." These attitudes supported a lifestyle and traditional society which existed in harmony with the forest. The peripheral geographical situation of the Toma in terms of communication, and the largely uncommercialized nature of past economy, supported these tendencies, so the argument goes.

Nevertheless, it is maintained that the Toma have lost their forest ways: "the forest has largely lost its customary importance, in favour of an essentially agricultural use of space. This evidences, without doubt, profound changes in economic orientation, especially among the Toma, ancient hunters and gatherers" (Baum and Weimer, 1992). The authors are surprised to find that women manage the principal crop, rice, and this serves to reinforce the idea that the Toma have only just learned to farm; it "reflects, without doubt the historical agricultural experience of a migratory farming, on small areas, only partially cleared." This view builds on colonial perceptions that Toma had "a very primitive agriculture, quite anarchic, centred on pluvial rice based on forest clearings . . . Those of the north have practically destroyed the cover of trees, those of the south, in the valleys and peneplanes, are still crushed by the forest" (Portères, 1965, pp. 688 and 726).

Changes in the Toma agricultural economy are linked to the opening-up of the area to

Table 2.1 Area of humid forest in Forest Guinea at different times

Period	Area (hectares)
At origin	1,930,000
c. 1958	1,300,000
c. 1980	1,075,000
1986	397,000

Source: République de Guinée (1990).

commerce and markets and to the need to feed growing populations. Both these trends are linked to the immigration and influence of Mandinka people from the north – immigration which is also central in explaining the area's demographic evolution. The authors present a picture of a long-term, very gradual peopling of the Ziama region through the immigration of Toma people and then brusque changes as Mandinka began to immigrate, now represented by second or third generation migrants. It is said that there were two villages present in the reserve when it was designated in 1932, Boo and Kpanya, having 542 and 370 persons at that time. Boo, which now has a population of some 1,600 is said to have had a population of 500 when it was founded, giving the impression that while the forest might have been lightly inhabited for long periods by forest people, it is only since the mid-19th century that it has been under a threat which is ever increasing. Immigration into the region is reported to have risen by four to sevenfold in 60 years. This rapid population growth is seen to have created severe land pressure in the areas neighboring the reserve. Assumptions about carrying capacity under shifting cultivation are used to argue that population:land ratios are now "fully saturated," and this largely accounts for farmers encroaching on the reserved land for farming.

This narrative – concerning a last remaining block of "pristine" natural forest, threatened by recent socioeconomic change and population pressure – provides a powerful justification for conservation. It also entails guidelines for conservation policy. "Original" forest is easily defined as a global or regional heritage, and its conservation by global and regional guardians a moral imperative. The narrative enables reserve administrations to list deforestation problems concerning climate and water as if they had never happened before, and to justify the urgency of conservation using arguments about their irreversibility. Within earlier, colonially derived approaches, the reservation of such forest, often as part of the state's domain, was acceptably justified with minimal regard for local interests in using reserved land and resources. In Ziama as elsewhere, "policing and patrolling" approaches characterized

early forest conservation. More recently, emphasis has been placed on the need to gain the participation, acceptance and support of local populations if conservation is to be sustainable. Since local resistance to and failure to respect the reserve are seen in terms of land shortage and economic pressure, the presumed policy needs are for socioeconomic development and agricultural intensification in the marginal area around the forest, accompanied by restricting of land tenure as necessary, to reduce current and future pressures on the reserve.

(b) The counternarrative

Once again, examination of historical data showing how vegetation, population and society have changed in this region reveal the extent to which the assumptions stabilized within this narrative are ill-founded. In the Ziama case, detailed descriptions come from the published writings of several highly educated Americo-Liberians who visited what is today the forest reserve in the mid-19th century (Anderson, 1870; Starr, 1912; Seymour, 1859/60). What they saw and described in no way conformed to the enduring image of sparse Toma hunter-gatherer populations living in harmony with an isolated high forest. The two "enclave" villages, now situated within the forests covering the wide Diani river plain, then lay in savannas. The Ziama mountain massif, now considered the heart of the primary forest, was either bare rock or covered "with cane grass and scarcely any tree but the palm" (Seymour, 1859/60). From the top of the massif, Seymour describes the plain as "covered with small bushes and grass, and it gives the country the appearance of an old farm, with palms standing scattered all over it." The ascription of 19th century identity as "forest people," however dubious in itself, seems highly inappropriate for these savanna-dwelling Toma of Ziama.

The region had large populations, by all accounts significantly larger, not smaller than today. Thus taking the enclave villages as an example, Anderson (in 1874) considered Kpanya as "very large" (when his account described 2,500 people as small) and Seymour (in 1859/60) estimated Boo to have 3,600 inhabitants. In addition, as the elders of the villages describe, these large villages had many smaller dependent settlements which no longer exist. The region was evidently highly agricultural. Seymour and Anderson describe large savanna farms of rice, maize and cassava stretching as far as the eye could see, and the short fallows necessary to sustain large populations. It was also commercially prosperous. Seymour noted 50 looms and five blacksmiths in Boo, and found some women wearing jewelery worth $20–30 at that time. A little further north, at Kuankan, people walked several miles from the mountains to the plain to sell firewood. As Seymour noted, "Firewood is scarce about this large city, but they have a good market, and it would do a person good to see the activity of the little boys, who are the principal traders in this line." Both enclave settlements had daily and weekly markets, as did all the major towns, distant some eight to 10 kilometers one from another, and these traded in foodstuffs, livestock, cash crops (such as cotton and kola), and artisanal goods of every description. The region was not economically or geographically marginal, but central to busy and long-established forest-savanna trade routes.

Thus in the mid-19th century the Ziama area clearly did not fit the images which today's policy narratives construct for it. Unsurprisingly, then, its subsequent history also overturns the conventional narrative's image of unilineal population increase and forest destruction. The story which explains how this region became a "primary forest" reserve within only 130 years of being heavily populated savanna turns, instead, on the wars which affected the area during 1870–1910 (Fairhead and Leach, 1994). Sustained military conflict first with Mandinka groups and then with the colonizing French caused major depopulation and economic devastation. It is this, not the extension of persistently low precolonial population densities, which explains the region's sparse populations at the turn of the century. On the abandoned settlements, fields and fallows, forest grew. By 1932 the French colonial administration recognized secondary forest worthy of reservation. That the forest grew so fast suggests that earlier intensive farming and savanna maintenance did not cause irreversible damage to forest vegetation potential; indeed it may indicate the positive legacy of previous local management practices, as in Kissidougou. By the early 1980s, conservationists were failing to distinguish Ziama's forest regrowth from primary forest. Populations since 1932 have not grown by the 400–700% suggested in the socioeconomic study. Using the study's own statistics, in the 41 villages in the vicinity of the reserve populations have increased by only 80% since 1932, or 120% if recent influxes of Liberian and Sierra Leonean refugees are taken into account,

It is clear that the stabilized assumptions which social science researchers are using to understand the nature and change of people-environment interactions in Ziama are completely at odds with a more demonstrable counternarrative centering on warfare, depopulation, forest regeneration and land alienation. The latter narrative better encompasses the experience and attitudes of today's Toma inhabitants, whose prominent display on village houses of portraits of ancestors who were killed or who fled during the wars testifies that these past events are not forgotten. It is largely this mismatch of narratives which underlies the failure of the reserve administration to build any constructive relationship with local inhabitants. Instead, their relationships are tense and have at times erupted into violence. Development activities around the reserve have seemed inadequate to calm this conflict and prevent "encroachment" on land within it. Achieving sustainable conservation, let alone of a participatory nature, remains a distant and unlikely goal, and much investment has been wasted in the effort.

When today's inhabitants "encroach" they are attempting both to reclaim ancestral lands, and to reestablish control over a once peopled and prosperous, now ex-social domain politically alienated from them. Recognizing this suggests alternative, potentially more fruitful guidelines for policy. If policy makers are to engage sensitively and productively with local communities, then local inhabitants' historical experiences need to be incorporated into policy dialogues and negotiations. Moreover, historically grounded claims to land and political authority need to be recognized and seriously addressed through conservation arrangements which, for example, cede tenurial control to local landholders, within the context of leasing or management agreements which fully recognize the value their lands now have for others.

4. The Regional Narrative and its Alternative

The specific narratives, concerning vegetation change and its social causes used to support policy in Kissidougou and Ziama, are examples of a broader narrative. This broader narrative contains and stabilizes assumptions which have been applied in the specific cases, but which are also written into national, regional and international policy documents.

Thus it was lamented in work incorporated into Guinea's agricultural development policy strategy that: "The north of forest Guinea (Beyla, Kissidougou and Gueckedou) is no longer a pre-forest region, but an 'ex-forest' or 'post forest' region!" Stating the narrative in its perhaps most succinct and pure form, it was asserted that:

This degradation of the natural environment . . . is the result of an evolution of rural societies little adapted to the rapid structural, demographic and economic changes this century, and above all, these last years . . . The problem today is the recession of traditional control of the orderly exploitation of space and its resources, which has not managed to follow or adapt to the recent and very rapid change in the rural world. This management becomes insufficient given a brutal increase in population [and] a progressive loss in the power of traditional control, due to the destructuration of rural society, the new amplitude of migration and the push towards agrarian individualism and the monetization of the local economy (République de Guinée, 1989, p. 8).

This narrative is the script of international donors, and one could fill shelves with its versions across Africa and beyond. Focusing on the population component, a recent World Bank policy review argues that:

. . . traditional farming and livestock husbandry practices, traditional dependency on wood for energy and for building material, traditional land tenure arrangements and traditional burdens on rural women worked well when population densities were low and population grew slowly. With the shock of extremely rapid population growth . . . these practices could not evolve fast enough. Thus they became the major source of forest destruction and degradation of the rural environment (Cleaver, 1992, p. 67).

This, it is argued, leads to vicious spirals of shortening fallows, land depletion, yield declines, and subsequent migration to marginal lands and forests. Environmental crisis results less from the overall effect of population pressure on resource availability, as a classic Malthusian position would have it, than from the multiple effects of population pressure on the institutions seeking to control resource access and use.

In exemplifying how inapplicable current regional narratives can be to local situations, the Kissidougou and Ziama cases invite a more fundamental examination of the origins and purposes of the regional narrative itself. More than empirical evidence, such narratives depend on – and expose – the field of Western imagination concerning African society; in particular, they show that stereotypes born of the colonial era are alive and well in the applied social sciences. Whether they are used to justify policies of external repression, or policies of social reorganization and "participatory" development, the narratives justify and make imperative a role for the outsider in the control of rural resources. The broader assumptions which the regional narratives contain can be summarized as follows:

(a) that African vegetation was once "original," consisting of a climax vegetation, i.e. the ultimate stage of plant succession which can exist under given ecological conditions. Prevailing ecological conditions are unchanging, so that what could exist today (e.g., humid forest in the forest and preforest region) did recently exist. Against this most natural vegetation one can judge levels of "degradation";

(b)   that African society can be seen, at origin, in terms of a traditional "functional order." Such order was once harmoniously integrated with "natural" vegetation (e.g., as epitomized in the idea of a "forest people" and a "savanna people"). African farming, land and resource-use practices degrade or are at best benign to the original vegetation. Degradation is thus limited only by functional social organization (regulation and authority). From environmental degradation one can diagnose the social ills of organizational dysfunction;

Not improve it [handwritten marginal note]

(c)   that African rural populations only increase, and do so fast. Population increase is as such environmentally and socially damaging;

(d)   that African society is essentially sedentary and subsistence oriented with an anti-commercial sentiment (e.g., in the popular imagery of "anti-commercial" traditional hunters). Money, mobility and trade are modern and lead to socioenvironmental dysfunction. African history consisted of the continuous reproduction of tradition until it began to become "modern," whether with markets and mobility, colonial intervention, or (in some work) the arrival of Islam.

The romantic links forged between these assumptions mean that vegetation change carries very profound moral messages. "Original climax vegetation" and "traditional functional society" provide fundamental baselines, so that whether the concern is about society or the environment, it is possible to judge that something is wrong and assess the extent of damage. From such a vantage point, the imperative is to intervene.

These assumptions, stabilized and sometimes hidden within social science analysis, are destructive and ultimately have no policy relevance. "The hard fact" as Sayer (1992) puts it, "is that most aid projects, and especially those in forestry fail." As the Kissidougou and Ziama cases exemplify, misleading narratives are fundamental to this failure. Moreover, just as for these cases there are counternarratives which better fit the facts of vegetation history, so at a more general level we follow the spirit of the articles in this special section to suggest other assumptions and a stabilizing narrative which better reflect realities surrounding African environments. The parameters of this counternarrative accord with recent developments in ecological and social theory and, significantly, they do not perpetuate the imperative for outside intervention in local resource control.

While the old narratives held within them a view of ecology which had to explain the disappearance of a natural climax vegetation, newer strands of ecological theory reject the idea of a single environmental maximum. When climate historians suggest that Africa has experienced both long-period, deep climatic fluctuations and changes in climatic variability, the history of vegetation begins to be seen as a history of continual transition, rather than of divergence from a single, once-extant climax. Recent theory suggests that such repeated transitions are likely to be between particular "stable" vegetation states, each determined by a multi-factor complex, rather than by trends in any particular variable. If the transition-causing factor reverts to its pretransition level, vegetation may move to another state, but need not return to its initial one (Sprugel, 1991; Scoones, 1994). Given the multiplicity of interacting factors influencing each state, shifts between them can be triggered by a particular, possibly unique, historical conjuncture of ecological factors. From this viewpoint, there is no basis for identifying a region's fundamental, archetypal vegetation. Vegetation is in continual transition, and its trajectory is determined by the legacy of past vegetation paths and present ecological conditions.

Ideas of environmental optima dovetailed neatly with ideas of static social maxima – of tradition and structure – typical of, but persisting beyond, colonial anthropology. But notions of society with a given social structure and order, maintained by functional adaptation and/or by rules and regulation, are challenged by more recent social theories giving weight to social action, processes and their capacity to shape and determine rules. Such continual structuration, over time and through social change, challenges the notion of a baseline "traditional" societal state. That African social forms have been in constant transition dovetails with the view of vegetation as in continual transition. There is no baseline in terms of how society values vegetation (and therefore no basis for the moral argument that indigenous values once preserved a more "natural" ideal). Vegetation values are shifting in accordance with social, economic and political changes, often of quite a conjunctural nature. The values placed on different vegetation types, conditioned by prevailing social conditions, are also socially differentiated: the high forest and wildlife priorities of today's global conservation planners are very different from the acricultural bush fallow priorities of today's Toma inhabitants.

In the West African context, these social and economic transitions have taken place within a long historical context of movement and migration, agriculture and commerce, and political and religious turbulence. The relationship between social and environmental change does not turn on the dramatic increase in any of these, but rather on people's responses to changing signals within this broader, dynamic continuity. Thus Kissidougou villagers have adapted forest island form to meet changing needs for fortification and different cash crops. Demographic change, rather than consisting always of unilinear population increase, involves periods of stability and decline, of shocks as well as secular trends. Depending on prevailing ecological and economic conditions, the effects of population growth periods can be positive as well as negative.

In the West African forest margin zones, climatic transition appears to have involved rehumidification since the mid-19th century, following a long relatively dry phase (Nicholson, 1979). Where the combination of ecological factors makes conditions marginal for forest, creating a precarious balance between forest vegetation and fire-maintained savanna, people's activities can make the difference, allowing forest vegetation to develop

in grassland. Where people have socioeconomic or political reasons to create forest they do so, in small patches, triggering transitions in small parts of the landscape, as has happened, for example, in Kissidougou. In open savanna and with low population densities, fire is harder to control, but as populations increase and transitions to forest are provoked in more places, fire is reduced and may eventually be eliminated. Agricultural priorities may mean large areas are maintained as bush fallow rather than allowed to develop into high forest. As populations increase further, fallow periods may need to be shortened and some resavannization can occur. But if population is removed at that point, and given the legacy of people's previous land use practices, the area may develop into high forest, as happened early this century in Ziama.

This regional counternarrative provides different, and more appropriate, guidelines for policy. In presenting socioenvironmental change in a way which better fits local experience, it provides a more effective basis for dialogue and participatory development work with local populations. In removing the baseline link between social and vegetation form, it removes the justification for external intervention in the organization of resource management to reestablish a lost social order, whether by replacement with external control or by the externally promoted "community reorganization" of recent more decentralized approaches. It suggests that more important priorities are to create the enabling policy and economic conditions in which local resource management constellations can act effectively, to support the diverse existing local institutional forms, and to build on the beneficial environmental implications of broader rural development and pricing policies – an approach which now finds support in some regional policy institutions (e.g., ENDA, 1992). Finally, as McNeely argues, "because chance factors, human influence and small climatic variation can cause very substantial changes in vegetation, [the biodiversity for] any given landscape will vary substantially over any significant time period – and no one variant is necessarily more 'natural' than the others" (1993). From this perspective, environmental policy can call on no moral high ground in recreating the natural (or the social that went with it). It becomes very clearly a question of social or political choice about what vegetation forms are desirable at any given time in social history, and about ensuring that conflicting perspectives on this – such as between local, global and intergenerational interests – are adequately articulated and addressed.

NOTES

1. This, like all subsequent quotations, has been translated from the original French by the authors.
2. More details of the following historical vegetation analysis are given in Leach and Fairhead (1994).
3. Such alternative social science analysis and its considerable evidence is documented fully elsewhere (Fairhead and Leach, [1996]; Leach and Fairhead, 1995).
4. For more on the management-use continuum (i.e. the way people use a resource in the way they manage it), see Roe and Fortmann (1982).
5. Further details concerning this case are given in Fairhead and Leach (1994).

REFERENCES

Adam, J. G., "Les reliques boisées et les essences des savanes dons le zone préforestière en Guinee fancaise," *Bulletin de la Société Botanique Francaise*, Vol. 98 (1948), pp. 22–26.

Anderson, B., *Narrative of a Journey to Musardu: capital of the western Mandigoes* (New York: S. W. Green, 1870).

Baum, G. A. and H-J. Weimer, "Participation et développement socio-économique comme conditions préalables indispensables d'une implication active des poulations riveraines dans la conservation de la forêt classée de Ziama," Report (Conakry: République de Guinée: Deutsche Forst-Consult/Neu-Isenburg. RFA/KfW, 1992).

Chevalier, A., "Les bois sacrés des Noirs de l'Afrique tropicale comme sanctuaries de la nature," *Revue de la Société de Biogéographie* (1933), pp. 37–42.

——, "Rapport sur les nouvelles recherches sur les les plantes a caouchouc de la Guinee francaise," IG276 (Dakar: Archives du Senegal, 1909).

Cleaver, K., "Deforestation in the western and central African forest: the agricultural and demographic causes, and some solutions," in K. Cleaver, M. Munashighe, M. Dyson, N. Egli, A. Peuker and F. Wencélius (Eds.), *Conservation of West and Central Africa's rainforests*, Environment Paper No. 1 (Washington, DC: World Bank, 1992), pp. 65–78.

Dupré G., "Les arbres, le fourré et le jardin: les plantes dans la société de Aribinda, Burkina Faso," in G. Dupré (Ed.), *Savoirs Paysans et Développement* (Paris: Karthala-ORSTOM, 1991), pp. 181–94.

ENDA, *Avenir des Terroirs: la ressource humaine* (Dakar: ENDA/GRAF, 1992).

Fairhead, J. and M. Leach, *Misreading the African Landscape: Society and Ecology in a Forest-Savanna Mosaic* (Cambridge: Cambridge University Press, 1996).

——, "Contested forests: modern conservation and historical land use of Guinea's Ziama reserve," *African Affairs*, Vol. 93 (1994), pp. 481–512.

Fofana, S., Y. Camaro, M. Barry and A. Sylla, "Etude relative au feu auprés des populations des bassins versants types du Haut Niger: Monographies des Bassins Kan I, Kan II, Kiss II," Report (Conakry: République de Guinée: Programme d' Aménagement des Bassins Versants Haut-Niger, 1993).

Green, W., "Lutte contre les feux de brousse," Report (Conakry République de Guinée: Projet DERIK, Développement Rural Intégré de Kissidougou, 1991).

Hair, P. E. H., "An account of the Liberian Hinterland c. 1780," *Sierra Leone Studies*, NS Vol. 16 (1962), pp. 218–26.

Holling, C. S., "Resilience and stability of ecological systems," *Annual Review of Ecology and Systematics*, No. 4 (1973), pp. 1–23.

Leach, M. and J. Fairhead, "The forest islands of Kissidougou: social dynamics of environmental change in West Africa's forest-savanna mosaic" (Report to ESCOR of the Overseas Development Administration, July, 1994).

——, "Ruined settlements and new gardens: gender and soil-ripening among Kuranko farmers in the forest-savanna transition zone," *IDS Bulletin*, Vol. 26, No. 1 (1995), pp. 24–32.

McNeely, J. A., "Lessons from the past: forests and biodiversity," Mimeo (Gland, Switzerland: IUCN, 1993).

Nicholson, S. E., "The methodology of historical climate reconstruction and its application to Africa," *Journal of African History*, Vol. 20, No. 1 (1979), pp. 31–49.

Ponsart-Dureau, M.-C., "Le pays Kissi de Guinée forestière: contribution a la connaissance du milieu; problematique de développement," Memoire (Montpellier: Ecole Superieure d'Agronomie Tropicale, 1986).

Portères, R., "Les noms des riz en Guinée: VI – Les noms des variétés de riz chez les Toma," *Journal d'Agriculture Tropicale et de Botanique Appliquée*, Vol. 12 (1965), pp. 687–728.

Programme d'Aménagement des Bassins Versants Haute Guinée (Projet Kan II), "Plan d'Opération," Report (Conakry, République de Guinée: Programme d'Aménagement des Hauts Bassins do Fleuve Niger, 1992).

Programme d'Aménagement des Hauts Bassins du Fleuve Niger, "Etude sociologique," Report (Conakry: République de Guinée: Programme d'Aménagement des Hauts Bassins do Fleuve Niger, n.d.).

République de Guinée (Jean, B.), "La gestion des ressources naturelles," Contribution to the lettre politique de développement agricole (Conakry: République de Guinée: Minstère d'Agriculture et des Ressources Animales, November, 1989).

République de Guinée and IUCN (Bourque, J. and R. Wilson), "Guinea forestry biodiversity Study – Ziama and Diecke Reserves," Report (Gland, Switzerland: IUCN for République de Guinée, September, 1990).

Roe, E., "Development narratives, or making the best of blueprint development," *World Development*, Vol. 19, No. 4 (1991).

Roe, E., and L. Fortmann, *Season and Strategy*, Special series on Resource Management, (Ithaca, NY: Rural Development Committee, Centre for International Studies, Cornell University, 1982).

Sayer, J. A., "Development assistance strategies to conserve Africa's rainforests," in K. Cleaver, M. Munashighe, M. Dyson, N. Egli, A. Peuker and F. Wencélius (Eds.), *Conservation of West and Central Africa's rainforests*, Environment Paper No. 1 (Washington, DC: World Bank, 1992), pp. 3–17.

Scoones, I. (Ed.), *Living with Uncertainty: new directions for pastoral development in Africa* (London: IT Publications, 1994).

Seymour, G. L., "The journal of the journey of George L. Seymour to the interior of Liberia: 1858," *New York Colonization Journal*, Vol. IX, No. 12, Vol. X, Nos. 6 and 8 (1859–60).

Sims, J. L., "The journal of a journey in the interior of Liberia by James. L. Sims, of Monrovia. Scenes in the interior of Liberia: being a tour through the countries of the Dey, Goulah, Pessah Barlain, Kpellay, Suloang, and the King Boatswain's tribes, in 1858," *New York Colonization Journal*, Vol. IX, No. 12, Vol. X, Nos. 6 and 8 (1859–60).

Sprugel, D. G., "Disturbance, equilibrium, and environmental variability: What is 'natural' vegetation in a changing environment?," *Biological Conservation*, Vol. 58 (1991), pp. 1–18.

Starr, F. (Ed.), *Narrative of the Expedition Despatched to Musahdu by the Liberian Government under Benjamin K. Anderson Esq. in 1874* (Monrovia: College of West Africa Press, 1912).

Stieglitz, F. V., "Exploitation forestière rurale et réhabilitation des forêts: Premièrs résultats d'un projet de recherche interdisciplinaire en Haute-Guinée (Janv – Mai 1990, République de Guinée)," Mimeo (Berlin: 1990).

Zerouki, B., "Etude relative au feu auprès des populations des bassins versants types du Haut Niger," Report (Conakry: République de Guinée: Programme d'Aménagement des Bassins Versants Types du Haut Niger, 1993).

3

Interest in Cattle

E. E. Evans-Pritchard

I

A People whose material culture is as simple as that of the Nuer are highly dependent on their environment. They are pre-eminently pastoral, though they grow more millet and maize than is commonly supposed. Some tribes cultivate more and some less, according to conditions of soil and surface water and their wealth in cattle, but all alike regard horticulture as toil forced on them by poverty of stock, for at heart they are herdsmen, and the only labour in which they delight is care of cattle. They not only depend on cattle for many of life's necessities but they have the herdsman's outlook on the world. Cattle are their dearest possession and they gladly risk their lives to defend their herds or to pillage those of their neighbours. Most of their social activities concern cattle and *cherchez la vache* is the best advice that can be given to those who desire to understand Nuer behaviour.[1]

The attitude of Nuer towards, and their relations with, neighbouring peoples are influenced by their love of cattle and their desire to acquire them. They have profound contempt for peoples with few or no cattle, like the Anuak, while their wars against Dinka tribes have been directed to seizure of cattle and control of pastures. Each Nuer tribe and tribal section has its own pastures and water-

supplies, and political fission is closely related to distribution of these natural resources, ownership of which is generally expressed in terms of clans and lineages. Disputes between tribal sections are very often about cattle, and cattle are the compensation for loss of life and limb that is so frequently their outcome. Leopard-skin chiefs and prophets are arbiters in questions in which cattle are the issue, or ritual agents in situations demanding sacrifice of ox or ram. Another ritual specialist is the *wut ghok*, the Man of the Cattle. Likewise, in speaking of age-sets and age-grades we find ourselves describing the relations of men to their cattle, for the change from boyhood to manhood is most clearly marked by a corresponding change in those relations at initiation.

Small local groups pasture their cattle in common and jointly defend their homes and herds. Their solidarity is most evident in the dry season when they live in a circle of windscreens around a common kraal, but it can also be seen in their wet season isolation. A single family or household cannot protect and herd their cattle alone and the cohesion of territorial groups must be considered in the light of this fact.

The network of kinship ties which links members of local communities is brought about by the operation of exogamous rules, often stated in terms of cattle. The union of marriage is brought about by payment of cattle and every phase of the ritual is marked by their transference or slaughter. The legal status of the partners and of their children is defined by cattle-rights and obligations.

Cattle are owned by families. While the head of the household is alive he has full rights of disposal over the herd, though his wives have rights of use in the cows and his sons own some of the oxen. As each son, in order of seniority, reaches the age of marriage he marries with cows from the herd. The next son will have to wait till the herd has reached its earlier strength before he can marry in his turn. When the head of the household dies the herd still remains the centre of family life and Nuer strongly deprecate breaking it up, at any rate till all the sons have married, for it is a common herd in which all have equal rights. When the sons are married they and their wives and children generally live in adjacent homesteads. In the early part of the dry season one sees a joint family of this kind living in a circle of windscreens around a common kraal, and in the big camps formed later in the year one finds them occupying a distinct section in the lines of windscreens. The bond of cattle between brothers is continued long after each has a home and children of his own, for when a daughter of any one of them is married the others receive a large portion of her bride-wealth. Her grandparents, maternal uncles, paternal and maternal aunts, and even more distant relatives, also receive a portion. Kinship is customarily defined by reference to these payments, being most clearly pointed at marriage, when movements of cattle from kraal to kraal are equivalent to lines on a genealogical chart. It is also emphasized by division of sacrificial meat among agnatic and cognatic relatives.

The importance of cattle in Nuer life and thought is further exemplified in personal names. Men are frequently addressed by names that refer to the form and colour of their favourite oxen, and women take names from oxen and from the cows they milk. Even small boys call one another by ox-names when playing together in the pastures, a child usually taking his name from the bull-calf of the cow

he and his mother milk. Often a man receives an ox-name or cow-name at birth. Sometimes the name of a man which is handed down to posterity is his ox-name and not his birth-name. Hence a Nuer genealogy may sound like an inventory of a kraal. The linguistic identification of a man with his favourite ox cannot fail to affect his attitude to the beast, and to Europeans the custom is the most striking evidence of the pastoral mentality of the Nuer.

Since cattle are a Nuer's most cherished possession, being an essential food-supply and the most important social asset, it is easy to understand why they play a foremost part in ritual. A man establishes contact with the ghosts and spirits through his cattle. If one is able to obtain the history of each cow in a kraal, one obtains at the same time not only an account of all the kinship links and affinities of the owners but also of all their mystical connexions. Cows are dedicated to the spirits of the lineages of the owner and of his wife and to any personal spirit that has at some time possessed either of them. Other beasts are dedicated to ghosts of the dead. By rubbing ashes along the back of a cow or ox one may get into touch with the spirit or ghost associated with it and ask it for assistance. Another way of communicating with the dead and with spirits is by sacrifice, and no Nuer ceremony is complete without the sacrifice of a ram, he-goat, or ox.

We have seen in a brief survey of some Nuer institutions and customs that most of their social behaviour directly concerns their cattle. A fuller study of their culture would show everywhere the same dominant interest in cattle, e.g. in their folklore. They are always talking about their beasts. I used sometimes to despair that I never discussed anything with the young men but livestock and girls, and even the subject of girls led inevitably to that of cattle. Start on whatever subject I would, and approach it from whatever angle, we would soon be speaking of cows and oxen, heifers and steers, rams and sheep, he-goats and she-goats, calves and lambs and kids. I have already indicated that this obsession – for such it seems to an outsider – is due not only to the great economic value of cattle but also to the fact that they are links in numerous

"Intoot("

social relationships. Nuer tend to define all social processes and relationships in terms of cattle. Their social idiom is a bovine idiom.

Consequently he who lives among Nuer and wishes to understand their social life must first master a vocabulary referring to cattle and to the life of the herds. Such complicated discussions as those which take place in negotiations of marriage, in ritual situations, and in legal disputes can only be followed when one understands the difficult cattle-terminology of colours, ages, sexes, and so forth.

Important though horticultural and piscatorial pursuits are in Nuer economy, pastoral pursuits take precedence because cattle not only have nutritive utility but have a general social value in other respects. I have mentioned a few situations in which this value is manifested, but have not recorded every role of cattle in Nuer culture, for they are significant in many social processes, including some I have mentioned, which lie outside the limited scope of this book [*The Nuer: A Description of the Modes of Livelihood and Political Institutions of a Nilotic People*]. It seemed necessary to give an introductory sketch on these lines in order that the reader might understand that Nuer devotion to the herdsman's art is inspired by a range of interests far wider than simple need for food, and why cattle are a dominant value in their lives. We shall ask later how this value is related to environmental conditions and how far the two, taken together, help us to explain some characteristics of Nuer political structure.

II

Before the present century Nuer were far richer in cattle than they are now and it is probable that they cultivated less millet. Their stock has been impaired by repeated outbreaks of rinderpest, which still decimate the herds. It was probably more destructive in the past than now, though the attacks I witnessed were severe; but in the past the warlike Nuer could always restore their losses by raiding Dinka. All Nuer agree that in the last generation their herds were more considerable and that the payments of bride-wealth and blood-wealth

were forty, and sometimes fifty to sixty, head of cattle, whereas today the kinsmen of a bride do not expect to receive more than twenty to thirty. At the present time I would say, on a general impression, that the Nuer are far richer in stock than the Shilluk, but not so prosperous as the more favoured of the Dinka tribes.

It was difficult to make a census of cattle, even in a small area, and Nuer would certainly have regarded such an attempt with repugnance. On the few estimates made I would reckon an average of ten head of cattle and five goats and sheep to the byre. A byre of the ordinary size cannot hold more than a dozen or so adult kine. As there are some eight persons to a byre the cattle probably do not greatly exceed the human population. Cows predominate and probably compose about two-thirds of the herds. Many plates in this book show the appearance of Nuer cattle. Nuer say that a very large hump shows Beir origin and that very long horns are evidence of Dinka stock.

Some tribes are richer in cattle than others. Lou country is considered especially suitable for raising stock and is renowned for its large herds. The Eastern Jikany were once very rich in cattle, but their herds are still recovering from losses in epidemics that forced the people to cultivate more extensively. Cattle are everywhere evenly distributed. Hardly any one is entirely without them, and no one is very rich. Although cattle are a form of wealth that can be accumulated, a man never possesses many more beasts than his byre will hold, because as soon as his herd is large enough he, or one of his family, marries. The herd is thereby reduced to two or three beasts and the next few years are spent in repairing its losses. Every household goes through these alternating periods of poverty and comparative wealth. Marriages and epidemics prevent accumulation of cattle and no disparity in wealth offends the democratic sentiment of the people.

When we come to examine the Nuer political system we shall keep in mind that till recent years they have probably been more exclusively pastoral, and more nomadic, than at the present time, and that the dwindling of their herds may partly explain their persistent aggressiveness.

III

Although cattle have many uses they are chiefly useful for the milk they provide. Milk and millet (sorghum) are the staple foods of the Nuer. In some parts of their country, especially among the Lou, the millet supply seldom lasts the whole year, and when it is exhausted people are dependent on milk and fish. At such times a family may be sustained by the milk of a single cow. In all parts the millet crop is uncertain and more or less severe famines are frequent, during which people rely on fish, wild roots, fruits, and seeds, but mainly on the milk of their herds. Even when millet is plentiful it is seldom eaten alone, for without milk, whey, or liquid cheese, Nuer find it stodgy, unpalatable, and, especially for children, indigestible. They regard milk as essential for children, believing that they cannot be well and happy without it, and the needs of children are always the first to be satisfied even if, as happens in times of privation, their elders have to deny themselves. In Nuer eyes the happiest state is that in which a family possesses several lactating cows, for then the children are well-nourished and there is a surplus that can be devoted to cheese-making and to assisting kinsmen and entertaining guests. A household can generally obtain milk for its little children because a kinsman will lend them a lactating cow, or give them part of its milk, if they do not possess one. This kinship obligation is acknowledged by all and is generously fulfilled, because it is recognized that the needs of children are the concern of neighbours and relatives, and not of the parents alone. Occasionally, however, after an epidemic or, to a lesser degree, after two or three youths of the group have married, an entire hamlet, or even a whole village may experience scarcity. Sometimes, also, shortage is caused by a tendency for the cows of a village to cease lactating at about the same time.

Nuer value their cows according to the amount of milk they give and they know the merits of each in this respect. The calves of a good milch cow are more highly prized than the calves of a cow that gives little milk. A cow is never to them just a cow, but is always a good cow or a bad cow, and a Nuer who is owed a cow will not accept in payment of his debt one that does not meet with his approval. If you ask a Nuer in a cattle camp which are the best and worst cows in the herd he can tell you at once. In judging their points he pays little attention to those aesthetic qualities which please him in an ox, especially fatness, colour, and shape of horns, but he selects those which indicate a good milch cow: a broad loose back, prominent haunch bones, large milk-veins, and a much-wrinkled milk-bag. In judging the age of a cow he notes the depth of the trenches which run on either side of its rump towards the tail, the number and sharpness of its teeth, the firmness of its gait, and the number of rings on its horns. Nuer cows have the familiar angular and thin-fleshed characteristics of dairy stock.

Milking is performed twice daily by women, girls, and uninitiated boys. Men are forbidden to milk cows unless, as on journeys or war expeditions, there are no women or boys present. The milker squats by the cow and milks a single teat at a time into the narrow mouth of a bottle-necked gourd balanced on her thighs. She milks with thumb and first finger but, the other fingers being closed, the teat is to some extent pressed against the whole hand. It is both a squeezing and a pulling motion. The gourd is kept in position by the downward stroke of the hands which press it against the thighs. When a pot, or a gourd with a wider mouth, is used it is held between the knees and the milker squeezes two teats at a time. Occasionally one sees two girls milking a cow, one at either side. If a cow is restless a man may hold it still by putting his hand in its mouth and gripping its muzzle, and if it kicks, a noose is placed round its hind legs and they are pulled together. I was told that sometimes they ring the nose of a cow that is habitually restless during milking.

The process of milking is as follows. The calf is loosened and with its tethering-cord round its neck runs at once to its dam and begins violently butting her udder. This starts the flow of milk, and Nuer hold that if the calf were not first to suck the cow would hold up its milk. They do not pat the udder with the hand unless the calf is dead, for this is

considered bad for the cow. When the calf has
sucked a little it is dragged away, resisting
stubbornly, and tethered to its dam's peg,
where it rubs against her forelegs and she licks
it. The girl now milks the first milking, known
as the *wic*. When the teats become soft and
empty the calf is again loosened and the
process is repeated. The second milking is
called *tip indit*, the greater *tip*. As a rule there
are only two milkings, but if it is a very good
milch cow at the height of her lactation period
the calf may once more be loosened and a
third milking, called *tip intot*, the lesser *tip*,
be taken. When the girl has finished milking
she wipes her thighs and the milk-gourd with
the cow's tail and loosens the calf to finish off
what milk is left. The first milking takes longer
time and produces more milk than the second,
and the second more than the third. The
morning yield is greater than the evening
yield.

Figure 3.1 *Churning gourd*

A series of measurements suggest that four to
five pints a day may be regarded as a general
average for Nuer cows during their lactation
period, which lasts, on an average, about seven
months. It must be remembered, however, that
this is an estimate of the yield for human consumption. The calf gets its share before, during,
and after the milking. It is possible, moreover,
that, as Nuer declare, some cows hold up their
milk for their calves, since the calves often suck
for several minutes after milking before their
dams refuse them by kicking them or moving
so that they cannot reach their udders. Sometimes a small boy drags the calf away and milks
the udders himself, licking the milk off his
hands, or shares the teats with the calf, but as a
rule the calf gets the remainder of the milk. The
total yield may, therefore, be as high as seven
to nine pints a day and it appears to be far richer
than milk given by English cows. It is not surprising that the yield is small, because Nuer
cows receive no artificial feeding, succulent pasturage is often difficult to obtain, and they have
to endure great hardship. It must, moreover, be
emphasized that whereas English dairy farmers
require only milk, Nuer herdsmen require milk
and also wish to preserve every calf. Human
needs have to be subordinated to the needs of
the calves, which are the first consideration if
the herd is to be perpetuated.

Milk is consumed in various ways. Fresh milk
is drunk, especially by children, and is also
consumed with millet-porridge. Fresh milk is
chiefly drunk by adults in the heat of the dry
season when a refreshing draught is most
appreciated and food is scarce. Some milk is
put aside, where it soon, very rapidly in hot
weather, sours and thickens, in which condition it is relished. Nuer like to have a gourd
of sour milk always at hand in case visitors
come. Part of the daily yield is kept for making
cheese, and if there are several cows in lactation one may be reserved for this purpose.
Milk for churning is drawn into a different
gourd to that used for drinking milk. It is then
transferred to a churning gourd (see Figure
3.1), in which it stands for several hours, and
as churning gourds are not cleaned, unless
they smell bad, the acids which remain from
the previous churning curdle the milk. After
standing it is churned by a woman, or girl,
who sits on the ground with her legs stretched
in front of her, and, raising the gourd, brings
it down with a jerk on her thighs where she
rocks it a few times before repeating her
actions: a simple but lengthy way of churning.
A small quantity of water is poured into the
gourd when the curds are beginning to form

to make them set well and to increase the quantity of whey, and some ox's urine may be added to give them consistency. When they have formed, the woman pours the milk into a cup-shaped gourd and scoops them out with a mussel shell into another gourd vessel which is hung up in a hut. The whey, mixed with fresh milk, is mainly drunk by women and boys. Every day they add to the supply of curds and now and again stir some ox's urine with them to prevent them from going bad. They may add to the supply for several weeks before the final boiling over a quick fire, which turns the curds, *lieth in bor*, into solid deep yellow cheese, *lieth in car*. After boiling for a time the liquid is poured into a gourd and the oil on top is removed, to be used as a flavouring for porridge. The cheese is suspended in a net from the roof of a hut in a round gourd, a piece of the shell of which has been cut out so that cords run through it and it acts as a sliding lid (see Figure 3.2), and, if air is excluded by a coating of cattle dung, it will keep in good condition for months. Milk may thus be stored in the form of cheese. It is eaten with porridge and is also used for anointing the body.

Sheep and goats are also milked in the mornings, but little importance is attached to their yield, which is drunk by small children and not used for dairy work. The woman milks and the kids and lambs finish what is left in the udders. As they run with their dams at pasture an evening milking is not taken; but during the day hungry herdboys often squeeze the udders and lick the milk off their hands.

Some points that arise from an account of milking and dairy-work deserve emphasis. (1) The present number and distribution of cattle do not permit the Nuer to lead an entirely pastoral life as they would like to do, and possibly did at one time. On a generous estimate the average daily yield to the byre is probably no more than twelve pints, or one and a half pints per person. A mixed economy is, therefore, necessary. (2) Furthermore the fluctuation in household resources, due to epidemics and transmission of bride-wealth, is further accentuated by the organic character of the staple diet, for cows only produce milk for a certain period after calving and the yield is not constant. It follows that a single family is

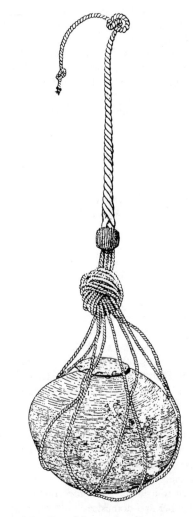

Figure 3.2 *Gourd for storing cheese*

not a self-sufficient unit, as far as milk is concerned, for it cannot always ensure an adequate supply. Therefore, since milk is considered essential, the economic unit must be larger than the simple family group. (3) Environmental conditions, as well as need for cereal food to supplement their milk diet, prevent Nuer from being entirely nomadic, but milk food enables them to lead a roving life for part of the year and gives them mobility and elusiveness, as their history shows and as has been recently demonstrated in the Government campaign against them. Milk requires neither storage nor transport, being daily renewed, but, on the other hand, involves a straight dependence on water and vegetation which not only permits, but compels, a wandering life. Such a life nurtures the qualities of the shepherd – courage, love of fighting, and contempt of hunger and hardship – rather than shapes the industrious character of the peasant.

IV

Nuer are also interested in their cattle for meat, boiled and roasted. They do not raise herds for slaughter, but sheep and oxen are frequently sacrificed at ceremonies. There are always ghosts and spirits in whose honour a sacrifice would at any time be appropriate, and such sacrifices are generally long overdue, so that there does not lack a proper excuse for a feast when people desire one. Fertile cows are sacrificed in mortuary rites, but, otherwise, only barren females are killed. At sacrifices most people are interested more in the festal than the religious character of the rites. Sometimes, as at marriage ceremonies, the people who perform the ritual are different from those who eat the meat, while at other ceremonies there is a general scramble for the carcass. Desire for meat is shown without shame on these occasions, and Nuer recognize that some men sacrifice without due cause. In some years it is a custom in the rains for young men to join together at a homestead with the purpose of slaughtering oxen and gorging themselves with meat. Except on such occasions, however, people ought not to kill an ox solely for food – it being even thought that the ox may curse them – and they only do so in severe famine. The Lou, who are rich in cattle, have a reputation, of which they are rather ashamed, for killing oxen for meat. Nevertheless, nowhere in Nuerland are cattle ordinarily slaughtered for food, and a man would never kill even a sheep or goat merely on the grounds that he desired meat. On occasions of minor importance sheep or goats are sacrificed rather than oxen, as they are less valuable.

Any animal which dies a natural death is eaten. Even when a youth's favourite ox dies he must be persuaded to partake of its flesh, and it is said that were he to refuse his spear might avenge the insult by cutting his foot or hand on some future occasion. Nuer are very fond of meat, and declare that on the death of a cow, "The eyes and the heart are sad, but the teeth and the stomach are glad." "A man's stomach prays to God, independently of his mind, for such gifts."

Though oxen are sacrificed and eaten they are not valued only for these purposes, but also for display and for the prestige their possession confers. Colour and shape of horns are significant, but the essential qualities are bigness and fatness, it being considered especially important that the haunch bones should not be apparent. Nuer admire a large hump which wobbles when the animal walks, and to exaggerate this character they often manipulate the hump shortly after birth.

Like other pastoral peoples in East Africa the Nuer extract blood from the necks of their cattle, and this is a supplementary article of diet in dry season camps, where one may generally see at least one cow bled each evening. Cows are bled for culinary purposes more frequently than oxen. The operation, called *bar*, consists of tying a cord tightly round a cow's neck so that the veins stand out and one of them can be stabbed, on the head side of the cord, with a small knife bound with cord or grass to prevent it entering too deeply. The blood spurts out, and when a large gourd has been filled they loosen the cord and it ceases to flow. Some dung is smeared over the wound. If one examines the neck of a cow one sees a row of small cicatrices. Cows appear to be a little giddy after the operation and may totter slightly, but otherwise seem none the worse for their experience. Indeed, it may well be, as Nuer assert, that they are the better for it, for they lead a sluggish life. The blood is boiled by women till it is fairly consistent and can be used as a meat flavouring with porridge; or the men let it stand till it coagulates into a solid block, and, after roasting it in the embers of a fire, cut it up and eat it.

Nuer do not regard the blood of cows as a staple article of diet and it does not play an important part in their cuisine. Indeed, they say that they do not perform the operation to acquire food, though they confess that roasted blood is delicious, but for the benefit of the cows. Bleeding is designed to cure a cow of any unfitness by letting out the bad blood of the sickness. Also, Nuer say, it makes the cow fat, for next day it will be more lively and graze avidly. Bleeding, moreover, in their opinion, decreases the desire of a cow to be served. Nuer say that if a cow is served too frequently it may eventually become barren, whereas, if it is bled now and again, it will only require to be served once and will be in calf. Cattle are sometimes bled for medical reasons in the rainy season, when people may be so replete that the blood is given to the boys of the kraal and to the dogs. Sometimes they make incisions in the noses of calves and let the blood flow to the ground in order to make them fat. I have seen Nuer scarify their own legs and the small of their backs to induce fleetness and strength.

The following two points seem to us to be significant. (1) Whilst Nuer normally do not kill their stock for food, the end of every beast is, in fact, the pot, so that they obtain sufficient meat to satisfy their craving and have no pressing need to hunt wild animals, an activity in which they engage little. (2) Except when epidemics are rife the usual occasions of eating meat are ritual and it is the festal character of rites which gives them much of their significance in the life of the people.

V

Apart from milk, meat, and blood, cattle furnish Nuer with numerous household necessities, and when we consider how few are their possessions we can appreciate the importance of cattle as raw material. The bodies and bodily products of cattle have the following uses:

Their skins are used for beds, trays, for carrying fuel, cord for tethering and other purposes, flails, leather collars for oxen (Figure 3.4), and for the tympana of drums. They are employed in the manufacture of pipes, spears, shields, snuff-containers, etc. The scrota of bulls are made into bags to contain tobacco, spoons, and other small objects (Figure 3.3). Tail-hairs are made into tassels used as dance ornaments by girls and to decorate the horns of favourite oxen. Their bones are used for the manufacture of armlets, and as beaters, pounders, and scrapers. Their horns are cut into spoons and are used in the construction of harpoons.

Their dung is used for fuel and for plastering walls, floors, and the outsides of straw huts in cattle camps. It is also employed as a plaster in minor technological processes and to protect wounds. The ashes of burnt dung are rubbed over mens' bodies, and are used to dye and straighten the hair, as a mouth wash and tooth powder, in the preparation of sleeping-skins and leather bags, and for various ritual purposes. Their urine is used in churning and cheese-making, in the preparation of gourd-utensils, for tanning leather, and for bathing face and hands.

The skins of sheep and goats are worn as loin garments by married women, used as rugs to sit on, made into bags for storing tobacco and millet, and are cut into strips to be tied round their ankles by youths when dancing. Their dung and urine are not utilized.

The Bedouin Arab has been called the parasite of the camel. With some justice the Nuer might be called the parasite of the cow. It may, however, seem that the list we have compiled does not cover a very wide range of uses, but so simple is Nuer material culture that it accounts for a very considerable part of their technology and contains items on which they are highly dependent, e.g. the use of dung as fuel in a country where it is difficult to obtain sufficient vegetable fuel for cooking, let alone for the large fires that burn day and night in every byre and windscreen.

We have seen that apart from their many social uses Nuer are directly concerned with cattle as producers of two essential articles of diet, milk and meat. We now perceive that the economic value of cattle is more extensive. Taking into consideration also the more general social value of cattle, briefly indicated in Section I, we may already note that there is over-emphasis on a single object, which dominates all other interests and is consistent with those qualities of simplicity, single-mindedness, and conservatism, so characteristic of pastoral peoples.

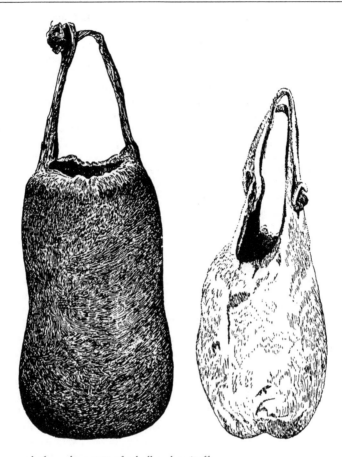

Figure 3.3 *Bags made from the scrota of a bull and a giraffe*

VI

In later chapters [of *The Nuer*] we shall describe how the needs of cattle, water, pasturage, protection from carnivorous beasts and biting insects, and so forth, are attended to, and show in what manner they determine human routine and affect social relations. Leaving these broader issues on one side, we ask here whether the Nuer, who are so reliant on their cattle and who value them so highly, are competent herdsmen. It is unnecessary to state that they give their beasts every attention that their knowledge allows, but it is pertinent to inquire whether their knowledge suffices. It was especially noted where Nuer practice is not in accord with the conventions of farming, and the reasons for the divergence were investigated. A few of the more evident difficulties and some general observations on Nuer husbandry are recorded below.

1. Since the cows are not brought back to the kraals at midday the smaller calves must go without nourishment for many hours each day. However, Capt. H. B. Williams, Director of the Sudan Veterinary Department, tells me that Nuer oxen have the reputation of being as good as any in the Sudan, so that their development as young calves cannot be seriously arrested. In the rains the cows are seldom milked before 9 to 10 a.m. and again at about 5 p.m., but in the dry season they may be taken to pasture as early as 8 a.m. and not return till about 5.30 p.m., so that they cannot

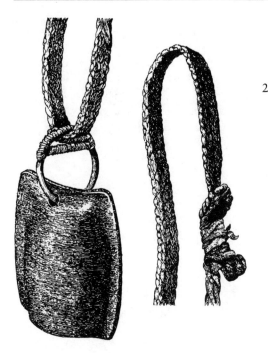

Figure 3.4 *Ox-bell and collar*

suckle their calves for about ten hours. However, this long interval is not easily avoided, for in the dry season the grazing grounds are often distant and owing to lack of good pasturage the cattle require longer to feed than in the rains. In the rains it would be a simple matter to pasture the herd at daybreak and bring it home at midday, as many East African peoples do, for the cows to suckle their calves and chew the cud. But Nuer say that when the cattle come out of their hot smoky byres they like to rest a while in the kraal before going to pasture, and their lethargy, which contrasts with their eagerness to graze after a night in the open in dry season camps, seems to justify this statement. Nuer realize that the heat and smoke of byres are bad for the cattle, but they consider mosquitoes worse. Also by waiting till the dew has evaporated they consider they lessen the risk of digestive troubles, for in the rains the ground is cold and damp till a late hour. A further reason for

keeping the cattle late in the kraals is that if they are loosened early they soon graze to repletion and begin to wander in all directions, since they are not usually herded in the rains.

2. It at once strikes a European that the condition of drinking water at periods of the dry season leaves much to be desired, especially if he has to drink it himself. Sometimes the pools have almost dried up and contain foul, even slimy, water which men and cattle drink. I have wondered why they do not move sooner from these small pools, around which they camp in the early drought, to the rivers and lakes where they make their final concentrations, but I do not distrust their judgement, for they are fully aware that dirty water is neither palatable to, nor good for, the cattle, and when circumstances permit they are at pains to ensure that they are supplied with clean water as often as they require it. In moving camp they have to take into account a number of desiderata: pasturage, fishing, the harvest of *Balanites aegyptiaca*, the second millet harvest, etc., besides conditions of water.

3. Unlike some East African peoples Nuer do not keep too many entire animals. If they err at all it is in keeping too few. On the limited observations made it was estimated that there is one adult bull to about thirty or forty adult cows. Nuer try to select as stud bulls the calves of their best milch cows so that they may breed good milch cows from them. They say that if they did not castrate most of the bull calves the cows would get no peace and there would be constant fighting in the kraals and commotion in the byres. A calf is not castrated till it is about eighteen months to two years old: "When its dam has had another calf and a third is in its womb." It is thrown, the scrotum is cut with a spear, and the testicles drawn out and severed. There is little loss of blood and the animal soon recovers. A calf may be castrated for sacrificial purposes at any time, but otherwise Nuer prefer to perform the operation in the dry season for there is less chance of inflammation than in the rains. Bulls

are not discouraged from fighting unless they belong to the same herd, and fights are often cited in tradition as the cause of fission and migration of lineages. A very large number of steers and oxen are slaughtered in sacrifices.

4. Heifers are not served till their third year. Nuer know when a cow is on heat by its behaviour in the kraal: it is restless, lows, swishes its tail, sniffs at the vulvas of other cows, and tries to mount them. If a cow has mated in the grazing grounds – for bulls run with the herd – the first signs of pregnancy are said to be vulvar changes. If you ask Nuer when a cow which has been served at a certain time will calve they can at once, and accurately, tell you. They say that if a cow has had no serious illness it will bear about eight calves.

In my experience there is very slight mortality among calves. Nuer give them every attention. When a cow is seen to be about to calve for the first time its owner sits up with it all night, or accompanies it to pasture, to assist delivery. An experienced cow is left to drop its calf itself, but a man is usually present to assist if it is in trouble. He must be present if it calves in the bush, because the calf is too weak to follow its dam, which will stay with it, and they may become separated from the herd and fall a prey to wild beasts. If a calf dies in the womb Nuer try to remove it, and when it is necessary to turn it in the womb they perform this operation. If the afterbirth does not fall, or if the cow does not lick its calf, they administer medicines. When a calf dies they resort to various devices to persuade its dam to give milk. They stuff the head with straw (see Figure 3.5), and rub some of the dam's urine on it; or, especially when a cow aborts, they stuff the whole calf, insert stumps of wood to act as legs, and place it in front of its dam and push its head against her teats, while they gently squeeze and pull them and a boy blows up the vagina.

Nuer say that if a calf is only a day or two old and its dam dies it will also die, but once it knows the *cak tin bor*, "the white milk" which follows the colostrum, it can be saved. It is fed by hand from a small gourd with a funnel mouth and efforts are made to get

Figure 3.5 *Stuffed calf's head*

another cow in lactation to suckle it. Since Nuer believe, erroneously it seems, that it is dangerous for a calf to drink the discoloured milk at the top of the colostrum, they milk this off before allowing the calf to suck, and if by inadvertence it sucks first they administer a purgative. They regard it as more serious if there is any blood in the milk.

For the first three or four days a calf sucks all its dam's milk except the part drawn off. Then close kinsmen, who live near by, are summoned to eat porridge over which is poured the first milk taken for human consumption. At this ceremony the end hairs of the calf's tail are cut off and its owner spits on them and waves them over the back of the dam, for otherwise the calf will sicken because it resents people stealing its milk. Afterwards, however, they can still say, "We do not yet share with its calf", for they take very little milk for the first fortnight in order to give it

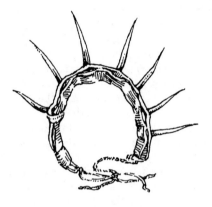

Figure 3.6   *Calf's weaning ring*

We shall have opportunities for noting further the attention Nuer give to their cattle and the wisdom of their methods. I have merely given in this section a few examples to illustrate a general conclusion reached in the course of my study: that Nuer cattle husbandry could not in any important particular be improved in their present oecological relations; that, consequently, more knowledge than they possess would in no way assist them; and that, as will be shown, were it not for their unceasing vigilance and care the cattle would not survive the harsh conditions of their environment.

<h2 style="text-align:center">VII</h2>

It has been remarked that the Nuer might be called parasites of the cow, but it might be said with equal force that the cow is a parasite of the Nuer, whose lives are spent in ensuring its welfare. They build byres, kindle fires, and clean kraals for its comfort; move from villages to camps, from camp to camp, and from camps back to villages, for its health; defy wild beasts for its protection; and fashion ornaments for its adornment. It lives its gentle, indolent, sluggish life thanks to the Nuer's devotion. In truth the relationship is symbiotic: cattle and men sustain life by their reciprocal services to one another. In this intimate symbiotic relationship men and beasts form a single community of the closest kind. In a few paragraphs I direct attention to this intimacy.

The men wake about dawn at camp in the midst of their cattle and sit contentedly watching them till milking is finished They then either take them to pasture and spend the day watching them graze, driving them to water, composing songs about them, and bringing them back to camp, or they remain in the kraal to drink their milk, make tethering-cords and ornaments for them, water and in other ways care for their calves, clean their kraal, and dry their dung for fuel. Nuer wash their hands and faces in the urine of the cattle, especially when cows urinate during milking, drink their milk and blood, and sleep on their hides by the side of their smouldering dung. They cover their bodies, dress their hair, and clean their teeth

a chance to get strong and for its teeth to harden. When the calf is stronger they take more milk and they then say that the calf shares *(buth)* the milk with men. It continues to suck till its dam is again in calf and refuses it. Weaning devices are not as a rule employed, but if the dam suckles when it is pregnant and it is found impracticable to keep it apart from its calf in the pastures they place a ring of thorns round the calf's muzzle (Figure 3.6), which allows it to graze but prevents it from sucking, for the thorns prick the dam's udder and she kicks it aside. It will be seen from this account how Nuer solve the herdsman's problem of making cows provide for their masters without depriving their calves of essential nourishment.

Small calves, after the adult herd has gone to the grazing grounds, are housed till the late afternoon in byres in wet-season villages, and tethered in the shade of a tree in dry-season camps.

They are watered during the afternoon, and boys bring them grasses, especially *poon (Oryza Barthii)*, which is very fattening. They begin to go to pasture with the older calves, under the care of herdboys, in about their third month and are kept apart from their dams by being driven in the opposite direction to that taken earlier in the day by the adult herd. They run with the herd when they are about a year old, by which time their dams are again in calf.

with the ashes of cattle dung, and eat their food with spoons made from their horns. When the cattle return in the evening they tether each beast to its peg with cords made from the skins of their dead companions and sit in the windscreens to contemplate them and to watch them being milked. A man knows each animal of his herd and of the herds of his neighbours and kinsmen: its colour, the shape of its horns, its peculiarities, the number of its teats, the amount of milk it gives, its history, its ancestry and its progeny. Miss Soule tells me that most Nuer know the points of the dam and grand-dam of a beast and that some know the points of its forebears up to five generations of ascent. A Nuer knows the habits of all his oxen, how one bellows in the evenings, how another likes to lead the herd on its return to camp, and how another tosses its head more than the rest are wont to do. He knows which cows are restless during milking, which are troublesome with their calves, which like to drink on the way to pasture, and so forth.

If he is a young man he gets a boy to lead his favourite ox, after which he takes his name, round the camp in the morning and leaps and sings behind it; and often at night he walks among the cattle ringing an ox-bell and singing the praises of his kinsmen, his sweethearts, and his oxen. When his ox comes home in the evening he pets it, rubs ashes on its back, removes ticks from its belly and scrotum, and picks adherent dung from its anus. He tethers it in front of his windscreen so that he can see it if he wakes, for no sight so fills a Nuer with contentment and pride as his oxen. The more he can display the happier he is, and to make them more attractive he decorates their horns with long tassels, which he can admire as they toss their heads and shake them on their return to camp, and their necks with bells, which tinkle in the pastures. Even the bull calves are adorned by their boy-owners with wooden beads and bells. The horns of young bulls, destined to be castrated later, are generally cut so that they will grow in a shape that pleases their masters. The operation, called *ngat*, is probably performed towards the end of their first year and usually takes place in the dry season, as it is said that a steer may die if its horns are cut in the rains. The animal is thrown

and held down while its horns are cut through obliquely with a spear. They grow against the cut. The beasts appear to suffer much pain during the operation and I have sometimes heard Nuer compare their ordeal to the initiation of youths into manhood.

When a Nuer mentions an ox his habitual moroseness leaves him and he speaks with enthusiasm, throwing up his arms to show you how its horns are trained. "I have a fine ox", he says, "a brindled ox with a large white splash on its back and with one horn trained over its muzzle' – and up go his hands, one above his head and the other bent at the elbow across his face. In singing and dancing they call out the names of their oxen and hold their arms in imitation of their horns.

The attitude towards cattle varies with varying situations in social life and with changes in social development. As soon as children can crawl they are brought into close intimacy with the flocks and herds. The kraal is their playground and they are generally smeared with dung in which they roll and tumble. The calves and sheep and goats are their companions in play and they pull them about and sprawl in the midst of them. Their feelings about the animals are probably dominated by desire for food, for the cows, ewes, and she-goats directly satisfy their hunger, often suckling them. As soon as a baby can drink animal's milk its mother carries it to the sheep and goats and gives it warm milk to drink straight from the udders.

The games of rather older children of both sexes centre round cattle. They build byres of sand in camps and of moistened ashes or mud in villages, and fill the toy kraals with fine mud cows and oxen (Figure 3.7), with which they play at herding and marriage. The first tasks of childhood concern cattle. Very small children hold the sheep and goats while their mothers milk them, and when their mothers milk the cows they carry the gourds and pull the calves away from the udders and tether them in front of their dams. They collect urine in gourds and wash themselves in it. When they are a little older and stronger they have to clean the byres and kraals, assist in the milking, and herd the small calves and the sheep and goats at pasture. Food and play

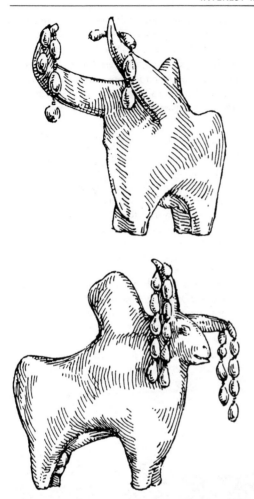

Figure 3.7 *Mud figures of oxen decorated with tassels*

they remain such when she grows up and is married and milks and churns for her husband's people, whereas to a boy they are part of the family herd in which he has property rights. They have entered the herd on the marriage of his kinswomen and one day he will marry with them. A girl is separated from the herd on marriage; a boy remains as its owner. When a boy becomes a youth and is initiated into manhood the cattle become something more than food and the cause of labour. They are also a means of display and marriage. It is only when a man marries and has children and an independent household and herd, when he has become an elder and man of position, that he often uses cattle as sacrifices, invests them with a sacred significance and employs them in ritual.

The Nuer and his herd form a corporate community with solidarity of interests, to serve which the lives of both are adjusted, and their symbiotic relationship is one of close physical contact. The cattle are docile and readily respond to human care and guidance. No high barriers of culture divide men from beasts in their common home, but the stark naked-ness of Nuer amid their cattle and the intimacy of their contact with them present a classic picture of savagery. I ask the reader to look at some of the illustrations, which will convey to him better than I can do in words the crudity of kraal life.

Cattle are not only an object of absorbing interest to Nuer, having great economic utility and social value, but they live in the closest possible association with them. Moreover, irrespective of use, they are in themselves a cultural end, and the mere possession of, and proximity to, them gives a man his heart's desire. On them are concentrated his immediate interests and his farthest ambitions. More than anything else they determine his daily actions and dominate his attention. We have remarked on the over-emphasis on cattle produced by their wide range of social and economic uses. So many physical, psychological, and social requirements can be satisfied from this one source that Nuer attention, instead of being diffused in a variety of directions, tends, with undue exclusiveness, to be focused on this single object and to be introvertive, since the

contacts with the cattle have changed to labour contacts. At this age the interests of the sexes in cattle begin to diverge and the divergence becomes more apparent as they grow up. The labour of girls and women is restricted to the byres and the kraals and is concerned mostly with the cows, while boys herd the calves at pasture, as well as assisting in the kraal, and after initiation they herd the adult cattle and in the kraal give their attention mainly to the oxen. The women are dairy-maids; the men herdsmen. Moreover, to a girl the cows are essentially providers of milk and cheese and object has a certain identity with themselves. We will now examine briefly some linguistic material wherein we shall perceive further evidence of this hypertrophy of a single interest and of the identification of men with cattle to which I have alluded.

VIII

Linguistic profusion in particular departments of life is one of the signs by which one quickly judges the direction and strength of a people's interests. It is for that reason, rather than for its intrinsic importance, that we draw the reader's attention to the volume and variety of the Nuer cattle vocabulary. Like all the pastoral Nilotes they use an enormous number of words and phrases about cattle and the tasks of herding and dairy-work, and from this vast assortment we select for comment a single class: the terms by which they describe cattle, chiefly by reference to their colours.[2] These terms are more than a linguistic technique which enables Nuer to speak of cattle with

precision in situations of practical husbandry and in the many social contexts in which they figure, for they establish associations on the one hand between wild creatures and cattle and on the other hand between cattle and their masters; they furnish certain ritual categories; and they greatly enrich the language of poetry.

In naming a Nuer cow one has to notice its colours and the way in which they are distributed on its body. When it is not of one colour the distribution of colours is the significant character by which one names it. There are ten principal colour terms: white *(bor)*, black *(car)*, brown *(lual)*, chestnut *(dol)*, tawny *(yan)*, mouse-grey *(lou)*, bay *(thiang)*, sandy-grey *(lith)*, blue and strawberry roan *(yil)*, and chocolate *(gwir)*. When a cow is of a single colour it is described by one of these terms. An animal may combine two or more colours, but a combination of more than two, known as *cuany*, is very rare. Normally there is a combination of white with one other colour and twelve common distributions of this combination are shown in Figure 3.8 and 3.9.

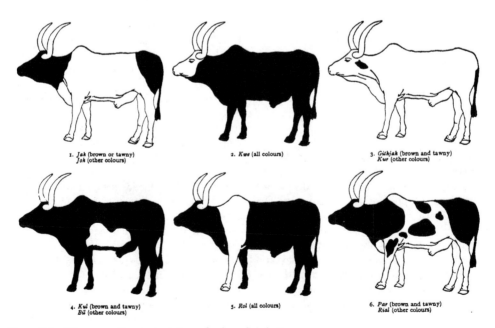

1. *Jak* (brown or tawny)
   Jok (other colours)

2. *Kwe* (all colours)

3. *Gŭhjak* (brown and tawny)
   Kur (other colours)

4. *Kul* (brown and tawny)
   Bŭ (other colours)

5. *Rol* (all colours)

6. *Par* (brown and tawny)
   Rial (other colours)

Figure 3.8 *Diagrammatic representation of colour distributions*

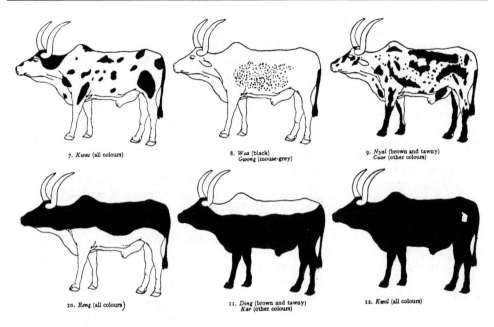

7. *Kwac* (all colours)

8. *Wea* (black)
   Gwong (mouse-grey)

9. *Nyal* (brown and tawny)
   Cuor (other colours)

10. *Reng* (all colours)

11. *Ding* (brown and tawny)
    Kar (other colours)

12. *Kwol* (all colours)

Figure 3.9   *Diagrammatic representation of colour distributions*

There are, however, many more combinations, at least twenty-seven, one of the commonest being varieties of a striped or brindled coat (*nyang*).

In describing a beast one often denotes both the form of distribution and the colour that is combined with white. Thus an ox may be entirely mouse-grey (*lou*); have a mainly mouse-grey colour with a white face (*kwe looka*): white back (*kar looka*), white splash on barrel (*bil looka*), white shoulder (*rol looka*), or white belly (*reng looka*): be brindled mouse-grey (*nyang looba*): be white with large mouse-grey patches (*rial looka*), medium mouse-grey patches (*kwac looka*), or a mouse-grey rump (*jok looka*), etc. There are at least a dozen terms describing different combinations of white and mouse-grey and there are a similar number of terms for a combination of white with each of the other colours. A further example is given to illustrate the wide range of variations: a white shoulder and foreleg (*rol*) may be found on a cow of any colour, e.g. *rol cara*, *rol yan*, *rol thiang*, *rol yili*, etc. There may also be a combination of one form of distribution with another and, in this case, the two combinations constitute the terms of reference and there is no need to denote the colouring that occurs in them, e.g. a white shoulder and foreleg (*rol*) may be combined with a white face (*kwe roal*), black spots (*rol kwac*), speckling (*rol cuor*), brown patches (*rol paara*), white back (*kar roal*), white face and black ears (*kur roal*), etc. There are at least twenty-five terms which include the *rol* distribution, and the other distributions likewise have wide ranges of combinations with colours and with one another.

As I shall elsewhere, and at length, analyse the principles of colour terminology and abstract the rules of nomenclature,[3] I need no more than remark here that it is evident from the few examples cited that there are several hundred colour permutations.

Some colours and combinations of colours are associated with animals, birds, reptiles, and fish, and this association is often indicated by secondary terms of reference and by ritual usages, e.g. *lou* (mouse-grey) is the bustard, *nyang* (striped) is the crocodile, *lith* (sandy-grey) is associated with *manlieth*, the grey kestrel, *thiang* (bay) is the tiang, *dwai* (brown with white stripes) is the female sitatunga, *kwe* (white-faced) is the fish eagle, *kwac* (spotted) is the leopard, *cuor* (speckled) is the vulture, *gwong* (spotted) is the guinea-fowl, *nyal* (brown-spotted) is the python, etc. These linguistic identifications and other colour associations lead to many fanciful elaborations of nomenclature, e.g. a black ox may be called *rual mim*, charcoal-burning or *won car*, dark clouds; a brown ox *riem dol*, red blood, or *rir dol*, red tree-cobra; a blue roan ox *bany yiel* after the blue heron; a mouse-grey ox *duk lou*, the shady gloom of forests, etc. These fancy names add greatly to the list of Nuer cattle terms.

Besides the vast vocabulary which refers to colours, distribution of colours, and colour associations, cattle can also be described by the shape of their horns and, as the horns of oxen are trained, there are at least six common designations in use besides several fancy names. Words denoting shape of horns add considerably to the number of permutations, for they can be combined with many of the colour and distribution terms, e.g. a sandy-grey cow with horns which almost meet in a curve above the head is a *duot lieth*, a shorthorn with *rial* markings is a *cot rial*, a brindled ox with one horn trained across its face is a *gut nyang*, etc. The ears of cattle, sheep, and goats are often cut in different shapes and it is permissible, and with sheep and goats usual, to describe them by reference to these incisions. Sheep and goats have very different mixtures of colours from those one finds among cattle, but the same terms can be used to cover all combinations, because they are never exact descriptions of colour dispositions but represent ideal distributions, to one or other of which any actual disposition approximates.

A further range of permutations is created by prefixes which denote the sex or age of an animal, e.g. *tut*, bull, *yang*, cow, *thak*, ox, *nac*, heifer, *ruath*, male calf, *dou*, female calf, *kol*, calf which has not yet begun to graze, and so forth. Thus one may speak of a *tut ma kar looka*, *dou ma rial*, *thak ma cuany*, etc. Indeed, if we were to count every possible mode of referring to animals of the flocks and herds they would be found to number several thousand expressions – an imposing and complicated system of ramifications which bears

eloquent witness to the social value of cattle.

Furthermore, as we have mentioned, every man takes one of his names from the term by which one of his oxen is described, and these ox-names are the preferred salutations among age-mates. A youth generally takes his first ox-name from the beast his father gives him at his initiation, but he may later take further names from any oxen of his herd which delight him. Men salute one another with these names and shower them, with many a fanciful elaboration, on their companions at dances. They also chant them when they display themselves with their oxen in camps, sing them in their poems, and shout them when they spear men, animals, or fish.

A man may be called by the identical name of his ox, e.g. Bi(l)rial, Kwac(c)uor, Werkwac, and so forth, but generally one part of the term is dropped and the other part is prefixed by a new term, usually descriptive of some ornament worn by the ox or some characteristic of it, not employed in defining its own name, e.g. *luth*, a large bell (Figure 3.4), *gier*, a small bell, *lue*, a long tassel, *dhuor*, a short tassel, *wak*, the tinkling of an ox-bell, *lang*, a brass ring attached to an ox's collar or tethering-cord, *rot*, bellowing of oxen, *cwai*, fatness, *boi*, shining whiteness, etc. Thus a man whose favourite ox has *rial* distribution of colours may be called Luthrial, Gierrial, Luerial, Dhuorrial, Boirial, and so on. When ox-names are used between age-mates at dances they are generally preceded by dance-names which are selected to harmonize with the ox-names, euphony being considered of great importance in all these word formations. Ox-names are voluminous and abstruse, and in describing them, as in describing cattle-colours, I have not only made a meagre selection from the wealth at my disposal, but have also chosen for illustration the simplest examples and neglected the more obscure.

Names of cattle, especially of oxen, and ox-names of men are used profusely in songs. The Nuer, like most pastoral peoples, are poetic and most men and women compose songs which are sung at dances and concerts or are composed for the creator's own pleasure and chanted by him in lonely pastures and amid the cattle in camp kraals. Youths break into song, praising their kinsmen, sweethearts, and cattle, when they feel happy, wherever they may be. I give a free translation of the first verses of two songs, the first sung by girls as they sit together in the evening after the day's work is done, and the second sung by its creator when he is happy.

1. The wind blows *wirawira*;[4]
    Where does it blow to?
    It blows to the river.
    The shorthorn carries its full udder to the
        pastures;[5]
    Let her be milked by Nyagaak;
    My belly will be filled with milk.
    Thou pride of Nyawal,
    Ever-quarrelling Rolnyang.[6]
    This country is overrun by strangers;
    They throw our ornaments into the
        river;
    They draw their water from the bank.[7]
    Blackhair my sister,
    I am bewildered.
    Blackhair my sister,
    I am bewildered.
    We are perplexed;
    We gaze at the stars of God.[8]

2. White ox good is my mother
    And we the people of my sister,
    The people of Nyariau Bul.
    As my black-rumped white ox,
    When I went to court the winsome
        lassie,
    I am not a man whom girls refuse.
    We court girls by stealth in the night,
    I and Kwejok
    Nyadeang[9]
    We brought the ox across the river,
    I and Kirjoak
    And the son of my mother's sister
    Buth Gutjaak.
    Friend, great ox of the spreading horns,
    Which ever bellows amid the herd,
    Ox of the son of Bul
    Maloa.[10]

It is not necessary to add more examples of cattle-terms and their uses to demonstrate that we are dealing with a galaxy of words in the arrangement of which a thesaurus of some magnitude might be compiled. I need only emphasize that this intricate and voluminous vocabulary is not technical and departmental but is employed by every one and in manifold situations of ordinary social life. I have only treated a fragment of a fragment of the linguistic field relating to cattle. I could enter into further detail, but, at best, I have only surveyed, and in an amateur way, that field, which invites broader and more specialist research. My purpose has been to draw attention to it and to show how a study of the dominant interest of Nuer might be approached from this angle. The subject is necessarily vast, because, as we have seen, it is not possible to discuss with Nuer their daily affairs, social connexions, ritual acts, or, indeed, any subject, without reference to cattle which are the core round which daily life is organized and the medium through which social and mystical relations are expressed. Nor is Nuer interest in cattle confined to their practical uses and social functions, but is displayed in their plastic and poetic arts, in which they are the chief theme. The over-emphasis on cattle is thus strikingly shown in language, which, moreover, by compelling reference to cattle, whatever be the subject of speech, continually focuses attention on them and makes them the superlative value of Nuer life.

IX

Another way in which Nuer engrossment in cattle can be illustrated – our last exemplification thereof – is by noting how readily and frequently they fight about them, for people risk their lives for what they greatly value and in terms of those values.

At the present time cattle are the main cause of hostility towards, and suspicion of, the Government, not so much on account of present taxation as of earlier tax-gathering patrols which were little more than cattle raids and of the avowedly plundering expeditions of the Egyptian Government era that preceded them. Nuer war with the Dinka has been almost entirely offensive and directed towards appropriation of herds and annexation of grazing grounds. Cattle have also been the chief occasion of strife among Nuer themselves. Indeed, after a successful raid on Dinka stock there is often further fighting over the booty. Moreover, Nuer tribes raid one another for cattle. Thus the Leek raid the Jikany,

Rengyan, and other western tribes, and cattle raids are of common occurrence along tribal boundaries elsewhere, for to "steal" (*kwal*) cattle from another tribe is regarded as laudable. Within a tribe, also, fighting frequently results from disputes about cattle between its sections and between individuals of the same section, even of the same village or homestead. Nuer fight on slight provocation and most willingly and frequently when a cow is at stake. On such an issue close kinsmen fight and homes are broken up. When ownership of cattle is in dispute Nuer throw over caution and propriety, showing themselves careless of odds, contemptuous of danger, and full of guile. As my Nuer servant once said to me: "You can trust a Nuer with any amount of money, pounds and pounds and pounds, and go away for years and return and he will not have stolen it; but a single cow – that is a different matter."

Nuer say that it is cattle that destroy people, for "more people have died for the sake of a cow than for any other cause". They have a story which tells how, when the beasts broke up their community and each went its own way and lived its own life, Man slew the mother of Cow and Buffalo. Buffalo said she would avenge her mother by attacking men in the bush, but Cow said that she would remain in the habitations of men and avenge her mother by causing endless disputes about debts, bridewealth, and adultery, which would lead to fighting and deaths among the people. So this feud between Cow and Man has gone on from time immemorial, and day by day Cow avenges the death of her mother by occasioning the death of men. Hence Nuer say of their cattle, "They will be finished together with mankind", for men will all die on account of cattle and they and cattle will cease together.

It must not, however, be supposed that Nuer live in continuous turmoil: the very fact that they are prepared to resist any infringement of their rights in cattle induces prudence in the relations between persons who regard themselves as members of the same group. It may be said, furthermore, that the great vulnerability of cattle coupled with the extensive living-space required for them are compatible only with a far recognition of conventions in the settlement of disputes, or, in other words, the existence of a tribal organization embracing a large territory, and of some feeling of community over yet larger areas.

Fighting about ownership of cattle and seizing cattle for what are claimed as debts and compensation for losses are of a somewhat different order to raiding for cattle over which no rights, other than the power of the strong, are asserted. War against foreign peoples, as distinct from warfare within a tribe, is almost entirely for plunder. Nuer war against the Dinka, therefore, differs from most primitive warfare in that its primary object is acquisition of wealth, for cattle are a form of wealth that not only lasts a long time and reproduces itself, but is, also, easily seized and transported. Furthermore, it enables invaders to live on the country without commissariat, Crops and dwellings can be destroyed, but cattle can be confiscated and taken home. This quality, which has given pastoral peoples a bias in favour of the arts of war rather than the arts of peace, has meant that the Nuer are not entirely dependent on their own cattle, but can augment their herds and restore the ravages of rinderpest, and have, in fact, for a long time increased their stock, and hence supplemented their food-supply, by raiding; a condition that has shaped their character, economy, and political structure. Skill and courage in fighting are reckoned the highest virtues, raiding the most noble, as well as the most profitable, occupation, and some measure of political agreement and unity a necessity.

We hasten to add that an explanation of warfare between Nuer and Dinka by reference to cattle and pastures alone is too simple a reduction. Hostility is expressed in terms of cattle, and desire for cattle accounts for some peculiarities of the struggle and some characteristics of the political organizations involved in it, but the struggle itself can only be fully understood as a structural process and we present it as such later.

We now pass to a brief examination of the oecological system of which Nuer and their cattle form part to discover the conditions in which cattle-husbandry is practised and how far its practice in a certain environment influences political structure.

NOTES

1. Nuer interest in their cattle has been emphasized by early travellers in their country. *Vide* Marno, op. cit., p. 343; Werne, op. cit., p. 439; du Couret, op. cit., p. 82.
2. I have recorded some information on this neglected subject among a neighbouring people in "Imagery in Ngok Dinka Cattle-Names", *Bulletin of the School of Oriental Studies*, 1934.
3. "Nuer Cattle Terms", to appear in *Sudan Notes and Records*. [Editors' note: We have been unable to locate details of this article and conclude that it was never published.]
4. Literally "My wind". The singer runs against it and seems by so doing to add to its strength. This is the north wind which blows at the time of rich pasture when the cows give plenty of milk: hence the connexion between the first three lines and those which follow them.
5. The cow has refused to suckle its calf or to be milked before going to graze.
6. Nyagaak is the sister of the poet. Pride *(gweth)* is the dance-name of a girl, Nyawal. Rolnyang is a youth's ox-name.
7. The strangers are Government forces. The reference to drawing water from the bank is obscure.
8. Blackhair is a girl's name. The Nuer are perplexed by foreign invasion and the last line is a prayer to God to help them in their adversity.
9. The ox referred to in the first and fourth lines is the poet's ox. Kwejok is a friend, whose mother is Nyadeang.
10. Buth is the birth-name of a friend whose ox-name is Gutjaak. The poet, who is a son of Bul Maloa, addresses his ox as his friend in the final lines.

REFERENCES

du Couret, C. L. (1854). *Voyage au Pays des Niam-Niams on Hommes à Queue.*

Marno, E. (1874). *Reisen im Gebiete des blauen und weissen Nil, in egyptischen Sudan und den angrenzenden Negerländern, in den Jahren 1869 bis 1873.*

Werne, F. (1848). *Expedition zur Entdeckung der Quellen des Weissen Nil (1840–1).*

4

The Cultural Ecology of India's Sacred Cattle

Marvin Harris

In this paper I attempt to indicate certain puzzling inconsistencies in prevailing interpretations of the ecological role of bovine cattle in India. My argument is based upon intensive reading – I have never seen a sacred cow, nor been to India. As a non-specialist, no doubt I have committed blunders an Indianist would have avoided. I hope these errors will not deprive me of that expert advice and informed criticism which alone can justify so rude an invasion of unfamiliar territory.

I have written this paper because I believe the irrational, non-economic, and exotic aspects of the Indian cattle complex are greatly overemphasized at the expense of rational, economic, and mundane interpretations.

My intent is not to substitute one dogma for another, but to urge that explanation of taboos, customs, and rituals associated with management of Indian cattle be sought in "positive-functioned" and probably "adaptive" processes of the ecological system of which they are a part,[1] rather than in the influence of Hindu theology.

Mismanagement of India's agricultural resources as a result of the Hindu doctrine of *ahimsa*,[2] especially as it applies to beef cattle, is frequently noted by Indianists and others concerned with the relation between values and behavior. Although different anti-rational, dysfunctional, and inutile aspects of the cattle complex are stressed by different authors, many agree that *ahimsa* is a prime example of how men will diminish their material welfare to obtain spiritual satisfaction in obedience to non-rational or frankly irrational beliefs.

A sample opinion on this subject is here summarized: According to Simoons (1961:3), "irrational ideologies" frequently compel men "to overlook foods that are abundant locally and are of high nutritive value, and to utilize other scarcer foods of less value." The Hindu beef-eating taboo is one of Simoons' most important cases. Venkatraman (1938:706) claims, "India is unique in possessing an enormous amount of cattle without making profit from its slaughter." The Ford Foundation (1959:64) reports "widespread recognition not only among animal husbandry officials, but among citizens generally, that India's cattle population is far in excess of the available supplies of fodder and feed . . . At least 1/3, and possibly as many as 1/2, of the Indian cattle population may be regarded as surplus in relation to feed supply." Matson (1933:227) writes it is a commonplace of the "cattle question that vast numbers of Indian cattle are so helplessly inefficient as to have no commercial value beyond that of their hides." Srinivas (1952:222) believes "Orthodox Hindu opinion regards the killing of cattle with abhorrence, even though the refusal to kill the vast number of useless cattle which exist in India today is detrimental to the nation."

According to the Indian Ministry of Information (1957:243), "The large animal population is more a liability than an asset in view of our land resources." Chatterjee (1960) calculates that Indian production of cow and buffalo milk involves a "heavy recurring loss of Rs 774 crores. This is equivalent to 6.7 times the amount we are annually spending on importing food grains." Knight (1954:141) observes that because the Hindu religion teaches great reverence for the cow, "there existed a large number of cattle whose utility to the community did not justify economically the fodder which they consumed." Das and Chatterji (1962:120) concur: "A large number of cattle in India are old and decrepit and constitute a great burden on an already impoverished land. This is due to the prejudice among the Hindus against cow killing." Mishra (1962) approvingly quotes Lewis (1955:106): "It is not true that if economic and religious doctrines conflict the economic interest will always win. The Hindu cow has remained sacred for centuries, although this is plainly contrary to economic interest." Darling (1934:158) asserts, "By its attitude to slaughter Hinduism makes any planned improvement of cattle-breeding almost impossible." According to Desai (1959:36), "The cattle population is far in excess of the available fodder and feeds."

In the *Report of the Expert Committee on the Prevention of Slaughter of Cattle in India* (Nandra, *et al.* 1955:62), the Cattle Preservation and Development Committee estimated "20 million uneconomic cattle in India." Speaking specifically of Madras, Randhawa (1961:118) insists, "Far too many useless animals which breed indiscriminately are kept and many of them are allowed to lead a miserable existence for the sake of the dung they produce. Sterility and prolonged dry periods among cows due to neglect add to the number of superfluous cattle . . ." Mamoria (1953:268–9) quotes with approval the report of the Royal Commission on Agriculture: ". . . religious susceptibilities lie in the way of slaughter of decrepit and useless cattle and hence the cattle, however weak and poor are allowed to live . . . bulls wander about the fields consum-

ing or damaging three times as much fodder as they need . . . Unless the Hindu sentiment is abjured altogether the Indian cultivators cannot take a practical view of animal keeping and will continue to preserve animals many of which are quite useless from birth to death." Despite his own implicit arguments to the contrary, Mohan (1962:54) concludes, "We have a large number of surplus animals." The National Council of Applied Economic Research (1963:51) notes in Rajasthan: "The scarcity of fodder is aggravated by a large population of old and useless cattle which share scant feed resources with working and useful cattle."

The Food and Agriculture Organization (1953:109) reports, "In India, as is well-known, cattle numbers exceed economic requirements by any standard and a reduction in the number of uneconomic animals would contribute greatly to the possibilities of improving the quality and condition of those that remain." Kardel (1956:19) reported to the International Cooperation Administration, "Actually, India's 180 million cattle and 87 million sheep and goats are competing with 360 million people for a scant existence." According to Mosher (1946:124), "There are thousands of barren heifers in the Central Doab consuming as much feed as productive cows, whose only economic produce will be their hides, after they have died of a natural cause." Mayadas (1954:28) insists "Large herds of emaciated and completely useless cattle stray about trying to eke out an existence on wholly inadequate grazing." Finally, to complete the picture of how, in India, spirit triumphs over flesh, there is the assertion by Williamson and Payne (1959:137): "The . . . Hindu would rather starve to death than eat his cow."

In spite of the sometimes final and unqualified fashion in which "surplus," "useless," "uneconomic," and "superfluous" are applied to part or all of India's cattle, contrary conclusions seem admissible when the cattle complex is viewed as part of an *eco-system* rather than as a sector of a national price market. Ecologically, it is doubtful that any component of the cattle complex is "useless," i.e., the number, type, and condition of Indian bovines do not per se impair the ability of the human population to survive and reproduce. Much more likely the relationship between bovines and humans is symbiotic[3] instead of competitive. It probably represents the outcome of intense Darwinian pressures acting upon human and bovine population, cultigens, wild flora and fauna, and social structure and ideology. Moreover presumably the degree of observance of taboos against bovine slaughter and beef-eating reflect the power of these ecological pressures rather than *ahimsa;* in other words, *ahimsa* itself derives power and sustenance from the material rewards it confers upon both men and animals. To support these hypotheses, the major aspects of the Indian cattle complex will be reviewed under the following headings: (1) Milk Production, (2) Traction, (3) Dung, (4) Beef and Hides, (5) Pasture, (6) Useful and Useless Animals, (7) Slaughter, (8) Anti-Slaughter Legislation, (9) Old-Age Homes, and (10) Natural Selection.

Milk Production

In India the average yield of whole milk per Zebu cow is 413 pounds, compared with the 5,000-pound average in Europe and the U.S.[4] (Kartha 1936:607; Spate 1954:231). In Madhya Pradesh yield is as low as 65 pounds, while in no state does it rise higher than the barely respectable 1,445 pounds of the Punjab (Chatterjee 1960:1347). According to the 9th Quinquennial Livestock Census (1961) among the 47,200,000 cows over 3 years old, 27,200,000 were dry and/or not calved (Chaudri and Giri 1963:598).

These figures, however should not be used to prove that the cows are useless or uneconomic, since milk production is a minor aspect of the sacred cow's contribution to the *ecosystem.* Indeed, most Indianists agree that it is the buffalo, not the Zebu, whose economic worth must be judged primarily by milk production. Thus, Kartha (1959:225) writes, "the buffalo, and not the Zebu, is the dairy cow." This distinction is elaborated by Mamoria (1953:255):

Cows in the rural areas are maintained for producing bullocks rather than for milk. She-buffaloes, on the other hand, are considered to be better dairy animals than cows. The male buffaloes are neglected and many of them die or are sold for slaughter before they attain maturity.

Mohan (1962:47) makes the same point:

For agricultural purposes bullocks are generally preferred, and, therefore, cows in rural areas are primarily maintained for the production of male progeny and incidentally only for milk.

It is not relevant to my thesis to establish whether milk production is a primary or secondary objective or purpose of the Indian farmer. Failure to separate emics from etics (Harris 1964) contributes greatly to confusion surrounding the Indian cattle question. The significance of the preceding quotations lies in the agreement that cows contribute to human material welfare in more important ways than milk production. In this new context, the fact that US cows produce 20 times more milk than Indian cows loses much of its significance. Instead, it is more relevant to note that, despite the marginal status of milking in the symbiotic syndrome, 46.7% of India's dairy products come from cow's milk (Chatterjee 1960:1347). How far this production is balanced by expenditures detrimental to human welfare will be discussed later.

Traction

The principal positive ecological effect of India's bovine cattle is in their contribution to production of grain crops, from which about 80% of the human calorie ration comes. Some form of animal traction is required to initiate the agricultural cycle, dependent upon plowing in both rainfall and irrigation areas. Additional traction for hauling, transport, and irrigation is provided by animals, but by far their most critical kinetic contribution is plowing.

Although many authorities believe there is an overall surplus of cattle in India, others point to a serious shortage of draught animals. According to Kothavala (1934:122), "Even with ... overstocking, the draught power available for land operations at the busiest season of the year is inadequate ..." For West Bengal, the National Council of Applied Economic Research (1962:56) reports:

> However, despite the large number of draught animals, agriculture in the State suffers from a shortage of draught power. There are large numbers of small landholders entirely dependent on hired animal labour.

Spate (1954:36) makes the same point, "There are too many cattle in the gross, but most individual farmers have too few to carry on with." Gupta (1959:42) and Lewis and Barnouw (1958:102) say a pair of bullocks is the minimum technical unit for cultivation, but in a survey by Diskalkar (1960:87), 18% of the cultivators had only one bullock or none. Nationally, if we accept a low estimate of 60 million rural households (Mitra 1963:298) and a high estimate of 80 million working cattle and buffaloes (Government of India 1962:76), we see at once that the allegedly excess number of cattle in India is insufficient to permit a large portion, perhaps as many as a third, of India's farmers to begin the agricultural cycle under conditions appropriate to their technoenvironmental system.

Much has been made of India's having 115 head of cattle per square mile, compared with 28 per square mile for the US and 3 per square mile for Canada. But what actually may be most characteristic of the size of India's herd is the low ratio of cattle to people. Thus, India has 44 cattle per 100 persons, while in the US the ratio is 58 per 100 and in Canada, 90 (Mamoria 1953:256). Yet, in India cattle are employed as a basic instrument of agricultural production.

Sharing of draught animals on a cooperative basis might reduce the need for additional animals. Chaudhri and Gin point out that the "big farmer manages to cultivate with a pair of bullock a much larger area than the small cultivators" (1963:596). But, the failure to develop cooperative forms of plowing can scarcely be traced to *ahimsa*. If anything, emphasis upon independent, family-sized farm units follows intensification of individual land tenure patterns and other property innovations deliberately encouraged by the British (Bhatia 1963:18 on). Under existing property arrangements, there is a perfectly good economic explanation of why bullocks are not shared among adjacent households. Plowing cannot take place at any time of the year, but must be accomplished within a few daylight hours in conformity with seasonal conditions. These are set largely by summer monsoons, responsible for about 90% of the total rainfall (Bhatia 1963:4). Writing about Orissa, Bailey (1957:74) notes:

> As a temporary measure, an ox might be borrowed from a relative, or a yoke of cattle and a ploughman might be hired ... but during the planting season, when the need is the greatest, most people are too busy to hire out or lend cattle.

According to Desai (1948:86):

> ... over vast areas, sowing and harvesting operations, by the very nature of things, begin simultaneously with the outbreak of the first showers and the maturing of crops respectively, and especially the former has got to be put through quickly during the first phase of the monsoon. Under these circumstances, reliance by a farmer on another for bullocks is highly risky and he has got, therefore, to maintain his own pair.

Dube (1955:84) is equally specific:

> The cultivators who depend on hired cattle or who practice cooperative lending and borrowing of cattle cannot take the best advantage of the first rains, and this enforced wait results in untimely sowing and poor crops.

Wiser and Wiser (1963:62) describe the plight of the bullock-short farmer as follows, "When he needs the help of bullocks most, his neighbors are all using theirs." And Shastri (1960:1592) points out, "Uncertainty of Indian farming due to dependence on rains is the main factor creating obstacles in the way of improvements in bullock labor."

It would seem, therefore, that this aspect of the cattle complex is not an expression of spirit and ritual, but of rain and energy.

Dung

In India cattle dung is the main source of domestic cooking fuel. Since grain crops cannot be digested unless boiled or baked, cooking is indispensable. Considerable disagreement exists about the total amount of cattle excrement and its uses, but even the lowest estimates are impressive. An early estimate by Lupton (1922:60) gave the BTU equivalent of dung consumed in domestic cooking as 35 million tons of coal or 68 million tons of wood. Most detailed appraisal is by National Council of Applied Economic Research (1959:3), which rejects H. J. Bhabha's estimate of 131 million tons of coal and the Ministry of Food and Agriculture's 112 million tons. The figure preferred by the NCAER is 35 million tons anthracite or 40 million tons bituminous, but with a possible range of between 35 and 45 million of anthracite dung-coal equivalent. This calculation depends upon indications that only 36% of the total wet dung is utilized as fuel (p. 14), a lower estimate than any reviewed by Saha (1956:923). These vary from 40% (Imperial Council on Agricultural Research) to 50% (Ministry of Food and Agriculture) to 66.6% (Department of Education, Health and Lands). The NCAER estimate of a dung-coal equivalent of 35 million tons is therefore quite conservative; it is nonetheless an impressive amount of BTU's to be plugged into an energy system.

Kapp (1963:144 on), who discusses at length the importance of substituting tractors for bullocks, does not give adequate attention to finding cooking fuel after the bullocks are replaced. The NCAER (1959:20) conclusion that dung is cheaper than coke seems an understatement. Although it is claimed that wood resources are potentially adequate to replace dung the measures advocated do not involve *ahimsa* but are again an indictment of a land tenure system not inspired by Hindu tradition (NCAER 1959:20 on; Bansil 1958:97 on). Finally, it should be noted that many observers stress the slow burning qualities of dung and its special appropriateness for preparation of *ghi* and deployment of woman-power in the household (Lewis and Barnouw 1958:40; Mosher 1946:153).

As manure, dung enters the energy system in another vital fashion. According to Mujumdar (1960:743), 300 million tons are used as fuel, 340 million tons as manure, and 160 million tons "wasted on hillsides and roads." Spate (1954:238) believes that 40% of dung production is spread on fields, 40% burned, and 20% "lost." Possibly estimates of the amount of dung lost are grossly inflated in view of the importance of "roads and hillsides" in the grazing pattern (see Pasture). (Similarly artificial and culture- or even class-bound judgments refer to utilization of India's night soil. It is usually assumed that Chinese and Indian treatment of this resource are radically different, and that vast quantities of nitrogen go unused in agriculture because of Hindu-inspired definitions of modesty and cleanliness. However, most human excrement from Indian villages is deposited in surrounding fields; the absence of latrines helps explain why such fields raise 2 and 3 successive crops each year (Mosher 1946:154, 33; Bansil 1958:104.) More than usual caution, therefore, is needed before concluding that a significant amount of cattle dung is wasted. Given the conscious premium set on dung for fuel and fertilizer, thoughtful control maintained over grazing patterns (see Pasture), and occurrence of specialized sweeper and gleaner castes, much more detailed evidence of wastage is needed than is now available. Since cattle graze on "hillsides and roads," dung dropped there would scarcely be totally lost to the *eco-system*, even with allowance for loss of nitrogen by exposure to air and sunlight. Also, if any animal dung is wasted on roads and hillsides it is not because of *ahimsa* but of inadequate pasturage suitable for collecting and processing animal droppings. The sedentary, intensive rainfall agriculture of most of the subcontinent is heavily dependent upon manuring. So vital is this that Spate (1954:239) says substitutes for manure consumed as fuel "must be supplied, and lavishly, even at a financial loss to government." If this is the case, then old, decrepit, and dry animals might have a use after all, especially when, as we shall see, the dung they manufacture employs raw materials lost to the culture-energy system unless processed by cattle, and especially when many apparently moribund animals revive at the next monsoon and provide their owners with a male calf.

Beef and Hides

Positive contributions of India's sacred cattle do not cease with milk-grazing, bullock-producing, traction, and dung-dropping. There remains the direct protein contribution of 25 million cattle and buffalo which die each year (Mohan 1962:54). This feature of the *eco-system* is reminiscent of the East African cattle area where, despite the normal taboo on slaughter, natural deaths and ceremonial occasions are probably frequent enough to maintain beef consumption near the ecological limit with dairying as the primary function (Schneider 1957:278 on). Although most Hindus probably do not consume beef, the *eco-system* under consideration is not confined to Hindus. The human population includes some 55 million "scheduled" exterior or untouchable groups (Hutton 1961:VII), many of whom will consume beef if given the opportunity (Dube 1955:68–9), plus several million more Moslems and Christians. Much of the flesh on the 25 million dead cattle and buffalo probably gets consumed by human beings whether or not the cattle die naturally. Indeed, could it be that without the orthodox Hindu beef-eating taboo, many marginal and depressed castes would be deprived of an occasional, but nutritionally critical, source of animal protein?

It remains to note that the slaughter taboo does not prevent depressed castes from utilizing skin, horns and hoofs of dead beasts. In 1956 16 million cattle hides were produced (Randhawa 1962:322). The quality of India's huge leather industry – the world's largest – leaves much to be desired, but the problem is primarily outmoded tanning techniques and lack of capital, not *ahimsa*.

Pasture

The principal positive-functioned or useful contributions of India's sacred cattle to human

survival and well-being have been described. Final evaluation of their utility must involve assessment of energy costs in terms of resources and human labor input which might be more efficiently expended in other activities.

Direct and indirect evidence suggests that in India men and bovine cattle do not compete for existence. According to Mohan (1962:43 on):

. . . the bulk of the food on which the animals subsist . . . is not the food that is required for human consumption, i.e., fibrous fodders produced as incidental to crop production, and a large part of the crop residues or by-products of seeds and waste grazing.

On the contrary, "the bulk of foods (straws and crop residues) that are ploughed into the soil in other countries are converted into milk" (p. 45).

The majority of the Indian cattle obtain their requirements from whatever grazing is available from straw and stalk and other residues from human food-stuffs, and are starved seasonally in the dry months when grasses wither.
[. . .]
In Bengal the banks and slopes of the embankments of public roads are the only grazing grounds and the cattle subsist mainly on paddy straw, paddy husks and . . . coarse grass . . . (Mamoria 1953:263–4).

According to Dube (1955:84, ". . . the cattle roam about the shrubs and rocks and eat whatever fodder is available there." This is confirmed by Moomaw (1949:96): "Cows subsist on the pasture and any coarse fodder they can find. Grain is fed for only a day or two following parturition." The character of the environmental niche reserved for cattle nourishment is described by Gourou (1963: 123), based on data furnished by Dupuis (1960) for Madras:

Il faut voir clairement que le faible rendement du bétail indien n'est pas un gaspillage: ce bétail n'entre pas en concurrence avec la consommation de produits agricoles . . . ils ne leur sacrifient pas des surfaces agricoles, ou ayant un potentiel agricole.

NCAER (1961:57) confines this pattern for Tripura: "There is a general practice of feeding livestock on agricultural by-products such as straw, grain wastes and husks"; for West Bengal (NCAER 1962:59): "The state has practically no pasture or grazing fields, and the farmers are not in the habit of growing green fodders . . . livestock feeds are mostly agricultural by-products"; and for Andhra Pradesh (NCAER 1962:52): "Cattle are stall-fed, but the bulk of the feed consists of paddy straw. . . ."

The only exceptions to the rural pattern of feeding cattle on waste products and grazing them on marginal or unproductive lands involve working bullocks and nursing cows:

The working bullocks, on whose efficiency cultivation entirely depends, are usually fed with chopped bananas at the time of fodder scarcity. But the milch cows have to live in a semi-starved condition, getting what nutrition they can from grazing on the fields after their rice harvest (Gangulee 1935:17).

At present cattle are fed largely according to the season. During the rainy period they feed upon the grass which springs up on the *uncultivated* hillsides. . . . But in the dry season there is hardly any grass, and cattle wander on the *cropless* lands in an often halfstarved condition. True there is some fodder at these times in the shape of rice-straw and dried copra, but it is not generally sufficient, and is furthermore given mainly to the animals actually *working* at the time (Mayer 1952:70, italics added).

There is much evidence that Hindu farmers calculate carefully which animals deserve more food and attention. In Madras, Randhawa, *et al.* (1961:117) report: "The cultivators pay more attention to the male stock used for ploughing and for draft. There is a general neglect of the cow and the female calf even from birth . . ."

Similar discrimination is described by Mamoria (1953:263 on):

Many plough bullocks are sold off in winter or their rations are ruthlessly decreased whenever they are not worked in full, while milch cattle are kept on after lactation on poor and inadequate grazing . . . The cultivator feeds

his bullocks better than his cow because it pays him. He feeds his bullocks better during the busy season, when they work, than during the slack season, when they remain idle. Further, he feeds his more valuable bullocks better than those less valuable . . . Although the draught animals and buffaloes are properly fed, the cow gets next to nothing of stall feeding. She is expected to pick up her living on the bare fields after harvest and on the village wasteland. . . .

The previously cited NCAER report on Andhra Pradesh notes that "Bullocks and milking cows during the working season get more concentrates . . ." (1962:52). Wiser and Wiser (1963:71) sum up the situation in a fashion supporting Srinivas' (1958:4) observation that the Indian peasant is "nothing if he is not practical":

Farmers have become skillful in reckoning the minimum of food necessary for maintaining animal service. Cows are fed just enough to assure their calving and giving a little milk. They are grazed during the day on lands which yield very little vegetation, and are given a very sparse meal at night.

Many devout Hindus believe the bovine cattle of India are exploited without mercy by greedy Hindu owners. *Ahimsa* obviously has little to do with economizing which produces the famous *phooka* and *doom dev* techniques for dealing with dry cows. Not to Protestants but to Hindus did Gandhi (1954:7) address lamentations concerning the cow:

How we bleed her to take the last drop of milk from her, how we starve her to emaciation, how we ill-treat the calves, how we deprive them of their portion of milk, how cruelly we treat the oxen, how we castrate them, how we beat them, how we overload them . . . I do not know that the condition of the cattle in any other part of the world is as bad as in unhappy India.

Useful and Useless Animals

How then, if careful rationing is characteristic of livestock management, do peasants tolerate the widely reported herds of useless animals?

Perhaps "useless" means one thing to the peasant and quite another to the price-market-oriented agronomist. It is impossible at a distance to judge which point of view is ecologically more valid, but the peasants could be right more than the agronomists are willing to admit.

Since non-working and non-lactating animals are thermal and chemical factories which depend on waste lands and products for raw materials, judgment that a particular animal is useless cannot be supported without careful examination of its owner's household budget. Estimates from the cattle census which equate useless with dry or non-working animals are not convincing. But even if a given animal in a particular household is of less-than-marginal utility, there is an additional factor whose evaluation would involve long-range bovine biographies. The utility of a particular animal to its owner cannot be established simply by its performance during season or an animal cycle. Perhaps the whole system of Indian bovine management is alien to costing procedures of the West. There may be a kind of low-risk sweepstake which drags on for 10 or 12 years before the losers and winners are separated.

As previously observed, the principal function of bovine cows is not their milk-producing but their bullock-producing abilities. Also established is the fact that many farmers are short of bullocks. Cows have the function primarily to produce male offspring, but when? In Europe and America, cows become pregnant under well-controlled, hence predictable, circumstances and a farmer with many animals, can count on male offspring in half the births. In India, cows become pregnant under quite different circumstances. Since cows suffer from malnutrition through restriction to marginal pasture, they conceive and deliver in unpredictable fashion. The chronic starvation of the inter-monsoon period makes the cow, in the words of Mamoria (1953:263), "an irregular breeder." Moreover, with few animals, the farmer may suffer many disappointments before a male is born. To the agriculture specialist with knowledge of what healthy dairy stock look like, the hot weather herds of walking skeletons "roaming over the bare fields and dried up wastes" (Leake

1923:267) must indeed seem without economic potential. Many of them, in fact, will not make it through to the next monsoon. However, among the survivors are an unknown number still physically capable of having progeny. Evidently neither the farmer nor the specialist knows which will conceive, nor when. To judge from Bombay city, even when relatively good care is bestowed on a dry cow, no one knows the outcome: "If an attempt is made to salvage them, they have to be kept and fed for a long time. Even then, it is not known whether they will conceive or not" (Nandra, et al. 1955:9).

In rural areas, to judge a given animal useless may be to ignore the recuperative power of these breeds under conditions of erratic rainfall and unpredictable grazing opportunities. The difference of viewpoint between the farmer and the expert is apparent in Moomaw's (1949) incomplete attempt to describe the life history of an informant's cattle. The farmer in question had 3 oxen, 2 female buffaloes, 4 head of young cattle and 3 "worthless" cows (p. 23). In Moomaw's opinion, "The three cows . . . are a liability to him, providing no income, yet consuming feed which might be placed to better use." Yet we learn, "The larger one had a calf about once in three years"; moreover 2 of the 3 oxen were "raised" by the farmer himself. (Does this mean that they were the progeny of the farmer's cows?) The farmer tells Moomaw, "The young stock get some fodder, but for the most part they pasture with the village herd. The cows give nothing and I cannot afford to feed them." Whereupon Moomaw's *non sequitur*: "We spoke no more of his cows, for like many a farmer he just keeps them, without inquiring whether it is profitable or not" (p. 25).

The difficulties in identifying animals that are definitely uneconomic for a given farmer are reflected in the varying estimates of the total of such animals. The Expert Committee on the Prevention of Slaughter of Cattle estimated 20 million uneconomic cattle in India (Nandra, et al. 1953:62). Roy (1955:14) settles for 5.5 million, or about 3.5%. Mamoria (1953:257), who gives the still lower estimate of 2.9 million, or 2.1%, claims most of these are males. A similarly low percentage – 2.5%

– is suggested for West Bengal (NCAER 1962:56). None of these estimates appears based on bovine life histories in relation to household budgets; none appears to involve estimates of economic significance of dung contributions of older animals.

Before a peasant is judged a victim of Oriental mysticism, might it not be well to indicate the devastating material consequences which befall a poor farmer unable to replace a bullock lost through disease, old age, or accident? Bailey (1957:73) makes it clear that in the economic life of the marginal peasantry, "Much the most devastating single event is the loss of an ox (or a plough buffalo)." If the farmer is unable to replace the animal with one from his own herd, he must borrow money at usurious rates. Defaults on such loans are the principal causes of transfer of land titles from peasants to landlords. Could this explain why the peasant is not overly perturbed that some of his animals might turn out to be only dung-providers? After all, the real threat to his existence does not arise from animals but from people ready to swoop down on him as soon as one of his beasts falters. Chapekar's (1960:27) claim that the peasant's "stock serve as a great security for him to fall back on whenever he is in need" would seem to be appropriate only in reference to the unusually well-established minority. In a land where life expectancy at birth has only recently risen to 30 years (Black 1959:2), it is not altogether appropriate to speak of security. The poorest farmers own insufficient stock. Farm management studies show that holdings below two-thirds of average area account for two-fifths of all farms, but maintain only a quarter of the total cattle on farms. "This is so, chiefly because of their limited resources to maintain cattle" (Chaudhri and Giri 1963:598).

Slaughter

Few, if any, Hindu farmers kill their cattle by beating them over the head, severing their jugular veins or shooting them. But to assert that they do not kill their animals when it is economically important for them to do so may be equally false. This interpretation escapes

the notice of so many observers because the slaughtering process receives recognition only in euphemisms. People will admit that they "neglect" their animals, but will not openly accept responsibility for the *etic* effects, i.e., the more or less rapid death which ensues. The strange result of this euphemistic pattern is evidenced in the following statement by Moomaw (1949:96): "All calves born, however inferior, are allowed to live until they die of neglect." In the light of many similar but, by Hindu standards, more vulgar observations, it is clear that this kind of statement should read, "Most calves born are not allowed to live, but are starved to death."

This is roughly the testimony of Gourou (1963:125), "Le paysan conserve seulement les veaux qui deviendront boeufs de labour ou vaches laitières; les autres sont écartés . . . et meurent d'epuisement." Wiser and Wiser (1963:70) are even more direct:

> Cows and buffaloes too old to furnish milk are not treated cruelly, but simply allowed to starve. The same happens to young male buffaloes. . . . The males are unwanted and little effort is made to keep them alive.

Obviously, when an animal, undernourished to begin with, receives neither food nor care, it will not enjoy a long life (compare Gourou 1963: 124). Despite claims that an aged and decrepit cow "must be supported like an unproductive relative, until it dies a natural death" (Mosher 1946:124), ample evidence justifies belief that "few cattle die of old age"[5] (Bailey 1957:75). Dandekar (1964:352) makes the same point: "In other words, because the cows cannot be fed nor can they be killed, they are neglected, starved and left to die a 'natural' death."

The farmer culls his stock by starving unwanted animals and also, under duress, sells them directly or indirectly to butchers. With economic pressure, many Indians who will not kill or eat cows themselves:

> are likely to compromise their principles and sell to butchers who slaughter cows, thereby tacitly supporting the practice for other people. Selling aged cows to butchers has over the centuries become an accepted practice alongside the *mos* that a Hindu must not kill cattle (Roy 1955:15).

Determining the number of cattle slaughtered by butchers is almost as difficult as determining the number killed by starvation. According to Dandekar (1964:351), "Generally it is the useless animals that find their way to the slaughter house." Lahiry (n.d.:140) says only 126,900 or .9% of the total cattle population is slaughtered per year. Darling (1934:158) claims:

All Hindus object to the slaughter and even to the sale of unfit cows and keep them indefinitely.... rather than sell them to a cattle dealer, who would buy only for the slaughter house, they send them to a *gowshala* or let them loose to die. Some no doubt sell secretly, but this has its risks in an area where public opinion can find strong expression through the *panchayat*.

Such views would seem to be contradicted by Sinha (1961:95): "A large number of animals are slaughtered privately and it is very difficult to ascertain their numbers." The difficulty of obtaining accurate estimates is also implied by the comment of the Committee on the Prevention of Slaughter that "90% of animals not approved for slaughter are slaughtered stealthily outside of municipal limits" (Nandra, *et al.* 1955:11).

An indication of the propensity to slaughter cattle under duress is found in connection with the food crisis of World War II. With rice imports cut off by Japanese occupation of Burma (Thirumalai 1954:38; Bhatia 1963:309 on), increased consumption of beef by the armed forces, higher prices for meat and foodstuffs generally, and famine conditions in Bengal, the doctrine of *ahimsa* proved to be alarmingly ineffectual. Direct military intervention was required to avoid destruction of animals needed for plowing, milking, and bullock-production:

During the war there was an urgent need to reduce or to avoid the slaughter for food of animals useful for breeding or for agricultural work. For the summer of 1944 the slaughter was prohibited of: (1) Cattle below three years of age; (2) Male cattle between two and ten years of age which were being used or were likely to be used as working cattle; (3) All cows between three and ten years of age, other

than cows which were unsuitable for bearing offspring; (4) All cows which were pregnant or in milk (Knight 1954:141).

Gourou (1963:124–5), aware that starvation and neglect are systematically employed to cull Indian herds, nonetheless insists that destruction of animals through starvation amounts to an important loss of capital. This loss is attributed to the low price of beef caused by the beef-eating taboo, making it economically infeasible to send animals to slaughter. Gourou's appraisal, however, neglects deleterious consequences to the rural tanning and carrion-eating castes if increased numbers of animals went to the butchers. Since the least efficient way to convert solar energy into comestibles is to impose an animal converter between plant and man (Cottrell 1955), it should be obvious that without major technical and environmental innovations or drastic population cuts, India could not tolerate a large beef-producing industry. This suggests that insofar as the beef-eating taboo helps discourage growth of beef-producing industries, it is part of an ecological adjustment which maximizes rather than minimizes the calorie and protein output of the productive process.

Anti-Slaughter Legislation

It is evident from the history of anti-slaughter agitation and legislation in India that more than *ahimsa* has been required to protect Indian cattle from premature demise. Unfortunately, this legislation is misinterpreted and frequently cited as evidence of the anti-economic effect of Hinduism. I am unable to unravel all the tangled economic and political interests served by the recent anti-slaughter laws of the Indian states. Regardless of the ultimate ecological consequences of these laws, however, several points deserve emphasis. First it should be recalled that cow protection was a major political weapon in Ghandi's campaign against both British and Moslems. The sacred cow was the ideological focus of a successful struggle against English colonialism; hence the enactment of total anti-slaughter legislation obviously had a rational base, at least among politicians who seized and retained power on anti-English and anti-Moslem platforms. It is possible that the legislation will now backfire and upset the delicate ecological balance which now exists. The Committee on the Prevention of Slaughter claimed that it

actually saw in Pepsu (where slaughter is banned completely) what a menace wild cattle can be. Conditions have become so desperate there, that the State Government have got to spend a considerable sum for catching and redomesticating wild animals to save the crops (Nandra, et al. 1955:11).

According to Mayadas (1954:29):

The situation has become so serious that it is impossible in some parts of the country to protect growing crops from grazing by wandering cattle. Years ago it was one or two stray animals which could either be driven off or sent to the nearest cattle pound. Today it is a question of constantly being harassed day and night by herds which must either feed on one's green crops, or starve. How long can this state of affairs be allowed to continue?

Before the deleterious effects of slaughter laws can be properly evaluated, certain additional evolutionary and functional possibilities must be examined. For example, given the increasing growth rate of India's human population, the critical importance of cattle in the *eco-system,* and the absence of fundamental technical and environmental changes, a substantial increase in cattle seems necessary and predictable, regardless of slaughter legislation. Furthermore, there is some indication, admittedly incomplete but certainly worthy of careful inquiry, that many who protest most against destructiveness of marauding herds of useless beasts may perceive the situation from very special vantage points in the social hierarchy. The implications of the following newspaper editorial are clear:

The alarming increase of stray and wild cattle over wide areas of Northern India is fast becoming a major disincentive to crop cultivation. . . . Popular sentiment against cow slaughter no doubt lies at the back of the

problem. People prefer to let their aged, diseased, and otherwise useless cattle live at the expense of *other people's crops* (Indian Express, New Delhi, 7 February 1959, italics added).

Evidently we need to know something about whose crops are threatened by these marauders. Despite post-Independence attempts at land reform, 10% of the Indian agricultural population still owns more than half the total cultivated area and 15 million or 22%, of rural households own no land at all (Mitra 1963:298). Thorner and Thorner (1962:3) call the land reform program a failure, and point out how "the grip of the larger holder serves to prevent the lesser folk from developing the land . . ." Quite possibly, in other words, the anti-slaughter laws, insofar as they are effective, should be viewed as devices which, contrary to original political intent, bring pressure to bear upon those whose lands are devoted to cash crops of benefit only to narrow commercial, urban, and landed sectors of the population. To have one's cows eat other people's crops may be a very fine solution to the subsistence problem of those with no crops of their own. Apparently, in the days when animals could be driven off or sent to the pound with impunity, this could not happen, even though *ahimsa* reigned supreme then as now.

Some form of anti-slaughter legislation was required and actually argued for, on unambiguously rational, economic, and material grounds. About 4% of India's cattle are in the cities (Mohan 1962:48). These have always represented the best dairy stock, since the high cost of feeding animals in a city could be offset only by good milking qualities. A noxious consequence of this dairy pattern was the slaughter of the cow at the end of its first urban lactation period because it was too expensive to maintain while awaiting another pregnancy. Similarly, and by methods previously discussed, the author calf was killed after it had stimulated the cow to "let down." With the growth of urban milk consumption, the best of India's dairy cattle were thus systematically prevented from breeding, while animals with progressively poorer milking qualities were preserved in the countryside (Mohan 1962:48; Mayadas 1954:29; Gandhi 1954:13 on). The Committee on the Prevention of Slaughter of Cattle (Nandra, *et al.* 1955:2) claimed at least 50,000 high-yielding cows and she-buffaloes from Madras, Bombay, and Calcutta were "annually sent to premature slaughter" and were "lost to the country." Given such evidence of waste and the political potential of Moslems being identified as cow-butchers and Englishmen as cow-eaters (Gandhi 1954:16), the political importance of *ahimsa* becomes more intelligible. Indeed, it could be that the strength of Gandhi's *charisma* lay in his superior understanding of the ecological significance of the cow, especially in relation to the underprivileged masses, marginal low caste and out caste farmers. Gandhi (p. 3) may have been closer to the truth than many a foreign expert when he said:

> Why the cow was selected for apotheosis is obvious to me. The cow was in India the best companion. She was the giver of plenty. Not only did she give milk but she also made agriculture possible.

Old-Age Homes

Among the more obscure aspects of the cattle complex are bovine old-age homes, variously identified as *gowshalas, pinjrapoles*, and, under the Five-Year Plans, as *gosadans*. Undoubtedly some of these are "homes for cows, which are supported by public charity, which maintain the old and derelict animals till natural death occurs" (Kothavala 1934: 123). According to Gourou (1963:125), however, owners of cows sent to these religious institutions pay rent with the understanding that if the cows begin to lactate they will be returned. The economics of at least some of these "charitable" institutions is, therefore, perhaps not as quaint as usually implied. It is also significant that, although the 1st Five-Year Plan called for establishment of 160 *gosadans* to serve 320,000 cattle, only 22 *gosadans* servicing 8,000 cattle were reported by 1955 (Government of India Planning Commission 1956:283).

Natural Selection

Expert appraisers of India's cattle usually show little enthusiasm for the typical undersized breeds. Much has been made of the fact that one large animal is a more efficient dung, milk, and traction machine than two small ones. "Weight for weight, a small animal consumes a much larger quantity of food than a bigger animal" (Marmoria 1953:268). "More dung is produced when a given quantity of food is consumed by one animal than when it is shared by two animals" (Ford Foundation 1959:64). Thus it would seem that India's smaller breeds should be replaced by larger, more powerful, and better milking breeds. But once again, there is another way of looking at the evidence. It might very well be that if all of India's scrub cattle were suddenly replaced by an equivalent number of large, high-quality European or American dairy and traction animals, famines of noteworthy magnitude would immediately ensue. Is it not possible that India's cattle are undersized precisely because other breeds never could survive the atrocious conditions they experience most of the year? I find it difficult to believe that breeds better adapted to the present Indian *eco-system* exist elsewhere.

> By nature and religious training, the villager is unwilling to inflict pain or to take animal life. But the immemorial grind for existence has hardened him to an acceptance of survival of the fittest (Wiser and Wiser 1963).

Not only are scrub animals well adapted to the regular seasonal crises of water and forage and general year-round neglect, but long-range selective pressures may be even more significant. The high frequency of drought-induced famines in India (Bhatia 1963) places a premium upon drought-resistance plus a more subtle factor: A herd of smaller animals, dangerously thinned by famine or pestilence, reproduces faster than an equivalent group of larger animals, despite the fact that the larger animal consumes less per pound than two smaller animals. This is because there are two cows in the smaller herd per equivalent large cow. Mohan (1962:45) is one of the few authorities to have grasped this principle, including it in defense of the small breeds:

Calculations of the comparative food conversion efficiency of various species of Indian domestic livestock by the writer has revealed, that much greater attention should be paid to small livestock than at present, not only because of their better conversion efficiency for protein but also because of the possibilities of bringing about a rapid increase in their numbers.

Conclusion

The probability that India's cattle complex is a positive-functioned part of a naturally selected *eco-system is* at least as good as that it is a negative-functioned expression of an irrational ideology. This should not be interpreted to mean that no "improvements" can be made in the system, nor that different systems may not eventually evolve. The issue is not whether oxen are more efficient than tractors. I suggest simply that many features of the cattle complex have been erroneously reported or interpreted. That Indian cattle are weak and inefficient is not denied, but there is doubt that this situation arises from and is mainly perpetuated by Hindu ideology. Given the technoenvironmental base, Indian property relationships, and political organization, one need not involve the doctrine of *ahimsa* to understand fundamental features of the cattle complex. Although the cattle population of India has risen by 38 million head since 1940, during the same period, the human population has risen by 120 million. Despite the anti-slaughter legislation, the ratio of cattle to humans actually declined from 44:100 in 1941 to 40:100 in 1961 (Government of India 1962:74; 1963:6). In the absence of major changes in environment, technology or property relations, it seems unlikely that the cattle population will cease to accompany the rise in the human population. If *ahimsa* is negative-functioned, then we must be prepared to admit the possibility that all other factors contributing to the rapid growth of the Indian human and cattle populations, including the germ theory of disease, are also negative-functioned.

NOTES

1. The author (1960) suggested that the term "adaptive" be restricted to traits, biological or cultural, established and diffused in conformity with the principle of natural selection. Clearly, not all "positive-functioned," i.e., useful, cultural traits are so established.
2. *Ahimsa* is the Hindu principle of unity of life, of which sacredness of cattle is principal sub-case and symbol.
3. According to Zeuner (1954:328), "Symbiosis includes all conditions of the living-together of two different species, provided both derive advantages therefrom. Cases in which both partners benefit equally are rare." In the symbiosis under consideration, men benefit more than cattle.
4. The U.S. Census of Agriculture (1954) showed milk production averaging from a low of 3,929 pounds per cow in the Nashville Basin sub-region to 11,112 pounds per cow in the Southern California sub-region.
5. Srinivas (1962:126) declared himself properly skeptical in this matter: "It is commonly believed that the peasant's religious attitude to cattle comes in the way of the disposal of useless cattle. Here again, my experience of Rampura makes me skeptical of the general belief. I am not denying that cattle are regarded as in some sense sacred, but I doubt whether the belief is as powerful as it is claimed to be. I have already mentioned that bull-buffaloes are sacrificed to village goddesses. And in the case of the cow, while the peasant does not want to kill the cow or bull himself he does not seem to mind very much if someone else does the dirty job out of his sight."

REFERENCES

Bailey, F. G. (1957). *Caste and the economic frontier.* Manchester: University of Manchester Press.

Bansil, P. C. (1958). *India's food resources and population,* p. 104. Bombay: Vora. p. 97 (if 1959).

Bhatia, B. M. (1963). *Famines in India.* New York: Asia Publishing House.

Black, John D. (1959). Supplementary to the Ford Foundation team's report: India's food crisis and steps to meet it. *The Indian Journal of Agricultural Economics* 14:1–6.

Chapekar, L. N. (1960). *Thakurs of the Sahyadri.* Oxford: Oxford University Press.

Chateerjee, I. (1960). Milk production in India. *Economic Weekly* 12:1347–48.

Chaudhri, S. C., and R. Giri. (1963). Role of cattle in India's economy. *Agricultural situation in India* 18:591–9.

Cottrell, Fred. (1955). *Energy and society.* New York: McGraw-Hill.

Dandekar, U. M. (1964). Problem of numbers in cattle development. *Economic Weekly* 16:351–5.

Darling, M. L. (1934). *Wisdom and waste in a Punjab village.* London: Oxford University Press.

Das, A. B., and M. N. Chatterji. (1962). *The Indian economy.* Calcutta: Bookland Private.

Desai, M. B. (1948). *The rural economy of Gujarat.* Bombay: Oxford University Press.

——. (1959). India's food crisis. *The Indian Journal of Agricultural Economics* 14:27–37.

Diskalkar, P. D. (1960). *Resurvey of a Deccan village Pimple Sandagar.* Bombay: The Indian Society of Agricultural Economics.

Dube, S. C. (1955). *Indian village.* Ithaca: Cornell University Press.

Dupuis, J. (1960). *Madras et le nord dii Coromatidel; étude des conditions de la vie indienne dans un cadre géografique.* Paris: Maisonneuve.

Food and Agriculture Organization. (1953). *Agriculture in Asia and the Far East: Development and outlook.* Rome: FAO.

Ford Foundation. (1959). *Report on India's food crisis and steps to meet it.* New Delhi: Government of India, Ministry of Food and Agriculture and Ministry of Community Development and Cooperation.

Gandhi, M. K. (1954). *How to serve the cow.* Edited by Bharaton Kumarappa. Ahmedabad: Navajivan Publishing House.

Gangulee, N. (1935). *The Indian peasant and his environment.* London: Oxford University Press.

Gourou, Pierre. (1963). Civilization et economie pastorale. *L'Homme* 123–29.

Government of India. (1956). *Second five-year plan.* Planning Commission. New Delhi.

——. (1957). *India.* Ministry of Information and Broadcasting. New Delhi.

——. (1962). *Statistical Abstract of the Indian Union* 11. Cabinet Secretariat. New Delhi.

——. (1963). *India.* Ministry of Information and Broadcasting. New Delhi.

Gupta, S. C. (1959). *An economic survey of Shamaspur village.* New York: Asia Publishing House.

Harris, Marvin. (1960). Adaptation in biological and cultural science. *Transactions of the New York Academy of Sciences* 23:59–65.

——. (1964a). *The nature of cultural things.* New York: Random House.

——. (1964b). *Patterns of race in the Americas.* New York: Walker.

Hutton, J. H. (1961). *Caste in India,* p. VII. London: Oxford University Press.

Kapp, K. W. (1963). *Hindu culture, economic development and economic planning in India.* New York: Asia Publishing House.

Kardel, Hans. (1956). *Community development in agriculture: Mysore State, India,* Washington, D.C.: International Cooperation Administration.

Kartha, K. P. R. (1936). A note on the comparative economic efficiency of the Indian cow, the half breed cow, and the buffalo as producers of milk and butter fat. *Agriculture and Livestock in India* 4: 605–23.

——. (1959). "Buffalo," in *An introduction to animal husbandry in. the Tropics.* Edited by G. Williamson and W. J. A. Payne. London: Longmans, Green.

Knight, Henry. (1954). *Food administration in India 1939–47.* Stanford: Stanford University Press.

Kothavala, Zal R. (1934). Milk production in India. *Agriculture and Livestock in India* 2:122–9.

Lahiry, N. L. (n.d.). "Conservation and utilization of animal food resources," in Proceedings of symposium on food needs and resources. *Bulletin of the National Institute of Sciences of India* 20:140–4.

Leake, H. Martin. (1923). *The foundations of Indian agriculture.* Cambridge: W. Heffer.

Lewis, Oscar, and Victor Barnouw. (1958). *Village life in northern India.* Urbana: University of Illinois Press.

Lewis, W. A. (1955). *The theory of economic growth.* Homewood, Ill.: R. D. Irwin.

Lupton, Arnold. (1922). *Happy India.* London: G. Allen & Unwin.

Mamoria, C. B. (1953). *Agricultural problems of India.* Allahabad: Kitab Mahal.

Matson, J. (1933). Inefficiency of cattle in India through disease. *Agriculture and Livestock in India* 1:227–8.

Mayadas, C. (1954). *Between us and hunger.* London: Oxford University Press.

Mayer, Adrian. (1952). *Land and society in Malabar.* Bombay: Oxford University Press.

Mishra, Vikas. (1962). *Hinduism and economic growth.* London: Oxford University Press.

Mitra, Ashok. (1963). "Tax burden for Indian agriculture," in *Traditions, values, and socio-economic development.* Edited by R. Braibanti and J. J. Spengler, pp. 281–303. Durham: Duke University Press.

Mohan, S. N. (1962). Animal husbandry in the Third Plan. *Bulletin of the National Institute of Sciences of India* 20: 41–54.

Moomaw, I. W. (1949). *The farmer speaks.* London: Oxford University Press.

Mosher, Arthur T. (1946). *The economic effect of Hindu religion and social traditions on agricultural production by Christians in North India.* Unpublished Ph.D. dissertation, University of Chicago. (Also microfilms T 566.)

Mujumdar, N. A. (1960). Cow dung as manure. *Economic Weekly* 12:743–4.

Nandra, P. N., *et al.* (1955). Report of the expert committee on the prevention of slaughter of cattle in India. New Delhi: Government of India Press.

National Council of Applied Economic Research. (1959). *Domestic fuels in India.* New York: Asia Publishing House.

——. (1960). *Techno-economic survey of Madhya Pradesh.* New Delhi.

——. (1961). *Techno-economic survey of Tripura.* New Delhi.

——. (1962a). *Techno-economic survey of Andhra Pradesh.* New Delhi.

——. (1962b). *Techno-economic survey of Punjab.* New Delhi.

——. (1962c). *Techno-economic survey of West Bengal.* New Delhi.

——. (1962d). *Economic atlas of Madras State.* New Delhi.

——. (1963). *Techno-economic survey of Rajasthan.* New Delhi.

Randhawa, M. S. (1962). *Agriculture and animal husbandry in India.* New Delhi. Indian Council of Agricultural Research.

Randhawa, M. S., *et al.* (1961). *Farmers of India.* 2 vols. New Delhi: Indian Council of Agricultural Research.

Roy, Prodipto. (1955). The sacred cow in India. *Rural sociology* 20:8–15.

Saha, M. N. (1956). Fuel in India. *Nature* 177:923–4.

Schneider, Harold. (1957). The subsistence role of cattle among the Pakot and in East Africa. *American Anthropologist* 59:278–300.

Shastri, C. P. (1960). Bullock labour utilization in agriculture. *Economic Weekly* 12:1585–92.

Simoons, F. J. (1961). *Eat not this flesh.* Madison: University of Wisconsin Press.

Sinha, R. P. (1961). *Food in India.* London: Oxford University Press.

Spate, Oskar Hermann. (1954). *India and Pakistan: A general and regional geography.* London: Methuen:

Srinivas, M. N. (1952). *Religion and society among the Coorgs of South India.* Oxford: Oxford University Press.

——. (1958). India's cultural values and economic development. *Economic Development and cultural change* 7:3–6.

——. (1962). *Caste in modern India.* New York: Asia Publishing House.

Thirumalai, Shri. (1954). *Post-war agricultural problems and policies in India,* p. 38. New York: Institute of Pacific Relations.

Thorner, Daniel, and Alice Thorner. (1962). *Land and labour in India*. New York: Asia Publishing House.

U.S. Census of Agriculture. (1954). "Dairy producers and dairy production." in *Farmers and farm production in the United States* 3, part 9, chap. V.

Venkatraman, R. B. (1938). The Indian village, its past, present, future. *Agriculture and Livestock in India* 7:702–10.

Williamson, G., and W. J. A. Payne. (1959). *An introduction to animal husbandry in the Tropics*. London: Longmans, Green.

Wiser, William H., and C. V. Wiser. (1963). *Behind mud walls: 1930–60*. Berkeley: University of California Press.

Zeuner, F. E. (1954). "Domestication of animals," in *A history of technology*. Edited by C. Singer, *et al.*, pp. 327–52. New York: Oxford University Press.

Part II

Ecology and Social Organization

5

Seasonal Variations of the Eskimo: A Study in Social Morphology

Marcel Mauss

- Morphology ↑?
- General relations about the Eskimo

Introduction

We propose to study here the social morphology of Eskimo societies. By this term, social morphology, we refer to the science whose investigations are intended not just to describe but also to elucidate the material substratum of societies. This includes the form that societies assume in their patterns of residence, the volume and density of their population, the way in which the population is distributed, as well as the entire range of objects that serve as a focus for collective life.

However, since this work deals with a specific geographical population, we want to avoid giving it the appearance of a purely ethnographic study. Our intention is not to collect, in one descriptive monograph, all sorts of diverse facts about Eskimo morphology. On the contrary, we intend to establish certain general relations about the Eskimo. We have chosen this remarkable people as the special object of our study precisely because the relations to which we wish to call attention are

exaggerated and amplified among them; because they stand out, we can clearly understand their nature and significance. As a result, it is easier to recognize them even in other societies where they are less immediately apparent or where a configuration of other social facts conceals them from the observer. The Eskimo offer such a privileged field of study because their morphology is not the same throughout the year. The way in which the Eskimo group together, the distribution of their population, the form of their houses and the nature of their settlements all change completely in accordance with the seasons. These variations which, as we shall see, are considerable, offer favourable conditions for a study of how the material form of human groups – the very nature and composition of their substratum – affects different modes of collective activity.

Seasons

We may perhaps find that only this one population provides the appropriate basis for a study whose aim is to establish propositions that are more widely applicable. But we must not lose sight of the fact that the Eskimo occupy an extensive coastal area. There exist, not one, but many Eskimo societies whose culture is sufficiently homogeneous that they may be usefully compared, and sufficiently diverse that these comparisons may be fruitful. Moreover, it is wrong to assume that the validity of a scientific proposition is directly dependent on the number of cases that can supposedly confirm it. When a relation has been established in one case, even a unique case but one that has been carefully and systematically studied, the result is as valid as any that can be demonstrated by resorting to numerous facts which are but disparate, curious examples confusingly culled from the most heterogeneous societies, races or cultures. John Stuart Mill states that a well-constructed experiment is sufficient to demonstrate a law; it is certainly infinitely more indicative than numerous badly-constructed experiments. Indeed this methodological rule applies just as much to sociology as to the other natural sciences. Hence, at the end of this work, we intend to refer to certain facts which indicate that the relations that we are about to establish for the Eskimo are more generally applicable.

In treating these questions, we should clarify our position in regard to the methods practised by that special discipline known as anthropogeography.[1] The facts that anthropogeography deals with are, in a sense, of the same sort as those with which we are going to be concerned. Anthropogeography also proposes to study the distribution of men on the surface of the earth and the material form of societies; and no one can rightly deny that the research undertaken in this direction has had important results. It is certainly not our intention to belittle the positive discoveries or the fruitful suggestions which we owe to this brilliant array of researchers. In conceiving of societies as groups of men organized at specific points on the globe, we are not going to make the mistake of considering them as if they were independent of their territorial base; clearly the configuration of the land, its mineral riches, its fauna and flora affect the organization of society. However, since the scholars of this school are specialists in geography, they are naturally inclined to see things from a particular angle; hence by the very nature of their studies they have attributed an almost exclusive preponderance to geographical factors. Instead of investigating all aspects of the material substratum of societies, they have concentrated their attention first and foremost on the factor of land. This is the prime consideration in their research; and the main difference between them and ordinary geographers is that they consider land particularly in relation to society.

They have, however, attributed to this factor a kind of perfect efficacy, as if land were capable of producing effects on its own without interacting with other factors that might reinforce or neutralize its effects either partially or entirely. We need only open the works of the most reputable of these anthropogeographers to see this conception translated into chapter headings; a successive discussion of land in relation to habitation, land in relation to the family, land in relation to the state, etc. Land, however, does not produce effects except in conjunction with thousands of other factors from which it is inseparable. The existence of mineral resources is an insufficient condition for determining human residence at a specific point in a region; a certain stage of industrial technology is needed to exploit them. For men to gather together, instead of living in a dispersed fashion, it is insufficient simply to assert that the climate or a configuration of the land draws them together; their moral, legal and religious organization must also allow a concentrated way of life. Although the geographical situation is an essential factor to which we must pay the closest possible attention, it still constitutes only one of the conditions for the material form of human groups. In most cases it produces its effects only by means of numerous social conditions which it initially affects, and which alone account for the result. In short, the land factor must be considered in relation to a social context in all its complex totality. It cannot be treated in isolation.

So, when we study its effects, we must trace their repercussions on all the categories of collective life. All these questions are not, therefore, geographical questions but proper sociological ones; and in this study we will approach them in a sociological spirit. If we prefer to refer to the discipline to which this study belongs as social morphology rather than anthropogeography, this is not because of some frivolous taste for neologisms but because these different labels define a difference in orientation.

[. . .]

Seasonal Morphology

[. . .]

Although the settlement is always the fundamental unit of Eskimo society, it still takes on quite different forms according to the seasons. In summer, the members of a settlement live in tents and these tents are dispersed; in winter, they live in houses grouped close to one another. Everyone, from the earliest authors onward, who has had a chance to follow the cycle of Eskimo life, has observed this general pattern. First, we are going to describe each of these two types of habitat and the two corresponding ways of grouping. We shall then endeavour to determine their causes and their effects.

reindeer, either as separate pieces or stitched together. These skins are held down at the base by large stones capable of withstanding the often severe force of the wind. Unlike Indian tents, Eskimo ones are not open at the top; there is no smoke that has to be allowed to escape, for their lamps produce none. The entrance can be closed tightly, and then the occupants are plunged in darkness.

[. . .]

Rather than all these technological details, it is more important to know what kind of group lives in the tent. From one end of the Eskimo area to the other, this group consists of a family defined in the narrowest sense of this word: a man and his wife (or, if there is room, his wives) plus their unmarried children including adopted children. In exceptional cases, a tent may include an older relative, or a widow who has not remarried and her children, or a guest or two. The relationship between the family and the tent is so close that the structure of the one is modelled on the structure of the other. It is a general rule, among all Eskimo, that there should be one lamp for each family; thus, ordinarily, there is only one single lamp to a tent. Similarly, there is only one bench (or raised bed of leaves and branches at the back of the tent) covered with skins for sleeping; this bed has no partition to separate the family from any guests. Thus the family lives perfectly united within this tightly closed interior; it builds and transports this summer dwelling which is made exactly to its measure.

Summer habitat

The tent

We begin by considering the tent, because it is a simpler construction than the winter house. *really?*

Everywhere, from Angmagssalik to Kodiak Island, the tent has the same name, *lupik*, and the same form. In structure it consists of poles arranged in the shape of a cone; over these poles are placed skins, mostly of

Winter habitat

The house

As summer turns to winter, there occurs a complete change in the morphology of Eskimo society, in its mode of livelihood and in the structure of its sheltered groups. Eskimo dwellings do not remain the same; their population is different, and they are arranged in a completely different settlement pattern.

Instead of tents, Eskimo build houses,[2] and indeed long-houses, as winter dwellings. We will begin by describing the external form of these houses and then proceed to discuss their content.

The Eskimo long-house is made up of three essential elements which serve to identify it: (1) a passage that begins outside and leads into the interior via a partially subterranean entrance; (2) a bench with places for lamps; and (3) partitions which divide the bench into a certain number of sections. These distinctive traits are specific to the Eskimo house; they are not found together in any other known type of house. In different localities, however, houses may have particular characteristics which give rise to a certain number of secondary varieties.

[. . .]

The contents of the house

Now that we know something about the arrangement of the house, we can consider the nature of the group living in it.

Just as the tent consists of a single family, so the winter dwelling, in all its forms, normally contains several families. We have already seen this from the previous discussion. The number of families who live together, however, is somewhat variable. There can be as many as six, seven or even nine families among the tribes of eastern Greenland, and formerly ten in western Greenland, though the number decreases to two for small snow-houses and for the tiny stone houses at Smith Strait. The existence of a certain number of families in the same house is so characteristic of Eskimo winter settlements that, wherever this begins to diminish, it is a sure sign that the culture itself is waning. Thus, in the census reports from Alaska, it is possible to distinguish Eskimo villages from Indian villages according to the number of families per house.

In the Greenland house, each family has its own set place. In the igloo, each family has its own special bench; similarly, the family has its own compartment in the polygonal house, a section of a partitioned bench in houses in Greenland and its own side in the rectangular house. There is thus a close relationship between the structure of the house and the structure of the group that it shelters. It is interesting, however, to note that the space occupied by each family is not proportional to the number of its members. Families are considered as separate units, each equivalent to the other. A family consisting of a single individual occupies as much space as a large one comprising more than two generations.

The kashim

Besides these private dwellings, there is another winter construction which deserves particular attention because it highlights particular features of Eskimo life during the winter season. This is the *kashim*, a European term derived from an Eskimo word meaning 'my place of assembly'.

The *kashim*, it is true, is no longer to be found in all areas. It is, however, still found throughout Alaska and among all the tribes of the western coast of America as far as Point Atkinson. According to the accounts we have of the most recent explorations, it is still found in Baffin Land, along the north-west coast of Hudson Bay and on the southern coast of Hudson Strait. Its existence was noted by the very first Moravian missionaries to Labrador. In Greenland, with one dubious exception, there is no trace of the *kashim* in the ruins of former settlements, nor is it mentioned by the early Danish writers; yet the *kashim* is still remembered in some Eskimo tales. There are good reasons, therefore, to regard it as a normal part of every primitive Eskimo settlement.

The *kashim* is an enlarged winter house. The connection between the two constructions is so close that the diverse forms of the *kashim* in different regions parallel the various forms of the winter house. There are two essential differences. First, the *kashim* has a central hearth, whereas the winter house does not, except in the extreme south of Alaska where the influence of the Indian house has its effect. This hearth is found not only where the use of firewood offers a good practical reason for its existence, but also in temporary *kashim* made of snow, as in Baffin Land. Second, there are usually no compartments, and often no benches but only seats, in the *kashim*. Even when it is built of snow and it is therefore impossible to construct a single large dome because of the nature of the material to hand, domes are joined together and walls are shaped to give the *kashim* the form of a large pillared hall.

These differences in the arrangement of the interior correspond to differences in function. There are no divisions or compartments but only a central hearth because the *kashim* is the communal house of the entire settlement. This, according to reliable sources, is where the ceremonies take place that reunite the community. In Alaska, the *kashim* is more specifically a men's house, where adult men, married or unmarried, sleep apart from the women and children. Among the tribes of southern Alaska, it serves as the sweat-house; but this use of the *kashim* is probably relatively recent and of Indian, or even Russian, origin.

The *kashim* is built exclusively during the winter. This is itself good evidence that it is the distinctive feature of winter life. Winter is characterized by an extreme concentration of the group. This is not only the time when several families gather together to live in the same house, but all families of the same settlement, or at least the men of the settlement, feel the need to reunite in the same place to live a communal life. The *kashim* was created in response to this need.

[. . .]

The Causes of Eskimo Seasonal Variations

It would be rather difficult to discover all the causes that resulted in the establishment of the various features of this twofold organization, for they happened in the course of a historical development that was probably quite long and during a migration of extraordinary scope. Yet we would like at least to indicate some of the factors that underlie this phenomenon, if only to distinguish social causes from

others of a limited and purely physical nature.

Most observers have usually been satisfied with simple explanations. They note that the communal house and the quasi-subterranean one retain heat better, that the presence of a number of individuals under the same roof is enough to raise the temperature, and that the clustering of several families economizes on fuel. They thus see in this organization nothing more than a means of fighting the cold. Yet, though there is some truth to these notions, they are only partial explanations. First, it is inaccurate to say that the Eskimo inhabit the coldest regions of the world. A certain number are settled in relatively temperate regions; for example, in the south of Greenland or Labrador, where the major difference between summer and winter is a result of the proximity of the inland ice or of the ice that is carried by the glacial stream rather than of any real lowering of temperature. Second, the Indians of the interior of Labrador, the Montagnais, the Cree of the Barren Grounds and the Indians of the Alaskan forest, live in higher latitudes and experience conditions of a continental climate that is basically harsher than that of their coastal Eskimo neighbours. Yet these Indians all live in tents throughout the year and though their tent is similar to that of the Eskimo, the opening at its top – the smoke-hole, with which the Eskimo are unacquainted – makes it a great deal less efficient against the cold, even in summer. It is thus surprising that the Indians have not borrowed from their neighbours an invention as useful as the house. This is just another piece of evidence to contradict those theories that suppose that they have accounted for a social institution by showing from whom it has been borrowed. Third, where there are good reasons for altering the form of the house, these alterations have not taken place; this can be taken as evidence that the winter house is, as it were, a distinctive feature of Eskimo society. Thus, in the forested districts of Alaska, some tribes have gone beyond the shores of the rivers and have their winter settlements closer to the woods than to the seal-hunting grounds. But instead of installing a hearth of wood and opening their roofs to allow the smoke to escape, these tribes prefer to purchase oil for their lamps, at considerable expense, from those of their neighbours who have some.

One explanation that shows an awareness of this problem and its complexity is that proposed by Steensby. He has argued that primitive Eskimo culture was once an Indian type of culture whose closest approximation can still be observed among the Eskimo during the summer; on the other hand, the form of the Eskimo house corresponds to the same type as that of the Plains Indians (from the Mandan to the Iroquois). The house is supposedly the result of primitive borrowing and was developed, along with the whole of the winter technology, at a time when the Arctic Ocean began to approach and overtake the Eskimo. But nowhere do we find a single trace of any Eskimo group whose principal occupation was hunting and whose only dwelling was the tent. From the moment that the Eskimo appear as a specific social group, they already have their well-established twofold culture. Thus the oldest summer settlements are always near the oldest winter settlements. Moreover, any comparison between an Indian long-house and an Eskimo house is relatively inexact, for in an Indian long-house there is neither a passage, nor benches, nor places for lamps – the three characteristic traits of an Eskimo house.

We must therefore put aside these explanations and see how we might otherwise account for the concentration of the Eskimo in the winter and their dispersion in the summer.

We have already seen how strongly the Eskimo are attached to their way of life, however poor it may be. They can hardly conceive of the possibility of leading another kind of existence. Never do they seem to have made an effort to modify their technology. Neither the examples they see of neighbouring peoples with whom they have contact, nor the clear prospect of a better life, is enough to induce in them the desire to change their ways. Some Eskimo in the northern part of America have carried on a steady commerce with their neighbours, the Athapascans and Algonquins. If they had adopted the snowshoe from these Indians instead of retaining their waterproof boot, small groups of Eskimo would have been able to pursue animals in the middle of the winter that they were unable to stop in their summer migration. But the Eskimo keep so much to their traditional organization that they hardly dream of changing.

It is by means of this technology, a social phenomenon, that Eskimo social life becomes a veritable phenomenon of symbiosis that forces the group to live like the animals they hunt. These animals concentrate and disperse according to the seasons. In winter, walruses and large numbers of seals assemble at certain points along the coast. The seal needs a sheet of ice to protect its young and also a spot where the ice is open for as long as possible in order to come and breathe easily at the surface; the number of these spots near shoals, beaches, islets and capes is fairly restricted, despite the great expanse of coastline. It is only at these points, at this time, that it is possible to hunt seal, given the technology of the Eskimo. On the other hand, as soon as the water is open and "leads" appear, the seals move and disperse to frolic in the sea, in the depths of the fiords and below the steep cliffs, and the hunters must spread out in the same way to reach them, for it is quite exceptional for seals to congregate. At the same time, the opportunities to fish in fresh water for salmon and other smaller sorts of fish and to hunt deer and reindeer in the high pastures or in the delta tundras lead to a nomadic life and a scattering in pursuit of game. During the summer, this dispersion is just as easy for the Eskimo as it is for their Indian neighbours, for they do not need snowshoes to follow and pursue the animals. As for river fishing, they do this precisely at those points where game are known to pass.

In summary, summer opens up an almost unlimited area for hunting and fishing, while winter narrowly restricts this area. This alternation provides the rhythm of concentration and dispersion for the morphological organization of Eskimo society. The population congregates or scatters like the game. The movement that animates Eskimo society is synchronized with that of the surrounding life.

Nevertheless, although biological and technological factors may have an important influence, they are insufficient to account for the total phenomenon. They provide an understanding of how it happens that the Eskimo assemble in winter and disperse in summer. But they do not explain why this concentration attains that degree of intimacy which we have already noted and which the rest of this study will confirm. They explain neither the reason for the *kashim* nor the close connection that, in some cases, seems to unite it to other houses. Eskimo dwellings could supposedly be grouped together without concentrating on this one point and without giving birth to the intense collective life which we will consider when we examine the effects of this organization. Neither need they have been long-houses. The natives could have placed their tents side by side, covered them better, or they could have constructed small houses instead of living in family groups under the same roof. One ought not to forget that the *kashim*, or men's house, and the large house where several branches of the same family reside are not confined to the Eskimo. They are found among other peoples and, consequently, cannot be the result of special features unique to the organization of these northern societies. They have to be related, in part, to certain characteristics that Eskimo culture has in common with these other cultures. These characteristics cannot be investigated here; the question, by its very generality, goes beyond the framework of this study. But the state of Eskimo technology can only account for the time of the year when these movements of concentration and dispersion occur, their duration and succession, and their marked opposition to one another.

The Effects of Eskimo Seasonal Variations

Now that we have described the seasonal variations of Eskimo morphology and have established some of their causes, we must study their effects. We will examine the way in which these variations affect the religious life of the group. This we consider to be a significant part of this study.

Effects on religious life

The religion of the Eskimo has the same rhythm as their social organization. There is, as it were, a summer religion and a winter religion; or rather, there is no religion during the summer. The only rites that are practised are private, domestic rituals: everything is reduced to the rituals of birth and death and to the observation of certain prohibitions. All the myths that (as we shall see) fill the consciousness of the Eskimo during the winter appear to be forgotten during the summer. Life is that of the layman. Even magic, which is often a purely private matter, hardly appears except as a rather simple sort of medical science whose rituals are minimal.

By contrast, the winter settlement lives in a state of continuous religious exaltation. This is the time when myths and legends are transmitted from generation to generation. The slightest event requires the more or less solemn intervention of the magicians, the *angekok*. A minor taboo can be lifted only by public ceremonies and by visits to the entire community. At every possible opportunity these events are turned into impressive performances of public shamanism to avert the famine that threatens the group, particularly during the months from March to May when hunting is unreliable and provisions are either dangerously low or have been exhausted. One can thus describe winter life as one long celebration. Earlier writers report perpetual dancing among the Eskimo of Greenland, dancing that was certainly mainly religious. Even if we take into account mistaken observations and comments, what these writers tell us is probably further evidence of this non-stop religious life. The religious mentality of the group is carried to such an extreme in several Eskimo societies that an exceptionally rigorous watch is kept for any religious failings. Any collective mishap – a storm that lasts too long, the escape of a game animal, an unfortunate break in the ice and so on – is attributed to the violation of some ritual prohibition. Such transgressions have to be publicly confessed so that their effects may be mitigated. The practice of public confession is indicative of the kind of holiness that marks the whole of winter social life.

Not only is this religious life intense, it also has a very special character which contrasts with life during the summer: it is pre-eminently collective. By this, we do not simply mean that festivities are celebrated in common, but that the feeling which the community has of itself and its unity suffuses all its actions. Festivities are not only collective in the sense that very many individuals assemble to take part; they are the object and the expression of the group.

This derives from the fact that they take place in the *kashim*, wherever there is one, and, as we have already seen, the *kashim* was once probably found everywhere. Whatever its other features may be, it is always essentially *a public place* that manifests the unity of the group. This unity is indeed so strong that, inside the *kashim*, the individuality of families and of particular houses disappears; they all merge in the totality of the society. In fact, in the *kashim*, individuals are not grouped by families or by houses but according to certain barely differentiated social functions which they perform.

[. . .]

The opposition between summer life and winter life does not, however, find expression simply in rituals, festivities and various sorts of religious ceremonies; it also profoundly affects ideas, collective representations and, in short, the entire mentality of the group.

In the course of a complex of festivities, among the Oqomiut of Baffin Land and the Nugumiut of Frobisher Bay, the population divides into two teams. The one comprises all those born during the winter; they have a special collective name and are called the *axigirn*, the "ptarmigans". The other is composed of all those born during the summer, who are called *aggirn*, the "ducks". The former represent the land; the latter the sea. Each team tugs on a rope and, depending on who is victorious, either summer or winter will prevail. This division of the population into two groups, according to the season when they were born, is not restricted to this special ritual; it forms the basis of other customs among all the central Eskimo. During their lifetime, but particularly during the festivities that we have just mentioned, individuals wear an amulet made from the skin of the animal, generally a bird, that presides over the month of their birth. It would seem from this tendency to classify people according to the season when they were born that the land birds are probably the winter birds and the sea birds are summer birds. At Angmagssalik (which is, however, far from where these other practices are observed) birth rituals certainly vary considerably depending on whether they involve a "winter" child or a "summer" child. If a child is born during the summer, his first meal consists of soup made from some land animal, or from a river fish cooked in fresh water; the "winter" child's first meal is soup from some sea animal cooked in salt water.

This division of people into two great categories appears indeed to be connected with an even greater and more general division that embraces all things. Without even discussing a number of myths in which all animals and important natural events are divided into two groups – one of winter, the other of summer – we can recognize this same idea as the basis of many ritual prohibitions. There are winter things and summer things, and the Eskimo feel the opposition between these two fundamental classes so deeply that to mix them in any way is forbidden. In the central regions, the skin of the reindeer (a summer animal) may not be brought into contact with the skin of the walrus (a winter animal); the same applies to the various objects used to hunt these two kinds of animals. When summer has begun, an Eskimo may not eat caribou (a summer animal) until he has put away all his winter clothes and put on new ones, or at the very least, until he has put on clothes that were not used during the walrus-hunting season. The small tents that shelter hunters during the summer are supposed to be buried under rocks along with the hunters' clothes; they are considered *shongeyew* or "taboo". No covering or thong of walrus-skin should be brought to any of the places where reindeer are hunted, on pain of returning empty-handed. Winter clothes, if made of caribou-skin, have to be completed before the men can leave to hunt walrus. Throughout the time the people are living on the ice, no one may work any skin, either caribou or reindeer. Neither should salmon meat, a product of summer fishing, come into contact with the flesh of any sea animal, not even in the stomach of the faithful. By contrast, contact with seal-meat is less strictly regulated since these animals are hunted throughout the year and at the same time as other animals. The violation of any of these taboos imparts to the offender a defilement that is visible to the game and is communicated by contagion to all who approach that person. Thus the game withdraw and famine follows throughout the land. In fact, the existence of these taboos has necessitated the formation of a special class of messengers whose task is to announce the capture of the first walrus. This is the sign that winter has begun. All work on caribou-skins immediately ceases. The way of life changes completely.

Thus the way in which both men and objects are classified bears the imprint of this fundamental opposition between the two seasons. Each season serves to define an entire class of beings and objects. We have already seen the basic role of this classification on the mentality of the people. One could say that the concept of summer and the concept of winter are like two poles around which revolves the system of Eskimo ideas.

[. . .]

Conclusion

The social life of the Eskimo assumes two clearly opposed forms which parallel a twofold morphology. Undoubtedly, between the two, there are transitions: a group does not always abruptly take up winter quarters nor leave them; similarly, a small summer camp is not always composed of one single family. But it still is generally true that the Eskimo have two ways of grouping, and that in accordance with these two forms there are two corresponding systems of law, two moral codes, two kinds of domestic economy and two forms of religious life. In the dense concentrations of the winter, a genuine community of ideas and material interests is formed. Its strong moral, mental and religious unity contrasts sharply with the isolation, social fragmentation and dearth of moral and religious life that occurs when everyone has scattered during the summer.

The qualitative differences that distinguish these successive and alternating cultural patterns are directly related to quantitative differences in the relative intensity of social life at these two times of the year. Winter is a season when Eskimo society is highly concentrated and in a state of continual excitement and hyperactivity. Because individuals are brought into close contact with one another, their social interactions become more frequent, more continuous and more coherent; ideas are exchanged; feelings are mutually revived and reinforced. By its existence and constant activity, the group becomes more aware of itself and assumes a more prominent place in the consciousness of individuals.

Conversely in summer, social bonds are relaxed; fewer relationships are formed, and there are fewer people with whom to make them; and thus, psychologically, life slackens its pace. The difference between these two periods of the year is, in short, as great as can possibly occur between a period of intense social activity and a phase of languid and depressed social life. This shows quite clearly that the winter house cannot be accounted for exclusively in technological terms. It is obviously one of the essential elements of Eskimo culture, appearing when the culture attains its maximum development; it becomes an absolutely integral part of it, and disappears when the culture begins to decline. The winter house is, therefore, dependent on this entire culture.

Social life among the Eskimo goes through a kind of regular rhythm. It is not uniform during the different seasons of the year. It has a high point and a low point. Yet though this curious alternation appears most clearly among the Eskimo, it is by no means confined to this culture. The pattern that we have just noted is more widespread than one would at first suspect.

First, among the American Indians, there is an important group of societies, quite considerable in themselves, that live in the same way. These are mainly the tribes of the northwest coast: Tlingit, Haida, Kwakiutl, Aht, Nootka and even a great number of Californian tribes such as the Hupa, and the Wintu. Among all these peoples there is an extreme concentration in winter and an equally extreme dispersion in summer, though there exist no absolutely necessary biological or technological reasons for this twofold organization. In keeping with this twofold morphology there are very often two systems of social life. This is notably the case among the Kwakiutl. In winter, the clan disappears, giving way to groups of an entirely different kind: secret societies or, more exactly, religious confraternities in which nobles and commoners form a hierarchy. Religious life is localized in winter; profane life is exactly like that among the Eskimo in summer. The Kwakiutl have an appropriate saying for expressing this opposition: "In summer, the sacred is below, the profane is on high; in winter, the sacred is above, the profane below." The Hupa show similar variations which were probably more marked than they are today. Many Athapascan societies, ranging from those in the far north such as the Ingalik and Chilcotin, to the Navaho of the New Mexican plateau, also have the same character.

These American Indian societies are not, however, the only ones that conform to this type. In temperate or extreme climates where the influence of the seasons is clearly evident, there occur innumerable phenomena similar to those we have studied. We can cite two particularly striking cases. First, there are the summer migrations of the pastoral mountain peoples of Europe which almost completely empty whole villages of their male population. Second, there is the seemingly reverse phenomenon that once regulated the life of the Buddhist monk in India and still regulates the lives of itinerant ascetics, now that the Buddhist *saṅgha* no longer has followers in India: during the rainy season, the mendicant ceases his wandering and re-enters the monastery.

What is more, we have only to observe what goes on around us in our western societies to discover these same rhythms. About the end of July, there occurs a summer dispersion. Urban life enters that period of sustained languor known as *vacances*, the vacation period, which continues to the end of autumn. Life then tends to revive and goes on to increase steadily

until it drops off again in June. Rural life follows the opposite pattern. In winter, the countryside is plunged into a kind of torpor; the population at this time scatters to specific points of seasonal migration; each small local or familial group turns in upon itself; there are neither means nor opportunities for gathering together; this is the time of dispersion. By contrast, in summer, everything becomes reanimated; workers return to the fields; people live out of doors in constant contact with one another. This is the time of festivities, of major projects and great revelry. Statistics reflect these regular variations in social life. Suicides, an urban phenomenon, increase from the end of autumn until June, whereas homicides, a rural phenomenon, increase from the beginning of spring until the end of summer, when they become fewer.

All this suggests that we have come upon a law that is probably of considerable generality. Social life does not continue at the same level throughout the year; it goes through regular, successive phases of increased and decreased intensity, of activity and repose, of exertion and recuperation. We might almost say that social life does violence to the minds and bodies of individuals which they can sustain only for a time; and there comes a point when they must slow down and partially withdraw from it. We have seen examples of this rhythm of dispersion and concentration, of individual life and collective life. Instead of being the necessary and determining cause of an entire system, truly seasonal factors may merely mark the most opportune occasions in the year for these two phases to occur. After the long revelries of the collective life which fill the winter, each Eskimo needs to live a more individual life; after long months of communal living filled with feasts and religious ceremonies, an Eskimo needs a profane existence. We know, in fact, that the Eskimo are delighted with this change, for it seems to come as a response to a natural need. Undoubtedly, the technological factors which we have noted account for the order in which these alternate movements succeed one another during the year; but if these factors did not exist, this alternation would still perhaps take place, though in a somewhat different way. One fact would tend to confirm this viewpoint. When favourable circumstances such as a major whale catch or the possibility of a large market bring the Eskimo of the Bering Strait and of Point Barrow together in the summer, the *kashim* temporarily reappears. And with it come all the ceremonies, wild dancing, feasts and public exchanges that usually take place there. The seasons are not the direct determining cause of the phenomena they occasion; they act, rather, upon the social density that they regulate.

The climacteric conditions of Eskimo life can be accounted for only by the contrast between the two phases of the year and the clearness of their opposition. As a result, among these people, the phenomenon is so easily observed that it almost springs to view, but very likely it can be found elsewhere. Furthermore, though this major seasonal rhythm is the most apparent, it may not be the only one; there are probably other lesser rhythms within each season, each month, each week, each day. Each social function probably has a rhythm of its own. Without wishing for a moment to offer these speculations as established truths, we believe that they are worth mentioning, for they offer serious possibilities for fruitful research.

Whatever the value of these remarks, however, there is another general conclusion to this work that deserves the same attention.

We have proposed, as a methodological rule, that social life in all its forms – moral, religious, and legal – is dependent on its mate-rial substratum and that it varies with this substratum, namely with the mass, density, form and composition of human groups. Until now, this hypothesis has been verified in only a few important cases. It has been shown, for example, how the respective evolution of criminal and civil law depends on a society's type of morphology; how individual beliefs develop or decline depending on the degree of integration or disintegration of familial, religious or political groups; and how the mentality of primitive tribes directly reflects their social organization. But the observations and comparisons upon which these laws depend allow some room for doubt that may apply *a fortiori* to the general principle that we initially stated. The phenomena we have studied could well be dependent on other unknown factors in addition to morphological variations. Eskimo societies, however, offer a rare example of a test case which Bacon would have regarded as crucial. Among the Eskimo, at the very moment when the form of the group changes, one can observe the simultaneous transformation of religion, law and moral life. This case has the same clarity and precision as an experiment would have in a laboratory and it is repeated every year with an absolute invariability. Henceforth we can say that this sociological proposition is relatively established. Therefore the present study has, at least, this methodological advantage: it has shown how the analysis of one clearly defined case can establish a general law better than the accumulation of facts or endless deduction.

NOTES

1. The founder of this discipline was Friedrich Ratzel, whose principal works, *Anthropogeographie* (vol. 1, 2nd ed., 1899; vol. 2, 1st ed., 1891) and *Politische Geographie* (1897), were reviewed in the *Année sociologique* along with other works of the same kind. See *Année sociologique*, vol. 2, 1899, pp. 522 ff.; vol. 3, 1900, pp. 550 ff.; vol. 4, 1901, pp. 565 ff.; vol. 6, 1903, pp. 539 ff.; vol. 8, 1905, pp. 613, 621. For a résumé by Ratzel, see *Année sociologique*, vol. 3, 1900, pp. 1–14.

2. The house is called an *iglu*.

6

The Great Basin Shoshonean Indians: An Example of a Family Level of Sociocultural Integration

Julian H. Steward

Cultural Ecology

The types of cultures and processes of development illustrated in this and following chapters [of *Theory of Culture Change: The Methodology of Multilinear Evolution*] are arranged in a sequence of successively higher levels of sociocultural integration.[1] This does not imply a unilinear evolutionary sequence of cultural development. Since particular cultures have unlike configurations and element content resulting from their distinctive origins, histories, and ecological adaptations, many different local or areal types of culture may represent the same level of sociocultural integration. Thus, the Shoshonean Indians of the Great Basin and the Eskimo illustrate an essentially family level of integration, although their respective ways of life and cultural types differed quite profoundly. Every level could be exemplified by several different cultures, some representing cross-culturally recurrent types and others unique developments.

The Shoshonean-speaking Indians – the Ute, Western Shoshoni, and Northern Paiute of western Colorado, Utah, Nevada, and eastern Oregon and California – acquired most of their hunting and gathering techniques from other peoples, but their general adaptation to the intermontane steppes and deserts was so distinctive that they constitute a special culture area usually called the Great Basin or Basin-Plateau area. In a quantitative sense, this culture was extremely simple. An "element list," which breaks the culture down into details such as basket weaves and shapes, religious beliefs, social practices, and other details, includes a total of about 3,000 items. By comparison, the U. S. forces landing at Casa Blanca during World War II unloaded 500,000 items of material equipment alone. The total "elements" of modern American culture would probably run to several million.

Shoshonean culture, however, is of interest for the nature of its organization as much as for its quantitative simplicity. Virtually all cultural activities were carried out by the family in comparative isolation from other families. A contrast with modern America helps clarify this point. In the United States today, people are highly specialized workers in an economic system geared to national and international patterns; education is increasingly standardized and the community or state takes over this function from the family when the child is six years old or younger; health practices are dictated largely by research carried out on an international scale and in part administered by the state and community; recreation more and more involves the consumption of products made by national organizations; religious worship is carried on in national or international churches. These growing functions of the community, state, and nation increasingly relieve the family of functions it performed in earlier historical periods. It is perhaps difficult to imagine that a family, alone and unaided, could obtain virtually all the food it consumed; manufacture all its clothing, household goods, and other articles; rear and train its children without assistance; take care of its sick except in time of crisis; be self-sufficient in its religious activities; and, except on special occasions, manage its own recreation. Why this was so in the case of the Shoshoneans is explainable largely in terms of their cultural ecological adaptations.

Owing to the nature of the natural environment of the Great Basin area and to the simple hunting and gathering techniques for exploiting it, it was inevitable that the individual family or at the most two or three related families should live in isolation during most of the year. "Family" in this case signifies the nuclear, biological or bilateral family, consisting of mother, father, and children. Unlike many primitive peoples, the Shoshoneans were not organized in extended family or lineage groups and, although, as we shall see subsequently, the immediate family was frequently enlarged through plural spouses and different families were closely allied by marriage, the functioning unit was the nuclear family, augmented only by a grandparent, aunt, or uncle who otherwise would be homeless.

Environment and Resources

The natural resources which were exploitable by Shoshonean culture were so limited that the population was extremely sparse. In the more fertile portions of this area there was perhaps one person to five square miles, while in the vast stretches of nearly waterless terrain the ratio was one to fifty or even one hundred square miles. The mean for the whole area was between one person to twenty or thirty square miles.

The territory once inhabited by the Shoshonean Indians is extremely arid, but technically most of it is classified as "steppe" rather than true "desert" although there are large areas devoid of vegetation. The country consists of large arid valleys lying between mountain ranges which run north and south. These valleys are from five to twenty miles wide and twenty to eighty miles long. The greater portion of the Shoshonean habitat lies within the Great Basin, a vast area of interior drainage between the Wasatch Mountains of Utah and the Sierra Nevada Range of California and Oregon, but it also includes portions of the Columbia River Plateau of Idaho and eastern Oregon and the Colorado River Plateau of eastern Utah and western Colorado.

The flora and fauna of all these areas are very similar. There are several biotic zones, which set the basic conditions for a society equipped only with very simple hunting and gathering techniques. In the valleys, which lie between 4,000 and 6,000 feet elevation, the low rainfall – five to twenty inches a year – together with high evaporation supports a predominantly xerophytic vegetation, that is, such drought-resisting plants as sagebrush and greasewood. This vegetation has very limited value to human beings or animals. Plants bearing edible seeds and roots occur in some abundance immediately along the stream banks, but, except in favored areas, such as the piedmont of the Wasatch Mountains and the Sierra Nevada Mountains, the streams are small and widely-spaced. In the Great Basin, the streams end in saline marshes or lakes. In the vast sandy areas between the streams, the quantity of edible plants depends directly upon rainfall, which varies from year to year and from place to place. These plants only afforded small quantities of food for the Indians, and they could not support game in herds comparable to the bison of the Great Plains or the caribou of the far north. The two species of greatest importance to the Indians were antelope and rabbits. These not only supplied meat and skins, but the communal hunts in which they were sometimes taken were among the few collective cultural activities. The numbers of both species, however, were limited, and the hunts were infrequent.

It is impossible to estimate the quantitative importance of different animal foods in the valley zone, but the Shoshoneans probably ate more rats, mice, gophers, locusts, ants, ant eggs, larvae of flies which breed in the salt lakes, snakes, and lizards than large game. In the rivers, such as the Owyhee, John Day, Crooked, Snake, Truckee, Carson, Walker, and Humboldt rivers, fish were an important supplement to other foods, but the runs were seasonal, the quantity did not compare with that of fish in coastal rivers, and the fish were evidently not suited for preservation and storage.

The zone of piñon and juniper trees lies between about 6,000 and 8,000 or 9,000 feet. This zone is largely restricted to the flanks of the mountain ranges since most valleys lie below this altitude. The juniper had little value to the Indians except for its wood, but the piñon (*Pinus monophylla* in the north, *Pinus edulis* in the south), which occurred throughout the Shoshonean area to a little north of the Humboldt River in Nevada, yielded pine nuts which were the most important of all food species. North of the piñon area, the seeds of certain other species of pines were eaten, but they were a relatively minor item in the diet. Since there was greater rainfall in the piñon-juniper belt than in the valleys, this zone afforded more seeds, roots, and grasses, and it had more game, especially deer. But it constitutes only a small portion of the total area, and the growing season is short. A few mountain ranges rise above 8,000 or 9,000 feet into the zone of the ponderosa pine, where vegetation is lush and where mountain sheep as well as deer were hunted.

The Shoshonean tribes were of necessity gatherers of vegetable foods and lower forms of animal life rather than hunters. They utilized nearly a hundred species of wild plants. The more important of these yielded small, hard-shelled seeds, which were collected in conical basketry containers, roasted with live coals in shallow baskets, ground on flat stones or metates, and eaten from basketry bowls. In the higher altitudes and latitudes where rainfall is greater, roots were relatively more important as food. When seeds and roots could not be had, especially in early spring, leafy vegetables or greens from many plants were eaten.

Socially Fragmenting Effect of the Cultural Ecology

All of the plant and animal foods had in common the extremely important characteristic that the place and quantity of their occurrence from year to year were unpredictable, owing largely to variations in rainfall. A locality might be very fertile one year and attract large numbers of families, but offer little food for several years thereafter. Few localities had foods in sufficient quantity and reliability to permit permanent settlements. Throughout most of the area, the families were concerned predominantly with warding off potential starvation by moving from place to place. These movements were determined by reports from friends or relatives about the probable quantities of foods to be had. Families from different localities would assemble at places where food was temporarily plentiful, but, owing to the impossibility of storing large quantities of food for the future, they soon dispersed to seek elsewhere.

The typical Shoshoni family living in the piñon area of Nevada traveled alone or with one or two related families during the spring and summer, seeking seeds, roots, various small mammals, rodents, insects, larvae, and other edible items. In the late summer when a family heard reports that the pine nuts seemed very promising in a certain portion of a mountain range, it arranged its travels so as to arrive in that locality in late October or early November, when the first frosts would have opened the cones and made the nuts ready to harvest. Other families who had also been foraging for food within a radius of perhaps twenty to thirty miles of that locality came there for the same reason.

In gathering the pine nuts, each family restricted itself by common understanding to a limited area, because there were so many pine nuts in the locality as a whole that no one could gather them all before they dropped and because each family could harvest more if it worked alone. The different families remained from several hundred yards to a mile or more apart. Each gathered pine nuts as rapidly as it could and stored them in earth caches. If the harvest was good, it might support the family throughout most of the winter.

The winter encampment consisted of perhaps twenty or thirty families within easy visiting distance of one another. Early spring generally found the people suffering more or less acutely from hunger. The families then had to go their separate ways to forage for greens, game, and any other foods they could find. Throughout spring and summer, the migrations of a particular family, although limited in general to the terrain it knew well, were determined almost week to week by its knowledge of available foods. It might learn that sand grass seeds were promising in one place, rabbits numerous elsewhere, fly larvae abundant in a certain lake, and antelope ready for a communal hunt under a shaman or medicine man over in the next valley.

Although the pine nut was perhaps the most important factor in determining the whereabouts of the winter encampment and which families would be associated in it, most other foods had a very similar effect in causing seasonal variations in interfamilial contacts. Owing to yearly and local variations in rainfall, the whereabouts of other wild seed and root crops and animal resources was unpredictable. Rabbits might be so numerous in a portion of a valley in a given year that people would assemble from considerable distances to hold a communal hunt. Several years might then follow before it was worthwhile to hold another such hunt in the same place, whereas rabbits were ready for a hunt in an adjoining valley the next year. The same was true of antelope. A co-operative hunt would so reduce the antelope that it required eight or ten years for their number to be restored. Even such foods as grasshoppers and locusts, or "Mormon crickets," were unpredictable. In certain years locusts occurred in such numbers as to be a major source of food to the Indians – and a plague to the modern farmers – and then

during several years they were of no importance.

A limitation of the value of animal products was the absence of preservation and storing techniques. Rabbits, antelope, and fish might afford more meat than the people who assembled to take them could eat, but after a few days or weeks, they spoiled. Fish, unlike other animal species, occurred with some annual regularity in fixed places. During runs, a considerable number of families came from far and wide to fish for a few weeks, after which they had to disperse in search of other foods. Had the Shoshoneans been able to dry and smoke fish, like the Northwest Coast Indians, it is possible that fairly large permanent populations might have developed along certain of the better fishing streams and lakes. In the absence of this possibility, the winter inhabitants of these areas were limited to the few families who used fish as a supplement to other foods. Consequently, the effect of fishing resources on social groups was like that of other foods: it permitted large aggregates of people to assemble for short periods and it helped tide a small number of local families over the winter.

Shoshonean society was affected not only by the erratic and unpredictable occurrence of practically all principal foods and by the limited technical skills for harvesting and storing most of them, but it was also shaped by the predominant importance of wild vegetable products, which put a premium upon family separatism rather than upon co-operation. Anyone who has gathered wild berries in a party knows that he can pick far more if he finds a patch of his own. Unlike certain forms of hunting – for example, collective rabbit drives or antelope hunts – participation of many persons in seed and root gathering not only failed to increase the per capita harvest, but it generally decreased it so greatly that individual families preferred to forage alone so as not to compete with other families.

The competitive aspect of seed and root gathering together with the erratic annual occurrence of practically all principal foods and the inability of the people to store foods in any locality in sufficient amount to permit considerable numbers of families to remain there for a major portion of the year, all contributed to the fragmentation of Shoshonean society into nuclear family units, which moved about the country seasonally and annually in a unpredictable itinerary.

Property

The concept of property rights among the Shoshoneans was directly related to their mode of life. These Indians assumed that rights to exclusive use of anything resulted from work expended by particular individuals or groups and from habitual use. This is a rather obvious, simple, and practical concept, and it seems to have entailed a minimum of conflict.

In most parts of the area, natural resources were available to anyone. The seeds gathered by a woman, however, belonged to her because she had done the work of converting a natural resource into something that could be directly consumed. If a man made a bow or built a house, these were his, although prior to making objects of them, the trees he utilized belonged to no one. Any family might fish in a certain river or stream, but if a group of families built a fish weir, it alone had the right to use that weir.

When a number of families came into potential conflict in the utilization of natural resources, the same principle held. In seed gathering, it was "first come, first served." The families which entered a seed plot or piñon grove selected the best portion and, by virtue of having started to work on it, had prior rights. Other families gathered pine nuts elsewhere, which was reasonable and necessary because if they gathered in competition with the first family, all would have harvested less. In rabbit drives, the person who clubbed or shot a rabbit or who owned the net which caught it had first claim. In deer or mountain sheep hunting, the man whose arrow first entered the game was entitled to the skin and the choice portions of the meat.

This principle of property rights was essential to survival in the Shoshonean area. Owing to the erratic annual and local occurrence of foods, the arbitrary exclusion of territorially delimited groups of families from utilization of other territories would have caused starvation and death. With few exceptions, the habitat of most families always provided such uncertain subsistence that the territorial interpenetration of families living in different localities was necessary to the survival of all. The absence of property claims of local groups to delimitable areas of natural resources upon which work had not been expended was the corollary of the fragmented nature of Shoshonean society.

In a few portions of the Great Basin, such as Owens Valley in eastern California, which was occupied by Northern Paiute, the many streams flowing from the high Sierra Nevada Range afforded food resources which were comparatively so abundant and reliable that each family could be reasonably certain of finding enough to eat within one or two days' travel from a permanent village. Instead of wandering an unpredictable course determined by the vicissitudes of nature, these families were able to make forays from permanent headquarters. Habitual use of resources within readily accessible portions of the terrain led to the concept that each local village or group of villages had exclusive rights to resources within bounded areas. This economic stability and permanent residence of a particular group of families provided a basis for association, leadership, and organization in band groups.

Co-operation and Leadership as Integrating Factors

The typical Shoshonean family was independent and self-sufficient during the greater part of the year, perhaps during 80 or 90 percent of the time. It subsisted and fulfilled most cultural functions with little assistance from other families. It probably could have survived in complete isolation.

But human history provides no instances in which nuclear families had progeny and perpetuated their culture without associating with and intermarrying with other families. Moreover, nuclear families have always co-operated with other families in various ways. Since this is so, the Shoshoneans, like other fragmented family groups, represent a family level of sociocultural integration only in a relative sense. It is relative in that most societies having a higher level of intergration possess patterns of co-operation and leadership among a permanent membership. I classify the Shoshoneans as an exemplification of a family level of sociocultural integration because in the few forms of collective activity the same group of families did not co-operate with one another or accept the same leader on successive occasions. By another definition, however, it might be entirely permissible to view this ever-changing membership and leadership as a special form of suprafamilial integration. While the Shoshoneans represent a family level of sociocultural integration in a relative sense, their suprafamilial patterns of integration involved no permanent social groups of fixed membership despite several kinds of interfamilial co-operation.

Collective hunting

The most important co-operation consisted of collective hunts. In these hunts, rabbits, antelope, deer, and mud hens were the principal species taken. Communal hunts could be held, however, only when there was sufficient game, when a considerable number of families could assemble, and when an appropriate leader was available. Under these circumstances, co-operation yielded many times the quantity of game that individuals, expending the same effort, could take alone.

The principal collective hunt was the rabbit drive. It could be held fairly often, and it yielded not only meat which could be consumed during a short period but furs which, cut into long strips and twisted, were woven into robes and blankets. The only distinctive technical feature of these drives was a net of about the height and mesh of a modern tennis net but often several hundred feet long. A number of these nets were placed end to end to form a huge semicircle. Men, women, children, and dogs beat the brush over a wide area, gradually closing in so that rabbits which were not clubbed or shot by the drivers became entangled in the nets, where they were killed.

Custom determined the several crucial aspects of the drive and the division of game. Experienced men – in recent years called rather appropriately "rabbit bosses" – were given supreme authority to co-ordinate all activities in this fairly complex operation. They chose the locality of the drive, directed disposition of nets, regulated the drivers, and divided the game according to customary understandings. Anyone who killed a rabbit with a bow or throwing stick in the course of the drive could claim it. Since, however, only a few families owned rabbit nets, net owners received a somewhat greater portion of the rabbits caught in the nets.

In spite of the rather rigid direction of these drives, there were several reasons why they did not bring about permanent integration or cohesion of territorial or social groups of fixed membership. First, drives were held only when rabbits were sufficiently numerous in a particular locality. Second, participants in the drive consisted of families who, because of the rather fortuitous annual occurrence of seeds and other foods in one place or another, happened to be in the locality where the drive was worth holding. Third, the drive was held only if an experienced leader and families owning nets happened to be present. Since the occurrence of these factors was rather haphazard, since the place, the participants, and the leaders were never quite the same in successive years, the drives provided only temporary bonds between independent families. A given family was under no obligation whatever to participate in a drive with a fixed group of families under a permanent leader. And, since the "rabbit boss" held authority only during the drive, the family paid little heed to him in other times, places, and contexts.

The communal antelope hunt had a social function like that of the rabbit drive. It was held in any given locality at intervals of several years and the participants consisted of those families which happened to be in the vicinity. It was held less frequently than the rabbit drive because it took much longer for the antelope herds to recover their number. A major difference in form rather than function between the rabbit drive and the antelope hunt is that whereas the former were led by men of experience and prestige – qualifications which anyone might develop – the latter were led by "antelope shamans." According to Shoshonean belief, these men were qualified less by their practical ability – though no doubt they were far from incompetent – than by their possession of supernatural power which enabled them to charm the antelope into a state of helplessness.

The practical procedures in the antelope drives were as appropriate to the situation as those in the rabbit hunts. The people built a brush corral from which wings, consisting of piles of brush or stones, extended outward a half mile or so. Drivers spread out several miles from the corral, formed a line across the valley, and slowly closed in, urging the antelope between the wings and into the corral. Antelope differ from rabbits in that they not only flee from something threatening but they are drawn by curiosity toward strange objects. The antelope shaman evidently became one of the chief functionaries in native Shoshonean culture because his role combined this peculiarity of antelope with a basic belief about sickness. It was thought by many primitive peoples, including the Shoshoneans, that sickness might be caused by loss of one's soul. While the antelope shaman was not a curer of human ills, he was thought to possess the power to capture the souls of antelope before the hunt began and thus irresistably to draw them into the corral, where he stood during the drive.

The shaman's authority was very great during these drives, but he had no voice in other activities. Moreover, even this socioreligious leadership like the lay authority found in rabbit drives failed to integrate social groups of fixed membership.

The other hunting activities involved much less co-operation than rabbit and antelope drives. Mud hen hunts were held only by small groups in the lake areas, while deer drives, held in the mountains, were infrequent and involved few persons.

Dancing, gambling, and visiting

The interfamilial associations of the Shoshonean Indians had to be adapted, as previously shown, to the exigencies of obtaining food by means of the techniques known to them. Although these families foraged throughout most of the year in isolation, their contacts with other families over many generations had contributed certain social patterns which strengthened bonds between them.

Whenever groups of Shoshonean families were together, they carried out certain recreational activities, such as dancing and gambling. Dancing, although popular, was originally limited to the circle dance, a performance in which men and women formed a circle and sidestepped to the accompaniment of singing. Gambling games were extremely numerous and included several forms of dice, the handgame, sports such as racing and hockey, and games of skill such as the hoop-and-pole game and archery. Both dancing and games, however, could be held only when local abundance of food, such as rabbits, locusts, antelope, or pine nuts, made large gatherings possible. After a rabbit or antelope drive, for instance, people might dance and gamble for several days until the meat supply was exhausted, when each family had to go its separate way in the unending food quest.

Interfamilial contacts were not limited to such formalized activities as hunting, dancing, and gambling. Visiting was an important integrating fact since people were always eager to associate with one another whether or not they danced and gambled. They preferred to visit with relatives, but when food was plentiful, a large number of unrelated families could assemble.

Hostilities and warfare

In aboriginal times most of the Shoshonean people had no national or tribal warfare. There were no territorial rights to be defended, no military honors to be gained, and no means of organizing groups of individuals for concerted action. When war parties of neighboring peoples invaded their country, the Shoshoneans ran away more often than they fought.

Hostilities generally consisted of feuds, not organized military action, and they resulted largely from the suspicion of witchcraft and from woman-stealing. They were therefore as often intratribal as intertribal. Death was generally ascribed to supernatural causes, especially to shamans, whose normally beneficent power had turned bad, perhaps even without the shaman's knowledge, and it was avenged by slaying the suspect. Usually, the malignant shaman was identified either as the person who had treated the deceased or as a member of a somewhat distant group. Accusations of witchcraft were rarely directed against relatives because kinship relations were too important to be endangered. It was, in fact, one of the most important kinship obligations to avenge the death of a relative. Once revenge had been taken, a series of reprisals and counter-reprisals might follow. These were purely personal and could not involve definable suprafamilial groups, for such groups did not exist.

The rise of predatory bands

After the Shoshonean tribes acquired horses and the territory was occupied by white settlers, warfare of a collective nature developed. Under aboriginal conditions, horses had little value because they consumed the very plants upon which the Indians depended while contributing little to the hunting of rabbits, antelope, or deer. The few horses acquired in early times were eaten. When immigrant trains crossed the area and when white settlers introduced irrigation, crops, and livestock into the country, horses enabled the previously dispersed families to amalgamate and remain fairly constantly together in *predatory bands*, which lived somewhat parasitically by raiding the whites. Warfare involved in raiding and in defense against white reprisals was the principal if not sole function of these bands, and the chiefs had authority over little other than raiding activities. It was only among the Northern Shoshoni of Wind River, Wyoming, and of eastern Idaho and the Bannock, who probably acquired horses by 1800, that bison hunting and native warfare of the Plains type were also functions of the native bands. The Ute received horses sometime after 1820, and their bands were essentially predatory, first in raiding people outside their territory and later in raiding the Mormons and other white settlers inside it. The Western Shoshoni and Northern Paiute continued to be dispersed in family units until about 1845, after which mounted bands rapidly developed. Mounted bands were dissolved among the Shoshonean peoples by 1870 or soon thereafter when the United States Army defeated them.

In understanding the quite specialized nature of these predatory bands and the restricted authority of the chiefs, it is important to note that the bands probably never involved all the people of any region. During the early phases of band operations, there were many families which had no horses and continued to live according to the older pattern of family separatism while some of their friends and relatives engaged in raiding. Later, when the United States Army opposed the raiders, the Indians had to decide whether to continue to fight or whether to accept peace, relinquish certain territory, and live on reservations. At this stage, there were two kinds of chiefs. The first were leaders of predatory bands which were now on the defensive. The second were spokesmen for those who advocated peace and the signing of treaties.

After the Indians were defeated, the division between peaceful and warring factions soon faded and the functions of war leaders were eliminated. Thenceforth, the principal need for leaders was to deal with the white men, especially with the officials of the United States government.

Religion

Religion integrated families with one another only to a minor degree. Shoshonean culture lacked collective social and economic activities and common interests, except the communal hunts, dancing, and gaming previously mentioned. There was no functional need for ceremonialism dedicated to group purposes and led by priests holding a definite office. The communal antelope hunt was directed by a special shaman, but this leader did not serve any permanent group.

The relationship between human beings and supernatural powers was conceived largely as a matter of individual concern. Every person hoped to acquire a supernatural power or guardian spirit. This power, manifest in the form of animals, plants, clouds, mountains, and other natural phenomena, came to him in dreams and gave him special abilities, such as gambling luck, hunting skill, endurance, and others of benefit to himself alone. Shamans' powers differed from those of ordinary persons mainly in the ability to cure sickness in other people. The shaman did not lead group ceremonies. His curing performances might attract large numbers of families which happened to be in the vicinity because they liked not only to watch his singing, dancing, trance, laying-on-of-hands, and other rites but to visit other families. Shamans were influential because their curing abilities gave them prestige while their presumed capacity for practicing black magic made them feared, but they carried no specific authority.

A minor collective religious activity designed for the common good was the circle dance, which, according to the belief of some of the Western Shoshoni, promoted general fertility and benefited everyone. Harris (1940) reported that the Tosavits or White Knife Shoshoni of northern Nevada held group ceremonies for general welfare. It is more likely, however, that the principal feature of such ceremonies was the circle dance, which was held by whatever families came together at various stages of their food quest, and that the religious aspect was secondary and incidental to the recreational purpose. The "dance boss" was certainly not a religious leader. Similarly, the bear dance of the Ute was primarily recreational and only secondarily religious in heralding the spring season and providing protection against bears. Its leader, like that of the circle dance, was a layman.

Winter encampments

The only prolonged accessibility of families to one another occurred in the winter encampments. These winter quarters have sometimes been called villages, but they were not tightly nucleated settlements which constituted organized communities. Instead, family houses were widely scattered within productive portions of the piñon zone. The location of each household was determined primarily by its pine nut caches and secondarily by accessibility to wood and water. The scattered families were able to visit one another to dance, gamble, and exchange gossip, and the men occasionally co-operated in a deer or mountain sheep hunt. Although dances and collective hunts required co-ordination, the leaders had no authority outside the particular activity.

Other interfamilial and interpersonal relationships were determined by customary usage. Disputes and hostilities arising from such matters as murder, theft, wife-stealing, and other violations of custom were settled between families. None of these was a "crime" against the community, for the community did not exist in any corporate or legal sense. Violations of custom threatened families, not larger socially integrated units. Thus, the very concept of crime presupposes some kind of suprafamily level of integration, some collectivity, which has a common purpose that must be protected against antisocial behavior by its members.

In addition to the leaders of special activities, each village or local area of scattered winter houses usually had a man of some importance whom modern Shoshonean informants frequently call the "village chief." So far as "chief" implies permanent authority over an identifiable group, this term is a complete misnomer, for this man had no authority and he served only one function. This function, however, was extremely important. It was to act as a clearing-house of information about where foods could be found. Since the Shoshoneans were constantly on the verge of starvation, especially at the end of winter, knowledge of where greens, seeds, rabbits, insects, and other foods were to be had made the repository of such information the most important person in the village.

The winter village cannot be considered a genuine suprafamilial form of social integration because it lacked permanent membership and even permanent location. Each year, families came from a general area to a locality of abundant pine nuts. Leaders were accepted by common consent to control such collective activities as required co-ordination. It was only in the few regions of uncommonly abundant and reliable food that a group of fixed membership occupied one or more permanent villages throughout most of the year and had a true village chief and permanent leaders of other activities.

Food-named groups

Considerable confusion concerning the nature of groups named according to special foods is found in the literature starting with the early accounts of the Shoshoneans and perpetuated in modern ethnographic studies.[2] It was the native custom throughout practically all of the area to name the people occupying different localities by some important or striking food found in them. Thus, several different and widely-separated groups were called Rabbit Eaters and Fish Eaters. Other names were Pine Nut Eaters, Ground Hog Eaters, Grass Seed Eaters, and the like. These names, however, did not designate definable groups but were merely applied to whoever happened to be in the locality. Since there were no bands and no territorial limitations on movements in search of food, families frequently traveled from one food area to another and were known by the local name in each. Just as a Washingtonian today becomes a New Yorker upon living in New York, so a Ground Hog Eater of western Idaho became a Salmon Eater if he moved to the Snake River.

Most of the early accounts of the Shoshoneans were written after wars with the whites began and predatory bands developed. Sometimes these bands were named after their leaders and sometimes after the food area from which the leader and many of his followers came. Writers therefore assumed that the inhabitants of these food-named localities constituted aboriginal, territorial bands under overall chieftainship. Data previously cited show clearly that this could not have been the case. The food-named areas were far too large for a foot people to associate in collective activities, even had the nature of Shoshonean subsistence not precluded integration in bands. After the whites entered the country, the "chiefs" of predatory bands not only failed to enlist the support of the peace faction in their own place of origin but their followers included persons from many other food-named areas.

Throughout the greater part of the area, therefore, food-names were a designation of people in a certain large region and nothing more. They implied no economic, recreational, religious, social, or political co-operation that would require collective action and lead to suprafamilial forms of integration.

Kinship Relations

The economic and social relations of Shoshonean families previously described may be likened to a net in that each family had occasional associations with families on all sides of it and these latter with families farther away and these with still others so that there were no social, economic or political frontiers. The entire area consisted of interlocking associations of family with family. So far as subsistence, recreational, and religious activities are concerned, however, the analogy of a net is not entirely apt because no family was necessarily and consistently associated with certain other families. The net lacked knots; each family was at liberty to associate with whom it pleased. Kinship relations, however, supplied the knots and made a fabric of what otherwise would have been a skein of loose threads, each of which shifted about somewhat randomly. This is not to say that Shoshonean society was based on extended ties of kinship which gave cohesion to any definable group. The activities of a given family month by month were dictated primarily by the food quest, which took precedence over every other consideration. But marriage bonds were fairly enduring, and they created a strong fabric of close relationships, which extended from one locality to the next. They also made interfamilial economic and recreational associations somewhat less random, for kin preferred to co-operate with one another when possible. Moreover, the very absence of socioeconomic unity among inhabitants of local areas made the kinship ties seem relatively more important.

The irreducible minimum of Shoshonean society was the nuclear or biological family. Isolated individuals could not well survive in this cultural-environmental or ecological situation, and unmarried or widowed persons generally attached themselves to a nuclear family. This family was able to carry out most activities necessary to existence, for husband and wife complemented each other in food-getting and together they procreated, reared, and socialized their children. Women gathered vegetable foods, made the baskets needed for this purpose, and prepared all food. Men devoted most of their time to hunting, which, though not very rewarding, was extremely important and time consuming. It was important not only because meat was a desired dietary item, but because hides and furs were needed for clothing. The scarcity of game and the difficulty of hunting is evidenced by the fact that few men were able to kill enough deer or antelope to clothe their families in skin garments or even to make moccasins. Many persons were naked and barefoot during the summer, and in winter had only a rabbit skin blanket which served both as a robe and as bedding.

In the household, women maintained the home and took care of the children. Men also played an important part in child-rearing. In the absence of toys and games designed expressly for children, boys played with small bows and arrows and other objects used by men, while girls imitated their mothers. In this way, children quickly learned the rudiments of adult functions and absorbed the attitudes, values, and beliefs of their parents. This learning was accomplished largely within the context of the family, for association with other families was limited.

In the course of the very uncertain wanderings and activities of Shoshonean life, the most frequent associates of the members of a nuclear family were members of families with which they had intermarried. These families were companions on seed and root gathering trips, when there was enough food for several families to travel together, and they co-operated in hunting. Relatives were the favored visitors, and often a few families would camp together and spend evenings gossiping and telling legends. Relatives were to be counted on for support if suspicion of witchcraft led to a feud. And they, more than others, were willing to share food in times of shortage.

These close interfamilial bonds were expressed in the marriage system. Marriage was more a contract between families than between individuals. The preferred arrangement was several marriages between the

children of two families. When a young man married, it was desired that his wife's brother marry his sister. Several brothers and sisters might marry several sisters and brothers. Shoshonean culture permitted plural spouses, wherein the same principle prevailed. If a man took several wives, custom prescribed that they be sisters, and penalties were imposed for failure to follow this custom. If a man's wife died, he was obligated to take her sister as his next wife. In a parallel way, a certain amount of polyandry, or plural husbands, was permitted. A woman might take a younger brother of her husband as a temporary spouse until he found a wife. If the husband died, his family was obligated to furnish a brother of the first husband if possible.

It was, of course, biologically impossible that the number and sex of siblings in two intermarrying families should be such that this cultural ideal could be met. Moreover, marriages of the parental and grandparental generation extended marital ties to many families. While marital ties often linked the younger generation of two families to one another somewhat more closely than either was linked to other families, the general pattern was one of innumerable interfamilial linkages extending over a wide area. It meant that a family in a given locality could probably find consanguinal or marital kin of one kind or another among a large proportion of the families which ranged its own territory and among many families farther afield.

These interfamilial marital and kinship bonds were not unbreakable, for, despite the contractual nature of marriage, separations or divorces were common. Individual temperament, incompatibility, and other factors were not to be discounted. Nonetheless, the cultural ideal ascribed these arrangements considerable importance. And this importance derived largely from the fact that these kinship bonds were the principal integrating factors in a cultural-environmental situation where the subsistence pattern prevented the development of bands, villages, or other social units consisting of permanent members having prescribed relationships to one another.

These marital and kinship ties were the knots of the social fabric of the various peoples in the Shoshonean area, but they did not constitute sociocultural frontiers. Marriage was contracted most often between families in contact with one another, but it was not governed by territorial or political units. While it united strands in the netlike fabric of Shoshonean society, it could not consolidate or integrate local groups in a political, social, or economic sense. To the contrary, it cut across local boundaries, making interfamilial ties diffuse and thus actually militating against band or community development.

The Theoretical Significance of the Shoshoneans

In a classification of cultures based on the concept of area, the Shoshoneans should probably be included in the Greater Southwest; for more of their culture elements, especially their material culture or technology, seem to have been derived from the Southwest than from any other area. Their economic, political, social, religious, and hostility patterns – general configurations which are not reducible to culture elements – were, however, wholly unlike those of the Southwest. Owing to the cultural ecological processes – to the exploitation of their particular environment by means of the techniques available to them – families functioned independently in most cultural activities, and the few collective interfamilial pursuits did not serve to give permanent cohesion to extended families, bands, communities, or other higher levels of sociocultural integration as in the Southwest.

The Shoshonean peoples were not unique in having a family level of integration. This level is also represented in North America by the Eskimo and in South America by the Nambicuara, Guató, Mura, and perhaps other groups. But this similarity of level does not mean that these tribes belonged to the same cultural type. In all cases, the food quest was of overwhelming importance, but, owing to the differences in environment and exploitative techniques, it entailed very unlike activities and associations between families. Perhaps there have been people similar to the Shoshoneans in other parts of the world; for the present, however, the Shoshoneans must be regarded as typologically unique.

This typological distinctiveness makes the Shoshoneans unique in cultural evolution. If the predecessors of any people who later developed to a community or state level were like the Shoshoneans, we have no way of knowing it. Even if all groups of mankind had begun their cultural evolution with sociocultural units integrated only on a family level, which is doubtful and certainly unprovable, it would not follow that they all had the same cultural configuration, that is, the same cultural type, as the Shoshoneans. Paleolithic data suggest that there were several major areas which differed in lithic technology, and within these areas many distinctive local cultural ecological adaptations must have taken place. So far as present evidence is concerned, therefore, the Shoshoneans represent a distinctive and non-recurrent line of development in a scheme of multilinear evolution.

The family type of organization found among the Shoshoneans should not be confused with that which developed after white contacts among several peoples in various parts of the world. For example, many Indians in the northeastern United States and Canada, who previously had some form of band organization, broke up into family groups after the fur trade had become virtually essential to their existence, and each family came to own a clearly delimited trapping territory. Social, economic, and religious patterns which had given cohesion to the bands were seriously disrupted or disappeared. This did not mean that the whole culture was actually reduced to a family level. The families ceased to be related to one another through band institutions and became partially integrated into the economic and to some extent into the religious and political institutions of the colonial or national states. These institutions were mediated to them through the trader, the missionary, and government officials.

The Mundurucú of the Cururá River in the Amazon Basin, according to Robert Murphy's recent, unpublished studies, have tended to lose their band and tribal organization and to split into family units for similar reasons. Since they have become gatherers of wild rubber, each family works the trees within delimited sections of the rivers. Family contacts are increasing with the rubber trader and to some extent with church and government officials rather than with one another. A similar pattern was found by Wagley among the rubber gathering Caboclos on the lower Amazon, although social and religious ties were stronger among them owing to their access to more developed communities (Wagley, 1953).

The Shoshoneans developed a higher level of sociocultural integration and a cross-culturally significant type only after the whites entered their country and horses were introduced. The multifamily, mounted, predatory bands depended upon raiding the new resources brought by the whites. In this respect they differed from the mounted Plains tribes, which subsisted by hunting bison, and resembled such peoples as the Apache, whose forays made them the scourge of the Southwest, the Puelche and certain tribes of the southern Gran Chaco in South America, and perhaps some of the Asiatic horse nomads, whose existence was at least quasiparasitic through raiding activities.

The full significance of the predatory band as a cultural type warrants detailed comparative study, for it is not now possible to say what people belong to this type. There is no doubt, however, that the type has conceptual validity. Moreover, it should be stressed that the cross-cultural significance of this type consists of form and function rather than element content. The Shoshoneans, Apache, Puelche, and Asiatics were very unlike in specific details of behavior. They belonged to different culture areas, but they had the same type of culture.

The final phase of Shoshonean culture history has been sketched in Chapter 3 [of *Theory of Culture Change*]. When the Indian wars ended, the people who did not enter reservations rapidly adapted themselves to the new white society by working for ranches, mines, or taking odd jobs in the new towns. The very absence of aboriginal band or community institutions made this adjustment easier. The principal obstacle to rapid and complete assimilation into the subculture of the local white American communities was and still is race relations, which bar the Shoshoneans from full participation in many crucial aspects of the American way of life.

NOTES

1. This chapter is essentially a condensation of "Basin-Plateau Sociopolitical Groups," *Bureau of American Ethnology Bulletin 120*, 1938.
2. O. C. Stewart, *Northern Paiute Bands* (Berkeley: University of California Press, 1939), p. 19, has mistaken food-named groups for aboriginal bands and leaders of post-white predatory bands for aboriginal chiefs.

REFERENCES

Harris, J. S. (1940). "The White Knife Shoshoni of Nevada," in *Acculturation in Seven American Indian Tribes*. Ed. Ralph Linton. New York.

Wagley, Charles. (1953). *Amazon Town. A Study of Man in the Tropics*. New York: Macmillan.

7

Ecologic Relationships of Ethnic Groups in Swat, North Pakistan

Fredrik Barth

The importance of ecologic factors for the form and distribution of cultures has usually been analyzed by means of a culture area concept. This concept has been developed with reference to the aboriginal cultures of North America (Kroeber 1939). Attempts at delimiting culture areas in Asia by similar procedures have proved extremely difficult (Bacon 1946, Kroeber 1947, Miller 1953), since the distribution of cultural types, ethnic groups, and natural areas rarely coincide. Coon (1951) speaks of Middle Eastern society as being built on a mosaic principle – many ethnic groups with radically different cultures co-reside in an area in symbiotic relations of variable intimacy. Referring to a similar structure, Furnivall (1944) describes the Netherlands Indies as a plural society. The common characteristic in these two cases is the combination of ethnic segmentation and economic interdependence. Thus the "environment" of any one ethnic group is not only defined by natural conditions, but also by the presence and activities of the other ethnic groups on which it depends. Each group exploits only a section of the total environment, and leaves large parts of it open for other groups to exploit.

This interdependence is analogous to that of the different animal species in a habitat. As Kroeber (1947:330) emphasizes, culture area classifications are essentially ecologic; thus detailed ecologic considerations, rather than geographical areas of subcontinental size, should offer the point of departure. The present paper attempts to apply a more specific ecologic approach to a case study of distribution by utilizing some of the concepts of animal ecology, particularly the concept of a *niche* – the place of a group in the total environment, its relations to resources and competitors (cf. Allee 1949:516).

Groups

The present example is simple, relatively speaking, and is concerned with the three major ethnic groups in Swat State, North-West frontier Province, Pakistan.[1] These are: (1) *Pathans* – Pashto-speaking (Iranian language family) sedentary agriculturalists; (2) *Kohistanis* – speakers of Dardic languages, practicing agriculture and transhumant herding; and (3) *Gujars* – Gujri-speaking (a lowland Indian dialect) nomadic herders. Kohistanis are probably the ancient inhabitants of most of Swat; Pathans entered as conquerors in successive waves between AD 1000–1600, and Gujars probably first appeared in the area some 400 years ago. Pathans of Swat State number about 450,000, Kohistanis perhaps 30,000. The number of Gujars in the area is difficult to estimate.

The centralized state organization in Swat was first established in 1917, and the most recent accretion was annexed in 1947, so the central organization has no relevance for the distributional problems discussed here.

Area

Swat State contains sections of two main valleys, those of the Swat and the Indus Rivers. The Swat River rises in the high mountains to the north, among 18,000 foot peaks. As it descends and grows in volume, it enters a deep gorge. This upper section of the valley is thus very narrow and steep. From approximately 5,000 feet, the Swat valley becomes increasingly wider as one proceeds southward, and is flanked by ranges descending from 12,000 to 6,000 feet in altitude. The river here has a more meandering course, and the valley bottom is a flat, extensive alluvial deposit.

The east border of Swat State follows the Indus River; only its west bank and tributaries are included in the area under discussion. The Indus enters the area as a very large river; it flows in a spectacular gorge, 15,000 feet deep and from 12 to 16 miles wide. Even in the north, the valley bottom is less than 3,000 feet above sea level, while the surrounding mountains reach 18,000 feet. The tributary valleys are consequently short and deeply cut, with an extremely steep profile. Further to the south, the surrounding mountain ranges recede from the river banks and lose height, the Indus deposits some sediment, and the tributary streams form wider valleys.

Climatic variations in the area are a function of altitude. Precipitation is low throughout. The southern, low-altitude areas have long, hot summers and largely steppe vegetation. The Indus gorge has been described as "a desert embedded between icy gravels" (Spate 1954:381). The high mountains are partly covered by permanent ice and snow, and at lower levels by natural mountain meadows in the brief summer season. Between these extremes is a broad belt (from 6,000 to 11,000 feet) of forest, mainly of pine and deodar.

Pathan–Kohistani Distribution

Traditional history, in part relating to place-names of villages and uninhabited ruins, indicates that Kohistani inhabitants were driven progressively northward by Pathan invaders (cf. Stein 1929:33, 83). This northward spread has now been checked, and the border between Kohistani and Pathan territories has been stable for some time. The last Pathan expansion northward in the Swat valley took place under the leadership of the Saint Akhund Sadiq Baba, eight generations ago. To understand the factors responsible for the stability of the present ethnic border, it is necessary to examine the specific ecologic requirements of the present Pathan economy and organization.

Pathans of Swat live in a complex, multi-caste society. The landholding Pakhtun caste is organized in localized, segmentary, unilineal descent groups; other castes and occupational groups are tied to them as political clients and economic serfs. Subsistence is based on diversified and well-developed plow agriculture. The main crops are wheat, maize, and rice; much of the plowed land is watered by artificial irrigation. Manuring is practiced, and several systems of crop rotation and regular fallow-field rhythms are followed, according to the nature of the soil and water supply. All rice is irrigated, with nursery beds and transplantation.

Only part of the Pathan population is actively engaged in agriculture. Various other occupational groups perform specialized services in return for payment in kind, and thus require that the agriculturalists produce a considerable surplus. Further, and perhaps more importantly, the political system depends on a strong hierarchical organization of landowners and much political activity, centering around the men's houses (*hujra*). This activity diverts much manpower from productive pursuits. The large and well-organized Pathan tribes are found in the lower parts of the Swat valley and along the more southerly tributaries of the Indus, occupying broad and fertile alluvial plains. A simpler form of political organization is found along the northern fringes of Pathan territory. It is based on families of saintly descent, and is characterized by the lack of men's houses. This simplification renders the economy of the community more efficient (1) by eliminating the wasteful pot-latch-type feasts of the men's houses, and (2) by vesting political office in saintly persons of inviolate status, thus eliminating the numerous retainers that protect political leaders in other Pathan areas.

Pathan territory extends to a critical ecologic threshold: the limits within which two crops can be raised each year. This is largely a function of altitude. Two small outliers of Pashto-speaking people (Jag, in Duber valley, and a section of Kalam) are found north of this limit. They are unlike other Pathans, and similar to their Kohistani neighbors in economy and political organization.

The conclusion that the limits of double cropping constitute the effective check on further Pathan expansion seems unavoidable. Pathan economy and political organization requires that agricultural labor produce considerable surplus. Thus in the marginal, high-altitude areas, the political organization is modified and "economized" (as also in the neighboring Dir area), while beyond these limits of double cropping the economic and social system can not survive at all.

Kohistanis are not restricted by this barrier. The Kohistani ethnic group apparently once straddled it; and, as they were driven north by invading Pathans, they freely crossed what to Pathans was a restricting barrier. This must be related to differences between Kohistani and Pathan political and economic organization, and consequent differences in their ecologic requirements.

Kohistanis, like Pathans, practice a developed plow agriculture. Due to the terrain they occupy, their fields are located on narrow artificial terraces, which require considerable engineering skill for their construction. Parts of Kohistan receive no summer rains; the streams, fed from the large snow reserves in the mountains, supply water to the fields through complex and extensive systems of irrigation. Some manuring is practiced. Climatic conditions modify the types of food crops.

Maize and millet are most important; wheat and rice can only be raised in a few of the low-lying areas. The summer season is short, and fields produce only one crop a year.

Agricultural methods are thus not very different from those of Pathans, but the net production of fields is much less. Kohistanis, however, have a two-fold economy, for transhumant herding is as important as agriculture. Sheep, goats, cattle, and water-buffalo are kept for wool, meat, and milk. The herds depend in summer on mountain pastures, where most of the Kohistanis spend between four and eight months each year, depending on local conditions. In some areas the whole population migrates through as many as five seasonal camps, from winter dwellings in the valley bottom to summer campsites at a 14,000 foot altitude, leaving the fields around the abandoned low-altitude dwellings to remain practically untended. In the upper Swat valley, where the valley floor is covered with snow some months of the year, winter fodder is collected and stored for the animals.

By having two strings to their bow, so to speak, the Kohistanis are able to wrest a living from inhospitable mountain areas which fall short of the minimal requirements for Pathan occupation. In these areas, Kohistanis long retained their autonomy, the main territories being conquered by Swat State in 1926, 1939, and 1947. They were, and still are, organized in politically separate village districts of from 400 to 2,000 inhabitants. Each community is subdivided into a number of loosely connected patrilineal lineages. The central political institution is the village council, in which all landholding minimal lineages have their representatives. Each community also includes a family of blacksmith-cum-carpenter specialists, and a few households of tenants or farm laborers.

Neighboring communities speaking the same dialect or language[2] could apparently fuse politically when under external pressure, in which case they were directed by a common council of prominent leaders from all constituent lineages. But even these larger units were unable to withstand the large forces of skilled fighters which Pathans of the Swat area could mobilize. These forces were estimated at

15,000 by the British during the Ambeyla campaign in 1862 (cf. Roberts 1898, vol. 2:7).

"Natural" Subareas

The present Swat State appears to the Kohistanis as a single natural area, since, as an ethnic group, they once occupied all of it, and since their economy can function anywhere within it. With the advent of invading Pathan tribes, the Kohistanis found themselves unable to defend the land. But the land which constitutes one natural area to Kohistanis is divided by a line which Pathans were unable to cross. From the Pathan point of view, it consists of two natural areas, one containing the ecologic requisites for Pathan occupation, the other uninhabitable.[3] Thus the Kohistanis were permitted to retain a part of their old territory in spite of their military inferiority, while in the remainder they were either assimilated as serfs in the conquering Pathan society or were expelled.

From the purely synchronic point of view, the present Pathan-Kohistani distribution presents a simple and static picture of two ethnic groups representing two discrete culture areas, and with a clear correspondence between these culture areas and natural areas: Pathans in broad valleys with a hot climate and scrub vegetation as against Kohistanis in high mountains with a severe climate and coniferous forest cover. Through the addition of time depth, the possibility arises of breaking down the concept of a "natural area" into specific ecologic components in relation to the requirements of specific economies.

Analysis of the distribution of Gujars in relation to the other ethnic groups requires such a procedure. Gujars are found in both Pathan and Kohistani areas, following two different economic patterns in both areas: transhumant herding, and true nomadism. But while they are distributed throughout all of the Pathan territory, they are found only in the western half of Kohistan, and neither reside nor visit in the eastern half. The division into mountain and valley seems irrelevant to the Gujars, while the mountain area – inhospitable to Pathans and usable to Kohistanis – is divided

by a barrier which Gujars do not cross. The economy and other features of Gujar life must be described before this distribution and its underlying factors can be analyzed.

Gujars constitute a floating population of herders, somewhat ill-defined due to a variable degree of assimilation into the host populations. In physical type, as well as in dress and language, the majority of them are easily distinguishable. Their music, dancing, and manner of celebrating rites of passage differ from those of their hosts. Their political status is one of dependence on the host population.

The Gujar population is subdivided into a number of named patrilineal tribes or clans – units claiming descent from a common known or unknown ancestor, but without supporting genealogies. There are sometimes myths relating to the clan origin, and these frequently serve as etymologies for the clan name. The clans vary greatly in size and only the smallest are localized. The effective descent units are patrilineal lineages of limited depth, though there is greater identification between unrelated Gujars bearing the same clan name than between strangers of different clans. These clans are irrelevant to marriage regulations. There is little intermarriage between Gujars and the host group.

The economy of the Gujars depends mainly on the herding of sheep, goats, cattle, and water buffalo. In addition to animal products, Gujars require some grain (maize, wheat, or millet) which they get by their own agriculture in marginal, high-altitude fields or by trade in return for clarified butter, meat, or wool. Their essential requirements may be satisfied by two rather different patterns of life – transhumance and true nomadism. Pathans differentiate persons pursuing these two patterns by the terms Gujar and Ajer, respectively, and consider them to be ethnic subdivisions. In fact, Gujars may change their pattern of life from one to the other.

Transhumance is practiced mainly by Gujars in the Pathan area, but also occasionally in Kohistan (see Figure 7.1). Symbiotic relationships between Gujars and Pathans take various forms, some quite intimate. Pathans form a multi-caste society, into which Gujars are assimilated as a specialized occupational caste

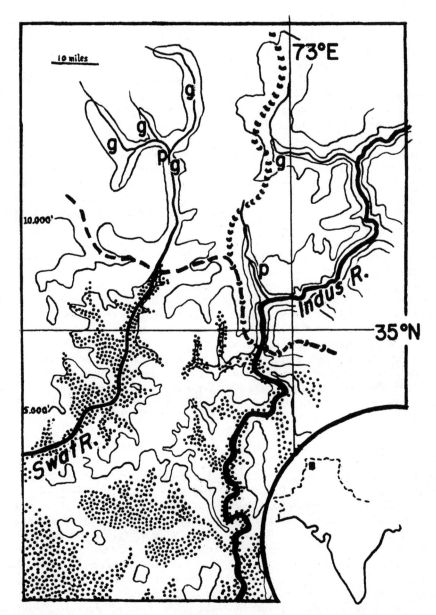

Figure 7.1 *Sketch map of area of Swat State, Pakistan. Stippled area: under cultivation by Pathans. Broken line: border between Pathan and Kohistani areas. Dotted line: border of area utilized by Gujars (the two borders coincide towards the southeast). p: outlying Pathan communities. g: outlying communities of transhumant Gujars. Gujar nomads spend the summer in the mountains central and north on the map, and winter in the southernmost area of the map. Inset: location of sketch map*

of herders. Thus most Pathan villages contain a small number of Gujars – these may speak Gujri as their home language and retain their separate culture, or may be assimilated to the extent of speaking only Pashto. Politically they are integrated into the community in a client or serf status. Their role is to care for the animals (mainly water buffalo and draft oxen) either as servants of a landowner or as independent buffalo owners. They contribute to the village economy with milk products (especially clarified butter), meat, and manure, which is important and carefully utilized in the fields.

In addition to their agricultural land, most Pathan villages control neighboring hills or mountain-sides, which are used by Pathans only as a source of firewood. The transhumant Gujars, however, shift their flocks to these higher areas for summer pasture, for which they pay a fixed rate, in kind, per animal. This rent supplies the landholders with clarified butter for their own consumption. Gujars also serve as agricultural laborers in the seasons of peak activity, most importantly during the few hectic days of rice transplantation. They also seed fields of their own around their summer camps for harvest the following summer.

In Kohistan there is less symbiosis between Gujars and their hosts but the pattern is similar, except that the few fields are located by the winter settlements.

The transhumant cycle may be very local. Some Gujars merely move from Pathan villages in the valley bottom to hillside summer settlements 1,000 or 1,500 feet above, visible from the village. Others travel 20 or 30 miles to summer grazing grounds in the territory of a different Pathan tribe from that of their winter hosts.

Nomads travel much farther, perhaps 100 miles, utilizing the high mountain pastures in the summer and wintering in the low plains. While the transhumant Gujars place their main emphasis on the water buffalo, the nomads specialize in the more mobile sheep and goats. Nonetheless, the two patterns are not truly distinct, for some groups combine features of both. They spend the spring in the marginal hills of Pathan territory, where they seed a crop. In summer the men take the herds of sheep and goats to the high mountains, while the women remain behind to care for the buffalo and the fields. In autumn the men return with the herds, reap the crops, and utilize the pastures. Finally, they store the grain and farm out their buffalo with Pathan villagers, and retire to the low plains with their sheep and goats for the winter.

The true nomads never engage in agricultural pursuits; they may keep cattle, but are not encumbered with water buffalo. The degree of autonomous political organization is proportional to the length of the yearly migration. Households of locally transhumant Gujars are tied individually to Pathan leaders. Those crossing Pathan tribal borders are organized in small lineages, the better to bargain for low grazing tax. The true nomads coordinate the herding of flocks and migrations of people from as many as 50 households, who may also camp together for brief periods. Such groups generally consist of several small lineages, frequently of different clans, related by affinal or cognatic ties and under the direction of a single leader. Thus, though migrating through areas controlled by other political organizations, they retain a moderately well-defined organization of their own.

Gujar Distribution

The co-existence of Gujars and Pathans in one area poses no problem, in view of the symbiotic relations sketched above. Pathans have the military strength to control the mountainous flanks of the valleys they occupy, but have no effective means of utilizing these areas. This leaves an unoccupied ecologic niche which the Gujar ethnic group has entered and to which it has accommodated itself in a politically dependent position through a pattern of transhumance. Symbiotic advantages make the relationship satisfactory and enduring. It is tempting to see the expansion of Gujars into the area as resulting from the Pathan expulsion of Kohistanis from the valley. The Kohistanis, through their own pattern of transhumance, formerly filled the niche and it became vacant only when the specialized agricultural Pathans conquered the valley bottom and replaced the Kohistanis.

But the co-existence of Gujars and Kohistanis poses a problem, since the two groups appear to utilize the same natural resources and therefore to occupy the same ecologic niche. One would expect competition, leading to the expulsion of one or the other ethnic group from the area. However, armed conflict between the two groups is rare, and there is no indication that one is increasing at the expense of the other. On the other hand, if a stable symbiotic or noncompetitive relationship may be established between the two groups, why should Gujars be concentrated in West Kohistan, and not inhabit the essentially similar East Kohistan area? The answer must be sought not only in the natural environment and in features of the Gujar economy, but also in the relevant social environment – in features of Kohistani economy and organization which affect the niche suited to utilization by Gujars.

East vs West Kohistan

As indicated, Kohistanis have a two-fold economy combining agriculture and transhumant herding, and live in moderately large village communities. Although most Gujars also practice some agriculture, it remains a subsidiary activity. It is almost invariably of a simple type dependent on water from the melting snow in spring and monsoon rains in summer, rather than on irrigation, and on shifting fields rather than manuring. The Kohistanis have a more equal balance between agriculture and herding. The steep slopes require complex terracing and irrigation, which preclude shifting agriculture and encourage more intensive techniques. The size of herds is limited by the size of fields, which supply most of the winter fodder, since natural fields and mountain meadows are too distant from the winter dwellings to permit haying. Ecologic factors relevant to this balance between the two dominant economic activities become of prime importance for Kohistani distribution and settlement density.

There are significant differences in this respect between East and West Kohistan, i.e. between the areas drained by the Indus and the

Swat Rivers respectively. While the Indus and the lowest sections of its tributaries flow at no more than 3,000 feet, the Swat River descends from 8,000 to 5,000 feet in the section of its valley occupied by Kohistanis. The higher altitude in the west has several effects on the economic bases for settlement: (a) Agricultural production is reduced by the shorter season and lower temperatures in the higher western valley. (b) The altitude difference combined with slightly higher precipitation in the west results in a greater accumulation of snow. The Indus bank is rarely covered with snow, but in the upper Swat valley snow tends to accumulate through the winter and remains in the valley bottom until April or May. Thus the sedentary stock-owner in West Kohistan must provide stored fodder for his animals throughout the four months of winter. (c) The shorter season of West Kohistan eliminates rice (most productive per land unit) as a food crop and reduces maize (most advantageous in return per weight of seed) in favor of the hardier millet.

These features serve to restrict the agricultural production of West Kohistan, and therefore the number of animals that can be kept during the winter season. No parallel restrictions limit the possibility for summer grazing. Both East and West Kohistan are noteworthy for their large, lush mountain meadows and other good summer grazing, and are thus rich in the natural resources which animal herders are able to exploit. However, these mountain pastures are only seasonal; no population can rely on them for year-round sustenance. Consequently, patterns of transhumance or nomadism are developed to utilize the mountain area in its productive season, while relying on other areas or techniques the rest of the year. True nomads move to a similar ecologic niche in another area. People practicing transhumance generally utilize a different niche by reliance on alternative techniques, here agriculture and the utilization of stored animal fodder. There appears to be a balance in the productivity of these two niches, as exploited by local transhumance in East Kohistan. Thus, in the Indus drainage, Kohistanis are able to support a human and animal population of sufficient size through the winter by means of agriculture and stored food, so as to utilize fully the summer pastures of the surrounding mountains. In an ecologic sense, the local population fills both niches. There is no such balance in the Swat valley. Restrictions on agricultural production limit the animal and human population, and prevent full exploitation of the mountain pastures. This niche is thus left partly vacant and available to the nomadic Gujars, who winter in the low plains outside the area. Moreover, scattered communities of transhumant Gujars may be found in the western areas, mainly at the very tops of the valleys. With techniques and patterns of consumption different from those of Kohistanis, they are able to survive locally in areas which fall short of the minimal requirements for permanent Kohistani occupation. The present distribution of Gujars in Kohistan, limiting them to the western half of the area, would seem to be a result of these factors.

A simple but rather crucial final point should be made in this analysis: why do Kohistanis have first choice, so to speak, and Gujars only enter niches left vacant by them? Since they are able to exploit the area more fully, one might expect Gujars eventually to replace Kohistanis. Organizational factors enter here. Kohistanis form compact, politically organized villages of considerable size. The Gujar seasonal cycle prevents a similar development among them. In winter they descend into Pathan areas, or even out of tribal territory and into the administered areas of Pakistan. They are thus seasonally subject to organizations more powerful than their own, and are forced to filter through territories controlled by such organizations on their seasonal migrations. They must accommodate themselves to this situation by travelling in small, unobtrusive groups, and wintering in dispersed settlements. Though it is conceivable that Gujars might be able to develop the degree of political organization required to replace Kohistanis in a purely Kohistani environment, their dependence on more highly organized neighboring areas still makes this impossible.

The transhumant Gujar settlements in Kohistan represent groups of former nomads who were given permission by the neighboring Kohistanis to settle, and they are kept politically subservient. The organizational superiority of the already established Kohistanis prevents them, as well as the nomads, from appropriating any rights over productive means or areas. What changes will occur under the present control by the State of Swat is a different matter.

This example may serve to illustrate certain viewpoints applicable to a discussion of the ecologic factors in the distribution of ethnic groups, cultures, or economies, and the problem of "mosaic" co-residence in parts of Asia.

(1) The distribution of ethnic groups is controlled not by objective and fixed "natural areas" but by the distribution of the specific ecologic niches which the group, with its particular economic and political organization, is able to exploit. In the present example, what appears as a single natural area to Kohistanis is subdivided as far as Pathans are concerned, and this division is cross-cut with respect to the specific requirements of Gujars.

(2) Different ethnic groups will establish themselves in stable co-residence in an area if they exploit different ecologic niches, and especially if they can thus establish symbiotic economic relations, as those between Pathans and Gujars in Swat.

(3) If different ethnic groups are able to exploit the same niches fully, the militarily more powerful will normally replace the weaker, as Pathans have replaced Kohistanis.

(4) If different ethnic groups exploit the same ecologic niches but the weaker of them is better able to utilize marginal environments, the groups may co-reside in one area, as Gujars and Kohistanis in West Kohistan.

Where such principles are operative to the extent they are in much of West and South Asia, the concept of "culture areas," as developed for native North America, becomes inapplicable. Different ethnic groups and culture types will have overlapping distributions and disconforming borders, and will be socially related to a variable degree, from the "watchful co-residence" of Kohistanis and Gujars to the intimate economic, political, and ritual symbiosis of the Indian caste system. The type of correspondence between gross ecologic classification and ethnic distribution documented for North America by Kroeber (1939)

will rarely if ever be found. Other conceptual tools are needed for the study of culture distribution in Asia. Their development would seem to depend on analysis of specific detailed distributions in an ecologic framework, rather than by speculation on a larger geographical scale.

NOTES

1. Based on fieldwork February to November 1954, aided by a grant from the Royal Norwegian Research Council.
2. There are four main Dardic languages spoken in Swat State: Torwali, Gawri, and Eastern and Western dialect of Kohistəi or Mayãn (Barth and Morgenstierne [1958]).
3. The Pathan attitude toward the Kohistan area might best be illustrated by the warnings I was given when I was planning to visit the area: "Full of terrible mountains covered by many-colored snow and emitting poisonous gases causing head and stomach pains when you cross the high passes; inhabited by robbers, and snakes that coil up and leap ten feet into the air; with no villages, only scattered houses on the mountain tops!"

BIBLIOGRAPHY

Allee, W. C. et al. (1949). Principles of animal ecology. Philadelphia, W. B. Saunders Company.

Barth, Fredrik. (1956). Indus and Swat Kohistan – an ethnographic survey. Studies honoring the centennial of Universitetets Etnografiske Museum Vol. II, Oslo.

Barth, Fredrik and Georg Morgenstierne. (1958). Vocabularies and specimens of some Southeast Dardic dialects. Oslo. Norsk Tidsskrift for Sprogvidenskap Vol. 18, pp. 118–36.

Bacon, Elizabeth. (1946). A preliminary attempt to determine the culture areas of Asia. *Southwestern Journal of Anthropology* 2:117–32.

Coon, Carleton S. (1951). Caravan. New York, Henry Holt & Co.

Furnivall, J. S. (1944). Netherlands India – a study of plural economy. Cambridge University Press.

Kroeber, A. L. (1939). Cultural and natural areas of native North America. Berkeley and Los Angeles, University of California Press.

——. (1947). Culture groupings in Asia. *Southwestern Journal of Anthropology* 3:322–30.

Miller, Robert J. (1953). Areas and institutions in Eastern Asia. *Southwestern Journal of Anthropology* 9:203–11.

Roberts, Field Marshal Lord. (1898). Forty-one years in India. London, Richard Bentley & Son.

Spate, O. H. K. (1954). India and Pakistan. London, Methuen.

Stein, Sir Aurel. (1929). On Alexander's track to the Indus. London, Macmillan & Co.

8

The Wet and the Dry: Traditional Irrigation in Bali and Morocco

Clifford Geertz

Introduction

The pioneer studies made by the anthropologist Julian Steward in what he later came to call cultural ecology were expressly comparative, either as between different sorts of hunting-gathering bands or different sorts of irrigation civilizations (Steward, 1955). More recent studies have tended to lose this dimension, however, and concentrate on monographic analysis of single societies in the conventional anthropological manner. Yet, as Steward realized, any attempt to discover broader generalities in the relationships between natural processes and cultural ones demands an at least implicitly (and, preferably, explicitly) comparative perspective. Any long-established adaptive regime considered only in itself tends to take on the look of not only inevitability but also optimality. The doctrine that whatever is is right is no more attractive in anthropology than it is in ethics. But it comes only too easily to hand when one looks too fixedly at a single case.

A comparative approach in human ecology restores the sense that things could quite easily be otherwise than they are, which is not the same as saying that they could be anything at all. It prevents the cultural aspects from decaying into a mere reflection of the ecological and the whole enterprise into another exercise in reductive materialism. When generally similar adaptive regimes are viewed in generally unlike cultural contexts, the recognition that those regimes are multiply determined is very difficult for even the most monomanic of theorists to escape. The original intent of Steward's program was to integrate physical and biotic variables into cultural analysis, not to segment them off as extrahuman determinants of culture within which unconditioned laws would then be sought. By dramatizing the fact that cultural presuppositions stemming from sources whose connections with adaptive constraints are (to the extent they exist at all) very distant can have a profound effect on adaptive responses, comparative analysis tends to keep that intent in the center of attention. Single case studies may, of course, do that as well, and a number have. But the proposition that landscape, weather, rice, or pigs make the man can be rendered much more readily plausible when there are no contrasting cases to challenge inferences from the exhaustively detailed immediate instance.

In this spirit, partly polemical, partly constructive, partly, I must admit, merely wistful, I will discuss here "traditional" irrigation in two settings – east central Morocco and southeastern Bali – about as different from one another as two settings can be. And I will attempt to show how the equally radically different ways in which water is handled in the two settings leads to some general insights into the again strikingly different cultures situated in them.[1]

Some General Contrasts between Morocco and Indonesia

Whatever Morocco and Indonesia have in common – Islam, poverty, nationalism, authoritarian rule, overpopulation, clean air, spectacular scenery, and a colonial past – the one thing they do not have in common is climate.

At base, the contrast is almost Lévi-Straussian in its simplicity: wet and dry.[2] The annual rainfall in central Java, the classical heartland of Indonesia, averages around 2,000 mm (i.e., about twice that of Chicago), while in parts of Sumatra and Borneo it gets up over 3,500 mm. In the Fez-Meknes-Marrakesh triangle, the classical heartland of Morocco, it averages about 500 mm (i.e., about half that of Chicago), while in the South, Pre-Sahara, it drops as low as 50 mm a year.

Further, not only are the annual mean totals near the opposite ends of the world scale, but also the rhythmicity with which rain falls is out near the extremes. In Indonesia, year-to-year variation is very small, as is variation in the shape of the rainfall regime from one year to the next. In Morocco, not only is year-to-year variation in rainfall enormous, but also is the within-year shape of it. To be a weatherman in monsoon Indonesia,

all you *do* need to know is which way the wind is blowing; in Morocco, to be one you need to be able to penetrate the mind of God.

In the Balinese area studied, the annual rainfall over a 10-year period varied between about 2,200 mm and about 2,500 mm, with a coefficient of variation of 5.8%. In the Moroccan area, over a similar period, the variation was from 350 mm to about 900 mm, for a coefficient of variation of 29.4%. Where the monthly Balinese totals over the same period – how much it rained in July, January, or whenever – were also extremely consistent, almost invariant, they were astonishingly unpredictable in Morocco. In January 1959 there were 15 mm of rain; in January of the following year, there were 190 mm. There was more rain in July (i.e., mid-summer of 1959) than in February (i.e., mid-winter) of 1961, though those two yearly totals happened to work out nearly identically.

One gets the same picture with all the other climatic measures – temperature (a constant 80 F in Bali year round, a 55 F mid-summer/mid-winter swing in Morocco, and similarly for diurnal variations), wind, sunshine, and so on. The same contrast could be extended throughout all the established metereological parameters: constancy, regularity, homogeneity in the one place; inconstancy, irregularity, and heterogeneity in the other.

Without going into the reasons for these systematic differences, nor into other environmental contrasts (soils, relief), it is clear that they are going to provide rather different sorts of habitats for agrarian man to live in. Bali is, of course, largely paddy country; central Morocco, largely wheat and olive (and, on the pastoral side, sheep) country. The thousands of small, squared off, carefully irrigated mud diked rice terraces sunk like ancient ruins into the sculptured landscape of the former, the thousands of narrow, little, medieval-like dirt-farming strips scratched on the baked surfaces of the latter can almost stand as paradigm images (and, in tourist posters, often do) of the two countries.

One can carry these contrasts forward in many directions – population density, cultivation methods, settlement patterns, trade.[3] But so far as our focus here is concerned (irrigation), the main difference is that there is a great deal of water in Bali, most of the time, and there is a great deal less – indeed, from the farmers' point of view, an absolute water shortage – irregularly distributed, both temporally and spatially, in Morocco.

Speaking generally, in south Bali irrigation is widespread to the point of being universal; in central Morocco it is confined to well-demarcated, commonly very constricted localities, micro-environments in the micro-est sense of the word. Where Bali, from this point of view, is a kind of giant outdoor aquarium, or, rather, a multitude of little aquariums pressed tightly up against one another, Morocco is – again from *this* point of view – a collection of scattered (or anyway discontinuous) oases, garden spots in a dessicate landscape.[4]

Balinese irrigation is a huge, homogeneous, very precisely calibrated, multi-leveled, extraordinarily effective system. Moroccan irrigation (and, again, to re-emphasize, the overwhelming bulk of Moroccan agriculture is not irrigated at all) is a small-scale, quite heterogeneous, broadly at best, calibrated, single-level, but, at best, moderately effective system. These general differences in long-established irrigation regimes are determinately related to similar differences in technological, sociological, and cultural patterns in such a way that two quite contrasting ecosystems with quite different properties are created. Environment is, therefore, and long has been, more than a passive, residual, limiting sort of factor in shaping Moroccan and Balinese life.[5] It is and has been an active, central, and creative one.

The Balinese *Subak*

The defining feature of the Balinese irrigation system, something which makes it, if not wholly unique, certainly unusual, is that it is organized into a separate, independent, completely autonomous social form, called the *subak*, and usually translated well enough, if awkwardly, as "the irrigation society."[6] A *subak* is, first and foremost, a differentiated, corporate, self-contained social organization, devoted specifically and exclusively to irrigated farming, mainly (though not exclusively) of paddy – a kind of "wet village," as opposed to the "dry" one in which people reside. Indeed, this idiom is commonly employed by the Balinese to refer to it.

In spatial terms, a *subak* consists of all the rice terraces irrigated from a single major water canal *(telabah gde)*. This canal runs down the steep volcano-to-beach slope of Bali from a single mud and stone river dam. (Southern Bali is laced with very deep cut gorges plunging down this slope every thousand yards or so, and it is across them that these dams, one every three or four miles, are thrown.) The dam *(empelan)*, which is usually five or ten miles, sometimes even more, upslope from the *subak* it serves, is the property of the *subak* as a corporate body. So also is the canal, which, often aided by underground tunnels, overhead aquaducts, and reservoirs, runs off from it to the fields proper.

The fields proper, the terraces, are contiguous and form a clearly bounded domain. (Like "dry" villages, *subaks* are individually named.) All people owning land, which they do in simple freehold fashion, in that domain are members of the *subak*. This membership is completely independent of any other social characteristic – residence (all *subaks* have people from various villages, and any one individual with much land at all will belong to several *subaks*), caste, kinship position, and so on.

Thus, the *subak* is at once a technological unit, marked out by the collectively owned dam and canal; a physical unit, an expanse of terraced land with a defined border around it; and a social unit, a corporation consisting of people owning land in that expanse, serviced by the dam and canal. It is also, as we shall see, a religious unit.

As the main canal approaches the fields, it usually is split by very ingenious bamboo water dividers into two smaller canals, and subsequently those smaller canals are again divided into halves or thirds by a second rank of dividers, a process which may, in large *subaks*, be repeated a third or even fourth time.[7] The final result of this before-the-terrace distribution is the creation of between six and twelve separate inlets to the terraces as a whole. Each such inlet defines a distinct sub-section of the *subak* as a whole called a *tempek*, which, if the *subak* is a water-village, would be the water-quarter or hamlet, and indeed is sometime thus referred to. This pre-terrace organization can get very intricate, but the essential point is that this dividing and redividing and thus water allocation by *tempek* is fixed and unchanging (or, at most, very, very gradually and marginally changing), embodied in hallowed custom, which here in fact is actually written down in palm-leaf *subak* constitutions (*awig-awig subak*). The technical grid, the crystalized canal and water gate structure, gives thus the form of the whole system, its skeleton. Alterations are occasionally made, but they are not done either easily or often.

After the water reaches the terraces proper it is further divided into halves, thirds, or fourths, occasionally sixths, to create yet smaller subunits (*ketjoran*), water neighborhoods, so to speak, which may consist of anywhere from six to seventy or eighty terraces and which is again named. And finally, within these subunits, smaller dividers, capable, given the mere rivulets they are by this stage faced with, of divisions as fine as a tenth, segment the water out into terminal canals defining the elementary unit of the *subak*, called a *tenah*.

Within any one *subak* (*not* between them, of course) such final *tenah* units represent, in theory, and given the technical precision involved, pretty much in fact as well, exactly the same share of the water supply, whatever that may be either in general or from moment to moment, the overall grid being very carefully arranged to produce such a result.[8]

This, then, is the physical structure of the *subak*. But it is, as I say, also the social structure, because the organization of the *subak*, and thus of wet rice agriculture generally, parallels this technical pattern with virtually perfect and explicit exactitude. The structure of the *subak* as a corporate body, as a social system, and as a cultivation regime is given by – or, if that is too deterministic a way to put it, is congruent with – the structure of the *subak* as a physical mechanism for moving water between rivers and fields.

The best way to see this is to look briefly at cultivation as such. The actual ploughing, planting, weeding, and harvesting of terraces is organized and carried out by the individual terrace owners, independently of the *subak* structure, *except*, and this is, as we shall see, a critical point, *with respect to timing. When* to plant is not a matter of individual choice: everyone in the *subak* must plant at the same time.[9]

As for irrigation proper, a technically complex matter here, it is wholly a collective *subak* matter. The upkeep of the various works, from the large main dam down to the smallest canal, is carried out by work groups of *subak* members, the details of whose formation, mode of operation, and compensation we can ignore here. The structure of the work group is socially extremely complex, and it is tiered like the grid itself into larger and smaller units devoted to tasks at different levels of the *subak*. The main point is that these are not mere ad hoc groups, but official arms of the *subak*. The opening and closing of water gates is similarly a *subak* matter Thus, except for work entirely confined to the individual terrace, and even indirectly there, cultivation is regulated, paced, if you will, by the *subak* as a set of larger and smaller groups of its members organized into work groups under appropriate officials.

At the peak of this political-social-technical hierarchy there is the *subak* chief (*klian subak*), elected by the members, and the *subak* council, consisting of all the members, each with a single vote irrespective of size of holding. The council sets general policy within limits of the written constitution and elects the various officials. It can, and does all the time, fine people for infraction. (For severe contumacy it can even take away a man's land, though matters but rarely come to such a pass.) It collects taxes for support of the *subak* and disburses moneys out of them for improvements. It appoints priests to conduct the appropriate rituals in the *subak* shrines. With a miniature bureaucracy, a parliament of the whole, specially focused task groups, police and tax powers, and a ritual encasement, the *subak* is not only a technically developed unit but also clearly a very organic social unit, a corporation, with a form and direction of its own.

Yet, at the same time, it must also be stressed that the *subak* is in no sense a collective farm. On his own land (which he can sell, rent, tenant, or whatever, as he wishes), within the regulations set by the *subak*, the individual peasant is his own master working in his own way, consuming (or selling) his own produce. The *subak* never engages in the actual process of cultivation as such, nor, as I say, of marketing; it regulates irrigation, and that's all that it does. And in order to do so (with results that for Southeast Asia are the most productive in the entire region), it exercises important constraints on the decisions of the individual cultivator. But the actual process of cultivation within those constraints has always been a matter specifically (and this too is written, like some agrarian bill of rights, into the palm-leaf constitutions) beyond both its competence and its interest. The *subak* is a technically specialized, cooperatively owned public utility, not a collective farm.

Since, as south Bali has, in simple quantitative terms, if not all the water it could conceivably use, then about all it can in fact effectively use, it is less the absolute amount of water overall that is at issue than the timing of its application to the fields. For this reason, the very elaborate ritual system, to which I have several times alluded, is as critical in the *subak's* operation as the technical, social-structural, and political aspects of it I have just reviewed.

The focus of this ritual system is a rice-goddess cult, whose precise content we need not go into here, and it is conducted at every level of the *subak* from the individual terrace, through the various subsections of the *subak*, to the *subak* as a whole.[10] At the higher levels there are specific temples, with assigned priests, special ceremonies at special times, and specific altars, gods, offerings, and prayers. These various ceremonies are symbolically linked to cultivation in a way which locks the pace of that cultivation into a firm, explicit rhythm.

Even more interestingly, however, the ritual system not only does this internally within the *subak*, but also reaches beyond the individual *subak* to ensure inter*subak* coordination within a given drainage region – a region, say, ten to fifteen miles wide and thirty-five or so long, fanning out as you descend from mountain to sea. To see how this occurs, it is necessary to give a very generalized and over-standardized description of the cult.

The cult consists of nine major named stages. These stages follow in a fixed order at a pace generally determined, *once the first stage is initiated*, by the intrinsic ecological rhythms of rice growing. This cult is uniform over the entire region and it refracts to all levels of the system from the terrace to the supra*subak*, i.e., concurrent rituals are conducted at all levels. The nine stages are: (1) water opening; (2) terrace opening; (3) planting; (4) purifying the water; (5) "feeding" the gods with holy water and other offerings; (6) budding of the rice plants (about a hundred days after planting); (7) "yellowing" (that is, approaching fruition) of the rice; (8) harvesting; (9) placing the harvested rice in the granary.[11]

Now, the "water opening" day, stage one, for the various *subak* in the drainage (i.e., the day on which, amid ceremonies at the dam temple, water is diverted at the river dam into the *subak's* main canal) is staggered in such a way that the higher the *subak* along the mountain-to-sea gradient, the earlier the opening day. *Subaks* at the top of the system begin the ceremonial cycle, and with it the cultivation sequence, in December; *subaks* at the bottom, near the coast, begin it in April; those in between topographically are in between temporally as well.

The result is that, at any one point in time, the drainage area as a whole shows a step-by-step progression in the cultivation sequence as one moves down-slope. When a higher *subak* is flooding its terraces preparatory to ploughing, a lower is clearing its. When a lower is flooding a higher is planting. When a lower is celebrating the yellowing of the rice and thus the promise about a month hence of harvest, the higher is already carrying the sheaves to the barns.

The temporal progression built into the ceremonial cycle (which is set off and continued by a kind of superpriest at a regional river cult temple at the volcanic lake at the very top) is thus laid out on the ground as well, and in addition to pacing the cultivation sequence in each *subak* separately, it also intermeshes those separate sequences in such a way as to provide for an overall sequence for the region as a whole.

The main ecological effect of this system is to stabilize the demands upon water over the crop year, rather than allowing it, as it would in the absence of such a system, to fluctuate widely. Simplifying somewhat, terraced wet rice growing requires maximum water input at or just after the initiation of the cycle, and then a steadily decreasing input as the cycle proceeds, until, at the end, harvesting is carried out in a fully drained, dry field. If the cycles of all the *subaks* in a single drainage, or, worse, along a single river, were coincident, the result would be that water resources would be enormously overtaxed during the earlier phases of the cycle and about as enormously underutilized during the later ones, especially as, again simplifying somewhat, the amount of water naturally available does not vary greatly over the year. Indeed, as water is the central limiting factor in the *subak* ecosystem, if *subak* cycles were not staggered, wet rice cultivation in Bali could never have attained, and could not maintain, a fraction of its actual extent, which is, as I have said, extremely great.

The Moroccan Irrigation System

In turning to the central Moroccan pattern, I am going to do something which, at the level of principle, I would prefer not to do: namely, describe it in opposition to something else, the Balinese pattern, rather than independently prior to comparison. As a developed, articulated, and in its own way and own place, not ineffective system, it deserves a more positive characterization, one in terms of what it is rather than in terms of what it is not. But for purposes of exposition it is nonetheless useful to describe it in a kind of negative design way. This is less than ideal, but even the negative design approach can bring out the main fea-

tures of the system, and in briefer compass, so long as it is remembered that the Moroccan irrigation system is not just a very inferior version of the Balinese. Indeed, it is not a version of the Balinese at all, which could never work in Morocco, but a particular adaptive form, a distinctive ecosystem of its own.

Having said that, the quickest way into the Moroccan system is to say that there is nothing like the *subak* here, no corporate group organization of irrigation at all. Indeed, the underlying principle in Morocco is individual personal ownership of water. This works out in a variety of ways, but underneath them all is the concept that water, like land, houses, clothing, women, children, friends, sheep, sanctity, and anthropologists, is *property*, something that someone owns.

As it is also, unlike land, women, anthropologists, and so forth, not a fixed entity but a fluid resource, this raises some important problems of coordination and even, in an agonistic sort of way, cooperation. But these problems are not met by any version of the public utility method, but by a precise and elaborate system of customary property law, a system of common-law type legal concepts defining individual rights in something which one can possess only as an agency, not as an object, but no less firmly for that.

In any case, rather than deep-cut ravines pouring water down the sides of volcanic slopes every thousand yards, what you have, at least in the area I studied, are irregularly scattered springs, some voluminous, some trivial, and a great many in between, irrigating sharply circumscribed areas – oases, in the broad sense of the term. There are other sources, but the spring sort of irrigation system is, in the region I am concerned with, overwhelmingly the main one, and I shall confine my attention therefore to it.[12]

The particular area involved – a small city plus its hinterlands about thirty kilometers south of Fez – is marked by three fairly distinct subregions. Behind the city, the Middle Atlas mountains rise immediately, and in them the major mode of adaptation is sheep and goat pastoralism. There is some extremely small-scale cultivation, mainly of maize, and even here and there in a favorable locality a spot of irrigation. But, in general, springs are few, scattered, and thin. Northward, toward Fez, the country is rolling prairie, prologue to the great Sais plain which forms the country's bread basket, and on the prairie there is a mixture of large capital intensive farms, formerly French, now mostly nationalized or bought up by members of the Moroccan elite, and hundreds of small strip farms, most of them (as are the large farms) in wheat. Though a few of the capital intensive farms have installed mechanical pumps for irrigation, this area also lacks more than a few scattered springs and depends almost entirely on rainfall for water. Between these two areas, in the piedmont, however, there is a thin band, ten to fifteen miles wide, where a very large number of springs, many of them sizeable, and what is even more important, reliable, exist. It is in this subregion where almost all the intensive irrigation in the area as a whole takes place, where there are intensive truck farming (vegetables, olives, grain), large villages, small garden-surrounded towns, and relatively dense population (though, of course, nothing like the Balinese).

Given the microenvironmental variation of this piedmont region particularly, each specific system differs somewhat from the next, because the problems it is faced with differ. But the family resemblance among them is for all that overwhelming. Thus, rather than using the ideal-type approach I employed for the *subak*, where there is also some variation, but less fitful in expression, I will describe, and that sketchily, a particularly well-developed specific example from this area, adding merely the remark that other systems in the area I could as well have described would have displayed little kinks of their own, but come, in general, to the same sort of thing.

The area involved consists of four or five, depending on how you count, clustered settlements, scattered several hundred yards apart down over five miles or so of the foothills to the mountains, just before they flatten out into the prairie.[13] The core of these settlements consists in four Arab-speaking lineages considered each to have descended from one of the sons of a famous seventeenth-century saint who is buried, so they say, in a shrine in the largest of the settlements. There is some tendency for the lineages to be correlated with the settlements, but this is far from absolute. There is also some tendency for them to be both separately and collectively endogamous, but that is not absolute either. In addition, there are other people living in the settlements who are not members of these saintly lineages.

It is unnecessary to go further into social structure here, except to say that though the area – the four or five settlements – is a rather well-defined one in kinship and religious terms (that is, essentially in terms of self-image), it is not as a whole a political unit of any reality, nor, for that matter, are the separate settlements; there is very little corporate quality to any of the social groupings – lineage, settlement, settlement cluster. Conceptually the area is an entity, socially it is rather profoundly not, a paradox, or apparent paradox, which tends to be characteristic of Morocco generally.

So far as irrigation is concerned, the important point is that, although the people of this area draw upon common water resources, they do so in a way about as far from the public corporation Balinese *subak* as it is possible to get and still not fall into a Hobbsean war.

Beginning, as I did with Bali, at the specifically technical level, the first point is that rather than a single irrigation source, the river dam, there are here a multiplicity, the various local springs. One of these, called "Sultan Spring" (*'ayn seltan*), is the most important, because it produces the most water and is the most reliable, but there are a number of others, large, small, and medium-sized as well. From these springs run canals, here hardly more than crude ditches as compared with the elaborate Balinese ones, whose form and direction can be changed, if not at will, at least relatively easily within a fairly wide range. It is not the structure of the grid that organizes the water distribution here, but rather the water distribution that organizes the grid.

There are, to be less aphoristic, two methods by which fields are irrigated from the springs. In some cases, here mostly the smaller ones irrigating local clumps of fields, there is an order of succession in terms of which individual fields are watered. That is to say, field A is watered until it has sufficient water, then B, C, ..., N, and then back to A. How fast the cycle goes around depends upon the amount of water, the number and size of the fields, and, not least, the rhetorical skills of the owners. In other cases, especially in connection with the larger springs, such as the Sultan Spring, water is rotated by the clock among various fields: section A gets three hours; B, three hours; then C, six; D, two; and so on, in a similarly cyclical fashion. Although the second pattern is more complicated, and now that there are clocks rather than prayer times to measure by, perhaps more precise, and probably more flexible, the underlying principle is the same: individual men have defined individual property rights in water.[14]

A man owns his place in the cycle, whether measured in hours or in queue terms, as he owns anything else, and though there are natural constraints on what he can do with these rights – for one thing Bali and Morocco do have in common is that water runs downhill in both places – there are none which stem from any overall community determination of the public utility sort. There is no "water village" here. There are rules; a very great many of them. But they are phrased in terms of individual rights, not collective necessities, as contractual, not civic, obligations.

In the first place, water rights and land rights are here not fused. One can sell either without the other, can own water rights from which one has no appropriate land, and can rent it to somebody who does. One also can – and it goes on constantly – borrow and lend water from one field to another, sometimes several miles away. (For example, a man who owns three hours downstream can as well apply it upstream if he wants and topography permits, and vice versa.) When a man dies, one of his heirs may get his land and another his water. And so on.

Second, there is no superordinate political structure of any significance connected with irrigation. There are a few, quite unimportant officials (*jarri*) to keep time and track (though everyone does this for himself as well), but there is no meeting, irrigation head, constitution, fines, taxation, organized collective labor, authorities with sanctioning power, etc. When canals (*sāqiya*) need to be cleaned, open, shut, or whatever, those concerned merely do it themselves: in the absence of elaborate works,

most jobs are minor and involve but a few people. On the rare occasion on which a larger task appears, some sort of ad hoc group is formed, or the owners pay laborers to do it. And where there are differences of opinion, which is just about all the time, people merely argue, occasionally even come to blows.

What *does* control this system is an elaborate property law. The simplest way to clarify this fact without getting into the formal details, which are numerous and intricate, of the matter is to give two quite typical examples from, on the one hand, the farmer's viewpoint, and on the other, from the viewpoint, so to speak, of the water.

As a prelude, it is necessary to know that all land plots, even uncultivated ones, and all water units have individual, proper, so to speak, "personal" names (Ḥariga, Ḥasun, etc.). In the water case, these units are shares in the output of a particular spring, say, Sultan Spring, determined, as I say, either in temporal or queue fashion; in the land case they are specific fields. For simplicity, I shall represent these named land or water units by letters A, B, . . . , Z.

Take, then, Muhammad. Muhammad has four irrigated plots, scattered in various parts of this miniregion.[15] He owns four-what can we call them? waters? One of these, A, is three nighttime hours in Sultan Spring which comes around to him once every six nights. Another, B, is four daytime hours in the same Spring which comes around to him every ten days. A third, C, is one daytime hour in another spring which comes to him every twelve days. Finally, for D, he has queue type rights in another small spring whose cycle depends upon how much water there is.

Now, Muhammad waters his four irrigated fields W, X, Y, and Z thusly: W – the four day-hours of B, once every four times they come around (i.e., every forty days) and one night-hour of the four of A every time it comes around; X – one night-hour of A's four each time it comes, the four day-hours of B once every four times they come around, and the queue right more or less as needed and/or available; Y – one night-hour of A's four every time around, the four day-hours of B every four times around, plus the one hour of C every other time it comes around (i.e., every twenty-four days); Z – the same as Y.

This is not only a quite ordinary example, but also a rather simpler than usual one. Further, I have ignored all the borrowing and lending of water, temporary renting in or out of rights, and so on, which goes on constantly. Indeed, how Muhammad deploys his resources differs according to time of year, what is planted where, and the like, so this is a rather reduced and too static version of Muhammad's actuality.

If you look at the situation the other way around, from the point of view of a water unit – call it N, a nighttime one which has a six-night cycle – the same complexity emerges. There are seven holders, owners, whatever you want to call them, owning, respectively, 3, ¾, ¾, 1, 1, 1, ½ of the total 8 hours. And this, too, is a simpler than average case.

The point of all this, again, is not the details as such: it is what they say, especially against the background of the *subak*, about what kind of system this is, what the social form of it is. It is a system in which individual private ownership of water is the organizing principle, a principle developed to levels of legal complexity which stand in marked contrast to the technical simplicity of the actual system which underlies it.

This whole area covers only a few hundred hectares, lying in three main discontinuous patches in this little cup of hills, but the number of major units of water rights involved in the main spring, the Sultan Spring, alone is twenty-three (ten "days"; thirteen "nights") and these, as we have seen, are then fractionated hour by hour, or even by half-, third-, or quarter-hours.[16] Add in the half dozen or so other springs, one of which at least is also quite large and complexly subdivided, and something of the social intricacy of this system can, I trust, at least be sensed.

Comparison of the Ballnese and Moroccan Irrigation Systems

On just about every dimension, the southeast Bali and east central Moroccan patterns contrast. Where the Balinese is technologically complex, the Moroccan is almost technologically embarrassing. Where the Balinese is enclosed in a tightly corporate, superordinate group which explicity and firmly enforces regulations, the Moroccan is entangled in an elaborate code of laws which provides as much a framework for disputation, a vocabulary of argument, as anything else. Where the Balinese system is exactly adapted and structurally very firmly fixed, the Moroccan is very generally and loosely adapted and structurally very flexible. Coordination, in the Moroccan system, is not only low in absolute terms, but also, insofar as it exists, it is confined to small well-demarcated systems, or even parts of systems, not extended to large regions, as the Balinese.

Even the religious dimensions, which I have not gone into in the Moroccan case, so contrast. There is nothing like the Balinese rice cult in Morocco. There are mass prayers at times of drought, certain symbolic connections between water sources, sacred places, gardens, and Paradise, too elusive and complicated to describe in short compass, and a highly developed, religiously supported (i.e., by Islam) sense for the objective reality of codified personal law.

So, what our two cases have in common is that physical, social, and cultural factors are integrated into quite distinctive ecosystems, ecosystems with human beings in them. What they differ in is how that system is organized and functions. But, even more interesting, however, is the fact that *this general order of difference within a single cultural dimension – adaptation to the setting – extends in an overall way to the two societies as a whole.*

The Balinese have a passion – that is the only word for it – for organizing everything into specifically focused, highly corporate, structurally articulate, mutually independent, autonomous groups and then seeking to adjust relations among them in terms of a highly developed ritual system. This way of "doing things" runs through the entire society, from kinship and village organization to temple worship and state structure. Similarly, the Moroccan passion for organizing everything in terms of the head-on encounter of individuals within a general, universalistic moral-legal code, which is used as a basis for forming contracts, arguing issues, deciding conflicts, maximizing options, and adjusting opportunistically to passing reality, runs through every aspect of local life there. Had I discussed family life, or the market, or the civil administration, a picture more than a little reminiscent of the one I have given for irrigation would emerge, and not solely because I was giving it.

Balinese social integration comes down to a matter of adjusting the relations among a sizeable number of differently based but similarly organized, highly corporate, cross-cutting membership groups – *subaks*, lineages, hamlets, castes, temple groups; Moroccan integration comes down to mediating relations among a field of competing individuals, each with a somewhat different basis of power and each scrambling to make his way within the general rules of the game by his own wit and resources. The pluralistic collectivism, as I have called it elsewhere, of Bali, is matched, as a pervasive theme, by, to have another phrase, the agonistic individualism of Morocco.

This is not geographical determinism. It is an argument that the kind of sociocultural analysis that applies to kinship, village politics, child raising, or ritual drama applies equally, and not just in these two societies, to human transactions with the environment. In the formation of Balinese and Moroccan civilization, environment is but one variable among many – or, better, one set of variables among many. And it is one whose actual force must be empirically determined, not a priori declaimed.

But it is one variable, or set of them, and the familiar split between nature and culture which renders the former a stage upon which the latter performs cannot any longer be maintained. As a chameleon tunes himself to his setting, growing into it as though he were part of it, just another dun rock or green leaf, a society tunes itself to its landscape, mountainside, river fan, or foothill oasis, until it seems to an outside observer that it could not possibly be anywhere else than where it is, and that, located where it is, it could not be otherwise than what it is. This is an illusion, of course, though certain kinds of Marxists and certain kinds of Romantics are habitually taken in by it. What this illusion arises from is the fact that an established society is the end point of such a long history of adaptation to its environment that it has, as it were, made of that environment a dimension of itself. If a people live in a place long enough the quality of it enters into the substance of their life.

To connect the restless irregularity of much of Moroccan life, the tense expectancy and aggressive opportunism of it, to the uncertain, capricious climate is not, therefore, to yield to a vulgar materialism, for it is in part that climate which projects the aura of irregularity and tension, at least to anyone with a sensuous imagination, in the first place. Similarly, the dogged, deliberate, unwavering – as they themselves say, "straight-line" – quality of Balinese peasant life, moving along one foot after the other in its fixed furrows, is not a mere product of the hanging monotony of the wet heat, but more a kind of comment on it, as it, the heat, in turn is upon that life. The environments of societies such as the Moroccan or Indonesian are no more external to them than the storms in *Lear* are external to the play or the moors in *Wuthering Heights* are external to what passes between Cathy and Heathcliffe.

Though perhaps more apparent in so-called "traditional" civilizations, this sort of infolding of setting and society is hardly confined to them. It used to be thought that, although environment might shape human life at primitive levels where men were, it was said, more dependent upon nature, culture-evolutionary advance, especially technical advance, consisted of a progressive freeing of man from such conditioning. But the ecological crisis has divested us all of that illusion; indeed, it may be that advanced technology ties us in even more closely with the habitat we both make and inhabit, that having more impact upon it we in turn cause it to have more impact upon us. It is not just the Balinese, looking out at the perfected geometry of their rice terraces, or the Moroccans, looking out on the ad hoc irregularity of their irrigation ditches, but us, looking out on the nervous, smoky confusion of our streets, who see the image of themselves.

NOTES

1. The fieldwork on which this article is based was carried out in Indonesia during 1957–58 and in Morocco during 1965–66 and 1968–69. Also, it should be noted that all vernacular terms, Balinese or Moroccan Arabic, are given in the singular form only, plurals being indicated by English endings.
2. For a general review of the Indonesian climate and natural setting, see Dobby (1954); for one of the Moroccan, see Martin *et al.* (1964).
3. For an attempt to pursue some of these matters for Indonesia generally, and Java particularly, see Geertz (1963).
4. It needs continually to be remembered in what follows that irrigation plays a role in only a small proportion, though the most productive, of Moroccan agriculture. In particular, nowhere does irrigated agriculture form the exclusive or even nearly exclusive basis of the subsistence regime, but is always set in a broader context of rainfull farming and/or pastoralism. The implication of this fact in a general assessment of the Moroccan adaptation is profound, but it cannot be pursued here.
5. Balinese irrigation, apparently organized along lines extremely similar to the present, is mentioned in inscriptions dating as early as 896 (Goris, 1954). For a description of Moroccan-introduced irrigation patterns substantially identical to those described below in medieval Valencia, see Glick (1970).
6. For other descriptions of the *subak*, see Grader, 1960: 268–88; Liefrinck, 1886–87: 1033–59, 1213–37, 1557–68, 17–30, 182–89, 364–85, 515–52; Geertz, 1959: 991–1012; and Geertz, 1967: 210–43. *Subak* terminology varies over the island; that given here is the Klungkung one.
7. In general, *subak* increase in size as one moves from the top of the drainage area downward toward the sea. The very highest are extremely small; those near

the strand, large and sprawling. A full description of the interaction of landscape, *subak* structure, and political organization is presented in a monograph on the traditional Balinese state [Geertz, 1980].
8. A *tenah* is, in fact, at once a water measure, a land measure, a seed measure, and a rice measure. A *tenah* of land is the amount a *tenah* of water irrigates; a *tenah* of seed, the quantity needed to plant that much land; and a *tenah* of rice, the yield thereby produced. For more of this, see Geertz (1967).
9. Traditionally, this was true only for rice, but with increased population pressure and crop diversification it is increasingly true for non-rice "dry" crops as well. For details, see Geertz (1967).
10. For general description of Balinese religious life see Swellengrebel (1960). For a description of the rice cult as such, see Wirz (1927).
11. The Balinese names for these ceremonies are: (1) *Amapeg Toja*; (2) *Njamu Ngempelin Toja*; (3) *Mubuhin*; (4) *Toja Sutji*; (5) *Ngerestiti* (or, more colloquially, *Ngrahinin*); (6) *Membiju Kukung*. Stages (7), (8), and (9) are all included under the general term *Ngusaba*, plus appropriate qualifiers, and are really, thus, seen as three phases of a single stage.
12. Elsewhere in Morocco both river-flooding and well irrigation are important, as are such technological inventions as the Persian water-wheel, dams, and the famous covered canals (*gana*). For a general review, see Martin *et al.* (1964).
13. For a full sociological description of this settlement, see Rabinow (1970).
14. The timed system is called *l-ma dyal s-sa'a* ("water by the hour") or *b-l magana* ("by the clock"; there is a large clock in the mosque which is the standard, though most men have watches of their own as well); the queue system is called *mubih*. For the same contrast between these two systems in old Spain, see Glick (1970).

15. Muhammad also has nine unirrigated plots. We will ignore them here, though he doesn't, and a full ecological analysis wouldn't either.

16. There are even 80- and 50-minute units on occasion. This hyperfractionation is most likely a recent development, brought on by population pressure and made possible by modern clocks.

REFERENCES

Dobby, E. H. G. (1954). *Southeast Asia* (4th edition). University of London Press, London.

Geertz, C. (1959). Form and variation in Balinese village structure. *American Anthropologist* 61: 991–1012.

———. (1963). *Agricultural Involution*. University of Chicago Press, Berkeley.

———. (1967). Tihingan: a Balinese village. In Koentjaraningrat, R. M. (ed.), *Villages in Indonesia*, Cornell University Press, Ithaca.

———. (1980). *Negara: The Theatre State in Nineteenth-Century-Bali*. Princeton, NJ: Princeton University Press.

Glick, T. F. (1970). *Irrigation and Society in Medieval Valencia*. Harvard University Press, Cambridge.

Goris, R. (1954). *Prasasti Bali*, Vol. 1. Kirtya Liefrinck-van der Tuuk, Bandung, Bali.

Grader, C. J. (1960). The irrigation system in the region of Jembrana. In Swellengrebel, J. L. (ed.), *Bali: Life, Thought and Ritual*, The Hague and Bandung.

Liefrinck, F. A. (1886–87). De Rijstcultuur op Bali. *Indische Gids*.

Martin, J., Sover, H., Le Coz, J., Mauver, G., and Woin, D. (1964). *Geographie du Maroc*. Hatier, Paris and Casablanca.

Rabinow, P. (1970). The social history of a Moroccan village. Unpublished doctoral dissertation in anthropology. University of Chicago.

Steward, J. (1955). *Theory of Culture Change*. University of Illinois Press, Urbana.

Swellengrebel, J. L. (1960). Introduction. In Swellengrebel, J. L. (ed.), *Bali: Life, Thought and Ritual*, The Hague and Bandung.

Wirz, P. (1927). Der Reisbau und die Reisbaukulte auf Bali und Lombok. In *Tijdschrift voor Indische Taal-, Land- en Volkenkunde*, G. Kolff and Co., Batavia.

9

Critical Pressures on Food Supply and their Economic Effects

Raymond Firth

Tikopia in 1952 was in a state of tension because of the threat of famine. This had arisen because of hurricane and drought and the effects became increasingly severe as the months went by. Sickness was common, the death rate increased and the social life of the people became governed very largely by the gnawing stringencies of their need to obtain and conserve food. It took more than a year before substantial fresh crops restored to the society its regular functions.

The implications of famine in social terms provide an interesting, if grim, example of the strength and weakness of a social system. Yet apart from Malinowski's brief examination of the concept of famine and of the reactions of the people to food shortage in the Trobriands, and observations by Richards, Fortes and others on African "hunger periods", there are hardly any investigations by anthropologists of the sociology of such critical situations.[1] The test of social relations as a working system is the extent to which they can withstand the strain of competing demands upon their agents. At a period of general hunger such demands are apt to be raised to a high pitch. Here is an empirical test of the power of integration of the social system – a test not dependent merely upon the anthropologist's personal evaluation.

When I left Tikopia in 1929 the population appeared to be increasing significantly. On the side of subsistence, the community was not self-sufficient in that a very important section of producer's goods – its steel tools – were obtained by sporadic trade with the rare vessels that called. But there was no import of food, the people being entirely dependent upon their own agriculture and fishing, with the limitations of both being fairly clearly perceptible. They themselves realized this situation. From my observations in 1929 I reported that pressure of population on land resources was potential rather than actual; it was not acute nor might be for another generation. But if the then rate of increase persisted pressure would come and in the case of hurricane or drought there would be a threat of famine. As I was planning my second Tikopia expedition I had thought I might find a situation in Tikopia where anxiety about subsistence had become more marked through population pressure on a *static* food supply. What I found was a rising population, and a severe intensification of pressure through the effects of hurricane in greatly *reducing* the food supply.[2]

Where such a lowering of the food supply takes place fairly rapidly, the strains on the social system are not simply nutritional – belly-gnawing; they depend on recognitions, sentiments, moral evaluations and symbols of social relations. They involve emotional attitudes to the hunger of wife, children and kinsfolk, moral attitudes towards giving food to starving neighbours; social attitudes to the presentation of food as symbol of social status and social relationships. In earlier accounts I have given a description of the "normal" workings of the Tikopia social and economic system; in 1952/3 we had to study as a major subject the "abnormal" workings – the sociology of crisis and disaster.

In this chapter I consider the problem of crisis from the point of view of the organization which coped with problems of procurement and conservation of food. In the next chapter [of *Social Change in Tikopia*] I consider the other ways in which the famine affected the Tikopia social system.

But how far was the crisis really abnormal? Answer to this question must be rather speculative. But if accounts of senior Tikopia can be taken as a guide, it seems that this particular famine and its social implications were only part of a long-term process affecting the development of the Tikopia population and Tikopia society. Ordinary seasonal food shortage seems to have been well known in Tikopia. In May and June 1929, there was a marked scarcity of food of all kinds there, and I understood that such shortage was not uncommon at this period of the year, in an interval between main crops. Moreover, according to Tikopia tradition, it was not by any means the first time that more severe hunger periods had occurred, owing to exceptional drought or hurricane.

Tropical cyclones (known more popularly as hurricanes or typhoons, being closed low pressure systems with winds exceeding seventy-five miles an hour) occur with some frequency in the south-west Pacific, in the period mid-December to mid-April. They are especially prevalent in the region between 15 deg. S. and 30 deg. S., averaging three or four a year for the region as a whole. Tikopia, lying a couple of hundred miles to the north of this region, suffers infrequently, but occasionally feels the destructive force of such a cyclone. W. H. R. Rivers noted that "a big hurricane" not long before 1908 was followed by "a great scarcity of food".[3] In 1929 I recorded from the Ariki Kafika and one of his elders that they had been through three severe hurricanes – i.e. on the

average, one every twenty years – in which not a roof had been left on houses in Ravenga and Namo, and even large trees had been torn up. About 1937 Dr C. E. Fox wrote to me, "I was lately at Tikopia, where they had had a hurricane and were short of food; and still increasing" (i.e. their population). The Tikopia term *onge*, a word I often heard, was applied to such situations of devastating food stringency. Stories of the past told how in their hunger people ate the bark of trees, and in their despair put off in canoes to sea to face quick death in the ocean rather than a lingering death on shore.

At first sight it looks as if the famine apt to follow such a hurricane is a case of a simple Malthusian check on population. In 1929, the population of Tikopia was approximately 1,300 people. By 1952 it had risen to approximately 1,750 – an increase of about 35 per cent. Already by 1929 the more responsible men had begun to view with disquiet the symptoms of population growth in terms of the limited food supply. The famine in 1952/3 may be regarded then as nature's way of cutting back the population to a manageable size in terms of the available resources.

But the situation was, of course, not so neat. In earlier times, with a greater degree of isolation than at present, the Tikopia demographic situation seems to have been characterized by an almost classical simplicity. A small but growing population[4] on a fertile but small island was singularly free (because of lack of contact with the outside world) from endemic disease. With the expansion of the population, pressure upon food supply resulted, and war and expulsion of some section of the people was the obvious solution. Traditionally this is what occurred. But increasing contact with the outside world brought both new – or at least intensified – disease on the one hand, and a greater acquaintance with medical facilities on the other. In the countries which have had already a full quota of endemic "killing" diseases, the introduction of Western medical facilities has stimulated the growth of population. This so far has not been the case in Tikopia; on the contrary, the introduced diseases have tended to check the growth of population and medical facilities have not been able, as yet, to alter this to any degree. Yet, even at the height of famine and epidemic disease, the population was not set back to the level of 1929.[5] The interrelation of factors was complex, but the expansion of population continued. Moreover, it was continuing as far as can be gathered at a rate greater than the expansion of the local food supply.

The situation was not a simple Malthusian one in other ways. At no time did the Tikopia appear to have been concerned with a balance between population and food supply in terms of mere subsistence. They would seem to have been always interested in quality as well as quantity of food, and indeed their estimate of the prosperity of the land is basically affected by this. Moreover, during the last century at all events, they had been interested in raising their level of living in terms not only of food, but also of other types of consumer goods. Hence any disposal of their resources has had to take into consideration changing demands for goods other than food and the tools to produce food. (This was illustrated even at the height of the 1952/3 famine when there was a question as to how far the export of labour should be for food alone, or for other consumer goods as well.) Moreover, for more than half a century the increasing interest of the external government and of the Melanesian Mission in the social order of the Tikopia has meant that war and expulsion have not been "free" solutions. However difficult it has been for these external agencies to help the Tikopia, they have been committed in the last resort to a search for methods of maintaining the community at some minimum level of health and comfort.

Speaking generally, then, one has the impression that though the famine of 1952/3 was abnormal in the short run, in the long run it represented a movement in a pendulum swing of relations between Tikopia population and food supply that has been going on for at least a century, and probably much more. In my opinion, such changes in demographic pressure on subsistence are far more responsible for much of the structure of primitive societies than anthropologists have generally allowed.

But what was the intensity of the crisis in Tikopia at this time, in particular in its eco-nomic aspects? And what action was taken to meet it?

Immediate Measures of Organization after Hurricane

Two hurricanes affected the economic and social life of the Tikopia during the period studied by the expedition, the first (occurring in two phases) in January 1952, and the second of somewhat less force, in March 1953. Both were severe, breaking down houses and tall trees, and affecting even ground crops. In the first hurricane, said the Ariki Taumako, the wind was so violent that the leaves of the giant taro, large, fleshy and spadelike, were as if someone had rubbed them between his hands until only the bare stalk was left. In this hurricane waves at the high tide swept inland, broke down many houses near the beach in Faea and scattered and buried property. Low-lying areas of cultivation were flooded by salt water which broke into the swamp area where much taro was grown. In neither hurricane was there any loss of life, but recovery of the crops was long delayed, partly owing in the first case to drought succeeding the hurricane and partly in both cases to the effects of salt spray which had a caustic action and retarded the growth of new shoots. The immediate effect of each hurricane was to shock the people and inhibit their activity. But in both cases they soon rallied to the many tasks demanding their attention. As I have noted, they were not without experience in this.

Directly after each hurricane, contrary to what one might have expected, food was extremely plentiful. People tried to save as much as possible of the crop which had been damaged, and so collected it at once. They either consumed it almost immediately, as in the case of manioc, or laid it down as paste to ferment, as in the case of banana and bread-fruit, to draw upon as required in the traditional way. All this necessitated considerable communal labour and domestic organization. Shortage of water impelled the organization of labour in another way. All drinking water is obtained from springs which flow into aqueducts down to the shore where the villages are located. These aqueducts, built of areca palm trunk, were almost completely destroyed, and for several days working parties were busy in reconstructing them and getting water flowing again. Housing was also affected seriously. Temporarily some people had to take refuge in the woods and others in shelters under the lee of cliffs, until their shattered dwellings could be rebuilt. But the repair and rebuilding of houses was inhibited owing to the shortage of sago fronds for thatch and of sinnet cord for lashing.[6] Because of shortage of materials although labour was available soon, at least a dozen houses damaged by hurricane or ensuing "tidal" wave were not rebuilt for months, and others were reconstructed on a reduced scale. On the other hand, some dwellings – "houses of the famine" – were built anew on ancient sites to allow their owners to cultivate inland and guard their growing crops with greater ease. All this was apart from the routine work of clearing up the debris.

The emergency measures put into operation after the second hurricane, in 1953, were, by Spillius's account, rather more delayed. In the intervening year the people had suffered great privation and this second hurricane seemed to them the last drop in their bitter cup. There was much talk about putting off to sea on suicide voyages and about asking the Government to remove all the population to another island. But after two or three days their leaders began to rally them again. Executive officers talked sharply to men lounging on the beach or in their houses, asking them why did they sit there like thieves who had full bellies instead of getting to work. Public meetings were called and instructions given by the leaders. At first people were apathetic but soon responded to exhortations and threats. Village working parties were organized to clear up wreckage so that people could pass quickly and safely along the paths. Children were set to collect firewood and dry it on the beach. Young men were directed to repair the aqueducts and adolescents were assigned to cut down areca palms and scoop out the pithy trunks to make flumes for them. The people of Namo were instructed to open the channel leading from lake to sea, to lower the level of the lake and provide fish; they were to let the Ravenga people know when they were ready so that all could help and share in the fish supply.

Prospects of Famine

When a disaster such as a hurricane strikes a Pacific island community, the full effects are rarely perceived at once. Retrospectively, their course can be traced in an apparently logical sequence from the initial situations, but as the events unfold a number of variables have, in fact, been in operation, including local estimates of prospects and local action in the light of the estimates and the chances of external aid.

One striking difference in the Tikopia situation from that of disaster in most Western or Oriental areas nowadays was the limitation which isolation set upon recovery. In the more accessible parts of the world there is almost immediate response from unaffected areas – goods and services flow in freely and speedily. But for a small isolated Pacific island community aid is distant and difficult to organize – it may be even difficult to finance. Hence all Tikopia planning for recovery had to be mainly local.

It was, therefore, of prime importance to the people to make close estimates of the damage and its effects, not only as an immediate measure, but also to give a long-term framework. They had to get a proper basis for their planning, for months ahead. From the anthropological point of view it was of major interest to see how far the Tikopia seemed to look ahead, how accurate their forecast was, what steps they took to remedy the situation and how far they had to revise their estimates and alter their procedure as time went on.

The crux of the matter lay in the conditions of the local food supply. How long would the reduced food supplies remaining after the hurricane last? How long would growing crops and crops newly planted take to come to maturity? Would there be enough available supplies to bridge the gap?

Normal vegetable food supplies in Tikopia were based on taro (*Colocasia antiquorum* – a ground crop) and breadfruit (*Artocarpus*, a tree fruit) as staples, with coconut as a regular emollient.[7] Supplemental to these were bananas, manioc, sago flour, yams and sweet potatoes. Pumpkin, Tahitian chestnut, aerial yam, cordyline roots and other foods were periodically drawn upon to eke out the menu. To all this food fish was regarded as a necessary supplement.

In mid-March 1952, six weeks after the first hurricane, consultations with leading men such as the Ariki Kafika, Ariki Taumako and Pa Fenuatara, produced the following estimate of the time needed for food supplies to recover. Taro then in the ground was estimated to take up to three months to begin to yield sizeable corms, sweet potato and pumpkin would take about the same time, and banana (which had only two or three leaves beginning to show on most plants) about six months. Coconuts, it was thought, would bear in four to five months, but only where palms were alive – people had noticed some new shoots but few mature leaves had yet appeared and many palms had died. Breadfruit would take at least a year, possibly two years, to recover and fruit; no fruit at all was showing and trees had been so blasted that many would die. Some other foods such as sago, cordyline and aerial yam which had survived the hurricane were being consumed already, but they were coarse and unpalatable – "simply wood".

As regards the immediate prospects, the leaders thought in March that the community might maintain itself, though at a minimum level, for the next most critical three months. They were not much interested in government proposals for gifts of seedlings from abroad, except as a token of sympathy. They said that men who had plots in the swamp had ample taro seedlings and others could borrow from them. Some seedlings of manioc and sweet potato might be welcome, they agreed, but there were really plenty already in Tikopia. The future depended on the rainfall, they emphasized. If the rain fell adequately, the island should be in fair condition for survival after two or three months, though good food – that is food prepared with coconut cream – could not be available before about six months. "Food is made palatable with coconut alone, as you know," they said. But if rain did not fall normally in the next few weeks, then the

situation would be very serious; actual famine might occur. They emphasized the gravity of the situation. At a later meeting of the chiefs in our house in an informal atmosphere the forcefulness and unanimity of their expressions were notable. They made much the same crop estimates as cited already, but stressed again that recovery would depend on the weather. For the ensuing couple of months, they said, conditions would be desperate. They wished a relief vessel to be sent immediately with food, but as a longer term measure they made suggestions for certain Tikopia men to recruit as labourers abroad, their wages to be paid in food to be sent to their families on the island.

Some weeks later the senior men revised their view; they put the period of recovery still further ahead. Taro, they reckoned now, would take six months to yield properly. Coconuts, coming on very slowly indeed, would need six months to a year to form, and even sweet potato would take some months to produce. They reckoned it would be a year at least before the island was on its feet again, and they talked of people putting off to sea in despair. This view was not unanimous. One very old man said rather cynically out of his previous experience, "They say they will die, but they will not die. They will dig for wild yam roots which will not be exhausted and they will go and search for early yams and for wild legume (aka)." But the more gloomy view was closer to what actually happened. (The old man himself died in the famine, though not specifically from hunger.)

Such early estimates show how the long-term concern of the Tikopia with their food supply manifested itself very quickly and in practical calculation. They needed no prompting from outside to survey their situation and judge its prospects. For the most part their appraisals were realistic. Polite about suggestions for help, they distinguished between them on grounds of their practicability. Moreover, the estimates of the most responsible Tikopia as to the gravity of the situation were proven in the upshot to have been more precise than those of Europeans, including the anthropologists, who judged with less experience.[8]

Course of the Famine

In the trend towards famine or away from it were two major imponderables – the weather as the months went by, and the behaviour of the mass of Tikopia when faced by acute food stringency. Unfortunately, Tikopia fears about the weather were realized. Though there was no marked drought at any time there was definite shortage of rain in April and May 1952, preventing crops from maturing properly. Moreover, not even the Tikopia seemed to have attached enough significance to the retarding effect of the salt spray blown up by the hurricane. And an intensifying factor as time went on was the growing prevalence of theft of immature crops in the ground, which still further retarded the period of recovery.

Fortunately, fish from the sea, and in some periods from the lake, continued to be available. There was an unprecedented length of run of mackerel off Faea, lasting from July 1952 to the beginning of November 1952, and an exceptional run of fingerlings in the lake in November and December 1952 and April and May 1953. Again, at the opening of the channel from the lake in Namo for two nights in May 1953, large quantities of fish were caught on their way to the sea. Apart from these bonuses, the regular seasonal fishing for flying-fish and other types continued. But the amount of reef around Tikopia is relatively small and is heavily worked daily and often by night as well. It had been a first thought of the Government that the Tikopia could make up by fishing the shortage of vegetable food caused by the hurricane. But this was quite a mistake. The amount of fish ordinarily available just suffices the Tikopia needs, and intensification of fishing by any existing Tikopia methods would not necessarily have resulted in any significant addition to the food supply.

But Tikopia was not completely cut off to work out its own fate. A factor which encouraged the recovery of the community was the relief supplies from the Government of the British Solomon Islands Protectorate. A shipment in June 1952 consisted primarily of nine long tons of rice, and gave the community as a whole rather more than two weeks' rations.

Another shipment in the beginning of October 1952 consisted of eighteen tons of rice (including about half a ton uneatable) and gave about four weeks' rations. A further shipment at the end of March 1953 consisted of various foodstuffs such as coconuts, rice and biscuits, as well as taro seedlings. These totalled about sixteen tons or nearly one month's relief. These relief supplies, from Spillius's account, cost the Government approximately £5,200. They were brought in with considerable difficulty owing to rice shortage in the Western Pacific as a whole; for instance, the second shipment was imported from Siam since no rice was available in Australia at that time, and the third shipment had to be gathered from the three territories of Fiji, New Hebrides and the Solomon Islands. These shipments of food, amounting in all to about two-and-a-half months' supply of the whole community, did not prevent the beginnings of a famine. But they were crucial to the alleviation of the general stringency because they gave food crops more opportunity to grow to maturity in the fields instead of being drawn upon in an immature state, and so intensifying the vicious circle. This extra time given by the relief food supplies made a great difference in the situation of many individual families. As it was, out of the total of eighty-nine deaths recorded by Spillius between March 1952 and March 1953, at least seventeen may be attributed to starvation; nearly all these cases were those of children under eighteen. But if it had not been for the relief supplies, undoubtedly the number of deaths directly attributable to starvation would have been greatly increased.

Receipt of these relief supplies in itself created some fresh problems. Many Tikopia, especially women and children, had not even tasted rice and foods prepared from flour. Contrary to what might have been expected, however, they all seemed to find these foods palatable[9] and, as far as we knew, there was no rejection of them. A serious problem, however, was how to cook them. The Tikopia ordinary methods of cooking were in earth ovens, in wooden bowls into which large red-hot stones were slid, and in leaf containers which were scorched over a fire. Most Tikopia then had no proper means of boiling rice or of

making flour into bread. Consequently, immediately after the arrival of the relief supplies,
we were besieged by requests for large containers to serve as boilers. Failing such utensils, the
Tikopia, acting partly on our suggestions,
partly on advice from their own young men
who had been abroad, and partly using their
own inventive talents, solved the problem in
other ways. They managed to boil rice by borrowing and sharing utensils. But flour, which
at first they hardly used, they began to treat
like a Tikopia food. Some households prepared flour pudding (*susua felaoa*). A large
amount of flour was put into a wooden bowl
and baking powder mixed with it. Water was
added and a thin paste prepared. Leaves of
giant taro with banana on top were then filled
with three or four handfuls of the dripping
paste, tied up and cooked in the earth oven as
for the Tikopia pudding (*kofu*). The result was
a heavy, doughy mass, semi-cooked by European standards, which the Tikopia ate with
apparent relish, convinced they were partaking
of a Western food.

Yet as the months went by the situation
became more acute. Fluctuations in food consumption between March 1952 and June 1953
can be followed from the chart (Figure 9.1). In
this the waxing and waning of the main food
supplies has been broadly indicated diagram-
matically, summarizing our entries made in
diary and notebook about the prevalence of
the various foods. It will be seen from this how
the famine mounted to a peak towards the
end of 1952, so that for three months the only
vegetable foods regularly available to the
Tikopia from their own supplies were manioc,
sweet potato and pumpkin, all nutritionally
very poor, consisting of little else than carbohydrate and water. Even these were not
available to all households.

A few examples of the straits to which the
people were reduced, even before the famine
had reached its peak, all indicate the strain
upon their economy and the disturbance in
their way of life through impoverishment of
their resources both for domestic consumption
and for hospitality and ceremonial presentation. After about two months from the first
hurricane, that is by about the beginning of
April, the finer foods had practically disap-

peared and even the stocks of paste of breadfruit, banana and taro, preserved in ground
pits, had begun to run very low. Giant taro left
standing in the ground as a general reserve had
been heavily drawn upon and was beginning
to be short. Fresh coconuts had practically
disappeared and dried coconuts were becoming rare. A good index of stocks was given by
the meals we recorded. In one of the more
wealthy households (Vangatau) towards the
end of April a meal offered to us consisted of
salmon trout from the lake, yam pudding
mixed with sago flour, breadfruit paste and
manioc root. This was very adequate, but significantly the householder said that his manioc
paste and his banana paste had been exhausted,
and that he had breadfruit paste enough only
for two more weeks. His yams and his sago
flour were nearly exhausted and the salmon
trout was a seasonal catch. This was the period
when people began to cull their orchards
for all the secondary food stuffs, e.g. aerial
yam (*soi, Dioscorea bulbifera*), spinach and
taro leaves, *fukau* berries (normally used as a
funeral food because of their poor quality) and
pandanus seeds (*fara*), which though standard
articles of diet in the Gilbert Islands are a
token of severe shortage when eaten in Tikopia.
Some people foraged for a particularly hard
root known as *aka*, looking like wood even
when cooked.[10] Some children cut down aerial
roots of a pandanus (*kie*) and chewed them
like sugarcane – there is a certain sweetness in
the sap. When I told a friend of mine that I
had seen a child with a piece of such root he
commented, "It is just the famine; they cut and
gnaw. When the land is secure again in food
they reject it."

In conformity with the general Tikopia
usage in times of food shortage, there was
great resort to sago pith and cordyline. At such
times sago palms are felled, the trunk chopped
up into baulks and cooked in huge earth
ovens.[11] Towards the end of April many of
these sago ovens had been already prepared,
so that in several villages all the sago of all the
householders had been exhausted. In Nuku,
for example, normally rich in sago palms,
there was not a single palm remaining among
any of the households. It takes five years for a
sago palm to grow to a state ready for felling,

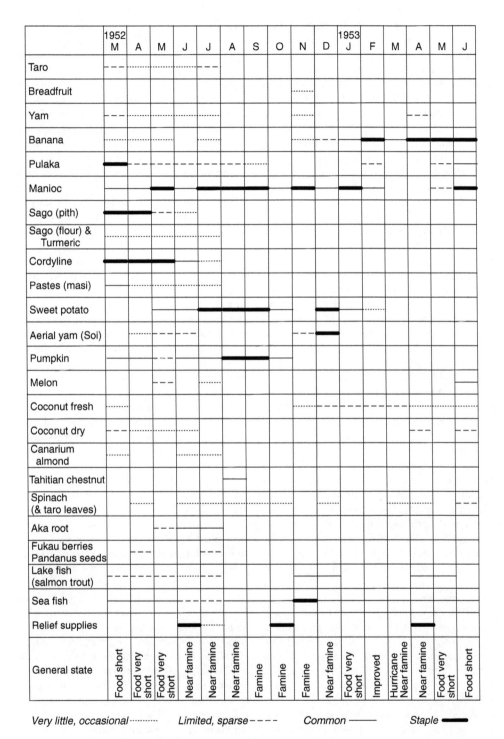

Figure 9.1 *Food Supplies in Tikopia, 1952–53*

and even then it is still small. So the drain upon resources can be seen. Into the oven with the baulks of sago the Tikopia put roots of *ti* (*Cordyline terminalis*), partly for flavour and partly to prepare from the roots a sweet thick syrupy liquid which they drink like soup. This liquid, known as *vai ti*, is prepared by hammering the roots between stones, putting the resultant juice into a bowl and mixing it with fresh water and turmeric flour (*tauo*). Then hot stones are slid in – steam-cooking the liquid. By May, few households had any turmeric flour left. As an alternative, manioc flour may be used, giving a more solid body. In famine times again the people may prepare *vai ti* with the turmeric pigment (*renga*), which they ordinarily use as dye or paint, but I did not see this done, presumably because the cordyline itself was exhausted soon. Some people, instead of drinking the cordyline liquor, extracted what extra nourishment they could from the root itself. The root was chopped into pieces, pulled apart by the fingers and chewed till the fibrous pith yielded no more sustenance. By the middle of the year households with few resources were already having a miserable diet in which some or all of the harsh foods mentioned were elements.

At the same time, the Tikopia were making strenuous efforts to restore agricultural production to normal levels. Almost immediately after the hurricane replanting of food supplies had begun and continued. By about May, the effects of this new planting were visible in the growing use of sweet potato and of manioc. But the growing prevalence of theft reduced the yield and prevented much of the crop from attaining full maturity. By August 1952, when real famine was close at hand, many families were eating sweet potato about the size of crab-apples and manioc about the size of carrots. (The usual length of a manioc root on Tikopia is about 2 feet.) The severity of the food shortage was by this time generally admitted. Towards the end of July, as we were sitting in a funeral gathering one day talking about the situation, Pa Fenuatara remarked, "There never was a famine on Tikopia like this one – the very posts in the middle of the orchards have been overturned." He meant by this that the last standby, the final reserve, the enormous giant taro left to grow in the heart of the orchard for years, were being dug up and consumed – by thieves as well as by their legitimate owners. On another occasion the Ariki Kafika and the Ariki Fangarere, discussing the famine, emphasized that this one was particularly bad because in former periods of stress only tree crops were affected, but now ground crops were suffering too. As I was writing down the conversation, the old Ariki Kafika turned to me and remarked, "Paper of the famine on Tikopia – great is the famine, write it on your paper," meaning that here was a record which should be carried to other lands and told there.

The period of most acute food shortage, properly to be described as famine, lasted approximately from some time in September until December 1952. For about three months the death rate on the island rose to three or two persons a week, or to about four times its normal level. Those most affected were the very old, and especially the very young, who were the least able to fend for themselves, in foraging for food scraps.

Towards the end of the year, according to Spillius's account, the situation showed some signs of improvement. Some breadfruit had matured by November and though the season was brief and not general, it inspired the people with hope of further crops soon. Coconuts had begun to appear in most orchards in Faea, though kept from consumption by a heavy taboo. Bananas were also showing. Theft had been much reduced by stern action by the men of rank, and the steady programme of planting ground crops had begun to have its effect. By February 1953 little manioc or sweet potato was now being drawn upon, and bananas had become a staple item of diet, with some giant taro and coconuts also being eaten. More fires were observable in the oven houses. Whereas the pattern had been that a household would prepare an oven only once every two or three days, now with the increasing quantities of food, some households had an oven every day. There were even some small surpluses of banana and manioc which were turned into paste (*masi*), and put down for storage.

Then came the hurricane of March 1953, which set back the food situation again for three months. Fallen fruits gave short-lived supplies, and the relief distribution of rice, biscuit and taro seedlings in April alleviated the worst distress. But the small stored surpluses were soon used up and theft again became rife. However, improvement was more rapid than before. By May, with bananas the staple food, there was also some manioc and giant taro, while by June some taro was being eaten and the breadfruit trees were budding everywhere. Coconuts were being used by most households, though sparingly, and again surpluses of banana and manioc were being made into paste for storage. Fish had continued to be fairly plentiful. By July, then, when the work of the expedition was closed and Spillius left Tikopia, the community was well on the way to recovery.

Organization for Food Procurement and Conservation

I have shown already how the Tikopia individually exercised considerable economic foresight in coping with the famine. They showed skill in searching out a wide range of food sources and in utilizing them. Some consumed their food carelessly and others did not plan adequately, but most husbanded their food supplies with great scrupulousness. When small surpluses became available, most at once began to lay down storage paste as reserves, and only a few indulged in gluttony, which would have been comprehensible after so long a period of privation. Without such individual care, the collective planning or centralized direction instituted by their leaders would have been ineffective. Such collective planning, too, showed a realistic appreciation of the situation and imaginative measures to meet it. In one respect, however, the Tikopia planners made some miscalculation. With the marginal yield of agricultural labour so low, they naturally wished to turn their labour power elsewhere and pursued most energetically requests

for recruiting vessels to take large numbers of the male population to work on plantations in return for food to be consumed on Tikopia. But apart from practical difficulties of transport, the Tikopia did not work out carefully the ratio of monthly wages of unskilled labour to food costs of rice, etc., per family per month. With many families, if all the males had been away at work it would have been unlikely that the wages would have been adequate to support the women and children at home.

How far was such foresight narrow and individual in its application and how far did it envisage interests of a wider group? What was the assumption of responsibility and how did it operate? What was its relation to structural considerations? There was no doubt that in practically every case individual interests were subordinated to the interests of the elementary family or individual household. Men and women were concerned not merely for themselves, but especially for their children, and the careful planning in the use of resources was in nearly every case intended to safeguard family interests. On the other hand the range of calculation rarely went beyond this. The limitations of economic foresight were seen especially in the widespread theft of growing crops. Nearly everyone in Tikopia spoke hotly against theft and thieves. But only in a very few cases was this apparently accompanied by personal canons of responsibility. Before the organization to cope with theft had got into its stride, stealing of food from the cultivations had become rife, there being no visible distinction as regards offenders between districts, clans, villages, Christians or pagans, commoners or members of chiefly families. The main obvious exceptions were the chiefs themselves, a few of their close senior kinsmen, and the principal executants (*maru*). In other words, they were mostly the men whose traditional structural position demanded the most acute sense of community needs. Moreover, their restraint was correlated with the active leadership they assumed, with which known theft would have been incompatible. Losses of food and the threat to morale became such that personal foresight had, therefore, to be supplemented by the sanction of force.

Control of Manpower

Ultimate Tikopia success in coping with the famine was due to their mechanisms for control of manpower. As may be the case in coping with any disaster, this was manifested in two main ways: control of labour power and control of movement. Tikopia control of labour power was assumed by the most active of the executive officers (*maru*), acting in the name of the chiefs in the last resort – in structural terms these executants are members of chiefs' lineages.[12] Initially these executants directed the labour power after the hurricane into clearing of paths, repairing of aqueducts and other essential tasks. Later they saw to it that a consistent planting policy was pursued and they followed the activities of individuals as well as those of the community at large. They reasoned thus: planting should be got under way at once after the hurricane and should be continued in order to replace foodstuffs drawn upon for subsistence. Moreover, they at once envisaged theft as probable and looked upon planting as one important means of later reducing it. There were many conversations about the necessity of the people planting new crops and enquiries were made about individuals not seen to plant. For instance, the Ariki Taumako asked about one member of his clan, "Pa Tekara who lives there, is he not planting food?" "No!" "What will he do, go and steal? What will his children eat? Will they die of starvation?" In this case the man was feckless and a thief; in due course some of his children did die. But in general, largely as a result of the supervision and injunctions of the chiefs and executives, expressed through the public assemblies (*fono*), supplies of sweet potato and manioc, the quick maturing bulk crops, became available as soon as feasible.

Control of movement was expressed in two main ways. One was to restrict economic opportunity in a sense by edicts to reduce the amount of fishing in favour of cultivation. It was thought that the most valuable use of labour was in the prime task of getting crops into the ground and for considerable periods sea fishing was discouraged for this reason.

The edict was relaxed during the flying-fish season (October to December 1952 and March to June 1953), but in general a man met with severe disapproval if he went fishing instead of working on his land. (Fishing off the north coast of the island was also discouraged because from that area it was very easy to land and steal food undetected.)

The other control of movement was the whole elaborate series of restrictions governing resort to cultivations and orchards in order to try and eliminate theft. The objections of the Tikopia authorities to theft in this situation were threefold. They had a moral reaction against the impropriety of taking food belonging to another person. They also saw the economic disincentive: if some people's crops were systematically raided they would cease to plant and if other people were allowed to use theft as an alternative to cultivation then their productive labour would be lost. Finally, the Tikopia authorities saw clearly that theft, leading to dispute and violence, would be a threat to the social order on a scale far wider than the immediate property loss, and might affect their own ultimate position. Ultimately, quite an elaborate set of rules dealing with a whole range of activities from bird netting to lake fishing, use of cultivations and movements of people at dance festivals was introduced.[13]

Despite the efforts at control, however, stealing did become a very acute problem once the famine became severe. Some people, especially women whose husbands were away at work, or members of poorer commoner families, stole because they simply did not have enough food. But in some cases theft took place by people who, having just enough food to scrape along, feared that another catastrophe in the form of drought or hurricane would reduce them to a starving condition. Such people then stole in order to safeguard their own resources and accumulate a margin of safety. Spillius estimated that only about forty or fifty households (out of a total of nearly 300) were actually in a starving condition, but there is no doubt that many others were in very severe straits. Almost the only people who did not steal at the height of the famine were the chiefs and members of their families.

Their restraint was primarily because on the one hand they were possessed of more land resources than most other people, and on the other because of the obligation still keenly felt that the people should support the chief. The slogan heard was "The chiefs must be the last to die". Yet, with typical human inconsistency, not even the orchards and gardens of the chiefs were respected by some thieves.

There was a still further way in which, by what was in effect the direction of labour, the Tikopia authorities reinforced their attempts to deal with the famine. This was by using their influence in the selection of men who were recruited for labour in the plantations in the Solomons. In theory, presumably, recruiting should have been completely free for each individual. But the exigencies of the famine were such that it was only reasonable for recruitment to be related to the major food needs of the community. Some men, therefore, were discouraged from signing on so that they could continue to provide agricultural labour power at home. In a few cases men who were well known to be arrant thieves were given a very broad hint that they must recruit. This was equivalent to exile for a time and was much milder than the traditional Tikopia punishment of being sent off to sea. Again, after initial experience had given the plantation managers a very poor idea of the efficiency of Tikopia labour and threatened to imperil the recruitment, which was a major factor in the recovery of the island, the chiefs selected good labourers who turned out to be of excellent quality.[14]

In coping with the difficulties of the famine in manpower terms Tikopia initiative was not uniformly directed towards increasing productivity. There was much gloomy talk, some of it concerned with suicide risk voyages. One man of apparently equable temperament announced his determination to seek recruitment: but should he be barred, either by Government order or by his chief, he said he would *forau* – go on a suicide voyage. "As it were I who sit here, I look on my children who are starving. I get my canoe ready to go. If a chief comes to block me I say 'Shall I stay here to steal from your orchards? Or are you prepared to feed me?' Then he is silent and lets me go.

..." This brings out the way in which the issues are conceptualized by the Tikopia in terms of choices: a man chooses between starvation on land and death at sea; his choice initially disallowed, he puts the situation in terms of a further choice by his chief. Note that the resolution is seen in a social compulsion – the chief, embarrassed at not having the wherewithal to feed his clansman, is compelled by shame to retract his ban on the suicide voyage. This conversation is patterned in type; it is the ideal mode. But the situation thus described is not merely an academic one. Voyages of this kind are said to have occurred in past famines. (Later the man quoted above *did* recruit.)

Migration Proposals

As an alternative to recruiting, or to possible suicide voyages, migration was also proposed.

Migration proposals for Tikopia have a long history. In 1934, "in view of the increasing population of Tikopia", the *Southern Cross* mission vessel took to the Solomons several men who hoped to get governmental approval to a proposal to form a colony on Vanikoro or Santa Cruz.[15] In 1939 a memorandum by a Government officer discussed the problem with great care, and suggested various alternative homes for the emigrants – including the south end of Ndeni, Utupua, the south-east corner of Vanikoro, and the Treasurers' islands of the Duff Group. Later suggestions included Bellona, the south coast of San Cristoval, Ugi, and an island in the Tonga group. But though much was talked of, by Government and by the Tikopia, no recruits came. In July 1948, at a meeting of chiefs in the house of the Ariki Kafika, the subject was raised again by a Government officer "and greeted with a refreshing laugh!", he reported. One difficulty on the Government side was to find a suitable home in which the Tikopia would not be immediately stricken with malaria. On the Tikopia side, while great enthusiasm was usually shown at the prospect of migration, when the time for action came, no one was actually willing to go. The Government in 1948 got the situation as far as to persuade the chiefs to allow a young

Tikopia man to visit Ugi and report, and themselves persuaded the Ugi people to allocate land to the Tikopia who would go. But again, when it came to the point there were no emigrants offering.

In 1953 there was much debate publicly (in the *fono*) and privately about the possibility of migration. There was much discussion with representatives of Government and a commercial firm about plans for establishing a substantial number of Tikopia families in the Russell Islands. The Tikopia themselves, after one public discussion, expressed the wish to have a settlement near Kirakira, the Government station at San Cristoval, their prime motive here being apparently to be located near someone in authority in whose hands they could place their future. But by July 1953,[16] as food again began to be abundant, interest in migration began to decline and for three years no move took place. What were the reasons for this reluctance?

In 1929 there was no disposition of any Tikopia to go and reside abroad; they hardly regarded it as conceivable.[17] But by 1952 there were several Tikopia who were permanently in residence away from the island. One, aged about thirty-two years, had become a mission teacher and gone to work at Star Harbour (San Cristoval) where he had married and settled down. Another, aged forty to forty-five years, I met as a boatboy at the British Residency at Vila (New Hebrides). He was unmarried and had no wish to be married; he said he did not want to return to Tikopia; his parents were both dead, and his brother had married and raised a family to inherit the ancestral lands. It is clear that by 1952 some Tikopia, though few, regarded it as quite feasible to make a life for themselves in a foreign land. There were others, men with special skills useful in a European environment, who were willing to spend the greater part of their working life abroad, and who might well decide to settle away from Tikopia in the end.

This is relevant to migration prospects, in that it has already established a pattern of *emigré* Tikopia. The reasons for the prolonged lack of response to the Government's tentative moves must have lain elsewhere than in total disinclination to live abroad.

One reason why earlier migration plans did not proceed was that they did not seem to have always been fully understood by the Tikopia chiefs. Without their support, the proposals withered. This was stated (by Robinson Vakasaumore to me) to have been the case with the proposed migration to Ugi. Rongoiteava, son of a mission teacher, Pa Rongotau, had been chosen by the *maru*, John Fararava, to survey the island and pick out a site. With him went Marukimoana (Remon), a son of Pa Fenuatara, and Marutukukimoana (Mark), a son of Pa Rangifakauvia. Despite the fact that both these young men were of chiefly family, one of Kafika and the other of Tafua, the proposals of the party were not acted upon. It may have been partly because they were too junior, but it was alleged that it was because the chiefs were ignorant of what was involved. Remon thought his father had been informed, but found that he had not. "The chiefs objected: they objected to people going. The root of their objection was that they did not know, and they objected to the land being divided."

A more basic reason was the highly integrated formal structure of Tikopia. It was with difficulty that the Tikopia as a body could be brought to contemplate the dismemberment of their society. That unnamed individuals should migrate was good. That a specific section of the community should go, and disturb the intricate social relations with the rest, was another matter. This was especially so when the proposed migrants would carry with them any particular symbolic values of Tikopia society. For instance, for such a migration to be successful, it was thought advisable for the migrants to have a leader, who could act as headman *vis-à-vis* the Government, and as chief according to the Tikopia pattern. One obvious suggestion would be that one of the chiefs should lead the migration. But any such suggestion was opposed flatly by the Tikopia.

There was also a third reason. Without the approval of the chiefs people could not migrate. But on the other hand, the chiefs were not prepared to indicate *who* should migrate. The reason for this is built upon the traditional relations between Tikopia chiefs and commoners. No chief would wish it to be thought that he was virtually expelling a commoner.

And however desirable the place of migration may be, such prolonged absence is a form of exile from Tikopia. Hence there had to be a technique of forming the migrating party by allowing people to nominate themselves with the approval of the chiefs. A final set of reasons was quite simply the great sentimental attachment the Tikopia had for their home and their specific way of life.

Hence it had required the pressures such as the famine provided to give to many people the final spur of decision to think of emigrating, and it was a solution easily postponed when local prospects improved.

This analysis has been based on my own experience in Tikopia. More recently some interesting details have become available of an actual resettlement.[18] In 1956 a pilot scheme was got under way to establish thirty Tikopia families in a village in the Russell Islands in association with Levers Pacific Plantation Pty. Limited, a company which recently had had good experience with Tikopia labourers and was anxious to secure such a regular labour supply. About seventy-five acres of land were made available by the Government, the subdivision of the land being left to the Tikopia themselves. During 1956/7 an advance party of about twenty men, mostly single, was engaged in building houses, clearing and planting the land in preparation for the arrival of kinsfolk from Tikopia. After about a year approximately thirty to thirty-five acres were already under intensive cultivation with coconuts, taro, yam, manioc and European vegetables and fruit. The cultivations included group areas to feed new settlers as they arrived and individual plots for the support of each man and his family.

The new settlement has been named Nukufero, from an ancient name for Tikopia. By 1958 it had about sixty persons.

For the time being the settlement was intended to be only semi-permanent and to be built up to a total of thirty families of whom some, from time to time, were to return to Tikopia and be replaced by others. The explanation of this is significant. "The reason is that when it came to the point, the settlers were reluctant to break all ties with Tikopia. They have insisted that social responsibilities require their periodic return to their homeland. Therefore, in the meantime, land interests in Tikopia will be used by close relatives but will not be extinguished. To this end the Tikopia chiefs have decided that in a family of four brothers, two will be allowed to settle in Nukufero. The two remaining in Tikopia will use the interests of the absentees which will be maintained alive. The passage of time and a steady development of Nukufero will perhaps result in the settlement being regarded as a new and permanent Tikopia. Any insistence on immediate extinction of land interests in Tikopia would have killed the settlement immediately. The compromise, unsatisfactory as it may be, offers a reasonable chance for its survival."

An important feature of the new settlement is that in the event of a further famine in Tikopia it could probably be extended rapidly. The success of this experiment may well depend upon the ability with which satisfactory communication between it and Tikopia can be maintained.

Land Use

The economic effects of the famine as regards land use in Tikopia were of four main kinds: shortening or abandonment of fallow period; closer definition of cultivation rights in the lands of others; restriction of collecting rights on the land of others; and intensified demarcation of land boundaries.

(i) Shortening of fallow period

It had formerly been Tikopia agricultural practice to allow a piece of ground used for taro or other important ground crop to lie fallow for at least a season after use. The theory was that the height of the succeeding crop would be roughly proportional to the wild vegetation it replaced.[19] As a result of the famine, this practice was often abandoned. With abandonment of fallowing was associated the planting of short-term crops. In one of the major growing areas, Rakisu, which was formerly devoted almost entirely to taro, and of which for each season more than half was usually fallow, the fallow area practically disappeared as the famine developed. It was completely planted with sweet potato, manioc and pumpkin. This was so contrary to traditional use that it led Pa Fenuatara to shake his head sadly and say, "Pumpkin in Rakisu!" Owing presumably to lack of fallowing, the soil in this area after a year of intensive planting came to be regarded by the Tikopia as being in very poor condition.[20]

Pressure was put upon people with fallow land, even upon chiefs, to allow it to be cultivated. In November 1952 a great deal of pressure was put upon the Ariki Taumako by members of his clan to allow planting to be undertaken on a strip of land in Rakisu which he had been reserving for taro in preparation for the initiation ceremonies of his sons and one of his brother's sons. He finally gave way. But ceremonial and religious claims were not completely disregarded. Lands above Te Roro which belonged to the Ariki Taumako, despite the shortage of food and tobacco, remained uncultivated until June 1953 when clearing of them began, to grow taro for the initiation mentioned above. Similarly, lands in the same area owned by the Ariki Kafika remained in fallow for crops which would be used for religious ceremonies. There seemed to be no pressure put on either chief to open up these lands, the most sacred *mara*, nor was any criticism of their policy heard by Spillius. In November 1952, however, the Ariki Taumako decided that other lands of his, near the peak of Reani, should be cleared and planted with manioc. Each lineage of his clan and others who requested permission were allowed to plant whatever ground they cleared. This decision was welcomed by the people since it made a great difference in food prospects to the households of commoners who had previously only very small patches of land.

(ii) Restriction of planting rights

At an early stage in the development of the food shortage after the hurricane, people began to impose restriction on the use of their land by others. One indication was a taboo sign – a coconut frond tied to a stick set up in a cultiva-tion or orchard as a warning that the owner did not wish the land used or any of the crop taken or the wild fruits collected. Such signs, known as *pi* (barriers), were to be seen commonly between April and June 1952, as on hibiscus near Tufenua, on a coconut palm with a couple of nuts on it in Uta, on giant taro in the swamp of Ropera, on manioc in Rotoaia and on taro ground at Nailopu.

But these were individual restrictions. As time went on they became less and less effective. Not only did thieves disregard them; close kinsfolk of the owners did so too, claiming that they had traditional right to do so. Indeed, these coconut frond signs came to be in the end protests after theft had occurred rather than warnings against it. Such individual signs came in time to be replaced by more general public rules supported by the chiefs and executant officers instead of being left to the owners to implement.

Before the famine it was still customary, as in 1929, to plant a crop where one pleased without asking the permission of the owner of the land – provided of course that the land was not already in use or being cleared for cultivation.[21] Two significant changes took place in the course of the famine. First, it was declared in the rules laid down in public assembly that people would have to ask permission from owners to plant on land that was not under cultivation. Very few people asked for this permission since by this time it was apparent that hardly anyone would grant it. Some people attempted to plant in plots which had been cleared by close kin. But there was more than one instance where the owner of the land, on discovering in his plot seedlings not his own, tore them up fiercely and threw them out on the public path, tying a taboo sign on his land to warn off anyone else who had similar intentions. Secondly, it was proclaimed in the public assembly that no food should be destroyed wantonly in the course of a quarrel over land, and indeed that no land disputes should take place at all. This placed in an awkward position those people on whose land others had planted short-term crops before the famine. It became the practice of such croppers not to take out the entire crop of manioc or sweet potato at once, but to take only as much as was needed for a meal or so and replant seedlings. Thus the land never went out of cultivation and the owner was never able to get back the use of it during this period. Sometimes, however, pressure of public opinion forced the user of such land to send some food over to the owner in recompense. As can be imagined, several land disputes did in fact occur.

(iii) Restriction of collecting rights

One source of friction and accusation of thefts lay in the utilization of wild plants which had formerly been available to all, regardless of the ownership of the land on which they grew. In August and September of 1952, after such plants had assumed major importance as food or as material for nets and mats, quarrels about them had become increasingly frequent. Several rules were then made in the public assembly. It was agreed that the wild yam with aerial tubers (*soi*) which grew in each person's orchard should be his own and that no one else should take it. This rule took a long time to materialize. Even at the end of April Pa Ngarumea said that *soi* tubers had been gathered as was customary from orchards without distinction of ownership and that while owners of orchards had been angry it had been too late. Asked if he himself had taken *soi* from other people's orchards, he said "No, because I give orders to others," meaning that he felt he had to exercise restraint. It was decreed also that only one person (normally a woman) could go in to pick the *soi*. The idea behind this was that a woman could carry at the most two baskets of *soi*, which is about the maximum one could expect from the available crop in one orchard. If a woman were found with more than two baskets of *soi* she would be suspected of having raided other people's orchards. Similar rules applied to breadfruit.

The rule was also made in public assembly that no person could wander about the cultivations looking for hibiscus bark for the manufacture of cord or nets. This was at a time when there was a taboo on fishing and it was argued, therefore, that no one needed hibiscus for nets or fishline; if people got in other gardens and said they were looking for hibiscus, they could only be using this as an excuse for stealing fruit. In addition to these changes in the customary rules for the use of land, it became suspect for an individual even to be seen near a plot of land away from his own.[22]

(iv) Demarcation of land boundaries

The increasing shortage of food made it imperative for most people to use to the full the amount of land available to them. It also intensified their interest in lands to which the title was in dispute or to which they could revive a claim. Another result was frequent quarrels between brothers, or other close agnatic kin holding a piece of land in common. In some cases land formerly used jointly by brothers was now divided and boundary marks set up to mark their respective properties. This process had been gaining ground in the intervening generation since my first visit, but it was sharply accentuated by the famine. In some land disputes there was argument over precise boundaries. Every small margin in either food or land that could be gained was of vital importance to some people. Stones marking boundaries were even moved surreptitiously during the night to gain an extra bit of land, measuring say a yard wide by twenty or thirty yards long.

Effects on Exchange

By ordinary Western reckoning a famine should have seen the poorer Tikopia selling off their most prized possessions to the richer Tikopia for food, and the Tikopia as a whole selling off their other material possessions to buy food from outside. Neither of these happened on any scale.

As far as selling to outside suppliers was concerned the Tikopia would have been quite willing to have done so; the difficulty was that for the most part they did not have the appropriate media. Their mats, bark-cloth and other goods were not acceptable in general exchange. It is true that in default of cash a European trader took a quantity of Tikopia goods in exchange for food, hoping to dispose of them at a profit, but the experiment was not a success. For the Government relief supplies, partly to get some recompense and partly to impress upon the Tikopia that they should not expect charity, it was suggested that a contribution of pandanus mats and (on one occasion) wooden bowls should be given in return. This was done, but the market for these Tikopia products was small and inelastic, and in no case can the Tikopia be said to have conducted a normal economic transaction as far as relief supplies were concerned. But why did not the Tikopia conduct such exchanges internally? To a Tikopia an additional supply of bowls, mats and bark-cloth could always be absorbed through the mechanism of ceremonial exchange later. Why would a starving Tikopia not barter food for such things?

There was in fact a small amount of barter of Tikopia goods for rice, and one case is reported of a man who stripped his house of all his goods in a gluttonous frenzy. Twice it seems he had "stolen" a pound or so of rice, leaving in its stead a knife or a hank of sinnet cord. But such cases were rare. The reason was essentially that the social norms did not provide for such kind of exchange. Probably not even the most wealthy Tikopia felt secure enough in the indeterminate conditions of the famine to barter away much food, and the poorer households may not have had much spare property. But the more wealthy Tikopia did dispense food – it went out in hospitality, support of kinsfolk and other dependants, and even in fulfilment of ceremonial obligations. Moreover, it would have been very difficult, and by convention impossible, for any ordinary Tikopia to acknowledge that he had taken a mat or other property specifically in direct exchange for a gift of food. Consequently, contrary to what outsiders might have expected, there was no significant flow of property in transactions involving transfer of food.

Exchange did take place, however, with one commodity, tobacco. The Tikopia tend to be obsessional about the use of masticants and about smoking. With the scarcity of areca nut, they had resort to various inferior substitutes – the inner bark of the breadfruit tree or of the natu (Spondias dulcis), or part of the coconut

shoot near the flower bract (roro niu) or unripe Calophyllum berries. All these, however, unsatisfactory, were chewed with lime and betel leaf. In default of tobacco, the more ardent smokers were reduced to substitutes such as papaya leaf or the dried fibres of cordyline root after the food material had been extracted from it. In 1952/3, as in 1928/9, the Tikopia demand for tobacco was very keen. It intensified as with time a real shortage of locally grown tobacco developed. By May 1952 we had ceased to give out sticks or half-sticks of trade tobacco (save in exceptional circumstances, as to chiefs who themselves dispensed it) and were niggardly even with the tiny inch-long plugs into which we cut the sticks and which we took with us on daily routine calls for census-taking and ordinary observation. An illustration of the fierce demand for native-grown tobacco was the bitterness engendered when it was found that the Mission priest had cornered the Anuta supply.[23] Towards the middle of the year one man said, half-jokingly, "Nowadays only chiefs smoke tobacco, others smoke leaves." It was an exaggeration, but had some truth. Apart from resort to substitutes, there was also much theft of immature tobacco from cultivations. Yet it was interesting to note that despite the fierce competition for tobacco women were able to smoke nearly as much as men. The Tikopia men heard from us with astonishment of the Victorian ban on English women smoking and laughed heartily at the idea which I had put forward to them as a joke that they should forbid their womenfolk from smoking in order to conserve the tobacco for themselves. Later on, Spillius noted that a source of many domestic quarrels between husband and wife was tobacco, but he would have been a hardy man who tried consistently to stop his wife from smoking.

Later in 1952 the new tobacco crop matured. By August almost every household had collected its tobacco and was preparing it in rolls for storage. The harvest had been meagre due to the hurricane and the supply began to run out about December 1952; by March of the following year the shortage was very acute indeed.[24] There was a famine not only in supplies for smoking but also in tobacco seedlings for replanting the future crop. Those people who had spare seedlings from their cultivations or who had bothered to plant them just outside their house, now demanded payment for them instead of giving them as before to kinsmen as an ordinary gesture of goodwill. They insisted not only on some equivalent at the time of handing over the seedlings, but also on a promise of tobacco when the harvest would have been reaped. A price asked was one stick of trade tobacco for twelve seedlings, or as a much larger quantity of seedlings was usually required, the equivalent demanded might be a piece of calico. In addition to this, the promise of at least one fathom of twist tobacco[25] was demanded against the time of harvest. If a person planted tobacco in another person's orchard, it was customary to give the owner a roll which came to fifteen or sixteen fathoms of twist tobacco. The Ariki Tafua, who owned the most productive land for tobacco, was the richest in this commodity and always had a supply on hand. To illustrate how great became the shortage of tobacco in the first few months of 1953, two exchanges may be cited: for half a fathom of tobacco, an axe or a knife; for a fathom of tobacco, a European blanket. There were no standard rates of exchange, but these examples – up to six times the normal rates – show how intense was the demand. By outside visitors a wide range of Tikopia goods was purchased with tobacco, e.g. the Captain of the SY *Southern Cross* bought many Tikopia war clubs as "curios".

From the growth of exchange rates for tobacco and not for food it might be argued that the quietening of their nervous excitation was more important to the Tikopia than the quietening of their pangs of hunger. But tobacco does not fit quite so closely into the Tikopia scheme of social conventions and ceremonial exchanges as does food, and therefore there was more freedom for direct exchange to develop for it.

Summary

From this analysis some general observations may be made on the economic reactions of the Tikopia to the famine, and the light these throw on their conceptions of the nature of their society and the proper choices to be made in time of crisis.

Hurricane and drought severely reduced the Tikopia food income to a level at which their survival was threatened. Their accumulated stocks of food were inadequate to raise the level of subsistence appreciably for any period, or even fully to bridge the gap until agricultural production could recover a minimum level of comfort. This lack of reserves was due partly to the lack of more efficient techniques of food preservation, and partly to the practice of consuming food amply in times of plenty, using it as a social instrument in ceremonial procedures. Tikopia capital stocks in other goods were small, not sufficient to purchase any quantity of food abroad, and for the measure of relief they received from outside they had to depend in part upon Government philanthropy and in part upon the sale of some of their male labour, for work elsewhere. For the most part, they had to cope with the crisis themselves, with their own forms of organization.

Three considerations seem outstanding in their economic proceedings. The first was their maintenance of the social framework of their exchange system. Traditionally, food in Tikopia is transferred from one person or economic unit to another by gift, not by barter, and even in the stringency of famine this procedure applied. There was no sale of food to the highest bidder, no profit-taking on small food surpluses, and almost no transfer of non-food items for food by direct exchange. In particular, no capital transfers of land, or canoes or tools occurred, giving fortunate possessors of spare food any increase of productive control for the future. Both the complex system of rights of ownership over such items and the general conventions about the uses of wealth inhibited this.

The second consideration was development of control of manpower in the interests of the community at large. There was conscription of some people for public works, and direction of many towards private production which would result in public benefit. In the effort to intensify production, leadership in the community assumed a more overt and mandatory form than usual, and more rigorous sanctions than usual were applied.

The third consideration was the contrast between the tendency to increased communal control of manpower and the increased limitation of communal rights in food and associated consumer goods. While there was some pooling of labour, there was no pooling of food. The rights of families and households were more carefully demarcated and promulgated than in ordinary times. While they were often not respected, this breach was given no public justification. Moreover, in fields in which communal exercise of rights had been regarded as appropriate, such as the collection of aerial yams from any orchard, new restrictions were introduced. Thus, while the individual's labour power was held to be at the disposal of the community, his food resources were held to be his own property, irrespective of his neighbour's plight.

This last proposition had one modification, in the case of the chiefs. The formula that "the chiefs must be the last to die" might seem from one point of view to be an archaic, feudal expression of inequality. In a sense this is true, in that the statement made for an intensification of unequal food distribution in two ways: it held that the food resources of chiefs ought to be inviolate; and that commoners, when both were in dire straits, should leave their food to the chiefs, and go out and perish that the chiefs should survive. It might even be argued that insofar as the Tikopia chiefs were richer in lands and food than commoners, the public insistence on private rights of consumption was an attitude fostered by the chiefs in their own interest. But this argument would ignore several points. One was that not every chief was so wealthy, certainly not richer than any commoner. Again, the public formula was not observed; theft from chiefs took place as much as from commoners. But the most important point is that a Tikopia chief is not simply a private person; he is also a symbol of the community and one of its acknowledged leaders. Hence the modification of the individualist rule – that each man was entitled to his own foodstuffs, without regard to the sufferings of others – in favour of the chiefs, was a real assertion in other terms, of the primacy of the community interest. The chiefs should survive, who else might perish, because they in the last resort were the representatives and directors of the community. Even though many people did not obey this rule, it was a factor in the choices of many, leading them to protect the interests of the chiefs on many occasions, to the possible detriment of their own.

NOTES

1. B. Malinowski, *Coral Gardens and Their Magic:* vol. 1, pp. 160 *et seq.*; (c.f. H. A. Powell, *An Analysis of Present-Day Social Structure in the Trobriand Islands,* PhD thesis, University of London, 1957, pp. 1–3, 515, 516, 548); A. I. Richards, *Land Labour and Diet in Northern Rhodesia,* 1939, pp. 35–7, 50; M. & S. L. Fortes, "Food in the Domestic Economy of the Tallensi," *Africa,* vol. ix, 1937. A recent study by David M. Schneider, "Typhoons on Yap", *Human Organization,* vol. 16, No. 2, pp. 10–15, offers especially interesting points for comparison with Tikopia.

2. See my detailed analysis *Primitive Polynesian Economy,* ch. 2, "Food and Population in Tikopia", esp. pp. 46–8; and *We, The Tikopia,* p. 416. My earlier prediction was thus borne out in general, but I was wrong in one particular – I assumed that in time of crisis there would be no possibility of food imports from outside. In 1952/3, however, partly owing to improved communications after the war and partly owing to our coincidental presence on the island with a radio-telephone, when the famine did

come after the hurricane and drought, relief imports of food were delivered. Even this relief could not avert a tragic crisis.

3. W. H. R. Rivers, *History of Melanesian Society*, vol. I, p. 317, 1914. For notes on food shortage see *Primitive Polynesian Economy*, pp. 73–5.

4. In 1828 D'Urville estimated the population at 400–500, and Gaimard at about 500. In 1862 Bishop Patteson said that it was probably not more than 300 or 400, and though this may well have been a gross underestimate even in view of the heavy mortality in the epidemic following D'Urville's visit, the true figure is unlikely to have been more than double. A figure of 1,100 people given by a missionary, apparently from the mission teacher, in November 1923, is very plausible (*M.M. Log*, June 1924, p. 85). A detailed examination of later figures is given by Borrie, Firth and Spillius, 1957. [Borrie, W. D., Raymond Firth, and James Spillius, "The Population of Tikopia, 1929 and 1952", *Population Studies*, vol. 3, 1957, pp. 229–52.]

5. The more severe epidemic of 1955 also does not seem to have been responsible for the deaths of more than about 200 people, leaving the population still about 20 per cent above the 1929 level.

6. The shortage of sago leaf later involved us in paying what would have been in normal times a stupendous price for sheets of thatch – two fishhooks per sheet – for the small shed used to house our petrol engine. Moreover, we were unable to have built the new house which we had planned.

7. *Primitive Polynesian Economy*, pp. 48–53, 64–73; see also *We, The Tikopia*, pp. 103–11, for food recipes.

8. The Tikopia attitude here seems to have been more realistic than that of the people of Yap, who seem to have exaggerated their food shortage after a typhoon, symbolizing in terms of famine their more general social anxieties. (See David M. Schneider, *op. cit.*).

9. The concentrated granular "Bournvita" was found sweet by many Tikopia and they liked it neat. One man ate six tins in an evening before its use could be explained to him.

10. Possibly the tuber of a legume known in Fiji as *yaka* and identified as *Pueraria lobata* by E. Massal and J. Barrau, *Food Plants of the South Sea Islands*, South Pacific Commission, Technical Paper No. 94, Noumea 1956, p. 40; see also "Pacific Subsistence Crops Cassava", *South Pacific Commission Quarterly Bulletin*, vol. 5, pp. 15–18, Noumea, 1955.

11. See *Primitive Polynesian Economy*, Plate 3b, p. 267; cf. my "Economics and Ritual in Sago Extraction in Tikopia", *Mankind*, vol. 4, No. 4, 1950, pp. 131–42.

12. Raymond Firth, "Authority and Public Opinion in Tikopia", *Social Structure: Studies presented to A. R. Radcliffe-Brown*. Ed. M. Fortes, Oxford 1949. Pp. 168–88.

13. For an account of the general type of control and the sanctions used to enforce it, see J. Spillius, 1957. [Spillius, James, "Natural Disaster and Political Crisis in a Polynesian Society: An Exploration of Operational Research", *Human Relations*, 1957, pp. 3–27, 113–25.]

14. J. Spillius, 1957, p. 26.

15. *The Melanesian Mission, Southern Cross Log*, London, vol. 41, May 1935, p. 70.

16. See J. Spillius, 1957, p. 21.

17. *We, The Tikopia*, pp. 18, 21.

18. Colin H. Allan, *Customary Land Tenure in the British Solomon Islands Protectorate* (Honiara, 1957, pp. 238–9).

19. *We, The Tikopia*, pp. 403–4; *Primitive Polynesian Economy*, pp. 93–4.

20. I have learned from Mr J. Tedder, District Commissioner at Vanikoro, that by mid-1956, while most of the area was still planted with manioc, there was no pumpkin and there were some taro gardens. It was stated that more taro would be planted again soon. Only a very small area was in fallow. By 1958 Rakisu was still under manioc.

21. See *We, The Tikopia*, pp. 400–4; *Primitive Polynesian Economy*, p. 261.
22. I owe information about all these rules to the observation of Spillius.
23. Raymond Firth, "Anuta and Tikopia", *Journal of Polynesian Society*, vol. 63, September 1954, pp. 118–19.
24. It was pointed out at this time that the atmosphere round the villages was usually quite free from the taint of tobacco smoke. Some young men used to walk sniffing round the houses at night to smell if tobacco was being smoked. If so, they would enter and demand a draw at the pipe. When Europeans came ashore children were immediately set on their trail to pick up at once any cigarette butts they might drop; these were then stuffed into pipes.

25. Local grown tobacco leaf is made up by the Tikopia into long lengths of twist about the thickness of one's finger, and these in turn are wound tightly into rolls about the thickness of one's arm. Measurement is as follows:

Te u paka na katoa, complete long roll;
Tutanga paka, large roll cut in half and re-wrapped;
Foi fetunga sokotasi, single arm-length of twist;
Ku rua ko foi fetunga, double arm-length, fathom;
Fetu paka sokotasi, a stick (trade tobacco);
Potu paka, a quid.

10

How the Enga Cope with Frost: Responses to Climatic Perturbations in the Central Highlands of New Guinea

Eric Waddell

Introduction

During 1972, the Central Highlands of Papua New Guinea experienced a prolonged drought that, through a combination of high altitude and stable weather conditions, generated a long series of frosts that did substantial damage to both the food gardens of the local population and the natural vegetation. In the worst-hit areas, above about 2300 m, in excess of 30 nights of ground frost were experienced between June and October, while individual frosts were recorded as low as 1,650 m, all this in a region where the subsistence food complex is almost exclusively of tropical lowland origin and therefore not frost tolerant.

Official response to this crisis was to declare a national emergency and mount a Famine Relief Program under the control of the Director of Civil Defense which had as its principal functions, first, to "maintain the existing nutritional status" of the estimated 130,000–150,000 people directly affected and, second,

to make available a variety of planting materials to facilitate their rapid return to a state of self-sufficiency. The program ran for about 8 months, cost an estimated 3 million dollars (Australian), and involved a very substantial commitment of human and material resources on the part of several government departments and Christian missions. It proved eminently successful in that no evident hardship or loss of life occurred as a direct result of the frosts and no cases of corruption or discriminating practices in the distribution of relief supplies were reported.

While the relief exercise could not be faulted, the assumptions that underlay it were of questionable validity. A fundamental premise was that the victims had no satisfactory means of their own to cope with the crisis. Hence if no action were taken to provide them with relief, "forced migration" of people out of the affected areas would result, and this would in turn generate a whole series of "secondary effects" of the crisis, identified specifically as

101

"social disorganization, a disruption of sanita-
tion, and the spread of infectious diseases"
(Ewald, 1972: 1). In this respect, officials
concerned with the relief effort sought simply
to follow guidelines established by the
World Health Organization on the basis of
famine relief experience elsewhere in actively
discouraging movement and initiating a
program of "replacement feeding" (Malcolm,
1972: 9) in disaster areas. Further reassurance
for the legitimacy of the approach was provided by the widespread conviction that this
particular climatic crisis was entirely without
precedent.

A few officials were, admittedly, vaguely
cognizant that a similar crisis had occurred
some 30 years previously (just prior to sustained European contact in this part of New
Guinea), but they were convinced that these
earlier frosts were milder and had nevertheless
resulted in widespread violence, starvation,
and death. Massive out-migration was known
to have occurred on this occasion but no one
considered it to have been a *structured* response
to the situation. Rather, it was interpreted
as a disorganized fleeing of starving victims
from the disaster area. The impression gained
was of a severely malnourished population that disputed for the few remaining
foodstuffs over a period of several weeks, and
then, as a last resort, fled across the mountains
in search of refuge at lower altitudes. The
further impression was that their poor physical
condition resulted in the death of many people
en route, while others suffered from the hostile
reception encountered at the end of their
journey.

Even as a partial solution to the problem,
such migration was discounted in 1972 on the
grounds that declining agricultural productivity and population increase since contact rendered it impossible for the customary host
areas to accommodate any additional population even for a short period. This long-term
trend was further aggravated by the fact that
this time these other areas were also experiencing the effects of the drought and even in some
cases frost.

These expatriate-held convictions were
not based on any formal evaluation of the
1972 frosts or investigation of previous

experiences. Rather, they arose out of casual
conversations with individual victims, plus
overt pressures placed by these latter on
expatriate organizations. Thus, on the one
hand, stories dramatizing the previous crisis
were eagerly preferred by a people well
known for their penchant for overstatement
– "Some died in their houses. Some died
on the way. Only the bones were left." On
the other hand, the local population was
acutely conscious of the presence of government and mission authorities and the fact
that they could be pressured into intervening on their behalf. So, for instance,
members of the Wabag Lutheran Church
knew the Lutheran mission to be actively
involved in relief work in other countries.
Why not here, too, then?[1]

A critical review of the Famine Relief
Program has been undertaken elsewhere and
conclusions have been drawn as to its inap-
propriateness (Waddell, 1972). The aim of this
article is to complement the former in demonstrating that the local population has a whole
series of mechanisms available to respond to
the kind of climatic hazard experienced in
1972 and that the response is structured, its
magnitude varying with the intensity of the
climatic perturbation. This concern is in conformity both with a current preoccupation in
human ecology – to investigate how people
adapt to departures from steady-state conditions – and with natural hazard research,
where there has been a shift in interest
from perception to response. At the same time,
this article seeks to challenge some of the
assumptions underlying relief work – of crisis,
unusual events, inadequate perception, and
incoherent response – and provide the
information necessary to assure more appropriate aid in the event of future frosts in the
region.

The Enga, Frost, and Agricultural Mounding

For most Enga – the people principally involved
in the 1972 crisis – frost is a fact of life. Indeed,
it provides the key to understanding the most

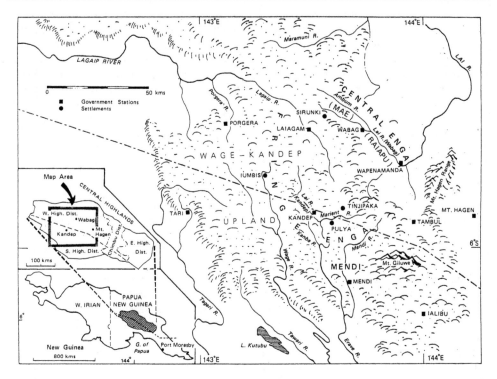

Figure 10.1 *Enga territory*

distinctive element of their adaptive strategy, agricultural mounding.

The Enga number about 150,000 and are located to the west of the Mount Hagen range in the Western Highlands District (Figure 10.1). They are concentrated principally in the Lagaip and Lai valleys in the vicinity of Wapenamanda, Wabag, and Laiagam government stations, but are also more widely distributed through the surrounding valleys and uplands over an altitudinal range of about 1,600 m, from 1,100 to 2,700 m MSL. Their "mean level of settlement" is unusually high for major New Guinea Highlands populations, being 1,900 m compared with about 1,700 m among the Chimbu.

As is widely recognized, the Enga cultivate their staple food, the sweet potato (*Ipomoea batatas*), and at higher altitudes most domestic crops, in large mulch mounds that average in the Middle Lai valley about 3.18 m in diameter and 0.6 m in height.[2] These mounds are designed to protect highly vulnerable crops from the particular type of frosts that are experienced in the Central Highlands, namely, radiation frosts. These occur on clear, still nights when outgoing radiation is excessive, and they are characterized by a marked inversion in the temperature regime close to the ground surface. Not surprisingly, they are restricted to the dry season in the highlands, and the inversions are generally of a moderate order. Thus recordings made at about 2,650 m in the Sirunki area indicate that when temperatures in a Stevenson screen fall to 5.5°C there is a slight risk of ground frost, while below 4.4°C the likelihood is very strong. Under such conditions, the mound serves to modify to a significant degree the microclimatic regime of cultivated areas by both elevating the sweet potato plants above the zone of lowest temperature and facilitating the drainage of dense, cold air downslope. Thus planting is concentrated in the upper part of the mound, while the whole mound surface and the "channels" between are clean-weeded. The experimental work carried out at Sirunki indicates that, under conditions of high frost risk, minimum temperature readings on cleared, un-mounded ground are of the order of 2°C lower than those on the upper part of the mound. Mulching further contributes to protecting the food plants from frost damage in that the heat generated by its decomposition raises soil temperature by about 1.2°C.

One striking confirmation of the functional significance of mounding is that the distribution of this practice through the highlands coincides closely with the distribution of the frost hazard. The Enga only mound above about 1,520 m. Below that altitude they practice casual mixed gardening where the staple is intercultivated with the subsidiary crops. More generally, as Brookfield (1962: 250) notes, mounding is restricted within the highlands to an area centering on the Wage-Kandep upland and forming an extensive area of unbroken country and broad valley flats at altitudes in excess of 1,825 m. Here topography, elevation, and a relative absence of cloud cover together actively encourage the concentration of cold air on agricultural land.

A phenomenon which is perhaps even more remarkable in the case of the Enga is the fact that certain attributes of the mound vary in relation to the intensity and frequency of the frost hazard. Generally speaking, the gravity of the hazard increases with altitude. Mound dimensions, minimum height above the ground at which the sweet potato vines are planted, and the degree of tillage of the soil similarly vary largely with altitude. A survey and classification according to similarity analysis of a large number of mounds through the Lai valley indicated the following. There is a general increase in mound height with altitude, from 0.55 m at 1,864 m through 0.79 m at 2,079 m to 0.85 m at 2,657 m, although dimensions are considerably modified by slope of the ground

surface to the extent that mounds on steeply sloping ground at high altitudes do not differ significantly from those at low. This presumably reflects the fact that conditions do not facilitate the settling of cold air. Minimum vine height varies much in the way that overall dimensions of the mound do, averaging 0.24 m above the ground surface at 1,864 m and rising to 0.64 m at 2,657 m. Indeed, the entire arrangement of planting changes. Thus at lower altitudes vines are planted over the whole upper surface of the mound, but above about 2,400 m a technique termed *moró* is used. Here the vines are arranged concentrically in such a way that tubers develop only within the circle and therefore at the very top of the mound. Both modifications are made in recognition of the fact that "ice" will destroy the sweet potato if it is planted too close to the ground surface. Finally, while at lower altitudes the soil is worked into a fine tilth, in the upper zone of settlement mounds are formed from coarse clods of earth which are then simply covered with a finer soil. This practice presumably serves, at least incidentally, to produce a soil which is less well aerated, therefore reducing the likelihood of significant fluctuations in surface temperature at altitudes where even slight variations might be critical to plant growth.

Mounding serves, then, as an effective adjustment to mild inversion frosts such as occur when screen temperatures drop to around freezing point. For the Central Enga (Mae and Raiapu) resident in the Syaka and Middle and Upper Lai valleys it is an entirely satisfactory means of coping with the hazard. At higher altitudes, however, frosts are occasionally much more intense, as well as being more persistent. During the recent series, for instance, in excess of 25 nights of ground frost[3] were experienced at Iumbis in the Upper Wage valley (about 2,620 m) and the lowest recorded screen temperature was −2.3°C. Under these conditions, mounding *per se* is rendered ineffective, the depth of the inversion frost greatly exceeding the dimensions of the mound. Thus the natural vegetation of the broad depressions in the Kandep area was damaged by frost up to 100 m above the valley floor. However, as the events of 1972 clearly illustrated, populations resident at these altitudes have additional ways of responding to the hazard.

The Fringe Enga: A Modified Adaptive Strategy to Cope with a more Persistent Hazard

From an ethnographic point of view, it is customary to draw a distinction between Central and Fringe Enga. The former are resident in the Wabag-Wapenamanda area (the Lai and Syaka valleys), are characterized by high population densities, and conform to what is generally recognized to be the New Guinea "norm" in that they can be viewed as comprised of a large number of locally organized populations – small discrete groups having intimate and exclusive relations with their immediate environment. They reside between about 1,500 and 2,200 m on dissected terrain and therefore experience only the occasional, mild frosts that are coped with in the manner described above, i.e., entirely within the bounds of their group territories. The Fringe Enga live, for the most part, at much higher altitudes (2,300–2,700 m) in the broader valleys of the Marient, Lai (Kandep), Wage, and Lagaip, centering on the government stations of Kandep and Laiagam. And conventional wisdom has it that they are for the large part simply refugees from the Central Enga: hapless individuals who eke out a miserable existence in a hostile environment.[4] That is, they live in essentially the same way as the Central Enga but much less successfully on account of the severity of the frost hazard. This view has been developed principally in the writings of the anthropologist M. J. Meggitt and subsequently reinforced by government officers (public health and agricultural officers) concerned with the area. While some of their observations, e.g., regarding Central Enga origin and inferior nutrition, are undoubtedly correct, the interpretations given tend to be highly ethnocentric (to the Central Enga) and therefore misleading. Thus at one level Fringe Enga nutrition must be viewed in light of the possibility that the prevailing environmental

conditions at higher altitudes reduce exposure to infectious diseases and therefore the need for more ample nutrition. More important, whatever the origins of the population, the events of 1972 clearly demonstrate that the high-altitude Fringe Enga adapt to their environment in a substantially different way than do their kinsmen at lower altitudes. In particular, in terms of strategy the notion of adaptation being achieved almost exclusively at the local level – of closed corporate communities – proves to be a highly inappropriate and misleading one. The reality is far more complex.

For these high-altitude populations, the frost hazard is much more persistent; minor frosts are experienced almost annually, while more serious, killing frosts occur every one to three decades. It is possible in turn to identify three distinct levels of coping with the problem – levels that may be called local, intraregional, and extraregional. The first refers to the strategy adopted within the boundaries of the group territory; the second refers to that within the immediate region, i.e., an area which shares similar ecological and particularly altitudinal characteristics; the third refers to the exploitation of resources at some distance from the local group territory and in a much more favorable ecological context, where the first hazard is nonexistent.

The local level

The fringe populations of the Kandep area (Marient, Lai, and Wage valleys) practice mounding as their exclusive method of cultivation. In this respect, they distinguish themselves markedly from the Raiapu (Central Enga), who have three types of gardens, only one of which is mounded. Further, virtually all food crops are planted on the mound, their actual arrangement over the surface reflecting variations in frost tolerance. Thus sweet potatoes are arranged concentrically around the top while the more quickly maturing and slightly frost-tolerant "Irish" potatoes (*Solanum tuberosum*) that have been introduced within the past 20 years or so are planted (or simply spring up) randomly over the whole surface. Similarly, other recent plant introductions with a moderate to high resistance to frost, such as peas (*Pisum sativum*), beans (*Phaseolus vulgaris*), and cabbage (*Brassica oleracea*), are confined to the lower parts of the mound below the circle of sweet potato vines. In this way, maximum advantage is derived from the cultivated area given the constraints under which agriculture is practiced.

In addition to this particular variation in cultivation techniques, gardens are generally maintained in two ecological niches. Within each group territory, there are two major terrain units of agricultural significance, the valley bottoms and the lower slopes of the dividing ranges, with settlement being concentrated along the margins of the two. The bottom lands are typically under grass while the slopes are under primary and secondary growth that is progressively being converted into grassland as a result of clearing for cultivation. From the point of view of agricultural productivity, it is the former that are preferred, the soil being more fertile and having less tendency to dry out. The land is in turn cultivated much more intensively, fallow periods being limited to one or two years' duration. Nevertheless, one serious disadvantage arises from the location of gardens in the bottom lands – they are very vulnerable to frost. Hence, while the vast majority of gardens are concentrated in the depressions, many households have one or two on the slopes. Here, elevation above the valley bottom, improved air drainage, and the shielding effect of the surrounding forest together significantly reduce the gravity of the hazard. These latter gardens, while mounded, are cultivated on a somewhat different cycle. There are two successive plantings, with emphasis in the first being placed on various minor greens (*Rorippa* sp., *Brassica ?campestris*, etc.) and in the second on the staple, sweet potato. In both, taro (*Colocasia esculenta*) is an important subsidiary crop. Thereafter, the gardens are abandoned more or less permanently, apparently because production falls off very rapidly. Since they are initially cleared from forest, this practice facilitates the progressive upward shift of the forest-grassland boundary.

This spatial arrangement of agricultural activity enables the population to cope with the minor killing frosts that are experienced every few years, because even though serious damage may be incurred in the depressions the slope gardens are left more or less unaffected. Thus in addition to food being continuously available there is, more importantly in the long run, a readily available source of planting materials, allowing recultivation of the damaged gardens to commence immediately.

Further, in addition to these long-term measures, a few people take preventive action immediately prior to an expected frost. A few mounds may be covered with grass or other plant material, all but the very tip of newly planted vines may be temporarily covered with earth, or the grassland in the center of the broad depressions may be set on fire. However, no one views these as satisfactory alternatives to serious agricultural planning. And here, because of the possibility of serious frosts occurring that will do massive destruction to foods and planting materials in both niches at the local level, most households are concerned with maintaining access to resources located at considerable distances beyond the boundaries of their particular group territories.

The intraregional level

Many members of each local group exercise outright and/or usufruct rights to land in two separate locations that may be as much as one day's walk from each other but still within the confines of the high frost risk area, i.e., within the same or adjacent valleys and at similar altitudes. Usufruct rights are obtained to land of affines and normally maintained by death compensation payments, while outright access reflects the fact that many clan territories are geographically fragmented. Thus those belonging to the Aimbirepe and Agulya phratries control land on both sides of the Marient basin, while members of Ku and Molopai, principally situated at the head of the Lai (Kandep), also have territory in the Upper and Middle Wage valley. In 1973, at least one-third of the members of Wesanda (at Tinjipaka in the Marient) and Bipe clans (at Iumbis in the Wage) were maintaining access to nonlocal land in this manner. On account of it, two houses are generally maintained and a great deal of time is spent in moving between the two locations in connection with garden work. However, under "normal" conditions gardens are not necessarily maintained in both areas.

Whatever the explanation for this territorial "splitting" at the clan level and parallel partial separation in agricultural activity, it makes good sense ecologically in spite of the fact that the frost hazard is uniformly high throughout the region. While there is little empirical evidence to support the fact, it is clear that severe frosts do have a variable impact; altitude is not the only factor determining their gravity. Both their intensity and duration are influenced by topographical considerations of slope and aspect, the one affecting the movement and accumulation of cold air and the other determining how long a given area is protected from the direct rays of the morning sun. In the case of the first, the flow of dense air is strongly influenced by watercourses which facilitate its concentration as it moves downslope, and by low ridges which permit movement from one valley to another. As far as aspect is concerned, nocturnal frosts probably persist longer on westward-facing slopes as a result of their being in the shade for half an hour or more after sunrise. Such minor intraregional variations as these may be of critical significance for plant growth under conditions in which temperatures drop only marginally below freezing and are of limited duration. Within a single altitudinal zone, serious damage may be inflicted on gardens in one locality while those in another remain largely untouched. Householders thus have every reason to maintain widely separated agricultural holdings.

Even in the case of total loss of food crops, this geographical separation often makes good sense. Given that most crops are vegetatively planted, in the long run it is the lack of planting materials which is the gravest problem the affected populations have to face. Failure to start reestablishing gardens immediately can mean extending the crisis by several months if not indeed also intensifying it. Thus, while the sweet potato tubers continue to be available for 1–2 months following killing frosts, the growing plants themselves are permanently affected.[5] In the circumstances, proximity to unaffected areas outside the region as alternative sources of planting materials becomes critical. In general, the maximum carrying distance for sweet potato vines is one day's walk. This is because, unless well protected by grass, they dry out very quickly and many are lost. More important, they are bulky, and an adult is unlikely to be able to carry more than enough to plant three or four mounds. However, not all the high-altitude zone is immediately adjacent to areas unaffected by intense frosts. For instance, Tinjipaka, on the northern side of the Marient, is at least two days' walk from the Syaka valley, an area that does not experience severe frosts. On the other hand, the other section of Wesanda clan's territory, at Pulya in the south-west corner of the basin, is within a day's walk of the Upper Mendi and Kanba valleys, both major sources of vines in the event of widespread killing frosts. Thus, on such occasions, many clansmen simply move to that part of their territory situated closest to the source of vines and commence replanting there. Significantly, all adults regardless of sex participate actively in the task. Six months or so later, as these new gardens approach maturity, vines are taken from them to the more remote territorial segment to initiate replanting there. The only alternative to this process of progressive reoccupation of the high-altitude areas is simply to wait until regrowth occurs in the damaged gardens. This is not always certain and involves extended dependence on an alternative supply of food.

In the event of extensive killing frosts, widely displaced clan holdings certainly facilitate rapid reestablishment of food gardens. However, there are inevitably several months when no major foodstuffs are available and an even longer period when they are in short supply by virtue of the time taken to replant with vines carried in exclusively by foot. Furthermore, at these high elevations the sweet potato takes at least 9 months to mature. In the circumstances, more direct recourse to extraregional resources is dictated, and this takes the form of out-migration.

The extraregional level

On at least three occasions within living memory (in the early 1920s, in 1941, and

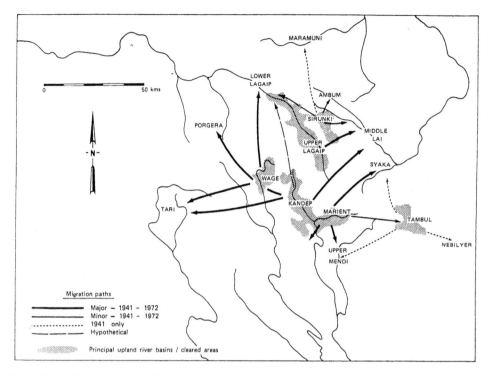

Figure 10.2 *Migration routes, 1941 and 1972*

again in 1972), a long series of frosts resulted in the massive movement of population down to lower altitudes. Entire families, together with their livestock, sought refuge in valleys sometimes situated as much as seven days' walk away across the mountains, namely, in the Syaka and Lai (Wabag), the Ambum, Maramuni, and the Lower Lagaip valleys, and in the Porgera, Tari, Mendi, and Tambul areas (Figure 10.2). While such out-migration represented, for those involved, a final recourse resorted to only some time after the certain destruction of food gardens, it was in no sense unplanned or haphazard.

The procedure on the first two occasions was, as repeated frosts resulted in increasing crop losses, to slaughter progressively most of the domestic pigs. This served both to reduce the demand for available resources (because pigs are partially dependent on cultivated foods, especially sweet potato tubers and vines) and to provide an important, if temporary

alternative source of food that was particularly valuable because of its high protein content. At the same time, household heads made gifts of meat and livestock to kinsmen and friends living at lower altitudes, and also made progressive forays out, with the aim of locating hosts. Then, 1–2 months after the final frosts, when remaining staple food supplies had been exhausted, massive out-migration occurred. Following the move, migrants were given food and rights to mature gardens. Then cultivation rights were granted, and, in the case of those intending to stay several years, an invitation to build their own houses was extended. Once the family and remaining livestock were established at lower altitudes, the men commenced moving constantly back and forth between the host and affected areas, to harvest pandanus nuts, check on the recovery of gardens, replant, etc. Occasionally they might be accompanied by other members of the family, but outright return occurred only when sufficient gardens were back in production. In the circumstances, they might remain with their hosts for as little time as 6 months or for as long as 3 years. On the other hand, they might never return.

The length of absence normally depended on such considerations as the extent of spontaneous recovery of gardens, the availability of planting materials, and the time taken for crops to mature, or, in other words, the altitude of the gardens, severity of the frosts, and proximity to unaffected regions.

From an adaptive point of view, what is significant about such out-migration is that it is a structured and carefully articulated respose to severe frosts founded on an elaborate fabric of social ties linking high- with low-altitude populations. The Fringe Enga differ from the Central Enga not only in terms of population size and density (both of which are low by comparison) but also in certain basic properties of their social system. As Lacey (1973) clearly illustrates, the former tend to be characterized by widely dispersed rather than compacted phratries. In other words, branched agnatic ties linking high- with low-altitude populations are common. Several clans in the southern Marient, for instance, have fraternal ties in the upper Mendi, others in the Kandep and Upper Lagaip with the Lai (Wabag), the Wage with Tari, Porgera, and the Lower Lagaip, and finally some Sirunki clans with the Ambum, Maramuni, and Lower Lagaip. In addition, marriage patterns tend to assume the same directional and altitudinal biases. Thus neither propinquity (distance decay) nor rules designed to spread affinal ties are so pronounced as among the Central Enga.

As may be expected, such ties are constantly being reinforced through exchange of various kinds, and they are in turn obligating for both parties. Thus, as far as the frosts are concerned, they greatly facilitate the occasional massive displacements of population, displacements that are seen to be crucial to the long-term occupation of the high-altitude areas. Indeed, they might almost be construed as designed to respond specifically to this need. However, if Meggitt's assessment of the "quality of life" at high altitudes is retained, it is difficult to understand why the more privileged lower-altitude populations should have any interest in developing and sustaining such links. On the one hand they are better endowed with resources and are not exposed to any serious environmental risks, while on the other they suffer from high population pressures. In effect, one would expect them to be actively concerned to prevent the development of any relationships that incur obligations.

In reality, the association is far from being one-sided: the frost-vulnerable populations possess or control access to a number of commodities that are highly valued by the Central Enga. The pandanus nut is a luxury vegetable food of major importance. The edible portion is of high nutritional value, particularly with respect to its protein and fat content, and is much relished by highlanders.[6] Depending on the variety, it may be eaten raw, cooked, or stored for many months if smoked. In consequence, it often enters into gift exchanges. Uncommon below 1,800 m, it forms extensive stands in the high-altitude depressions and surrounding forests, while domesticated forms are planted in groves adjacent to settlements. The pandanus normally fruits during the period December-January-February, at which time entire households will take up residence adjacent to their stands, subsisting almost exclusively on the nut. Relatives are frequently invited to assist in the harvest. From the point of view of severe frosts, the timing of the harvest is extremely significant, for it tends to coincide with the period of maximum food scarcity, and those that have sought refuge at lower altitudes will commonly return for the harvest with their hosts, who are only too keen to supplement their own protein-deficient diets.

Although the pigs bred in the high-altitude fringe areas are relatively few in comparison with the situation among the Central Enga, they are well known for their superior body weight and the quality of their meat. The common explanation provided for this qualitative difference is the excellent foraging provided by the swamplands situated in the center of the depressions. It is in turn believed that, on account of their improved nutrition (they are dependent on domestic foods to only a limited extent), the pigs mature more rapidly. Lower numbers – pig: human ratios probably never exceed 1:1 among the Fringe Enga compared with a peak in excess if 3:1 among the Central Enga – may well reflect a situation where major distributions occur with comparative frequency (every 2–3 years) and there is no complex and more infrequent ceremonial exchange cycle, analogous to the *te*, operating at the regional level.

Irrespective of whether it is grounded in myth or reality this reputation that the high-altitude pigs have results in a constant and insatiable demand for them among the Central Enga. Because of it, refugees find no difficulty in obtaining hospitality in exchange for livestock.

Apart from having resources of their own which are highly desired by the Central Enga, people of the Kandep area have until recently acted as middlemen in the distribution of certain major traditional trade goods through the Western and Southern Highlands Districts. Four commodities that were, and to some extent still are, handled by Kandep people are sodium salt, "tree oil,"[7] a wide variety of sea shells, and stone axes. The first is obtained from springs at Murisosa near Sirunki and serves as the exclusive source for the Southern Highlands. The second originates from the Lake Kutubu area, and the third from the Gulf of Papua, where both are passed on to the Enga by Mendi speakers. Finally, stone axes were obtained from Ialibu. In terms of the proportion of total trade of tree oil and salt, the Enga speakers of the Marient, Kandep, and Wage valleys undoubtedly handled a major share. In the case of the other trade goods, the Central Enga obtained most of their supplies through the Tambul and Minyamp valleys. However, in all cases, demand was never satisfied and hence, even in cases in which their role was a minor one, the high-altitude populations profited from serving as agents in the distribution of essential commodities.

Yet to the Central Enga the most elementary and perhaps the most vital commodity offered by the high-altitude groups was people, or, in other words, potential allies and recruits to the local group. As I have stressed elsewhere (Waddell, 1973), local groups among the Central Enga are small in size and the lineage

system renders membership potentially restrictive. Viewed against the perspective of a quasi-anarchic political environment, high population pressure on resources, and the obvious fact that natality and mortality rates vary significantly from one group to another over time, it is evident that the survival and good functioning of individual local groups are continually being threatened. Invariably there are some which are short of people, and for them it is axiomatic that equilibrium (in terms of population size and density relative to that of their neighbors) must be restored as quickly as possible. Here, an event such as severe frost at higher altitudes provides a welcome opportunity. In effect, individual groups among the Central Enga *actively* solicit immigrants in spite of the fact that overall densities and pressures on resources are high compared with the fringe areas.

Because of this potential or actual, *continuing* value of maintaining close relations with high-altitude populations, migrants are invariably well received when they move down to lower altitudes. The violence and warfare that characterize highland populations and are often stressed for the Enga are in fact confined essentially to relations with immediate neighbors where each group is posing a constant threat to the survival of the other. Such threats do not characterize long-distance relationships, since there is no risk of one group expanding its territory at the expense of another.

Both parties then are interested in developing and maintaining ties, each for different reasons. But while for the Central Enga only a few (the most wealthy) seek systematically to develop long-distance connections and others are content to interact with their immediate neighbors, *every* Fringe Enga is explicitly concerned to "open roads." The reasons for this desire are obvious. Those without ties must pay dearly for their hospitality in the event of having to seek refuge elsewhere. It is not surprising, then, that most household heads in the high-altitude areas can claim among their primary kin at least one individual who is resident in or originates from an area not subject to serious frosts.

Discussion

The obvious conclusion to be derived from this overview of Fringe Enga adaptive strategies is that they possess a diversity of mechanisms designed more or less explicitly to cope with frosts of varying intensities. These several mechanisms may be conceptualized as a three-phased series built into the structure of the adaptation. Of these, the lowest (local) level is in constant operation, whereas the other two become progressively operational as the intensity of the climatic perturbation (frosts) increases. This situation is thus analogous to that described for war processes by Vayda (1974) and lends itself to analysis on the basis of the assumption that "successful human populations, like successful animal species, have evolved mechanisms for achieving at least rough correspondences between magnitudes of perturbations and magnitudes of responses to them" (Vayda, 1974: 190).

Such mechanisms permit the Fringe Enga to deal more or less effectively with even the severest of frosts that seem to be experienced about once every generation. Thus, of those individuals directly affected by them, about three-quarters can, it is estimated, readily migrate to lower altitudes and at least some of the remainder can "get by" while remaining behind.[8]

Because of their ability to "manage" the effects of severe frosts, linked in turn with the fact that historically they controlled access to a variety of highly valued resources, the Fringe populations do not share Meggitt's view of their being comparatively disadvantaged vis-à-vis the Central Enga, at least prior to and in the early stages of contact. Their adaptation is simply different: the frost-coping mechanisms demand a degree of mobility that is unknown among the Central Enga. Only "development" has endowed them with this inferior status because much traditional trading has been eliminated through the provision of more favored commercial substitutes and because, in the eyes of at least one resident of the Marient valley, the benefits are trickling through to them by a very circuitous route – "If only the

Europeans had come directly to us from Moresby instead of via Hagen, Wabag, Laiagam, and Kandep!"

The traditional strategy as modified by developments since contact

What I have outlined thus far is essentially the customary strategy for coping with frosts, i.e., the traditional strategy as modified by certain changes in the subsistence economy but unaffected by direct intervention on the part of government and mission. In fact, this strategy was only partially implemented in 1972 at the extraregional level in spite of the fact that the gravity of the crisis certainly warranted massive out-migration. As indicated at the beginning of this article, the limited scale of migration was due in large part to the mounting of a relief program which envisaged fundamentally different solutions to the problem.[9] However, both the viability of and necessity for the extraregional strategy have been affected by various other developments in recent years.

As noted, migration has been greatly facilitated by widespread trade and exchange activities which in turn have served to create and sustain kinship ties. However, the progressive substitution of manufactured for traditional goods over the past 20 years or so has led to a very real attrition in these activities. The Fringe Enga no longer play an enviable middleman role in the distribution of stone axes and shells. Sodium salt trade has also experienced a major decline, while only tree oil has no obvious counterpart in the modern commercial world. In consequence, the Fringe Enga have less of interest to offer to their potential hosts resident at lower altitudes, and there is grave danger of declining interaction for all but a few. Affinal ties may in turn be weakened. All of this is making it more difficult to "open roads." On the other hand, the construction of an extensive road network and the operation of an increasing number of "business cars" (passenger-carrying commercial vehicles) on it certainly renders movement easier. Now, should the circumstances require, public transport can move large numbers of people to lower altitudes, and those who had hitherto been denied the opportunity of migrating because of poor physical condition can be included. Thus on the one hand some of the constraints on mobility have been removed, and on the other it is probably becoming somewhat more difficult to find hosts.

However, the traditional adaptive strategy has been more directly affected by certain plant introductions of varying degrees of frost tolerance. These render the resource complex as a whole less vulnerable and thus make migration less necessary or reduce its duration. Two plant introductions in particular are important, one for the pig population and the other for the human. Kikuyu grass (*Pennisetum clandestinum*), originally introduced into the highlands by the government to cover airstrips and road cuttings and, because of its high protein content, now used by the Department of Agriculture in cattle projects, grows widely through the high-altitude areas. Initially impressed by its suitability for covering ceremonial grounds, the Enga now value it highly as pig feed. Tolerant of the severest frosts experienced, it provides an excellent alternate food source for the livestock in the event of a crisis, and women systematically harvest it. In this manner, large-scale slaughtering of pigs becomes unnecessary, while any sweet potatoes that survive the frosts can be used exclusively for human consumption instead of having to be shared with the pigs, as was normally the case previously.

"Irish" potatoes probably entered the high-altitude areas through customary trade routes in the early 1950s. They now assume an important role in the subsistence economy as a supplement to the sweet potato; their principal advantages are a tolerance of mild frosts and a maturation period of 3–4 months, compared with 9 or more for the staple. So well adapted are they to local conditions that they are treated as a semi-cultigen, planted systematically only in new gardens or ones being cleared from a long fallow. Elsewhere, a substantial harvest from self-sown potatoes is obtained after the various greens and before the sweet potatoes reach maturity. The severest of the 1972 frosts killed the growing plants

but left the tubers undamaged.[10] As a result, they continued to be available for consumption, and spontaneous recovery (through resprouting) led to a new crop within 3 months of the final frosts at the time when, otherwise, the crisis would have been at its worst.

In addition to the Irish potato, there are several greens of admittedly limited importance that have diffused widely through the region in the past 20 years or so, again largely as a result of Enga initiative. These are the common cabbage (*Brassica oleracea*), Chinese cabbage (*?Brassica chinensis*), and a semi-cultigen, watercress (*Nasturtium officinale*). Finally, there are several "European vegetables" which are grown for sale but are as of yet of limited appeal for domestic consumption, namely, parsnips, peas, and beans. All these greens were unaffected by the 1972 frosts.

These various developments since contact have served collectively to diversify and strengthen the Fringe Enga subsistence food complex, which prior to contact consisted essentially of a sweet potato staple, some taro, sugarcane (*Saccharium officinarum*), *Setaria palmifolia*, and a few minor greens. The damage done to it by severe frosts is no longer quasitotal, and, much more important, the period without a major food source available is much reduced. This serves to mitigate what Scoullar (1972: 7) refers to as "the most critical period of food supply" which may be expected to occur "between 5 and 8 months after the frost." Previously, there was migration by all who were able to migrate, while those obliged to remain behind subsisted for many months on a starvation diet comprised of a few greens (both wild and cultivated) that recover within a month or so of the frosts,[11] plus the product of hunting and foraging in the forest. With an increase in the numbers being able to remain behind and subsist on a more adequate diet and with a reduction of several months in the *necessary* period during which the majority must resort to out-migration, a relative, although as yet limited, decline in the importance of the extraregional level of coping with the frost hazard is occurring.

Since the Fringe Enga themselves are entirely responsible for these modifications to their subsistence resource base, it can be assumed that this trend toward increasing sedentarization of the adaptive strategy will continue, irrespective of the form that any government intervention may take in the event of a crisis. To date, however, these observed changes, while indicative of future trends, are of no great material significance. With the sweet potato still the staple and most of the major subsidiary crops not frost-resistant, mobility at the intra- and extraregional levels continues to serve as a vital mechanism for coping with all but the mildest of frosts.

The incompatibility of customary coping mechanisms with modernization

While the Fringe Enga themselves are changing their subsistence economy in ways that are reducing the necessity for the most extreme forms of mobility, externally induced developments are also contributing to a greater sedentarization of the population.

Since contact, a new institutional structure has been created and initial steps have been taken to integrate the local population into a cash economy. Postcontact political units comprise much larger populations than the traditional clan. These units are at once responsible to and served by a government – initially, an Australian administration and, since 1974, an independent government – concerned primarily with law and order, and health and welfare. In recent years, a degree of regional autonomy has been achieved in the form of local government councils and representation at the national House of Assembly. Christian missions, concerned principally with evangelization, have created similar but separate institutional structures centering on "mission" rather than "government" stations. Attempts have been made by both institutions to stimulate commercial crop production at the local level, in the form of cattle raising, pyrethrum production, and the sale of a variety of vegetables. Outlets for the money so acquired are provided largely through a developing network of local trade stores as well as a system of annual tax collection by the local government council.

Clearly, if these various enterprises are to function efficiently, the population must not be constantly shifting. Its stabilization is necessary for development. In view of this fact, it is not surprising that government and missions actively sought to discourage out-migration in 1972. Irrespective of World Health Organization guidelines, they, as institutions, had a personal stake in retaining the affected populations in the disaster areas.

While this trend toward sedentarization may be irreversible, it is nevertheless important that the pressures exerted by external agencies do not exceed the capacity of the population itself to sustain the process. From an adaptive point of view, acting quickly to discourage mobility is not only unnecessary but also very expensive, as illustrated by the 1972 experience wherein the government had to assume full responsibility for the support of those victims of frost that they had persuaded to remain behind. Strictly speaking, to administrate and to proselytize are largely self-justifying acts. They bring limited tangible benefits to the population, and frost victims are in no sense denied these benefits in the event of their migrating elsewhere since all Enga are served by the government and one or another of the Christian missions. It is rather the commercial economy which, in a *measurable* sense, suffers from migration, through an immediate curtailing of production and entrepreneurial activities and through longer-term effects on the investments already made. As far as the Fringe Enga are concerned, however, this sector remains very poorly developed. Thus in the Lagaip subdistrict, pyrethrum is the principal local source of revenue, yet sales over the year 1971–72 amounted to only about $120,000, with an additional $25,000 or so being earned from vegetable and beef cattle production. Even by highlands standards, such a level of commercial activity is slight for a population of 65,000.

It may reasonably be assumed from this that the form of intervention adopted in 1972 was inappropriate.[12] More seriously, in systemic terms its long-term effects are likely to have been disruptive rather than constructive on account of the active discouragement of the third phase of the response to the hazard, that of extraregional migration. Further, the gestures, along with other general transformations associated with the contact experience, are leading to the progressive attrition of the infrastructure that permits this extreme response.

It is evident that, in the event of future environmental crises, relief should be designed to supplement and strengthen customary mechanisms for coping with the frost hazard, rather than to undermine them. This requires familiarity with these mechanisms to a degree rarely found among government and scientific personnel. It requires also some commitment to improving the effectiveness of the mechanisms

in the context of an evolving political and economic environment. The challenge is considerable, because we are only now developing the conceptual tools for gaining understanding of the relationships between the temporal dimensions of stresses and responses, and a colonial and Third World situation is not propitious to acting on the basis of such understanding. Thus the very disruptions inherent in a colonial situation mean that intervention is invariably geared more directly to the interests of the institutional structures and commercial enterprises than to the interests of the population at large.

NOTES

1. It is interesting to note in this context the sequence of events following the major, terminal frosts, as recounted by E. Bloos, lay missionary at Laiagam: "and then they started coming onto the station and saying, 'Everything is buggered up finish. Look at the ice.' They brought in sheets of ice. 'All our gardens are finished. What are we going to do for food?' And so here on our station several hundred people, most of the local head people got together and said, 'What are we going to do? We want you to go and talk to the Kiap who is the government administrator, and tell him about this.' So I did a patrol around the area on the main roads, on the motor bike; and this was pretty widespread, so we went down to the main government station and got them all out, the Agriculturalists, the Administrators and we agreed that it was a serious thing, so we notified Hagen" (ABC broadcast "Look Back at Famine," June 14, 1973).

2. The following discussion of the functional significance of sweet potato mounding represents a summary of the material presented in Waddell (1972) in the section dealing with "land use techniques in response to environmental constraints" (pp. 138–68). The same source contains a detailed discussion of the Enga

agricultural system as well as a comparative analysis of the agricultural practices of other highlands populations.

3. Calculated on the assumption that ground frosts were experienced whenever screen temperatures fell below 4.4°C.

4. Meggitt (1972: 117) writes, for instance, that the Kandep was "until the recent construction of roads little more than a vast series of cold swamps at about 7,500 ft [2,313 ml above sea level, punctuated by drier hillocks on which small communities huddled and grew inferior sweet potatoes."

5. In a survey carried out through the Kandep area immediately following the killing frosts of October 1972, informants repeatedly made statements similar to the following (in Pidgin English): "olsem mipela kisim inap kaikai nau, tasol taim bilong ol pipel i dai long hangri ino yet. Dispela taim nau ino taim bilong ol pipel i dai. Taim bilong pipel i dai ino kam yet" (Lacey, n.d.:1). ("We nevertheless get enough sweet potatoes at present; this isn't yet the time when people die from starvation. Now isn't the time when people die. The time when people die hasn't come yet.")

6. The estimated food value for *Pandanus julianetti* is 588 calories, 10.7g protein, and 59.0g fat per 100g (quoted in Waddell, 1972: 232).

7. A vegetable oil obtained from *Campnosperma* sp.

8. Scoullar (1971) arrived at similar conclusions for a specific population, namely, some groups in the Lagaip subdistrict that experienced a localized but fairly intense frost in 1971. He estimated that of the 12,500 affected some two-thirds could readily migrate, while of the 3,800 expected to remain behind over half would be able to survive on remaining food resources. In sum, less than 13% of the entire population would require government relief.

9. See Waddell (1974) for a detailed treatment of this point.

10. This contrasts with sweet potato tubers, where rot quickly sets in, rendering them inedible within 1–2 months of the killing frosts, and earlier if rain occurs.

11. The most important of these greens were *Solanum nigrum, Oenanthe javanica, Brassica ?campestris*, and *Commelina diffusa*. People also scavenged through the abandoned food gardens.

12. I have argued this point at some length in Waddell (1974).

REFERENCES

Brookfield, H. C. (1962). Local study and comparative method: An example from Central New Guinea. *Annals of the Association of American Geographers* 52: 242–54.

Ewald, E. (1972). Presentation to frost relief committee. New Guinea Lutheran Mission, Wabag, 16 pp., mimeographed.

Lacey, R. (1973). A question of origins: An exploration of some Enga oral traditions. Department of History Seminar, University of Papua New Guinea, 22 pp., mimeographed.

Lacey, R. (n.d.). Toktok biong pipel Kandep. 9 pp., typescript.

Malcolm, L. A. (1972). The famine situation in the Western and Southern Highlands of Papua and New Guinea – Estimated food needs and health surveillance. District Health Office, Lae, 10 pp., mimeographed.

Meggitt, M. J. (1972). System and subsystem: The *te* exchange cycle among the Mae Enga. *Human Ecology* 1: 111–23.

Scoullar, B. (1971). Frost damage – Subsistence gardens, Lagaip subdistrict. Summary report and recommendations, Department of Agriculture, Stock and Fisheries, Papua New Guinea, Laiagam, 7 pp., typescript.

——. (1972). The effect of frost on sweet potato production at higher altitudes in the highlands of Papua New Guinea. Department of Agriculture, Stock and Fisheries, Papua New Guinea, Laiagam, 8 pp., mimeographed.

Vayda, A. P. (1974). Warfare in ecological perspective. *Annual Review of Ecology and Systematics* 5: 183–93.

Waddell, E. (1972). *The Mound Builders: Agricultural Practices, Environment and Society in the Central Highlands of New Guinea*, University of Washington Press, Seattle.

——. (1973). Raiapu Enga adaptive strategies: Structure and general implications. In Brookfield, H. C. (ed.), *The Pacific in Transition: Geographical Perspectives on Adaptation and Change*, Edward Arnold, London, pp. 25–54.

——. (1974). Frost over Niugini: A retrospect on bungled relief, *New Guinea* 8(4): 39–49.

Part III

Methodological Challenges and Debates

11

An Ethnoecological Approach to Shifting Agriculture

Harold C. Conklin

Methods of shifting cultivation, while unfamiliar to many of us living in temperate latitudes, are typical of vast areas in the tropics. Such methods account for approximately one third of the total land area used for agricultural purposes in southeast Asia today (Dobby, 1950:349). In some countries, including the Philippines, it has been estimated (Pelzer, 1945:29) that shifting cultivation produces food for up to 10 per cent of the total population. In these regions the economy of large segments of the upland population is based solely on such means. Nevertheless, shifting agriculture is still only inadequately understood. It is often categorically condemned as primitive, wasteful, or illegal, with little or no regard for such pertinent local variables as population density, available land area, climate, or native agricultural knowledge. For most areas, detailed field reports against which such statements might be tested are totally lacking. There is a definite need for ascertaining what are the real facts about shifting agriculture.

In this paper, I shall attempt to throw some light on the nature of such methods of upland farming and to draw our attention to certain important problems in this area of research. First we shall review some of the more frequent statements made by writers on the subject. Then we shall examine the pertinent ethnographic data for a specific culture,

emphasizing not only the local environmental conditions and their apparent modification, but especially the determination of how these conditions and modifications are culturally interpreted.

For our purposes we may consider shifting cultivation, also known by such designations as field–forest rotation (Pelzer, 1945:17) or slash-and-burn agriculture, as always involving the impermanent agricultural use of plots produced by the cutting back and burning off of vegetative cover. We shall call such a field a *swidden*. This term, like its by-forms *swithen* or *swivven*, is an old dialect word from northern England (Northumberland, Yorkshire, Lancashire, and elsewhere) meaning "burned clearing" or "to burn, sweal, or singe, as heather" (Hallowell, 1847:838; Wright, 1904, 5:881–2). It has been revived recently, and in an ethnographic description, by a Swedish anthropologist (Izikowitz, 1951:7). There are many vernacular terms for swidden, but few are widely known or used in the literature except in reference to limited geographical regions: *kaingin* (*caiñgin*) in the Philippines, *ladang* in Indonesia, *taungya* in Burma, and terms (see Pelzer, 1945:16) such as *djum* in India, *chitemene* in parts of Africa, and *milpa* in Central America.

Swidden agriculture, of course, involves more than is stated in our minimal definition, but before we attempt greater precision, let us examine some of the characteristics which various authors have attributed to it. The following list is not intended to be complete, but does include the most frequent and problematic statements and assumptions I have encountered.

(1) Swidden farming is a haphazard procedure involving an almost negligible minimum of labor output. It is basically simple and uncomplicated.

(2) Usually, and preferably, swiddens are cleared in virgin forest (rather than in areas of secondary growth). Tremendous loss of valuable timber results.

(3) Swidden fires escape beyond cut-over plots and destroy vast forest areas. One author states that from 20 to more than 100 times the swidden area itself are often gutted by such fires (Cook, 1921:313).

(4) Swidden techniques are everywhere the same. Such features as the lack of weeding and the use of a single inventory of tools are practically universal.

(5) Stoloniferous grasses such as "notorious *Imperata*" (Gourou, 1953:18) are abhorred as totally useless pests by all groups whose basic economy is swidden agriculture.

(6) Swiddens are planted with a single (predominant) crop. Any given swidden can thus be said to be a rice or a maize or a millet field or the like. Hence, it is possible to gauge the productivity of a swidden by ascertaining the harvest yield of a single crop.

(7) Furthermore, it is possible to gauge the efficiency (i.e., relative to some other method of agriculture) of a given swidden economy in terms of its one-crop yield per unit of area cultivated (Hutton, 1949).

(8) Swiddens are abandoned when the main crop is in. "The harvest ends the series of agricultural operations" (Gourou, 1953:28).

(9) There is no crop rotation in swidden agriculture. Instead, soil fertility is maintained only by the rotational use of the plots themselves. The duration of the rotational cycles can be determined by the time interval between successive clearings of the same plot.

(10) Not only is fertility lost, but destructive erosion and permanent loss of forest cover result from reclearing a once-used swidden after less than a universally specifiable minimum number of years of fallowing (set by some authors at 25 years, e.g., Gourou, 1953:31). It is claimed that "dangerous" consequences of more rapid rotation often result from native ignorance.

On these and many other points there is frequently an overall assumption that the standards of efficiency in terms of agricultural economy in the United States or Western Europe are attainable and desirable among any group of swidden farmers.

Field Observations

From November 1952 until January 1955 I lived with the Yāgaw Hanunóo of southeastern Mindoro Island in the Philippines. The Hanunóo, numbering approximately 6,000, are pagan mountaineers who occupy about 800 square kilometers of forest and grass-covered hinterland, and whose primary economic activity is swidden agriculture (Conklin, 1953:1–3). I was able to observe and participate in more than a full annual cycle of agricultural activities. Since most of my efforts during this time were directed toward an ethnographic analysis of the relation between Hanunóo culture and the natural environment (Conklin, 1954), I was drawn toward an increasingly closer examination of Hanunóo concepts of the ecology of the Yāgaw area and of Hanunóo methods of swidden farming.

The following brief statements summarize the preliminary results of my investigation of Hanunóo swidden agriculture. Except where otherwise noted, these remarks apply specifically to the Hanunóo on the upper eastern slopes of Mt. Yāgaw (Figure 11.1). The six settlements in this area comprise an unstratified, unsegmented, neighborhoodlike community,

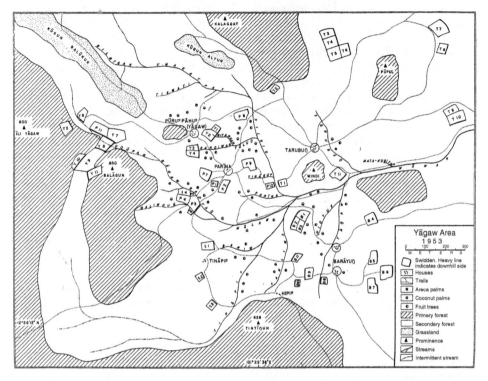

Figure 11.1 *Yāgaw area, Mindoro. (Sources: field data; Coast and Geodetic Survey, 1935.)*

which has a total of 128 inhabitants. The average population density for the entire Hanunóo territory is 10 per square kilometer, but in the more heavily settled areas, such as Yāgaw, there are from 25 to 35 persons per square kilometer.

The Hanunóo do not have a general term for swidden or for swidden cultivation, but do employ a set of terms distinguishing developmental stages of potential, actual, or used swidden areas. These are based on changes – natural or artificial – in the vegetational cover. Swidden activities are best outlined by taking these stages in sequence, indicating the significant human activities and plant changes occurring at each:

First year

(1) Activities resulting in a slashed clearing, a *gāmasun* (January–February): Possible

swidden locations are discussed within the settlement group. Final decision depends on location augury, dreams, the local omens, as well as an intimate knowledge of the local forms of vegetation. The cultivator marks his plot with bamboo stakes and, using a large bolo, cuts down the underbrush and small saplings. Men and women participate in this initial clearing, family units making up the usual work teams. The average size of a Hanunóo swidden is two fifths of a hectare. This area averages about one hectare of cultivated swidden cleared each year for every eight people. The total area of productive swidden land in a given area, however, is always several times that of the most recently cleared fields, because of intercropping (see below). As shown in Figure 11.1, 48 new swiddens (numbered serially for each settlement) were cleared in the Yāgaw area in 1953. Of these only four were cut partly from virgin forest (amounting to less than 10 per cent of the total area cleared). Second-growth forest areas are preferred because the clearing of primary forest requires much more man power for a given area, and demands a longer drying period before burning can take place than can profitably be allotted to such tasks.

(2) Activities resulting in a cut clearing, a *buklid* (February-March): Using the same bolos and a few single-bladed axes, men begin the more arduous task of felling large trees. Women continue to clear undergrowth and begin planting root crops (such as taro) which can survive the intense heat of swidden burning. Instead of being felled, a number of larger trees are pollarded, not only to remove unwanted shade branches, but also to provide firewood and promote seeding of other trees in the first fallow year. Smaller branches and cut underbrush are spread over the whole area so that complete burning will occur and exposed patches of earth will be protected from the dry season sun. These cutting, trimming, and drying activities may take more than a month, especially in a primary forest clearing. Group labor parties, repaid with feasts of rice, are usually needed to finish this stage.

(3) Activities resulting in a burned clearing, a *tūtud* (March-April-May): While the field dries, the Hanunóo farmer removes cut timber suitable for fence building or other construction purposes and clears a 4-meter-wide safety path around the entire clearing to prevent the fire from escaping into surrounding forest or fallow swidden areas. Firing starts at the upward and windward margins. A steep hectare of dry, second-growth vegetation will burn up in an hour or less, depending on the wind. While secondary burning is being completed, men begin fencing the entire swidden to prevent wild and domestic mammals (especially the zebu) from getting at young crop plants. Constant guarding against daytime animal

marauders is facilitated by the construction of scarecrows of straw, wind-blown dangling objects, and small field houses from which children can jerk lines leading to distant parts of the swidden.

(4) Activities resulting in, and necessary for the maintenance of, a planted swidden, a *tanman* (May through October): Maize is planted soon after the swidden is burned. The main rice planting comes at the end of the dry season, in May or early June. It is an important social and religious event and involves special spirit offerings, large work parties in gala attire, feasting, and the participation of men, women, and children. Men make the seed holes (ca. 5 cm deep and 25 cm apart) with 2-meter long, pointed dibbles. Women and children follow, dropping a small handful of prepared seed (often from a mixture containing small quantities of pigeon pea, cucumber, melon, and sorghum seeds as well as rice). The Yāgaw average for planted rice seed is 40 gantas (1 3/5 cavans) per hectare. Other important swidden crops are planted less ceremoniously (e.g., sweet potatoes, in August), as are many secondary (i.e., nonstaple) crops. During the rice growing season, other swidden activities include: completion of fences, continued guarding against destructive animals and birds, constant thinning and weeding (the entire swidden area being cleaned of weeds, shoots, and noncultivated vines at least three times), building of granaries, and the almost continuous planting and harvesting of other crops in both new and old swiddens (see discussion of intercropping below).

(5) Activities resulting in a riceless field, a *dayamihan* (October-November): The most important harvest in a new swidden is that of short-growing-season maize (in July and August). This is usually performed (including minor magical rites) by the cultivator himself, with only one or two helpers. The main rice harvest, in late October and early November, involves elaborate arrangements for group labor, feasts, magical rites, and religious offer-

ings. It is the most important agricultural event of the year. Harvesting rice is done by hand (usually without knives) by men, women, and older children. The normal yield in rice ranges from 25 to 40 times the volume of the seed planted. One hectare of swidden land may give more than 30 cavans of unhusked rice. After threshing, drying, hulling, cooking, and other preparations, a settlement-wide celebration is held, after which the rigid observance of many rice-connected taboos, such as that which forbids one to eat new rice from another's swidden, are removed.

(6) Activities resulting in a cleaned swidden, a *lūmun bagʔūhan!* (November-December): After gleaning, all rice stalks are cut, piled, and burned. Group labor, with compensatory rice feasts, are necessary to finish this task in less than two months. Other cultigens, especially leguminous crops and sweet potatoes, are now the focus of attention.

Dry season swiddens, always cut in second-growth areas, are cleared in September and October, planted in early November, and harvested unceremoniously in February, March, and April. They are usually small and are planted with corn and root crops only, never with rice. Some dry-season crops (including maize, certain beans, and sugar cane) are planted in main swiddens a few weeks before the rice harvest.

After the first year

(7) Activities resulting in a recleaned (used, but still productive) swidden, a *lūmun dāʔan*: Fruit trees, and other perennial cultivates planted in new swiddens continue to provide edible food products if the plot is systematically weeded and cleaned. By interplanting cultigens other than the principal grain staples, the Hanunóo practice a kind of limited crop rotation. Such intercropping results in successive harvests of different primary and secondary crops for at least two years, frequently extended to five or six

years, especially where the cultivation of banana plants is continued. The many leguminous crops so interplanted incidentally return significant amounts of nitrogen to the soil (Wernstedt, 1954:65). Single-crop swiddens are nonexistent. Up to 40 separate crops have been observed growing in one Hanunóo swidden at the same time (cf. Anderson, 1952:84; Merrill, 1906:179–180; Hester, 1953:290; Segawa, 1953). One informant drew a map of an "ideal" swidden containing 48 basic kinds of plants (over 250 subsumed specific types) including: 41 cultigen crop foods (including varieties of rice, sweet potatoes, yams, taro, maize, squash, sugar cane, and beans); 1 noncultigen food plant (papaya); and 6 nonfood cultigens, namely: tobacco, for chewing with betel, areca, and lime; betel vine, for leaves used in the betel chew; cotton, for spinning and weaving into garments; indigo, for dyeing cotton yarn; derris, for its fish-stupifying roots; and vetiver, for its scented roots (sachet).

Once productive cultivates give out – but usually not for two or three years after the main rice harvest – fallowing begins. After five years, fallow second-growth forest (*talun*) types are readily distinguishable by their predominant plant forms. The most common types are either some kind of tree or bamboo. Bamboo second growth is preferred for swidden making, because it dries uniformly and burns quickly and completely. If not recleared, of course, *talun* eventually reverts to primary forest (*pūruʔ*). Swidden areas are not recut before at least five years of fallowing – after the last cultigens give out – and this period is extended preferably to more than ten. In 1953, most Yāgaw swiddens had been fallowed for more than eight years. The Yāgaw area is in a rain belt and thus fallowing usually means the growth of replacement forest and a continuing natural refertilization of the land. In areas where there is a long dry season – aided by frequent burning for hunting purposes – tough grasses tend to dominate the replacement vegetation. Without artificial manuring and draft animals, productive swidden cultivation then becomes difficult. Damper areas seem more suited to continued swidden making. Despite an apparently long history of occupation by swidden farmers – there are more than a dozen groves of coconut palms in the area (see Figure 11.1) – the Yāgaw region today includes very little grassland. And *kūgun* (*Imperata* spp.), the predominate grass, is highly valued for livestock pasturage and especially for roof thatching. It is a persistent weed, but in other respects it is an important economic necessity.

Swidden activities require from 500 to 1000+ hours of work per year on the part of the average adult Hanunóo. In addition to swiddens, houseyard gardens are kept for experimentation with new cultigens, and for the individual cultivation of medicinal, ritual, aromatic, and ornamental plants.

The Hanunóo recognize innumerable natural and artificial factors as variables affecting swidden agriculture. Ecologically speaking, climatic factors, while closely observed, can be modified least by the Hanunóo. Edaphic factors, though not practically amenable to artificial change, can be dealt with in a more concrete manner. A study of Hanunóo soil classification and associated ideas regarding suitability for various crops – other variables being equal – checked well with the results of a chemical analysis of soil samples. Ten basic and 30 derivative soil and mineral categories are distinguished by the Hanunóo farmer. He may not know of the minute degree of lime disintegration and low pH value of *nāpunāpuʔ*, but he does know that certain beans and sugar cane (considered "high lime" crops, technically) will not thrive in such soil as they will in *baragʔaŋ* (which has a higher lime content and pH value). Effects on soil quality of erosion, exposure, and over-swiddening are well understood. They are topics of frequent discussion, and preventive measures are often taken. Biotic factors are most subject to control and experimentation by the Hanunóo, and are of the greatest concern to them. More than 450 animal types and over 1,600 plant types are distinguished. The floral component is the more significant, especially in regard to swidden agriculture. Of Some 1,500 "useful" plant types over 430 are cultigens (most of which are swidden-grown), existing only by virtue of the conscious domestication of the Hanunóo. Partly as a result of this intensified interest in plant domestication and detailed knowledge of minute differences in vegetative structures, Hanunóo plant categories outnumber, by more than 400 types, the taxonomic species into which the same local flora is grouped by systematic botanists (Conklin, 1954).

Conclusions

Much of the foregoing is fragmentary and perhaps more suggestive than conclusive. There is certainly a need for continued research in other areas (Leach, 1949:28), and for field observations covering greater periods of time. However, by using what recent ethnographic materials are available, we may tentatively rephrase the statements made earlier, so that a more accurate picture of swidden agriculture will emerge. Most of the changes we shall make indicate that the swidden farmer sometimes knows more about the interrelations of local cultural and natural phenomena than ethnocentric temperate zone writers realize.

(1) Swidden farming follows a locally determined, well-defined pattern and requires constant attention throughout most of the year. Hard physical labor is involved, but a large labor force is not required.

(2) Where possible, swidden making in second-growth forest areas (rather than in primary forests) is usually preferred.

(3) Swidden fires are often controlled by firebreaks surrounding the plot to be burned. Accidents happen, but greater damage may result from hunting methods employing fire in an area having a long dry season than from swidden clearing *per se*.

(4) Many details of swidden technique differ from area to area, and with changing conditions. Weeding is assiduously accomplished in some regions. Fencing is considered requisite if domestic cattle

are kept, less so where such animals are rare. Wooden hand implements are very simple and are used only once. Metal cutting implements and harvesting equipment, however, vary greatly from region to region.

(5) Even the most noxious weeds, in one context, may serve the local economy admirably in another. *Imperata*, if dominant, restricts swidden opportunities, but its total loss causes similar hardships for those depending on it for pasture and thatch.

(6) Swiddens are rarely planted with single or even with only a few crops. Hence, the productivity of a swidden can be determined only partially by an estimate of the harvest yield of any one crop.

(7) It appears that the efficiency of swidden farming can be ascertained – relative to some other type of economy – only by taking into account the total yield per unit of labor, not per unit of area (Hutton, 1949; Leach, 1949).

(8) Because of intercropping, the harvest of one main swidden crop may serve only to allow one or more other crops to mature in turn. Plantings and harvests overlap usually for more than a full year, and frequently continue for several years.

(9) Swidden intercropping, especially if wet season cereals are alternated with dry season leguminous crops, amounts to a type of crop rotation, even if on a limited scale. Cycles of field "rotation" cannot be meaningfully assessed by merely determining the number of years which lapse between dates of successive clearings. The agricultural use of the swidden plot following initial clearing may have continued for one, several, or many years.

(10) It is difficult to set a minimum period of fallowing as necessary for the continued, productive use of swidden land by reclearing. Many variables are at work. A reasonable limit seems to be somewhere between 8 and 15 years, depending on the total ecology of the local situation. Swidden farmers are usually well aware of these limitations.

REFERENCES

Anderson, E. (1952). Plants, Man and Life. Little, Brown & Co. New York, N.Y.

Coast and Geodetic Survey. (1935). Philippines: Mindoro. [Map] No. 10, scale 1:200,000. Manila.

Conklin, H. C. (1953). Hanunóo-English Vocabulary. Univ. of California Publications in Linguistics. Vol. 9. Berkeley and Los Angeles, Calif.

——. (1954). The Relation of Hanunóo Culture to the Plant World. Doctoral dissertation in Yale University. New Haven, Conn.

Cook, O. F. (1921). Milpa agriculture, a primitive tropical system. Annual Report of the Smithsonian Institution 1919: 307–26.

Dobby, E. H. G. (1950). Southeast Asia. Univ. of London Press. London, England.

Gourou, P. (1953). The Tropical World: Its Social and Economic Conditions and Its Future Status. Longmans, Green and Co. New York, N.Y.

Hallowell, J. 0. (1847). A Dictionary of Archaic and Provincial Words . . . from the Fourteenth Century. Smith. London, England.

Hester, J. A., Jr. (1953). Agriculture, economy, and population densities of the Maya. Carnegie Inst. Wash. Year Book No. 52, 1952–53: 288–92.

Hutton, J. H. (1949). A brief comparison between the economics of dry and of irrigated cultivation in the Naga Hills and some effects of a change from the former to the latter. *Advancement of Sci.* 6(21): 26.

Izikowitz, K. G. (1951). Lamet, Hill Peasants in French Indochina. Etnologiska Studier 17. Göteborg, Sweden.

Leach, E. R. (1949). Some aspects of dry rice cultivation in North Burma and British Borneo. *Advancement of Sci.* 6(21): 26–8.

Merrill, E. D. (1907). The ascent of Mount Halcon, Mindoro. *Philippine J. Sci.* 2(3): 179–203.

Pelzer, K. J. (1945). Pioneer Settlement in the Asiatic Tropics. American Geographical Society, Special Publication No. 29. International Secretariat, Institute of Pacific Relations. New York, N.Y.

Segawa, K. (1953). The means of subsistence among the Formosan aborigines. *Japan. J. Ethnol.* 18(1–2): 49–66.

Wernstedt, F. (1954). The role of corn in the agricultural economy of Negros Oriental. Silliman J. 1(1): 59–67. Dumaguete.

Wright, J. (1904). The English Dialect Dictionary. Frowde. London, England.

12

Slash-and-Burn Agriculture: A Closer Look at its Implications for Settlement Patterns

Robert L. Carneiro

Primitive peoples in forested areas throughout the world practice a system of agriculture which is known variously as slash-and-burn, milpa, and shifting cultivation. Its general features are as follows. Early in the dry season an area of forested land selected as a garden site is cut, and the trees and undergrowth left on the ground to dry. A few months later the dried vegetation is burned. At the beginning of the rainy season the crops are planted. The wood ashes that remain on the ground restore some minerals to the soil, but otherwise no fertilizer is used.

The same plot is replanted until a decrease in the fertility of the soil, or, especially, the invasion of weeds and grass, makes it uneconomical to do so any longer. At this point it is abandoned, and a new area of forest is cut down, burned, and planted as before. An abandoned plot becomes so overrun with weeds and grass that even if its fertility soon recovers, its recultivation by such simple means as digging sticks or hoes is made almost impossible. To be able to recultivate a once-abandoned plot a milpa farmer must generally wait until a new cover of forest has grown up and shaded out the smaller vegetation. This usually takes many years.

Since under this system of agriculture land is exhausted at a faster rate than it recovers, the area of arable land held in reserve for future cultivation must be several times larger than that currently planted. Therefore, only a fraction of the habitat can be exploited agriculturally at one time.

In a number of societies practicing milpa agriculture it has been observed that villages sometimes have to be moved because the nearby arable land is exhausted. The occasional relocation of the village because of soil depletion has been taken by many writers to be a necessary consequence of slash-and-burn cultivation – something inherent in the system itself. To give but one example, V. Gordon Childe[1] has written:

> Under . . . [slash-and-burn] cultivation any plot will become exhausted after one or two croppings. The simplest reaction is to start again on a fresh plot. The repetition of this process soon uses up all the land conveniently accessible from a single settlement. Thereupon, the whole settlement is transferred to a new location and the cycle repeated here (p. 198).

Although many students are quite ready to assume that the depletion of the land inevitably brings about the relocation of villages, no one, to my knowledge, has ever attempted to demonstrate this in a rigorous way. A proposition with such important implications certainly bears testing in the light of the data at hand. This is what I propose to do here.

My interest in this problem was aroused during field work carried out among the Kuikuru Indians of the Upper Xingú region of central Brazil. I discovered that the Kuikuru, who subsist very largely by the slash-and-burn cultivation of manioc, have maintained their village in the same locale for the last ninety years. It is true that during that time they have had four different village sites, but all of them have been within a few hundred yards of each other. Furthermore, what thrice has prompted the Kuikuru to move their village was not the depletion of the soil at all, but rather supernatural reasons of one sort or another.

The Waurá, a neighboring tribe with a mode of subsistence like that of the Kuikuru, also have shown the same pattern of settlement. Writing about them Pedro de Lima[2] has said:

> According to information that we obtained, the Waurá have lived in the same place for many years, having had a number of village sites, all near the present one. In the course of time [probably 100 years at least] they have built no less than 10 villages, each new one being 100 or 200 meters distant from the previous one. These moves are motivated by superstitious beliefs. (p. 5; my translation.)

Thus, to all intents and purposes, the Kuikuru and the Waurá, shifting cultivators *par excellence,* have nevertheless been able to remain sedentary. We see, therefore, that slash-and-burn agriculture *can* be compatible with permanent settlements.

This conclusion in no way denies the kernel of truth contained in the commonly accepted theory about the implications of slash-and-burn farming. Under certain circumstances shifting cultivation may indeed bring about periodic relocations of the village. What is needed is some technique for evaluating the various factors involved in order to determine how, by their interplay, they either permit or prevent fixity of settlement. This problem is not only soluble, but lends itself to precise,

even mathematical formulation as do very few others in ethnology.

The significant variables are six in number, and all of them are capable of being quantified. These six variables, with appropriate symbols for each, are the following:

A the area of cultivated land (in acres) required to provide the average individual with the amount of food that he ordinarily derives from cultivated plants per year.

P the population of the community.

Y the number of years that a plot of land continues to produce before it has to be abandoned.

R the number of years an abandoned plot must lie fallow before it can be recultivated.

T the total area of arable land (in acres) that is within practicable walking distance of the village.

L the length of time (in years) that a village can remain in a single location in so far as the requirements of agriculture are concerned.

Using these variables it is possible to construct several formulas[3] each of which enables us to solve for a particular unknown when the values of the other variables are known. Thus,

formula (1): $P = \dfrac{\frac{T}{(R+Y)} \times Y}{A}$, will tell us how

large a population can be supported permanently in one locale given certain values for the terms on the right-hand side of the equation.

If, on the other hand, we wish to determine the smallest area of cultivable land that will support a village of a given size in the same locale indefinitely, we make use of a different

formula, (2): $T = \dfrac{P \times A}{Y} \times (R+Y)$.

And if we wish to know how long a community can remain in the same place before soil depletion forces it to move (if it ever does),

we use formula (3): $L = \dfrac{T}{(P \times A)/Y}$, where L

is less than $(R+Y)$. If L turns out to be equal to or greater than $(R+Y)$, then, for reasons to be made clear in a moment, the locale in question can be occupied indefinitely.

Having exhibited some of the formulas that can be derived from the variables, I would like to try to prove mathematically what we already know historically: namely, that the practice of slash-and-burn cultivation by the Kuikuru has not made it necessary for them to change the location of their village. In order to do this we must be able to substitute actual numbers for the symbols. The values assigned to the variables were determined during the course of fieldwork, and later refined with the help of aerial photographs. They are as follows:

A   (the acreage of manioc required to support the average person for one year) = .7
P   (the population of the community) = 145
Y (the number of years a manioc field produces before being abandoned) = 3
R   (the number of years the plot must lie fallow before it can be recultivated) = 25
T (the acres of cultivable land lying within practicable walking distance of the village) = 13,350
L   (the length of time in years that the village may remain in the same locale), is what we are solving for in this problem.

The appropriate equation to use is (3):

$$L = \frac{T}{(P \times A)/Y}, \quad \text{if } L < (R+Y).$$
(If $L \geq (R+Y)$, L ∞).

Substituting numbers for the symbols we have:

$$L = \frac{13,350}{(145 \times .7)/3}; \quad (R+Y) = 28.$$

Solving the equation we get L = 395, and since L is greater than (R + Y), L is infinite. Let me try to clarify the meaning of this answer. The value 395 for L represents the number of years it would take the Kuikuru to plant and exhaust successively all of the arable land conveniently available to them. Since this period is much longer than the 25 years it takes for a plot to be exhausted and recover, it is clear that at the end of the 395 years the Kuikuru could simply go back to the first plots and start all over.

Thus we have succeeded in demonstrating mathematically that under a system of shifting

cultivation the Kuikuru have been able to remain permanently settled.

The fact that L turned out to be so much larger than (R + Y) indicates that the Kuikuru are sedentary by a wide margin. In order to find out just how ample this margin is, let us calculate the size of the smallest area which, under prevailing conditions, would permit a village of 145 persons to stay indefinitely in the same locale. The appropriate formula in this case is (2): $T = \frac{P \times A}{Y} \times (R+Y)$. When we substitute the actual figures we have $T = \frac{145 \times .7}{3} \times (25+3)$. Solving the equation through we get an answer of 947.25 acres. This means that by utilizing only 950 acres, or about 7% of the arable land within an accessible radius, the Kuikuru could still remain completely sedentary.

Another question of interest is how large a village population, subsisting under the same conditions, could be permanently supported in the habitat of the Kuikuru. To arrive at an answer we use formula (1): $P = \frac{\frac{T}{(R+Y)} \times Y}{A}$, which, once substitutions are made, gives us $P = \frac{\frac{13,350}{(25+3)} \times 3}{.7}$. This yields as an answer, P = 2,041. That is to say, with slash-and-burn agriculture as the only limiting factor, a village of some 2,000 persons could live on a permanent basis where the Kuikuru do now.

The various formulas used here are of course perfectly general. They can be applied to any group practicing shifting cultivation, provided there are figures to insert in place of the symbols.

We have seen that the Kuikuru and the Waurá at least, do not have to relocate their villages periodically because of soil exhaustion. Now the major objective of this paper is to determine whether or not the same is true for the *average* community practicing shifting cultivation. In trying to answer this question I will use the Tropical Forest of South America as a proving ground, not only because I am most familiar with it, but also because it is a large and, I think, typical area of slash-and-burn farming.

The procedure will be first, to ascertain what the average horticultural conditions are for the Tropical Forest; second, to compute by means of one of the formulas how large a sedentary village could be supported under such conditions; and third, to match the figure thus obtained against an independent estimate of average village size for the Tropical Forest. The data that are needed to determine average horticultural conditions for this area are difficult to find in sufficient completeness or detail. For this reason the safest course is to take the figures we have for the Kuikuru, assume that they represent optimal conditions, and scale them down in order to arrive at "average" conditions. Since the figures for the Kuikuru appear to be much nearer average than optimal, the "average" Tropical Forest conditions we obtain by scaling them down will be a *low* average. This gives us the assurance that we are not presenting an overly favorable picture of horticultural conditions in the area.

I will begin by assuming that while the Kuikuru are willing to go 4 or 5 miles to till a field of manioc, the average Amazonian cultivators find it impracticable to walk farther than 3 miles. Taking 3 miles as a radius, I will assume further that of the area of the circle generated by swinging this radius a full 360°, only a third is suitable for cultivation. This is an area of 5,971 acres, compared to the 13,350 acres of the Kuikuru.

Next, whereas a field of manioc yields for about 3 years among the Kuikuru, I will assume that the average Tropical Forest Indians abandon a plot after 2.5 years. Furthermore, instead of allowing 25 years as the period of necessary fallow for abandoned plots, I will arbitrarily raise that figure to 30 years. Lastly, I shall assume that 1 acre (instead of .7 acre) is needed to grow the amount of manioc required per person per year. This is indeed a high figure; de Fauterau[4] has estimated that among the Indians of French Guiana, for example, the area needed for this is only .2 acre.

We now have the following numerical values:

$T = 5,971$
$R = 30$
$Y = 2.5$
$A = 1$

Substituting these numbers into formula (1) we have $P = \dfrac{\dfrac{5,971}{(30 + 2.5)} \times 2.5}{1}$, which yields as an answer $P = 459$. Thus, under distinctly low average conditions of agricultural subsistence, it would still be possible in a Tropical Forest environment for an Indian village of nearly 500 people to remain completely sedentary. (One can readily appreciate that if the figures used as average values had been nearer the true average, P would have come out substantially higher than 500.)

The next facet of the problem is to ascertain the average size of villages in the Tropical Forest to see whether it is larger or smaller than 459. This can be determined with reasonable accuracy by referring to a map compiled by Julian Steward[5] for Volume 5 of the *Handbook of South American Indians*. This map shows the distribution of community size for all of native South America broken down into the following class intervals: 1–50, 51–150, 151–500, 500–3,000, and 3,000–plus. It is quite evident from the map that the most typical community size in the Tropical Forest – typical in the sense of covering the largest portion of this culture area – falls into the class interval 51–150. Thus average village size in the Tropical Forest is well below the size that average horticultural conditions would permit.

On the basis of these findings I would venture the following suggestion: If the ethnographic or archeological record reveals periodic relocations of villages of 500 persons or less, causes *other than soil depletion* should be assumed to have been responsible unless there is clear and conclusive evidence to the contrary. What these other causes are constitutes an interesting problem in itself, but one which falls outside the scope of this paper.

Let me say again that under certain conditions – which formula (1) would reveal to us – soil exhaustion may indeed force a society to move its village. However, I am led to conclude that for primitive peoples in general permanence of settlement is certainly compatible with slash-and-burn agriculture.

The conclusions which I have reached in this paper are by no means novel. They were understood and expressed in the earliest systematic treatment of slash-and-burn agriculture that I know of, O. F. Cook's "Milpa Agriculture, A Primitive Tropical System."[6] Writing in 1919 Cook said:

Milpa agriculture is a permanent system if the intervals between successive clearings of the same land are very long and the forest has time to restore the land to its original condition. [In this case] a few people can live indefinitely in the same region. . . . (p. 323.)

What I have done is simply to isolate the relevant factors, reduce them to variables which can be quantified, and arrange these into mathematical formulas. These formulas provide us with a means of answering several questions of interest. They also serve to emphasize that local conditions pertinent to shifting cultivation must be known in detail before statements concerning the permissible size or duration of a village can be made with finality.

NOTES

1. V. Gordon Childe, "Old World Prehistory: Neolithic." In A. L. Kroeber (Ed.), *Anthropology Today,* Chicago, University of Chicago Press, 1953, pp. 193–210.

2. Pedro E. de Lima, "Os Índios Waurá: Observações Gerais. A Cerâmica." *Boletim do Museu Nacional. Nova Série. Antropologia.* No. 9. Rio de Janeiro, 1950.

3. The formulas presented in this paper are modifications of those contained in the paper as originally read. For pointing out the slight inaccuracies in the original formulas and for suggesting how they might be revised I am indebted to Dr Albert C. Spaulding.

4. Eric de Fauterau, *Etudes d'Ecologie, Humaine dans l'Aire Amazonienne.* FontenayLeComte. Vendée, 1952, p. 3.

5. Julian H. Steward, "South American Cultures: An Interpretative Summary." In Julian H. Steward (Ed.), *Handbook of South American Indians,* Volume 5: *The Comparative Ethnology of South American Indians,* pp. 669–772. (*Bureau of American Ethnology Bulletin,* No. 143). Washington, D.C., Government Printing Office, 1949, p. 676.

6. O. F. Cook, "Milpa Agriculture, A Primitive Tropical System." *Smithsonian Institution Annual Report,* 1919, pp. 307–26. Washington, D.C., Government Printing Office, 1921.

13

Ritual Regulation of Environmental Relations among a New Guinea People

Roy A. Rappaport

Most functional studies of religious behavior in anthropology have as an analytic goal the elucidation of events, processes, or relationships occurring within a social unit of some sort. The social unit is not always well defined, but in some cases it appears to be a church, that is, a group of people who entertain similar beliefs about the universe, or a congregation, a group of people who participate together in the performance of religious rituals. There have been exceptions. Thus Vayda, Leeds, and Smith (1961) and O. K. Moore (1957) have clearly perceived that the functions of religious ritual are not necessarily confined within the boundaries of a congregation or even a church. By and large, however, I believe that the following statement by Homans (1941: 172) represents fairly the dominant line of anthropological thought concerning the functions of religious ritual:

Ritual actions do not produce a practical result on the external world – that is one of the reasons why we call them ritual. But to make this statement is not to say that ritual has no function. Its function is not related to the world external to the society but to the internal constitution of the society. It gives the members of the society confidence, it dispels their anxieties, it disciplines their social organization.

No argument will be raised here against the sociological and psychological functions imputed by Homans, and many others before him, to ritual. They seem to me to be plausible. Nevertheless, in some cases at least, ritual does produce, in Homans' terms, "a practical result on the world" external not only to the social unit composed of those who participate together in ritual performances but also to the larger unit composed of those who entertain similar beliefs concerning the universe. The material presented here will show that the ritual cycles of the Tsembaga, and of other local territorial groups of Maring speakers living in the New Guinea interior, play an important part in regulating the relationships of these groups with both the nonhuman components of their immediate environments and the human components of their less immediate environments, that is, with other similar territorial groups. To be more specific, this regulation helps to maintain the biotic communities existing within their territories, redistributes land among people and people over land, and limits the frequency of fighting. In the absence of authoritative political statuses or offices, the ritual cycle likewise provides a means for mobilizing allies when warfare may be undertaken. It also provides a mechanism for redistributing local pig surpluses in the form of pork throughout a large regional population while helping to assure the local population of a supply of pork when its members are most in need of high quality protein.

Religious ritual may be defined, for the purposes of this paper, as the prescribed performance of conventionalized acts manifestly directed toward the involvement of non-empirical or supernatural agencies in the affairs of the actors. While this definition relies upon the formal characteristics of the performances and upon the motives for undertaking them, attention will be focused upon the empirical effects of ritual performances and sequences of ritual performances. The religious rituals to be discussed are regarded as neither more nor less than part of the behavioral repertoire employed by an aggregate of organisms in adjusting to its environment.

The data upon which this paper is based were collected during fourteen months of field work among the Tsembaga, one of about twenty local groups of Maring speakers living in the Simbai and Jimi Valleys of the Bismarck Range in the Territory of New Guinea. The size of Maring local groups varies from a little over 100 to 900. The Tsembaga, who in 1963 numbered 204 persons, are located on the south wall of the Simbai Valley. The country in which they live differs from the true highlands in being lower, generally more rugged, and more heavily forested. Tsembaga territory rises, within a total surface area of 3.2 square miles, from an elevation of 2,200 feet at the Simbai river to 7,200 feet at the ridge crest. Gardens are cut in the secondary forests up to between 5,000 and 5,400 feet, above which the area remains in primary forest. Rainfall reaches 150 inches per year.

The Tsembaga have come into contact with the outside world only recently; the first government patrol to penetrate their territory arrived in 1954. They were considered uncontrolled by the Australian government until 1962, and they remain unmissionized to this day.

The 204 Tsembaga are distributed among five putatively patrilineal clans, which are, in turn, organized into more inclusive groupings on two hierarchical levels below that of the total local group.[1] Internal political structure

is highly egalitarian. There are no hereditary or elected chiefs, nor are there even "big men" who can regularly coerce or command the support of their clansmen or co-residents in economic or forceful enterprises.

It is convenient to regard the Tsembaga as a population in the ecological sense, that is, as one of the components of a system of trophic exchanges taking place within a bounded area. Tsembaga territory and the biotic community existing upon it may be conveniently, viewed as an ecosystem. While it would be permissible arbitrarily to designate the Tsembaga as a population and their territory with its biota as an ecosystem, there are also nonarbitrary reasons for doing so. An ecosystem is a system of material exchanges, and the Tsembaga maintain against other human groups exclusive access to the resources within their territorial borders. Conversely, it is from this territory alone that the Tsembaga ordinarily derive all of their foodstuffs and most of the other materials they require for survival. Less anthropocentrically, it may be justified to regard Tsembaga territory with its biota as an ecosystem in view of the rather localized nature of cyclical material exchanges in tropical rainforests.

As they are involved with the nonhuman biotic community within their territory in a set of trophic exchanges, so do they participate in other material relationships with other human groups external to their territory. Genetic materials are exchanged with other groups, and certain crucial items, such as stone axes, were in the past obtained from the outside. Furthermore, in the area occupied by the Maring speakers, more than one local group is usually involved in any process, either peaceful or warlike, through which people are redistributed over land and land redistributed among people.

The concept of the ecosystem, though it provides a convenient frame for the analysis of interspecific trophic exchanges taking place within limited geographical areas, does not comfortably accommodate intraspecific exchanges taking place over wider geographic areas. Some sort of geographic population model would be more useful for the analysis of the relationship of the local ecological population to the larger regional population of which it is a part, but we lack even a set of appropriate terms for such a model. Suffice it here to note that the relations of the Tsembaga to the total of other local human populations in their vicinity are similar to the relations of local aggregates of other animals to the totality of their species occupying broader and more or less continuous regions. This larger, more inclusive aggregate may resemble what geneticists mean by the term population, that is, an aggregate of interbreeding organisms persisting through an indefinite number of generations and either living or capable of living in isolation from similar aggregates of the same species. This is the unit which survives through long periods of time while its local ecological (*sensu stricto*) subunits, the units more or less independently involved in interspecific trophic exchanges such as the Tsembaga, are ephemeral.

Since it has been asserted that the ritual cycles of the Tsembaga regulate relationships within what may be regarded as a complex system, it is necessary, before proceeding to the ritual cycle itself, to describe briefly, and where possible in quantitative terms, some aspects of the place of the Tsembaga in this system.

The Tsembaga are bush-fallowing horticulturalists. Staples include a range of root crops, taro (*Colocasia*) and sweet potatoes being most important, yams and manioc less so. In addition, a great variety of greens are raised, some of which are rich in protein. Sugar cane and some tree crops, particularly *Pandanus conoideus*, are also important.

All gardens are mixed, many of them containing all of the major root crops and many greens. Two named garden types are, however, distinguished by the crops which predominate in them. "Taro-yam gardens" were found to produce, on the basis of daily harvest records kept on entire gardens for close to one year, about 5,300,000 calories[2] per acre during their harvesting lives of 18 to 24 months; 85 per cent of their yield is harvested between 24 and 76 weeks after planting. "Sugar-sweet potato gardens" produce about 4,600,000 calories per acre during their harvesting lives, 91 per cent being taken between 24 and 76 weeks after planting. I estimated that approximately 310,000 calories per acre is expended on cutting, fencing, planting, maintaining, harvesting, and walking to and from taro-yam gardens. Sugar-sweet potato gardens required an expenditure of approximately 290,000 calories per acre.[3] These energy ratios, approximately 17:1 on taro-yam gardens and 16:1 on sugar-sweet potato gardens, compare favorably with figures reported for swidden cultivation in other regions.[4]

Intake is high in comparison with the reported dietaries of other New Guinea populations. On the basis of daily consumption records kept for ten months on four households numbering in total sixteen persons, I estimated the average daily intake of adult males to be approximately 2,600 calories, and that of adult females to be around 2,200 calories. It may be mentioned here that the Tsembaga are small and short statured. Adult males average 101 pounds in weight and approximately 58.5 inches in height; the corresponding averages for adult females are 85 pounds and 54.5 inches.[5]

Although 99 per cent by weight of the food consumed is vegetable, the protein intake is high by New Guinea standards. The daily protein consumption of adult males from vegetable sources was estimated to be between 43 and 55 grams, of adult females 36 to 48 grams. Even with an adjustment for vegetable sources, these values are slightly in excess of the recently published WHO/FAO daily requirements (Food and Agriculture Organization of the United Nations 1964). The same is true of the younger age categories, although soft and discolored hair, a symptom of protein deficiency, was noted in a few children. The WHO/FAO protein requirements do not include a large "margin for safety" or allowance for stress; and, although no clinical assessments were undertaken, it may be suggested that the Tsembaga achieve nitrogen balance at a low level. In other words, their protein intake is probably marginal.

Measurements of all gardens made during 1962 and of some gardens made during 1963 indicate that, to support the human population, between .15 and .19 acres are put into cultivation per capita per year. Fallows range from 8 to 45 years. The area in secondary forest comprises approximately 1,000 acres, only 30 to 50 of which are in cultivation at any time. Assuming calories to be the limiting factor, and assuming an unchanging population structure, the territory could support – with no reduction in lengths of fallow and without cutting into the virgin forest from which the Tsembaga extract many important items – between 290 and 397 people if the pig population remained minimal. The size of the pig herd, however, fluctuates widely. Taking Maring pig husbandry procedures into consideration, I have estimated the human carrying capacity of the Tsembaga territory at between 270 and 320 people.

Because the timing of the ritual cycle is bound up with the demography of the pig herd, the place of the pig in Tsembaga adaptation must be examined.

First, being omnivorous, pigs keep residential areas free of garbage and human feces. Second, limited numbers of pigs rooting in secondary growth may help to hasten the development of that growth. The Tsembaga usually permit pigs to enter their gardens one and a half to two years after planting, by which time second-growth trees are well established there. The Tsembaga practice selective weeding; from the time the garden is planted, herbaceous species are removed, but tree species are allowed to remain. By the time cropping is discontinued and the pigs are let in, some of the trees in the garden are already ten to fifteen feet tall. These well-established trees are relatively impervious to damage by the pigs, which, in rooting for seeds and remaining tubers, eliminate many seeds and seedlings that, if allowed to develop, would provide some competition for the established trees. Moreover, in some Maring-speaking areas swiddens are planted twice, although this is not the case with the Tsembaga. After the first crop is almost exhausted, pigs are penned in the garden, where their rooting eliminates weeds and softens the ground, making the task of planting for a second time easier. The pigs, in other words, are used as cultivating machines.

Small numbers of pigs are easy to keep. They run free during the day and return home at night to receive their ration of garbage and substandard tubers, particularly sweet potatoes. Supplying the latter requires little extra work, for the substandard tubers are taken from the ground in the course of harvesting the daily ration for humans. Daily consumption records kept over a period of some months show that the ration of tubers received by the pigs approximates in weight that consumed by adult humans, i.e., a little less than three pounds per day per pig.

If the pig herd grows large, however, the substandard tubers incidentally obtained in the course of harvesting for human needs become insufficient, and it becomes necessary to harvest especially for pigs. In other words, people must work for the pigs and perhaps even supply them with food fit for human consumption. Thus, as Vayda, Leeds, and Smith (1961: 71) have pointed out, there can be too many pigs for a given community.

This also holds true of the sanitary and cultivating services rendered by pigs. A small number of pigs is sufficient to keep residential areas clean, to suppress superfluous seedlings in abandoned gardens, and to soften the soil in gardens scheduled for second plantings. A larger herd, on the other hand, may be troublesome; the larger the number of pigs, the greater the possibility of their invasion of producing gardens, with concomitant damage not only to crops and young secondary growth but also to the relations between the pig owners and garden owners.

All male pigs are castrated at approximately three months of age, for boars, people say, are dangerous and do not grow as large as barrows. Pregnancies, therefore, are always the result of unions of domestic sows with feral males. Fecundity is thus only a fraction of its potential. During one twelve-month period only fourteen litters resulted out of a potential 99 or more pregnancies. Farrowing generally takes place in the forest, and mortality of the young is high. Only 32 of the offspring of the above-mentioned fourteen pregnancies were alive six months after birth. This number is barely sufficient to replace the number of adult animals which would have died or been killed during most years without pig festivals.

The Tsembaga almost never kill domestic pigs outside of ritual contexts. In ordinary times, when there is no pig festival in progress, these rituals are almost always associated with misfortunes or emergencies, notably warfare, illness, injury, or death. Rules state not only the contexts in which pigs are to be ritually slaughtered, but also who may partake of the flesh of the sacrificial animals. During warfare it is only the men participating in the fighting who eat the pork. In cases of illness or injury, it is only the victim and certain near relatives, particularly his co-resident agnates and spouses, who do so.

It is reasonable to assume that misfortune and emergency are likely to induce in the organisms experiencing them a complex of physiological changes known collectively as "stress." Physiological stress reactions occur not only in organisms which are infected with disease or traumatized, but also in those experiencing rage or fear (Houssay *et al.* 1955: 1096), or even prolonged anxiety (National Research Council 1963: 53). One important aspect of stress is the increased catabolization of protein (Houssay *et al.* 1955: 451; National Research Council 1963: 49), with a net loss of nitrogen from the tissues (Houssay *et al.* 1955: 450). This is a serious matter for organisms with a marginal protein intake. Antibody production is low (Berg 1948: 311), healing is slow (Large and Johnston 1948: 352), and a variety of symptoms of a serious nature are likely to develop (Lund and Levenson 1948: 349; Zintel 1964: 1043). The status of a protein-depleted animal, however, may be significantly improved in a relatively short period of time by the intake of high quality protein, and high protein diets are therefore routinely prescribed for surgical patients and those suffering from infectious diseases (Burton 1959: 231; Lund and Levenson 1948: 350; Elman 1951; 85ff; Zintel 1964: 1043ff).

It is precisely when they are undergoing physiological stress that the Tsembaga kill and consume their pigs, and it should be noted that they limit the consumption to those likely to be experiencing stress most profoundly. The Tsembaga, of course, know nothing of physiological stress. Native theories of the etiology and treatment of disease and injury implicate various categories of spirits to whom sacrifices must be made. Nevertheless, the behavior which is appropriate in terms of native understandings is also appropriate to the actual situation confronting the actors.

We may now outline in the barest of terms the Tsembaga ritual cycle. Space does not permit a description of its ideological correlates. It must suffice to note that Tsembaga do not necessarily perceive all of the empirical effects which the anthropologist sees to flow from their ritual behavior. Such empirical consequences as they may perceive, moreover, are not central to their rationalizations of the performances. The Tsembaga say that they perform the rituals in order to rearrange their relationships with the supernatural world. We may only reiterate here that behavior undertaken in reference to their "cognized environment" – an environment which includes as very important elements the spirits of ancestors – seems appropriate in their "operational environment," the material environment specified by the anthropologist through operations of observation, including measurement.

Since the rituals are arranged in a cycle, description may commence at any point. The operation of the cycle becomes clearest if we begin with the rituals performed during warfare. Opponents in all cases occupy adjacent territories, in almost all cases on the same valley wall. After hostilities have broken out, each side performs certain rituals which place the opposing side in the formal category of "enemy." A number of taboos prevail while hostilities continue. These include prohibitions on sexual intercourse and on the ingestion of certain things – food prepared by women, food grown on the lower portion of the territory, marsupials, eels, and, while actually on the fighting ground, any liquid whatsoever.

One ritual practice associated with fighting which may have some physiological consequences deserves mention. Immediately before proceeding to the fighting ground, the warriors eat heavily salted pig fat. The ingestion of salt, coupled with the taboo on drinking, has the effect of shortening the fighting day, particularly since the Maring prefer to fight only on bright sunny days. When everyone gets unbearably thirsty, according to informants, fighting is broken off.

There may formerly have been other effects if the native salt contained sodium (the production of salt was discontinued some years previous to the field work, and no samples were obtained). The Maring diet seems to be deficient in sodium. The ingestion of large amounts of sodium just prior to fighting would have permitted the warriors to sweat normally without a lowering of blood volume and consequent weakness during the course of the fighting. The pork belly ingested with the salt would have provided them with a new burst of energy two hours or so after the commencement of the engagement. After fighting was finished for the day, lean pork was consumed, offsetting, at least to some extent, the nitrogen loss associated with the stressful fighting (personal communications from F. Dunn, W. MacFarlane, and J. Sabine, 1965).

Fighting could continue sporadically for weeks. Occasionally it terminated in the rout of one of the antagonistic groups, whose survivors would take refuge with kinsmen elsewhere. In such instances, the victors would lay waste their opponents' groves and gardens, slaughter their pigs, and burn their houses. They would not, however, immediately annex the territory of the vanquished. The Maring say that they never take over the territory of an enemy for, even if it has been abandoned, the spirits of their ancestors remain to guard it against interlopers. Most fights, however, terminated in truces between the antagonists.

With the termination of hostilities a group which has not been driven off its territory performs a ritual called "planting the *rumbim*." Every man puts his hand on the ritual plant, *rumbim* (*Cordyline fruticosa* (L.), A. Chev; *C. terminalis*, Kunth), as it is planted in the ground. The ancestors are addressed, in effect, as follows:

> We thank you for helping us in the fight and permitting us to remain on our territory. We place our souls in this *rumbim* as we plant it on our ground. We ask you to care for this *rumbim*. We will kill pigs for you now, but they are few. In the future, when we have many pigs, we shall again give you pork and uproot the *rumbim* and stage a *kaiko* (pig festival). But until there are sufficient pigs to repay you the *rumbim* will remain in the ground.

This ritual is accompanied by the wholesale slaughter of pigs. Only juveniles remain alive. All adult and adolescent animals are killed, cooked, and dedicated to the ancestors. Some are consumed by the local group, but most are distributed to allies who assisted in the fight.

Some of the taboos which the group suffered during the time of fighting are abrogated by this ritual. Sexual intercourse is now permitted, liquids may be taken at any time, and food from any part of the territory may be eaten. But the group is still in debt to its allies and ancestors. People say it is still the time of the *bamp ku*, or "fighting stones," which are actual objects used in the rituals associated with warfare. Although the fighting ceases when *rumbim* is planted, the concomitant obligations, debts to allies and ancestors, remain outstanding; and the fighting stones may not be put away until these obligations are fulfilled. The time of the fighting stones is a time of debt and danger which lasts until the *rumbim* is uprooted and a pig festival (*kaiko*) is staged.

Certain taboos persist during the time of the fighting stones. Marsupials, regarded as the pigs of the ancestors of the high ground, may not be trapped until the debt to their masters has been repaid. Eels, the "pigs of the ancestors of the low ground," may neither be caught nor consumed. Prohibitions on all intercourse with the enemy come into force. One may not touch, talk to, or even look at a member of the enemy group, nor set foot on enemy ground. Even more important, a group may not attack another group while its ritual plant remains in the ground, for it has not yet fully rewarded its ancestors and allies for their assistance in the last fight. Until the debts to them have been paid, further assistance from them will not be forthcoming. A kind of "truce of god" thus prevails until the *rumbim* is uprooted and a *kaiko* completed.

To uproot the *rumbim* requires sufficient pigs. How many pigs are sufficient, and how long does it take to acquire them? The Tsembaga say that, if a place is "good," this can take as little as five years; but if a place is "bad," it may require ten years or longer. A bad place is one in which misfortunes are frequent and where, therefore, ritual demands for the killing of pigs arise frequently. A good place is one where such demands are infrequent. In a good place, the increase of the pig herd exceeds the ongoing ritual demands, and the herd grows rapidly. Sooner or later the substandard tubes incidentally obtained while harvesting become insufficient to feed the herd, and additional acreage must be put into production specifically for the pigs.

The work involved in caring for a large pig herd can be extremely burdensome. The Tsembaga herd just prior to the pig festival of 1962–3, when it numbered 169 animals, was receiving 54 per cent of all of the sweet potatoes and 82 per cent of all of the manioc harvested. These comprised 35.9 per cent by weight of all root crops harvested. This figure is consistent with the difference between the amount of land under cultivation just previous to the pig festival, when the herd was at maximum size, and that immediately afterwards, when the pig herd was at minimum size. The former was 36.1 per cent in excess of the latter.

I have estimated, on the basis of acreage yield and energy expenditure figures, that about 45,000 calories per year are expended in caring for one pig 120–150 pounds in size. It is upon women that most of the burden of pig keeping falls. If, from a woman's daily intake of about 2,200 calories, 950 calories are allowed for basal metabolism, a woman has only 1,250 calories a day available for all her activities, which include gardening for her family, child care, and cooking, as well as tending pigs. It is clear that no woman can feed many pigs; only a few had as many as four in their care at the commencement of the festival; and it is not surprising that agitation to uproot the *rumbim* and stage the *kaiko* starts with the wives of the owners of large numbers of pigs.

A large herd is not only burdensome as far as energy expenditure is concerned; it becomes increasingly a nuisance as it expands. The more numerous pigs become, the more frequently are gardens invaded by them. Such events result in serious disturbances of local tranquillity. The garden owner often shoots, or attempts to shoot, the offending pig; and the pig owner commonly retorts by shooting, or attempting to shoot, either the garden owner, his wife, or one of his pigs. As more and more such events occur, the settlement, nucleated when the herd was small, disperses as people try to put as much distance as possible between their pigs and other people's gardens and between their gardens and other people's pigs. Occasionally this reaches its logical conclusion, and people begin to leave the territory, taking up residence with kinsmen in other local populations.

The number of pigs sufficient to become intolerable to the Tsembaga was below the capacity of the territory to carry pigs. I have estimated that, if the size and structure of the human population remained constant at the 1962–3 level, a pig population of 140 to 240 animals averaging 100 to 150 pounds in size could be maintained perpetually by the Tsembaga without necessarily inducing environmental degradation. Since the size of the herd fluctuates, even higher cyclical maxima could be achieved. The level of toleration, however, is likely always to be below the carrying capacity, since the destructive capacity of the pigs is dependent upon the population density of both people and pigs, rather than upon population size. The denser the human population, the fewer pigs will be required to disrupt social life. If the carrying capacity is exceeded, it is likely to be exceeded by people and not by pigs.

The *kaiko* or pig festival, which commences with the planting of stakes at the boundary and the uprooting of the *rumbim*, is thus triggered by either the additional work attendant upon feeding pigs or the destructive capacity of the pigs themselves. It may be said, then, that there are sufficient pigs to stage the *kaiko* when the relationship of pigs to people changes from one of mutualism to one of parasitism or competition.

A short time prior to the uprooting of the *rumbim*, stakes are planted at the boundary. If the enemy has continued to occupy its territory, the stakes are planted at the boundary which existed before the fight. If, on the other hand, the enemy has abandoned its territory, the victors may plant their stakes at a new boundary which encompasses areas previously occupied by the enemy. The Maring say, to be sure, that they never take land belonging to an enemy, but this land is regarded as vacant, since no *rumbim* was planted on it after the last fight. We may state here a rule of land redistribution in terms of the ritual cycle: *If one of a pair of antagonistic groups is able to uproot its rumbim before its opponents can plant their rumbim, it may occupy the latter's territory.*

Not only have the vanquished abandoned their territory; it is assumed that it has also been abandoned by their ancestors as well. The surviving members of the erstwhile enemy group have by this time resided with other groups for a number of years, and most if not all of them have already had occasion to sacrifice pigs to their ancestors at their new residences. In so doing they have invited these spirits to settle at the new locations of the living, where they will in the future receive sacrifices. Ancestors of vanquished groups thus relinquish their guardianship over the territory, making it available to victorious groups. Meanwhile, the *de facto* membership of the living in the groups with which they have taken refuge is converted eventually into *de jure* membership. Sooner or later the groups with which they have taken up residence will have occasion to plant *rumbim*, and the refugees, as co-residents, will participate, thus ritually validating their connection to the new territory and the new group. A rule of population redistribution may thus be stated in terms of ritual cycles: *A man becomes a member of a territorial group by participating with it in the planting of rumbim.*

The uprooting of the *rumbim* follows shortly after the planting of stakes at the boundary. On this particular occasion the Tsembaga killed 32 pigs out of their herd of 169. Much of the pork was distributed to allies and affines outside of the local group.

The taboo on trapping marsupials was also terminated at this time. Information is lacking concerning the population dynamics of the local marsupials, but it may well be that the taboo which had prevailed since the last fight – that against taking them in traps – had conserved a fauna which might otherwise have become extinct.

The *kaiko* continues for about a year, during which period friendly groups are entertained from time to time. The guests receive presents of vegetable foods, and the hosts and male guests dance together throughout the night.

These events may be regarded as analogous to aspects of the social behavior of many nonhuman animals. First of all, they include massed epigamic, or courtship, displays (Wynne-Edwards 1962: 17). Young women are presented with samples of the eligible males of local groups with which they may not otherwise have had the opportunity to become familiar. The context, moreover, permits the young women to discriminate amongst this sample in terms of both endurance (signaled by how vigorously and how long a man dances) and wealth (signaled by the richness of a man's shell and feather finery).

More importantly, the massed dancing at these events may be regarded as epideictic display, communicating to the participants information concerning the size or density of the group (Wynne-Edwards 1962: 16). In many species such displays take place as a prelude to actions which adjust group size or density, and such is the case among the Maring. The massed dancing of the visitors at a *kaiko* entertainment communicates to the hosts, while the *rumbim* truce is still in force, information concerning the amount of support they may expect from the visitors in the bellicose enterprises that they are likely to embark upon soon after the termination of the pig festival.

Among the Maring there are no chiefs or other political authorities capable of commanding the support of a body of followers, and the decision to assist another group in warfare rests with each individual male. Allies are not recruited by appealing for help to other local groups as such. Rather, each member of the groups primarily involved in the hostilities appeals to his cognatic and affinal kinsmen in other local groups. These men, in turn, urge other of their co-residents and kinsmen to "help them fight." The channels through which invitations to dance are extended are precisely those through which appeals for military support are issued. The invitations go not from group to group, but from kinsman to kinsman, the recipients of invitations urging their co-residents to "help them dance."

Invitations to dance do more than exercise the channels through which allies are recruited; they provide a means for judging their effectiveness. Dancing and fighting are regarded as in some sense equivalent. This equivalence is expressed in the similarity of some pre-fight and pre-dance rituals, and the Maring say that those who come to dance come to fight. The size of a visiting dancing contingent is consequently taken as a measure of the size of the contingent of warriors whose assistance may be expected in the next round of warfare.

In the morning the dancing ground turns into a trading ground. The items most frequently exchanged include axes, bird plumes, shell ornaments, an occasional baby pig, and, in former times, native salt. The *kaiko* thus facilitates trade by providing a market-like setting in which large numbers of traders can assemble. It likewise facilitates the movement of two critical items, salt and axes, by creating a demand for the bird plumes which may be exchanged for them.

The *kaiko* concludes with major pig sacrifices. On this particular occasion the Tsembaga butchered 105 adult and adolescent pigs, leaving only 60 juveniles and neonates alive. The survival of an additional fifteen adolescents and adults was only temporary, for they were scheduled as imminent victims. The pork yielded by the Tsembaga slaughter was estimated to weigh between 7,000 and 8,500 pounds, of which between 4,500 and 6,000 pounds were distributed to members of other local groups in 163 separate presentations. An estimated 2,000 to 3,000 people in seventeen local groups were the beneficiaries of the redistribution. The presentations, it should be mentioned, were not confined to pork. Sixteen Tsembaga men presented bridewealth or childwealth, consisting largely of axes and shells, to their affines at this time.

The *kaiko* terminates on the day of the pig slaughter with the public presentation of salted pig belly to allies of the last fight. Presentations are made through the window in a high ceremonial fence built specially for the occasion at one end of the dance ground. The name of each honored man is announced to the assembled multitude as he charges to the window to receive his hero's portion. The fence is then

ritually torn down, and the fighting stones are put away. The pig festival and the ritual cycle have been completed, demonstrating, it may be suggested, the ecological and economic competence of the local population. The local population would now be free, if it were not for the presence of the government, to attack its enemy again, secure in the knowledge that the assistance of allies and ancestors would be forthcoming because they have received pork and the obligations to them have been fulfilled.

Usually fighting did break out again very soon after the completion the ritual cycle. If peace still prevailed when the ceremonial fence had rotted completely – a process said to take about three years, a little longer than the length of time required to raise a pig to maximum size – *rumbim* was planted as if there had been a fight, and all adult and adolescent pigs were killed. When the pig herd was large enough so that the *rumbim* could be uprooted, peace could be made with former enemies if they were also able to dig out their *rumbim*. To put this in formal terms: *If a pair of antagonistic groups proceeds through two ritual cycles without resumption of hostilities their enmity may be terminated.*

The relations of the Tsembaga with their environment have been analyzed as a complex system composed of two subsystems. What may be called the "local subsystem" has been derived from the relations of the Tsembaga with the nonhuman components of their immediate or territorial environment. It corresponds to the ecosystem in which the Tsembaga participate. A second subsystem, one which corresponds to the larger regional population of which the Tsembaga are one of the constituent units and which may be designated as the "regional subsystem," has been derived from the relations of the Tsembaga with neighboring local populations similar to themselves.

It has been argued that rituals, arranged in repetitive sequences, regulate relations both within each of the subsystems and within the larger complex system as a whole. The timing of the ritual cycle is largely dependent upon changes in the states of the components of the local subsystem. But the *kaiko*, which is the culmination of the ritual cycle, does more than reverse changes which have taken place within the local subsystem. Its occurrence also affects relations among the components of the regional subsystem. During its performance, obligations to other local populations are fulfilled, support for future military enterprises is rallied, and land from which enemies have earlier been driven is occupied. Its completion, furthermore, permits the local population to initiate warfare again. Conversely, warfare is terminated by rituals which preclude the reinitiation of warfare until the state of the local subsystem is again such that a *kaiko* may be staged and completed. Ritual among the Tsembaga and other Maring, in short, operates as both transducer, "translating" changes in the state of one subsystem into information which can effect changes in a second subsystem, and homeostat, maintaining a number of variables which in sum comprise the total system within ranges of viability. To repeat an earlier assertion, the operation of ritual among the Tsembaga and other Maring helps to maintain an undegraded environment, limits fighting to frequencies which do not endanger the existence of the regional population, adjusts man-land ratios, facilitates trade, distributes local surpluses of pig throughout the regional population in the form of pork, and assures people of high quality protein when they are most in need of it.

Religious rituals and the supernatural orders toward which they are directed cannot be assumed *a priori* to be mere epiphenomena. Ritual may, and doubtless frequently does, do nothing more than validate and intensify the relationships which integrate the social unit, or symbolize the relationships which bind the social unit to its environment. But the interpretation of such presumably *sapiens*-specific phenomena as religious ritual within a framework which will also accommodate the behavior of other species shows, I think, that religious ritual may do much more than symbolize, validate, and intensify relationships. Indeed, it would not be improper to refer to the Tsembaga and the other entities with which they share their territory as a "ritually regulated ecosystem," and to the Tsembaga and their human neighbors as a "ritually regulated population."

NOTES

1. The social organization of the Tsembaga will be described in detail elsewhere.
2. Because the length of time in the field precluded the possibility of maintaining harvest records on single gardens from planting through abandonment, figures were based, in the case of both "taro-yam" and "sugar-sweet potato" gardens, on three separate gardens planted in successive years. Conversions from the gross weight to the caloric value of yields were made by reference to the literature. The sources used are listed in Rappaport (1966: Appendix VIII)
3. Rough time and motion studies of each of the tasks involved in making, maintaining, harvesting, and walking to and from gardens were undertaken. Conversion to energy expenditure values was accomplished by reference to energy expenditure tables prepared by Hipsley and Kirk (1965: 43) on the basis of gas exchange measurements made during the performance of garden tasks by the Chimbu people of the New Guinea highlands.
4. Marvin Harris, in an unpublished paper, estimates the ratio of energy return to energy input on Dyak (Borneo) rice swiddens at 10:1. His estimates of energy ratios on Tepotzlan (Meso-America) swiddens range from 13:1 on poor land to 29:1 on the best land.
5. Heights may be inaccurate. Many men wear their hair in large coiffures hardened with pandanus grease, and it was necessary in some instances to estimate the location of the top of the skull.

BIBLIOGRAPHY

Berg, C. (1948). Protein Deficiency and Its Relation to Nutritional Anemia, Hypoproteinemia, Nutritional Edema, and Resistance to Infection. Protein and Amino Acids in Nutrition, ed. M. Sahyun, pp. 290–317, New York.

Burton, B. T., ed. (1959). The Heinz Handbook of Nutrition. New York.

Elman, R. (1951). Surgical Care. New York.

Food and Agriculture Organization of the United Nations. (1964). Protein: At the Heart of the World Food Problem. World Food Problems 5. Rome.

Hipsley, E., and N. Kirk. (1965). Studies of the Dietary Intake and Energy Expenditure of New Guineans. South Pacific Commission, Technical Paper 147. Noumea.

Homans, G. C. (1941). Anxiety and Ritual: The Theories of Malinowski and Radcliffe-Brown. *American Anthropologist* 43: 164–172.

Houssay, B. A., *et al.* (1955). Human Physiology. 2nd ed. New York.

Large, A., and C. G. Johnston. (1948). Proteins as Related to Burns. Proteins and Amino Acids in Nutrition, ed. M. Sahyun, pp. 386–96. New York.

Lund, C. G., and S. M. Levenson. 1948. Protein Nutrition in Surgical Patients. Proteins and Amino Acids in Nutrition, ed. M. Sahyun, pp. 349–63. New York.

Moore, O. K. (1957). Divination – a New Perspective. *American Anthropologist* 59: 69–74.

National Research Council. (1963). Evaluation of Protein Quality. National Academy of Sciences – National Research Council Publication 1100. Washington.

Rappaport, R. A. (1966). Ritual in the Ecology of a New Guinea People. Unpublished doctoral dissertation, Columbia University.

Vayda, A. P., A. Leeds, and D. B. Smith. (1961). The Place of Pigs in Melanesian Subsistence. Proceedings of the 1961 Annual Spring Meeting of the American Ethnological Society, ed. V. E. Garfield, pp. 69–77. Seattle.

Wayne-Edwards, V. C. (1962). Animal Dispersion in Relation to Social Behaviour. Edinburgh and London.

Zintel, Harold A. (1964). Nutrition in the Care of the Surgical Patient. Modern Nutrition in Health and Disease, ed. M. G. Wohl and R. S. Goodhart, pp. 1043–64. Third ed. Philadelphia.

14

Why Hunters Gather: Optimal Foraging and the Aché of Eastern Paraguay

Kristen Hawkes, Kim Hill, and James F. O'Connell

In the recent literature, there are some differences of opinion about the determinants of hunter-gatherer subsistence patterns. Richard Lee (1968, 1979), among others, has observed that plant resources are often the dominant element in the diets of mid- to low-latitude hunter-gatherers. He argues that this is because plant resources are more dependable than animal foods and, in most cases, more efficiently exploited. He suggests that meat will provide the bulk of hunter-gatherer diets only where plant foods are unavailable. Marvin Harris (1977, 1979) implicitly rejects this position by maintaining that animal foods are the more efficiently exploited resources. He attributes the predominance of plant foods in the diets of many modern hunters to the depletion of large mammal populations through a combination of late-Pleistocene climatic change and overhunting. In Harris's view, modern hunters take plants *in spite of* the fact that they "cost" more than meat, primarily because meat is scarce. Yet a third line of argument has been offered by Marshall Sahlins (1976) and others, who reject economic and ecological factors as the principal determinants of subsistence patterns.

In our view, Harris is essentially correct, though for reasons that remain inadequately appreciated. We argue here that hunter-gatherer subsistence patterns can be explained largely, if not entirely, in cost/benefit terms, specifically as these are expressed in models derived from the theory of optimal foraging (Pyke et al. 1977). We support this argument by an analysis of foraging among the Aché of eastern Paraguay, who are notable for the very high proportion of meat in their diet. We also briefly consider how the same principles may be used to explain the rather different mix of plant and animal foods taken by the !Kung. We conclude with some comments on the general implications for our approach.

The Problem

The array of resources taken by hunter-gatherers and the determinants of that array have long been matters of concern to anthropologists, particularly because of their implications for the form and evolution of other aspects of human behavior (e.g., Dart 1953;

Steward 1936, 1955; Lee and DeVore 1968). Several somewhat contradictory approaches to this problem are represented in the recent literature. One, pursued initially by Lee (1968, 1969, 1979), is based on the observation that plant foods are often the dominant element in modern hunter-gatherer diets. Lee argues that plant foods are favored because they are abundant, reliable, and readily located, and therefore more efficiently exploited than are animal foods. Plants are said to be low-risk/high-return resources, while animals are high-risk/low-return resources. Animals are taken in spite of the inefficiencies involved because of the taste appeal of meat and the prestige that accrues to successful hunters. Still, Lee contends, given a choice, hunter-gatherers will always rely more heavily on plants. Only when this option is unavailable (e.g., at high latitudes) will animals make up the bulk of hunter-gatherer diets (for similar views, see Gould 1969, 1980; Meehan 1977; Jones 1980; Flannery 1968; see Bettinger 1980 and Hayden 1981 for comprehensive reviews of opinion).

Harris (1977, 1979) also appeals to cost/benefit relationships in explaining hunter-gatherer subsistence patterns, but sees them in a different way. He contends that meat is the favored (if not dominant) element in hunter-gatherer diets because of its nutritional value and because heavy reliance on meat is the more efficient strategy where meat resources are abundant. Only when these have been depleted (e.g., through long-term climatic change or overexploitation) does it become more efficient to add a greater proportion of plant foods to the diet.

Yet a third line of argument identifies cultural preference as the principal determinant of subsistence. In referring to a particular ethnographic case, Sahlins (1976:171) makes an observation he evidently takes to be generally true: "Specific valuations of edibility and inedibility [are] themselves qualitative and in no way justifiable by biological, ecological, or economic advantage." While this is an extreme position, the idea that traditional preferences frequently nullify biological or economic costs and benefits is widely held by anthropologists of very different theoretical persuasions (e.g., Douglas 1975; Jochim 1981).

We reject this third argument because of the archaeological record of near-synchronous changes in hunter-gatherer diets in many parts of the world over the past 30,000 years. These changes occur independently in at least some areas, yet are similar in that they involve significant increases in the relative proportions of plant foods and other sessile resources (such as shellfish) in local diets (e.g., Flannery 1969; MacNeish 1967; Allen 1974). They are often closely correlated with periods of major climatic change. In light of this, it seems quite likely that "biological, ecological and economic" factors *are* critical determinants of subsistence strategy, even if the details of this relationship remain unclear. Moreover, appeals to cultural preference or systems of meaning beg precisely the question with which we are concerned, namely, the explanation of the preferences themselves.

By contrast, it seems to us that in spite of the inconsistencies that separate their positions, Lee, Harris, and others who treat this problem in terms of ecological costs and benefits are on the right track. Still, some important problems remain to be resolved. Lee's argument may be faulted in that it involves a miscalculation of the relative costs of plant and animal foods (Hawkes and O'Connell 1981) and is inconsistent with the archaeological record. If Lee were right, plants should always have been the dominant element in hunter-gatherer diets, at least at low latitudes. Harris's argument seems much closer to the mark but needs a conceptual framework to account for the mix of resources exploited in any particular setting.

We propose that variation in hunter-gatherer subsistence patterns can be explained largely in terms of models derived from the theory of optimal foraging (Pyke et al. 1977). These models are designed to describe and explain foraging behavior in nonhuman organisms and are based on the assumption that, all else being equal, foraging strategies that are more efficient will be favored by natural selection and will spread at the expense of those that are less efficient. Examples of the use of such models with reference to human (especially hunter-gatherer) behavior are found in Winterhalder and Smith (1981), Hames and

Vickers (1983), and Earle and Christenson (1980). We are concerned here with two models that seem particularly useful: the *optimal diet model*, which describes prey selection in a uniform or "fine-grained" environment, where resources are encountered at random; and the *patch choice model*, which describes the movement of predators where resources display a nonrandom or "coarse-grained" distribution. We apply these models in the analysis of foraging practices observed among the Aché of eastern Paraguay. This case is of some interest because of the surprising success the Aché enjoy as hunters and because the research reported here was designed specifically to assess the utility of optimal foraging models in analyzing hunter-gatherer subsistence. We begin with a descriptive account of Aché foraging and then turn to the analysis of diet and patch choice.

Background

The Aché (or "Guayaki") speak a language of the Guarani family and have lived as hunters in the forests of eastern Paraguay since before the arrival of the Spanish. They divide themselves into three groups on the basis of differences in dialect, customs, and geographical range. Two of these groups have been described ethnographically by Clastres (1968, 1972). Earlier descriptions are in Vellard (1939) and in the references in Metraux and Baldus (1946). Our experience has been with the third group, the Northern Aché, who have come into unarmed contact with outsiders only within the past decade (Hill 1979).

The traditional range of the Northern Aché covers some $5,000 \text{ km}^2$ between the Río Paraná and the Río Paraguay, about 240 km northeast of Asunción. This area is characterized by gently rolling hills covered with broadleaf evergreen forest and by flat-floored valleys filled with tall broadblade grasses. The climate is marked by hot summers (October–February) and cool winters (March–September). Average daily temperatures in July are about 17°C, with minima as low as −3°C; temperatures in January average about 27°C, with maxima as high as 41°C. Annual rainfall averages about 1,600 mm but varies greatly from year to year in both total amount and seasonal distribution. The Aché divide the year broadly into "hot time" and "cold time" and mark finer divisions by reference to the particular resources then in season.

The fauna and flora of this region are poorly described (but see Hill and Hawkes [1983]). We have identified 33 mammals hunted by the Aché and have Aché names for several others. The Aché also eat at least 10 species of reptiles and amphibians, more than 15 species of fish, and a seemingly endless list of birds. They take the adult forms of more than 5 insects, at least 10 types of larvae (notably cerambicid larvae), and at least 14 kinds of honey, most commonly that of *Apis melifera*. In addition, they collect the edible products of more than 40 species of plants, the most important of which is the palm (*Cocos romanazoffiana*).

More than 130 Aché now live at a Catholic mission established in 1978 as an agricultural colony. Under the supervision of the mission staff of five, they grow manioc, sugarcane, corn, and sweet potatoes, and they keep a few pigs, goats, chickens, and burros. The mission provides additional resources in the form of milk, sugar, rice, flour, noodles, and salt, as well as cast-off clothing, tools, and agricultural implements. Some Aché reside full time at the mission, but others spend more than half their time in the jungle on long-range foraging trips, sometimes of several weeks' duration.

Two of us accompanied the Aché on seven such trips and recorded all subsistence-related activity (Table 14.1). Hawkes stayed with the women, noting time spent in travel, search, and collecting and processing resources, weighing the latter whenever possible. Hill made comparable observations of the men's activities. The complete record covers 61 gathering days and 58 hunting days, for a total of 457 woman-gathering days, 794 man-gathering days, 674 man-hunting days, and 1,570 consumer days.[1] Each day's report includes information on all game animals taken (species, number, and weight of individuals), the composition of the hunting party (including identities of those who made kills) and the time spent in a sample of pursuits, a partial tally of insect and plant resources taken, and a record

Table 14.1 Quantitative data on seven Aché foraging trips

TRIP NUMBER	1[a]	2[b]	3[c]	4	5[d]	6[e]	7[f]
TRIP DATES	Mar 31–Apr 3	Apr 5–Apr 16	Apr 25–May 3	May 15–May 20	May 30–Jun 13	Jun 21–Jun 29	Jul 5–Jul 16
STARTING COMPOSITIONS							
Men	8	18	27	20	5	19	11
Women	4	10[g]	15	8[g]	5	9[g]	8[g]
Children	1	4	14	2	2	3	7
Infants	2	8	8	3	3	3	2
RESOURCES COUNTED							
Number of individuals							
white-lipped peccary (avg. 30 kg)	4	3	2	2	2	4	–
armadillo (avg. 4.3 kg)	4	9	12	5	20	23	17
monkey (avg. 2.5 kg)	4	20	53	20	24	67	33
paca (avg. 7.5 kg)	2	4	13	8	1	8	5
coati (avg. 3.5 kg)	1	19	18	19	11	21	2
collared peccary (avg. 20 kg)	1	9	2	–	–	1	–
deer (avg. 30 kg)	1	7	1	1	–	1	–
fish	–	–	200+	–	–	–	–
bird (avg. 1 kg)	–	11	2	4	6	5	3
snake (avg. 1.4 kg)	3	3	–	1	–	–	–
In kilograms							
palm fiber	28	191	213	177	220	280	270
oranges (avg. 0.18 kg)	68	188	192	54	254	323	205
honey	5.6	25.0	7.4	2.3	9.2	5.5	1.6
palm larvae (small:avg. 0.003 kg; large:avg. 0.01 kg)	8.0	4.8	4.6	1.3	15.0	4.2	4.5
palm heart (avg. 0.33 kg)	5	44	30	11	19	31	30
palm fruit (avg. 0.005 kg)	92	57	125	11	18	10	15

[a] Shotgun used.

[b] Shotgun used; some palm nuts taken.

[c] The initial target was fish on April 28; 14 adults left the foraging band after this.

[d] On June 13 one man left the foraging band.

[e] On June 25 the group split; it reunited on June 28.

[f] On July 11 the group split.

[g] One man taking a woman's role is included here.

of time spent collecting and processing them. Because groups commonly disperse throughout most of the day, these tallies represent a minimum count of resources taken. This qualification applies most strongly to gathered resources, because the Aché eat as they travel. Since game animals come in tidy packages that require processing before they can be consumed, we are fairly confident that our tally includes almost all those taken. In addition to the animals listed in Table 14.1, several baby monkeys (*Cebus apella*), a few coatis (*Nasua nasua*), a tamandua (*Tamandua tetradactyla*), and a fawn (*Mazama americana*) were taken as pets.

Resources and Subsistence Techniques

The list of plant foods exploited by the Aché during the study period is a short one. The most important are oranges and palm products. Oranges occur in groves of varying size and are taken by climbing trees and shaking the fruit loose. Branches or entire trees may be cut down if climbing is difficult and the fruit is out of reach. Both men and women are adept climbers, but usually it is the men who do the climbing and the women who gather the fallen fruit.

Palm products (usually *Cocos romanazoffiana*) include the moist, starchy fiber of the trunk, the terminal bud (or "heart"), and the fruit. The fiber is taken by felling the tree, cutting a section from the trunk, and beating loose the exposed inner fiber with the butt of an ax. The fiber may be picked out by the handful, sucked dry, and discarded, or else bound in palm leaves and carried to camp, where its moisture is squeezed out and the fiber is cooked separately or with meat. Some kinds of fiber are sifted to separate the flour, which may be eaten alone, mixed with meat, and/or roasted in balls in the fire. The terminal bud of a palm is cut from the fallen tree with an ax and removed from its inedible outer husk. The palm heart is large, the edible portion averaging about 0.33 kg. It is usually eaten immediately but may be carried to camp and cooked in palm broth, sometimes with

larvae or meat. The apricotlike fruit of *Cocos romanazoffiana* grows in huge clusters and is sometimes taken in larger quantities, then mashed and mixed with water. Ripe fruit is often collected from the ground and eaten, almost without pause, while walking.

Insect products taken by the Aché include larvae and several kinds of honey. The Aché harvest cerambicid larvae, which grow in rotting palm trunks, by cutting chunks of the logs free with an ax, then breaking the soft wood further by hand, sometimes using a twig to dislodge larvae from their burrows. Some of the larvae are always eaten immediately; others are either lightly toasted in hot ashes or boiled in palm broth. Honey is taken by men with fire and axes. The honey tree is usually cut down, the bees quieted with smoke, and the comb extracted. Honey produced by other insects is also collected, although less frequently.

Aché hunting techniques are varied. Collared peccaries (*Pecari tajacu*), white-lipped peccaries (*Tayassu pecari*), red brocket deer (*Mazama americana*), capuchin monkeys (*Cebus apella*), tapir (*Tapirus terrestris*), and birds of many species are always hunted with bows and arrows or shotguns. Of these animals, the white-lipped peccary and capuchin monkey are pursued by groups of men, the others by solitary hunters.

Armadillos (usually *Dasypus novemcintus*), pacas (*Cuniculus paca*), and coatimundis (*Nasua nasua*) are taken without bows and arrows. Armadillos are dug from their burrows with machetes, with bows, or by hand, often by solitary hunters. Pacas are always hunted by groups of men. The several entrances of an occupied paca burrow are located and each is guarded by a hunter. A log is then pushed into one of these to send the animal running out. The nearest hunter falls on the large rodent and smothers it. Troops of coatis in the forest canopy are surrounded on the ground below by groups of hunters. When all hunters are in place, arrows are shot until the animals try to escape by leaping out of the trees. The hunters grab the fleeing animals and slam them against the ground. Snakes are killed quickly with a bow or machete. Often this is a matter of self-defense, for snake bite is one of the most frequent causes of death mentioned in Aché folklore. Fishing is done in large groups. Tree branches are piled across a lagoon to form a dam, which is then rolled or pushed down from one end of the lagoon to the other, trapping fish behind it. The cornered fish jump with increasing frequency as the space is constricted, and as they do, they are grabbed and tossed onto the bank.

Most food processing is done after camp is made for the night. While women tend to process the plant food they collect, it is unusual for a hunter to butcher, cook, or distribute his own game. Although this varies with different kinds of animals, one person rarely carries out all the processing steps. Men perform these tasks more often than women, especially the distribution of cooked meat. In accordance with an explicit prohibition, a hunter almost never eats an animal he has killed with an arrow, but everyone else is likely to get some. Cooked meat is cut into pieces and these are distributed to all the men, who pass them on to their wives and children.

Aché Foraging Trips

Trips reported here began at about 8:00 a.m. when men left the settlement carrying only bows and arrows and machetes (on the first two trips some took shotguns). The direction of departure was usually guided by expectations about peccary hunting. Women (usually wives) and children followed, the women carrying infants and children up to age four, as well as axes, carrying baskets, and sometimes a pet (usually a monkey or coati). Each basket held all the household gear brought by a single family, including one or more knives and pots, a plate or cup, matches, a sewing kit, extra clothing, and a mat or blanket. Most women began these trips with several kilos of manioc or corn, and someone always brought sugar and salt.

After about an hour's walk, the group stopped for a brief rest and some discussion about the direction of the hunt. Serious foraging seemed to begin only after this stop. When the party moved again, men set the pace as they walked ahead looking for signs of game.

Women followed at some distance, tracking the men through the jungle. When men were in active pursuit of animals, women stopped to await the result. They might eat a bit from their baskets or scout the area nearby for palms, often taking hearts or fiber and eating them on the spot. When a hunting episode was finished, women packed the game in their baskets while the men took off in search of other prey.

Women were sometimes more actively involved in the hunt. If monkeys or coatis were the target, women might act as spotters and noisemakers, keeping track of the animals and trying to direct their movement through the canopy. When pacas were hunted, women might guard a burrow exit.

Oranges and honey typically brought men and women together. Orange groves provided an occasion for all to eat and for women to fill their baskets with fruit. When honey was found, all waited while one or two men extracted it. Most of it was generally eaten immediately, but often some was carried away, later to be mixed with water and drunk. Women took insect larvae whenever they encountered them. Men also stopped for this resource, although it did not produce the group aggregation that formed for oranges and honey.

An hour or so before dark, a camp was established by the women, who collected huge fire logs. On arriving at a camp, a man might take an ax and go off to cut palms and take palm hearts; on his return he would report the location of those with good fiber to the women. On rainy days when there was little or no hunting, or after an early stop, husbands and wives might exploit palms as a team, the husband cutting them and testing the fiber, the wife then pounding the fiber in the good ones and/or collecting ripe palm fruit.

Throughout the day, plant and insect food was eaten as it was collected, although some larvae or honey might remain to be finished in the evening. Only rarely was game not cooked on the day it was killed. Most of the meat would be consumed that evening, with some remaining for the next day's breakfast. The Aché do not store or preserve anything. Seldom did any food remain two days after it was acquired.

Nuclear families slept at the same fire, women pillowing their husbands and children, sometimes more than one couple to a hearth. The extra men scattered among these fires to sleep, men laying against each other.

The next morning, people awakened just before first light. Meat and perhaps palm broth or oranges not finished the night before were eaten. Men sharpened their arrows. People talked about the prospects for the day, where to go, what they were hungry for. Unless it was raining or very cold, the men were off within two hours, usually together in a sudden, quiet exodus. The only days that the men did no hunting (two) and the only days (with two exceptions) that we did not move camp were days of heavy rain. After the men departed, the women finished packing their baskets and followed.

This pattern was repeated each day as the Aché walked through the jungle in search of food and other necessities, including material for their bows, arrows, baskets, and mats. When they finally returned to the colony, they almost always brought meat, oranges, and sometimes honey taken on the last day or two of the trip to share with those who had remained behind.

Foraging Returns

Our sample of seven foraging trips represents about 1,570 consumer days, counting all the Aché who took part in each trip (except infants) and including Hawkes and Hill as equivalent consumers. Over this period, the average daily per capita intake from foraging was about 3,600 Cal (Table 14.2). Eighty percent of this total (ca. 150 g per day) came from game animals. Both the high Calorie total and the large proportion of meat are quite surprising in view of recent generalizations about lowland South America and low-latitude hunters in general.

It is often said that hunting returns in lowland South America are poor by comparison with other parts of the world (Meggers 1971). Lathrap (1968:29) has remarked that the "hunting cultures of the tropical forest zone of South America offer highly explicit examples of the cultural and demographic effects of a dependence on hunting in an area where hunting is neither profitable nor easy." Harris (1974, 1977), Gross (1975), and Ross (1978) have held that the limited availability of animal protein places serious constraints on human population density, community size, and organizational complexity throughout this region. These views are widely disputed (Chagnon 1975, 1977; Lizot 1977; Beckerman 1979; Chagnon and Hames 1979; Hames 1980). The unexpected richness of the Aché diet represents another exception to the generalization that lowland South America is a poor place to hunt.[2]

The Aché figures are also exceptional for mid- to low-latitude hunter-gatherers in general. Lee (1969:72) reports that the Dobe !Kung take in approximately 2,140 Cal per consumer day, only about 60 percent of the total available to the Aché, who are about the same height (158 cm for a sample of ten adult men, 150 cm for a sample of nine adult women) as the !Kung (Howell 1979). Meehan (1977) calculates a figure of 2,150 Cal for the Anbara of coastal Arnhem Land, who, by her reckoning, are relatively well fed in comparison with other Australian Aborigines. Certainly, the high proportion of meat in the Aché diet is quite inconsistent with Lee's (1968) widely cited generalization that hunting dominates hunter-gatherer subsistence only at latitudes higher than about 60 degrees above the equator.

Circumstances that might have altered Aché hunting success in this area during these four months of 1980, making the results unrepresentative of traditional returns, should be considered. One factor is the use of firearms. On the first two trips, some Aché hunters carried shotguns, but at our request they used only bows and arrows on all succeeding trips. (Hill always carried a .22 caliber rifle.) On the 43 hunting days when shotguns were *not* used, the return rate from hunting fell from 2,755 to 2,657 Cal per consumer day, a drop of less than four percent. Guns *do* make a difference in hunting efficiency (Hill and Hawkes [1983]), but shotgun hunting is so small a component of this data set that the difference in meat per consumer is insignificant.

Table 14.2 Total caloric return, total time invested, and average caloric return per consumer day

AVERAGE CALORIES PER CONSUMER DAY (N = 1,570 consumer days)

Animal Resources		Plant Resources	
white-lipped peccary	568	oranges	209
armadillo	479	honey	109
monkey	441	palm fiber	105
coati	436	palm larvae	86
paca	381	palm heart	65
collared peccary	288	palm fruit	55
deer	156		
fish	117	Subtotal	710
bird	28		
snake	6		
Subtotal	2,900		

Grand total   3,610 Cal per consumer day

TOTAL CALORIES
Animal Resources	4,555,625
Plant resources	1,113,041
Total	5,668,666

TOTAL FORAGING HOURS
Animal resources	4,086
Plant resources	1,405
Carrying	1,024
Toal	6,515

Notes: Caloric values for plant food and larvae are from the Ford Chemical Laboratory, Salt Lake City, Utah, analysis of samples we collected in the field. Since standard drying procedures were impossible, we preserved our collections by adding 25 ml methanol to each 100 g of food.

The Aché eat every edible bit of an animal. We have estimated this to be 65 percent of the live weight for mammals and birds, 70 percent for reptiles and fish. Caloric values for most mammals are estimated at 300 Cal/100 g edible portion (Meehan 1977; Lee 1979). Deer and monkey are estimated at 125 Cal/100 g and 200 Cal/100 g edible portion, respectively; birds at 190 Cal/100 g; reptiles and fish at 150 Cal/100 g and 137 Cal/100 g. All of these estimates are derived from the USDA Agricultural Handbook No. 456, or Meehan (1977); the former is also the source of our caloric figure for honey. The caloric content of palm fiber may be inaccurately estimated – we have used the result from an analysis of the nutritional constituents of the liquid squeezed by hand (sucking may extract more from the fiber).

The second factor that may increase hunting success is the reduced dependence on foraging due to the mission's agricultural and provisioning activities. Since the Aché are not entirely dependent on hunting and gathering as they were in the past, each individual takes less from the jungle. While in one sense this reduces pressure on resources, the effect is countered by the size and permanence of the mission colony. More hunters cover less area, thereby increasing the pressure on local resources (Hill and Hawkes [1983]). There is also a growing Paraguayan population in this region, which has the twin effect of raising the number of competing hunters and decreasing the size of the game habitat. We cannot sum these effects in any precise way, but it seems unlikely that they could combine to increase current hunting success very much.

The extremely high Calorie totals remain to be explained. Two things should be noted here. First, foraging parties almost always brought food back to share with those remaining at the mission colony. Thus the returns of the last day or two were spread over more consumers (although mission provisions carried into the jungle balance this to some extent). Second, the bias in the population profile of these groups is in a direction that raises average dietary requirements as well as food totals. The very high sex ratio and the small number of children in these foraging groups elevate the Calories per consumer figures by inflating the proportion of hunters and reducing the proportion of dependents (Table 14.1).

Is Gathering a Supplementary Practice?

Since the Aché do so well hunting, why do they gather? The notion that plants are a low-risk/high-return food source while game is a high-risk/low-return resource (Lee 1968) suggests that gathering provides insurance against hunger if hunting fails. If, as Lee generalizes from the Dobe !Kung, *"people eat as much vegetable food as they need, and as much meat as they can"* (1968:41, original italics), we might expect a significant inverse correlation between the amount of meat and the amount of gathered food in each day's menu, especially in the Aché case, where the pattern of movement allows men and women to exchange information during the day, so that the success of the hunters is usually known by all as the day proceeds. A supplementing pattern would be obscured by storage where daily acquisition did not provide daily fare, success rates being averaged out over longer periods. But since the Aché do not store, they provide a particularly good test of this expectation.

The correlation coefficient for total Calories from plant and insect food to total Calories from meat over 61 foraging days (r = −.04) shows *no* correlation between the two. The view of plant and insect resources as supplements to cover failures in high-risk hunting is not supported. Why then do the Aché gather? An answer to this question is provided by optimal foraging theory.

The Optimal Diet Model

Optimal foraging models predict certain features of the set of resources foragers will exploit so as to maximize the returns they get for their work. The underlying assumption is simple: people will continue to use or adopt foods and techniques that give them greater returns (measured conventionally as Calories) to cost (measured conventionally as time); and they will stop using, or fail to copy the use of, foods and techniques that decrease their returns to cost. A series of nonintuitive propositions flow from models built on this assumption.

Consider the optimal diet model (Charnov and Orians 1973; MacArthur and Pianka 1966; MacArthur 1972; Pulliam 1974; Pyke et al. 1977; Emlen 1966; Schoener 1971; Charnov 1976a). Resources may be ranked according to the ratio of returns they provide (Calories) to the cost (handling time) of acquiring and processing the resources once they have been encountered.[3] The model shows that returns will be maximized if foragers take those resources for which this ratio is equal to or higher than the average returns they get for foraging in general *and* if they ignore all potential resources for which this ratio is lower than their average returns. Thus, whether or not a potential resource is in the optimal diet does not depend on its abundance: an item that is out of the optimal diet is out no matter how abundant it becomes; an item that is in the optimal diet is not excluded no matter how rare it becomes.[4]

We can state this more formally, following Charnov and Orians (1973), given the simplifying assumption that the energetic costs per unit of time do not differ significantly for exploiting different resource types:

Define: E = total Calories acquired foraging
  T = foraging time
  E_i = Calories available in a unit of resource i
  $T = T_s + \Sigma h_i$
  T_s = search time
  h_i = handling time per unit of resource i
  λ_i = the number of units of resource i encountered in a unit of search time (T_s)

Table 14.3 Costs and benefits of Aché resources

Resource	Total kg	Cal/kg[a]	No. of measured pursuits	Pursuit hr/kg	Processing hr/kg[b]	Handling hr/kg[c]	Calc. total handling time	E/h[d]	Rank
Collared peccary	232	1,950	none[e]	~.01	.02	.03	7.0	65,000	1
Deer	300	819	none[e]	~.01	.02	.03	9.0	27,300	1
Paca	307	1,950	33	.24	.04	.28	86.0	6,964	2
Coati	351	1,950	20	.22	.06	.28	98.3	6,964	2
Armadillo	386	1,950	20	.27	.06	.33	127.4	5,909	3
Snake	10	1,000	none[e]	~.01	.16	.17	1.7	5,882	3
Oranges	1,283	355	34			.07	89.8	5,071	4
Bird	35	1,240	none[e]	~.01	.25	.26	8.75	4,769	5
Honey	57	3,037	48			.93	52.5	3,266	6
White-lipped peccary	457	1,950	13	.69	.02	.71	324.5	2,746	7
Palm larvae	43	3,124	41			1.32	56.8	2,367	8
Fish	189	975	3	.45	.01	.46	86.9	2,120	9
Palm heart	171	595	13			.39	66.7	1,526	10
Monkey	533	1,300	37	.97	.10	1.07	570.3	1,215	11
Palm fiber	1,377	120	83			.10	137.7	1,200	11
Palm fruit	249	350	31			.37	94.6	946	12

[a] We assume the edible portion to be 65 percent of the live weight.
[b] We assume 0.5 hr for large and 0.25 hr for small animals.
[c] This is average pursuit time plus processing time per kg.
[d] This is Calories per handling hour.
[e] These animals are shot immediately upon encounter: a miss or a near miss means the target escapes; a good hit ends the pursuit in a few seconds.

An optimal forager will maximize: $E/T =$

$$\frac{\sum \lambda_i \cdot E_i \cdot T_s}{T_s + \sum \lambda_i \cdot h_i \cdot T_s} = \frac{\sum \lambda_i E_i}{1 + \sum \lambda_i h_i}$$

Thus, an item j will be included in the diet only

if: $E/T \leq \dfrac{E_j}{h_j}$

since, for some item a *not* in the optimal set, the following inequality must hold:

$$\frac{\sum \lambda_i E_i}{1 + \sum \lambda_i h_i} > \frac{\sum \lambda_i E_i + \lambda_a E_a}{1 + \sum \lambda_i h_i + \lambda_a h_a}.$$

which implies that

$$E/T > \frac{\lambda_a E_a}{\lambda_a h_a} \quad \text{or} \quad E/T > \frac{E_a}{h_a}.$$

In the following application we treat carrying time as a fixed cost, like search time. This would be reflected in the preceding algebra if T_s were defined as the sum of search time *plus* carrying time.

Note that the resource rankings of this model say nothing about the quantitative importance of a resource to optimal foragers. High-ranked items may be so rarely encountered that they represent only a very small proportion of the diet; low-ranked items in the optimal set may be encountered with sufficient frequency to contribute the bulk. The ranking shows instead which resources are more likely to enter or leave the diet and in what order. If the encounter rate with high-ranked resources fluctuates widely, the optimal diet will fluctuate, with the very highest ranked resources being the only ones that never go out.

Table 14.3 shows the resources taken by the Aché ranked in order by the ratio of caloric returns to handling time (E_i/h_i). Average returns per forager-hour ($E/_T$) include time spent searching for resources. These are calculated as total Calories (5,668,666) divided by the sum of total hunting hours (4,086) plus gathering hours (1,405) plus carrying hours (1,024), or 870 Cal per foraging hour.

Figure 14.1 shows the ratio of Calories returned to handling time (E_i/h_i) for each of the resources ordered by rank and the average returns for foraging in general ($E/_T$) that result from the addition of each of these resources. The latter numbers are derived as follows: 3,673 forager-hours were spent searching during the 61 foraging days (this is the total 5,491 hunting and gathering hours minus 1,818 total resource handling hours – column

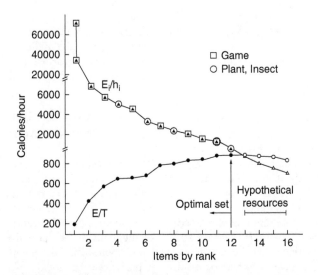

Figure 14.1 *An optimal foraging model of Aché resources*

8, Table 14.3). If only the top-ranked resources (i.e., collared peccaries and deer) were taken, average returns would be 148 Cal/hr (452,400 Cal plus 245,700 Cal for these resources, respectively, divided by 3,673 hours of search plus 1,024 hours of carrying plus 16 hours of handling peccaries and deer). Adding the second-ranked resources changes the average, as the total Calories for pacas and coatis are added to the numerator, the handling time for these animals added to the denominator. The result is 405 Cal/hr. The foraging returns gained after the addition of resources of each rank are as follows: 1st-ranked resources only – collared peccaries and deer = 148 Cal/hr; add 2nd-ranked – paca and coati = 405 Cal/hr; add 3rd-ranked – armadillo and snake = 546 Cal/hr; add 4th-ranked – oranges = 625 Cal/hr; add 5th-ranked – bird = 632 Cal/hr; add 6th-ranked – honey = 660 Cal/hr; add 7th-ranked – white-lipped peccary = 783 Cal/hr; add 8th-ranked – palm larvae = 799 Cal/hr; add 9th-ranked – fish = 821 Cal/hr; add 10th-ranked – palm hearts = 829 Cal/hr; add 11th-ranked – monkeys and palm fiber = 871 Cal/hr; add 12th-ranked – palm fruit = 872 Cal/hr. Four hypothetical resources with E_i/h_i ratios of 850, 800, 750, and 700, respectively, would *reduce* rather than increase average foraging returns. Assuming that each was encountered at a rate to constitute 1,000,000 Cal during this foraging period, the cumulative addition of these items would result in averages of 868, 859, 845, and 828 Cal/hr.

As the figure illustrates, the inclusion of the plant and insect resources that the Aché take *increases* their ratio of Calories returned for time invested. Changes in the encounter rate with higher-ranked resources alter the position of the $E/_T$ curve. If encounter rates increase, search time is reduced and this curve shifts up, intersecting the descending E_i/h_i line at a higher point; and conversely if encounter rates are depressed. Thus, low-ranked resources move in and out of the optimal diet.

It is interesting to note that on several occasions, reports of nearby palm fruit (ranked 12) were ignored, something that did not happen with oranges. On several other occasions people discussed the relative merits of hunting

monkeys (ranked 11), reaching consensus that monkeys should not be pursued "because they are not fat." While we observed that monkeys once encountered were actually ignored only twice, this ambivalence was not expressed toward any other game animal. This suggests an alternative to the idea that monkeys are often excluded as game because they are so "like humans." Such an alternative would have the virtue of accounting for the differential treatment of monkeys from one region to another. The Aché, after all, find monkeys to be humanlike, but they hunt them all the same.[5]

Note that size is not the only factor that affects return ratios. Differences in the habits of the animals and in hunting techniques are very important. The white-lipped peccary is the larger of the two peccaries in this area, but its return ratio is lower than that of the collared peccary by more than an order of magnitude. White-lipped peccaries travel in larger groups. Usually several men track them over long distances, investing a relatively large amount of time in pursuit. The smaller peccaries, by contrast, travel quickly in smaller groups. Hunters, alone or in pairs, try to take them immediately upon encounter, only pursuing animals they judge to be mortally wounded. Although the suggestion will not be explored here, the optimal foraging perspective suggests that differences in hunting techniques, for example, group or solitary hunting, the use of bows and arrows, or hunting by hand – which the Aché practice in hunting pacas, coatis, and armadillos – may themselves be accounted for by optimality criteria.

Hunting, Gathering, and Optimal Patch Choice

The optimal diet model just considered assumes a "fine-grained" environment, that is, one in which resources are randomly distributed. If this array of Aché resources were encountered at random, optimal foragers would take any of the items in the optimal set whenever they came upon them. For example, anyone finding a palm tree that looked likely to have good fiber would cut down the tree, take the palm heart, and pound out the fiber. Yet as hunters search for game, they pass by innumerable palm trees and ignore them, turning to this resource only in late afternoon after camp has been established.

The distribution of tools suggests itself as an explanation for this. To take palm fiber, palm larvae, palm hearts, and honey, the Aché use axes. When they are hunting the men usually carry only bows and arrows. Still, the availability of the tool does not account satisfactorily for the hunters' treatment of nonmeat resources, since they pass palms throughout the day but almost always stop and call for an ax to take honey. Why stop hunting for oranges and for honey but not for palm hearts and palm fiber? Optimal foraging models that deal with the use of patchy environments, that is, those in which resources are clumped, are relevant here.

The patch choice model predicts that where resources are differentially distributed in kind and quantity, foragers will operate on that spatial set or patch which produces the best energy return for time spent traveling to the patch, searching it, and gathering and processing the resources found there (Charnov and Orians 1973; MacArthur and Pianka 1966; Pyke et al. 1977; Schoener 1971; Charnov 1976b). Note that while the ranking of diet items *excludes* the cost of search, the return figures for a patch *include* the cost of searching it. Among other things, this means that high-ranked resources may be avoided by a forager if they occur in patches with high search costs and low return rates.

The patch choice model can be applied to the Aché as follows. The average energy return for hunting, including search, pursuit, and processing of animals, is 4,555,625 total Cal divided by 4,086 total hunting and processing hours, or about 1,115 Cal per hunter-hour. If game animals are conceptualized as a patch, optimal foragers will exploit that patch in preference to patches with lower average returns and leave it for patches with higher average returns.

Consider oranges as a patch. When an orange grove is encountered, search time within it is effectively zero. The time required to exploit the patch is almost entirely time required to scale trees, shake the fruit loose, and gather the fallen oranges. Once in a grove, average returns are 355 Cal/kg divided by the sum of ~0.01 hr/kg in patch search time plus 0.07 hr/kg handling time, or 4,438 Cal per forager-hour. Since returns for the orange patch are higher than the hunting patch, foragers should leave the hunting patch for the orange patch.

Honey, considered as a patch, has similar characteristics. When a honey tree is located, the patch and its resources are encountered at the same time. Occasions on which trees were cut but produced only dry combs have been included in the calculations of average handling costs as "failed pursuits": 3,037 Cal/kg divided by the sum of ~0.01 hr/kg in patch search plus 0.93 hr/kg handling yields 3,231 Cal/hr. Foragers should leave the hunting patch for honey.

Palm larvae patches are rotting palm logs that usually occur in clumps. These clumps may be conceptualized as patches. Some search time is required within patches of logs because they may be meters apart in dense jungle and because not every one contains larvae. On one occasion a husband and wife spent 64 minutes each, or 2.14 foraging hours, exploiting several clusters of logs from which they took 1.26 kg of larvae. Included here is the time (1.69 hr) spent finding and checking new logs after they had started exploiting the patch. This means that the return for the patch was about 1,849 Cal per forager-hour. Hunters should stop for larvae.

The palm patch contains palm hearts, palm fiber, and palm fruit. As with palm larvae and honey, encountering the palm patch is not the same as encountering its resources; some investment in search is necessary. Trees must be cut and the fiber tested before one can be certain whether this resource is "good." No doubt the Aché can often judge fiber quality on standing trees, but it is still frequently the case that fiber is found unacceptable after a tree has been felled. Similarly, palm hearts are not available on every tree cut. On one occasion one of us requested the heart from a palm being pounded for fiber. Remarking that it would be no good, one of the women eating the fiber cut the terminal bud, which proved

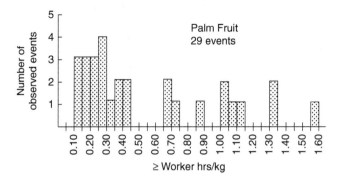

Figure 14.2 *Variation in costs and benefits of exploiting palm fruit*

to be less than half the average size of those usually taken.

We can make a very tentative approximation of the return rate for the palm patch in the following way.[6] On the basis of 25 observed events in which fiber was taken from several trees and time spent searching (including evaluation of the trees) estimated, an average return in fiber for this patch type is 74.63 hr/379 kg, or 0.20 hr search and handling per kilogram. Subtracting from this the 0.10 hr/kg handling cost for fiber (Table 14.3) gives 0.10 hr/kg average search cost. Using this figure we can estimate 1,377 kg × 0.10 hr/kg = 137.7 total search hours in the palm patch during the foraging period under study.

Viewing the *patch* as a fine-grained environment, the optimal diet model may be applied. If only palm hearts were taken, returns in the patch would be (171 kg × 595 Cal/kg) ÷ (137.7 hr search + 66.7 hr processing) = 498 Cal per forager-hour. Adding fiber raises hourly returns to (171 kg × 595 Cal/kg + 1,377 kg × 120 Cal/kg) ÷ (137.7 hr search + 66.7 hr processing + 137.7 hr processing) = 780 Cal per forager-hour. Finally, adding palm fruit raises returns to 810 Cal per forager-hour.

It is important to note that the returns for patches and resources vary considerably. This is illustrated by the returns for palm fruit presented as event averages in Figure 14.2. We expect that such fluctuations will affect both patch choice and resource exploitation within patches. Individual foraging practices may be expected to differ depending on features of particular context – including differences in skill. It will be of interest to determine which averages, long-term or short-term, individual or group, are the best predictors of various sorts of foraging behavior.

The average value for the palm patch shows that optimal foragers should not stop hunting for that patch unless hunting returns had fallen to about 800 Cal per forager-hour. It may be that hunting returns decline as the day wanes so that the palm patch enters the optimal set. This possibility remains to be investigated. Still, this tentative treatment suggests that hunters may well be maximizing their foraging efficiency in bypassing palms.

One patch is still to be considered: the fishing patch. On the two days of the third trip in which fishing was the main activity, 85 forager-hours fishing and about 2 forager-hours processing were spent for 189 kg of fish. The group fishing technique of the Aché includes no search. The return ratio for the fishing patch is equivalent to the returns to handling time for the resource. Since this is over 2,000 Cal per forager-hour, markedly higher than the average returns for the hunting patch, why don't the Aché fish more often?

Two events may shed some light on this. On April 11, during the second trip, five women spent 2.25 hr each fishing a small lagoon and stream. Their returns were negligible: less than 2 kg of fish. This seemed to be viewed more as play than foraging. On April 20, at the mission colony, 38 adults spent 5 hr each fishing the lagoon and took about 25 kg of fish. The addition of these two incidents to the figures for April 26 and 27 (trip 3) results in a total of 288 forager-hours for 216 kg of fish, which is 1.3 hr/kg or about 733 Cal per forager-hour. These figures suggest that the Aché fish infrequently because they do better hunting. We suspect that in a larger data set returns in the fishing patch will be lower on average than those in the hunting patch.

Where the patches exploited by optimal foragers are randomly encountered, they may be treated as formally equivalent to the set of individual resources in the optimal diet. Patches for which the ratio of energy gained to time invested equals or exceeds the average ratio for foraging in the environment as a whole should be included in the set of exploited patches. Patches with ratios that fall below this average should be excluded. Low-ranked patches move in and out of the optimal set as average foraging returns fluctuate with the depletion and renewal of high-ranked patches. High-ranked patches always stay in the optimal set. Applying this model[7] to the Aché exploitation of oranges, honey, palm larvae, game animals, palm trees, and fish does two things. First, it accounts for some general features of the patterns, including the tendency for hunters to stop for oranges, honey, and (usually) larvae, but not palms or (provisionally) fish. Second, it raises questions and poses hypotheses for further research: Why do the Aché take palms when they do? Why do they fish when they do?

What about the !Kung?

Aché hunting and gathering appears to be consistent with predictions derived from optimal foraging theory. If these predictions are truly general in character, then they should enable us to explain the mix of resources taken by other hunter-gatherers. In particular, they might be expected to resolve what now seems an anomaly: Lee's (1968, 1969, 1979) influential conclusion that the !Kung devote substantial time to hunting in spite of the fact that it is less rewarding in terms of energy yield than is gathering. If Lee is right, optimal foraging predictions are violated by the !Kung.

Lee's data allow a brief exploration of this. The returns for gathering suggested by his figures are about 670 Cal per forager-hour (as recalculated by Hawkes and O'Connell [1981] to include processing time). Each man-day of hunting produces about 7,230 Cal (Lee 1979:262). The cost in time is about 8 hr hunting plus 1.12 hr processing the kill (Lee 1979:278), or about 9.12 hr, which indicates a return rate of about 793 Cal per hunter-hour. This makes hunting the optimal choice for anyone doing as well as the average hunter. Thus, the foraging models that fit the Aché may also account for the hunting and gathering behavior of the !Kung.

Conclusions

The question raised initially was why hunter-gatherers take the set of resources they do from among the available array. Our answer is that such choices are determined largely by cost/benefit considerations as expressed in optimal foraging theory. We have supported this argument by showing that Aché foraging behavior is consistent with predictions derived from the optimal diet and patch choice models.

The result has important implications. We suspect that game animals, especially large game animals, will often be high ranked in optimal diet terms and because of this will frequently be identified by hunter-gatherers as preferred foods, regardless of their local abundance or quantitative contribution to the total diet. Conversely, plant foods, especially those that require extensive processing (e.g., roasting, grinding, or leaching), will often be relatively low ranked. Indeed, they may move in and out of local diets depending on the abundance of higher-ranked foods relative to the number of potential consumers but regardless of their own abundance or nutritional quality. We do not mean to imply here that *all* animals are high ranked and *all* plants are low ranked. Still, the available data indicate that many large and medium-sized mammals are high ranked and many seeds and nuts are low ranked (Keene 1981; Earle and Christenson 1980; Winterhalder and Smith 1981; Jones 1981; Simms 1981).

If we are correct in this, then optimal foraging models may account for the broad spatial and temporal patterns in hunter-gatherer diet noted by Lee, Harris, and others. We note, for example, that present-day mid- and low-latitude hunters often compete with pastoralists and agriculturalists in situations where large-mammal populations have been depleted (e.g., Schrire 1980). In such circumstances, it should be not surprising that they often rely heavily on high-cost plant resources in spite of an expressed preference for meat. It is interesting (and consistent with optimal foraging theory) that such resources may be among the first to be dropped from the diet when higher-ranked items become more abundant (O'Connell and Hawkes 1981).

It also seems likely that the same processes account for broad patterns of dietary change widely noted from the late Paleolithic through the development of agriculture. Certainly, the coincidence between the disappearance of large mammals and other fauna at or near the end of the Pleistocene and the emergence of "broad spectrum" or mesolithic subsistence economies is consistent with this idea.

We conclude with the caution that optimal foraging theory need not necessarily explain all the variation in hunter-gatherer subsistence. Nevertheless, its value lies in its capacity to provide testable hypotheses about foraging behavior and about the changes that behavior is likely to sustain under different circumstances. Whatever the outcome of any particular test, our knowledge of hunter-gatherer subsistence will have been enhanced by the use of such theory.

NOTES

1. Data collection techniques are further described in Hill and Hawkes [1983].
2. Since they do so well as hunters, it is not surprising that the Aché have persisted as such in a neighborhood of farmers. The material presented here in no way contradicts the historical observation that refugee populations often remain nomadic because the depredations of stronger enemies make the cost of resettling too high. They may thus take great cuts in "standard of living" and suffer by comparison with their stronger neighbors. Nevertheless, the Aché data dispute the view that all South American hunters have been pushed into environments where they must pursue a demanding food quest.
3. Some anthropologists (e.g., Reidhead 1980; Keene 1981) have constructed optimal foraging models based on assumptions about nutritional requirements. We recognize that such requirements may constrain foraging behavior in some circumstances (see Belovsky 1978 for an example), but prefer to use Calories as a currency, primarily because this simplifies analysis and facilitates cross-cultural comparisons. The addition of other nutritional parameters to these models inevitably increases analytical complexity. The more variables included in an analysis, the more difficult it becomes to perform; yet, conversely, any attempt to keep the list within manageable limits requires difficult, often arbitrary, decisions about which variables to include and which to omit. This also puts the general utility of the models at risk in that different investigators may often use quite different parameters, thereby inhibiting comparison with other cases. Finally, incorporating more than a very few nutritional parameters may reduce accuracy by requiring precise estimates of intake requirements for which data are at best equivocal (Dubos 1980; Wing and Brown 1979:25–6). The power of optimal foraging models lies in their simplicity and generality. It seems appropriate to take advantage of these attributes by using simple, general currencies, at least initially.

4. These generalizations are modified to the extent that abundance or scarcity alters handling cost. But it is the change in handling cost, not abundance, that has the effect.

5. Further analysis by Hill and Hawkes [1983] shows that monkeys are excluded from the optimal diet of shotgun hunters.

6. We use this estimate because it gives results that fit the model. The problem of distinguishing search time from other activities remains far short of solution.

7. More knowledge about the background ecology and more detailed analysis of the foraging data should allow a fuller application of the patch choice models. Like plant and insect resources, animals are patchily distributed; for example, pacas tend to live along rivers.

REFERENCES

Allen, H. (1974). The Bagundji of the Darling Basin: Cereal Gatherers in an Uncertain Environment. *World Archaeology* 5:309–22.

Beckerman, Steven. (1979). The Abundance of Protein in Amazonia: A Reply to Gross. *American Anthropologist* 81:533–60.

Belovsky, G. E. (1978). Diet Optimization in a Generalist Herbivore. *Theoretical Population Biology* 14:100–34.

Bettinger, Robert. (1980). Explanatory/Predictive Models of Hunter-Gatherer Adaptation. *Advances in Archaeological Method and Theory* 3:189–262.

Chagnon, Napoleon. (1975). Response to Marvin Harris' "Protein Theory of Warfare." *Psychology Today* 8:6–7.

——. (1977). Yanomamö. New York: Holt, Rinehart and Winston.

Chagnon, Napoleon, and Raymond Hames. (1979). Protein Deficiency and Tribal Warfare in Amazonia: New Data. *Science* 203:910–13.

Charnov, Eric L. (1976a). Optimal Foraging: Attack Strategy of a Mantid. *American Naturalist* 110:141–51.

——. (1976b). Optimal Foraging: The Marginal Value Theorem. *Theoretical Population Biology* 9:129–36.

Charnov, Eric L., and Gordon Orians. (1973). Optimal Foraging: Some Theoretical Explorations. Mimeograph. Department of Biology, University of Utah.

Clastres, Pierre. (1968). Ethnographie des Indians Guayaki (Paraguay-Brésil). *Journal de la Société des Americanistes de Paris* 57:9–61.

——. (1972). The Guayaki. *In* Hunters and Gatherers Today. M. B. Bicchieri, ed. pp. 138–74. New York: Holt, Rinehart and Winston.

Dart, Raymond. (1953). The Predatory Transition from Ape to Man. *International Anthropological and Linguistic Review* 1:207–8.

Douglas, Mary. (1975). Implicit Meanings: Essays in Anthropology. London: Routledge and Kegan Paul.

Dubos, Rene. (1980). Nutritional Ambiguities. *Natural History* 7:14–21.

Earle, Timothy K., and Andrew L. Christenson, eds. (1980). Modeling Change in Prehistoric Subsistence Economies. New York: Academic Press.

Emlen, J. M. (1966). The Role of Time and Energy in Food Preference. *American Naturalist* 100:611–17.

Flannery, Kent V. (1968). Archaeological Systems Theory and Early Mesoamerica. *In* Anthropological Archaeology in the Americas. B. Meggers, ed. pp. 67–87. Washington, DC: Anthropological Society of Washington.

——. (1969). Origins and Ecological Effects of Early Domestication in Iran and the Near East. *In* The Domestication and Exploitation of Plants and Animals. P. J. Ucko and G. W. Dimbleby, eds. pp. 73–100. Chicago: Aldine.

Gould, Richard A. (1969). Subsistence Behaviour among the Western Desert Aborigines of Australia. *Oceania* 39:252–74.

——. (1980). Living Archaeology. Cambridge: Cambridge University Press.

Gross, Daniel. (1975). Protein Capture and Cultural Development in the Amazon Basin. *American Anthropologist* 77:526–49.

Hames, R., ed. (1980). Studies of Hunting and Fishing in the Neotropics. Working Papers on South American Indians, No. 2. K. M. Kensinger, ed. Bennington, VT: Bennington College.

Hames, Raymond, and William Vickers, eds. (1983). Adaptive Responses of Native Amazonians. New York: Academic Press.

Harris, Marvin. (1974). Cows, Pigs, Wars, and Witches. New York: Random House.

——. (1977). Cannibals and Kings. New York: Random House.

——. (1979). Cultural Materialism: The Struggle for a Science of Culture. New York: Random House.

Hawkes, Kristen, and James F. O'Connell. (1981). Affluent Hunters? Some Comments in Light of the Alyawara Case. *American Anthropologist* 83:622–6.

Hayden, Brian. (1981). Subsistence and Ecological Adaptations of Modern Hunter-Gatherers. *In* Omnivorous Primates: Gathering and Hunting in Human Evolution. R. S. O. Harding and Geza Teleki, eds. pp. 344–421. New York: Columbia University Press.

Hill, Kim. (1979). The Aché of Eastern Paraguay: Current Conditions and Recent History. Ms. Department of Anthropology, University of Utah.

Hill, Kim, and Kristen Hawkes. (1983). Neotropical Hunting among the Aché of Eastern Paraguay. *In* Adaptive Responses of Native Amazonians. R. Hames and W. Vickers, eds. pp. 139–88. New York: Academic Press.

Howell, Nancy. (1979). Demography of the Dobe Area !Kung. New York: Academic Press.

Jochim, Michael A. (1981). Strategies for Survival: Cultural Behavior in an Ecological Context. New York: Academic Press.

Jones, Kevin T. (1981). Patch Choice Models and the Study of Prehistoric Hunter-Gatherers. Ms. Department of Anthropology, University of Utah.

Jones, Rhys. (1980). Hunters in the Australian Coastal Savanna. *In* Human Ecology of Savanna Environments. D. R. Harris, ed. pp. 107–46. New York: Academic Press.

Keene, Arthur S. (1981). Optimal Foraging in a Non-Marginal Environment: A Model of Prehistoric Subsistence Strategies in Michigan. *In* Hunter-Gatherer Foraging Strategies: Ethnographic and Archaeological Analyses. B. Winterhalder and E. A. Smith, eds. pp. 171–93. Chicago: University of Chicago Press.

Lathrap, Donald. (1968). The "Hunting" Economies of the Tropical Forest Zone of South America: An Attempt at Historical Perspective. *In* Man the Hunter. R. B. Lee and I. DeVore, eds. pp. 23–9. Chicago: Aldine.

Lee, Richard B. (1968). What Hunters Do for a Living; Or, How to Make Out on Scarce Resources. *In* Man the Hunter. R. B. Lee and I. DeVore, eds. pp. 30–48. Chicago: Aldine.

——. (1969). !Kung Bushmen Subsistence: An Input-Output Analysis. *In* Environment and Cultural Behavior. A. P. Vayda, ed. pp. 47–79. New York: Natural History Press.

——. (1979). The !Kung San: Men, Women, and Work in a Foraging Society. Cambridge: Cambridge University Press.

Lee, Richard B., and Irven DeVore, eds. (1968). Man the Hunter. Chicago: Aldine.

Lizot, Jacques. (1977). Population, Resources and Warfare among the Yamomami. *Man* (NS) 12:497–517.

MacArthur, Robert. (1972). Geographical Ecology. New York: Harper & Row.

MacArthur, Robert, and Eric Pianka. (1966). On Optimal Use of a Patchy Environment. *American Naturalist* 100:603–9.

MacNeish, Richard. (1967). A Summary of Subsistence. *In* The Prehistory of the Tehuacan Valley. Vol. 1: Environment and Subsistence. D. S. Byers, ed. pp. 290–309. Austin: University of Texas Press.

Meehan, Betty. (1977). Hunters by the Seashore. *Journal of Human Evolution* 6:363–70.

Meggers, Betty. (1971). Amazonia: Man and Culture in a Counterfeit Paradise. Chicago: Aldine.

Metraux, Albert, and Herbert Baldus. (1946). The Guayaki. *BAE Bulletin* 143(1):435–44.

O'Connell, James F., and Kristen Hawkes. (1981). Alyawara Plant Use and Optimal

Foraging Theory. *In* Hunter-Gatherer Foraging Strategies: Ethnographic and Archaeological Analyses. B. Winterhalder and E. A. Smith, eds. pp. 99–125. Chicago: University of Chicago Press.

Pulliam, H. R. (1974). On the Theory of Optimal Diets. *American Naturalist* 108:59–74.

Pyke, Graham, R. Pulliam, and E. L. Charnov. (1977). Optimal Foraging Theory: A Selective Review of Theory and Tests. *Quarterly Review of Biology* 52:137–54.

Reidhead, Van A. (1980). The Economics of Subsistence Change: Test of an Optimization Model. *In* Modeling Change in Prehistoric Subsistence Economies. T. K. Earle and A. L. Christenson, eds. pp. 141–86. New York: Academic Press.

Ross, Eric. (1978). Food Taboos, Diet and Hunting Strategies: The Adaptation to Animals in Amazon Cultural Ecology. *Current Anthropology* 19:1–36.

Sahlins, Marshall. (1976). Culture and Practical Reason. Chicago: University of Chicago Press.

Schoener, T. W. (1971). Theory of Feeding Strategies. *Annual Review of Ecology and Systematics* 2:369–404.

Schrire, Carmel. (1980). An Inquiry into the Evolutionary Status and Apparent Identity of San Hunter-Gatherers. *Human Ecology* 9:9–32.

Simms, Steven R. (1981). Optimal Foraging, Pine Nut Use and Settlement Patterning in the Great Basin. Ms. Department of Anthropology, University of Utah.

Steward, Julian H. (1936). The Economic and Social Basis of Primitive Bands. *In* Essays in Anthropology Presented to A. L. Kroeber. R. H. Lowie, ed. pp. 331–345. Berkeley: University of California Press.

———. (1955). Theory of Culture Change: The Methodology of Multilinear Evolution. Urbana: University of Illinois Press.

Vellard, J. (1939). Une Civilization du Miel. Paris: Gallimard.

Wing, Elizabeth S., and Antoinette B. Brown. (1979). Paleonutrition: Method and Theory in Prehistoric Foodways. New York: Academic Press.

Winterhalder, Bruce, and Eric Alden Smith, eds. (1981). Hunter-Gatherer Foraging Strategies: Ethnographic and Archaeological Analyses. Chicago: University of Chicago Press.

15

Foragers, Genuine or Spurious?: Situating the Kalahari San in History

Jacqueline S. Solway and Richard B. Lee

One of the dominant themes of critical anthropology in the 1970s and 1980s has been the critique of ethnographic models that depict societies as isolated and timeless. Where an older generation of anthropologists tended to see societies as autonomous and self-regulating, the newer generation has discovered mercantilism and capitalism at work in societies hitherto portrayed as, if not pristine, then at least well beyond the reach of the "world system." Thus the Nuer (Gough 1971, Newcomer 1972, Sacks 1979, Kelly 1985), Samoans (Freeman 1983), Tallensi (Worsley 1956), Kachin (Friedman 1975, 1979; Nugent 1983), Maya (Lewis 1951, Wasserstrom 1982), and many other "classic" cases have been the subject of critical scrutiny. These studies have sought to resituate these peoples in the context of wider regional and international economies, polities, and histories (see Wolf 1982).

Studies of hunting-and-gathering peoples have been strongly influenced by this revisionism (see, e.g., Endicott 1988; Woodburn 1988; Ingold, Riches, and Woodburn 1988; Headland and Reid 1989; Howell, cited in Lewin 1989; Bower 1989; Lewin 1989). It was in the spirit of this endeavor that we produced a critical analysis of the impact of the fur trade on the 19th-century Kalahari San (Solway and Lee 1981). A number of other scholars have focussed on the San, uncovering the early interactions between San foragers and Bantu farmers, herders, and traders within the complex historical dynamics of the Kalahari Desert (Schrire 1980, 1984a; Wilmsen 1983; Gordon 1984; Denbow 1984, 1986; Parkington 1984; Denbow and Wilmsen 1986).[1] In their zeal to discover links and to dispel myths of pristinity, however, these scholars are in danger of erecting new straw men and of doing violence of a different kind to the data – imputing links where none existed and assuming that where evidence exists for trade it implies the surrender of autonomy. What is perhaps most troubling about the Kalahari revisionism is its projection of a spurious uniformity on a vast and diverse region.

In this paper we present two case studies that demonstrate the varied nature and consequences of San contact with non-San in the Kalahari. By examining the different historical experiences of two San groups, one largely dependent on its Bantu-speaking neighbours and the other (until recently) substantially autonomous, we intend to make clear that contact may take many forms, not all of which lead to dependency, abandonment of foraging, or incorporation into "more powerful" social formations.

The attribution of dependency to societies formerly considered autonomous resonates with other themes in the culture of late capitalism. Borrowing an image from the popular film *The Gods Must Be Crazy*, we call this view the "Coke Bottle in the Kalahari Syndrome," whereby modernity falls mysteriously from the sky, setting in motion an inevitable spiral of cultural disintegration that can only be checked by the removal of the foreign element. This is clearly a caricature, but it reveals the common and unstated perception of foraging societies as so delicately balanced and fragile that they cannot accommodate innovation and change. Sahlins's (1968:2) summary law "Cultural dominance goes to technological pre-dominance" could be the foragers' epitaph. The "Coke Bottle in the Kalahari" imagery also bears a subtext, the rueful recognition of the unlimited capacity of "advanced societies" to consume everything in their path.

We challenge the notion that contact automatically undermines foragers and that contemporary foragers are to be understood only as degraded cultural residuals created through their marginality to more powerful systems. We consider the possibility that foragers can be autonomous without being isolated and engaged without being incorporated. And we follow Marx (1977 [1887]:89–92) in proposing that exchange can occur in the absence of "exchange value." Further, our argument calls into question any model of social change that implies linearity; the historical record reveals protracted processes, with fits and starts, plateaus and reversals, and varied outcomes. While many historical foragers have assimilated to other societies, a number, such as the African Pygmies and the foragers of South and South-east Asia, have developed stable forms of interaction with agricultural neighbours and persisted alongside them, sometimes for centuries (see, e.g., Leacock and Lee 1982, Endicott 1988, Petersen 1978). The fact that foragers have coexisted with farmers for so long is testimony to the resilience of their way of life. The position adopted here is that 20th-century foragers are neither pristine nor totally degraded and encapsulated. The historical status of African foraging peoples must be seen as the complex product of the dynamics of the foraging mode of production itself, of long interaction between foragers, farmers, and herders, and finally of dynamics growing out of their linkages with world capitalism.

The Problem

By the mid-20th century, San societies in Botswana exhibited a wide range of "adaptations." Along the Nata, Botletli, and Okavango Rivers there were "black" San who fished, owned cattle, and practiced agriculture (Cashdan 1987, Tlou 1985, Hitchcock 1987); in the Ghanzi freehold zone of western Botswana many San had become farm labourers, dependent squatters on their traditional lands (Guenther 1986, Russell 1976); in the Game Reserve areas of Khutse and the Central Kalahari, the /Gwi and other San groups lived relatively independent lives, hunting and gathering, raising small stock, and gardening (Kent 1989a, Tanaka 1980, Silberbauer 1981); and in the central sandveld many San lived clustered around Tswana cattle posts, where the men were employed as herders (Hitchcock 1978).

The historical antecedents of this diversity have been difficult to discern. Until the 1970s the available archaeological evidence indicated that the Kalahari had been a stronghold of hunter-gatherer societies and the diversity was the product of the last few hundred years (Phillipson 1977). Recent excavations, however (Denbow 1980, 1984, 1986; Wilmsen 1983, 1988; Denbow and Wilmsen 1983, 1986), have demonstrated a much earlier Iron Age presence, in parts of the Kalahari as early as AD 500. Later Stone Age (LSA) sites, commonly associated with populations ancestral to San hunter-gatherers, are present as well and in some areas remain predominant, but a number of these sites have Iron Age materials indicating contact between farmers and foragers. Thus the time depth of contact with non-hunters has increased from a few centuries to a millennium or more, and the presence of "exotic" goods is evidence for regional trade between hunters and non-hunters.

A second line of evidence for the revisionists springs from rereadings of 19th-century accounts of exploration and trade in the

Kalahari interior. Gordon (1984), for one, has argued that the interior San were so deeply involved in trade, warfare, and diplomacy that they bore little resemblance to the "autonomous" societies described by 20th-century ethnographers. A closely related issue is the question of San servitude for black overlords. Indeed, many 19th- and 20th-century sources describe the San as living in a condition close to serfdom, a perception that has coloured observations of them.

The revisionists have used these lines of evidence to call into question the claims to authenticity of a number of foraging peoples studied by Marshall (1976), Lee and DeVore (1976), Lee (1979), Silberbauer (1981), Tanaka (1980), and others. Schrire (1980, 1984b), for example, argues that the San are not hunter-gatherers at all but failed pastoralists who oscillate between herding and foraging from century to century.[2] Labelling recent ethnographies of the San "romantic accounts of Bushman isolation and independence," Denbow (1986:1) dismisses them as "an ahistorical and timeless caricature." He suggests that whatever hunters persisted through the long period of contact did so not as autonomous societies but as "part of long-standing regional systems of interaction and exchange involving neighboring peoples with quite different economic and sociopolitical orientations" (p. 27). Wilmsen (1983), the most outspoken critic, referencing the perspective pioneered by Wolf, challenges the idea that the flexible egalitarian sharing documented for several San groups has anything to do with the dynamics of a foraging mode of production, concluding that "it is more than merely possible that the San are classless today precisely because they are the underclass in an intrusive class structure" (p. 17). In the same vein, Schrire (1984b:18) asks,

Are the common features of hunter-gatherer groups, be they structural elements such as bilateral kinship systems or behavioral ones such as the tendency to share food, a product of interaction with us? Are the features we single out and study held in common, not so much because humanity shared the hunter-gatherer lifestyle for 99% of its time on earth, but because the hunter-gatherers of today, in

searching for the compromises that would allow them to go on doing mainly that, have reached subliminal consensus in finding similar solutions to similar problems?

The questions raised by the revisionists are challenging ones, and the claims they make go well beyond the reinterpretation of Kalahari archaeology. Yet it is an open question how much of their revision arises from the data and how much rests on unexamined inference and assumption. It will be useful to set out their claims as a series of propositions in order to clarify the boundary between fact and interpretation. They propose that (1) the Iron Age settlement of the Kalahari is earlier than previously thought, and therefore (2) hunter-gatherers were absorbed into regional economic networks and (3) ceased to exist as independent societies well before the historic period. They go on to argue that (4) if these societies continue to exhibit characteristics associated with hunting and gathering it is because of (a) their poverty (Wilmsen) or (b) their resistance to domination by stronger societies (Schrire). Of these only Point 1 can be considered well established; Points 2 and 3 draw unwarranted conclusions from scanty data while Point 4 relies heavily on discourses that are as ideological as they are analytical.

What kinds of questions need to be asked in order to evaluate the conflicting claims of the Kalahari ethnographers and their critics? It is necessary, first, for both parties to attend to issues of regional variation. Some foragers certainly were drawn into farming and herding centuries ago, and some of these became part of regional economic systems, but, as we spell out below, both archaeology and ethnohistory contradict the view of a uniform grid of economic interdependency throughout the Kalahari. Second, we need to sensitize ourselves to the assumptions we make about the nature of "contact." For some "contact" appears to be unconsciously equated with "domination." The possibility of trade or exchange *without* some form of domination is excluded from the range of outcomes. When considering the Kalahari we need to ask further whether the conditions for domination existed there before, say, 1850. Were the societies with which the foragers came in contact after AD 500 sufficiently powerful to compel San servitude? Again the evidence shows that outcomes were variable and that in a number of areas the foraging life persisted. Third, and related, we need to examine our assumptions about the transformative power of the commodity – the view that when a society is linked to another by trade or tribute that linkage will necessarily transform social organization and create dependency. Are there other outcomes possible in which exchange relations do not undermine existing relations of production? Finally, we need to assess the evidence for San servitude; the contradictions in the literature suggest that appearances may be deceiving and in some cases San subordination may be more apparent than real. We wonder whether the current vogue for projecting unequal tributary and mercantile power relations into the past and for debunking the "myth of the primitive isolate" has not created a climate of scholarly opinion in which contact with domination is accepted as the normative or inevitable condition – thus making it impossible to examine actual cases treating the impact of trade as problematic rather than as given. It seems prudent not to exclude a priori the possibility of societal and cultural autonomy.

Case Studies

The Western Kweneng San

Many San peoples today live on the fringes of Bantu communities or white-owned farms;[3] the Western Kweneng San are one example. In contrast to the Dobe San, whose contact with non-San has traditionally been intermittent, these Southern San have lived amongst Bantu-speaking peoples for at least 200 years. The peoples of the Dutlwe area, in the southern Kalahari 250 km west of Gaborone (Figure 15.1), include three intermarrying San groups (Tshassi, Kwa, and Khute) and the Bantu-speaking Kgalagadi. The Kwena, a Tswana chiefdom, occupy the better-watered eastern edge of the desert.[4] The dominant Tswana-Kgalagadi cultural model posits a hierarchical social order in which the San and other servile peoples occupy the social and physical margins.

This "Tswanacentric" model does not, however, fit everywhere with the same precision, nor has it fit equally through time. The historical record reveals a variety of linkages between San and their neighbours, with a variety of consequences. San encapsulation within the orbit of Bantu-speaking peoples and loss of autonomy have been neither automatic nor, in most instances, complete. The San of Western Kweneng have not always worked for their Bantu neighbours, nor, in spite of the pronouncements of current Kalahari residents, is there anything "natural" about the state of affairs that exists today.

The pre- and protohistoric period

Oral traditions obtained from current residents indicate that relations between Kgalagadi and San were largely symbiotic in the early period.[5] All were nomadic and lived primarily by hunting and gathering, although the Kgalagadi may have practiced some horticulture. After 1820 new waves of Kgalagadi, refugees of the wars of the turbulent period known as the Difaqane, retreated into the desert with their goats, sheep, and dogs. The Kgalagadi credit the San with having taught them desert skills, and the San made use of Kgalagadi animals, especially hunting dogs. According to the Kgalagadi, their ancestors were able to migrate to western Kweneng with their goats and sheep in the early 19th century because the animals could obtain virtually all of their moisture from melons during the trek. These new immigrants chose a more sedentary life than their predecessors, and the pans on which they settled were also San water sources. In a Mokgalagadi's words, "The Basarwa [San] were already here. They just move around a lot. . . . They were not driven away."

The fur-trade period

In the period following 1840 the Kwena, who themselves had fared badly during the Difaqane (Thompson 1975:396), were attempting to reassert and consolidate their hold on the Kalahari periphery. Threatened from the east by the Boers, they were eager to accumulate Western trade goods, particularly guns (Livingstone 1857:39).[6] To do so they needed

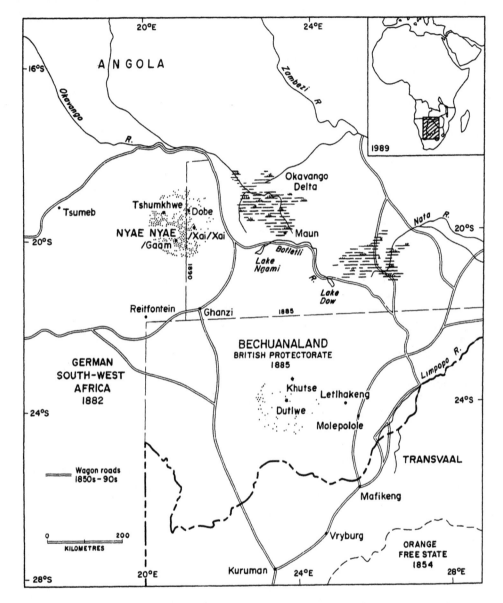

Figure 15.1 *The 19th-century Kalahari, with relevant contemporary boundaries and political divisions superimposed*

desert products such as furs, ostrich feathers, skins, and ivory, and vast quantities of these were obtained from the peoples of the area as tribute; Livingstone writes (p. 50) that while he was living among the Kwena he observed "between twenty and thirty thousand skins . . . made up into karosses; part of them were worn by the inhabitants and part sold to traders."

The San participated only indirectly in the tribute system; they and the Kgalagadi were the primary producers, hunting and preparing skins, but in most cases it was the Kgalagadi (and usually only the elite among them) who dealt with the Kwena.[7] The San hunted with dogs and occasionally with guns owned by others; they brought the hides and often some of the meat to the owners and kept a portion of the meat for themselves (see, e.g., Silberbauer and Kuper 1966, Hitchcock 1987, Schapera and van der Merwe 1945, Stow 1964 [1905]). Tobacco, grown and/or obtained by trade, was a central commodity in the system, exchanged for skins and labour. Contact between Kgalagadi and San was concentrated in the winter months, when the fur-bearing animals were most desirable and water most scarce. In this period there was little difference in the objective conditions of life of San and Kgalagadi. Their relations were less coercive than Kwena-Kgalagadi relations and resembled trade more than tribute.

Towards the end of the 19th century the Kwena's control over the periphery began to break down. The desert was difficult to police; Kwena rule was thin and maintained largely through periodic displays of force. The Kgalagadi as a result were able to begin to accumulate property, especially cattle (see Okihiro 1976; Schapera and van der Merwe 1945:5), thus laying the groundwork for an agro-pastoral base that did not develop among the Kweneng San. Inequalities between the San and some Kgalagadi also began to grow. The Kgalagadi attempted to replicate in their relations with the San the Tswana hierarchical model that subordinated them to the Kwena, but the material conditions for institutionalized servitude were absent.

In 1885, with the imposition of British colonial rule, the tribute system was officially disbanded; the Kgalagadi were allowed to trade their goods, and instead of tribute a tax, of which Kwena chiefs received 10%, was collected (although in practice the transition from tribute to tax was not automatic) (Schapera and van der Merwe 1945:6). The colonial state was intrigued by the San and voiced concern over their condition, but in fact the new government had little direct impact on their life.

A colonial officer travelling through western Kweneng in 1887 considered the San the Kgalagadi's "slaves pure and simple," but at the same time he reported, "They have no fixed residence, often living miles from water and living on the melons and roots, changing their abode, as these are scarce or plentiful" (Botswana National Archives 1887a:17). (If the San had truly been slaves they would not have been following the melons but would have been working for the Kgalagadi.) This apparent contradiction emerges repeatedly; the San are described as slaves and yet as "scoundrels, snakes, and rascals" who will not stay in one place and move about as they wish (Botswana National Archives 1887b; cf. MacKenzie 1871:128–32 for the Central district). Again, an 1899 report states that the Masarwa (San) "lives a nomadic life in a wild state and hunts for the masters" (HC. 24, quoted in Schapera and van der Merwe 1945:4), thus portraying them as simultaneously enserfed and nomadic foragers.[8]

In part this contradiction may reflect European observers' response to the contempt in which the San were held by the eastern tribes. The San's disregard for the pastoral values of preservation and accumulation, their nomadism, and their lack of a hereditary chiefly line went against the grain of Tswana society, inverted the natural order, and were, in certain respects, incomprehensible and frightening to the Bantu-speaking peoples and many Europeans. In speaking of the San some European observers romanticized them for their free-spiritedness and lack of material desires; others, heeding the Tswana standards of a proper life, more resonant with their own, looked upon them as candidates for civilizing. According to the latter and predominant view, the San were the victims in southern Africa, and their Bantu-speaking neighbours bore some responsibility for that state of affairs.[9] It is also possible that administrators were told exaggerated stories and lacked the breadth of experience that would have placed these in a more realistic light. Lack of experience might also have made it difficult for them to distinguish between the claims of Bantu overlords to their "serfs" and the degree of real servitude in the Kalahari. The evidence does seem to indicate that some San were subservient to some Bantu, but we argue that the institutionalization of San subordination came later.

Agro-pastoralism

The fur trade remained for some time the primary link between San and Kgalagadi. The Kgalagadi elite who owned cattle in the early 20th century relied upon their poorer relatives rather than San for herding labour. At the same time, the development of agro-pastoral production was beginning to undermine the San's foraging base. Permanent settlement, population increase, cattle herding, and agriculture combined to reduce the environment's hunting-and-gathering potential. The desertification noted by elderly residents and by ecologists alike can be traced not simply to overhunting but to human habitation (Campbell and Child 1971, Leistner 1967). Every bush or tree cleared to make way for cultivation, especially plowing, reduces the ground cover, disrupts root systems, facilitates erosion, and reduces the soil's ability to absorb and retain moisture. It was increasingly only in the bush, away from the better water sources, that the San could maintain their autonomy. The Central Kalahari has remained (by law) free of large-scale village and livestock development and served as a "hinterland" for the San, a place where their culture and mode of subsistence have persisted and where many Western Kweneng San claim roots, refuge, and restoration. Many of the elder San now living in western Kweneng were born in the bush, had a youth of mostly hunting and gathering, and only came to spend most of their time in the village later, in their own words because of "fear of lions and thirst." The integrity of the San's own flexible social organization and communal property arrangements permitted fluidity between village and bush. The existence of the hinterland, in spite of its diminished productivity and diminished appeal for some San, provided them with a hedge against complete subordination.

The organic link

By the 1940s, local agro-pastoralism was well established. With trading revenues and migrant labourers' wages, the Kgalagadi accumulated cattle and plows and imported new well-digging techniques that permitted expansion of the livestock sector. Cultivated water sources such as wells and boreholes came to be considered the private property of the group that dug them,[10] and eventually many of the better-watered pans (which probably had been dry-season homes of the San [Vierich 1977]) were associated with the Kgalagadi; now to obtain drinking water the San had to enter into unequal relations with the Kgalagadi. Plow agriculture and animal husbandry increased the workload at precisely the time when able-bodied young Kgalagadi men were leaving for contract work on the South African mines, and it was San labour that filled the gap (Solway 1987). By the 1950s the San had become the Kgalagadi's casual labour force. The Kgalagadi today frequently try to minimize the importance of San labour and like to think of themselves as humanitarian for "helping" them, but when pressed many will quietly admit, "We are lucky, we have Bushmen."

That the Kgalagadi's greater demand for labour occurred in concert with the growing precariousness of foraging in the area was not a result of conscious conspiracy, but neither was it a coincidence. The Kgalagadi's new productive base altered the environment; it changed their labour demands, transformed property relations over water sources, and increasingly distinguished the Kgalagadi from the San. In the 19th century differences in material conditions between the groups were small, but by the mid-20th century the hierarchical model in which the San occupy a marginal and servile position more closely matched reality than it had in the past. Hunting for the Kgalagadi had not undermined the San's foraging subsistence strategy; it is doubtful whether the Kgalagadi of the 19th century had the resources or power to compel San servitude, except in the very short term. The Kgalagadi of the 20th century, in contrast, had control of water, milk, grain, and purchased items such as tobacco, clothing, guns, and wagons, and these resources, in the face of diminishing returns from foraging, tied the San to them more thoroughly than in the past. New kinds of work that followed the rhythm of the agricultural and livestock cycle resulted in more intimate and regular association than that created by the hunting arrangements. With the expansion of Kgalagadi agriculture,

San women entered the workforce in greater numbers, which meant that San social reproduction increasingly took place in the Kgalagadi's domain. Today, a few San live permanently as domestic servants with Kgalagadi; the Kgalagadi claim to "take these San as our children," but they are children who never achieve adult status. There are a number of San homesteads on the periphery of the villages, their populations waxing and waning with the seasons. The spatial marginality neatly reflects the San's social marginality and positioning somewhere between village and bush.

Although the hinterland persists and some San forage full-time in it (Kent 1989, Silberbauer 1981), most Western Kweneng San work for the Kgalagadi at least during the agricultural season, arriving "after the flowers appear on the melon plants." Sixty years ago, coming to the village and working for the Kgalagadi was seen as a "break" from foraging in an increasingly unproductive environment. Now the village end of the cycle has taken precedence, and most San are resigned to the fact that they can make a living only by working for the Kgalagadi, begging, or accepting government aid. Foraging offers only an occasional supplement. Some San still return to the bush in the wet season. According to one woman, "We are happy to be away from the Kgalagadi. There are water roots and berries. If we come upon a tortoise or a dead animal we will eat and dance all night. We only come back because of thirst."

The Dobe San

The Dobe area, 700 km north of Dutlwe, was far from the turmoil of 19th-century colonial southern Africa.[11] The Dobe people were not affected by the Difaqane, though they had heard about it, and they were not subject to tribute. More important, the wave of black settlement did not reach them until 1925. Surrounded by a waterless belt 70–200 km in depth, the Dobe area is difficult of access even today; it would have been accessible to Iron Age peoples with livestock for only a few months in years of high rainfall, and even then only after an arduous journey. It would be risky to assume that contemporary patterns of contact (or lack of contact) were characteristic of all periods of prehistory. Fortunately, the data of archaeology can be brought to bear on this kind of question.

The pre- and protohistoric period

Despite the abundant evidence of Iron Age settlement elsewhere in northwestern Botswana dating from AD 500 or earlier and despite concerted efforts to find the same in the Dobe area, there is *no archaeological evidence of Iron Age occupation of the area until the 20th century* (Brooks 1989, Yellen and Brooks 1989). What does exist in Later Stone Age archaeological deposits, along with a classic stone tool kit, is a few fragments of pottery and a few iron implements, items best interpreted as evidence of intermittent trade with Iron Age settlements to the east and north.

!Kung oral traditions reinforce this view. Elders speak of their ancestors' maintaining long-term trade relations with "Goba" while maintaining their territorial organization and subsistence as hunter-gatherers in the Dobe area and to the west of it. Some have gone so far as to insist that the first visitors on a large scale to their area were whites rather than blacks. According to !Xamn!a, who was born at the end of the [19th] century, "The first outsiders to come to /Xai/Xai were /Ton [European] hunters. . . . They used to shoot guns with bullets one and one-half inches thick. But this was before I was born. My wife's father, Toma!gain, worked for the /Tons." When asked which of the Tswana ruling clans had first arrived in the Dobe area in the last century, a !Goshe elder emphatically replied, "None! The /Tons [Europeans] were first." And when asked if his "fathers" knew of blacks of any origin in the area, he replied, "No, we only knew ourselves."

The picture that emerges from the archaeological, ethnohistorical, and oral-historical evidence can be sketched as follows: The Dobe area has been occupied by hunting-and-gathering peoples for at least several thousand years. The evidence of unbroken LSA deposits 100 cm or more in depth, with ostrich eggshells and indigenous fauna from bottom to top, with a scattering of pottery and iron, and with European goods in surface levels supports a picture of relative continuity.[12] At some point between AD 500 and 1500, the interior !Kung established trade relations with "Goba" to the east and northeast and carried on trade with them in which desert products – furs, honey, and ivory – were exchanged for iron, tobacco, ceramics, and possibly agricultural products. It is unclear whether the Goba made reciprocal visits to the Dobe area or even whether the ceramics that are found are of outside origin.[13]

Thus, on the eve of the European colonial incursions, the !Kung were evidently occupying the interior on their own as hunter-gatherers and producing a small surplus of furs and other desert products for barter with agriculturalists on the western margins of the Okavango swamps. The few accounts from the precolonial era that do refer to the !Kung of the interior – called KauKau or MaKowkow – treat them with respect as a fierce and independent people (a reputation that has persisted to the present among neighbouring blacks). Chapman (1971 [1868], vol. 1:165), travelling through the Ghanzi area in 1855, had this to say:[14]

The inhabitants of these parts are a much finer race of Bushmen than we had generally met with. Freedom, and the enjoyment of their own game for food and the skins for clothing, are the main causes. They acknowledge no chief and are in the habit of defending themselves against oppressors and intruders, either from Lake Ngami or the Namaqua region; in former times they have often combined to resist marauding parties sent out by the Batuana and other tribes. Their minds are free from apprehension of human plunderers, and the life they lead is a comparatively fearless one. The population is numerous, and they are more attached to each other than in other parts.

The fur-trade period

Two kinds of economic networks were involved in the San articulation with the "world system": indirect involvement through black intermediaries – the Goba and later the Tswana – and direct contact with European

hunters and traders. The indirect form resembled the precolonial African trade that the San had carried on for centuries and therefore involved no basic restructuring of relations of production. The direct European trade, while intense and disruptive, did not last very long. It was not until the 1920s and 1930s, with the arrival of black settlers in the Dobe area, that basic production relations began to be modified and incorporative processes set in motion.

Several accounts exist of the lively trade that went on in the "Gaamveld" between the "Bushmen" and Afrikaner, German, and English hunter-traders in the period 1870–90 (Lee 1979:78; Solway and Lee 1981). The first European known to have visited the Dobe-Nyae/Nyae area was Hendrik van Zyl, whom Ramadjagote Harry, a Tswana born in 1903, describes as "the hunter who was responsible for killing all the elephants and rhinos in the west." Tabler (1973:114) confirms that in 1877 alone van Zyl's party killed 400 elephants in the Gaamveld and took out 8,000 lb. of ivory. !Kung recall the period with a great deal of affection as a time of intense social activity and economic prosperity. They were provided with guns and ate enormous quantities of meat. One could find no trace of regret in these accounts for the carnage and diminution of wildlife; elephants, regarded as pests by the !Kung, are rarely hunted today. The legacy of this brief but intense irruption for the Dobe-area people can be briefly set out. One small family of !Kung, fully integrated into the Dobe community, is acknowledged to be descended from a member of van Zyl's party and a local !Kung woman. Few other impacts are evident. Even though firearms were widely distributed to African populations (Marks and Atmore 1971) and though many 19th-century-vintage weapons remained in African hands into the 1960s, only a single !Kung man, a tribal constable who had purchased his weapon with wages, possessed a gun in 1963.

A second instance of European presence, also short-lived, was the cattle drives sent by a group of Afrikaner trekkers from Angola to the Transvaal via Lewisfontein (!Kangwa), a large perennial spring in the centre of the Dobe area. The "Dorsland" Trekkers reached

Angola only in 1880, and according to Clarence-Smith (1979:59–60) the trek route had fallen into disuse by 1900 (see also Gordon 1984:202).

Since most European goods – iron pots, beads, etc. – continued to be obtained through Bantu intermediaries, one would be hard put to argue that the sporadic European presence from 1870 to 1900 had transformed !Kung society. On the other hand, it is likely that the European penetration of the !Kung interior was the catalyst for incursions by Tswana and others.

!Kung call the period after the departure of the Europeans and before the arrival of permanent black settlers *koloi* (wagon), a reference to the ox-carts used by the Tswana from the 1880s to about 1925. A number of Tswana had been employed on the European hunting parties as hunters, trackers, and gun bearers. After 1880 Tswana hunter-traders with wagons began making their own trips to the Dobe area; this was part of the general expansion of the Tawana state after 1874 (Tlou 1985:49). In the !Kung oral traditions it is the !Kung and not the Tswana who are the initiators of this trade. As !Xamn!a tells it,

When the Europeans left, the Zhu/twasi were all alone. My ≠*tum* [father-in-law] said, "Let's go to the Tswana, bring their cattle here and drink their milk." So then my ≠*tum* organized the younger men and went east to collect the cattle. . . . Then they chopped a brush-fence kraal under the camel thorn trees and kraaled them there. The Tswana came up to visit and hunt, then they went back leaving the San drinking the milk. Then my ≠*tum* got *shoro* [tobacco] from the Tswana and smoked it. When the *shoro* was all finished the young men collected all the steenbok skins and went east to bring back more *shoro*. The boys shouldered the tobacco and brought it back. Later they drove the cattle out to Hxore Pan where they built a kraal and ate the *tsin* beans of Hxore while the cattle drank the water. So they lived, eating *tsin*, hunting steenbok and duiker, and drinking milk. When Hxore water was dry, they loaded the pack oxen with sacks of *tsin* [for the !Kung to eat] and drove them back to /Xai/Xai. At the end of the season the cattle boys loaded the pack oxen with bales

and bales of eland biltong and went east with it to collect the balls of *shoro* and sometimes bags of corn. These they would deliver to my ≠*tum*.

This account provides a good description of two forms of economic linkage: the barter system, in which desert products are exchanged for agricultural and manufactured products, and the *mafisa* system, whereby well-to-do Tswana farm out cattle to others – fellow tribesmen or members of subordinate groups. The first form of linkage does not lead to incorporation and loss of autonomy, especially when the level of trade is modest and the element of coercion is absent. *Mafisa*, by contrast, does alter the character of production at the levels of both forces and relations. Animal husbandry places foragers in a different relation to land and to predators and necessitates a shift in the patterns of labour deployment. Energy is drawn away from hunting and reallocated to herding, and in return the producers are rewarded with a more secure food source, at least in the short run. At the level of production relations, *mafisa* is a form of loan-cattle–labour exchange set in the context of a patron-client relationship.

Briefly, the *mafisa* system in northwestern Ngamiland operated as follows (see also Tlou 1985:52): The San client maintained the herd on behalf of the Tswana patron, who retained ownership of the beasts. In return San could consume all the milk the herd produced and the meat of any animal that had died of natural causes, including predation. A tally was kept of beasts lost, and all animals had to be accounted for when the patron made a periodic visit. If he was satisfied with the performance of the *mafisa* holder he might pay him a calf, but this was not obligatory. If he was not satisfied he could withdraw his animals and seek another client. Similarly, the client was free to withdraw his services – with notice – and either leave *mafisa* entirely or seek another patron and a new herd of cattle.

On the face of it, *mafisa* appears to resemble a system of agrarian dependency: ownership of the means of production, in this case cattle, is in the hands of the overlord, who at his whim can withdraw the herd and thus deprive the client of his livelihood. Clients therefore existed, it would seem, in a highly vulnerable state of dependency. Only a minority of Dobe-area people became involved in *mafisa*, however, and families with cattle retained links with families fully immersed in hunting and gathering, which remained viable as an alternative economic strategy throughout the *koloi* period and beyond. Had *mafisa* been the only means of subsistence for the people of the Dobe area, then the withdrawal of the cattle would have caused a crisis in subsistence and the threat of it would have been sufficient to produce a condition of virtual serfdom. But the *mafisa* families were not peasants; they were islands of pastoralism in a sea of hunting and gathering, with benefits flowing in both directions. When cattle were withdrawn, as they often were, the bush was there to fall back on, and that same bush beckoned as an alternative if the responsibilities of keeping cattle grew too onerous.

Thus we have to consider seriously the !Kung's view of *mafisa* as something that operated in their favour. Far from having the system forced upon them or being forced into it by circumstance, !Kung who entered into it did so voluntarily, for the opportunity it provided to supplement a foraging diet with milk and occasional beef. Some of the men who went into *mafisa* did become "big men" of a sort, acting as brokers in transactions between San and black. But a large majority of !Kung remained hunter-gatherers and never relinquished their claims to foraging *n!ores,* the collectively owned hunting lands that were the foundations of their communal mode of production (see Lee 1979:333–69; 1981). In fact, many of the ranges where cattle were grazed were superimposed on these *n!ores,* and the herds were managed by members of the groups that held them. Thus the niche that had sustained the communal foraging mode of production was modified and expanded to encompass *mafisa* cattle husbandry without destroying the preexisting adaptation.[15]

Agro-pastoralism

Permanent settlement by non-San came late to the Dobe area. Starting in the mid-1920s, Herero pastoralists moved into the area at cattle posts both east and west of the Namibian border.[16] The Herero began to deepen the waterholes and dig new ones to accommodate increased numbers of cattle. At first only a handful – about 50 – came, but their herds grew rapidly and created a growing need for labour. After 1954, when an influx of Herero immigrants increased the area's non-San population fivefold, the demand for !Kung labour rose still further. Dobe-area Herero remained oriented to subsistence pastoralism rather than moving into production for market; the market was distant and the price for cattle low. Except for a few cattle sold to pay for special purchases, such as guns, horses, or sewing machines, the Herero preferred to let their herds expand and to draw additional !Kung labour as necessary into the work of managing them. By the late 1950s the job of herdboy had become normative for Dobe-area !Kung men between the ages of 15 and 25.[17] In 1963 there were about 460 !Kung in the Dobe area, 340 Herero and other non-San, and about 2,000 head of cattle. About half of the !Kung young men of the age-category called ≠doiesi (adolescents) were working on the cattle at any one time. Eventually most men returned to their camps to marry and raise families, but some married men stayed on in a semi-permanent arrangement with Herero families.

By the 1960s an alternative economy had begun to crystallize, and the Dobe !Kung were found distributed between two kinds of living groups. About 70% lived in camps – bandlike multifamily units whose members engaged in a mixed economy of foraging, *mafisa* herding, and some horticulture. The rest lived in client groups consisting of retainers and their families attached to black cattle posts. Despite the variety of economic strategies that supported them, camps continued to exhibit the characteristic patterns of collective ownership of resources and food sharing that have been documented for hunter-gatherers around the world (Lee 1979, Leacock and Lee 1982). The client groups offered an instructive contrast, being in effect appendages of the domestic economy of their Herero masters. The men worked alongside their Herero counterparts herding the cattle, while the !Kung women shared in the domestic tasks with the Herero women. Some client groups consisted of a !Kung woman married to a Herero man and her relatives, and a few involved a !Kung man, his (!Kung) wife, and their children and relatives (Lee 1979:54–61). The camp-living !Kung also maintained ties to the cattle posts; Dobe residents frequently went to Mahopa to ask for milk, meat, or other items. The cattle-post !Kung acted as conduits for the transmission of Herero goods to the population at large.

The stage was now set for the final act in the transformation of the Dobe-area !Kung from a relatively autonomous people with long-standing but non-decisive linkages to the larger regional pastoral, tributary, and mercantile economy to a people bound to the region and the world by ties of dependency. Having survived long-distance trade, contacts with European hunters, Tswana overlordship, *mafisa* herding, direct employment on cattle posts, even forced resettlement in Namibia, the !Kung became dependent largely as a consequence of the inability of their land to support a foraging mode of production. The bush had always been the backdrop to economic change, giving the !Kung security and a degree of freedom not available to the great majority of the agrarian societies of southern Africa. Tlou (1985:54) speaks of the Tawana's difficulties in exacting tribute or service from the "BaSarwa" (San) and concludes, "The sandbelt BaSarwa rarely became serfs because they could easily escape into the Kgalagadi Desert." By 1970, however, four decades of intensive and expanding pastoralism had begun to take their toll on the capacity of the environment to support hunting and gathering. Cattle grazing and the pounding of hooves had destroyed the grass cover over many square kilometers and reduced the available niches for dozens of species of edible roots and rhizomes. Goat browsing had destroyed thousands of berry bushes and other edible plants. The reduction or removal of these food sources placed added pressure on the remaining human food sources; for example, mongongo nut harvests noticeably diminished in the 1980s. The drilling of a dozen boreholes in Bushmanland, Namibia, just to the west of Dobe, in the early 1980s aggravated these trends by lowering the water table. Hunting remained viable but became subject to much stricter controls by the Game Department, and many men, fearing arrest, stopped hunting.[18] The effect of these changes was seriously to undermine the foraging option and to force the Dobe-area !Kung into dependency on the cattle posts and particularly the state. The latter responded with large-scale distribution of food relief between 1980 and 1987, which further deepened dependency.

Discussion

What common and contrasting patterns of change can be discerned by a comparative analysis of the two case studies?

In the earliest period for which we have information, the pre- and protohistoric (ca. 1820), the Western Kweneng San were already sharing their land with Bantu-speaking Kgalagadi, who mediated their contact with the wider world. The Dobe San, by contrast, were in unmediated though distant and intermittent contact with riverine peoples to their east and north. A second point of difference concerns the nature of social formations on the San peripheries after 1830. The Kwena in the south became more mobile and expansive, ranging widely in search of trade and tribute, while the neighbours of the northern !Kung were sedentary, river-oriented peoples who did not expand into the arid interior.

The fur-trade period (mid-19th century) was marked by social, political, and economic turbulence, yet by the time its ripple effects reached the interior of the Kalahari the impact was often attenuated.[19] If in Parsons's (1977:119) terms the 19th-century Tswana economies were becoming the "periphery of the periphery" of European capitalism, then surely the Kalahari must have been the "deep periphery." Driven by trade and external threat, strong chiefdoms arose in the south. The Kwena's need for guns to defend themselves against the Boers was a powerful impetus for the articulation of tributary and mercantile systems. Guns could only be obtained in exchange for desert products. The Kwena subjugated the Kgalagadi, who in turn enlisted the San to aid in primary production. While unequal exchange characterized British-Kwena and Kwena-Kgalagadi relationships, the Kgalagadi-San relationship was symbiotic if not entirely equal. In contrast, Dobe was part of a much more tenuous and extended trade network. The Ngwato occupied the pivotal position between mercantile and tributary networks. Their junior partners were the Tawana, nominal overlords of Ngamiland, who in turn relied on Yei and Mbukushu ("Goba") intermediaries to accumulate desert products from the San, including the distant !Kung. The Tawana's power was contested by other chiefs, and they were never able to consolidate their hold on the hinterland as effectively as the Kwena (Parsons 1977; Livingstone 1857; Tlou 1985:66–7). As a consequence there was less pressure on the !Kung to enter the system, and when they did they were able to retain more control over the terms of trade. In neither instance, however, did the fur trade have much impact on the internal organization of San societies. San exchanged their products after the completion of the productive process. Linkage was predominantly through the sphere of exchange, not production, and intervention in San society remained limited (see Bonner 1983 and Harries 1982 on similar processes elsewhere).

The expansion of herding and farming to the remoter Kalahari did not signal the end of the fur trade, but the incorporation of cattle into the desert economy shifted the priorities in the deployment of land and labour. Western Kweneng San and Dobe San entered the cattle economy under different circumstances and with different statuses. In Dutlwe, Kgalagadi acquired cattle and rendered them as *mafisa* to their poorer relatives; eventually San became their herdboys. Because cattle were kept in the village, not at distant cattle posts, San herders were in regular interaction with their employers and had their subordinate status frequently reinforced. In Dobe it was the San themselves who entered into *mafisa*, a privilege they held exclusively until the 1920s. The Tawana were absentee cattle owners; the Dobe San bore responsibility for the productive enterprise, made routine decisions, and determined their daily activities. This arrangement was much more compatible with foraging than the

Western Kweneng San's situation. In neither case did even a majority of the San enter into cattle service. Many relatively independent groups remained on the peripheries of villages and cattle posts, subsisting on wild foods and continuing to provide furs for the trade. Reciprocity between foraging and non-foraging San allowed each group to enjoy the fruits of the other's labour. In lean years the foraging San would provide a safety net and alternative subsistence for their "employed" relatives, and even in good years San contact with pastoralists was largely limited to certain seasons. At all times the hinterland provided a cultural point of reference and locus of reproduction. Thus in both cases the complete incorporation, as dependents, of the San into the agropastoral system was delayed as long as the bush held the possibility of an alternative livelihood.[20] An important source of the continued viability of the San's foraging option was the strength of the egalitarian and reciprocal communal relations of reproduction that characterized life in the bush. As even the revisionists (e.g., Wilmsen 1989:66) acknowledge, this way of life, while far from ideal, provides an extraordinarily rich and meaningful existence for those who practice it. Communally based societies offer their members a sense of social security, entitlement, and empowerment (Lee 1988, 1990; Rosenberg 1990). Aspects of this quality of life persist in both Dutlwe and Dobe even today.[21]

Several factors combined to undermine the viability of the dual subsistence economy of the Dutlwe and Dobe San. Expansion of the numbers of cattle through natural increase, purchase with wages from other areas, and migration of cattle keepers (as in Dobe after 1954), along with expanding opportunities for migrant wage labour, especially in the 1960s, created a rapidly increasing need for San labour. It is fair to say that without the availability of a reservoir of San labour to replace absentee blacks the Kgalagadi and Herero could not have enjoyed the prosperity they experienced in the 1960s and 1970s. (San men also went to the mines but in much smaller numbers; in 1969 7% of Dobe San men and in 1978 25% of Dutlwe San men had done so.) At the same time, plow agriculture was expanding, especially in the south, increasing the demand for both male and female labour.

The retreat from foraging by the San began as the agro-pastoral complex drew larger and larger numbers of labourers, male and female, into its employ. In the last analysis, however, a critical factor in moving the San into a position of dependency has been environmental degradation, which has, like an unintended scorched-earth policy, deprived them of an alternative means of livelihood. In the south, dependency increased throughout the [20th] century, and many San entered into a relationship of perpetual minor status. Cultivated food and water have a powerful attraction for people foraging in a degraded environment, and it was the possession of cultivated food and water sources that distinguished the haves from the have-nots. In the north, where the local blacks have a healthy respect for the San's determination to protect their water claims, in the last century by force of arms and today through the courts, the organic link came later. For the Dobe San comparable levels of dependence and integration were approached only in the 1970s and 1980s, and it was the government, not neighbouring blacks, that provided the material incentive in the form of wells, schools, grain, and other forms of aid.

Foragers Genuine and Spurious: The Limitations of World Systems

What kinds of socioeconomic arrangements characterized the Kalahari San in the 19th and 20th centuries, and what kinds of explanatory frameworks best account for them? These questions must be approached at two levels: the level of fact, in which the archaeological, ethnohistoric, and ethnographic evidence is set out and interrogated, and the level of discourse, in which the explanatory frameworks themselves become the focus of interrogation.

The archaeological record shows a diversity of economic adaptations in the 19th century and earlier. The interaction of Stone Age with Iron Age cultures resulted in dramatic economic shifts in some areas, while in other areas the effects were more subtle. Kalahari trade was widespread, and in many instances when tributary formations emerged in the 19th century ties of domination/subordination were superimposed on preexisting linkages. But not all San groups experienced this pattern of early linkage and later subordination. Interrelationships were strongest on the river systems and the margins of the desert and weaker as one moved into the interior. Thus there were large areas of semi-arid southern Africa that lay outside tributary orbits, where trade was equal, non-coercive, and intermittent and where independent – but not isolated – social formations persisted into the 20th century.

In attempting to explain this situation, it is important, first, to recognize that trade and exchange cannot simply be equated with domination and loss of autonomy. Exchange is a fundamental part of human life and appears in all cultural settings (Mauss 1925, Lévi-Strauss 1949). Hunter-gatherer peoples have participated in exchange with farming and market societies for hundreds of years (in India, Southeast Asia, and East Africa) while maintaining a foraging mode of production (Leacock and Lee 1982). Even with "hunters in a world of hunters," exchange was part of social life (see, e.g., Thomson 1949, Wilmsen 1974, Earle and Ericson 1977, Ericson 1977, Torrence 1986). The evidence for long-established trade relations between foragers and others has been glossed by some as evidence for the fragility of the foraging mode of production. But if it was so fragile, why did it persist?

Throughout these debates about the status of Kalahari and other foragers there has been a lack of attention to the meanings of key terms. Just what is meant by "autonomy," "dependency," "independence," "integration," and "servitude" is rarely made clear. Without consistent, agreed-upon definitions it will be difficult or impossible to resolve the issues with which we are concerned. "Autonomy," for example, has a wide range of uses. Given its currency, it is remarkable how unreflexive its anthropological uses have been. We will confine our discussion to economic autonomy, since much of the debate in hunter-gatherer studies seems to revolve around it.

One of the rhetorical devices of the revisionist view of hunter-gatherers is to equate autonomy with isolation – a definition so stringent that no society can possibly satisfy it. But autonomy is not isolation and no social formation is hermetically sealed; we take it as given that all societies are involved in economic exchanges and political relations with their neighbours.

As an economic concept, autonomy refers to economic self-sufficiency,[22] and self-sufficiency in turn hinges not on the *existence* of trade – since all societies trade – but on whether that trade is indispensable for the society's survival. To demonstrate autonomy one must demonstrate self-reproduction. Dependency therefore may be defined as the inability of a society to reproduce itself without the intervention of another.[23]

Politically, two kinds of autonomy may be provisionally defined: imposed and asserted.[24] In the former, the economic autonomy of a subject group may serve the interests of the dominant group. Subordinates are encouraged to pursue their habitual activities at their own pace while providing goods or services – often on equitable terms – to the dominant group. In the latter, the autonomous group asserts its claims through its own strengths and political will. In practice these two forms may be difficult to distinguish, and which form is considered to be present will depend heavily on subjective judgements both by the peoples involved and by observers.[25] Thus the Mbuti pygmies observed by Turnbull (1962) appear to be entirely subservient to their black neighbours while they are in the villages but quite autonomous in the forest.

Autonomy is best regarded not as a thing or a property of social systems but as a relationship – between social groups and between a group and its means of production. At any given moment a society may exhibit elements of both autonomy and dependency, and it should be possible to assess the degree of each through empirical investigation.

The camp-dwelling people of the Dobe area were economically self-sufficient during the 1960s. They owned the bulk of their means of production and paid no rent, tribute, or taxes in money or kind. They hunted and gathered for the large majority of their subsistence requirements and for the rest tended *mafisa* cattle or worked as herdboys for their Herero neighbours. The latter tasks provided income that was a welcome supplement but not essential to survival. How can we demonstrate its non-essentiality? First, San *mafisa* holders and herdboys were observed to leave "service" without visible detriment to their well-being. In fact, it was common for young men to work on cattle for a few years and then return to the bush at marriage (Lee 1979:58, 406–8). More compelling, in the drought of 1964 Herero crops failed and cows were dry yet the San persevered without evident difficulty. In fact, the Herero women were observed gathering wild foods alongside their San neighbours (Lee 1979:255). Since the San carried on through this period without visible hardship (Lee 1979:437–41) despite the withdrawal of Herero resources, it is clear that the latter were not essential to their reproduction.

These lines of evidence argue for the economic autonomy of some Dobe !Kung in the 1960s. Obviously a great deal more could be said on the question of autonomy, especially from the cultural and political points of view. Even the simplest historical judgements will involve a series of mediating judgements concerning economy, polity, voluntarism and coercion. Automatically classifying 2d-millennium San societies as dependent, incorporated, or "peasant-like" seems no more legitimate than classifying them as "primitive isolates."

Turning to "servitude," we are confronted with a literature replete with reports of San "dependency," "serfdom," "slavery," "vassalage," and the like.[26] In contrast to the early sources cited above (and see Wilson 1975:63), which tended to portray all San as dominated, recent ones such as Silberbauer and Kuper (1966), Tlou (1977), Russell and Russell (1979), Hitchcock (1987), and Motzafi (1986) employ these terms more critically, but even here usage tends to be imprecise. Silberbauer and Kuper (1966), for example, use the term "serfdom" but note its inapplicability – the San being bound neither to the soil nor to a particular master. Guenther (1986:450) reinforces the ambiguity when he speaks of a "benignly paternalistic form of serfdom" that departs from the European pattern. Tlou (1977), Wilson (1975), and Biesele et al. (1989) use the term "clientship" to refer to a loose association between peoples with unequal access to resources that they distinguish from the classic patron-client relationship. Russell and Russell (1979:87) further qualify the term "clientship" by contrasting the rights and obligations of "employed" San with those of "client" San. The latter are said to maintain a "foot in both worlds," one in the bush and one on the farm. Thus in their terms clientship is a partial relationship from which San can disengage.

Difficulties on several levels are encountered when we try to pin down the forms and content of San servitude and dependence. First, it is obvious that terms such as serfdom and chattel slavery, developed in a specific European context, are not easily grafted onto Kalahari social relations. More specifically, the language that is used in the Kalahari itself appears to overstate the degree of dependence. Both Vierich (1982) and Solway were struck by the exaggerated descriptions of servitude by San and black alike. The cultural vocabulary of superior/subordinate relations further illustrates the difficulty of translating words that lack cognates in the language of the observer. Silberbauer and Kuper, for example, show that the Sekgalagadi term *munyi*, used for "master" in San-black relations, is also used for the senior in asymmetrical kin relations, i.e., "elder brother." It denotes authority but falls short of our concept of mastership or ownership. Similarly, they note that the Tswana "jural model" of *bolata* (hereditary servitude) signifies something stricter than actually exists. This misunderstanding, they assert, may be the reason social commentators from 19th-century missionaries to 20th-century anthropologists have assumed that *bolata* was worse in the past and only recently has become more humane. They argue that "the practice of serfdom in Bechuanaland is much more humane than the indigenous jural model would lead one to expect: in the past some observers may have been led into assuming that the jural model represented the past, while the easy-going actuality was equated with the enlightened present" (p. 172).

At the level of concrete social relations, there is a puzzling incongruity between the exaggerated degree of inequality described by Kalahari residents and the relative ease (and frequency) with which the San "serfs" disappear into the desert for periods of time, leaving their "masters" high and dry. Vierich (1982:282) has argued that "interdependence" more accurately describes the relationship between San and non-San and that San simply "play the beggar" to get handouts. While this may be overstating the case, clearly there is a disjunction between model and practice. In no instance in which hereditary serfdom has been asserted by Kgalagadi in theory has it been observed in practice. The Dutlwe-area San may be dependent and have to work for someone at some time, but they retain some choice of when to work and for whom. An observer will find some San in relations of dependency and others not, but closer examination will reveal that the same individuals will move into clientship, out to the bush, and back again to clientship. Wealthy blacks will have full-time San labourers living in their compounds while their neighbours rarely or never retain San clients.[27] The full-time labourers living with blacks will be the most conspicuous to casual observers, and this may account for the prevalence of this kind of report in both the early and the more recent literature, but such reports fail to do justice to the complexity and fluidity of the situation. We certainly do not want to minimize the degree of San dependence and subjection to discrimination, but we would suggest that this is best seen as a product of underdevelopment and not a primordial condition.

Hunter-Gatherer and Agrarian Discourse: Making the Transition

We have traced in some detail the historical pathways followed by the Dutlwe and Dobe San as they changed from autonomous foragers to clients and labourers increasingly subject to and dependent upon local, national, and world economies. In order to understand these processes it is necessary to make a second transition, from discourse about hunter-gatherers to discourse about agrarian societies and the emerging world system.

In agrarian discourse structures of domination are taken as given; it is the *forms* of domination and the modes of exploitation and surplus extraction that are problematic (Amin 1972, Hindess and Hirst 1975, Shanin 1972). In the literature on the agrarian societies of the Third World, stratification, class and class struggle, patriarchy, accumulation, and immiseration constitute the basic descriptive and analytical vocabulary. In hunter-gatherer discourse it is not the forms of domination that are at issue but *whether domination is present*. This question is often side-stepped or ignored.

We are not alone in our concern about the tendency for the discourse of domination to be imposed on precapitalist societies. Beinart (1985:97), for example, dealing with the Eastern Cape – an area under far greater pressure than the Kalahari – cautions against granting omnipotence to capitalism or the state or assuming that the migrant-labour system automatically destroys the integrity of rural societies:

Even in so coercive an environment as South Africa, the patterns of domination were constrained – in part by fear of the consequences of other routes and in part by the defensive responses of the dominated. Certainly, capital and the state . . . had only limited power to shape social relationships in those areas which were left under African occupation . . . the fact that a migrant works for a wage, even for a number of years, does not necessarily determine the totality of his, much less his family's, class position and consciousness. The importance of defensive struggles in the rural areas, amongst communities which included seasoned migrants, has generally been underestimated.

Silberbauer (1989:206–7) challenges the view that hunter-gatherer contacts with other societies necessarily preclude autonomy:

[The] concept of coexisting states, tribes, and hunter-gatherer bands can be found accurately documented in any authoritative history of the appropriate part of Africa. It does not require that any of the coexisting societies be in a state of compulsory, day-to-day mutualism with all others. Interaction can occur at sufficiently low intensity and be of such a quality as to allow hunters and gatherers (for instance) to retain cultural, social, and political, and economic autonomy (i.e., in the philosophical sense, not in that of isolated, complete independence). At least in southern Africa and Australia that state of affairs persisted only when the hunter-gatherers were able to retain control of enough resources of sufficient variety to be largely . . . self-sustaining.

Perhaps the most serious consequence of imposing agrarian discourse on hunter-gatherers is that it robs the latter of their history. What is at issue here is an intellectual neo-colonialism that seeks to recreate their history in the image of our own. This revisionism trivializes these people by making their history entirely a reactive one. Even at its best revisionism grants historical animation and dignity to the San only by recasting their history as the history of oppression. But is their oppression by us the only thing, or even the main thing, that we want to know about foraging peoples? The majority of the world's foragers are, for whatever reason, people who have resisted the temptation (or threat) to become like us: to live settled lives at high densities and to accept the structural inequalities that characterize most of the world. Many former foragers – and that includes most of us – now live in stratified, entrepreneurial, bureaucratic society, but not all have followed this route, and the presence or absence of inequality and domination can be investigated empirically.

Ultimately, in understanding the histories of Third World societies or of our own, we will have to rely on the histories of specific instances and not allow preconceptions to sway us. This caveat applies equally to those who would place the hunter-gatherers in splendid isolation and those who would generalize the power relations of contemporary capitalism to most of the world's people through most of their historical experience.

NOTES

1. Lee (1965) had already noted the diversity of non-foraging adaptations among the contemporary San.
2. Schrire's model in turn is drawn from Elphick's (1977) studies of the 17th-century Cape San, who were observed to move into herding as opportunities arose and back to foraging when the livestock was lost or stolen.
3. For some the fringes are more social than physical, and San live, as servants, in Tswana, Kgalagadi, or Herero households. At the same time, many San live literally on the outskirts of Bantu communities or, in the case of the Ghanzi district, of white-owned farms and oscillate between client-like relations with their Bantu employers, hunting and gathering, and stock raising and agriculture. Such arrangements are described for much of Botswana (see, e.g., Silberbauer and Kuper 1966, Guenther 1986, Solway 1987, Vierich 1982, Hitchcock 1987, Kent 1989, Biesele et al. 1989). In the densely settled eastern regions of Botswana, San tend to be tightly linked to Tswana communities and have little opportunity to hunt and gather or to claim a "hinterland" area to which to retreat (Motzafi 1986). In the southern and central Kalahari, where settlement is relatively sparse, San generally maintain more options and greater cultural integrity and economic diversity.
4. The southern Kalahari, drier than the north, has no year-round standing water, but the pans that dot the desert have high water tables and hold water, often salty, for varying periods of time after the rains.
5. Ethnohistorical data on the western Kweneng for the 19th century are limited. Maps in Livingstone (1857), MacKenzie (1971 [1871]), and Chapman (1971 [1868]) exclude the area, and Leistner (1967:30) notes that the mid-19th-century explorers avoided the "inhospitable southern wastes." Oral traditions collected in the field by Solway in 1977–

9 and 1986 (Solway 1987) and by Okihiro (1976) contain few specific data on transactions between the ethnic groups in the 19th century. We know of no archaeological work in the region.
6. In 1852 the Boers attacked the Kwena capital and killed 60 Africans. Livingstone (1857:121), whose home was destroyed in this raid, notes that African refugees from the Boers came to Kwena afterward, buttressing their power. In terms of trade, the Kwena capital remained the center and launch point to the north until the 1860s (Parsons 1977:119).
7. Like the San of the Central district described by Hitchcock (1987:234), the Dutlwe-area San may well have engaged directly in trade with Europeans, but there is little evidence to support this view. Few traders ventured into western Kweneng.
8. Russell's (1976) analysis of Ghanzi San subordination contains similar contradictions. It is reported that "in the Bushman view [the Boers' arrival] presented an alternative to Tswana overlordship" (p. 189), yet a 1910 Boer petition is quoted as requesting that "the Bushmen be placed in a location . . . for being in such a wild state they are very little use as servants." Motzafi (1986) notes that in the Tswana world view the San's "wild" qualities emerge as much from their lack of social standing as from their association with the bush. Thus, for the Tswana, "wildness" and servility are not necessarily incompatible. It is doubtful that this cultural understanding can be attributed to the European view.
9. There was a strong ideological component to this; by showing how Africans could mistreat other Africans the Europeans could feel less culpable about their own treatment of the Africans.
10. Peters (1983, 1984) presents a structurally similar case in which common property (pasture) surrounding private property (borehole) becomes identified with the private and treated as such. Again, for the Ghanzi area it is reported

that "Boer skill at digging wells gave them an economic advantage over Bushmen for the first time. The further decline of the water table necessitated the more complex technology and capitalization of borehole and pump, and Bushman dependence accelerated" (Russell 1976: 190).

11. Although the !Kung San of the Dobe-Nyae/Nyae area are arguably the most thoroughly documented hunting-and-gathering society in this century, they are markedly underrepresented in the historical literature. Tabler's (1973) definitive compendium contains only 10 references (out of 334) to Europeans who entered the area prior to 1900. Thus the classic accounts of Baines (1973 [1864]), Chapman (1971 [1868]), Galton (1889), Anderson (1856), and Livingstone (1857) refer only elliptically to the peoples of the central !Kung interior. The earliest firsthand account, that of Passarge, dates from 1907, while Wilhelm's observations from the period 1914–19 were not published until 1954.

In his ethnohistorical examination of !Kung exchange, Gordon (1984) uncritically conflates accounts from all over northern Namibia, distorting the picture of 19th-century !Kung San by portraying a number of highly acculturated and distant San peoples as if they were San of the central !Kung interior; less than 20% of his material refers to the !Kung of the Dobe-Nyae/Nyae area. For example, he refers to a group of San controlling a rich copper mine near Tsumeb and marketing 50–60 tons of ore each year as if they were !Kung (pp. 212–13), but the San in question are the Nama-speaking Heikum and Tsumeb is located 400 km west of Dobe.

Sources of data for this case study consist of extensive interviews with San, Tswana, and Herero informants between 40 and 80 years of age, mainly during three years of fieldwork between 1963 and 1969. A number of the older informants had been alive at the end of the

[19th] century. All informants drew upon older oral histories and oral traditions. Individual accounts were checked for consistency against the growing corpus of material, and follow-up visits were made to resolve discrepancies wherever possible. These accounts were placed in the context of the growing historical literature for the region, including Tlou (1985), Tlou and Campbell (1984), Vedder (1966 [1938]), Drechsler (1980), Parsons (1982), Palmer and Parsons (1977), and Clarence-Smith (1979).

12. For example, at Nxai Nxai, excavated by Wilmsen (1978), Levels 6–10 (60–100 cm) produced 4 sherds, Levels 1–5 (10–50 cm) 32, and the surface levels 348. Fragments of a single bovine maxilla found in the 60-cm level were identified as domesticated cow. That no further examples of domesticates have been found has led some archaeologists to suggest that this specimen was intrusive (Yellen and Brooks 1989).

13. Some !Kung insisted that their ancestors had made the pottery from local clays. With the advent of European iron pots, the art was lost.

14. As this passage indicates, the !Kung's willingness to defend themselves may be involved in the persistence of their autonomy. Chapman's reference to their fierceness is echoed by many of the !Kung's non-San neighbours today. The Herero see them as unpredictable and prone to flare-ups, an image at odds with some anthropological views of !Kung temperament (Lee 1979:370–400).

15. The *mafisa* cattle may well have degraded the environment, but the appearance of these effects was delayed.

16. The Herero had been driven out of Namibia by the German colonists in 1904–5, and, cattleless, had sought refuge among the Tswana in Bechuanaland. Through *mafisa* they had quickly rebuilt their herds.

17. The gradual shift of the Dobe-area !Kung onto the cattle posts contrasted sharply with developments in the adjacent Nyae/Nyae area. In 1960, 800–1,000 !Kung

were rapidly recruited to a South African settlement scheme at Tsumkhwe (Volkman 1983, Marshall 1980). The effects of the settlement on the Dobe !Kung are discussed in Lee (1979).

18. In 1987, after an aerial survey indicated that game was plentiful, the administration eased the game regulations, and hunting increased but still without guns.

19. Exceptions, of course, exist. Tlou and Campbell (1984:109) describe a battle between the Ngwaketse and the Amandebele in the Dutlwe area ca. 1830. The skirmish was brief, and neither group remained in the area, nor had either been resident there for any appreciable length of time.

20. Both the Kgalagadi and the Herero were "devolved" pastoralists with the socioeconomic infrastructure to facilitate the rapid reabsorption of livestock into the cultural system. If, as is suggested by Schrire (1980), the San were also "devolved" pastoralists, why did they not follow in their neighbours' path and become predominantly pastoralists in the 20th century?

21. These qualities may coexist with dependency, but we see no reason to believe that they are caused by it. For a recent statement of what primitive communalism is and is not, see Lee (1990).

22. Political autonomy, by contrast, hinges not on a society's capacity to reproduce itself but on the willingness of other (dominating) societies to let it remain autonomous. Neither Dutlwe nor Dobe could be said to have been politically autonomous in the 1960s.

23. For example, Memmi's (1984:185) definition of dependence as "a relationship with a real or ideal being, object, group, or institution that involves more or less accepted compulsion and that is connected with the satisfaction of a need" is consistent with our own usage.

24. We are indebted to Gerald Sider for this suggestion and some of the discussion that follows.

25. The subjectivity involved in determining whether a given autonomy is asserted or imposed has been a major problem in articulation theory (e.g., Foster-Carter 1978, Clarence-Smith 1985) regarding whether a given "tribal" communal social formation was preserved because its maintenance was "functional" for capitalism (Wolpe 1972) or because the local system and the local people were strong enough to resist (Beinart 1985).

26. The issue received international attention in the late 1920s and 1930s, when a series of reports was commissioned by the London Missionary Society, the British, and the Ngwato chief concerning the status of the San in the Ngwato Reserve. The question was whether the San were in a state of slavery. As might have been predicted, there was no consensus, and while instances of hereditary servitude were noted it was clear that this condition was not general and that many San persisted in their "miserable nomadic existence" (Tagart 1933, quoted in Miers and Crowder 1988:188).

27. Ethnic boundaries may also be blurred, and in many instances poorer blacks and San live similar lives, intermarry, and defy any neat ethnic categorization or hierarchy.

REFERENCES

Amin, S. (1972). Underdevelopment and dependence in black Africa: Origins and contemporary forms. *Journal of Modern African Studies* 10:503–24.

Anderson, C. (1856). *Lake Ngami*. London: Hurst.

Baines, T. (1973 [1864]). *Explorations in South West Africa*. Salisbury: Pioneer Head.

Beinart, W. (1985). Chieftaincy and the concept of articulation: South Africa ca. 1900–1950. *Canadian Journal of African Studies* 19(1):91–8.

Biesele, M., M. Guenther, R. Hitchcock, R. Lee, and J. MacGregor. (1989). Hunters, clients, and squatters: The contemporary socioeconomic status of Botswana Basarwa. *African Studies Monographs* 9:109–51.

Bonner, P. (1983). *King, commoners, and concessionnaires: The evolution and dissolution of the 19th-century Swazi state.* Cambridge/New York: Cambridge University Press.

Botswana National Archives. (1887a). HC 14/2 Despatch, Administrator, British Bechuanaland to Governor, Capetown, forwarding copy of a report and a map by Captain Goold-Adams of a police patrol from Molepolole to Lehututu.

———. (1887b). HC 153/1 High Commission for South Africa. On Bakgalagadi and Bushmen slavery.

Bower, B. (1989). A world that never existed. *Science News* 135:264–6.

Brooks, A. (1989). Past subsistence and settlement patterns in the Dobe area: An archaeological perspective. Paper presented at the 88th annual meeting of the American Anthropological Association, Washington, D.C., November.

Campbell, A., and G. Child. (1971). The impact of man on the environment of Botswana. *Botswana Notes and Records* 3:91–110.

Cashdan, Elizabeth. (1987). Trade and its origins on the Botetli River. *Journal of Anthropological Research* 43:121–38.

Chapman, J. (1971 [1868]). *Travels in the interior of South Africa (1849–1863): Hunting and trading journeys from Natal to Walvis Bay and visits to Lake Ngami and Victoria Falls.* Edited by E. Tabler. Cape Town: Balkema.

Clarence-Smith, W. (1979). *Slaves, peasants, and capitalists in southern Angola 1840–1926.* Cambridge and New York: Cambridge University Press.

———. (1985). "Thou shall not articulate modes of production." *Canadian Journal of African Studies* 19:19–23.

Denbow, J. (1980). Early Iron Age remains in the Tsodilo Hills, northwestern Botswana. *South African Journal of Science* 76:474–75.

———. (1984). "Prehistoric herders and foragers of the Kalahari: The evidence for 1500 years of interaction," in *Past and present in hunter-gatherer studies.* Edited by C. Schrire, pp. 175–93. Orlando: Academic Press.

———. (1986). A new look at the later prehistory of the Kalahari. *Journal of African History* 27:3–28.

Denbow, J., and E. Wilmsen. (1983). Iron Age pastoral settlements in Botswana. *South African Journal of Science* 79:405–8.

———. 1986. Advent and the course of pastoralism in the Kalahari. *Science* 234:1509–15.

Drechsler, H. (1980). *Let us die fighting: The Nama and Herero war against Germany.* London: Zed.

Earle, T., and J. E. Ericson, eds. (1977). *Exchange systems in prehistory.* New York: Academic Press.

Elphick, R. (1977). *Kraal and castle: Khoikhoi and the founding of white South Africa.* New Haven: Yale University Press.

Endicott, K. (1988). Can hunter-gatherers survive in the rain forest without trade? Paper presented at the University of Toronto, April.

Ericson, J. E. (1977). "Egalitarian exchange systems in California: A preliminary view," in *Exchange systems in prehistory.* Edited by T. Earle and J. E. Ericson, pp. 109–206. New York: Academic Press.

Foster-Carter, A. (1978). The modes of production controversy. *New Left Review* 107:44–77.

Freeman, D. (1983). *Margaret Mead in Samoa.* Cambridge: Harvard University Press.

Friedman, J. (1975). "Tribes, states, and transformations," in *Marxist analyses in social anthropology.* Edited by M. Bloch, pp. 161–202. London: Tavistock.

Galton, F. (1889). *Narrative of an explorer in tropical Africa.* London: Ward and Lock.

Gordon, Robert J. (1984). "The !Kung in the Kalahari exchange: An ethnohistorical perspective," in *Past and present in hunter-gatherer studies.* Edited by C. Schrire, pp. 195–224. Orlando: Academic Press.

Gough, K. (1971). "Nuer kinship: A re-examination," in *The translation of culture.* Edited by T. O. Beidelman, pp. 79–120. London: Tavistock.

Guenther, M. (1986). "Acculturation and assimilation of the Bushmen," in *Contemporary studies on Khoisan.* Edited by I. R. Vossen and K. Keuthmann, pp. 347–73. Hamburg: Helmut Buske Verlag.

Harries, P. (1982). "Kinship, ideology, and the nature of precolonial labour migration," in *Industrialism and social change in South Africa*. Edited by S. Marks and R. Rathbone. London: Longman.

Headland, T., and L. Reid. (1989). Hunter-gatherers and their neighbors from prehistory to the present. *Current Anthropology* 30:43–66.

Hindess, B., and P. Hirst. (1975). *Precapitalist modes of production*. London: Routledge and Kegan Paul.

Hitchcock, Robert K. (1978). *Kalahari cattle posts: A regional study of hunter-gatherers, pastoralists, and agriculturalists in the Western Sandveld Region, Central District, Botswana*. 2 vols. Gaborone: Government Printer.

——. (1987). Socioeconomic change among the Basarwa in Botswana: An ethnohistorical analysis. *Ethnohistory* 34:219–55.

Howell, Nancy. (1979). *The demography of the Dobe !Kung*. New York: Academic Press.

——. (1988). The Tasaday and the !Kung: Reassessing isolated hunter-gatherers. Paper presented at the annual meeting of the Society for American Archaeology, Tucson, Ariz., April.

Ingold, T., D. Riches, and J. Woodburn, eds. (1988). *Hunters and gatherers*. Vol. 1. *History, evolution, and social change*. Oxford: Berg.

Kelly, R., (1985). *The Nuer conquest*. Ann Arbor: University of Michigan Press.

Kent, S. (1989a). The cycle that repeats: Shifting subsistence strategies among Kalahari Basarwa. Paper presented at the 88th annual meeting of the American Anthropological Association, Washington, D.C., November.

——. (1989b). And justice for all: The development of political centralization among newly sedentary foragers. *American Anthropologist* 91:703–11.

Leacock, E., and R. Lee, eds. (1982). *Politics and history in band societies*. Cambridge and New York: Cambridge University Press.

Lee, R. (1965). Subsistence ecology of !Kung Bushmen. Ph. D. diss University of California, Berkeley, Calif.

——. (1979). *The !Kung San: Men, women, and work in a foraging society*. Cambridge: Cambridge University Press.

——. (1981). Is there a foraging mode of production? *Canadian Journal of Anthropology* 2:13–19.

——. (1988). "Reflections on primitive communism," in *Hunters and gatherers*, vol. 1. Edited by T. Ingold, D. Riches, and J. Woodburn, pp. 252–68. Oxford: Berg.

——. (1990). "Primitive communism and the origins of social inequality," in *The evolution of political systems*. Edited by S. Upham. Cambridge and New York: Cambridge University Press.

Lee, R. B., and I. Devore. (1976). *Kalahari hunter-gatherers*. Cambridge: Harvard University Press.

Leistner, O. (1967). *The plant ecology of the southern Kalahari*. Pretoria: Government Printer.

Lévi-Strauss, C. (1949). *The elementary structures of kinship*. Boston: Beacon Press.

Lewin, R. (1989). New views emerge on hunters and gatherers. *Science* 240:1146–8.

Lewis, O. (1951). *Life in a Mexican village: Tepoztlán restudied*. Urbana: University of Illinois Press.

Livingstone, David. (1857). *Missionary travels and researches in South Africa*. London: John Murray.

Mackenzie, J. (1971 [1871]). *Ten years north of the Orange River: A story of everyday life and work among the South African tribes from 1859 to 1869*. Edinburgh: Edmonston and Douglas.

Marks, S., and A. Atmore. (1971). Firearms in southern Africa: A survey. *Journal of African History* 7:517–30.

Marshall, L. K. (1976). *The !Kung Bushmen of Nyae/Nyae*. Cambridge: Harvard University Press.

——. 1980. *N!ai: The story of a !Kung woman*. Watertown, Mass.: Documentary Education Resources.

Marx, Karl. (1977 [1887]). *Capital*. Vol. 3. New York: International Publishers.

Mauss, M. (1925). Essai sur le don. *Année Sociologique* 1:30–186.

Memmi, A. (1984). *Dependence*. Boston: Beacon.

Miers, S., and M. Crowder. (1988). "The politics of slavery in Bechuanaland: Power struggles and the plight of the Basarwa on the Bamangwato Reserve, 1926–1940," in *The end of slavery in Africa*. Edited by S. Miers and R. Roberts, pp. 172–202. Madison: University of Wisconsin Press.

Motzafi, P. (1986). Whither the "true Bushmen": The dynamics of perpetual marginality. *Sprache und Geschichte in Afrika* 7:295–328.

Newcomer, P. (1972). The Nuer and the Dinka: An essay on origins and environmental determinism. *Man* 7:5–11.

Nugent, D. (1983). Closed systems and contradiction in the Kachin in and out of history. *Man* 17:508–27.

Okihiro, G. (1976). Hunters, herders, cultivators, and traders: Interaction and change in the Kgalagadi, nineteenth century. Ph.D. diss., University of California, Los Angeles, Calif.

Palmer, R., and N. Parsons. (1977). Editors. *The roots of rural poverty in central and southern Africa*. Berkeley: University of California Press.

Parkington, J. (1984). "Soaqua and Bushmen: Hunters and robbers," in *Past and present in hunter-gatherer studies*. Edited by C. Schrire, pp. 151–74. Orlando: Academic Press.

Parsons, N. (1977). "The economic history of Khama's country in Botswana, 1844–1930," in *The roots of rural poverty in central and southern Africa*. Edited by R. Palmer and N. Parsons, pp. 113–42. Berkeley: University of California Press.

——. (1982). *A new history of southern Africa*. Gaborone: Macmillan, Boleswa.

Peters, P. (1983). Cattlemen, borehole syndicates, and privatization in the Kgatleng District, Botswana: An anthropological history of the transformation of a commons. Ph.D. diss., Boston University, Boston, Mass.

——. (1984). Struggles over water, struggles over meaning: Cattle, water, and the state in Botswana. *Africa* 54(3):29–49.

Peterson, J. T. (1978). Hunter-gatherer/farmer exchange. *American Anthropologist* 80:335–51.

Phillipson, D. (1977). *The prehistory of southern and central Africa*. London: Heinemann.

Rosenberg, H. (1990). "Complaint discourse, aging, and caregiving among the Kung San of Botswana," in *The cultural context of aging: World-wide perspectives*. Edited by J. Sokolovsky. Boston: Bergin and Garvey.

Russell, M. (1976). Slaves or workers? Relations between Bushmen, Tswana, and Boers in the Kalahari. *Journal of Southern African Studies* 2:178–97.

Russell, M., and M. Russell. (1979). *Afrikaners of the Kalahari: White minority in a black state*. Cambridge: Cambridge University Press.

Sacks, K. (1979). Causality and change on the Upper Nile. *American Ethnologist* 6:437–48.

Sahlins, M. (1968). *Tribesmen*. Englewood Cliffs: Prentice Hall.

Schapera, I., and D. F. Van Der Merwe. (1945). *Note on tribal groupings, history, and customs of the Bakgalagadi*. Communications for the School of African Studies, n.s., 13.

Schrire, Carmel. (1980). An enquiry into the evolutionary status and apparent identity of San hunter-gatherers. *Human Ecology* 8:9–32.

——, ed. (1984a). *Past and present in hunter-gatherer studies*. Orlando: Academic Press.

——. (1984b). "Wild surmises on savage thoughts," in *Past and present in hunter-gatherer studies*. Edited by C. Schrire, pp. 1–25. Orlando: Academic Press.

Shanin, T., ed. (1972). *Peasants and peasant societies*. New York: Penguin Books.

Silberbauer, George B. (1981). *Hunter and habitat in the central Kalahari Desert*. Cambridge: Cambridge University Press.

——. (1989). On the myth of the "savage other." *Current Anthropology* 30:206–7.

Silberbauer, G. B., and A. Kuper. (1966). Kgalagadi masters and their Bushmen serfs. *African Studies* 25:171–9.

Solway, J. (1987). Commercialization and social differentiation in a Kalahari village. Ph.D. diss., University of Toronto, Toronto, Ont.

Solway, J., and R. B. Lee. (1981). The Kalahari fur trade. Paper presented at the 80th annual meeting of the American Anthropological Association, Los Angeles, Calif.

Stow, G. W. (1964 [1905]). *The native races of South Africa.* Cape Town: C. Struik.

Tabler, E. (1973). *Pioneers of South West Africa and Ngamiland.* Cape Town: Balkema.

Tagart, E. S. B. (1933). *Report on the conditions existing among the Masarwa in the Bamangwato Reserve of the Bechuanaland Protectorate and certain other matters appertaining to the natives living therein.* Pretoria: Government Printer.

Tanaka, J. (1980). *The San hunter-gatherers of the Kalahari: A study in ecological anthropology.* Tokyo: University of Tokyo Press.

Thompson, L. (1975 [1969]). "Co-operation and conflict: The High Veld," in *The Oxford history of South Africa,* vol. 1. Edited by M. Wilson and L. Thompson, pp. 391–446. Oxford: Oxford University Press.

Thomson, D. (1949). *Economic structure and the ceremonial exchange cycle in Arnhem Land.* Melbourne: Angus and Robertson.

Tlou, T. (1977). "Servility and political control: Botlhanka among the Batawana of northwestern Botswana, ca. 1750–1906," in *Slavery in southern Africa.* Edited by S. Miers and I. Kopytoff, pp. 367–90. Madison: University of Wisconsin Press.

——. (1985). *A history of Ngamiland, 1750 to 1906: The formation of an African state.* Gaborone: Macmillan.

Tlou, T., and A. Campbell. (1984). *A history of Botswana.* Gaborone: Macmillan.

Torrence, R. (1986). *Production and exchange of stone tools.* Cambridge: Cambridge University Press.

Turnbull, C. (1962). *The forest people.* New York: Simon and Schuster.

Vedder, H. (1966 [1938]). *South West Africa in early times.* London: Frank Cass.

Vierich, H. (Esche). (1977). *Interim report on survey of Basarwa in Kweneng.* Gaborone: Ministry of Local Government and Lands.

——. (1982a). The Kua of the southeastern Kalahari: A study of the socio-ecology of dependency. Ph.D. diss., University of Toronto, Toronto, Ont.

——. (1982b). "Adaptive flexibility in a multi-ethnic setting: The Basarwa of the southern Kalahari," in *Politics and history in band societies.* Edited by Eleanor Leacock and Richard Lee, pp. 213–22. Cambridge: Cambridge University Press.

Volkman, T. (1983). *The San in transition.* Vol. 1. Cambridge: Cultural Survival.

Wasserstrom, R. (1982). *Class and society in Chiapas.* New York: Columbia University Press.

Wilhelm, J. (1954 [1914–19]). *Die !Kung Buschleute.* Jahrbuch des Museums für Völkerkunde zu Leipzig 12.

Wilmsen, E. (1974). *Lindenmeier: A Pleistocene hunting society.* New York: Harper and Row.

——. 1978. Prehistoric and historic antecedents of a contemporary Ngamiland community. *Botswana Notes and Records* 10:5–18.

——. (1983). The ecology of illusion: Anthropological foraging in the Kalahari. *Reviews in Anthropology* 10:9–20.

——. (1988). The antecedents of contemporary pastoralism in western Ngamiland. *Botswana Notes and Records* 20:29–39.

——. (1989a). "Those who have each other: San relations to land," in *We are here: Politics of aboriginal land tenure.* Edited by Edwin Wilmsen, pp. 43–67. Berkeley: University of California Press.

——. (1989b). *Land filled with flies: A political economy of the Kalahari.* Chicago: University of Chicago Press.

Wilmsen, E., and D. Durham. (1988). "Food as a function of seasonal environment and social history," in *Coping with uncertainty.* Edited by G. Harrison and I. de Garine, pp. 52–87. Cambridge: Cambridge University Press.

Wilson, M. (1975). "The hunters and herders," in *The Oxford history of South Africa,* vol. 1. Edited by M. Wilson and L. Thompson, pp. 40–75. Oxford: Oxford University Press.

Wolf, E. (1982). *Europe and the people without history.* Berkeley: University of California Press.

Wolpe, H. (1972). Capitalism and cheap labour-power in South Africa: From segregation to apartheid. *Economy and Society* 1(4).

Woodburn, J. (1988). "African hunter-gatherer social organization: Is it best understood as a product of encapsulation?" in *Hunters and gatherers*, vol. 1. Edited by T. Ingold, D. Riches, and J. Woodburn, pp. 31–64. Oxford: Berg.

Worsley, P. (1956) The kinship system of the Tallensi: A reevaluation. *Journal of the Royal Anthropological Institute* 86: 37–77.

Yellen, John E., and Alison S. Brooks. (1989). The Late Stone Age archaeology of the !Kangwa and /Xai/Xai Valleys, Ngami-land Botswana. *Botswana Notes and Records*.

16

Links and Boundaries: Reconsidering the Alpine Village as Ecosystem

Robert McC. Netting

In occasionally referring to the Swiss mountain village of Törbel as an "island in the sky" and describing the intricate economic and social means by which its inhabitants over the centuries struck a balance with their alpine environment (Netting 1981), I may well have been guilty of the ecosystematic fallacy. This common anthropological error involves an overemphasis on functional integration, stability, and regulatory mechanisms within the community and a relative neglect of disequilibrium, changes emanating from more inclusive political-economic systems, and instances of evolutionary maladaptation. The solid specificity of terrain and climate may appear as a fundamental set of constraints on human activity, especially when ethnological comparison with communities in similar environments is lacking. The nature of long-term resident field research, our anthropological reverence for a holistic perspective, and the romantic mystique of the self-sufficient, autonomous, emotionally rewarding "little community" all perpetuate our proclivity to learn a lot about a very limited group.

Ecological anthropologists with their commitment to gathering a wider range of non-cultural data and organizing these variables into systems models often focus on small units of interaction for both practical and theoretical reasons. Biologists have told us comfort-ingly that ecosystem is an accordion concept, applying equally well to a drop of pond water or the entire biosphere. If indeed the ecosystem may be delimited at any magnitude appropriate for a particular investigation, and if natural boundaries are desirable but not essential (Fosberg, personal communication), we can continue to study those convenient social entities where we have always worked – the band, the village, or the tribe. The boundaries are, of course, recognized as artificial or drawn for "heuristic" purposes. We vigorously deny that we still labor in the expiring vineyard of neo-functionalism (Vayda and McCay 1975; Orlove 1980). Nevertheless, we remain concerned with more or less closed systems whose internal processes are regulated by negative feedback loops and we tend to make common cause with the biologists who stress the idea of ecosystems rather than of natural selection as an organizing concept (Richerson 1977). Distinguishing between local and regional ecosystems (Rappaport 1971a) recognizes part of the problem, but the sheer complexity of charting energy flows in local food production and consumption (Rappaport 1971b) may be so demanding that exchanges of goods, services, and people in the wider network over long periods of time cannot be adequately handled.

The appearance of biological orthodoxy and objective comparability that comes from selecting "populations" rather than "cultures" as units of investigation (Vayda and Rappaport 1968) is often illusory. Lacking species distinctiveness and geographical isolation, questions of where to bound a population as ecosystem may rely on endogamous groups or other ethnic bars to mating whose creation and effective maintenance are based on cultural rules of acceptable marriage. The fact is that human populations must be typified and analyzed by demographic means, but we necessarily begin with localized, co-resident, on-the-ground groups that identify themselves by name and tell us about the links of kinship, cooperation, and citizenship that bind their members together. Without hard information on such biosocial factors as diet and disease, warfare mortality and migration, and changing age-specific fertility (Buchbinder 1978; Morren 1977; Hassan 1978), ecological approaches to human cultures, populations, or ecosystems, however defined, can hardly rise above the level of explanatory sketches.

Jochim (1981:4) has pointed out that the boundary definition of human ecosystems is even harder than that of biological ones because of the more diverse interactions and because humans establish cultural boundaries that may or may not coincide with any natural ones. It seems to me now that I was led down the garden path of the independent population subsisting on its own resources in a clearly defined geographical area by the extraordinarily definite and enduring congruence between the Swiss folk model of the community and the historic realities of peasant village economy in the Alps. But in the very process of finding out how orderly, effective, self-correcting, and responsive the local system had been in sustaining a self-conscious, corporate population through time in an unremittingly difficult mountain environment, I became aware of the often concealed interdependencies that sustained the system at its points of weakness and rectified its dangerous imbalances. We will consider some of the ways in which a culturally and materially defined local community ecosystem survived by means of significant economic and demographic flows back and forth across its boundaries.

Self-Sufficiency and the Market

Anthropologists coming from technologically complex, occupationally specialized, economically interdependent societies may be attracted to groups where the entire labor process from raw natural resource to finished product and consumption is visible and comprehensible. We are devotees of mechanical solidarity for whom small has always been beautiful and ecological homeostasis in traditional societies is assumed until proven otherwise. It was with a sense of considerable satisfaction that I settled on the community of Törbel in the Visp valley of Valais Canton as a site for field research. Törbel seemed by all accounts a representative alpine village whose peasants had lived since at least the eleventh century AD on the returns of agro-pastoral subsistence pursuits carried on within their own demarcated territory. A contiguous area of 1,545 ha. (including 967 ha. of field, meadow, and pasture, 455 ha. of forest, and 123 ha. of unproductive land in 1924) sloped from the Mattervispa river at 770 meters above sea level to the peak of Augsbordhorn at 2,972 meters (Netting 1981:2). Various altitudinal zones were used for vineyards, hay meadows, grainfields, gardens, and summer grazing grounds (Netting 1972), so that almost the entire supply of wine, rye bread, dairy products, potatoes, vegetables, and meat were locally produced. Wood for building and fuel, slate for roofs, and wool for textiles also came from village lands, and the mountain stream powered grist mills, a saw mill, and a fulling mill. Every farm family had access to the various types of land and other means of production such as barns and livestock (Netting 1981:10–41). Climatic fluctuations were cushioned by the scatter of individually-owned fields with various degrees of slope and sun exposure (Netting 1976), an extensive system of meadow irrigation (Netting 1974), and effective techniques for the storage of hay, grain, bread, cheese, and dried meat. The provision of adequate food, clothing, and shelter from within the village territory by subsistence methods that changed little from at least the fourteenth century does not appear to have degraded the local environment. Soil fertility was maintained by manuring. Terracing and uphill transport of earth limited erosion, and carefully controlled timber cutting prevented deforestation (Netting 1981:46, 67). The localized ecosystem seemed to epitomize a well articulated, self-sustaining interdependence of physical environment, subsistence techniques, and human population.

Both the Swiss inhabitants of Törbel and the outsider ecologist are inclined to stress a peasant past in which comparative independence and autarchy distinguished the community from other European rural societies. But economic isolation was probably never the rule. A path through the Törbel hamlets of Burgen and Feld is part of the ancient trail connecting the Rhone valley with Italy. Roman coins found on the Theodul Pass indicate early connections, and a hill fort in Zeneggan near Törbel dates to the Iron Age (Netting 1981:8). Trails of this kind were perhaps less important than the Simplon or St. Bernard routes in linking northern Europe with the Mediterranean, but the alpine traffic could only be interrupted and the passes closed when a disaster like the bubonic plague caused medieval Valais to quarantine itself. Mountain agriculture is hardly imaginable without axes and other woodworking tools, hoes, and caldrons for cheese making. Metals have always necessarily been imported. Salt for the dairy cattle and for preserving cheese had also to be brought in from a distance. Indeed, the trade in salt from either France or Italy was a cantonal monopoly around which the late medieval international relations of the mountain districts revolved (Dubois 1965). Sixteenth century documents record an annual wagonload of salt delivered to Törbel, and in the nineteenth century it was estimated that an ordinary household with cattle used 70 kg of salt per year (Franscini 1848:139).

From the time of the earliest parchment documents relating to the community, land sales have required money, and both churchly tithes and personal debts with interest are given cash values. Törbel had to participate in the market, but it is not completely clear how this was done. To this day, Törbel has a reputation for raising milk cows, and most families sell some breeding or slaughter stock every year. Animals were driven to the lower Rhone valley, across the passes into Italy, or disposed of at the annual markets in Visp and Stalden. Live sheep and goats as well as raw wool and cheese may also have been traded in former times, but the alpine herding pattern was more oriented to subsistence than exchange, and it seems likely that an appreciable surplus was not regularly produced. Cash income may have been dependent more on the export of labor than of agricultural goods. The trans-alpine trade required the seasonal work of drivers, mule skinners, and guards, and Törbel men may have taken such jobs as they did when the tourist industry began in the late nineteenth century. They also served for longer periods as mercenary soldiers in the armies of France, Spain, Naples, and the Pope (Netting 1981:54). If more recent accounts of wage labor outside the community as miners, craftsmen, and waitresses represent past practices, the earnings of such workers were returned in large part to parents or conjugal families in the village. The export of labor power allowed the community to meet its needs for commodities and manufactured goods, pay taxes, and conduct internal exchange on a cash basis. Though the typical farming village was something of a commercial *cul de sac*, its continued existence on the alpine margins has always required active exchange with the capitalist European centers of the world system.

Just how porous is the membrane separating the peasant economy from wider spheres is demonstrated by two processes. In the first place, self-sufficiency in food has been both aided and diminished by contact with external agricultural sources. There is evidence that mountain agriculture was made substantially more productive and dependable by the adoption of the potato in the late eighteenth century (Netting 1981:159–68). On the other hand, the purchase of cheap maize meal from Italian sources in the early 1900s decreased Törbel's reliance on its own rye crop. Construction of a road and daily bus service with valley towns more recently allowed the buying of bread made from imported wheat. The price and convenience of the white loaves spelled the quick demise of local grain *Aecker*, grist mills, and bake ovens.

In the course of our research, it also became clear that a model of village wealth built on inheritance of agricultural resources within a closed system did not adequately represent reality. If the major determinant of an individual's property in farm land and buildings was the holdings of his parents (and the parents of his spouse) to which he was heir, then there should have been an association between father's and son's wealth. Quantitative data from tax valuations between 1851 and 1915 failed to disclose significant correlations between father's and son's property measured by average wealth, maximum wealth, wealth at marriage, or wealth at age 40 (McGuire and Netting 1982). Even controlling for the number of siblings with whom the partible inheritance was shared brought no better prediction of the wealth of the son. This considerable mobility up and down the village wealth spectrum suggested that inherited resources were less of an influence than we had thought, and that differences resulting from cash earned outside the village context and then invested in agricultural property were substantial. The hard summer work on the mule train postal transport or on railway construction tapped funds from the national economy that allowed peasant households to prosper without leaving the land.

Population Growth and Self-Regulation

Ecological anthropologists have found it difficult to resist the attractions of a hypothesized human ecosystem in which population was somehow regulated without direct imposition of Malthusian sanctions, and growth rates, if present, were extremely low. Simple models of populations maintaining themselves below carrying capacity have been criticized (Street 1969; Brush 1975; Hayden 1975; Jochim 1981), and theoretical constructs of "group selection" in adjusting numbers so as to maintain local resource stability have been

questioned (Lewontin 1970; Bates and Lees 1979; Orlove 1980). My choice of a Swiss village with adequate vital records and our major effort to reconstruct 300 years of local historical demography were motivated in part by the wish to determine (1) if population equilibrium with fixed resources had in fact been achieved and (2) what was the role of social factors in influencing population growth. The more extensive the quantitative data to be analyzed, the more complex and partial become the answers to simple questions. We have found that the population of Törbel went through periods of quite marked growth as well as times of relative stability (Netting 1981:90–108). These dynamics have been responsive to a variety of internal factors, both biological, such as life expectancy, seasonality of conception, lactation, and nutritional patterns, and socio-cultural variables, such as age of marriage, celibacy, and inheritance (Netting 1981:109–58). But at no time could the fluctuations of local population be understood in isolation from surrounding populations.

Törbel's demographic distinctiveness from its neighbors was due less to topographical barriers than to the conscious imposition of legal and political barriers that successfully barred most in-migration. Unlike the rapid turnover of population characteristic of most European rural settlements (Schofield 1970; Gaunt 1977; Macfarlane 1978), Törbel family lines showed remarkable continuity over time, and no new family names took root in the village from before 1700 to 1970 (Netting 1981:70–89). Village citizenship descended in the male line, and local statutes first written down in 1483 prohibited outsiders from enjoying communal rights in the forests or the Alp. Without such resources to supplement privately owned farm lands, alpine agropastoralism would not have been possible. Formulation and enforcement of these rules was explicitly an activity of the corporate community (Wiegandt 1978) which thereby "closed" itself and effectively resisted population expansion due to immigration.

Village boundaries were, however, permeable to the movement of people in the other direction. It is possible that mountain populations have long followed a type of gravity model – that is, flows set up by birth rates higher than the replacement level and a comparatively isolated and healthy situation have taken surplus people from the highlands down to the valleys and plains. Törbel citizens have always left their homes permanently as mercenaries, farm laborers, artisans, and clerics, but new opportunities such as the colonizing of the Argentine interior, hotel jobs, or the construction industry in Swiss cities led to increased departures (Netting 1981:101–7). Without this safety valve, local population would have outstripped the potential of the territory to provide viable household subsistence holdings. The late nineteenth century demographic growth would have resulted in both rapid impoverishment and even higher than observed rates of celibacy if everyone had been forced to remain within the village. As it was, Törbel's export of people was one means by which the creation of a landless proletariat was avoided.

Does the conception of a community rejecting settlement by outsiders and allowing its own excess bodies to migrate mean that Törbel remained a homogeneous isolate in biological terms? Again, the self-contained ecosystem proves a poor analogy. Analysis of 917 marriages since 1703 shows that 14% of these were with women from other villages who took up residence in Törbel (Hagaman, Elias, and Netting 1978). Though this represents a very low rate of exogamy (cf. Levine 1977:39), the comparison of genetic contributions shows that in-migrants accounted for nearly 38% of the 1970 gene pool, while the more numerous Törbel ancestors were responsible for only 62% of the living population's genetic constitution. It appears that, for reasons not entirely clear, the fertility of children of in-migrants was significantly higher than that of Törbel natives. A high endogamy rate evidently does not create the conditions of a genetic isolate. The social and economic constraints on marriage between Törbel men and women from other villages have not prevented a substantial flow of "foreign" genetic materials into the local population.

The Ghost of Environmental Determinisms Past: Comparing Alpine Ecosystems

One of the attractions of fitting a structural-functional model of a social system into a more inclusive ecological system is that the significant aspects of the physical environment can be held constant. Where altitude, slope, water availability, and seasonal climate seemed to dictate the possible types and extent of agropastoral production under traditional technology in the European Alps, there has been a tendency to conceive of a similarly constrained set of social institutions and demographic patterns. Though I would have heatedly denied the charge that my explanation of Törbel's economic self-sufficiency and the adaptive advantages of its inheritance, marriage, and common property institutions smacked of environmental determinism, it is clear in retrospect that I sought to emphasize the neatness of fit between fixed natural conditions and more malleable human means of organization. If I had some measure of success in this endeavor, it was in part because my picture of an autarchic, closed corporate community with low fertility, emigration as a safety valve, and resource ceiling set by the marginality of mountain agriculture tallied well with the "canonical image of the upland community" in the growing anthropological literature (Viazzo 1989:11–14). In claiming some more than idiosyncratic significance for their work, anthropologists at least implicitly put their village studies forward as representative of an entire region. Without ever having set foot in a French, Italian, or Austrian alpine village, I may have done just that.

The great corrective to the tacit overgeneralization of any local model of ecosystem functioning is, of course, comparison. What might be termed the new, ecologically-informed ethnology examines spatially distinct populations through time in similar alpine environments, using the methods of historical demography and political economy to measure and analyze variation in a series of controlled comparisons (Eggan 1954). Pier Paolo Viazzo

(1989) has rigorously applied these methods, demonstrating that the Italian community of Alagna, sharing the same habitat, material culture, legal tradition, language, and ethnicity with Törbel was in many respects strikingly different. Rather than being relatively closed, isolated, and economically marginal, this village displayed an enormous amount of migration, with men up to the 1930s going out every summer as skilled plasterers to France, and outsiders entering the village as miners, beginning in the 1530s. These activities were heavily dependent on international economic conditions and on national trade and emigration policies. Women and hired laborers maintained the agro-pastoral subsistence economy, but there was no communal pasture, no irrigation, and food grains were imported (Viazzo 1989:110–15). Mining fluctuated with both the external market and the stock of exploitable ore resources, and the immigrant wage-labor population had differing interests from those of the local land-owning peasantry.

Low marital fertility was combined with late age of marriage, considerable celibacy, and partible inheritance as in the Törbel case, but there is in Alagna evidence of conscious family limitation. A low pressure demographic regime with restraints on local population growth could evidently be maintained by checks on nuptiality as in Törbel, by emigration as in the Western Alps of France and Italy, or by birth control (Viazzo 1989:219). A system of elevated ages of marriage and high celibacy such as I described for Törbel does appear to act as a crucial homeostatic mechanism in population growth, but levels of nuptiality can vary regionally and over time, and other factors may produce similar effects. The picture of a single pattern of traditional alpine nuptiality rests on the postulates "that similar ecological imperatives must invariably produce similar responses and that recent changes must have been preceded by a long period of static equilibrium" (Viazzo 1989:220). I would agree that formulations stressing the close functional integration of environmental and demographic factors in a stable ecosystem are too rigid and in the last analysis untenable, but I have taken pains to avoid suggesting the applicability of

the specific ecological analysis of Törbel to other alpine cross-cultural situations.

Complex multiple and extended family households in northern Italy contrasted with the Valaisan pattern. Though proportions of household types show some adaptive variation through time (Netting 1979; Viazzo 1989:96–8), it is possible that the stem family in Alagna was well suited to the periodic absence of younger migrant males (Viazzo 1989:245–50) as it was in French Savoy households with early marriage and low fertility rates (Siddle and Jones 1983; Viazzo 1989:202). There are, however, regional similarities in the prevalence of stem family organization that occur in northern Portugal and Spain, southern France, northern Italy, and Austria in a variety of farming systems and landscapes. Peter Laslett (1984) refers to this as the Mediterranean pattern of domestic organization and suggests that it may have considerable antiquity in this extensive area. There are also political factors that favor the maintenance of stem family households and impartible inheritance in the Austrian Alps. The nobles who colonized this mountainous region wanted to ensure the persistence of landed holdings capable of producing a surplus to be marketed in the lowlands (Viazzo 1989:264). The Hapsburg state also wished to promote a stable tax base and prevent fragmentation of peasant farms. These policies contributed to pronounced inequalities between the heir to a household farmstead and his landless siblings (Khera 1972). The Törbel corporate community of relatively egalitarian citizen smallholders (McGuire and Netting 1972) resident in independent nuclear family households contrasts sharply with the hierarchical class structure of upland Austrian society.

Even the degree of economic self-sufficiency or "autarchy" in Törbel, and by extension in Valais, Grisons, and Ticino cantons that supported a certain peasant autonomy from the market did not characterize other northern Swiss communities. By the mid-eighteenth century, villages of the *Hirtenland* or pastoral region had given up grain cultivation to specialize in summer pasture for commercial livestock or dairy production. Richer farmers leased the Alp and bought out the meadows and gardens of the poorer citizens (Viazzo 1989:184–5, 272–3). In some agricultural villages, a slow growth of population could continue with the new subsistence opportunities offered by the potato, while in other areas, the proliferation of cottage industry among the landless allowed a rapid demographic increase. In both areas, greater dependence on the market and the control of land by a large-farmer elite introduced greater stratification and pauperized a section of the population (Viazzo 1989:274). The closed corporate community that gave rights in the commons to all its citizens, allowing a rational exploitation of the diffuse summer grazing and forest resources, and at the same time protecting them from overuse and degradation (Netting 1976), may have been an institutional bastion against such differentiation. But even this historic and egalitarian system of local government is not a constant in alpine social organization (Viazzo 1989:280). The intricate and interlocking factors in even the most aesthetically compelling ecosystem model are not inevitable. Environment and history show regularities and causal relationships, but they are never unitary or necessary.

Tilting the Environment/ Population Balance

The variety of regional and national economic and political arrangements that have influenced local alpine production and social organization historically suggest that a diversity of viable ecosystems may exist. Some measure of stability may be reached at different levels of population, under contrasting fertility and nuptiality regimes, and with variable modes of land tenure and wealth distribution. It is possible, for instance, that a single private owner could stock and manage an alpine summer pasture with more efficiency and in a more optimal manner than does a corporate community with common property rights. Non-communal Alps do exist, and about one-fifth of Swiss Alp territory belongs to a Kanton or to a private owner or group of owners (Picht 1987). It is possible that corporate groups may put less than the optimal or maxi-

mally sustainable number of cows on the Alp. Milk yields from common property Alps fall below those of private property Alps (though production and transaction costs may be higher), and grazing pressure on the Swiss commons is *lower* than on private land (Stevenson 1990, cited in Ostrom 1990).

In the early years of this century, surveys of the management of all the alpine pastures in upper Valais recommended that Törbel reduce the number of cow-rights to prevent over stocking and that a series of improvements be made. Specifically, the tasks of cleaning the Alp of loose stones, removing brush such as raspberries and wild roses (a job estimated at a total of 800 man days of work), draining a swampy area, and constructing a 100 m protective wall were suggested (Schweizerische Alpstatistik 1900, 1909). The inspectors of the Swiss Alp Economy Association appeared to feel that conservative communities like Törbel were unwilling to invest the labor that could intensify the husbandry of local resources and substantially raise production (Schweizerische Alpstatistik 1909:4).

It is also difficult to reach an objective scientific judgment of the forestry practices on communal lands. A rising demand for timber in the market led to significant deforestation of many Swiss mountainous areas in the nineteenth century (Picht, personal communication). Törbel itself had to provide firewood by the 1870s for twice as many people as it had a hundred years before, and one authority expressed dismay about the scraping of the forest floor for livestock stall bedding material (Stebler 1922). Despite rigid controls on cutting live trees and the public auction of windfalls and dead standing timber by the forest steward (*Waldvogt*) after Sunday mass (Netting 1981:68), major house construction in Törbel for more than a century has been possible only with timber purchased outside the community. But communally managed forest cutting and the accompanying protection against avalanche and slope erosion damage seem to have remained an optimal solution to threats of environmental deterioration. Where Swiss commonly-owned forests were divided among villagers to become individually owned woodlots, "the lots were generally too small for effective management and degenerated until [government] intervention occurred in the nineteenth century" (Ostrom 1990; citing Ciriacy and Bishop 1975). Admirable as the institution arrangements may be for allocating rights to scarce resources, the question of whether they maintain optimal, sustainable yields remains a matter of empirical determination. It is also difficult to reconstruct past patterns of resource use, and the contemporary appearance of equilibrium may conceal historic episodes of overuse and environmental degradation.

Cultural Conception, Folk Model, and Ecosystem

In order to adequately conceptualize the ecological relationships of human groups, it may be necessary to treat them *as if* they were parts of a functionally integrated, persisting, homeostatic, isolatable ecosystem. Since Geertz (1963:9) cogently recommended the biologists' term ecosystem, ecological anthropologists have used it with characteristic alacrity and looseness. The danger was not so much in the flexible inclusiveness by which ecosystem could embrace a wide range of cultural, biological, and physical variables as in the tendency for heuristically-drawn boundaries to harden into the familiar shapes of geographical regions or self-conscious social groups. The tendency is strong for the anthropologist to accept the

members of a peasant closed corporate community at their word and emphasize the historic identity, economic self-sufficiency, population continuity, and socio-political autonomy that they claim for their village. The direct reality of participant observation combines with the villagers' own behavioral spheres of kinship, neighborliness, farm labor, and religious participation to emphasize everything that is bounded, familiar, and parochial. Living in Törbel, the very mountains and streams and serpentine road to the valley became for me identified with 600-year-old log houses and parchment documents and peasant genealogies vanishing into medieval mists (Reader 1988: Fig. 29). The marvel that any people had lived so long and so well on these alpine slopes led me to see and describe Törbel as an ecosystem. But for all the intricate adaptive mechanisms and the balance between human needs and environmental potentials, the village was never encapsulated or cut off. Subtly variable flows of goods and money and people tied it to a wider world. The significance of these movements of salt, iron, cattle, soldiers, coins, New World migrants, and in-marrying wives was often hidden from me and from my Törbel friends. But without these surges and trickles of energy in both directions, the local system could never have survived. The concept of a human ecosystem, like the idea of a niche or a lineage or a community, does not help us to create an airtight case but to model a useful, well-wrought urn of the imagination.

REFERENCES

Bates, Daniel G. and Susan H. Lees. (1979). The Myth of Population Regulation. *Evolutionary Biology and Human Social Behavior: An Anthropological Perspective,* Edited by N.A. Chagnon and W. Irons, North Scituate, Mass.: Duxbury, pp. 273–89.

Brush, S. B. (1975). The Concept of Carrying Capacity for Systems of Shifting Cultivation. *American Anthropologist* 77:799–811.

Buchbinder, Georgeda. (1978). Nutritional Stress and Post-contact Population Decline among the Maring of New Guinea. *Malnutrition, Behavior, and Social Organization,* Edited by L. S. Greene, New York: Academic.

Ciriacy-Wantrup, S. V. and R. C. Bishop. (1975). Common Property as a Concept in Natural Resource Policy. *Natural Resources Journal* 15:713–27.

Dubois, A. (1965). *Die Salzversorgung des Wallis 1500–1610: Wirtschaft und Politik.* Winterthur: P. G. Keller.

Eggan, F. (1954). Social Anthropology and the Method of Controlled Comparison. *American Anthropologist* 56:743–63.

Franscini, Stephan. (1848). *Neue Statistik der Schweiz.* Bern: Haller'schen.

Gaunt, David. (1977). Pre-Industrial Economy and Population Structure. *Scandanavian Journal of History* 2:183–210.

Geertz, Clifford. (1963). *Agricultural Involution: The Process of Ecological Change in Indonesia.* Berkeley: University of California Press.

Hagaman, Roberta M., Walter S. Elias. Robert McC. Netting. (1978). The Genetic and Demographic Impact of In-Migrants in a Largely Endogamous Community. *Annals of Human Biology* 5:505–15.

Hayden, B. (1975). The Carrying Capacity Dilemma. *Population Studies in Archaeology and Biological Anthropology*, A. C. Swedlund, ed. Memoir 30, pp. 11–21. Washington: Society for American Archaeology.

Howell, Nancy. (1979). *Demography of the Dobe Area !Kung.* New York: Academic.

Jochim, Michael A. (1981). *Strategies for Survival: Cultural Behavior in an Ecological Context.* New York: Academic.

Khera, Sigrid. (1972). An Austrian Peasant Village Under Rural Industrialization. *Behavioral Science Notes* 7:9–36.

Laslett, Peter. (1984). The Family as a Knot of Individual Interests. *Households: Comparative and Historical Studies of the Domestic Group*, Edited by R. McC. Netting, R. R. Wilk, and E. J. Arnould, Berkeley: University of California Press, pp. 353–79.

Levine, David. (1977). *Family Formation in an Age of Nascent Capitalism.* New York: Academic Press.

Lewontin, R. C. (1970). Units of Selection. *Annual Review of Ecology and Systematics* 1:1–18.

Macfarlane, Alan. (1978). *The Origins of English Individualism: the Family, Property and Social Transition.* New York: Cambridge University Press.

McGuire, Randall and Robert McC. Netting. (1982). Levelling Peasants? The Demographic Implications of Wealth Differences

in an Alpine Community. *American Ethnologist* 9:269–90.

Morren, G. E. B. (1977). From Hunting to Herding Pigs and the Control of Energy in Montane New Guinea. *Subsistence and Survival: Rural Ecology in the Pacific*, Edited by T. P. Bayliss-Smith and F. G. Feachem, New York: Academic Press.

Netting, Robert McC. (1971). Of Men and Meadows Strategies of Alpine Land Use. *Anthropological Quarterly* 45:132–44.

——. (1974). The System Nobody Knows: Village Irrigation in the Swiss Alps. *Irrigation's Impact on Society,* Edited by T. E. Downing and M. Gibson, Tucson: University of Arizona Press, pp. 67–75.

——. (1976). What Alpine Peasants Have in Common: Observations on Communal Tenure in a Swiss Village. *Human Ecology* 4:135–46.

——. (1979). Household Dynamics in a Nineteenth Century Swiss Village. *Journal of Family History* 4:39–58.

——. (1981). *Balancing on an Alp: Ecological Change and Continuity in a Swiss Mountain Community.* Cambridge: Cambridge University Press.

Orlove, Benjamin S. (1980). Ecological Anthropology. *Annual Review of Anthropology* 9:235–73.

Ostrom, Elinor. (1990). *Governing the Commons: the Evolution of Institutions for Collective Action.* Cambridge: Cambridge University Press.

Picht, Christine. (1987). Common Property Regimes in Swiss Alpine Meadows. Paper presented at the Conference on Advances in Comparative Institutional Analysis at the Inter-University Center of Post Graduate Studies, October 19–23, Dubrovnik, Yugoslavia.

Rappaport, Roy A. (1971a). Nature, Culture, and Ecological Anthropology. *Man, Culture, and Society*, Edited by H. L. Shapiro, London: Oxford University, pp. 237–67.

——. (1971b). The Flow of Energy in an Agricultural Society. *Scientific American* 244:116–23.

Reader, John. (1988). *Man on Earth: A Celebration of Mankind.* New York: Harper and Row.

Richerson, P. J. (1977). Ecology and Human Ecology: A Comparison of Theories in the Biological and Social Sciences. *American Ethnologist* 4:1–26.

Schofield, R. S. (1970). Age-Specific Mobility in an Eighteenth Century Rural English Parish. *Annales de Demographie Historique*, pp. 261–74.

Schweizerische Alpstatistik. (1900). *Schweizerische Alpstatistik: Die Alpwirtschaft im Ober-Wallis*. Solothurn: Schweizerische alpwirtschaftlichen Verein.

——. (1909). *Bericht über die Alpen-Inspektionen in Kanton Wallis im Jahre 1909*. Vol. 1, Ober-Wallis. Solothurn: Schweizerischen alpwirtschaftlichen Verein.

Siddle, D. J. and A. M. Jones. (1983). Family Household Structures and Inheritance in Savoy, 1561–1975. *Liverpool Papers in Human Geography*, No. 11.

Stebler, F. G. (1922). *Die Vispertaler Sonnenberge. Jahrbuch des Schweizer Alpenclub*. Sechsundfunfzigster Jahrgang. Bern: Schweizer Alpenclub.

Stevenson, G. G. (1990). *The Swiss Grazing Commons: The Economics of Open Access, Private, and Common Property*. Cambridge: Cambridge University Press.

Street, J. (1969). An Evaluation of the Concept of Carrying Capacity. *Professional Geographer* 21:104–7.

Vayda, A. P. and B. McCay. (1975). New Directions in Ecology and Ecological Anthropology. *Annual Review of Anthropology* 4:293–306.

Vayda, A. P. and R. A. Rappaport. (1968). Ecology, Cultural and Non-Cultural. *Introduction to Cultural Anthropology*, Edited by J. A. Clifton, Boston: Houghton Mifflin, pp. 476–98.

Viazzo, Pier Paolo. (1989). *Upland Communities: Environment, Population, and Social Structure in the Alps Since the Sixteenth Century*. Cambridge: Cambridge University Press.

Wiegandt, Ellen. (1978). Past and Present in the Swiss Alps. *Hill Lands: Proceedings of an International Symposium*, Edited by J. Luchok, J. D. Cawthon, M. J. Breslin, Morgantown: West Virginia University Books, pp. 203–8.

Part IV

The Politics of Natural Resources and the Environment

17

Forest Knowledge, Forest Transformation: Political Contingency, Historical Ecology, and the Renegotiation of Nature in Central Seram

Roy Ellen

Countering Threats

eroded by colonialism

Argument

Since the mid-1980s Nuaulu living on the edge of lowland rainforest[1] in central Seram, Maluku, have become increasingly active in countering threats to their traditional resource base. This latter has been dramatically eroded, mainly through government-sponsored settlement and logging. Nuaulu have successfully defended land claims in the courts, there have been violent incidents at a nearby transmigration area leading to their imprisonment, and in their representations to outsiders they have become articulate about the damage done to their environment. However, Nuaulu have a long history of interaction with "the outside world", of forest modification and participation in the market. They were politically engaged as early as the Dutch wars of the late seventeenth century and have been indirectly, and, more recently, directly subject to the oscillations and economic fall-out of the spice trade ever since. The seventies and eighties of the present [20th] century have seen the expansion of cash-cropping, together with accelerated rates of land sale and forest extraction.

I shall argue in this chapter that as different material and social changes take place, so Nuaulu have renegotiated their conceptual relationship with forest. In particular, I seek to ask why, given an apparent historic readiness to accept environmental change, they have now adopted a rhetoric which we would recognise as "environmentalist". I claim that part of the explanation is that older, local forms of knowledge which underpin subsistence strategies are qualitatively different from knowledge of macro-level processes – "environmental consciousness" in the abstract – which only comes with a widening of political and ecological horizons.

The Nuaulu in
the World System

The patterns of ecological change which have
accompanied Nuaulu interaction with the
rainforest cannot be understood properly
except in relation to the history of contact
(direct and indirect) between the forest peoples
of Seram and various groups of outsiders: the
rulers and subjects of various traditional
coastal polities; the Dutch East India Company,
its heirs and successors; various agencies of the
colonial Dutch government, and thereafter of
the government of an independent Indonesia
(local district officers, police, military, and the
personnel of assorted provincial level departments); and finally traders and settlers of
diverse ethnic origins, but predominantly
Chinese, Butonese and Ambonese.

The details of the early phase of the movement of biological species in and out of Seram
(Ellen 1993b) is not relevant to the specific
argument put forward in this chapter, but that
it happened is a part of the general background
picture. Thus, the circulation of valuables,
upon which the reproduction of Nuaulu social
structure became effectively dependent over
several hundreds of years (Ellen 1988a) was
based on articles traded in from the Asian
mainland (porcelain from China and elsewhere, and cloth from India) and from other
parts of the archipelago (including textiles
from Timor and Java); and what we know of
the dynamics of the regional Moluccan system
suggests contact which goes back much further
than this, and which must have involved the
export of forest products.

The most important single factor affecting
Moluccan forests during the early period was
the rise in the international demand for spices,
which by the early sixteenth century had led to
the spread of production from the northern
to the central Moluccan islands. Expansion
and fluctuation in growing clove in particular
from this time onwards (Ellen 1985, 1987:
39–41) played a crucial role – both directly and
indirectly – in the lives of inland and coastal
peoples alike. Although there is no evidence
that the Nuaulu planted cloves or collected
wild cloves for sale until the twentieth century,

they did have an identifiable role in relations
with politically significant trading polities and
Europeans as early as the Dutch wars of the
late seventeenth century, as we know from the
VOC archives and from the *Landbeschrijving*
of Rumphius (Ellen 1988b: 118, 132n2). We
have a remarkably clear idea of the general
location of their settlements in the mountains
of central Seram from this time to the end of
the nineteenth century through oral histories,
corroborated by surface archaeology, botanical evidence and eighteenth century maps (Ellen
1978, Ellen 1993a: frontispiece). By the end of
the nineteenth century, most Nuaulu clans had
relocated around Sepa on the south coast
(Figure 17.1), largely as a result of Dutch pressure, though they have continued an essentially
highland, interior-oriented way of life down to
the present, relying on historic zones of extraction. In the eyes of official agents of the present
Indonesian government, other coastal peoples,
and in terms of their own self-definition, they
have never ceased being uplanders and people
of the forests.

During the twentieth century there has been
renewed clearance, on Seram as a whole, for
clove, nutmeg and other tree crops, such as
coconut, cacao and coffee. The seventies and
eighties have seen the expansion of market
participation and cash-cropping (of clove,
nutmeg and copra in particular), the planting
of fast-growing pulp trees, together with accelerated rates of land sale and forest extraction.
This has mainly taken place through logging
and in-migration, first spontaneous and then
official. Forest is being destroyed through
unplanned slash and burn cultivation by
non-indigenous pioneer settlers, and by the
expansion of transmigration settlements into
surrounding areas. There is no doubt that
rapid forest clearance of this kind is damaging,
and that long-standing swiddening practices
which modify the forest, increase its genetic
diversity and usefulness, and permit extraction
on a sustainable basis, are being eroded by
technological innovation, population pressure
and market forces. Local populations are
encouraged by government to deliberately cut
mature forest for cash crops, and commercial
estate plantations are spreading widely.
Logging is a particularly serious threat in the

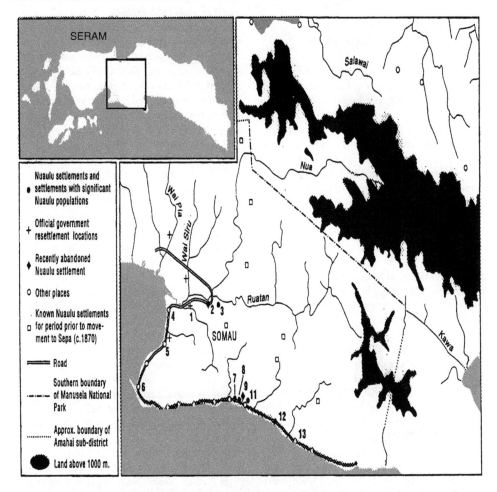

Figure 17.1 *The eastern part of the Amahai sub-district, Seram, showing historical, recent and present Nuaulu settlements, and other places mentioned in the text (as of 1994). The numbered locations are as follows (Nuaulu settlements in roman): 1. Wai Ruatan transmigation zone (kilo 5–kilo 11), 2. Simalouw (kilo 9), 3. Tahena Ukuna (kilo 12), 4. Makariki, 5. Masohi, 6. Amahai, 7. Bunara, 8. Watane, 9. Aihisuru, 10. Sepa, 11. Hahuwalan, 12. Rohua, 13. Tamilouw*

area where the Manusela National Park meets the Samal transmigration zone. Here and elsewhere so-called "selective" logging of *Shorea selanica* has led to water shortages, serious gully erosion and soil compaction. It has undermined existing forest ecology, resulting in more open canopy structures, *Macaranga* dominance, a greater proportion of dead wood, and herbaceous and *Imperata* invasions. In terms of fauna, there has been an

obvious reduction in game animals. These effects have been systematically inventoried in the Wahai area by Ian Darwin Edwards (1993: 9, 11), but it is instructive to compare his description with that provided in the Nuaulu text discussed later, and which is appended to this chapter. However, it has been transmigration and its various knock-on effects which – more than anything else – have been responsible for forest transformation.

Nuaulu Responses to Intrusion since 1970

The phasing and character of indigenous responses to the kinds of change I have highlighted have depended very much on local perceptions of government policy and on the ways in which law and policy are interpreted by officials and translated into action. It is now widely acknowledged, for example, that the Basic Agrarian Law of 1960 and the Basic Forestry Law of 1967 are fundamentally contradictory and overlapping, and are viewed differently by different government departments and in different situations. Sometimes they are used to defend the rights of indigenous peoples, but more often they override *adat*, legitimating the confiscation of land, and criminalising those local inhabitants who insist on asserting long-established rights of use (Colchester 1993: 75; Hurst 1990; MacAndrews 1986; Moniaga 1991; SKEPHI 1992; SKEPHI and Kiddell-Monroe 1993; Zerner 1990). Where there are doubts, national interest is invariably placed above local interests (Hardjono 1991: 9). Up until recently, Nuaulu have been beneficiaries of an, on the whole, advantageous interpretation of the law (Ellen 1993c), though as I go on to explain, this may now be changing.

During the period covered by my own fieldwork, the Nuaulu population has continued to grow dramatically: from 496 in 1971 to an estimated 1,256 in 1990. This has led to greater pressure on existing land, intensified by competition along the south Seram littoral with people from traditional non-Nuaulu villages, and due to unplanned immigration, mainly of Butonese. Growth along the south coast has been facilitated by the extension of a metalled road during the early 1980s. At about the same time the government began to establish transmigration settlements along the Ruatan valley (Figure 17.1).

The overtures by provincial government authorities to the Nuaulu with respect to these developments, were, at least initially, benign and paternalistic. In part they have been guided by the special administrative status of the Nuaulu as *masyarakat terasing* (Koentjaranin-grat 1993: 9–16; Persoon 1994: 65–7). Thus, local government officers (*camat, bupati*) have recognised uncut forest in the vicinity of transmigration settlements as "belonging" to the Nuaulu, following the widely-held view of many non-Nuaulu inhabitants of south Seram. They then encouraged them to move into one of the new transmigration zone settlements along the Ruatan river, at Simalouw (Figure 17.1), an area which abutted sago swamps long claimed and utilised by Nuaulu. Although by 1990 only the villages of Watane and Aihi-suru had moved permanently from their earlier locations on the south coast (about a quarter to one-third of all Nuaulu households), many Nuaulu established temporary dwellings, used the improved transport facilities to reach ancestral sago areas, and began to cut land for cash crop plantations. Moreover, two clans (Matoke-hanaie and Sonawe-ainakahata) moved even further inland, out of the original transmigration zone altogether to a place called Tahena Ukuna. Many Nuaulu saw these shifts as a return to traditional land, and for outsiders it confirmed Nuaulu status as upland forest peoples rather than lowland and coastal. Although Nuaulu had been located around the Muslim coastal domain of Sepa for the best part of one hundred years, and subject to the tutelage of its Raja, their self-image and the image of them held by non-Nuaulu, had never been otherwise. Moreover, implicit government recognition of Nuaulu preferential rights to over one-and-a-half thousand square kilometres enabled them to sell land in the Ruatan area to other incomers. This unusually positive approach was reflected in a successfully defended land claim in the courts at Masohi, the capital of Kabupaten Maluku Tengah.

The practical consequences of all this were alleviation of the growing pressure on Nuaulu land generally, and an opportunity to sell land along the more crowded south coast, most of which was sold to the inhabitants of Sepa itself and to incoming Butonese. This latter land, mainly old garden land and secondary forest, was a mixture of land gifted by the Raja of Sepa since the late nineteenth century, and land further inland which had always been regarded as Nuaulu. As I have argued elsewhere (Ellen 1993c), altogether, this created a

Laus =
Colonialism

rarely reported situation whereby an indigenous forest people appeared to be endorsing further forest destruction (both in the interior and along the south coast) by themselves and by others, for short-term gain.

Nuaulu cash incomes certainly increased through sale of land and trade with immigrants. Moreover, the practices which accompanied this were not dramatically contrary to any locally-asserted principles of indigenous ecological wisdom. However, there has recently been increased conflict with other autochthonous villages over rights to land, disenchantment with the effects of logging, and, since 1990, serious conflict with settlers resulting in convictions for the murders of two Saparuan migrants being brought against three residents of Rohua. This incident was widely reported in the local press, who made much of the manner of death (decapitation), and of removal of the heads back to the village and their burial near a *rumah adat*. The episode has understandably been viewed by some government officials and other observers as a reversion to head hunting, or confirmation that it had never ceased, though the protagonists themselves strenuously deny such interpretations. Whatever the case, this narrative amply highlights the fundamental ambiguity in the concept *masyarakat terasing*, seemingly indicating both the vulnerability of a people so labelled, their need of special protection and advancement by the state, as well as their primitive threatening character, which the state must subject and change. Either way, Nuaulu are frequently viewed as prime candidates for *pembangunan* (development) in its moral and ideological sense (Grzimek 1991: 263–83). Moreover, recent events reinforce a particularly pejorative local Ambonese stereotype of interior peoples as *Alifuru*, and have made it easier for the government to explicitly expropriate territory when the occasion arises.

How the Nuaulu have Changed their Environment

Conventional Western conceptions of nature are usually of some unaltered other, of wilderness; and conventional views of traditional peoples living on forest margins or biotopes, of tribes benignly extracting from an essentially pristine ecosystem. Such a view is, of course, now wholly unacceptable and there is mounting evidence of the ways in which humans dependent on forest actively change it. Much tropical lowland rainforest – in Indonesia as elsewhere – is the product of many generations of selective human interaction and modification (deliberate and inadvertent), optimising its usefulness and enhancing biodiversity. The outcome is a co-evolutionary process to which human populations are crucial. Indeed, particular patterns of forest extraction and modification are often seen as integral to its sustainable future. For some authorities, the evidence for intentional rather than serendipitous human influence is so compelling as to invite the description of "managed" forest (Clay 1988; Schmink, Redford and Padoch 1992: 7–8).

The empirical work supporting these claims comes mainly from the Amazon (e.g. Balée 1993, 1994; Posey 1988; Prance, Balée, Boom and Carneiro 1987); but there is emerging evidence that it also applies to large parts of Malaysia and the Western Indonesian archipelago (Aumeeruddy and Bakels 1994; Dove 1983; Maloney 1993; Peluso and Padoch 1996; Rambo 1979). My own work, supported by recent botanical research, suggests that it is no less true for the forests of Seram, which have long been a focus of subsistence extraction, and where human agency has had decisive consequences for ecology. This has been largely through the long-term impact of small-scale forest-fallow swiddening and the extraction of palm sago over many hundreds of years (Ellen 1988a), but also through the introduction and hunting of deer, selective logging and collection for exchange in more recent centuries (Ellen 1985:563). Since sago is a frequent reason for venturing into forest beyond the limits of the most distant gardens, and since it illustrates so well the kind of co-evolutionary relationship I have just been discussing, it is helpful to say a bit more about it here.

Sago (*Metroxylon sagu*) is currently extracted by Nuaulu both from extensive swamp forest reserves along major rivers and from planted groves much nearer to settlements. Certain swamp forest zones, such as at Somau, appear to have been continuously important for several hundred years, though smaller patches in the vicinity of the south coast villages may be the artifacts of more recent settlement histories. Smaller inland sago groves have been abandoned since coming to the coast, or are extracted from only occasionally.

Nuaulu manipulate vegetative reproduction of sago by replanting and protecting suckers from recently cut palms, selecting suckers from some palms rather than others, and transferring root stocks to village groves. The result is an interchange of genetic material between cultivated and "non-cultivated" areas, even though there is no particular evidence of domestication through selective planting of seeds. Although most reproduction of sago palms in the lowland riverine forest areas of Seram occurs quite independently of human interference, in certain areas human involvement is highly significant, and the contemporary phenotypes of Southeast Asian sago palms are best seen as the outcome of a long-term process of human-plant interaction. Indeed, the historic spread of *Metroxylon* from its assumed centres of dispersal in New Guinea or Maluku suggest very strongly anthropogenic factors. Ecologically, the heavy reliance placed by Nuaulu and other indigenous peoples of Seram on sago has, over some hundreds of years, reduced the necessity to cut forest for swiddens. This has an important bearing on Nuaulu changing conceptions of their environment, as we shall see.

The distribution of many other useful trees throughout the lowland forests of Seram reflects patterns of human modification, and serves as a convenient botanical indicator of settlement histories. Many are certain or probable domesticates and semi-domesticates. One of the most culturally salient of these is the *kenari (Canarium indicum = commune)*. This is found so widely in lowland areas, and in particular configurations, that its distribution must almost certainly be explained as a consequence of human interference, both motivated and inadvertent (Ian Edwards, personal communication). Kenari provides nuts rich in protein and essential oils, which are an impor-

tant ingredient in local diet, but which for the Nuaulu also have a salient symbolic role, the precise character of which I shall return to later.[2]

Nuaulu practices of swidden cultivation and movement have, over several centuries, altered the character of forest vegetation in measurable ways: increasing the proportion of useful species, increasing the numbers of stands of particular useful species, decreasing the proportion of easily-extracted timber trees against those which are resistant to extraction, creating patches of culturally productive forest in more accessible areas, and creating dense groves of fruit trees in old village sites. Many of the trees nowadays found in areas otherwise not obviously modified by humans represent species introduced historically, and even prehistorically, for their useful timber, fruits, and other properties (Ellen 1985). Indeed, approximately 78% of the 319 or more forest trees identified by the Nuaulu have particular human uses which make them potentially subject to manipulation through forms of protection and selective extraction. No wonder, then, that the distinctions between mature forest, different kinds and degrees of secondary regrowth and grove land are often difficult to establish. Although the contribution of non-agricultural activities, narrowly-defined, to overall Nuaulu energy expenditure and production is not to be under-estimated, and by comparison with other Indonesian swiddening peoples is rather high, my earlier contrast (Ellen 1975) between "domesticated" and "non-domesticated" resources was, in retrospect, drawn too starkly.

→Argument

Renegotiating Nature

My main argument in this chapter is that as different material and social changes have occurred – changes which have accelerated over the last 20 years – so Nuaulu have renegotiated their relationship with forest, and with "nature" more generally. How people conceptualise nature depends on how they use it, how they transform it, and how, in so doing, they invest knowledge in different parts of it. I have argued in another paper that concepts of nature have underlying pan-human cognitive roots, all people appearing to derive them from imperatives to identify "things" in their field of perception, situate these in terms of a calculus of self and other, and identify in discrete bits and aggregations essential inner properties (Ellen 1996). However, identifying these commonalities is not to deny that such concepts are everywhere ambiguous, intrinsically moral in character and a *condition* of knowledge (Strathern 1992: 194). Nature is not a *basic* category in the sense specified by Pascal Boyer (1993), and means different – often contradictory – things in different contexts. It is constantly being reworked as people respond to new social and environmental situations (Croll and Parkin: 1992: 16), and provides in the guise of something all-encompassing what I have elsewhere (Ellen 1986: 24) called a "theory of selective representations". Ambiguity itself, as Bloch (1974) has pointed out, can be socially useful. In the Nuaulu case there is an evident underlying tension between an oppositional calculus of forest and "village" or "house", and a non-oppositional calculus which draws much more on the lived experience of particular strategies of subsistence which unite what we loosely call nature and culture. Such an ambivalent conception of nature is wholly consistent with the difficulties faced in classifying the Nuaulu mode of subsistence according to conventional anthropological criteria (Ellen 1988a).

Before examining how these different concepts and their relative balance might be the outcome of a particular sequence of past events, and before highlighting contemporary patterns of change, it is necessary to sketch out in general terms the substance of the two apparently competing models or orientations. I do so on the basis of ethnographic data acquired by me at various times between 1970 and 1990. Since it is so obviously central, I start with the Nuaulu category of forest.

The Nuaulu use the term *wesie* to refer to forest of most kinds, but the term belies a complex categorical construction. Nuaulu relate to different parts of the forest – indeed to different species – in different ways. This mode of interaction is inimical to a concept of forest as some kind of void or homogeneous

entity, and certain parts require different responses and evince different conceptualisations. Some bits of forest are protected, others destroyed without thought. Forest is never experienced as homogeneous, but is much more of a combination (rather than a *mixture*) of different biotopes and patches. As such it well reflects the complex historical ecology which I referred to at the beginning of this paper. With its emphasis on human acculturation, it fits comfortably into a non-oppositional model of the kind we more usually associate with hunting and gathering peoples (Ingold 1996).

On the other hand, the generic term *wesie* exists, and is linked into general symbolic schemes such that it stands for some kind of conceptual exterior, a natural other. In some significant respects it is rather like the received twentieth-century English concept of nature. Although subject to degrees of effective control through practical and supernatural mastery, *wesie* is associated with essential qualities of danger and otherness, and opposed to an unmarked category of "culture", most palpably evident in – but certainly not restricted to – the category *numa*, "house". As such it is intricately linked with gender imagery (c.f. Valeri 1990). This forest : house : nature : culture logic is evident in a whole raft of rituals, and in the symbolic organisation of space. In some ways it is not what we might expect given Nuaulu lived subsistence, with its heavy reliance on extracting forest resources, where gardening is traditionally rudimentary, swiddening practised on a forest-fallow basis, where regenerated growth supplies many "forest" resources over the longer term, and where – consequently – there is a definite blurring of anthropogenic and other forest.

The two somewhat contradictory models we find with respect to forest are repeated at the level of interactions with specific parts of nature. Thus, Nuaulu are (and have been continuously so for many centuries) primarily vegetative rather than seed propagators, and most of their starchy garden crops are tubers (taro, manioc, yam, *Xanthosoma*). Such agricultural regimes are widely associated in the ethnographic literature with notions of continuity between nature and culture, in contrast to seed

[handwritten margin notes: "Nature"]

[handwritten note at bottom: "Non - Homogenous view of forest"]

propagators who tend to emphasise a sudden transition between nature and culture (Coursey 1978; Haudricourt 1962, 1964). In particular, Nuaulu place great practical and symbolic emphasis on sago palm starch extraction, and as we have seen, this species is ambiguously wild and domesticated. Such a view is reinforced by the highly reliable character of palm starch as a staple, with a stable output subject to little fluctuation, lack of economically significant pests (Flach 1976) and considerable potential as a food reserve. In these ways, not only does sago contrast with grain domesticates, but is superior to tubers such as yams and taro, and is, therefore, an even better symbol of the continuity between nature and culture.

Given that many "forest" trees show evidence of human manipulation, occur simultaneously in cultivated and uncultivated areas, and provide long-term supplies of particular resources without continuous human attention and susceptibility to hazard, they too reinforce the applicability of the non-oppositional model. However, "trees" are only homogeneous as a category if we ruthlessly simplify it to some common cognitive morphotype (woody, foliaceous, rigid). Different modes of extraction, use and characteristics involve different relationships with people, different social profiles and potential symbolic values. This often leads to classificatory patterns which appear to cut across conventional logics, and which are almost provocatively ambiguous. I have already indicated that two extremely important sources of food – the sago palm and the kenari tree – are ambiguous in terms of the forest : village (house) logic, and in terms of the unlabelled "nature/wild" and "culture/ tame" categories of which forest and house are, respectively, the most dominant expression. Both species show evidence of protodomestication, incipient cultivation, and their distribution is heavily affected by human use, despite the fact that they are for the most part culturally "of the forest" and reproduce without much human interference. The problem is accentuated by the symbolic complementarity of the two: sago is the everyday starch staple and the product of – almost always – male labour, while kenari is collected

for special festive occasions, when it is combined with sago by females to make *maiea* (Ellen and Goward 1984: 32). Thus, in certain contexts sago and kenari are linked together in opposition to products of the garden; in others they are contrasted in terms of an implicit gender distinction. Similarly, in the sphere of interaction with forest animals, I have (Ellen 1996: 116–18) been able to demonstrate how a single ritual associated with killing (*asumate*) can simultaneously reflect a perspective which stresses the unity of all living things, and one which stresses human opposition through killing (c.f. Wazir-Jahan Karim 1981: 188). Nature, I repeat, is not a basic category in the sense that it has a rooted perceptual salience, but though it may be symbolically deployed in radically different ways, it is still able to convey notions of logical primacy.

In developing a model which will help us understand how social and ecological changes have influenced Nuaulu conceptions and representations of forest and nature, we also need to recognise that in almost every instance this will have been motivated by an alteration in the character and intensity of relationships with non-Nuaulu, and how the Nuaulu deal with this socially. As I have indicated, ecological change has almost always been a consequence of exogenous factors: whether this involves the introduction of new species, outside appropriation of endemic resources or clearance of forest for extraction, or agriculture. But whenever there is an environmental interface of this kind, there is also a cultural and social one. Transfer of new cultigens is not just about the movement of genetic material, but of cultural knowledge as well, knowledge which always carries a social burden. Contact with outsiders, in particular, seldom involves actors operating on equal terms, and the relationship is always mediated by considerations of power and control. For their part, the Nuaulu repeatedly represent changes of all kinds in terms of the interplay of principles of opposition and continuity, complementarity and hierarchy[3], symbolic schemes as opposed to practical experiences, outside influence versus persisting tradition. To show how this might work, we can, I think, provisionally identify three historical periods which are likely to have been associated with somewhat different conceptualisations of the natural world: pre-European contact, the VOC and early colonial period until about 1880, 1880 to 1980, and 1980 to the present.

From what we can reconstruct of pre-European Nuaulu social organisation, clans appear to have occupied separate dispersed settlements and had considerable autonomy, entering into loose alliances only for the purpose of intermittent political negotiation and to manage hostilities with outsiders. Thus, that subsistence placed less stress on gardening than became the case later on was wholly in keeping with what we know of political arrangements. We might, therefore, expect here a concept of nature which focuses much more on the symbolic logic of vegetative propagation and the systematic harvesting of forest trees, and which involves a less oppositional conception of *wesie*. Moving around in forest is not conducive, after all, to developing an enduring opposition with it. Historically, we know gardening on Seram to be very underdeveloped, and even at the present time gardens are relatively unimportant in many areas, while in describing Nuaulu subsistence the distinction between "gathering" and "cultivation" is very fuzzy (Ellen 1988a: 117, 119, 123, 126–7). There is no new evidence, as yet, ethnobotanical or archaeological (Stark and Latinus 1992), to suggest that horticulture amongst the native peoples of Seram was once more important than it is now (c.f. Balée 1992), except the general ethnological observation that pioneer migrant Austronesian speakers, their linguistic if not directly genetic precursors, depended on domesticates, including – in all probability – seed cultigens (Blust 1976; Bellwood 1978: 141).

The new embeddedness in the world system which developed from the sixteenth century onwards opened up new pan-Pacific links, cut out intermediary connections, and intensified exchange with Oriental, Asiatic and European centres. It also had immediate economic consequences in terms of spice production, and longer term implications for subsistence ecology. With the introduction of maize, manioc, *Xanthosoma* and *Ipomea*, reliable garden yields increased making these cultigens competitive with sago in their reliability and superior in the effort required to harvest them. This appears to have led to a greater dependence on gardens (Ellen l988a: 123). Almost all the new garden crops were vegetatively propagated tubers, therefore sustaining a pre-existing conceptualisation of reproductive process and its metaphoric transformations; but they were also the harbingers of a longer-term process of decentering sago from people's conceptions of nature. Although sago is still culturally salient for the Nuaulu, amongst many present-day peoples of the central Moluccas sago (an indigenous crop) is nutritionally crucial but widely seen as inferior to (imported) rice. The same crops, because they decreased dependency on sago and other forest resources, encouraged greater emphasis on the symbolic opposition between gardens and forest. Increasing attention to cash-cropping, which both required high yield cultigens to offset the reduction of time and land available for subsistence extraction, and which provided opportunities to purchase – for example – rice, further accentuated this division.

The next major change came when the peripheral areas of Seram were formally drawn into the administrative system of the Dutch East Indies in the 1880s. From this time onwards environmental and social distinctions which had hitherto been implicit became underscored by administrative fiat. We have seen that from at least the late seventeenth century, the Nuaulu have had a distinct political identity in the eyes of outsiders. They had identifiable leaders, and were drawn into various alliances, always including Sepa. Indeed, this long history of interaction has made Nuaulu ultra-sensitive to questions of identity vis-à-vis other cultural groups, even though that identity has not always been reflected in any degree of permanent political centralisation. Formal incorporation into the Dutch administrative system, however, required that this identity and arrangement of traditional alliances of mutual advantage be regularised (Ellen 1988b: 118–19), both for administrative convenience and to provide the Nuaulu themselves with an effective channel of political communication. It is not therefore surprising that, at the time when the Nuaulu clans were relocating around Sepa, when Sepa was – in Dutch eyes – becoming administratively responsible for Nuaulu *rust, orde en belasting*, there emerges a line of Nuaulu *rajas*. This, in turn, changes the terms of the oppositional relationship between Nuaulu and Sepa into a more hierarchical one. Clans begin to lose some of their autonomy, even though the line of rajas effectively terminated after only a few generations. And ever since, the question of a Nuaulu raja and his possible reinstatement has been an issue which has periodically become the subject of heated debate, most recently at the time of the establishment of the Nuaulu presence at Simalouw. The same necessity for formal mechanisms to communicate with the holders of administrative power in Sepa, Amahai, Masohi, Amboina or Jakarta is reflected in Nuaulu involvement in rituals of the Indonesian state (Ellen 1988b).

Nuaulu movement to the coast meant a shift from a pattern of dispersed clan-hamlets and swiddens to concentrated multi-clan villages with large connected areas of garden land. This, in turn, led to a reconceptualisation of the forest : village (house) boundary, contrasting owned land (*wasi*) with unowned forest (*wesie*), and gardens (*nisi*) with uncleared forest (*wesie*); the first distinction juridical, the second technical. The changes in Nuaulu social relations of land use which accompanied this (Ellen 1977, 1993c) – land sale, cash-cropping, individualisation, permanent occupancy – emphasised still further a view of the natural world in which dualistic and contrastive properties predominated, even though sago continued to dominate their lives as their most important source of carbohydrate and as a cultural symbol.

So, it is at least plausible that the apparent contradiction between oppositional and non-oppositional models, the one more concordant with external relations of exchange, the other with internal subsistence experience, is a dialectical function of a particular transitional history. It might also be connected with the historic emphasis on exchange of valuables for forest products (see above, and Ellen 1988a), and the influence and internalisation of Austronesian symbolic schemes otherwise more

amenable to seed-cultivation. Whatever the case, the balance is tipping in favour of an emergent, more oppositional, reified concept of "forest/nature". Amongst the coastal peoples of Seram (such as the inhabitants of Sepa) the enduring perception of the Nuaulu has been of a forest people – the opposite of themselves. Forest is a much stronger exteriority for coastal Muslims than it has traditionally been for animist Nuaulu, but it is towards this view that the Nuaulu are now progressing. Similarly, the Dutch colonial government, and thereafter the Indonesian government, created forest as a strong official category, establishing bureaucracies to manage it, a component in a wider state administrative division of labour which encouraged implicit linkages between the geographical designation of forest and the social category *masyarakat terasing*.

Moreover, as forest has been reduced in extent, so its representation as some kind of ether in which humans are suspended has been transformed into a much more restricted environmental category, as just one ever-diminishing part of a wider non-afforested dwelling space. Not only does the small size of Moluccan islands make the forest more vulnerable physically, but also, as forest disappears, so it is reconceived as a fundamentally limited, rather than limitless, good. Thus, both material experience of environmental change and the necessity to participate in a state level of discourse are reifying Nuaulu concepts of forest, just as environmental degradation and the ecological movement have done in the West. In order to protect their own lives, Nuaulu find themselves adopting the discourse of officialdom and national politics, responding to agendas dictated by the state. From a history of commitment to environmental change, they have now adopted a rhetoric which we would recognise as broadly "environmentalist".

New Rhetorics and Rapid Social Change

What I have in mind by this new Nuaulu conception of nature and its relation to a more reflexive, globally-situated understanding of their own identity, is well exemplified by two empirical cases: the first is a video-recording (cassette 90-2, 8-3-90) which I was asked to make by the people of Rohua in 1990 and which was prompted by Nuaulu concerns of state non-recognition of their religion; the second is a text recorded and transcribed in 1994 by Rosemary Bolton addressed as a personal appeal to me.

The first – the video-recording – consists of three parts, all of which refer to performances which occurred on 8 March. The first is a formal address given by Komisi Soumori (the kepala kampung and most senior secular clan head). It is an impassioned assertion of the legitimacy of Nuaulu core beliefs, showing how many Nuaulu believe their cultural identity to be, quite literally, "rooted" in land, forest and sago. The spoken words and the visual imagery used (and this would be well understood by the local Nuaulu witnessing the event) evoke – though not explicitly – widely-shared mythologies of origin. All this is unashamedly broadcast to an outside, unseen, audience. What is significant about the event is in part its presentation: it is given in Nuaulu, because to speak of such things in any other language is to deny Nuauluness, but also because Komisi is most comfortable in Nuaulu. But the oratorical style and the physical props – rostrum etc. – indicate the acceptance that discourse should assume formats appropriate to engagement with the state, and a notion that it is possible to communicate with an unseen audience, not indirectly through a human mediator, but directly employing an electronic medium to which they have only recently had access. The second part is a short dramatic performance by adolescents about discrimination against Nuaulu customs and religion at school and in the labour market. This is conducted entirely in terms of the kind of performance rhetoric which is, again, associated with government institutions, and which is, appropriately, spoken in Indonesian – the language of the state. Paradoxically, such conventions (and the education through which they are acquired) inevitably result in the further attrition of Nuaulu distinctiveness as perceived by non-Nuaulu, and perhaps the eventual disappearance of certain cultural

markers which were once salient. This is, of course, not to rule out the likelihood that Nuaulu "cultural identity" is anyway in transformation, subject to continual re-negotiation, and might emerge as strong as ever, but in a slightly different guise. The third part of the video-recording is a speech by the *ia onate* (*kepala*) *pemuda*, Sonohue Soumori, again in Indonesian, which pulls the various themes together. Such reflections can also be cast in a more traditional idiom, such as the *kepata arariranae* (a ritual verse form associated with male-female tug-of-war) and *kepata Sepa* (a ritual verse form associated with workplace routines and domestic relaxation), though on this occasion they were not.

The transcribed text, the English language version of which is provided here as an appendix, is a rather different kind of document. It was dictated by a long-standing acquaintance to Rosemary Bolton, and is separated in time from the 1990 performance by the harrowing events of 1993 in the Ruatan transmigration area, to which I have already referred. These events are structurally significant in Nuaulu representations of themselves because an attempt to defend legitimate interests resulted in defeat. The rugged independence and assertiveness so typical of the 1970s and 1980s, and so well exemplified in the 1990 videotaped events, has – it would seem – been replaced by a new quiescence and passivity: "we are quiet and obeying them" (section 5). From a position in which Nuaulu saw themselves negotiating *with* the Indonesian state, they are now simply citizens *of* that same state. There is an acceptance that events are no longer under their own control, that they can no longer take them or leave them. As it happens, Nuaulu have a history of accommodating certain kinds of pragmatic change. This may explain their cultural survival, when most other groups of tribal animists on Seram have all but disappeared. But Nuaulu now claim not to want anything to do with the outside agents of change: government or logging companies. There is a realisation that the government does not keep its promises (7).

We can also see from this text how it is that the rapidity of environmental change has forced the Nuaulu to redefine their relationship with the natural world, to see connections between microclimatic change, deforestation and erosion, and game depletion; between land clearance, river flow, impacting caused by logging vehicles, and fish depletion. We can see in it how Nuaulu now identify their forest as a whole as a commodity, something which has exchange value, when previously it was inalienable. We find an equation between big trees and profit (5, 6), and governmental prohibition on sale. To begin with, Nuaulu accepted the advantages brought by the lumber companies: vehicles used the tracks and kept them clear, the tracks and trucks facilitated hunting (1, 2). We also find recognition that replacement of large stands is in a time scale that is beyond the use of Nuaulu, that sustainable use has been superseded by something which Nuaulu would never seek to sustain (6), that old secondary forest, based on the cutting of patches and individual stands (Ellen 1985) has been replaced by wholesale clearance, which results in quite different patterns of regeneration, including more noxious vegetation (e.g. thorns). And the blame for these changes is placed quite squarely at the feet of logging companies and the state.

So, recent Nuaulu reworking of their conceptions and responses to those things which we designate as "nature", show that the patronage of various government departments, levels of organisation, and types of parastatal agency, as well as official categories, are no less central to an understanding of what is going on at the forest frontier than they are for lowland agrarian processes (c.f. Hart 1989: 31). "Bringing the state into the analysis . . . entails understanding how power struggles at different levels of society are connected with one another and related to access to and control over resources" (Hart 1989: 48). As the forest frontier reproduces the inequalities of the wider state and its economically dominant groups, and as short-term production for use arises and is sustained by production for exchange (Gudeman 1988: 216), as Nuaulu move from being semi-independent "tribesmen", relying on sago and non-domesticated forest resources, to being dependent peasant farmers, increasingly reliant on introduced

cultigens and cash crops, so their conceptions of nature reflect this. There is, in an important sense, an ecological, economic and conceptual continuity between forest modification and farming, and redefining forest extraction as a kind of farming may help us appreciate its similarities with the agrarian process.

In the Nuaulu case, intensification of subsistence agriculture, cash-cropping, forest extraction, commercial logging and transmigration combine to threaten an existing relationship with the forest. But Nuaulu attitudes have always been tactical, depending on their perceived material interests, and it is therefore not surprising that their conceptualisations of nature should mirror this. Their initial response to forest destruction and consequent land settlement reflected perceived advantages in terms of a traditional model of forest interaction, based on implicit notions of sustainability of reproductive cycles of tree growth and animal populations. When this logic failed, complacency was replaced by uncertainty and bewilderment, eventually translating into hostility and decisive actions to defend their subsistence interests. Punitive actions taken by the state in response to this have engendered further uncertainty and bewilderment.

Conclusion

What I have tried to demonstrate in this chapter is that there is a connection between shifting Nuaulu constructions and representations of nature (particularly of environmental change), their social identity and the way they interact with the outside world.

There is nothing intrinsically problematic about environmental change for the Nuaulu. As we have seen, their cultural history is full of it. There is no overarching "ecocosmology" or "cosmovision" which rules it to be culturally illegitimate. Indeed, during the early phase of transmigration and logging in the 1980s, it was regarded wholly positively. What we need to recognise, however, is that there are different kinds of environmental change. The crucial distinctions here are between change which you can control, and change which is outside your control (and more specifically, is controlled by outsiders); and between change which is readily recognised as bearing unacceptable detrimental risks and that which is not so recognised. In terms of both distinctions it is the *scale* of change which provokes direct or delayed political responses and conceptual rejigging. The older, local, embedded forms of knowledge which underpin Nuaulu subsistence strategies are qualitatively different from knowledge of higher-order processes, "environmental consciousness" in the abstract, which only comes with a widening of political and ecological horizons to a national and global level. In some ways this process is similar to how articulate Nuaulu have come to re-conceptualise their ritual practice as *agama* (religion), and their distinct way of life as *kebudayaan* (culture); agama, kebudayaan, *lingkungan hidup* (living space, milieu, environment) are – in Indonesian officialese – secondary abstractions of a comparable order. Forest, they now understand, is subject to pressures of in-migration, expropriation and economic exploitation in many places other than their own.

This quasi-global[4] consciousness is no better symbolised than by the arrival of electronic means of communication in Nuaulu villages, first radio and then television. Television has not only enabled Nuaulu to keep in touch with the world by watching English league soccer matches and Thomas Cup badminton, but – and this is the reflexive twist – to watch David Attenborough eulogise tropical rainforest in its death throes. Despite a long history of interaction with outsiders of various origins, changing patterns of environmental modification, patterns of subsistence and the conceptual modulation of these things, it is the major changes associated with cultural globalisation which have forced a really radical response from them. It could be said that the aggressive individualism of the 1980s, the selling of land and market engagement, represented both the end of an old small-scale conception of nature in which resources and forest are infinite, and the beginning of a new conception of participation in an open global ecology of limited goods. The changes, therefore, are a response to a different problematic, to a different social and political agenda, rather than a rejection of environmental change itself or an a priori endorsement of ecological holism. Nuaulu constructions of environment are changing to accommodate a new *level* of discourse, and it is no coincidence that those who currently complain that their schooled children are unable to obtain appropriate employment in the Indonesian state because they are told that the doctrine of *Pancasila* is an impediment, also – though paradoxically – adopt an environmentalist rhetoric which seeks to keep the state from their land.

APPENDIX: THE CONSEQUENCES OF DEFORESTATION – A NUAULU TEXT FROM ROHUA, SERAM, 1994

1. About we Nuaulu people. Our own government here in Indonesia allowed large lumber companies to come here looking for timber. Like *onia* [Malay *kayu meranti, Shorea* spp.]. So they leveled the tops of mountains, digging them all up. At the heads of rivers they cut down *punara* [*Octomeles sumatrana*] trees, they cut down onia along the edges of rivers, vehicles leveled and filled in the heads of rivers. While they lived here it was still good. We got around well because they were working.

2. Vehicles went up and down the roads so they were clear. Or if we went hunting we rode on their vehicles with them. But when they went home, our roads were covered up, trees started to grow on them and then we couldn't travel about well because when it rained landslides covered the roads. Game animals moved far away as did cuscus. Land slid into the rivers because they cut down the big trees along the edges of the rivers.

3. Therefore we are really suffering because we have to go around the roads. Before they came here we knew when it was

rainy season and when it was dry season. But when they leveled our lands and rivers here in our forest it wasn't the same when it rained and when it was sunny. It was sunny all the time so land slid into all the rivers. Therefore we do not feed good because it is no longer like before.

4. Before, the rivers flowed well and the sun shone well so they looked good to us. But now that the vehicles leveled them so much the fish in the rivers and the game animals in the forest have moved far away. They electrocuted all the fish in the rivers so there are no more fish. So where can we look for our food? Even if we look for our food in rivers that are far away we do not find any fish. We do not find any game animals. The deer have moved far away.

5. Therefore we want to ask for money to cover the price of our forest but the government in Masohi and Amahai forbid us from doing so. So we are quiet and are obeying them. But because of our village and forest we are suffering. We suffer when it is so difficult to go to our forest and look for our food because they leveled all the rivers. They leveled all the mountains. The rivers do not flow well. It is difficult to find game animals. Therefore, we do not feel well about this.

6. They destroyed the lands and rivers. They took away all the big trees. They sold them and made a profit but they did not give any of it to us. Therefore the Nuaulu elders do not want anything to do with them because they did not think of us. We let them take the wood because they said that they would plant new trees to replace those they cut down. But when will those trees grow? They will never grow like the trees before. How will they grow like those big trees? And when will they plant the trees to replace them? It will be a long time before those little trees are big.

7. Therefore the elders do not want anything to do with them because the lumber companies came here making things dif-

ficult for us with our forest. Our lands and rivers are no good at all. They have been gone a long time like the Filipinos. When we go to the river Lata Nuaulu or Lata Tamilou we have to cut the thorns that have grown with our machetes until we are almost dead because they block the path. If it rains just a little there are landslides cutting off the path and then we have to go far around them before we can find a straight path. Therefore, we are suffering a lot just because of this.

8. Therefore if there is any help or any word that can be given here in Indonesia that would help the officials here in Indonesia. Help quickly so that they will not agree that all our lands, rivers, and trees be taken. So the heads of rivers would not be leveled so we cannot eat well or find food well.

9. We people find our food in the forest. There are a lot of Nuaulu people who do not fish well so they look for food in the forest. This is just us Nuaulu people. Other people look for food and have a lot of people who fish but there are only a few of us who fish. Therefore these people look for food but do not find it. We are all dead from hunger [hyperbole]. Before the lumber companies came we got around well. We found food well because the deer slept nearby, pigs lived nearby, and cassowaries lived nearby. But when they leveled and destroyed these animals' places and caves they ran away. So it is very hard for the Nuaulu people to find food because they chased away all the pigs and deer so that they are now far away.

10. Therefore if Roy (Ellen) can find a little help and wants to talk to the officials here in Indonesia I ask that he help us a little so that they do not come here and work again. We do not want them to because we are already suffering a lot.
   That is all.

[Text recorded and translated by Rosemary Bolton, 1994.]

NOTES

1. Lowland is used here to refer to a forest type generally dominated by the dipterocarp *Shorea selanica*, in contrast to the montane vegetation of higher altitudes. In fact, the lowland forest of Seram covers, on the whole, hilly country and may extend to an altitude of some 1,000 meters.

2. Another striking case of human management of forest trees (though not one which I have observed in the Nuaulu area) is reported by Soedjito *et al.* (1986) for higher altitude forests in west Seram. Here, seedlings of the resin-producing *Agathis dammara*, important as a source of cash, are systematically planted to replace older, less productive, trees.

3. Nuaulu symbolically represent their relations with outsiders, dialectically, in two ways: in terms of relations of complementarity, and in terms of hierarchy. The first is exemplified in the relationship between most local clans, in *pela* partnerships (that is between individuals linked through historical blood siblinghoods between villages) and through common membership of the *patalima* grouping (Valeri 1986). The second is reflected in their relations with Sepa and the Indonesian state. Here they manage to assert, simultaneously, a mythic superiority (usually expressed in the conventional older-younger sibling metaphor) and a pragmatic political submissiveness. The articulation of the two principles, however, is on their terms. They insist that they are prepared to accept the benefits of a good raja, but equally prepared to withdraw into their own autonomy when it suits them.

4. I use the term "quasi-global" to avoid any accusation that Nuaulu consciously conceive of themselves as global actors and consumers in the sense which has entered the consciousness of many in the West. It would be more accurate to say that they have become increasingly conscious of the degree of connectedness between their lives and those in remote places with whom they share common experiences (such as televised football matches) and material products (such as cassette players).

REFERENCES

Aumeeruddy, Y. and J. Bakels. (1994). "Management of a sacred forest in the Kerinci valley, central Sumatra: an example of conservation of biological diversity and its cultural basis". *Journal d'Agriculture Tropicale et de Botanique Appliquée*, 36(2), 39–65.

Balée, W. (1992). "People of the fallow: a historical ecology of foraging in lowland south America" in *Conservation of neotropical forests: working from traditional resource use*, edited by K.H. Redford and C. Padoch, pp. 35–57. New York: Columbia University Press.

——. (1993). "Indigenous transformation of Amazonian forests: an example from Maranao, Brazil". *L'Homme*, 33(2–4), 231–54.

——. (1994). *Footprints of the forest: Ka'apor ethnobotany – the historical ecology of plant utilization by an Amazonian people.* New York: Columbia University Press.

Bellwood, P. (1978). *Man's conquest of the Pacific: the prehistory of southeast Asia and Oceania.* London: Collins.

Bloch, M. (1974). "Symbols, song, dance and features of articulation: is religion an extreme form of traditional authority?" *European Journal of Sociology*, 15(1), 55–81.

Blust, R. (1976). "Austronesian culture history: some linguistic inferences and their relations to the archaeological record". *World Archaeology*, 8(1), 19–43.

Boyer, P. (1993). *Cognitive aspects of religious symbolism.* Cambridge: Cambridge University Press.

Clay, J.W. (1988). *Indigenous peoples and tropical forests.* New York: Cultural Survival Inc.

Colchester, Marcus. (1993). "Forest peoples and sustainability" in *The struggle for land*

and the fate of the forests, edited by Marcus Colchester and Larry Lohmann, pp. 61–95. Penang, Malaysia: World Rainforest Movement, The Ecologist, Zed Books.

Coursey, D.G. (1978). "Some ideological considerations relating to tropical root crop production" in *The adaptation of traditional agriculture: socio-economic problems of urbanisation*, edited by E.K. Fisk, pp. 131–41. Development Studies Centre Monogr. 11. Canberra: Australian National University.

Croll, E. and D. Parkin. (1992). "Cultural understandings of the environment" in *Bush base: forest farm : culture, environment and development*, edited by E. Croll and D. Parkin, pp. 11–36. London: Routledge.

Dove, M.R. (1983). "Theories of swidden agriculture and the political economy of ignorance". *Agroforestry Systems*, 1(3), 85–99.

Edwards, I.D. (1993). "Introduction" in *Natural history of Seram, Maluku, Indonesia*, edited by I.D. Edwards, A.A. Macdonald and J. Proctor, pp. 1–12. Andover: Intercept.

Ellen, R.F. (1975). Non-domesticated resources in Nuaulu ecological relations". *Social Science Information*, 14(5), 51–61.

——. (1977). "Resource and commodity: problems in the analysis of the social relations of Nuaulu land use". *Journal of Anthropological Research*, 33, 50–72.

——. (1985). "Patterns of indigenous timber extraction from Moluccan rain forest fringes". *Journal of Biogeography*, 12, 559–87.

——. (1986). "Microcosm, macrocosm and the Nuaulu house: concerning the reductionist fallacy as applied to metaphorical levels". *Bijdragen tot de Taal-, Land- en Volkenkunde*, 142(1), 1–30.

——. (1988a). "Foraging, starch extraction and the sedentary lifestyle in the lowland rainforest of central Seram" in *History, evolution and social change in hunting and gathering societies*, edited by J. Woodburn, T. Ingold and D. Riches, pp. 117–34. London: Berg.

——. (1988b). "Ritual, identity and the management of interethnic relations on Seram" in *Time past, time present, time future:* *essays in honour of P. E. de Josselin de Jong*, edited by D.S. Moyer and H.J.M. Claessen, Verhandelingen van het Koninklijk Instituut voor Taal-, Landen Volkenkunde 131, pp. 117–35. Dordrecht-Holland, Providence-U.S.A.: Foris.

——. (1993a). *Nuaulu ethnozoology: a systematic inventory of categories*. CSAC Monogr. 6. Centre for Social Anthropology and Computing and Centre for Southeast Asian Studies: University of Kent at Canterbury.

——. (1993b). "Human impact on the environment of Seram" in *Natural history of Seram, Maluku, Indonesia*, edited by I.D. Edwards, A.A. Macdonald and J. Proctor, pp. 191–205. Andover: Intercept.

——. (1993c). "Rhetoric, practice and incentive in the face of the changing times: a case study of Nuaulu attitudes to conservation and deforestation" in *Environmentalism: the view from anthropology*, edited by K. Milton, pp. 126–43. London: Routledge.

——. (1996). "The cognitive geometry of nature: a contextual approach" in *Nature and society: anthropological perspectives*, edited by G. Pálsson and P. Descola, pp. 103–23. London: Routledge.

Ellen, R.F. and N.J. Goward. (1984). "Papeda dingin, papeda dingin . . . Notes on the culinary uses of palm sago in the central Moluccas". *Petits Propos Culinaires*, 16, 28–34.

Flach, M. (1976). "Yield potential of the sago-palm and its realisation" in *Sago-76: First international sago symposium: the equatorial swamp as a natural resource*, edited by K. Tan, pp. 157–77. Kuala Lumpur: Kemajuan Kanji.

Grzimek, Benno R. (1991). *Social change on Seram: a study of ideologies of development in eastern Indonesia*. Thesis submitted for the Degree of Doctor of Philosophy: London School of Economics and Political Science, University of London.

Gudeman, Stephen. (1988). "Frontiers as marginal economies" in *Production and autonomy: anthropological studies and critiques of development*, edited by John W. Bennett and John R. Bowen, Monographs in Economic Anthropology 5, pp. 213–16. Lanham: University Press of America.

Hardjono, J. (1991). "The dimensions of Indonesia's environmental problems" in *Indonesia: resources, ecology and environment,* edited by J. Hardjono, pp. 1–16. Oxford: Oxford University Press.

Hart, G. (1989). "Agrarian change in the context of state patronage" in *Agrarian transformations: local processes and the state in Southeast Asia,* edited by G. Hart, A. Turton and B. White, pp. 31–49. Berkeley: University of California Press.

Haudricourt, André. (1962). "Domestication des animaux, culture des plantes et traitement d'autrai". *L'Homme,* 2(1), 40–50.

——. (1964). "Nature et culture dans la civilsations de l'igname: l'origine des clones et des clans". *L'Homme,* 4(1), 93–104.

Hurst, P. (1990). *Rainforest politics: ecological destruction in southeast Asia.* London: Zed Books.

Ingold, T. (1996). "Hunting and gathering as ways of perceiving the environment" in *Redefining nature: ecology, culture and domestication,* edited by R. Ellen and K. Fukui, pp. 117–55. Oxford, New York: Berg.

Karim, W.A. (1981). "Mah Betisek concepts of humans, plants and animals". *Bijdragen tot de Taal-, Land- en Volkenkunde,* 137, 135–60.

Koentjaraningrat. (1993). "Pendahuluan" in *Masyarakat terasing di Indonesia,* edited by Koentjaraningrat, Seri Etnographi Indonesia 4, pp. 1–18. Jakarta: Gramedia Pustaka Utama.

MacAndrews, C. (1986). *Land policy in modern Indonesia.* Boston: Lincoln Institute of Land Policy.

Maloney, B.K. (1993). "Climate, man and thirty thousand years of vegetation change in north Sumatra". *Indonesian Environmental History Newsletter,* 2, 3–4.

Moniaga, S. (1991). "Toward community-based forestry and recognition of adat property rights in the outer islands of Indonesia" in *Voices from the field: Fourth Annual Social Forestry Writing Workshop,* edited by J. Fox, O. Lynch, M. Zimsky and E. Moore, pp. 113–33. Honolulu: East-West Center.

Peluso, N. and C. Padoch. (1996). "Changing resource rights in managed forests of West Kalimantan" in *Borneo in transition: people, forests, conservation and development,* edited by C. Padoch and N. Peluso. Kuala Lumpur: Oxford University Press.

Persoon, G.A. (1994). *Vluchten of Veranderen: processen van verandering en ontwikkeling bij tribale groepen in Indonesie.* Leiden: Riksuniversiteit te Leiden, Faculteit der Sociale Wetenschappen.

Posey, Darrell. (1988). "Kayapo Indian natural-resource management" in *People of the tropical rainforest,* pp. 89–90. Berkeley: University of California Press.

Prance, Ghillean T., William Balée, B.M. Boom and Robert L. Carneiro. (1987). "Quantitative ethnobotany and the case for conservation in Amazonia". *Conservation Biology,* 1, 296–310.

Rambo, A. Terry. (1979). "Primitive man's impact on genetic resources of the Malaysian tropical rainforest". *Malaysian Applied Biology,* 8(1), 59–65.

Schmink, M., K.H. Redford and C. Padoch. (1992). "Traditional peoples and the biosphere: framing the issues and defining the terms" in *Conservation of neotropical forests: working from traditional resource use,* edited by K.H. Redford and C. Padoch, pp. 3–13. New York: Columbia University Press.

SKEPHI and R. Kiddell-Monroe. (1993). "Indonesia: land rights and development" in *The struggle for land and the fate of the forests,* edited by M. Colchester and L. Lohmann, pp. 228–63. Penang, Malaysia: World Rainforest Movement.

SKEPHI (1992). "Logging and the sinking island". *Inside Indonesia,* 33, 23–5.

Soedjito, H., A. Suyanto and B. Sulaeman. (1986). *Sumber daya alam di pulau Seram Barat, Propinsi Maluku.* Jakarta: Lembaga Biologi Nasional.

Stark, Ken and Kyle Latinus. (1992). "Research report: the archaeology of sago economies in central Maluku". *Cakalele: Maluku Research Journal,* 3, 69–86.

Strathern, Marilyn. (1992). *After nature: English kinship in the late twentieth century.* Cambridge: Cambridge University Press.

Valeri, V. (1989). "Reciprocal centers: the Siwa-Lima system in the central Moluccas" in *The attraction of opposites*, edited by D. Maybury-Lewis and U. Almagor, pp. 117–41. Ann Arbor: University of Michigan Press.

Valeri, V. (1990). "Both nature and culture: reflections on menstrual and parturitional taboos in Huaulu (Seram)" in *Power and difference: gender in island Southeast Asia,* edited by J.M. Atkinson and S. Errington, pp. 235–72. Stanford, California: Stanford University Press.

Zerner, C. (1990). *Community rights, customary law and the law of timber concessions in Indonesia's forests: legal options and alternatives in designing the commons.* Jakarta: FAO Forestry Studies TF/INS/065.

18

Articulating Indigenous Identity in Indonesia: Resource Politics and the Tribal Slot

Tania Murray Li

[handwritten: → Erasure of INDG PPLs]

[handwritten right margin: → The 'slot']

It was the official line of Suharto's regime that Indonesia is a nation which has no indigenous people, or that all Indonesians are equally indigenous.[1] The internationally recognized category "indigenous and tribal peoples" (as defined in International Labour Organization convention 169) has no direct equivalent in Indonesia's legal system, nor are there reservations or officially recognized tribal territories. Under Suharto the national motto "unity in diversity" and the displays of Jakarta's theme park, Taman Mini, presented the acceptable limits of Indonesia's cultural difference, while development efforts were directed at improving the lot of "vulnerable population groups," including those deemed remote or especially backwards. The desire for development was expressed by rural citizens through the approved channels of bottom-up planning processes and supplications to visiting officials. National activists and international donors who argued for the rights of indigenous people were dismissed as romantics imposing their primitivist fantasies upon poor folk who wanted, or should have wanted, to progress like "ordinary" Indonesians. Nevertheless, a discourse on indigenous people took hold in activist circles in the final years of Suharto's rule, and its currency in the Indonesian coun-tryside is still increasing. With the new political possibilities opened up in the post-Suharto era, now seems an appropriate time to reflect on how Indonesia's indigenous or tribal slot is being envisioned, who might occupy it, and with what effects.[2]

[handwritten right margin: → Li engaged in a comparativo study]

A comparative perspective stimulated this inquiry, and forms its focus. My attention was drawn by the contrast between two locations in the hilly interior of Central Sulawesi.[3] In earlier centuries, these two locations were inhabited by rather similar people: scattered swidden farmers loosely organized into family groups, threatened by slave raiders and by sometimes hostile neighbours, and involved in important but tense and unstable trade and tribute relationships with coastal powers. Today, one of these regions is peopled by prosperous, literate, Christian farmers growing irrigated rice and coffee, whose children aspire to government jobs, while in the other, very few people can read or speak the national language, swidden cultivation is the norm, housing and nutrition are poor, and livelihoods and health precarious. Yet it is in the former location – Lake Lindu – that a collective, indigenous identity has been persuasively articulated. The immediate context of this articulation was a national and international campaign to

[handwritten bottom: Context of articulation]

oppose the construction of a hydro-power plant at the lake, but the preconditions which enabled it have deep historical roots. In the Lauje area, by contrast, while no one would question that the hill farmers are the original inhabitants of their land, the specificity of their identity has not been made explicit, nor does it serve to conjoin local projects to national or global ones.

The comparison of these two locations raises a political problem. In view of the still-powerful official line that indigenous people are figments of an NGO imagination unduly influenced by imported ideas, the contrast between the two sites could be taken to imply that the indigenous identity articulated at Lindu has been adopted strategically – that it is opportunistic and inauthentic. Mention of the "invention of tradition" presents a similar risk. So too might academic discussions of ethnic identity framed in individualist terms, which seem to suggest that maximizing, goal-oriented "actors" switch or cross boundaries in pursuit of their ends, approaching questions of identity in consumer terms, as a matter of optimal selection. Equally problematic from another perspective are theoretical positions which might suggest that one or other of the groups is suffering from false consciousness: the Lindu perhaps for articulating a tribal position rather than one defined in class terms, or the Lauje for their apparent failure to mobilize at all.

My goal in this article is to set out an alternative approach to the question of indigenousness that is theoretically more adequate to the diversity of conditions and struggles in the Indonesian countryside, and alert to the political risks and opportunities posed by particular framings. I use the terms "indigenous" and "tribal" interchangeably in my general discussions, while drawing attention to nuances in the deployment of these terms and the meanings they invoke in particular contexts. For reasons of history and social structure which I discuss later, anthropologists have not tended to use the term "tribe" in reference to Indonesia, and legal scholars (e.g., Kingsbury 1998) are uncertain about whether the term "indigenous people," framed in the context of white settler colonies, fits the Asian scenario.[4]

But these are mobile terms which have been reworked and inflected as they have traveled, and as they have been used to engage with, and envision alternatives to, the models of development promoted by Indonesia's New Order regime. They have taken on new meanings in relation to quite specific fields of power.

My argument is that a group's self-identification as tribal or indigenous is not natural or inevitable, but neither is it simply invented, adopted, or imposed. It is, rather, a *positioning* which draws upon historically sedimented practices, landscapes, and repertoires of meaning, and emerges through particular patterns of engagement and struggle. The conjunctures at which (some) people come to identify themselves as indigenous, realigning the ways they connect to the nation, the government, and their own, unique tribal place, are the contingent products of agency and the cultural and political work of *articulation*. Other conjunctures have a different resonance, but are no less political in character. The Lauje who do not currently see themselves in the "indigenous peoples" slot nevertheless engage with routine, everyday forms of power. This point is important because one of the risks that stems from the attention given to indigenous people is that some sites and situations in the countryside are privileged while others are overlooked, thus unnecessarily limiting the field within which coalitions could be formed and local agendas identified and supported.

The concepts of articulation and positioning, which I draw from Stuart Hall, are central to my analysis, and I discuss them in the next section. I then go on to describe the fields of power within which the discourse on indigenous people is taking shape in Indonesia, focusing upon the ways in which government departments and NGOs characterize, and seek to transform, the rural populace of frontier spaces potentially envisaged as indigenous or tribal. Following this I explore the historical and contemporary processes at work in the formation of collective identities in the two study areas, seeking the reasons why the discourse on indigenous people has taken hold in one place but not another. Finally, I discuss issues of risk and opportunity, indicating what is at stake for those who might occupy Indonesia's tribal slot, as well as for those who seek to support their struggles and frame alternatives to the New Order development regime.

Articulation and Positioning

Stuart Hall alerts us to the dual meaning of the term "articulation." It is the process of rendering a collective identity, position, or set of interests explicit (articulate, comprehensible, distinct, accessible to an audience), and of conjoining (articulating) that position to definite political subjects. For Hall,

An articulation is . . . the form of the connection that *can* make a unity of two different elements, under certain conditions. It is a linkage which is not necessary, determined, absolute and essential for all time. You have to ask under what circumstances *can* a connection be forged or made? So the so-called 'unity' of a discourse is really the articulation of different, distinct elements which can be rearticulated in different ways because they have no necessary 'belongingness.' The 'unity' which matters is a linkage between that articulated discourse and the social forces with which it can, under certain historical conditions, but need not necessarily, be connected. Thus, a theory of articulation is both a way of understanding how ideological elements come, under certain conditions, to cohere together within a discourse, and a way of asking how they do or do not become articulated, at specific conjunctures, to certain political subjects . . . [It] asks how an ideology discovers its subject rather than how the subject thinks the necessary and inevitable thoughts which belong to it; it enables us to think how an ideology empowers people, enabling them to begin to make some sense or intelligibility of their historical situation, without reducing those forms of intelligibility to their socio-economic or class location or social position (1996:141–2).

Hall's formulation offers a framework for addressing both the empirical and the political dimensions of my problem. In relation to the empirical question of how the tribal slot is defined and occupied, the concept of articulation usefully captures the duality of positioning which posits boundaries separating within from without, while simultaneously selecting the constellation of elements that characterize what lies within. Further, it suggests that the articulation (expression, enunciation) of collective identities, common positions, or shared interests must always be seen as provisional. Cultural identities, as Hall argues elsewhere, "come from somewhere, have histories. But far from being eternally fixed in some essentialised past, they are subject to the continuous 'play' of history, culture and power" (Hall 1990:225). They are "unstable points of identification or suture . . . Not an essence but a *positioning*" (1990:226). While the "cut" of positioning is what makes meaning possible, its closure is arbitrary and contingent, rather than natural and permanent. This feature renders any articulation complex, contestable, and subject to rearticulation. Positively asserted on the one hand, articulations are also limited and prefigured by the fields of power or "places of recognition" which others provide (c.f. Hall 1995:8,14).

In relation to the political dimensions of my problem, Hall's argument that identities are *always* about becoming, as well as being, but are never simply invented, offers a way out of the impasse in which those who historicize the identities or traditions of "others" are accused of undermining subaltern political projects founded upon originary, perhaps essential truths.[5] In rejecting the idea of a necessary correspondence between social or class position and the discourses through which people make sense of their lives, Hall moves beyond the concept of false consciousness. At the same time, his attention to history and structure suggests a notion of agency quite different from that found in transactionalist accounts (e.g., Barth 1981). While there is a tactical element in the cut of positioning which may become explicit at times of heightened politicization and mobilization, the flow of meaning from which an articulation is derived and the fields of power with which it is engaged transcend that temporary fixity. The concept of articulation is thus alert to the unevenness of conjunctures and conditions of possibility, but offers no simple recipe for assessing degrees of determination or the points at which everyday understandings and practices shade into consciously selected tactics. It points rather to the necessity of teasing out, historically and ethnographically, the various ways in which room for maneuver[6] is present but never unconstrained. Finally, rather than focus on the identity dilemmas of the individual subject, Hall draws attention to those articulations which have the potential to define broad constellations of shared or compatible interests, and mobilize social forces across a broad spectrum.[7]

Locating the Tribal Slot in Shifting Fields of Power

Simplification and stereotyping are characteristic modes of apprehending the symbolic and material space of a nation's frontiers, the space at the cutting edge of capitalist expansion and state territorial control (Watts 1992:116–7; Shields 1991). Indonesia is an archipelagic state, whose frontiers are the hilly and forested interiors of the larger islands and the smaller islands of Eastern Indonesia. The populations that occupy these spaces are classified by the state according to two rather distinct frames of meaning and action, and classified by social and environmental activists according to a third, competing frame. Each of these frames narrows or simplifies the field of vision in its own particular way, highlighting some aspects of the landscape and its inhabitants and overlooking others. The tribal slot, like the savage slot described by Trouillot (1991), is a simplified frame of this sort. As my comparative study will later demonstrate, the predominance of a particular frame at a particular time and place depends not upon essential differences between the populations themselves, but upon the regimes of representation or "places of recognition" that preconfigure what can be found there, together with the processes of dialogue and contestation through which identifications are made on the ground.

State programs for interior and upland frontiers

The New Order government unilaterally classified about one million rural people as "estranged and isolated" (*masyarakat terasing, masyarakat terpencil*, Department of Social Affairs 1994). The official program designed to civilize such people views them as generic primitives, occupants of a tribal slot which is negatively construed. Their ethnic or tribal identities, cultural distinctiveness, livelihood practices, and ancient ties to the places they inhabit are presented in program documents as problems, evidence of closed minds and a developmental deficit that a well-meaning government must help them to overcome. This is to be accomplished by means of a resettlement program, a successor to Dutch efforts, which attempts to narrow the distance (in time, space, and social mores) between *masyarakat terasing* and the "normal average Indonesian citizen" (Koentjaraningrat 1993). The cultural distinctiveness they are encouraged to retain is of the song and dance variety.

Resettlement program guidelines specify that *masyarakat terasing* can be recognized by their tendency to move from place to place, as well as by their lack of a world religion, strong commitment to local customs and beliefs, and deficient housing, clothing, education, diet, health, and transportation facilities (Department of Social Affairs 1994). But there is, as I have argued elsewhere (Li 1999b), a problem with this list. Elements of the description could apply to almost all the rural population outside Java, especially to the tens of millions engaged in swidden agriculture or living in or near forests.[8] Identifying suitable subjects to be classified as *masyarakat terasing* is, therefore, a matter of interpretation and negotiation. Considerations include the need for the department responsible for resettlement to meet its quota; the distribution of construction contracts and associated forms of state largesse; pressures to reallocate land to more lucrative ventures; and the interest of the subjects themselves in access to the short or long-term benefits promised to them.

In contrast to the few classified as *masyarakat terasing* whose ethnic distinctiveness is acknowledged, and whose unique cultural characteristics are officially marked (albeit negatively), the majority of people occupying forested, mountainous, or other types of frontier land are classified simply as village folk, *orang kampong*. The development programs designed for such people ignore ethnic differences and assume, at the same time as they seek to create, homogenous forms of family and village life and a common administrative structure throughout the archipelago.[9] Many of these programs encourage or enforce mobility across the rural landscape. In the past few decades Indonesians have moved from one place to another as migrants, transmigrants, or workers attracted to, or ejected from, boom/bust industries (Brookfield et al. 1995). They have been forced to move when the state, which claims control over most of Indonesia's land (approximately seventy-five percent of it under the Ministry of Forestry), allocates their lands to other uses and users (Evers 1995; Zerner 1990; Moniaga 1993b). Few rural people outside Java have formal title to their lands. Regardless of the depth of their attachments to a particular place, most of the people who are rural and poor are deemed to be illegal squatters, subject to expulsion and other sanctions (Departmen Kehutanan 1994). To be an "ordinary villager" is, therefore, to belong to a homogenized or simplified category of people whose ethnic identity, distinctive forms of social organization, and localized commitments are officially unrecognized and often seen as contrary to national laws, policies, and objectives. In keeping with this official view of the countryside, national census data contains no information about the numerical size of ethnic or linguistic groups, their regional concentrations, or the relative proportions of migrants and original inhabitants in a particular area (Peluso 1995:399).

NGO visions and agendas

Counterposed to these two official frames for defining and managing rural space and populations is the category of indigenous people whose presence in the Indonesian countryside has been highlighted by social and environmental activists, especially in the past decade.

Activists draw upon the arguments, idioms, and images supplied by the international indigenous rights movement, especially the claim that indigenous people derive ecologically sound livelihoods from their ancestral lands and possess forms of knowledge and wisdom which are unique and valuable. But the discourse on indigenous people has not simply been imported. It has, rather, been inflected and reworked as it has traveled. While it is significant that some Indonesian activists writing in their own language continue to leave the English term "indigenous people" untranslated, others use a range of terms such as *masyarkat adat, masyarakat tradisional, masyarakat asli,* and *penduduk asli,* each of which is contextualized in particular struggles, some of them decades old.

Support for indigenous or tribal people is widespread in the Jakarta activist community, where their plight is seen as one among many ways in which the promises of Indonesian democracy and nationhood remain unfulfilled. The population that is envisaged to fit the indigenous or tribal slot differs according to the agenda and activities of the NGO in question.[10] For urban activists concerned to critique and redirect Indonesian modernity, indigenous people are the embodiment of pure forms of Indonesian cultural heritage unsullied by encounters with colonialism, westernization, and city life.[11] Some activists focus their concern upon especially isolated or exotic groups, who conform to the slot imagined by international promoters of tribal environmental wisdom. These are the same people who would readily be classified by the government as *masyarakat terasing*: some NGOs refer to the number published by the Department of Social Affairs (i.e., about one million) to identify the subjects of their concern. Their goal is to reverse the negative valorization that the government has placed upon the traditions of those in the tribal slot, and defend their right to maintain their distinctive ways of life, rejecting state-defined environmental and developmental imperatives that involve displacement or forced and rapid change.[12]

For other activists, the term "indigenous people" can be applied not only to especially isolated or exotic groups, but to the majority of Indonesia's rural citizens outside Java. At their most radical, these broader definitions amount to an attempt to roll back the state's territorial, social, and political control over the countryside, and empower tens of thousands of rural communities to manage their own affairs.[13] A key objective for many activists is implementation of the provisions in the Basic Agrarian Law of 1960, which recognizes rights to land based upon *adat,* or custom. They do not restrict their attention to those groups formally recognized by the Dutch as "adat law communities," but rather argue that any rural community can qualify under the provisions of the Basic Agrarian Law if their rights to land derive from and are recognized under local custom. Distinctive cultural styles which substantiate the idea of "a customary law community," and local sites and signs which provide proof of ancient ties to a place strengthen a claim but, according to some activists at least, are not essential to it. As one activist explained, "Adat is dynamic. So long as local people manage their land and resources in an orderly way, they can be said to have a customary tenure system."

Within this array of state and activist positions, there are many criteria for specifying which groups fill the tribal or indigenous slot, just as there are many agendas for their future. Rural people in Indonesia have some room to maneuver as they situate themselves in relation to the images, discourses, and agendas that others produce for or about them. On the one hand, if they are to fit the preconfigured slot of indigenous people they must be ready and able to articulate their identity in terms of a set of characteristics recognized by their allies and by the media that presents their case to the public. But the contours of the tribal slot are themselves subject to debate, as I have shown. Agency is involved in the selection and combination of elements that form a recognizably indigenous identity, and also in the process of making connections. Under some conditions, the room for maneuver may be quite limited. Struggles over resources, which are simultaneously struggles over meaning, tend to invoke simplified symbols fashioned through processes of opposition and dialogue, which narrow the gaze to certain well-

established signifiers and traits. In contests that pit marginalized populations against the state it may be the case that only one story can be presented. Whichever story this is, its audibility increases to the extent that it fits a familiar, preestablished pattern.[14] But power is seldom so singular, and articulations are correspondingly complex. They are contingent but not random; provisional and indeterminate, but not without form. It is not possible, just by surveying the rural scene, to predict which articulations will in fact be made. Nevertheless, it is possible to gain some understanding of the processes involved. To this end, I focus upon particular conjunctures – in this case, the two contrasting sites in the Sulawesi hills.

Articulating Indigenous Identity: Where an Ideology Finds its Subject

Power and the production of cultural difference

In the Western popular imagination fed by *National Geographic,* and also in the minds of some activists, tribes are naturally bounded, culturally distinct groups occupying spatially continuous and usually remote terrain. Tribes so imagined are hard to find in Indonesia, where analysis of history and social structure points, rather, to the political nature of group formation processes. The bilateral kinship system found in much of the archipelago lends itself more easily to the inclusion of others than to their exclusion. While there are some unilineal and hierarchical groups at the western and eastern extremes of Indonesia, in most areas kin loyalties are diffuse and residence patterns flexible. More common than sharp ethnic boundaries are patterns of continuous variation on familiar themes (Kahn 1999, Kipp and Rodgers 1987:8). Therefore, when tribal or ethnic boundaries *are* clearly marked, they can usually be traced to specific histories of confrontation and engagement.[15] Kipp and Rodgers (1987:1) argue that the distinctive ancestral customs claimed by Indonesia's more ethnicized groups are often "less ancestral than exquisitely contemporary . . . a system of symbols created through the interaction of small minority societies, their ethnic neighbours, colonial administrations, the national governments, and the world religions, Islam and Christianity."

Precolonial coastal kingdoms were not much interested in the details of cultural variation and ethnic affiliation in the uplands and interiors of their domains. Their principal goal was to monopolize trade and, in some cases, to control labor through direct enslavement or debt bondage. Coastal powers were often thwarted in both these endeavors by the capacity of interior peoples to subsist on their swidden fields, avoid trade engagements, and retreat to inaccessible areas when faced with violence or unreasonable demands. Muslim coastal powers therefore relegated most of the inhabitants of the interior to a tribal slot which they characterized by animism, backwardness, and savagery. Interior peoples, meanwhile, developed positive identities stressing independence, autonomy, and their capacity to carve a livelihood out of their hilly, forested terrain.[16] Domination and difference therefore emerged within a single political and cultural system, as distinctive identities began to be attributed to, imposed upon, and forged by interior populations through a complex and resistance-permeated process, which Gerald Sider (1987:17) terms "create and incorporate." Where definite, tribe-like social units were found in the interior, their emergence could often be traced to conditions of warfare and conflict.[17] In the absence of such encounters and confrontations, loosely structured, decentered, often scattered populations did not view themselves as distinct ethnic groups or tribes, and their identities remained only vaguely specified.[18]

The Dutch colonial authorities played an important role in ethnicizing or traditionalizing the Indonesian interior. In frontier areas where the indigenous political structures were amorphous, they set about consolidating people into tribe-like groups under centralized, hierarchical leadership.[19] They used the notion of tradition quite deliberately to legitimate colonial policies of indirect rule, and to help consolidate the authority of the Dutch-

appointed "traditional" leaders through whom this rule would be exercized.[20] To this end, local practices or customs (adat) were codified by scholars and officials.[21] The Dutch concept of the adat law community (*masyarakat hukum adat*) assumed, as it simultaneously attempted to engineer named, bounded, and organized groups. It was a concept that resonated differently with the local social formations that existed across the archipelago.[22] Ironically, but not surprisingly, it corresponded better to the formations that arose as *result* of colonial interventions (including the adat codification process itself) than it did to those that existed prior to Dutch control. In regions of little interest to the Dutch, the process of traditionalization did not occur or was incomplete, and identities, practices, and authority in matters of custom remained – and in some cases still remain – flexible and diffuse.[23]

Dutch efforts to systematize adat preconfigured the contemporary "indigenous peoples" slot, and their uneven reach continues to be reflected in the differential capacity of frontier peoples to articulate collective identities and positions. In the precolonial period, both of the highlands I am describing were peripheral to the concerns of the coastal chiefdoms that claimed nominal control over them. It was in the colonial period that a marked divergence occurred in their historical trajectories, laying the basis for the distinct spatial, political, and social configurations that characterize them today.

The mountain Lauje: development supplicants, cynics, or tribe manquée?

The Lauje, currently numbering about thirty thousand, occupy the hilly interior and the narrow coastal strip of the peninsula to the north of Tomini Bay. They are concentrated in the present day subdistricts of Tomini and Tinombo. Their language (Lauje) shades gradually into Tiaolo and Tajio, the languages of their neighbors, and no ethnicizing signs mark the borders of the Lauje domain. The Lauje hills are fairly densely settled and cultivated but not especially fertile, so they have not attracted outsiders. The Lauje have therefore not been provoked into articulating collective identities and associated boundaries in order to claim or defend their territory (Li 1996).

According to Nourse's (1989) account of local history, in precolonial times most Lauje kept to the hills for fear of slave raiders and pirates, although they traded jungle produce. Those occupying the drier lower slopes produced tobacco for regional markets. Lauje who moved down to the coast during the nineteenth century constituted themselves as a class of aristocrats, and intermarried with traders who moved in from other parts of Sulawesi: mainly Bugis, Mandar, and Gorontalo. The Lauje area was of only peripheral interest to the Dutch. It contained little natural wealth, and the coastal aristocrats were quiescent and easily co-opted, posing no threat to Dutch authority. A halfhearted attempt was made early this century to move the interior population to the coast, but it was clear that the land base was insufficient and they were soon allowed to return to their scattered mountain homes. Some undertook forced labor service, working on the construction of the coastal road and bridges, while others moved further inland to evade such obligations. Dutch revenues from the area, such as they were, came from taxing the owners of coconut groves that had been planted along the coast at Dutch insistence.

The coastal chiefs' minimal obligation to their Dutch overlords was to keep peace in the interior, and prevent feuding and bloodshed. Their model for governance was to select highlanders of renown and make them responsible for maintaining order. Since the expectations associated with rule over the interior were relatively light, the Dutch had no need to discover, constitute, or record Lauje customary practices or traditional law (adat). The mechanisms for accomplishing rule in the postcolonial period became somewhat more systematic but did not fundamentally change. Since the borders of the lowest level administrative units (desa) were defined to crosscut the terrain from the coast to the hills, the coastally-based desa heads continued the practice of appointing hillside leaders to be responsible for the maintenance of order in their vicinity. These leaders occupy the official positions of

hamlet chief (kepala RT) and chief of customary affairs (kepala adat). The task of the latter is to adjudicate marriage arrangements and local disputes in the hillside hamlets to which they belong.

According to several of those holding responsibility for "customary affairs," the procedures, rules, and fines they administer in their hillside hamlets were not handed down by the ancestors but, rather, established by the coastal authorities earlier this century in order to overcome the anarchy and feuding that previously prevailed in the hills. They consider their own authority to settle disputes to be a power granted by the desa administration, ultimately backed by the civil, police, and military authorities of the district. They do not articulate a sense of adat as something distinctive, autochthonous, locally derived, or essential to Lauje identity. There are, of course, many beliefs and practices of a spiritual nature relating to ancestors as well as to features of the landscape, but these are described as matters of personal, family, or at most hamlet-wide conviction, rather than pan-Lauje tradition.

Desa officials regard the hill people and their farming practices as backward, and generally show little interest in them. Desa maps portray the hills in spatially compressed form, while depicting the houses and public facilities on the narrow coastal strip in minute detail. Some desa officials describe the hilly interior as "empty," even when more than half the desa population lives up above (see Li, 1996). When pressed to discuss the mountain population, they emphasize their primitive, unruly nature and their status – not as noble savages, but as awkward and annoying ones. They sometimes refer to the mountain dwellers as orang dayak, a term they have picked up through media exposure to the apparently wild and primitive people of the Kalimantan interior, and now use to label and characterize their own backwoods. Many desa officials are themselves Lauje, but they, like the rest of the coastal Lauje elite, regard their shared ancestry with the heathen and backwards interior as a source of embarrassment. Some coastal Lauje have tried to highlight distinctions between Lauje and "foreigners" (Bugis, Mandar, and others), but their goal has been to bolster their own claims to aristocratic status, rather than to foster an overarching Lauje identity uniting coast and hills (c.f. Nourse 1989, 1994). Meanwhile, officials from the Ministry of Education and Culture bemoan their assignment to an area of Indonesia so patently lacking in the kinds of songs, dances, and handicrafts that they are expected to identify and turn into emblems of the local, for display in provincial or national fora. No sympathetic outsiders have yet come looking for indigenous people.

Engagements between the state and the Lauje people have been framed within, rather than outside or in opposition to, the state's discourse of development. This does not mean that there is consensus on who or what needs to be developed, or how development should be accomplished. For their part, desa officials readily classify the mountain Lauje as *masyarakat terasing* when planners from the provincial capital visit to ask about local development needs. In so doing, they seek to absolve themselves of responsibility for the onerous tasks of trying to count, monitor, or control, let alone provide services to, a mountain population which, they stress, is continuously on the move. They also hope to attract resettlement projects to their desa – massive deployments of state attention and expenditure which would help to resolve their administrative difficulties and potentially their financial ones. To this end they have helped to generate long lists of names of people who should be resettled; the Department of Social Affairs (1994:89–92) has it on record that there are 912 households of Lauje *masyarakat terasing* in need of government attention, in addition to the eighty that have already been resettled under the Department's program. But the Department receives many more requests for resettlement programs than it can handle. Numbers alone do not make a compelling case. The Department was already exposed to embarrassment when all the Lauje abandoned a resettlement site and returned to the hills within a year. Moreover, the Lauje are considered rather dull folk, lacking in the paint and feathers expected of true primitives. As one senior official observed in an interview, "sometimes we look at them and say these are not indigenous people, they are village people."[24] There are other groups in Central Sulawesi,

such as the Wana, who better fit the bill.[25] The mountain Lauje, who are not especially exotic and have no serious competitors for their hilly terrain, have therefore been left pretty much to their own devices.[26]

Generally, the mountain Lauje agree that their part of the province, and the hills in particular, suffer from a development deficit. This is a deficit they mostly attribute not to their own primitiveness or recalcitrance, but to the indifference, corruption, and greed of local elites, who direct state facilities, programs, and benefits away from them. Those who have heard about the official resettlement program oppose it on practical grounds. While they would be happy to receive new houses and rice rations as gifts from the government, they are rightly skeptical about livelihood prospects on the coast, and insist that they would have to remain where they are.[27] Not having been exposed to the overtly coercive dimensions of state power, nor to the threat of having land and livelihoods removed from them in the name of development, they have not articulated collective positions on these matters. Their engagements with state authority and development occur mostly through unremarked, "everyday" patterns of action and inaction. Some participate in mandatory public works days (*kerja bakti*), while others do not. Some hike down to the desa office when called to pick up free cocoa seedlings, while others surmise that any handouts offered to them will probably be of poor quality or purloined by coastal elites, and make their own arrangements. Some pay land taxes, while others claim they are too poor to pay, and count on officials to be lenient. Like the coastal elites, they bring a well-honed cynicism to these everyday encounters. They have learned the parameters of what can be requested from the government, the list of things (schools, seedlings, roads, or footpaths) that fit within the official purview of development. These are indeed things that many Lauje feel they want and need, although they do not define their lives as chronically deficient in the absence of such things, nor do they sit passively waiting for the government to secure their futures. They are, however, willing to adopt the position of supplicants in the hope that some of the desired goods and facilities will come their way.

So far, there has been no conjuncture, no context, site, event, or encounter, in which the mountain Lauje have articulated a collective position as indigenous people. So far no hillside leaders have been interested in, or capable of, articulating territorial claims beyond the level of their own hamlet, still less a generic Lauje identity. There are respected shamans living both in the hills and on the coast, but their agendas do not appear to be political. The pretensions of coastal Lauje "aristocrats" are largely unheard or ignored. The main authority hill folk acknowledge is that of desa officials, but, as noted above, the mountain Lauje are rightly suspicious of this group's motives and resent the unfair treatment they receive at their hands. The mountain Lauje are not anti-development. Indeed, they are taking their own initiatives to improve their chances of being *included* in state development agendas which have hitherto passed them by. They engage with the state in a discourse consistent with their knowledge of themselves, their needs and aspirations, and their understanding of what it is possible to demand and expect in that relationship. The ideology of indigenous people has not found its subject in the Lauje hills because, under current conditions, it would not help people to make sense of their situation, nor would it help them to improve it.

Sulawesi Tribe Opposes Lake Lindu Dam Project

So stated a headline in the Jakarta Post (an English-language daily) on September 11, 1994. The article quoted Gesadombu, "Tribal Chief of the Lindu plains," on the centrality of the lake to the Lindu tribe's livelihood; the "strong traditional and practical ties the Lindu people had with the land they live on"; and the certain loss of traditional values should the people be forced to move out. Accompanying the Chief were "23 other fellow Lindu indigenous people, non-governmental activists, students and nature-lovers from Central Sulawesi." They were visiting Jakarta to meet with state officials and present their case against the construction of a hydropower plant at the lake.

The article also quoted activists on the ecological soundness of the Lindu people's traditional resource management practices, on the need for the government to learn about land and water management from the people, and on the right of the Lindu people to express their culture.

Every component of this news story is familiar: the presence of tribes, tribal leaders, tribal ecological wisdom, and a specific tribal place central to the group's identity and culture, plus the presence of allies and sympathizers, and of a massive external force poised for destruction. It is a story for which the conceptual frame or "place of recognition" already exists, and for which the intended readership has been prepared. Nevertheless, the telling of this story in relation to Lindu or any other place in Indonesia has to be regarded as an accomplishment, a contingent outcome of the cultural and political work of articulation through which indigenous knowledge and identity were made explicit, alliances formed, and media attention appropriately focused.

The historical preconditions for this situation were established at Lindu at the turn of the century, when, according to Acciaioli (1989), the area was subjugated by the Dutch, and the scattered hill farmers (numbering about six hundred) were forced to form three concentrated settlements beside the lake. There they were converted to Christianity by the Salvation Army mission, educated in mission schools, and encouraged to view custom as matter for display at celebrations overseen by an officially recognized "customary" leadership, the adat council. The subsequent arrival of migrants from neighbouring districts and Bugis from the south gave the Lindu people some (often bitter) experience in articulating claims to their "ancestral, customary or village land" (Acciaioli 1989:151). Resource struggles thus provided the stimulus to articulate (select, formulate, and convey) a set of Lindu adat rules which *ought* to be acknowledged by outsiders – a process which in turn reworked the significance, and substance, of Lindu knowledge and identity. Even before the discourse of indigenous people became available to them, the preconditions that would suggest its relevance were firmly in place. Moreover, unlike the mountain Lauje, whose aristocratic elite and desa administrators are located far away on the coast, in a distinct class position and ecological niche, the leaders of the consolidated lakeside villages at Lindu experienced the threat posed by newcomers in the same way as their covillagers. Thus mission-educated, literate desa officials, schoolteachers, and prosperous farmers played a central role in the articulation of Lindu identity, rights, and claims.[28]

The identity of the Lindu as indigenous people with valuable knowledge and ancestral rights to their land was firmly established in the context of opposition to the hydro plan and the threat of forced resettlement. According to Sangadji's account (1996), the campaign involved confrontational encounters with the authorities, media attention, collaboration with national and international NGOs, and activities organized by Lindu leaders to heighten awareness within the community. NGO campaigning and support began in 1988. In 1992, at a dialogue with NGOs in Palu, a Lindu leader stated that he and his people would rather die than be removed from their ancestral lands. A youth group was formed at Lindu to research Lindu tradition and work for its preservation. Many journalists and officials visited the site, and adat leaders reiterated the preference to die rather than lose their culture. Security forces warned the people that activists, whose values were Western and contrary to the official national ideology (*pancasila*), were misleading them. An environmental assessment was carried out by consultants in 1993, but invited no public input. The delegation mentioned above then visited Jakarta to meet with top officials, and was told that an amended design would avoid the necessity for resettlement. Currently, the hydro plan is on hold, though the Lindu and their supporters remain vigilant.[29]

The scale of the threat to local lives and livelihoods, the dramatic nature of a dam as a stage for NGO action, the location of the dam within a national park, and the massive economic implications of the project explain why Lindu attracted so much attention. But it remains to be explained how and why

the Lindu have come to articulate their identity, present themselves, and be represented by their supporters in terms consistent with both national and international expectations concerning indigenous people or tribes.

The news coverage and documents prepared in the course of the campaign shed some light on the "how" question. Members of the NGO coalition worked with Lindu leaders to produce documents informing the public and policy makers about the Lindu people and the negative impacts of the dam. These documents present Lindu as a unique, tribal place, its integrity basically intact. They note that the Lindu are the only speakers of the Tado language (related to Kaili), and that they are an autonomous group who have managed their own affairs (*hidup mandiri*) for hundreds of years (Sangadji 1996:19; Laudjeng 1994:150–2). There is little mention of the impact of Dutch rule, or of the presence of Bugis and other non-Lindu at the lake. The documents focus upon cultural features which confirm the uniqueness of the Lindu people, their environmental wisdom, and their spiritual attachment to the landscape. Culture is substantiated through a focus upon "traditional" costumes, major annual feasts, and marriage arrangements. Lindu capacities for environmental management are demonstrated through the existence of the adat council, which is said to have jurisdiction over the Lindu people's collective territory – an area extending to the peaks of all the mountains surrounding the lake. Management rules include the exclusion of outsiders from the use of Lindu resources except with permission from the adat chiefs, and the zoning of land according to specified uses. The documents pay considerable attention to the existence of named zones for farming, hunting, and grazing, and of sacred sites in which all forms of activity (tree cutting, gathering, etc.) are strictly forbidden (Laudjeng 1994:155–60). They also state that each clan – and within the clan, each household – has fishing rights over specific portions of the lake. Filtered and interpreted through a "green lens" (Zerner 1994), these land use categories are presented as similar to, but more efficient than, the land use zones imposed by the state through its forest and national park regulations (Sangadji 1996:26–8). Finally, the documents emphasize Lindu people's attachment to their place by naming features of the landscape: hills, sacred spots, grazing areas, and the sacred island in the lake, which is associated with the magical culture hero Maradindo. Although these place names mean nothing to a reader without a map, they assert and confirm that the Lindu are thoroughly familiar with their territory. Between the named zones and the specific named places, the point is made that there is no undifferentiated or unclaimed space, but rather an orderly system of land use designed and managed by the indigenous people of Lindu.

A finer reading reveals many subtleties in these accounts. They present a selective picture, but one which is complex rather than simple, positioning the Lindu in relation to multiple fields of power. They emphasize that the Lindu are "traditional" people, but in no sense are they primitive. The mention of Christianity confirms their nationally acceptable religious standing, yet little is made of the influence of ninety years of missionary work upon their "traditional" rituals and practices. They are shown to be in touch with nature and bearers of tribal wisdom, but by emphasizing the orderliness of the Lindu land use system it is made clear that there is nothing wild about this scene. The accounts emphasize subsistence uses of the forest, such as the collection of building materials and medicinal plants (Sangadji 1996:44). They make less of the presence within these forests of the hillside coffee groves that provide the Lindu people with a significant source of cash. It is noted that the Lindu people are not poor. They have an adequate standard of living, though not luxurious, and are satisfied with their lot. Thus they are sufficiently similar to "ordinary villagers" not to be in need of drastic changes or improvements (framed as development), still less the civilizing projects directed at *masyarakat terasing*. Yet they are unlike "ordinary villagers" in their uniqueness, their special knowledge, and their attachment to their place.

When these documents are read through the prism of the Lindu history presented in Acciaioli's thesis (researched prior to the dam

conjuncture), and in relation to the fields of power and opportunity presented by the Lindu people's NGO and government interlocutors, they reveal how group boundaries were defined, and how elements from the local repertoire of cultural ideas and livelihood practices were selected and combined to characterize the group. They reveal, that is, the "cut" of positioning, its arbitrary closure at a highly politicized moment. They point to the uniqueness and contingency of articulation, and its necessary occlusion of the larger flows of meaning and power, the practices of everyday life and work, the differences according to gender or class position, and the structures of feeling which form the larger canvas within which positioning occurs.

The efficacy of framing Lindu people's position in terms of the arguments and images associated with indigenous people was not guaranteed. It was effective in the NGO campaign, as activists were able to use the environmental soundness of the Lindu's livelihood practices to argue against the dam and also to support their arguments on behalf of other indigenous people in Indonesia. In activist circles, Lindu became an exemplary case, which was framed within – and helped to frame – broader struggles.[30] But not all nongovernment organizations recognized the tribal uniqueness of Lindu. In 1992, while the Lindu campaign was underway, a parks-focused international conservation NGO described the population in the many villages bordering the national park as ethnically diverse, with a mix of "local" or "traditional" people and newcomers. It observed that the area's inhabitants were subsistence farmers, only weakly integrated into markets, and often exploited and displaced by aggressive immigrants. It also noted that they were rather lacking in handicrafts with a tourist potential (Schweithelm et al. 1992:39–47). So described, they fit the state category of "ordinary villagers." But the NGO's report contains no suggestion that the border villages in general, or Lindu in particular, are populated by tribal people who have ancient ties to the forest, or who possess unique environmental wisdom.

Media receptiveness to the idea of Lindu as indigenous people was also mixed. The

English-language news coverage cited earlier picked up the tribal angle, as the headline clearly shows. The coverage of opposition to the dam in a major Indonesian language newspaper (*Kompas*) was more equivocal. An article ("Masyarakat Lindu," 11 September 1993) described the Lindu people not as a tribe but as a subgroup of Kaili. It acknowledged their environmental wisdom, but observed that – the satisfaction expressed by residents notwithstanding – the area does suffer from a development deficit, signaled by the seventeen kilometer hike from the nearest road, the muddy village paths, and the incomplete electrical service. Most of the media coverage skillfully analyzed by Sangadji (1996) supported the hydro plan on the grounds of development, and did not address the issue of indigenous people.

Throughout the campaign, the government agencies promoting the power plant neither accepted nor rejected the notion that the Lindu are indigenous people: they simply did not engage with it. Refusing, or not recognizing, the discursive terrain developed by the Lindu people and their allies, officials maintained their focus upon the need for electricity to promote modernization and industrial development in the Palu valley (Sangadji 1996:54). They also made the argument that the resettlement of the Lindu would make them more developed, but this was difficult to justify. Livelihoods at Lindu are, in provincial terms, rather good, as the government itself previously acknowledged when it brought new settlers into the area to share in its prosperity and help develop the potential for irrigated rice production (Sangadji 1996:44). For these reasons, the development argument was consistently rejected by Lindu spokesmen. Indeed, it was their overt rejection of the idea that they were in need of any form of state-directed development, as much as their emphasis upon the unique character of their tribal place, that was notable in their campaign.

In view of the weak case made by the state, various approaches could have been used to frame opposition to the project. A materialist case, focusing upon the loss of good livelihoods, and a political case, focusing upon the rights of the Lindu people to fair treatment as

citizens, were indeed argued. But the most prominent form of articulation – that which clarified positions and made connections – was focused upon the loss of a unique tribal identity and way of life. The reasons for this had to do with the fields of power and opportunity surrounding the concept of indigenous people at that juncture. The possibility of articulating local concerns with national and international agendas was clearly present. Situations which set indigenous people up against big projects and the state are guaranteed attention, and they set up predictable alliances (Sangadji 1996:13, 16). Also significant is the way in which an indigenous or tribal identity asserts the unity of people and place, addressing an issue at the heart of state-society relations in the Indonesian countryside. According to the state model, which sees rural people as "ordinary villagers," those that must be moved to facilitate national development can be compensated in cash, or given new land to replace the old. If the Lindu people were simply villagers, their livelihoods could, in theory, be recreated elsewhere. Indeed, the future planned for them was to join the (technically troubled) transmigration scheme at Lalundu (Sangadji 1996:20) as homogenized quota-fillers, names on a list. Only indigenous or tribal people can claim that their very culture, identity, and existence are tied up in the unique space that they occupy (Cohen 1993). There can be no compensation. This was the point argued repeatedly by the Lindu and their supporters (Sangadji 1996:16).

Finally, the tribal slot opens up some maneuvering room unavailable to ordinary villagers. Obstinate peasants can be labeled communists, as they often are in Java (Sangadji 1996:15), but communist tribesmen are somehow less plausible. Their concerns seem to be somewhat different from those of the mass of rural people reacting to the contempt and arrogance with which they are treated by their government. Indigenous people and their nature-and-culture loving supporters are differently positioned in relation to the field of power. The sacred shrine of the Lindu's heroic and supernatural ancestor Maradindo is located on an island within the lake. When Maradindo is angered he causes accidents, bizarre events of which the

Lindu can cite recent examples (Sangadji 1996:32, 41–2). The Lindu tell a powerful story: ignore Maradindo at your peril.[31]

Articulating Indigenous Identity: Conditions, Risks and Opportunities

Conditions for articulation

The contrast between my two examples highlights some of the conditions and conjunctures that have enabled the articulation of "indigenous" identity in contemporary Indonesia. A summary of the factors present at Lindu, but not in the Lauje case, includes the following: competition for resources, in the context of which group boundaries were rendered explicit and cultural differences entrenched; the existence of a local political structure that included individuals (elders, leaders) and an adat council mandated to speak on behalf of the group; a capacity to present cultural identity and local knowledge in forms intelligible to outsiders – an activity undertaken in this case by a literate elite of teachers, local officials, prosperous farmers, and entrepreneurs; an interest on the part of urban activists in discovering and supporting exemplary indigenous subjects, and documenting indigenous knowledge which fit the niche preconstituted in national and international environmental debates; and, finally, heightened interest in a particular place, arising from a conflict which pit locals against the state or state-sponsored corporations.[32]

My comparative study also illustrates the contingent aspects of articulation and the significance of human agency. It was not predetermined which articulations would be made at the conjunctures described: by some of the obvious criteria, the Lauje were more qualified for the tribal slot. Every articulation is a creative act, yet it is never creation *ex nihilo*, but rather a selection and rearticulation of elements structured through previous engagements. It is also, as Hall points out, subject to contestation, uncertainty, risk, and the possibility of future rearticulation.

Contestation and risk

The potential for contestation is easy enough to identify, since the different interests at play in any articulation could always lead to its unraveling. At Lindu, for example, the Bugis and other settlers who currently go along with the indigenous position could object to, or find themselves threatened by, the potential exclusivism of "the Lindu tribe," and identify alternative positions and alliances from which to oppose the dam. Lindu people themselves have different stakes in adat and its contemporary articulations, and are situated unevenly in relation to the power of adat chiefs.[33] NGOs do not always agree on visions, priorities, or the forms in which connections should be made and actions taken. Many activists are aware of the differential benefits that would accrue from a strengthening of customary land rights. Losers would include those who fail to fit a clear-cut ethnic and territorial niche, whose family background or patterns of geographic and class mobility have removed them from any material connection to a specific tribal place. Several observers have noted that it is displaced, landless people – mainly Javanese, not indigenous people – who are Indonesia's most vulnerable group (Brookfield et al. 1995; Evers 1995:11). The whole concept of indigenous people, and the idea that they have particular rights, can be – and is, in some quarters – contested on these grounds. Others see the possibility of broadening and redefining interests and visions to create even stronger alliances.

Risk is apparent at many levels. Under Suharto, risk was endemic to any form of political organizing. The government commonly saw activists as fomenting trouble, or, in the standard language used to refer to subversive activities, acting as an (unspecified) "third party," misleading and manipulating simple rural folk, and creating "politics" where there is none. But, despite the risk, support for indigenous people provided activists with an opportunity, a space where they could act. The grounding of association and mobilization in culture and tradition, and its affinity with conservation agendas, became crucial to the (precarious) political acceptability of community organizing in the Indonesian countryside (Zerner 1994). It also provided a space in which some rural people could affirm positive identities, and articulate, substantiate, and defend their claims.

Conjunctures at which rural people have identified themselves, and become identified, as indigenous people are moments at which global and local agendas have been conjoined in a common purpose, and presented within a common discursive frame. But the tribal slot fits ambiguously with the lives and livelihoods of people living in frontier areas. It is not an identity space that every local group is able or willing to occupy. They may present themselves as indigenous people, or they may emphasize their standing as ordinary villagers. Too much like primitives and they risk to be classified as *masyarakat terasing*, to be resettled by the Department of Social Affairs. On the other hand, as "ordinary villagers," they are vulnerable to arbitrary removal under another set of government programs. Candidates for the tribal slot who are found deficient according to the environmental standards expected of them must also beware.[34] The majority of Indonesia's swidden farmers have long been committed to producing for the market, and many are more interested in expanding commercially-oriented agriculture than in conserving forests. Some are interested in profits from the sale of timber, and not just the non-timber forest products usually deemed appropriate to them (Dove 1993). Neither good tribes nor good peasants, they are in an ambiguous position which, rather than allowing them room for maneuver, may instead restrict their scope, and make it difficult to isolate opponents and identify allies and arenas for action.

Uncertainty and contingency

One of the most significant uncertainties in the articulation of indigenous identities concerns whether or not connections can actually be made. At Lindu, government officials refused to engage with the issue of indigenousness. They simply repeated the development argument regardless of evidence that it was inappropriate. Environmentalists, journalists, or other social and political activists searching for indigenous knowledge find it more easily in some places than others, as the contrast between Lauje and Lindu clearly reveals. For people in a hurry, it is easier to seek out conjunctures at which the articulations they seek are readily forthcoming and connections easily made. Such places then become exemplars, visited by many people, and are increasingly reified as they are written about, quoted, and cited in ever-broadening circuits of knowledge and action (c.f. Keck 1995; Rangan 1993). The process is similar to that which Robert Chambers has dubbed "rural development tourism" (1983), although in the case of tribes the main issue drawing outsiders is not development success but conflict, especially when it pits locals against the state. Struggles over access to mundane resources like schools and roads, and the strategies of those who seek to position themselves closer to the state, go relatively unremarked.

The circumstances of my research at Lake Lindu and in the Lauje hills can usefully illustrate the uneven channels through which outsiders connect to "the local." I point this out not in confessional mode, but because reflexivity, in this instance, brings to light issues of a general nature (Herzfeld 1997). NGO friends in Jakarta who were active in the campaign against the hydro project suggested I should visit Lindu, and put me in touch with their partner NGO in Palu. Contacts easily made, I was able to make a two-day visit to Lindu at the end of a five-week stint in the Lauje hills. When I arrived at Lindu, a group of community leaders gathered to talk to me. The contrasts with the Lauje area I had just left were palpable: a much higher standard of living, an educated, Indonesian-speaking population, and a leadership with a clearly articulated collective position. Moreover, the clarity of their discourse, together with the set of documents and press clippings given to me by the NGO, made it possible for me to write about them even without conducting field research. Connecting with the hillside Lauje is much more difficult. Very few people speak

Indonesian, illiteracy is almost total, and there are precious few documentary sources. The hillside population has no obvious spatial or social center, no hierarchy of leadership that would suggest to a visitor (especially one in a hurry) where they should go, or whom they should talk to. The historical reasons for this are deep but contingent, as I have shown. The possibilities for research, writing, and connecting are also preconfigured, and have real political effects. While I can protest that more attention should be paid to the Lauje and people like them, as well as to the historical contexts of meaning and action and the more subtle workings of power, it was usually the dramas at Lindu that captured the imagination of readers of this paper in its earlier drafts. My accounts of the Lauje are more nuanced, but also fuzzier, more equivocal, less easily picked up and read by outsiders in search of a tribal place.

Articulation versus imposition

Many locally produced images, counterimages, inversions, and inventions receive little attention on the global stage as a result of the unequal power relations within which processes of representation occur. One could mention here the shaman/leader described by Tsing (1993), whose project for defining Meratus identity and reordering community life enthralled local audiences, although it would surely be dismissed by outsiders as the ravings of a madwoman. Her articulations fail to forge connections to wider circuits of meaning. Thomas (1994:89) also draws attention to the problem of uneven privileging: "Constructions of indigenous identities almost inevitably privilege particular fractions of the indigenous population who correspond best with whatever is idealized: the chiefly elites of certain regions, bush Aborigines rather than those living in cities, even those who appear to live on ancestral lands as opposed to groups who migrated during or before the colonial period."[35] As my studies in Central Sulawesi suggest, "correspondence" is itself a product of articulation. Few places could be more "bush" than the Lauje hills, and yet, as I have shown, the people and their concerns do not easily connect.

There has been much written about how subaltern struggles are distorted by representations created and imposed by outsiders. DuPuis and Vandergeest (1996) decry the simplified spatial images (wilderness, countryside) imposed upon rural people through policy processes (and their green counterpoints) pursued in ignorance of the complexity of local histories, livelihoods, and aspirations. Similarly, Fisher (1996) and Hecht and Cockburn (1990) are troubled by the way political space for Amazonians has been circumscribed by contemporary antidevelopment in the shape of environmentalism. Lohmann (1993:203) argues that "green orientalism" compels locals to act out assigned roles which they can, at best, only "twist and subvert" to their own advantage. Similar effects result from *indigenismo* and images of the "hyperreal Indian" (Ramos 1994). Rangan (1993) has recounted the damage done by an externally generated image of the Garhwal Himalayas, home of Chipko, as an ecological utopia.

This is an important critique. However, it treats representation as a one-sided imposition. By paying attention to the process of articulation it is possible to appreciate opportunities as well as constraints, and the exercise of agency in these encounters. Simplified images may be the result of collaborations in which "natives" have participated for their own good reasons. According to Eder (1994), Batak highlanders in the Philippines see themselves simultaneously as a deprived underclass lacking the resources (but not the desire) to pursue lowland Filipino lifeways, and also as proud bearers of a tribal identity. The latter has become emphasized through their collaboration with NGO allies, as they have discovered the value of ethnic claims for obtaining desired outside resources. Neumann (1995) describes the way Tanzanian pastoralists have made productive political use of an environmentalist rhetoric even as it was deployed to displace them. Jackson (1995) describes Tukanoans in the Vaupes "orientalizing themselves" to acquire more Indianness. Complexity, collaboration, and creative cultural engagement in both local and global arenas, rather than simple deceit, imposition, or reactive opportunism, best describe these processes and relationships.

Connecting social forces

As Hall observed, the most important articulations go beyond the "cut" through which localized groups position themselves, to connect with broader social forces. Like a localized group, a social movement also needs to select some issues from a broader canvas if it is to position itself and build alliances. From this point of view, images of environmentally friendly tribes in exemplary places may be necessary, at least as a starting point. But there are limitations to a social movement built around such images. To the extent that they highlight primordial otherness, separating us from them, traditional from modern, and victim from aggressor or protector, they reinforce differences and channel alliances along binary pathways. Moreover, ideal candidates for the tribal slot are difficult to find in Indonesia, and their identification is, as I have indicated, a contingent matter. Taking advantage of such ambiguities, the government could set out new rules to identify and accommodate a few "primitives" or traditional/indigenous people, and even acknowledge their rights to special treatment, without fundamentally shifting its ground on the issue that affects tens of millions: recognition of their rights to the land and forest on which they depend. Some people would gain from official recognition of their "indigenous peoples" status, but the result might be heightened tensions as neighbouring or intermingled populations find themselves differently affected.

On the other hand, too much fuzziness, or too broad an agenda, makes it difficult to forge connections. It is not obvious to me, for example, that substituting a discourse of class for one about indigenous identities and practices, as proposed by Rouse (1995), would necessarily have formed a broader coalition or more effectively "found its subject" in the Indonesian countryside over the past decade. Rouse exposes the politics of identification in the US as the effect of routinized micropower and attempts by the ruling regime to deflect opposition potentially formulated in broader, class terms. In Indonesia under the New Order, in contrast to the US and also in contrast to the adat-making endeavors of the Dutch colo-

nial period, ethnic identity has most decidedly *not* been the chosen ideological terrain of the state. Although colorful cultural signs have always been acceptable, localized identities, histories, and commitments have been consistently unmarked and derecognized in favour of a homogenizing discourse of development. Positioned in relation to this particular field of power, an articulation that focuses attention on the tribal slot has been able to make important connections. But articulations are, as Hall argues, not given or fixed for all time.

The broader visions framed by the discourse on indigenous people have been attempts to rework the meanings of democracy, citizenship, and development. These are visions which could incorporate Lauje, Lindu, and millions of other rural Indonesians. Often they note, but then proceed to blur the distinctions between indigenous people, local people, and other rural folk, including migrants, stressing the common concerns that arise from the grounding of livelihoods in particular places, and the need to contest arbitrary state power to displace and impoverish. These visions do not reject the idea of development, but hold the state accountable. They engage with the state at its most vulnerable point: when its promises are tested by routine or spectacular development failures, and its raison d'être called into question. The Lindu rejected the idea that the state could or would bring them development, and mobilized accordingly. The cynical reflections of the Lauje are the product of decades of experience with official greed, incapacity, and indifference. They know full well that their future does not lie in state handouts – a knowledge which renders the exaggerated claims of state programs vulnerable to exposure and critique.

Conclusion

The discourse on indigenous people in Indonesia has emerged from new visions and connections that have created moments of opportunity, but there are no guarantees. There is the potential for the development of a broad social movement, in which urban activists and rural people can begin to articulate shared interests.

There are also risks. Articulation, in Hall's formulation, is a process of simplification and boundary-making, as well as connection. The forms it takes are not predetermined by objective structures and positions, but emerge through processes of action and imagination shaped by the "continuous play of history, culture and power."

Seeking to negotiate the political dangers of attributing either too much, or too little, agency to those who would claim the tribal slot as their own, I explored contrasting conjunctures to expose the conditions and processes which made particular articulations possible. The Lindu came to position themselves in the tribal slot at a moment of crisis, but their articulations drew upon experiences of boundary-making and selection, sedimented over more than a century. The Lauje have engaged with more diffuse forms of power, and their positions have not been collectively defined. They do not easily fit into the tribal slot defined for them in some activist agendas. In their work on behalf of tribal and indigenous people, NGOs have also articulated their positions to engage quite specific fields of power. As agendas and positions are recalibrated in the post-Suharto era, no doubt the risks and opportunities associated with the tribal slot will be reassessed by those it potentially engages as subjects, and by those who seek to place the resource struggles and aspirations of Indonesia's frontier peoples at the center of a broad social movement.

NOTES

1. Sarwono Kusumaatmadja (1993), Minister of State for the Environment, addressing an NGO forum.

2. This paper was first submitted to CSSH in November 1997. It was revised and resubmitted in November 1998, after the fall of Suharto, during a period when hopes for progressive change and skepticism about *reformasi* were present in equal measure. The situation in November 1999, as I make final revisions before the journal goes to press, has changed again in ways that I cannot fully explore. Most notably, the indigenous peoples' platform was highlighted by a national congress held in Jakarta in March 1999, and the founding of an indigenous peoples' organization, AMAN (*Aliansi Masyarakat Adat Nusantara*). See the special issue of *Down to Earth,* October 1999. Improved prospects for some kinds of legal recognition under the new government make reflection on the issues I raise in this article even more important.

3. In one of these locations, the Lauje area, I have carried out fieldwork for a total of about seven months, spread over a period of seven years. For the other,

Lake Lindu, I rely mainly on secondary sources.

4. While acknowledging the desire of some parties to pin the category down, Kingsbury (1998:450) takes a "constructivist" position on indigenousness, arguing that this identification will emerge and shift in relation to international discourses, national policies, and local dynamics. Gray (1995) argues that the term "indigenous" lacks descriptive coherence in relation to Asia, but signals a process and phenomenon which occurs in struggles that pit localized groups against encompassing states. Therefore, millions of people in Asia who actually or potentially experience this scenario fall within its compass.

5. See the polemics over this matter in the journal *Identities* (1996, volume 3,1–2). See also Friedman (1992).

6. For an elucidation of the phrase "room for maneuver" and an insightful ethnographic account, see Tsing (1999).

7. The formulation of articulation in the "modes of production" literature of the 1970s focused upon the process of conjoining, but not on that of "giving expression to" (Foster-Carter 1975:53). For an account of how Hall positions his concept of articulation in relation to the work of

Althusser, Foucault, Lacan, and others, see Hall (1985).

8. Lynch and Talbott (1995:22) estimate that Indonesia has eighty to ninety-five million people directly dependent upon forest resources, of whom forty to sixty-five million live on land classified as public forest.

9. See Colchester (1986a and b) for a discussion of transmigration and other programs which are explicitly designed to homogenize the rural population and eliminate ethnic distinctions. Much criticism has focused upon the Desa Administrative Law No. 5 (1979), which seeks to standardize villages and weaken adat institutions concerned with social organization and leadership. See Moniaga (1993a:33–5).

10. I draw here upon a set of interviews I carried out with the staff of Jakarta NGOs in 1996, as well as upon their published documents. Where the subject matter might be sensitive, I do not identify the organizations to which I am referring in my discussion.

11. See, for example, Moniaga (1993b) and "Ekistensi Hukum" (*Kompas* 27 March 1996).

12. Simply reversing the images is also problematic, as NGOs increasingly recognize. An NGO campaign against transmigration and large-scale plantations on the island of Siberut argued that the island's residents were so traditional they could not mix with newcomers, or adapt to rapid and major change. But the very same image of an extreme gulf between an isolated and primitive "them" and a modern Indonesian "us" was used by Transmigration Minister Siswono to argue that development must proceed, because the Siberut people cannot be left in a stone-age state. See "Siberut Island" (*Jakarta Post* 14 February 96) and "Skephi opposes" (*Jakarta Post* 17 February 96).

13. See critiques of the government for its refusal to recognize customary land rights in Moniaga (1993a, b); Skephi and Kiddell-Monroe (1993); "Semoga"

(*Kompas* 29 March 93), "Indigenous Peoples" (*Kompas* 29 April 93), and "Eksistensi Hukum Adat" (*Kompas* 27 March 96). See Evers (1995) for an overview of the legal status of customary land rights, the difficulties of specifying who should be included in the category of indigenous people in Indonesia, and an attempt to reconcile these questions with World Bank policies. For a discussion of the difference between the Dutch colonial concept of a traditional-law society (*masyarakat hukum adat*) and the internationally recognized concept of indigenous people, and the (lack of) resonance of these concepts with forestry law, see Safitri (1995).

14. See O'Brien and Roseberry (1991:13); Cohen (1993:203).

15. See Thomas (1992:65), Scott (1992:376), and Gupta and Ferguson (1992:16) for general arguments along these lines; see Kahn (1993:23) and Tsing (1993) for Indonesian examples.

16. For a summary of the large literature on upland-lowland relations in the pre-colonial era, see Li (1999a), and references cited therein.

17. In Northern Sulawesi, for example, Henley characterizes the indigenous political geography in terms of "aterritoriality, fluidity and fragmentation" (1996:143). He notes that local kin-based groups, or *walak*, became more strongly bounded and endogamous under warlike conditions, although they could still fragment and realign (1996:26,35).

18. See, for example, Tsing's (1993) description of the mountain dwellers of Southeast Kalimantan, for whom she had to coin a singular name, the Meratus.

19. For Sulawesi examples, see Acciaioli (1989:66,73); Henley (1996).

20. See Kahn (1993), Benda-Beckmann and Benda-Beckmann (1994), Ruiter (1999); for a more general discussion of colonial practices of discipline and rule, see Cooper and Stoler (1997).

21. See Kahn (1993:78–110) for an extended discussion of the intellectual, economic,

and political rationales for the Leiden School of adat law associated with van Vollenhoven, influential in the codification of adat in the period 1911–55. See also Ellen 1976.

22. For example, Kahn (1993:180; 1999) observes that in the nineteenth century the term "Minangkabau" did not have the sense of a discrete, bounded, distinctive cultural unit; this developed in the colonial period and subsequently.

23. See, for example, the discussion of Meratus identity, leadership and ad hoc adat-making processes in Tsing (1993).

24. Thanks to Dan Paradis for access to transcripts of interviews with provincial officials in 1994. Because the transcripts had been translated, I do not know which Indonesian expression was translated here as "indigenous people."

25. To illustrate his point, the official showed photos of a Wana medicine man conducting a ritual. Prominently displayed in the Palu office are "before and after" pictures of near-naked Wana who are subsequently clothed, revealing the contradictory impulses of nostalgia and development.

26. This situation has begun to change in the past five years, as coastal elites see the economic potential for hillside cocoa and clove gardens. For a discussion of the local and regional class dimensions of this process, see Li (1996 and 1997).

27. Many people were reluctant to talk to me when I first started field work in the Lauje hills because they feared my research would lead to their resettlement. They were especially nervous about anything that looked like a list of names.

28. This did not mean they always spoke with one voice: disputes arose over the issue of who among "the Lindu" had the right to confer upon outsiders permission to use Lindu resources.

29. The redesign would still require a green belt around the lake, restricting access to both fisheries and farmland. Sangadji's (1996) research continues to highlight the ways in which the Lindu are, and must remain, anchored to very specific spots on the landscape, including fishing spots that are the preserve of particular families. During my visit to Lindu, an NGO was facilitating a community mapping process in which the Lindu leaders who had traveled to Jakarta were key participants. They had been informed by the Minister of State for Environment that their case would be strengthened by representing their customary zones and places on maps which outsiders could read. On the politics of mapping and countermapping in Indonesia, see Peluso (1995).

30. See Moniaga (1993a:33) and "Kearifan Masyarakat" (Kompas 13 September 1993). The Institute of Dayakology also presents generic Dayak as environmentalists (Bamba 1993). For critiques of the claim that natives are naturally nurturant of nature, see Ellen (1986) and Stearman (1994).

31. Opposition to the hydro project at Lindu was widespread in the community, so there was a common interest in the success of the campaign. On other matters, including the relevance of indigenous environmental knowledge to everyday lives and practices, and the role of the adat council in controlling resources, there are bound to be differences of opinion among people differently situated by class, gender, and ethnic origins. Since I have not carried out field research at Lindu, I am not in a position to discuss these.

32. For other Indonesian conjunctures in which some or all of these factors were also relevant, see Tsing (1999) and Zerner (1994).

33. On the non-egalitarian aspects of adat, see Benda-Beckman and Benda-Beckman (1994); on "lairdism" or the risks associated with concentrating power in the hands of adat chiefs, Colchester (1994:87); on the ways in which concentrated adat power becomes more easily enmeshed in or subverted by the projects of the colonial and postcolonial states, Zerner (1994).

34. For a good discussion of this point in the Philippine context, see Brown (1994).

Note that ecological soundness is a relative matter: smallholders expanding into old-growth forests may threaten biodiversity, but the resulting mosaic of land uses is vastly more biodiverse than the industrial-scale oil palm or timber plantations programmed to displace small holdings under state-sponsored schemes.

35. See also Carrier (1992), Friedman (1987), and Scott (1992:387).

REFERENCES

Acciaioli, Gregory. (1989). "Searching for Good Fortune: The Making of a Bugis Shore Community at Lake Lindu, Central Sulawesi." PhD Thesis, Australian National University.

Bamba, John. (1993). "The Concepts of Land Uses among the Dayaks and Their Contribution to the Sustainable Management of the Environment," in Arimbi, H. P. ed. *Proceedings, Seminar on the Human Dimensions of Environmentally Sound Development*. Jakarta: WALHI and Friends of the Earth, 37–49.

Barth, Frederick. (1981). *Process and Form in Social Life*. London: Routledge and Kegan Paul.

von Benda-Beckmann, Franz and Keebet von Benda-Beckmann. (1994). "Property, Politics, and Conflict: Ambon and Minangkabau Compared." *Law and Society Review* 28(3):589–607.

Brookfield, Harold, Lesley Potter and Yvonne Byron. (1995). *In Place of the Forest: Environmental and Socio-economic Transformation in Borneo and the Eastern Malay Peninsula*. Tokyo: United Nations University Press.

Brown, Elaine. (1994). "Grounds at Stake in Ancestral Domains," in James Eder and Robert Youngblood, eds. *Patterns of Power and Politics in the Philippines*. Tempe: Arizona State University, 43–76.

Carrier, James. (1992). "Occidentalism: the World Turned Upside-Down." *American Ethnologist* 19(2):195–212.

Chambers, Robert. (1983). *Rural Development: Putting the Last First*. New York: Longman.

Cohen, Anthony. (1993). "Culture as Identity: An Anthropologist's View." *New Literary History* 24:195–209.

Colchester, Marcus. (1986a). "Unity and Diversity: Indonesian Policy towards Tribal Peoples." *The Ecologist* 16(2–3):89–97.

——. (1986b). "The Struggle for Land: Tribal Peoples in the Face of the Transmigration Programme." *The Ecologist* 16 (2–3): 99–110.

——. (1994). "Sustaining the Forests: The Community-based Approach in South and South-East Asia." *Development and Change* 25(1):69–100.

Cooper, Frederick and Ann Stoler, eds. (1997). *Tensions of Empire: Colonial Cultures in a Bourgeois World*. Berkeley: University of California.

Department of Social Affairs. (1994). *Isolated Community Development: Data and Information*. Jakarta: Directorate of Isolated Community Development, Directorate General of Social Welfare Development, Department of Social Affairs.

Departmen Kehutanan. (1994). *Pentujuk Teknis Inventarisasi dan Indentifikasi Peladang Berpindah dan Perambah Hutan*. Jakarta: Direktorat Reboisasi.

Dove, Michael. (1993). "A Revisionist View of Tropical Deforestation and Development." *Environmental Conservation* 20(1): 17–24, 56.

Dupuis, E. Melanie and Peter Vandergeest. (1996). "Introduction," in E. Melanie Dupuis and Peter Vandergeest, eds. *Creating the Countryside: The Politics of Rural and Environmental Discourse*. Philadelphia: Temple University Press, 1–25.

Eder, James. (1994). "State-Sponsored 'Participatory Development' and Tribal Filipino Ethnic Identity." *Social Analysis* 35: 28–38.

Ellen, R. F. (1986). "What Black Elk Left Unsaid: On the Illusory Images of Green Primitivism." *Anthropology Today* 2(6): 8–12.

——. (1976). "The Development of Anthropology and Colonial Policy in the Netherlands: 1800–1960." *Journal of the*

History of the Behavioural Sciences 12:303–24.

Evers, Pieter. (1995). "Preliminary Policy and Legal Questions about Recognizing Traditional Land in Indonesia." *Ekonesia* 3:1–24.

Fisher, William. (1996). "Native Amazonians and the Making of the Amazonian Wilderness: From Discourse of Riches to Sloth and Underdevelopment," in E. Melanie Dupuis and Peter Vandergeest, eds. *Creating the Countryside: The Politics of Rural and Environmental Discourse*. Philadelphia: Temple University Press, 166–203.

Foster-Carter, Aidan. (1975). "The Modes of Production Controversy." *New Left Review* 107:47–77.

Friedman, Jonathan. (1987). "Beyond Otherness: The Spectacularization of Anthropology." *Telos* 71:161–70.

——. (1992). "The Past in the Future: History and the Politics of Identity." *American Anthropologist* 94(4):837–59.

Gray, Andrew. (1995). "The Indigenous Movement in Asia," in R. H. Barnes, Andrew Gray and Benedict Kingsbury, eds. *Indigenous Peoples of Asia*. Michigan: Association for Asian Studies, 35–58.

Gupta, Akhil and James Ferguson. (1992). "Beyond 'Culture': Space, Identity, and the Politics of Difference." *Cultural Anthropology* 7(1):6–23.

Hall, Stuart. (1996). "On Postmodernism and Articulation: An Interview with Stuart Hall," edited by Lawrence Grossberg, in David Morley and Kuan-Hsing Chen, eds. *Stuart Hall: Critical Dialogues in Cultural Studies*. London: Routledge, 131–50 (reprinted from Journal of Communication Inquiry (1986) 10(2):45–60).

——. (1995). "Negotiating Caribbean Identities." *New Left Review* 209:3–14.

——. (1990). "Cultural Identity and Diaspora," in Jonathan Rutherford, ed. *Identity: Community, Culture, Difference*. London: Lawrence and Wishart, 222–37.

——. (1985). "Signification, Representation, Ideology: Althusser and the Post-Structuralist Debates." *Critical Studies in Mass Communication* 2(2):91–114.

Hecht, Susanna and Alexander Cockburn.

(1990). *The Fate of the Forest*. London: Penguin.

Henley, David. (1996). *Nationalism and Regionalism in a Colonial Context: Minahasa in the Dutch East Indies*. Leiden: KITLV Press.

Herzfeld, Michael. (1997). "Anthropology: A Practice of Theory." *International Social Science Journal* 153:301–18.

Jackson, Jean. (1995). "Culture, Genuine and Spurious: The Politics of Indianness in the Vaupes, Colombia." *American Ethnologist* 22(1): 3–27.

Kahn, Joel. (1993). *Constituting the Minangkabau: Peasants, Culture and Modernity in Colonial Indonesia*. Providence: Berg.

——. (1999). "Culturalising the Indonesian Uplands," in Tania Murray Li, ed. *Transforming the Indonesian Uplands: Marginality, Power and Production*. Amsterdam: Harwood Academic Publishers, 79–101.

Keck, Margaret. (1995). "Social Equity and Environmental Politics in Brazil: Lessons from the Rubber Tappers of Acre." *Comparative Politics* 27(4):409–24.

Kingsbury, Benedict. (1998). " 'Indigenous Peoples in International Law: A Constructivist Approach to the Asian Controversy." *The American Journal of International Law* 92(3):414–57.

Kipp, Rita Smith and Susan Rodgers. (1987). "Introduction: Indonesian Religions in Society," in Rita Smith Kipp and Susan Rodgers, eds. *Indonesia Religions in Transition*. Tucson: University of Arizona Press, 1–31.

Koentjaraningrat. (1993). "Pendahuluan" and "Membangun Masyarakat Terasing" in Koentjaraningrat, ed. *Masyarakat Terasing di Indonesia*. Jakarta: Gramedia and Departemen Sosial, 1–18, 344–50.

Kusumaatmadja, Sarwono. (1993). "The Human Dimensions of Sustainable Development," in Arimbi H. P., ed. *Proceeding, Seminar on the Human Dimensions of Environmentally Sound Development*. Jakarta: WALHI and Friends of the Earth, 12–15.

Laudjeng, Hedar. (1994). "Kearifan Tradisional Masyarakat Adat Lindu" in Arianto Sangadji, ed. *Bendungan Rakyat dan Ling-*

kungan: Catatan Kritis Rencana Pembangunan PLTA Lore Lindu. Jakarta: WALHI, 150–63.

Li, Tania Murray. (1996). "Images of Community: Discourse and Strategy in Property Relations." *Development and Change* 27(3): 501–27.

———. (1997). "Producing Agrarian Transformation at the Indonesian Periphery," in Richard Blanton et al., eds. *Economic Analysis Beyond the Local System.* Lanham: University Press of America, 125–46.

———. (1999a). "Marginality, Power and Production: Analysing Upland Transformations," in Tania Murray Li, ed. *Transforming the Indonesian Uplands: Marginality, Power and Production.* Amsterdam: Harwood Academic Publishers, 1–44.

———. (1999b.) "Compromising Power: Development, Culture, and Rule in Indonesia." *Cultural Anthropology* 14(3): 1–28.

Lohmann, Larry. (1993). "Green Orientalism." *The Ecologist* 23(6):202–4.

Lynch, Owen J. and Kirk Talbott. (1995). *Balancing Acts: Community-Based Forest Management and National Law in Asia and the Pacific.* Washington, D.C.: World Resources Institute.

Moniaga, Sandra. (1993a). "The Systematic Destruction of the Indigenous System of Various Adat Communities throughout Indonesia," in Arimbi H.P. ed. *Proceeding, Seminar on the Human Dimensions of Environmentally Sound Development.* Jakarta: WALHI and Friends of the Earth, 31–6.

———. (1993b). "Toward Community-Based Forestry and Recognition of *Adat* Property Rights in the Outer Islands of Indonesia," in Jefferson Fox, ed. *Legal Frameworks for Forest Management in Asia: Case Studies of Community-State Relations.* Honolulu: Environment and Policy Institute, East-West Center, 131–50.

Neumann, Roderick. (1995). "Local Challenges to Global Agendas: Conservation, Economic Liberalization and the Pastoralists' Rights Movement in Tanzania." *Antipode* 27(4):363–82.

Nourse, Jennifer. (1989). "We are the Womb of the World: Birth Spirits and the Lauje of Central Sulawesi." PhD Dissertation, University of Virginia.

———. (1994). "Textbook Heroes and Local Memory: Writing the Right History in Central Sulawesi." *Social Analysis* 35: 102–21.

O'Brien, Jay and William Roseberry. (1991). "Introduction," in Jay O'Brien and William Roseberry, eds. *Golden Ages, Dark Ages.* Berkeley: University of California Press, 1–18.

Peluso, Nancy. (1995). "Whose Woods Are These? Counter-Mapping Forest Territories in Kalimantan, Indonesia." *Antipode* 27(4):383–406.

Ramos, Alcida Rita. (1994). "The Hyperreal Indian." *Critique of Anthropology* 14(2): 153–71.

Rangan, Haripriya. (1993). "Romancing the Environment: Popular Environmental Action in the Garhwal Himalayas," in John Friedmann and Haripriya Rangan, eds. *In Defense of Livelihood: Comparative Studies on Environmental Action.* West Hartford: Kumarian Press, 155–81.

Rouse, Roger. (1995). "Personhood and Collectivity in Transnational Migration to the United States." *Critique of Anthropology* 15(4):351–80.

Ruiter, Tine. (1999). "Agrarian Transformations in the Uplands of Langkat: Survival of Independent Karo Batak Smallholders," in Tania Murray Li, ed. *Transforming the Indonesian Uplands: Marginality, Power and Production.* Amsterdam: Harwood Academic Publishers, 279–310.

Safitri, Myrna. (1995). "Hak dan Akses Masyarakat Lokal pada Sumberdaya Hutan: Kajian Peraturan Perundang-undangan Indonesia." *Ekonesia* 3:43–60.

Sangadji, Arianto. (1996). *Menyorot PLTA Lore Lindu.* Palu: Yayasan Tanah Merdeka.

Schweithelm, James et al. (1992). *Land Use and Socio-Economic Survey Lore Lindu National Park and Morowali Nature Reserve.* Sulawesi Parks Program, Directorate-General of Forest Protection and Nature Conservation, Ministry of Forestry, and the Nature Conservancy.

Scott, David. (1992). "Criticism and Culture: Theory and Post-colonial Claims on

Anthropological Disciplinarity." *Critique of Anthropology* 12(4):371–94.

Shields, Rob. (1991). *Places on the Margin: Alternative Geographies of Modernity.* London: Routledge.

Sider, Gerald. (1987). "When Parrots Learn to Talk, and Why They Can't: Domination, Deception, and Self-deception in Indian-White Relations." *Comparative Studies in Society and History* 29:3–23.

SKEPHI and Rachel Kiddell-Monroe. (1993). "Indonesia: Land Rights and Development," in Marcus Colchester and Larry Lohmann, eds. *The Struggle for Land and the Fate of the Forests.* Penang: World Rainforest Movement, 228–63.

Stearman, Allyn MacLean. (1994). "Revisiting the Myth of the Ecologically Noble Savage in Amazonia: Implications for Indigenous Land Rights." *Culture and Agriculture* 49:2–6.

Thomas, Nicholas. (1992). "Substantivization and Anthropological Discourse," in James Carrier, ed. *History and Tradition in Melanesian Ethnography.* Berkeley: University of California Press, 64–85.

——. (1994). *Colonialism's Culture.* Cambridge: Polity Press.

Tsing, Anna Lowenhaupt. (1999). "Becoming a Tribal Elder and other Green Development Fantasies," in Tania Murray Li, ed. *Transforming the Indonesian Uplands: Marginality, Power and Production.* Amsterdam: Harwood Academic Publishers, 159–202.

——. (1993). *In the Realm of the Diamond Queen.* Princeton: Princeton University Press.

Trouillot, Michel-Rolphe. (1991). "Anthropology and the Savage Slot: The Poetics and Politics of Otherness," in Richard Fox, ed.

Recapturing Anthropology. Santa Fe: School of American Research, 17–44.

Watts, Michael. (1992). "Space for Everything (A Commentary)." *Cultural Anthropology* 7(1):115–29.

Zerner, Charles. (1990). Community Rights, Customary Law, and the Law of Timber Concessions in Indonesia's Forests: Legal Options and Alternative in Designing the Commons, Forestry Studies UTF/INS/065.

——. (1994). "Through a Green Lens: The Construction of Customary Environmental Law and Community in Indonesia's Maluku Islands." *Law and Society Review* 28(5):1079–122.

NEWSPAPER REPORTS

"Eksistensi Hukum Adat Dewasa Ini" *Kompas* 27 March 1996 (Achmad Sodiki).

"'Indigenous Peoples' dan Penguasaan atas Tanah" *Kompas* 29 April 1993 (Tim Babcock and Maria Ruwiastuti).

"Kearifan Masyarakat Adat dalam Konservasi Alam Sangat Tinggi" *Kompas* 13 September 1993 (Anon).

"Masyarakat Lindu Menolak Rencana Pembangunan PLTA" *Kompas* 11 September 1993 (Anon).

"Semoga Hak Ulayat Dihargai" *Kompas* 29 April 1993 (Masri Singarimbun).

"Siberut Island Likely to have New Settlement Areas" *Jakarta Post* 14 February 1996 (Anon).

"SKHEPI Opposes Siberut Resettlement" *Jakarta Post* 17 February 1996 (Stevie Emilia).

"Sulawesi Tribe Opposes Lake Lindu Dam Project" *Jakarta Post* 11 September 1994 (Anon).

19

Green Dots, Pink Hearts: Displacing Politics from the Malaysian Rain Forest

J. Peter Brosius

1999

[E]thnography is crucial in a world in which the domination of privileged discourse . . . threatens to make other discourses inaudible or unintelligible. [Rappaport 1993:301]

Recent years have witnessed the rapid proliferation and growth of numerous local, national, and transnational environmental movements. Most often today, they appear in the guise of what have become known as Non-Governmental Organizations (NGOs). These movements, representing new forms of political agency, stand at the forefront of a fundamental shift in the distribution of power – or at least they *appear* to do so.

Accompanying this process of proliferation, we have witnessed a dramatic upsurge in interest among anthropologists (and others) in analyzing these movements (Dizard 1994; Fisher 1997; Milton 1993, 1996; Taylor 1995; Wapner 1996). This is in part a product of the fact that environmental NGOs have become such highly visible players in a terrain that anthropologists once thought they could claim as their own – the rural/remote field site, most likely occupied by indigenous communities of one sort or another.

There are, however, other reasons for our interest in these movements, reasons that have more to do with recent theoretical trends within our discipline. Most obvious, perhaps, has been the trend since the mid-1980s toward what Marcus and Fischer refer to as "the repatriation of anthropology as cultural critique" (1986:111). Uncomfortable with the way we see otherness essentialized in indigenous rights campaigns, acculturative processes disguised in an effort to stress the authenticity of indigenous peoples, and concepts such as "wilderness" deployed in environmentalist campaigns, we have taken it as our task to provide critical commentary.[1] A factor of equal importance in contributing to our interest in the study of environmental movements has been the way in which post-Foucauldian insights into the intersections of discourse/power/knowledge have likewise come to converge with a series of critiques of traditional anthropological conceptions of culture and ethnographic fieldwork (Clifford 1988; Fox 1991; Gupta and Ferguson 1992, 1997; Marcus 1995; Rosaldo 1989) and with an interest in transnational processes and globalization (Appadurai 1990, 1991; Featherstone 1990; Kearney 1995). Finally, a broader, transdisciplinary florescence in environmental scholarship in the last decade has had a decisive influence in alerting us to the importance of recognizing the cultural and historical contingency of "nature" and the significance of this contingency for understanding the ways in which various kinds of political agents construct and contest nature (Bennet and Chaloupka 1993; Cronon 1995; DuPuis and Vandergeest 1996; Escobar 1996, 1999; Herndl and Brown 1996; Soper 1995; Takacs 1996; Zerner 1996).

This brief attempt to suggest some sources for our interest in the study of environmental movements is far from complete: an adequate account of factors that are of significance in stimulating our interest in the study of environmental movements would require a much more lengthy discussion (see Brosius [1999]). What is important for the present discussion, however, is the direction in which this has led us. We can discern three very conspicuous trends in the study of environmental movements today: (1) a sustained critique of romantic, essentialized images (Brosius 1997a; Cronon 1995; Lewis 1992; Slater 1995; Sturgeon 1997; Zerner 1994); (2) an emphasis on contestation (Dizard 1994; Fairhead and Leach 1994; Hawkins 1993; Mason 1992; McManus 1996; Moore 1993; Morehouse 1996; Proctor 1995; Rangan 1995; Schmink and Wood 1992; Zimmerman 1994); and (3) an interest in the transnationality of environmental movements and discourses (Brysk 1994; Conklin and Graham 1995; Lipschutz and Conca 1993; Princen and Finger 1994; Schwartzman 1991; Turner 1991).

I introduce all of this by way of wanting to argue that I think we are missing the mark. To the extent that we equate "environmentalism" with environmental movements and focus our attention on subaltern social movements as objects of ethnographic research, we ignore a contemporary development that is in many respects more crucial: the progressive envelopment of environmental movements within institutions for local, national, and global environmental surveillance and governance.

I want to frame my argument in terms defined by Roy Rappaport in "The Anthropology of Trouble," first delivered as the Distinguished Lecture in General Anthropology at the 1992 American Anthropological Association meetings and subsequently published in the *American Anthropologist* in 1993. In the process of articulating what he means by

"trouble," Rappaport expresses concern about "the subordination of the fundamental to the contingent and instrumental." In particular, he laments the way in which economics (the contingent and instrumental), in its attempt to "bottom line" the world, has come to supply contemporary "society with its dominant social discourse" (1993:298) at the expense of basic ecological concerns (the fundamental). Rappaport poses this "deformation of . . . 'the order of viability'" (p. 299) as something characteristic of the encounter between two domains: the ecological and the economic. I want to draw attention to something perhaps even more pernicious: the way in which this deformation has been able to insinuate itself into that which is considered to be more purely ecological. It does this through what have been termed "Institutions for the Earth" (Haas et al. 1993).

Institutionalizations

Escobar (1995), Ferguson (1994), and others have recently produced a series of remarkable critical accounts of international development institutions and their local manifestations (see Apffel-Marglin and Marglin 1990; Pigg 1992; Redclift 1987; Sachs 1992). Escobar in particular provides a detailed historical account of the post–World War II emergence of development discourse and of the subjects and forms of institutional intervention that this discourse has conjured into being.

One of Escobar's primary goals is to describe "how the 'Third World' has been produced by the discourses and practices of development since their inception in the early post–World War II period" (1995:4). Development discourse, Escobar argues, "has created an extremely efficient apparatus for producing knowledge about, and the exercise of power over, the Third World. . . . In sum, it has successfully deployed a regime of government over the Third World, a 'space for "subject peoples"' that ensures certain control over it" (p. 9).

In something of a sideline discussion, Escobar briefly examines how, as a result of the 1987 Brundtland report *Our Common Future* published by the World Commission on Environment and Development in 1987, environmental concerns came to be incorporated – institutionally and discursively – into the field of development through the concept of "sustainable development." This has promulgated a regime of "environmental managerialism" (1995:194). wherein the "Western scientist continues to speak for the Earth" (p. 194), aided by a bevy of planners and administrators in an ongoing process of professionalization and bureaucratization. According to Escobar:

> The resignification of nature as environment; the reinscription of the Earth into capital via the gaze of science; the reinterpretation of poverty as effect of destroyed environments; and the new lease on management and planning as arbiters between people and nature, all of these are effects of the discursive construction of sustainable development. [p. 202]

To illustrate his argument, Escobar briefly examines the role of the World Bank's Global Environmental Facility (GEF) in Colombia. In explicating the discursive contours of sustainable development in this particular context, what Escobar's analysis points to is the degree to which an immense institutional/managerial apparatus is presently descending on "the environment," much as it once did on development.

The scale at which this is occurring is remarkable indeed. It takes many forms: the Montreal Protocol, the Convention on Biological Diversity, and Agenda 21, to name just a few. Acronyms proliferate: UNEP (United Nations Environment Programme), UNCED (United Nations Conference on Environment and Development), CSD (Commission on Sustainable Development), WCMC (World Conservation Monitoring Centre), TFAP (Tropical Forest Action Plan), IPCC (Intergovernmental Panel on Climate Change), ICDPs (Integrated Conservation and Development Programs), NEAPs (National Environmental Action Policies), and so on ad infinitum. Each of the above represents or supports regimes for the institutionalization of environmental surveillance and governance.

One of the clearest indicators of the scale of contemporary environmental institutionaliza-

tion has been the accelerating pace of professionalization – indicated, for instance, in the remarkable growth of the field of environmental management and in the proliferation of Environmental Studies programs at universities. These represent efforts to train a transnational cadre of planners to design and execute various forms of environmental intervention. Yet another indicator, more oblique perhaps, has been the growth of scholarly interest in international environmental politics, primarily as this concerns the establishment of regimes for environmental management. Significantly, this is a field of study dominated by political scientists and other scholars of international relations.[2] With very few exceptions, anthropologists have not contributed to research in this area.[3]

This process of environmental institutionalization can be viewed as a positive development in many respects, apparently representing progress in raising environmental concerns to a level of legitimacy that was previously lacking. There have been a number of concrete successes, most notably perhaps the Montreal Protocol, which has had a significant effect in reducing the destruction of atmospheric ozone.

Nevertheless, there are reasons to be concerned about this process of institutionalization. Such institutions, whatever else they may do, inscribe and naturalize certain discourses. While they create certain possibilities for ameliorating environmental degradation, they simultaneously preclude others. They privilege certain actors and marginalize others. Apparently designed to advance an environmental agenda, such institutions in fact often obstruct meaningful change through endless negotiation, legalistic evasion, compromise among "stakeholders," and the creation of unwieldy projects aimed at top-down environmental management. More importantly, however, they insinuate and naturalize a discourse that excludes moral or political imperatives in favor of indifferent bureaucratic and/or technoscientific forms of institutionally created and validated intervention.

This process of institutionalization and political displacement is occurring across a range of environmental concerns. I have observed it in my own work on the international environmental campaign that focused on rain forest destruction and indigenous rights in the East Malaysian state of Sarawak (see Bevis 1995; Colchester 1989; Hong 1987; Hurst 1990; INSAN 1989; World Rainforest Movement and *Sahabat Alam Malaysia* 1990). In the following discussion I trace the history of the Sarawak campaign in order to elucidate this process of institutionalization and displacement. After briefly describing several points of articulation among Penan, the state, and the timber industry, I consider the formative stages of the campaign in which both Malaysian and Northern environmentalists[4] succeeded in bringing the issue of rain forest destruction in Sarawak to world attention by focusing on the plight of indigenous communities. Malaysian authorities, in turn, responded with a vigorous series of condemnations of Northern environmentalists. I then examine several significant rhetorical shifts that occurred as Malaysian authorities, joined by Malaysian NGOs, began to articulate persuasive counterarguments to Northern environmental rhetoric, and as Northern environmentalists themselves began to incorporate those counterarguments into the Sarawak campaign. These rhetorical shifts had real effects. Northern consumption of tropical timber began to decrease and Malaysian authorities were compelled to respond by embracing the idea of timber certification and by waging a public relations campaign aimed at demonstrating their adherence to the principle of sustainable forest management. By finding what seemed to be common ground with Northern environmentalists in their acceptance of timber certification, Malaysian authorities were able to shift the discursive contours of the Sarawak campaign away from the moral/political domain and toward the domain of institutionalized environmental managerialism. As a result, the momentum that had built up over opposition to logging in Sarawak began to dissipate. Elucidating this complex history of negotiations and displacements, of shifting definitions of interest and shifting forms of agency, provides a number of important insights into how regimes of governmentality[5] are established and amplified, to the exclusion

of other forms of engagement in the politics of nature.[6]

The International Sarawak Campaign

Situating Penan

In interior central Borneo there exist two broad classes of people: longhouse-dwelling swidden agriculturalists and hunting and gathering forest nomads such as the Penan. While agriculturalists live along the main rivers, Penan and other hunter-gatherers are found in interior headwaters.[7] The Penan of Sarawak are divided into two distinct populations, Eastern and Western Penan (Needham 1972:177), together numbering some 7,000 individuals. The Eastern Penan inhabit the Baram and Limbang watersheds, while the majority of the Western Penan are found in the Balui watershed (see Figure 19.1).[8] Though in broad outline the forest adaptations of Eastern and Western Penan are very similar, and though the Eastern and Western Penan speak mutually intelligible subdialects of the same language, there are significant differences between these two groups with regard to subsistence technology, settlement patterns, and social organization.

Government policy toward Penan and other indigenous communities in Sarawak is directed by a thoroughly modernist ideology of development.[9] Since joining Malaysia in 1963, the Sarawak state government has made a concerted effort to bring the Penan into what is termed the "mainstream" of Malaysian society by persuading them to settle. The ideology of development, and the associated concept of the "mainstream," have an imperative force that leaves little latitude for Penan to continue existing within the rain forest. This is evident in any number of official pronouncements about the Penan way of life and the benevolent role that the government should play in ameliorating their "plight" as forest dwellers. Sarawak Chief Minister Taib Mahmud, for instance, stated:

> That's why we want to slowly settle them and it is our responsibility. We are belted with one

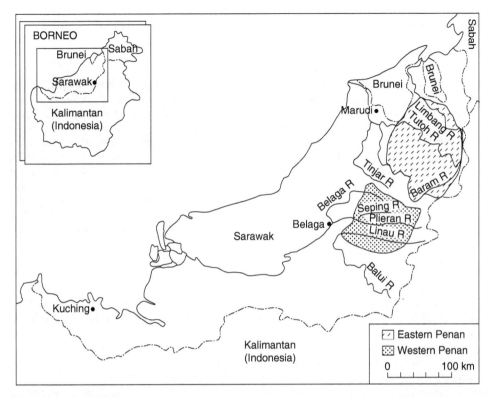

Figure 19.1 *Distribution of Eastern and Western Penan in Sarawak (from a map by Ellen Walker)*

philosophy and this is to build an equal society. How can we have an equal society when you allow a small group of people to behave like animals in the jungle. . . . I owe it to the Penans to get them gradually into the mainstream so that they can be like any other Sarawakian. [Siva Kumar 1991:178–9]

Government efforts to bring Penan into the mainstream have had a transformative effect on their lives. During the 1960s, Penan began to settle in increasing numbers. Today fewer than 400 Eastern Penan in the vicinity of the upper Tutoh and upper Limbang River areas remain fully nomadic, approximately 5 percent of the total. In persuading Penan to settle, the state government has provided them with all manner of goods: corrugated roofing, piped water systems, chainsaws, outboard motors, and the like. Most Penan settlements have heli-

copter pads to facilitate visits by medical personnel, civil servants, and politicians, and a number of schools and model villages have been built. Altogether, most forms of government intervention have been relatively benign and Penan have remained on ancestral lands.

Even more consequential for the lives of Penan has been the advent of logging. In the 1980s, Sarawak became a major supplier of tropical hardwoods on the international market and experienced one of the highest rates of deforestation in the world. The speed with which logging progressed was remarkable. Although timber companies only began to penetrate the interior in the late 1970s, by the 1980s they had moved into areas occupied by Penan, and have now nearly reached the Indonesian border in several places. Today the pace of logging has diminished, as timber is much depleted and as timber companies from

Sarawak have moved to Papua New Guinea, Surinam, Guiana, and elsewhere.

Logging has a dramatic effect on the lives of Penan. Sago palms (*Eugeissona utilis*), which form the basis of traditional subsistence, are uprooted by bulldozers; fruit trees and rattan are destroyed; game disappears; severe river siltation occurs; and graves are obliterated. Logging not only undermines the basis of Penan subsistence but, by transforming sites with biographical, social, and historical significance, also destroys those things that are iconic of their existence as a society.

Although Sarawak is notable within Malaysia for the degree to which it has historically recognized the land rights of indigenous communities, Sarawak state law does not recognize Penan principles of land tenure. According to Sarawak land law, communities can only claim land that they cultivated before 1958. Because the majority of Penan settled after that, their claims to land are without legal basis.

In response to logging, Penan have attempted to defend their claims to land in the most profoundly moral terms. They view the way they are treated by government officials, camp managers, police, and others as indicating an utter disregard for their humanity. Penan characterize government officials as people who "don't know how to pity." As one woman stated, "When they [the government or company people] look into our eyes, they see the eyes of a monkey, the eyes of a dog." The Penan express overwhelming frustration at the apparent inability of government officials to hear them. Indeed, state officials most often attribute Penan disaffection either to the fact that they have been instigated by foreign environmentalists or that they have been "neglected": if only the government had done more to help Penan develop, one hears officials say, they would not be so "confused" and unruly. These officials present logging as a key facet of their efforts to achieve development.[10]

Although Penan are almost uniformly opposed to logging, the ways in which Eastern and Western Penan have responded contrasts markedly. While Western Penan have been conspicuously acquiescent to the activities of logging companies, Eastern Penan have responded with the erection of blockades.[11]

The campaign unfolds

The Sarawak campaign began in 1987 when Eastern Penan hunter-gatherers in the Baram and Limbang Districts of Sarawak (see Figure 19.1) erected a series of over a dozen blockades against logging companies that were encroaching on their lands (Brosius 1997a, 1997b). Within a very short time, images of these blockades, accompanied by transcripts of Penan statements, made their way to Japan, Australia, Europe, and North America. The result, at a time when concern about rain forest destruction was increasing among environmentalists and the Euro-American public alike, was a dramatic upsurge in interest in the Penan among Northern environmental NGOs. The campaign that developed was very high profile indeed, covered widely by media in North America, the UK, Europe, and Australia. For a while at least, the Penan became icons of resistance for environmentalists worldwide. This was not to last.

The history of this campaign can in part be written as one of increasing and then decreasing momentum. Environmentalists who were involved recount that there were periods when the possibility of success seemed certain, enthusiasm was high, and events followed one after the other. At some point in the early 1990s, this momentum began to dissipate. Different participants have varying interpretations of why this was so. Some are puzzled about where it went, some attribute it to cumulative frustration over the lack of any progress, while still others suggest that "every campaign exists on a bell curve" (Wade Davis, pers. comm.). There is, I would argue, more to it than that.

The early part of the campaign focused on the civil disobedience of the Penan – blockades, arrests, and trials – as well as on the efforts of the Malaysian environmental organization Sahabat Alam Malaysia (SAM [Friends of the Earth Malaysia]) to support the Penan struggle both locally and internationally. It also focused on the charismatic figure of Swiss environmentalist Bruno Manser, who lived with nomadic Penan for some six and a

Need for development

half years (from 1984 to 1990) and who was instrumental in helping them to organize.[12] There was also a sustained series of direct actions and other campaign activities in the US, UK, Japan, Australia, and Europe that served to keep a focus on the situation in Sarawak.

In the early years of the campaign – from 1987 to 1990 – the threat facing the Penan and the rain forest was constructed by environmentalists according to what might be termed the *Fern Gully* allegory, after the animated film. The image presented was of pristine indigenous innocents living a timeless existence in the depths of the rain forest, as bulldozers churned toward them, devouring everything in their path. Such an image had the effect of producing a sense of great urgency: little time remained and it was imperative that the bulldozers be stopped. The statement that logging in Sarawak was going on 24 hours a day was repeated again and again in campaign literature, along with statements to the effect that the Penan had only a few months left or that the forests of Sarawak would be gone in just a few years.

Declarations such as these lent great force to the imperative that logging must be stopped, and the starkness of the image purveyed through the *Fern Gully* allegory had a galvanizing effect. In the face of a threat represented in such harsh terms, the campaign gained wide support among Northern environmentalists, as well as among numerous public figures. In 1989, members of the Grateful Dead testified before the US Congress on behalf of the Penan. In 1990 and 1992, then Senator Al Gore held two press conferences with Bruno Manser and with Penan, and in *Earth in the Balance* he wrote the following:

Two thousand miles northwest of PNG [Papua New Guinea] . . . thousands of indigenous people in Sarawak, Malaysia linked arms in human barricades to block the logging roads deep inside the tropical rain forest in a desperate effort to stop indiscriminate and destructive logging. . . . Although these resistance fighters had little chance against the powerful forces arrayed against them, their courage inspired international protests that are still continuing.

One of the Sarawak peoples, the Penan, sent a delegation to the United States with the help of an environmental group, the Friends of the Earth. They walked into my office one winter day, looking a little like visitors from another millennium, their straw headgear and wooden bracelets the only remnants of the culture they left behind, wearing borrowed sweaters as protection against the unaccustomed cold. Using a translator . . . the Penans described how the logging companies had set up floodlights to continue their destruction of the forest all through the night as well as the day. Like the shell-shocked inhabitants of a city under siege, they described how not even the monsoon rains slowed the chain saws and logging machinery that was destroying the ancestral home of their people. [Gore 1992:283–84]

In a speech at Kew Gardens in 1990, Prince Charles made the following statement:

It seems to me important that any discussion about the tropical forests should start by looking at the people who depend directly on them for their livelihood. . . . Ever since the first explorers from Spain and Portugal set foot in South America, and the British visited the Caribbean, the people of the so-called developed world have always treated tribal people as total savages, be it to enslave them, subdue, civilise them or convert them to our way of religious thinking. . . . Even now, as the Penan in Sarawak are harassed and even imprisoned for defending their own tribal lands . . . that dreadful pattern of collective genocide continues.

As the campaign gained momentum, extensive media coverage served to raise the profile of the Penan even further. The Sarawak situation received coverage on *NBC Evening News*, National Public Radio, CNN, and *Primetime Live* and in *Newsweek*, *Time*, *The New Yorker*, *The Wall Street Journal*, and *Rolling Stone* (for example, see Linden 1991 and Sesser 1991). BBC and *National Geographic* both produced documentaries on the Penan. The Australian film *Blowpipes and Bulldozers* and the Swedish film *Tong Tana* both reached large audiences and received wide acclaim. Universal Studios began development of an action/adventure ecohorror script in which the forest wisdom of the Penan saves the world from catastrophe, and Warner Brothers has been developing a script on the Bruno Manser story. Meanwhile, Penan were awarded the Reebok Human Rights Award and the Sierra Club-sponsored Chico Mendez Award, and SAM activist Harrison Ngau was awarded the Goldman Prize for his work against logging in Sarawak.

Malaysia responds

In responding to the Sarawak campaign as it was becoming rapidly internationalized through the late 1980s, Malaysia broke new ground in defining how Southern (that is, "Third World") governments could react to the criticisms of Northern environmentalists. Their response, while somewhat haphazard, was immediate and vigorous. Among other things, the Malaysian government criticized Northern environmentalists for romanticizing the Penan, for ignoring their own histories of subjugating indigenous peoples, and for behaving as imperialists. They further accused environmentalists of using the Penan issue to raise funds for their organizations or to promote the interests of the temperate forest industry.

By far the harshest and most outspoken critic of Northern environmentalism was Malaysian Prime Minister Dr Mahatir Mohamed. In 1992, Dr Mahatir referred to the Sarawak campaign as a form of "Eco-imperialism" and stated that "when we achieved independence we thought we would be free. But the North is still subjecting us to imperial pressures" (Mahatir bin Mohamed 1992). The intensity of Dr Mahatir's disdain for Northern environmentalists was perhaps most forcefully expressed in his widely publicized 1987 response to the letter of a ten-year-old English boy who had written to him to express his concern about rain forest destruction in Sarawak. The boy's letter was as follows: "I am 10 years old and when I am older I hope to study animals in the tropical rain forests. But if you let the lumber companies carry on there will not be any left. And millions of animals will die. Do you think that is right just so one rich man gets another million pounds or more. I think it is disgrace-

ful" (INSAN 1989:75). The Prime Minister responded with the following:

> It is disgraceful that you should be used by adults for the purpose of trying to shame us because of our extraction of timber from our forests. . . . The timber industry helps hundreds of thousands of poor people in Malaysia. Are they supposed to remain poor because you want to study tropical animals? . . . If you don't want us to cut down our forests, tell your father to tell the rich countries like Britain to pay more for the timber they buy from us. . . . I hope you will tell the adults who made use of you to learn all the facts. They should not be too arrogant and think they know how best to run a country. They should expel all the people living in the British countryside and allow secondary forests to grow and fill these new forests with wolves and bears, etc. so you can study them before studying tropical animals. . . . [pp. 76–8]

Dr Mahatir was not alone in his condemnation of Northern environmentalists. Numerous Malaysian government ministers and other senior officials, inspired by Dr Mahatir's example, were equally critical, characterizing the campaign against logging in Sarawak as nothing more than a self-interested "smear campaign" against Malaysia. In a 1992 statement published in the *Los Angeles Times*, Malaysian trade minister Rafidah Aziz declared angrily that "anybody who's too concerned about what happens in other countries better not venture out of their own country. . . . We don't want people to impose their human rights values on us. These great busybodies of the world, who don't bother with their own problems, their back yards are full of dirt" (Schoenberger 1992).

Such criticisms were also often expressed in editorials in the government-controlled press. In a 1988 newspaper editorial, Sarawak Chief Minister Taib Mahmud was quoted as criticizing foreign environmentalists for being "even more dangerous than the communists" (Ngu 1988). He was further quoted as stating, "These people were nobodies who tried to become gods in our midst. They are not our friends because they were actually making a laughing stock of our communities" (Ngu 1988). A 1991 editorial in the *Sarawak Tribune* entitled "Crude Interference" criticized a group of Euro-American environmentalists who had staged a protest action in Sarawak in the following terms:

A group of scruffy foreigners, including some grotesquely fat women, mindlessly chained themselves to metal structures belonging to a timber company in Kuala Baram. . . . The bizarre behavior is their weird way of protesting against logging in Sarawak. . . . The self-proclaimed environmental pariahs are plain foreign political agitators who use the Penans and the environment as political issues against the State of Sarawak. . . . They came from organizations and countries which had, decades ago, depleted their own forests. . . . The Penans are [the] perfect smokescreen to camouflage double-standard[s] and double-talk. [July 14, 1991]

These, then, were the polarized terms around which the debate over rain forests and indigenous rights in Sarawak unfolded as the Sarawak campaign was gaining momentum and becoming increasingly internationalized through the late 1980s. On the one hand, Malaysian and Northern environmentalists drew attention to the situation in Sarawak by framing it in the starkest of terms: rampant forest destruction, the devastation of indigenous communities, an environmental and indigenous rights disaster demanding urgent action. Responding vigorously, Malaysian authorities accused Northern environmentalists of "ecoimperialism" and focused upon what was portrayed as the utter hypocrisy of Northern environmentalists for criticizing Malaysia's environmental and indigenous rights record. What is significant here is that both sides of the debate were framed in the most resolute moral and political terms. As the campaign continued, however, a series of striking rhetorical shifts began to occur.

The shifting contours of critique

When they began the Penan campaign, Northern NGOs, convinced that they had the moral high ground, never expected that their actions would be met with such a sustained, aggressive response from Malaysia. This was not a case where landless peasants were forced to clear rain forest for the sake of survival. The line between good and bad seemed evident; through a complex system of political patronage a group of corrupt officials were devouring Sarawak's forests for short-term profit at the expense of rural peoples. Even more compelling was the fact that these were *indigenous* peoples, bravely and unflinchingly staring into the face of power as they stood at their blockades.

When Malaysia began to respond, Northern environmentalists were surprised at the audacity of its response. For some time it was quite easy to dismiss this response as the most base form of defensiveness. This was particularly easy to do because, as the Sarawak campaign began to accelerate in 1987 and 1988, many of Malaysia's early responses were quite crude. For instance, Sarawak Minister of Environment and Tourism James Wong stated to a delegation of European environmentalists, in response to a concern raised that deforestation may affect climate, "We get too much rain in Sarawak – it stops me playing golf." Claims to the effect that environmentalists were a front for Northern softwood interests or that they only wanted to hobnob with celebrities appeared to be little more than clumsy attempts at deflection.

With time, however, it became less easy for environmentalists to dismiss Malaysian responses to the campaign. Increasingly through the early 1990s, Malaysian officials began to make compelling counterarguments about the linkages between North and South. They raised questions, for instance, about the place of temperate forests in the global forest equation: why should the North impose standards of sustainability for logging in tropical forests when no such efforts are made in their own countries? Linked to this were compelling arguments concerning the relationship between forest destruction in the South and Northern consumption. Again, it was Dr Mahatir who most forcefully argued this position. In a 1992 article, for instance, he stated,

The North should begin to clean up its own backyard and stop scapegoating the South for the ecological sins it committed on the road to prosperity. The North should resist the temptation to lock up the tropical forests and other natural resources, which are critical for our development, in the name of a "common heritage." Eco-imperialism should be brought to an end once and for all. [Mahatir bin Mohamed and Lutzenberger 1992:56]

Sentiments such as those expressed by Dr Mahatir were reflected by other Malaysian officials as well. In a 1993 speech in Atlanta, Minister of Primary Industries Lim Keng Yaik stated, "As a response to Rio, the time has come to address not just tropical forests but also temperate and boreal forests. I am sure that the world does not think that everything is going well and fine in temperate and boreal forest management and that tropical forests is [sic] the only wayward child that needs to be brought under control" (1993). Criticizing Northern environmentalists, he continued, "These so-called champions have for their own reasons chosen to ignore the problems in their own backyards and are only interested in pointing their fingers and directing world attention at tropical forest [sic], as if that is the be all and the end all of all environmental ills" (1993). In a 1995 interview, an official from the Malaysian Timber Council told me that in the period leading up to the 1992 Rio Summit, "Malaysia played a big role in broadening the forestry debate." If forestry is to play a role in biodiversity conservation, climate change, and the search for new medicines, he said that "then it is imperative that the debate be opened to all forest types. . . . We have been able to be very forceful in arguing that temperate forests matter too. We convinced them [the North] that not only tropical forests have management problems."

Such arguments were compelling to Northern environmentalists because they were being articulated not only by Malaysian government officials, but also by a number of Malaysian activists who had participated in the earliest stages of the Sarawak campaign and who Northern environmentalists considered to be allies. Most conspicuous among these was economist Martin Khor Kok Peng, who for several years had been a prominent voice in Malaysian environmental politics. In a 1991 article Khor argued,

The North must recognise that it has already depleted most of its own forests and that it is now also responsible for consuming a very large share of tropical forest products. To facilitate forest conservation, it must drastically reduce its wasteful use of products derived from natural forests. . . . Moreover the Northern countries should acknowledge its responsibility for forest loss and now correspondingly for facilitating and saving of remaining forests. [p. 24]

In a 1995 interview, Martin Khor asked me rhetorically, "What if Northern elites define what is a global environmental problem, with sanctions? Should we allow the North to implement this? That is unfair, a new kind of colonialism."

The arguments put forth by Malaysian officials and activists were compelling to Northern environmentalists for other reasons as well. At a time when controversies about the logging of old-growth forest were gaining greater prominence in Australia, the US, Canada, and Scandinavia, Northern environmentalists viewed Malaysia's criticism that more focus needed to be placed on temperate and boreal forests as essentially valid. Indeed, many viewed it as a valuable tool for lobbying their governments to conserve old-growth forests within their own countries. Further, Malaysia's argument that Northern consumption was the real source of tropical forest destruction was consistent with critiques that Northern environmentalists had themselves leveled for many years against industrial society. Northern environmentalists also recognized as a strategic matter that, unless acknowledged and seriously engaged with, Malaysia's arguments could be very effective in blunting much of the moral/political force of the arguments deployed in the campaign. They recognized that, in order for them to retain any degree of moral authority in their encounter with Malaysia and to avoid appearing hypocritical, arrogant, or heavy-handed, they had to be willing to position themselves as taking an even-handed view of the problem of forest destruction on a global scale. This was particularly the case among environmentalists from mainstream organizations such as the World Wide Fund for Nature (WWF), who, because of their institutional affiliations, tended to take a longer-term, more global view as to what the most appropriate strategies might be for halting tropical forest destruction. Thus, while Northern environmentalists had misgivings about the messenger, Malaysia, they could not ignore the message being conveyed.

Most Northern environmentalists eventually realized that this had ceased to be a simple morality play. No longer was it merely an issue of stopping bulldozers and saving endangered forest dwellers. Given Malaysia's sustained critique of "eco-imperialism" and its arguments about Northern consumption, no longer did demands that Malaysia reduce its rate of logging – expressed in letter-writing campaigns, demonstrations, and direct actions such as ship blockades – have much salience. British environmentalist Koy Thompson described to me what he saw as a remarkable shift in attitude among Northern environmentalists. What had changed, he suggested, was the idea that the South was bad, and that the North could "bash them on the head." All the things that contribute to ecological degradation – debt, trade, and aid flows – are, he asserted, the fault of the North rather than the South.

Increasingly, too, in the face of growing political pressure from their own government, Malaysian NGOs (Sahabat Alam Malaysia in particular) indicated to Northern environmentalists that they should only undertake campaign activities directed at Malaysia when specifically requested to do so by their Malaysian counterparts and that in the meantime, they should concentrate their efforts in the North. As one Penang-based Malaysian activist put it,

We began to understand that Sarawak is a North/South issue. . . . The best way [to make headway] was for Northern NGOs to coordinate national campaigns – how each country is connected to this [deforestation] and what can they do locally [in their own countries]. How can things be coordinated? How can they tie in and be effective and not be drawn into sensitivities [within Malaysia].

The result of these developments was that, through the early 1990s, Northern environmentalists turned their attention increasingly toward temperate and boreal forests and toward a focus on the Northern role in tropical deforestation. Mainstream organizations such as WWF took a leading role in defining the temperate forest issue, exemplified by the 1992 publication of *Forests in Trouble: A Review of the Status of Temperate Forests Worldwide* (Dudley 1992). Organizations such as Friends of the Earth, Greenpeace, and the Japan Tropical Forest Action Network (JATAN) soon followed suit, and organizations such as the Taiga Rescue Network began to emerge. There was considerable debate (and a fair degree of ambivalence) within the movement as to whether it was prudent to shift away from an exclusive focus on tropical forests. With only some minor exceptions, however, there developed a consensus that this was the best way to proceed. As Austrian Greenpeace activist Martin Frimmel explained, they recognized the similarity between the tropics and the situation in places such as Canada and Siberia, and it was important to their credibility to focus on temperate and boreal forests. At the same time, they also recognized that it was necessary politically. As British rain forest activist George Marshall bluntly put it, "Southern countries are ready to say 'Piss off' unless we are willing to look at our own forests." In the summer of 1994, the European Rainforest Movement changed its name to Forest Movement Europe in direct response to these concerns.

Northern environmentalists turned their efforts not only toward temperate and boreal forests, but also toward reducing tropical timber consumption in their own countries. Describing JATAN's switch toward a focus on timber consumption within Japan, JATAN founder Yoichi Kuroda explained that the "ideology of forest use is from North to South. The problem is one of industrial consumption. Thus, we need to fundamentally rethink forest issues." The simple truth, he asserted, is that Northern consumption "drives basic land use in other countries."

Certainly efforts to pressure Malaysia through various kinds of threats to its markets for timber were initiated fairly early in the campaign through the efforts of environmentalists and indigenous rights advocates. For instance, the European Parliament unanimously passed a resolution in 1988 stating that all EC (European Community) member nations should suspend the import of timber from Sarawak, and in 1990 the Austrian Parliament voted unanimously to ban the import of tropical timber except that from sustainable sources. However, such efforts gained new impetus in the early 1990s with the shift toward a focus on consumption among Northern NGOs. This shift reverberated throughout the rain forest movement, with often remarkable results. In Japan the Sarawak Campaign Committee (SCC) lobbied local governments to declare a moratorium on the use of tropical timber in municipal projects; by 1994, some 50 or 60 municipal councils had agreed to comply. Because of pressure by Greenpeace in Germany, many large home-improvement (DIY or "do it yourself") store chains were forced to stop selling tropical timber. Austria experienced a 50 percent decrease in the import of tropical timber (Martin Frimmel, pers. comm.). In 1992 the Austrian Parliament enacted a law (rapidly overturned due to Malaysian pressure) that required the labeling of all tropical timber sold in Austria. In Belgium, Brussels declared itself a tropical timber-free city. In the Netherlands, where over 300 local groups were working on tropical timber issues through the early 1990s, DIY store chains signed agreements with Friends of the Earth not to sell tropical timber, scores of local municipal councils committed themselves to not using it, and the Dutch government declared that after 1995 it would use only tropical timber that was sustainably produced. Nationally, the consumption of tropical timber is down by almost 50 percent (Puan Adawiah Zakaria, Under Secretary, Ministry of Primary Industries, Malaysia, pers. comm.). In the UK, Friends of the Earth, the World Wide Fund for Nature UK, and Survival International joined together in 1992 to launch a nationwide campaign calling for a comprehensive national forest policy to restrict the import of tropical timber.

This focus on consumption, however, had another effect on the forms of advocacy taken by Northern environmentalists. Throughout the years since 1987, Northern NGOs, as they devised national campaigns, lobbied political leaders, and engaged in direct actions in order to increase awareness of the logging issue in Malaysia, debated the question of whether they should campaign for a complete boycott of tropical timber or whether they should seek ways to promote the use of timber that was produced sustainably. Some felt that to seek a complete boycott would penalize those few cases where genuine efforts to create systems of sustainable forestry were in progress, others denied there was such a thing as sustainable logging in tropical forests, while yet others felt that their ability to influence both the commercial sector and national governments depended upon their ability to provide constructive alternatives to existing forms of forest exploitation. Now, as Northern NGOs began to see results from their campaign efforts in the form of declining consumption of tropical timber, and as they had greater success in initiating conversations with timber retailers and with their governments, they had to face the issue of how to define their engagement with business and government directly. In order to continue making progress in reducing tropical timber consumption, they had to foster their relationships with the commercial sector in particular. The only way to do so was to provide a viable alternative.

The experience of Friends of the Earth (FOE) in the Netherlands is typical. According to Dutch environmentalist Saskia Ozinga, when DIY stores in the Netherlands signed pledges with Friends of the Earth not to use tropical timber, they also made very clear that they wanted to be able to say in their pledges that they would be able to sell sustainably produced timber in the future. The Dutch government also pledged to use only sustainably produced tropical timber after 1995. This, Ozinga said, had forced FOE and other environmental organizations to shift from a position of urging a complete boycott of tropical timber to calls to sell and use only sustainably produced tropical timber. This in turn demanded that organizations such as FOE participate in the process of devising a system to insure that tropical timber was sustainably produced.

As a result, through the early 1990s a consensus began to build among Northern NGOs that they should move away from simple boycotts and instead participate in efforts to define sustainability, a strategy that would allow them to declare moratoria on timber that was not certified to have been sustainably harvested. There ensued an extended debate as to how they should participate in the process of developing or promoting sustainable forestry. Here they faced a dilemma. The most pressing question for them was how far they should go in endorsing particular initiatives, given the potential that their participation might legitimize systems that, while representing progress, did not adequately meet their criteria, whether in terms of harvesting practices or because they did not take sufficient account of the rights of local communities. Negative experiences with the Tropical Forest Action Plan (TFAP) in the 1980s and with the International Tropical Timber Organization (ITTO) in the late 1980s and early 1990s made Northern NGOs very cautious about what sorts of systems they might be willing to endorse (see, for instance, Colchester 1990; Colchester and Lohmann 1990; Friends of the Earth and World Rainforest Movement 1992; Gale 1996; Humphreys 1996; Marshall 1991). Yet they realized that, if they wanted to continue to make progress in cooperation with national governments, timber importers, and retailers, they had to be willing to participate in some kind of process to certify timber.

What we observe as both Malaysian authorities and NGOs began to articulate a series of compelling counterarguments to Northern environmental rhetoric and as Northern environmentalists began to incorporate those counter-arguments into their own assessments of how to respond to Malaysia's apparent intransigence, is a conspicuous shift in the discursive contours of the Sarawak campaign. Far from being merely rhetorical, this shift had a number of very real strategic and institutional implications.

Sustainable forest management and certification

When Northern environmentalists shifted their focus to the issue of tropical timber consumption, and when timber consumption subsequently began to decline, concern mounted within the Malaysian timber industry and government. Malaysian authorities recognized that they faced a new challenge and that criticizing Northern environmentalists in Malaysian newspapers or in press conferences at international media events would never have much of an effect on countering the effects of the campaign against tropical timber consumption. They realized that a new response was required if they were to counter effectively the efforts of Northern environmentalists. One of the more significant shifts in Malaysia's response to the campaign was rhetorical. Increasingly through the 1990s, Malaysia began to deploy a rhetoric of "sustainable forest management."

Scientific forestry has a long history both in peninsular Malaysia and in the state of Sarawak.[13] For most of this century forestry discourses and practices in Malaysia have focused on the harvest of timber. In the period after Malaysia's independence, the timber industry was regulated under the principle of "sustained yield management" through the Selective Management System (Kumar 1986:77). In the earliest stages of the Sarawak campaign, one of the points made with great frequency by Malaysian officials in response to criticisms that the forests of Sarawak were being rapidly destroyed was that Malaysia had in place a well-established system of laws and practices regulating timber extraction.[14] This was supported by an extensive research apparatus, most visibly in the form of the Forest Research Institute of Malaysia near Kuala Lumpur. Given that Northern environmentalists had constructed the issue as one of urgency over the rapid destruction of Sarawak's forests, Malaysia had only to demonstrate that it in fact had a long-standing tradition of environmental stewardship and that its forests continued to be well managed.[15]

It was with this latter goal in mind that, through the early 1990s, Malaysian officials began to speak ever more frequently of their commitment to the principle of "sustainable forest management." While never foreclosing the possibility that forests should be managed primarily for the harvest of timber, an idea inherent in the concept of "sustained yield management," the term "sustainable forest management" was intended to project a more benign, caring image of Malaysia's environmental stewardship. The "sustainability" of "sustainable forest management" was not that of "sustained yield management": it displaced (or appeared to displace) an economistic focus on timber yields, substituting instead the softer, greener discursive contours of post-Brundtland "sustainability." That the two terms were lexically (if not semantically) similar allowed Malaysia to assert that its commitment to the idea of sustainability was a long-standing one, an assertion that was supported by reference to its forest codes.

It is remarkable to see how thoroughly the rhetoric of sustainable forest management has today insinuated itself into official Malaysian environmental discourse. A widely distributed publication by the Ministry of Primary Industries entitled *Forever Green: Malaysia and Sustainable Forest Management* (Ministry of Primary Industries 1992) is an extended commentary on Malaysia's commitment to this principle. In his introductory message to this publication, Dr Mahatir states that "sustainable forest management has long been accepted as the concept and the principle of Malaysia's National Forest Policy" (p. 1). In a 1993 speech in Atlanta, Minister of Primary Industries Lim Keng Yaik stated, "Malaysia is doing all it can to ensure that policies on sustainable forest management are effectively implemented." Likewise, a paid insert published in *Scientific American* in April 1994 stated,

> Malaysia is one country that has embarked on sustainable forest management long before the concern on [*sic*] global environmental degradation became a burning issue. . . . Malaysia has striven to strengthen sustainable forest management, policy-wise and implementation-

wise. . . . The Malaysian leadership and its citizenry are committed to the long-term management of its rich and varied resources, ensuring that the forest will be there to stay from generation to generation. [MTIDC 1994: M57–M59]

It is one thing to declare support for sustainable forest management but another thing altogether to be able to specify what that means. Whatever their disagreements, Northern NGOs, the Malaysian government, and the International Tropical Timber Organization had in common the fact that none was sure what "sustainable" meant. In an interview, Dr B. C. Y. Freezailah, the Malaysian Executive Director of ITTO, lamented that "we really don't know what sustainability is, and what it costs," and went on to describe the efforts of the ITTO to define this. Similar concerns were expressed to me by a senior official in the Ministry of Primary Industries who, in stressing her government's commitment to sustainable forest management, also emphasized just how difficult it was to define it. For instance, she asked, should sustainable management be measured at the national level or at the level of actual harvesting units? Likewise, Dutch environmentalist Saskia Ozinga, referring in 1994 to the Dutch government's decision to use only "sustainably produced" tropical timber after 1995, stated that the real issue was what that meant. Within the Dutch government itself, she noted, there was disagreement among different ministries as to how "sustainability" should be defined, primarily due to differences over the degree to which economic considerations should be weighed in specifying the parameters of sustainability.

On the assumption that criteria for defining sustainability could eventually be specified, the next step was to provide some means to communicate this to consumers (that is, *Northern* consumers) so that they would have some means to determine that the timber they purchased was harvested in a sustainable manner. The impetus to develop some market-oriented timber certification or "ecolabelling" system was provided in the early 1990s by the efforts of NGOs such as the Woodworkers Alliance for Rain Forest Protection and the Rain Forest Alliance (Elliott 1995). In 1992, the Forest Stewardship Council (FSC) was founded by representatives from a range of conservation NGOs, national forestry institutes, aid agencies, forest industry representatives, timber retailers, and others. At first the ideas proposed by the FSC, coming as they did from mainstream environmental organizations, were viewed with suspicion by many Northern environmentalists, by producer countries such as Malaysia, and by many within the timber industry. Among Northern environmentalists, discussion about whether or not to support timber certification was debated vigorously. Most pressing was the question of whether the existence of a few good examples of sustainably harvested timber should negate calls for a total ban. Only when they were able to move beyond this issue were Northern environmentalists able to address the questions of what constituted "good" timber and "bad" timber and how this should be communicated to consumers seriously.

It was only as the efforts by environmental NGOs in the UK, Europe, and Australia to target the consumption of tropical timber began to have a real effect on consumption that producer countries such as Malaysia began to embrace the idea of timber certification. Today, it has become a central feature of their efforts to counter the effects of the Northern environmentalist tropical timber campaign.

The effort to establish a timber certification scheme has brought into being an extensive research/conference apparatus comprised of multilateral institutions such as the World Bank and ITTO, donor agencies such as the McArthur Foundation, representatives of producer countries, the business community, and environmental NGOs. The technical literature has proliferated as the effort continues to define "sustainable forest management" in tropical forests scientifically and to translate this into a viable system of certification.[16] Just starting to take shape is a complex set of institutions concerned with establishing and enforcing basic standards, assessing logging operations, providing accreditation to producers, and insuring a secure "chain of custody" from forest concession to market.[17]

Obviously much is at stake for all those involved in the effort to implement a system of timber certification. Producer countries such as Malaysia, interested primarily in promoting their timber to Northern consumers, argue for a definition of sustainability that is largely technical, based on the principles of scientific forestry, and focused on matters such as annual rates of harvest. The International Tropical Timber Organization, representing timber interests from both producer and consumer countries, focuses its efforts on the development of criteria that reflect the principles of scientific forestry as well but also devotes a great deal of attention to estimating the economic costs of adherence to various criteria for defining sustainability. Though environmental NGOs have approached the issue of certification from a variety of perspectives, most have argued for consideration of other than technical and economic criteria in defining sustainability: criteria such as the impact of logging on local communities. This is reflected in an anecdote I recently heard about an exchange between an Indonesian environmental activist and a government official. They were discussing the efforts underway by the Indonesian government to institute timber certification. The NGO member raised a concern about whether the government was taking into account the welfare of indigenous communities in its certification scheme. In response the official said, "Remember, this is a green dot, not a pink heart." Frustrated that many of the criteria they have proposed have not been incorporated into any definitions of sustainability and concerned that their presence not be exploited to legitimize any regime of certification that they feel lacks any meaningful consideration of environmental or social criteria, many environmental NGOs have removed themselves from the ITTO certification process. Nevertheless, enough remain involved to keep it moving ahead without the legitimacy of the process being challenged in any serious way.

Public relations and the imagineering of sustainable forest management

Even as the effort to define sustainable forest management proceeded, Malaysian officials continued to be concerned with the effect that the Sarawak campaign was having on the market for Malaysian timber. Observing continued declines in European timber consumption, Malaysian officials realized that it was not enough for them to simply speak about sustainable forest management in reaction to environmentalist campaign efforts. As one Malaysian official noted in an interview, as the Malaysian timber campaign gained momentum in the 1980s, there was no single coordinating body to respond to what Malaysia considered to be unfounded allegations. Whatever efforts to respond were made – most often by Malaysian embassy officials or by government ministers – tended to be haphazard and often created additional problems. A disastrous 1993 broadcast of the television program *Primetime Live*, in which reporter John Quinones confronted the Malaysian ambassador to the United States, Abdul Majid, was a case in point. The Malaysian government was persuaded that it had to try to shape the discursive contours of the debate more actively, that its message had to be packaged more effectively and communicated more broadly.

With this in mind, Malaysia stepped up its efforts to develop its international public relations capabilities. The Malaysian Timber Industry Development Council (MTIDC) – later shortened to the Malaysian Timber Council (MTC) – was founded in 1992 as the primary agent designated for this task. The semiofficial Malaysian Timber Council acted as the public relations arm of the Malaysian timber industry, concerned primarily with promoting Malaysian timber and countering environmentalist rhetoric, especially in the UK and Europe. Its activities were funded by a levy on the export of timber. Although precise figures are difficult to come by, the Malaysian Timber Council had collected some US$24 million (RM$63 million) by 1995 and was spend-

ing approximately US$3.8 million (RM$10 million) per year.[18]

The Malaysian Timber Council had its work cut out for it as it undertook the effort to contain the campaign. An official from the Ministry of Primary Industries complained in a 1995 interview that, though certification was the primary issue, "Our concern is if we address this issue, then other issues will come up. It is always like that." He observed, for instance, that environmentalists started with calls to boycott Malaysian timber, then pushed for labeling, and "now they go down to consumers. We are responding to changes – a bit behind. The stigma [against tropical timber] is there in the consumer's mind. It's not easy to get it out of their mind. . . . We are fighting that." An official with the Malaysian Timber Council admitted in an interview that the one major mistake they had made was that they responded too late to the Sarawak campaign, adding that they were trying to correct this. Likewise, a senior official with the Ministry of Primary Industries described how, in the late 1980s, there was considerable criticism of how they had responded to the campaign: "We didn't really know the issue on the ground. We were responding. That became a problem." Because of this failure to respond adequately, the Malaysian government faced a series of minor crises, such as the Austrian effort to restrict imports of tropical timber. European consumption of tropical timber continued to decline.

Malaysian officials viewed the problem as one of disinformation: that Northern environmentalists were deliberately misinforming the Euro-American public for their own selfish reasons. According to the former Chief Executive Officer of the Malaysian Timber Council, Mr. Wong Kum Choon, Northern environmentalists, in organizing their campaign against Malaysia, had been exploiting the Penan from "an emotional and sentimental viewpoint . . . They make use of this for the issue of saving the rain forest . . . [and] give the impression that the Penan are treated like dirt."

The Sarawak Timber Association (STA) also played an active role in countering the campaign against Malaysian timber. The Sarawak Timber Association was actually founded in the early 1970s. It began to engage actively in public relations efforts in the late 1980s, though it lacked the international reach that the Malaysian Timber Council was able to maintain. Reflecting on the history of Malaysia's response to the campaign, Sarawak Timber Association manager Barney Chan stated that when they first encountered the campaign, they saw it as just

a bunch of adolescents yapping, who were saying things that were just incredible. Originally we just thought these were rantings. We didn't take them seriously. People were saying things like that a 14 year old Penan girl was raped. Then the campaign just got out of control. Bruno [Manser] lost control of it, Greenpeace lost control. In the meantime, it infiltrates all of Western society, even getting into preschool books. There were many fronts opening up before me.

He went on to describe his frustration at being unable to identify any single "enemy" and at the way in which the rhetoric constantly shifted as environmentalists would "open up new fronts, new ideas just to keep themselves going" and "fuel the campaign." He explained how, for instance. Northern environmentalists began with the "mantra" that 50 football fields-worth of forest were being destroyed every second. "We discovered that if we were to overturn their arguments, they would quickly switch it. So difficult to whack it." He went on to describe how environmentalists would switch to arguments about global warming, indigenous rights, human rights violations, and the loss of genetic resources. Mr Chan said he thought it enough that he "started an information flow to the west," placing particular emphasis on the sharing of scientific research results on logging. With time, however, his frustration grew as he realized that this was not enough: "These guys [environmentalists] can't appreciate it."

It was clearly not sufficient simply to criticize Northern environmentalists either within Malaysia or in their own countries, where they enjoyed considerable support and where the Malaysian government and timber industry were viewed as corrupt. The appropriate response for Malaysia, therefore, was to better communicate what they considered to be accu-

rate information to the audience that they were most concerned about: European consumers. Even with the Malaysian Timber Council and Sarawak Timber Association in place, however, reaching consumers was not easy. Reflecting on Malaysian efforts to reach a European audience, a senior official in the Ministry of Primary Industries stated that "it is not easy to counter the campaign – we are dealing with consumers, the public, not just governments: a very dispersed, diverse target." Speaking of the Sarawak Timber Association's efforts to "go down to buyers, as close as we can," Barney Chan described how frustrating this was because "NGOs know their local people much better than STA does. They can go to the Rotterdam city council and get a tropical timber ban instituted."

To assist it in reaching this target audience, Malaysia engaged the services of two major international public relations firms in the early 1990s: Burson-Marsteller and Hill and Knowlton. Coordinating this effort through the Malaysian Timber Council, but with substantial input from the Ministry of Primary Industries, these firms provided the expertise necessary for the Malaysian government and timber interests to reach European consumers. Commenting on the Malaysian Timber Council's relationship with these firms, one senior official with the MTC stated that "it is impossible to reach Europe alone.... Before Rio, NGOs were having a field day. No more." Furthermore, he stated "We can't be present [at all times], so we employ them to assist us in putting across our message. When there are problems in the market, [or] NGOs criticize [Malaysia], make accusations, they are there to respond, there to pass on information to relevant parties."

The coordinated efforts of the Malaysian Timber Council, the Sarawak Timber Association, Burson-Marsteller, and Hill and Knowlton have taken a number of forms. One of the most visible efforts is the monthly publication and distribution of some 20,000 copies of the *Malaysian Timber Bulletin*. This publication contains news of Malaysian efforts to manage its forests, promote its forest industries, and implement certification. It often features reports describing Malaysian positions on various international conventions relating to timber, particularly as those positions are articulated by Minister of Primary Industries Lim Keng Yaik. This and other publications are sent out to municipal governments, trade organizations, the media, NGOs, corporations, and "friends." Additionally, the Malaysian Timber Council organizes trade missions to Europe and elsewhere, where they meet with legislators and municipal government officials, and attend conferences of trade groups (architects, furniture industry representatives) and local governments (the US Conference of Mayors, for example). Typically these delegations – travelling to cities such as Hanover, Antwerp, and San Diego – hold a series of seminars to which local officials, the press, and other interested parties are invited. The primary goal is to stress Malaysia's long history of environmental stewardship and its commitment to sustainable forest management, and to reassure audiences that they need not heed the alarmist statements of what they portray as irresponsible radical environmentalists.

Where public relations firms have been most useful to Malaysia has been in the effort to help it shape a coherent message. Rather than simply respond post facto to every environmentalist statement or action, these firms impressed upon Malaysia the need to develop and deploy a consistent and coherent message that offered an alternative version of Malaysia's record of environmental stewardship. That message had (and has) as its centerpiece the concepts of sustainable forest management and certification. Not only did this allow Malaysian authorities to project a more environmentally friendly image, it also provided a way for them to strategically admit to past, and even present, problems with forest management, accompanied by assurances that they are working hard to resolve them.

Equally central to Malaysia's efforts to soften its image have been declarations of openness and willingness to work together with who ever has a sincere desire to help Malaysia work toward sustainable forest management. Malaysian officials today speak incessantly of "transparency" and of their efforts to work cooperatively with anyone to realize this goal. In his 1993 speech in Atlanta, Minister of Primary Industries Lim Keng Yaik stated:

> Now I am not saying that forest management in Malaysia has reached a state of sublime perfection. We know that despite our best will and intention there are still deficiencies and weaknesses. We have not tried to hide these. They are widely publicized, discussed and addressed in international fora and in our news media. We have also welcomed observers and interested parties to come to Malaysia and see for themselves.

In a 1995 interview, an official from the Malaysian Timber Council complained that "Westerners say we are not transparent.... The West looks at negative things, while not talking about the positive, in perspective.... We need to join hands to work together, that would help." Speaking of a 1995 meeting with several Northern NGOs in the Hague, he added that they "had productive discussions. We said we were open. We gave facts and figures. If they want facts and figures, we give them. As long as they are willing to share views, and not be polemic, we are happy to talk to NGOs."

This rhetoric of transparency and openness can be viewed as a form of wedge politics, intended to create in the eyes of the Euro-American public a distinction between "sincere" environmentalists willing to work together with Malaysia and irresponsible "radicals" interested only in confrontation. Thus, for instance, the government publication *Forever Green* states:

> Unfortunately radical environmental pressure groups have failed to understand what sustainable forest management is all about, let alone how it is being practised in its spatial, temporal, and holistic dimensions. Acting under the banner of NGOs, environmental radicals appear interested only in making the issue of tropical forests the "scapegoat" of global environmental ills and turning it into a highly successful fund-raising campaign. [Ministry of Primary Industries 1992:3]

Speaking of Northern environmental NGOs, a senior official in the Ministry of Primary Industries stated: "Some groups are genuine, others are more extreme, and are only making use of the Penan. They have an agenda to pursue. Some groups we can work with. But more often than not they use our problem for their own purposes – to raise money."

Although they still express certain frustrations with Northern environmentalists, governments, and consumers, Malaysian officials today consider their efforts to confront the Sarawak campaign to have been largely successful. Indeed, in recent years, the momentum of the Sarawak campaign has diminished considerably as Malaysia has extended its efforts to reconfigure the discursive contours of the debate.

What we observe in Malaysia's response to the Sarawak campaign is a remarkable fusion of three elements: the emergence of an official rhetoric of "sustainable forest management," the development of a transnational technoscientific apparatus to certify timber, and the evolution of a sophisticated network of Malaysian government ministries and semiofficial organizations (the Ministry of Primary Industries, the Malaysian Timber Council, the Sarawak Timber Association) and international public relations firms (Burson-Marsteller, Hill and Knowlton) charged with the responsibility of countering the campaign against tropical timber. In short, Malaysia's efforts to institute the appearance of a certifiable regime of "sustainable forest management" became an extension of an elaborate public relations apparatus focused on dissipating concern about the fate of Malaysia's rain forests among Northern governments and consumers, and diverting attention from the political to the technical and institutional.

It has been one of the tangible effects of this fusion that media interest in the Sarawak campaign, particularly in coverage of environmentalist direct actions and other grassroots efforts, has diminished considerably. This lessening of media interest, undoubtedly a major element in the loss of momentum in the campaign, has been the result of a remarkable discursive shift set in motion and sustained by Malaysia: between the late-1980s and the mid-1990s the debate over logging in Sarawak shifted from a focus on stopping forest destruction and securing the rights of indigenous

communities – the *Fern Gully* allegory – to a focus on sustainable forest management and certification.

This shift, I suggest, can be seen as a process of displacement. At the center of the early Sarawak campaign were arresting images (in the most literal sense) of Penan and charismatic figures such as Bruno Manser and indigenous activists Harrison Ngau and Anderson Mutang. However, as Northern NGOs began participating in the process of defining sustainable forest management, and as the institutional foundations of certification were established, the role that such images and individuals could play was diminished. At an ITTO meeting in which "criteria and indicators" of sustainability are on the agenda, images of blockades and arrests are not merely irrelevant but disruptive, and there is no place whatever for figures such as Harrison Ngau or Bruno Manser.

The issue, then, is not whether sustainable forest management or timber certification is desirable. Rather, it is the potential for such efforts to become part of an elaborate public relations scheme, designed to obscure a highly destructive system of resource extraction and to assuage consumer and government concerns, that makes them problematic. The larger message being conveyed is that the problems of rain forest destruction and indigenous rights can be solved by some combination of technically grounded institutional interventions.

Conclusions

My intention in the foregoing has been to illustrate a process common to virtually all environmental issues today: the process by which the discursive and institutional contours of such issues are simultaneously shifted – not innocently – away from the moral/political domain and toward the domain of governmentality, managerialism, and bureaucratization. We see it also, for instance, in the domain of community-based natural resource management. What began as a series of critiques of top-down environmental management (and as a diversity of local movements formed in response to those critiques [Bonner 1993;

Broad 1994; Gadgil and Guha 1993; Gray 1991; Guha 1989; Hitchcock 1995; Kemf 1993; Kothari and Parajuli 1993; Peluso 1993; Shiva 1993]) is increasingly being appropriated as multilateral aid agencies, and even extractive industries, adopt community-based natural resource management into their agendas and increasingly envelop local communities and grassroots social movements in a rhetoric of participation (see Brosius et al. 1998).

Accompanying this is another critical dynamic: a shifting pattern of marginalizations and privilegings that occurs as the terms of a debate shift. Who is listened to, ignored, or regarded as disruptive, and in which contexts? Who is it useful to be engaged with and who is it necessary to establish distance from? This is very much bound up with the question of the institutional space of environmental praxis. Institutions are both enabling and limiting. Defining themselves as filling particular spaces of discourse and praxis, they in effect define (or redefine) the space of action; they privilege some forms of action and limit others; they create spaces for some actors and dissolve spaces for others.

Each of these dynamics represents a broader process of the displacement of the political from the domain of the "environment." It is a process akin to that described by James Ferguson in his landmark work on development in Lesotho (Ferguson 1994). Describing the development apparatus as an "anti-politics machine," Ferguson argues that:

> by uncompromisingly reducing poverty to a technical problem, and by promising technical solutions to the sufferings of powerless and oppressed people, the hegemonic problematic of "development" is the principal means through which the question of poverty is depoliticized in the world today. At the same time, by making the intentional blueprints for "development" so highly visible, a "development" project can end up performing extremely sensitive political operations involving the entrenchment and expansion of institutional state power almost invisibly, under cover of a neutral, technical mission to which no one can object. The "instrument-effect," then, is two-fold: alongside the institutional

effect of expanding bureaucratic state power is the conceptual or ideological effect of depoliticizing both poverty and the state. [p. 256]

This is an altogether interesting time in environmental affairs as an institutional apparatus such as that I have described descends upon the environment much as it once did on development, and as we witness the increasing displacement of grassroots environmental movements, both by "moderate" environmental organizations (WWF, IUCN) and by large transnational institutions that have appropriated environmental rhetoric. It is essential that anthropologists attend to the task of elucidating the dimensions of this institutional envelopment and the forms of environmental surveillance and intervention it promotes.

Rappaport's discussion of "the anthropology of trouble" provides a useful topology for undertaking this task. In describing the aforementioned "deformation of ... 'the order of viability,' " Rappaport points not merely to the "subordination of the fundamental to the contingent and instrumental" but to the way in which the contingent and instrumental can claim the place of the fundamental (1993:300). This conjuring trick is, as often as not, the work of institutions that treat moral/political imperatives as "externalities" and that make it "possible for ever-more narrowly defined interests to become regnant in larger socioeconomic systems ..." (p. 300). Rappaport's argument here closely parallels a point made by Visvanathan (1991:381) in a pointed critique of the idea of "sustainable development" inspired by his understanding of Brundtland ecology:

> The entire discourse of bureaucrats is still written in the language of a monetized economy. Consider the word 'ecology.' In the bureaucrat's world, it becomes bastardized because money and market dissolve real ecologies. Ecology – true ecology – should be an attempt to liberate the imagination of democracy from the constraints that "big science," the nation-state, and development have imposed. It seeks a notion of a good life, an idea of restraint and self-limits that cannot be reduced to economic audits and goes beyond a world that values obsolescence as godhead.

In Brundtland, ecology is merely a search for managerial efficiency.

The concern I want to raise here is that this process of subordinating the fundamental to the contingent is too often the work of ostensibly *environmental* institutions: not the Shell Oil Corporation, but the Forest Stewardship Council and the International Union for the Conservation of Nature. Such institutions, I suggest, too often promulgate – or are, at the very least, complicit in promoting – what Rappaport called "institutional deafness": "the unwillingness or inability of authorities to understand messages encoded in terms other than those of the dominant economic discourse" (1993:300). In this respect, Rappaport's argument parallels Kuehls's extension of Deleuze and Guattari's essay on nomadology, published in *A Thousand Plateaus*, to environmental politics (1993, 1996). Kuehls describes the opposition between the "striated space" of state forms of governmentality – a space in which I would include environmental institutions – and the nonstate, nomadic practices of rhizomatic actors arrayed in unregulatable "smooth space" – grassroots groups constituting themselves outside the space of institutional sovereignty. From this perspective, environmental institutions such as the FSC and IUCN might be viewed as engaged in projects of domestication, attempting to seduce or to compel nomadic actors to participate in statist projects of environmental governmentality. Consider, for instance, how often today we see environmental institutions describe sites of struggle in terms of (or rather reduced to) the affectless, faux-inclusive language of "participation," in which a range of "stakeholders" are brought together to work toward the resolution of some environmental concern.

It is not my intention to suggest that we should embrace a simplistic environmental moralism, or that "rhizomatic" grassroots actors provide an intrinsically better alternative to all forms of governmentality. Nor should my argument be understood as a blanket condemnation of all forms of institutionalization or state intervention. One need not look far to find cases where both human suffering and environmental degradation have

been wrought in the name of moral/political imperatives, or cases in which the results of institutional or state intervention can be judged to have been beneficial. What the foregoing analysis points to is the danger of displacing the moral/political – discursively and institutionally – to such an extent that it is regarded as disruptive or irrelevant, or can no longer be heard at all.

The argument I am making here has a close parallel in James Scott's *Seeing Like a State* (1998). Scott examines the ways in which states "attempt to make a society legible, to arrange the population in ways that simplified the classic state functions of taxation, conscription, and prevention of rebellion" (p. 2). This effort extends to the natural world as well – to agriculture and forestry – which are all "calculated to make the terrain, its products, and its workforce more legible – and hence manipulable – from above and from the center" (p. 2). For Scott, *legibility* – achieved through a series of "state simplifications" designed to reduce the opacity of the local – is the "central problem of statecraft" (p. 2). The state, Scott is careful to point out, is not the only such agent of simplification: capitalism, too, is an agent of "homogenization, uniformity, grids, and heroic simplification" (p. 8). To these – the state and capitalism – one could add the process of institutionalization such as I have described above.

Although Scott develops a "case against the *imperialism* of high-modernist, planned social order" (p. 6), he is very clear that he is "not making a blanket case against either bureaucratic planning or high-modernist ideology." He is not "uncritically admiring of the local, the traditional, and the customary" (p. 7), nor is he making

an anarchist case against the state itself. The state . . . is the vexed institution that is the ground of both our freedoms and our unfreedoms. My case is that certain kinds of states, driven by utopian plans and an authoritarian disregard for the values, desires, and objections of their subjects, are indeed a mortal threat to human well-being. . . . We are left to weigh judiciously the benefits of certain state interventions against their costs. [p. 7]

Much the same could be said of the dilemma that faces us in the encounter between grass-roots environmentalism and institutionaliza-tion. The question is not whether we should make a choice between one or the other, or whether one is an intrinsically better alterna-tive than the other. Rather, it is a call for us to weigh carefully the terms under which insti-tutionalization occurs, and to make an effort to discern what is gained and what is lost, who is heard and who is silenced, as the process continues.

NOTES

1. While critiques such as this may not appear to be very good examples of "repatriation," they are often premised on the assumption that the forms of rep-resentation that local social movements partake of incorporate discursive ele-ments that are derived from Western/metropolitan contexts and are therefore not truly autochthonous. That the mes-sages deployed by these movements are often conveyed to Western audiences by Western environmental organizations only reinforces this assumption.

2. For instance: Brenton (1994), Caldwell (1996), Conca et al. (1995), Haas (1990), Hurrell and Kingsbury (1992), Kuehls (1996), Lipschutz and Coca (1993), Litfin (1994), McCormick (1989), Miller (1995), and Porter and Brown (1991).

3. See Thompson and Rayner (1998). Also worth noting is the work of Myanna Lahsen, a graduate student at Rice Uni-versity who is presently conducting dis-sertation research on the scientific debate over climate change.

4. In speaking of "Northern environmental-ists," I am following current usage, wherein the "North" refers to the indus-trialized countries of Europe, North America, Japan, and Australia (while the "South" refers to the "third world").

5. Sec Manser (1996) and Ritchie (1994). It should be stressed that the Penan are only one of many ethnic groups in Sarawak. The question of whether the campaign should focus only on the Penan or on the issue of indigenous rights in Sarawak more generally was debated extensively among both Malaysian and Northern environmentalists. Whatever the position taken, the images used by both were overwhelmingly those of Penan, photogenic and very obviously "indigenous," with loincloths and blowpipes.

6. I use the term *governmentality* in the Foucauldian sense of "governmental rationality" (Gordon 1991). In speaking of governmentality, Foucault was refer-ring not only to the domain of civil/polit-ical government as it is conventionally understood but to a broader domain of discourses and practices that create and administer subjects through the presence of a variety of knowledge-making apparatuses. See Foucault ([1978]1991). For other recent attempts to extend the concept of governmentality into the realm of the environment, see Darier (1996) and Luke (1995).

7. See King (1993) and Rousseau (1990) for overviews of the societies of Borneo.

8. In Sarawak there are also several small, scattered groups of long-settled Penan with close linguistic affinities to Eastern and Western Penan. For more informa-tion on Penan in Sarawak, see Arnold (1958), Brosius (1986, 1988, 1991, 1992, 1993a, 1993b, 1995, 1995–96, 1997a, 1997b), Harrisson (1949), Huehne (1959), Kedit (1982), Langub (1972a, 1972b, 1974, 1975, 1984, 1989, 1990), Needham (1954a, 1954b, 1965, 1972). Nicolaisen (1976a, 1976b, 1978), and Urquhart (1951).

9. In referring to the "government," it is important to keep in mind the disjunc-tion between the Sarawak state govern-ment and the Malaysian federal government. Sarawak agreed to join

Malaysia in 1963, some six years after Malaysia's independence in 1957. It was able to negotiate the terms of its entry into Malaysia and therefore, more so than any other state in Malaysia, has a considerable amount of control over its internal affairs. The policies of the state and federal governments are often at odds. This is a matter of considerable frustration to the federal government, which has consistently attempted to establish greater control over Sarawak. For instance, in Sarawak (as in all of Malaysia) timber policy is established entirely at the state level. Because of the negative attention that logging in Sarawak has brought to Malaysia, the federal government has attempted (unsuccessfully) to persuade the Sarawak state government to control logging. Despite the apparent differences between the state and federal governments (differences which are rarely acknowledged publicly), they have displayed a remarkably unified front with respect to their response to domestic and foreign critics of contemporary logging practices.

10. The rhetoric of development is therefore used to obscure purely monetary interests on the part of prominent politicians. It is politicians and their families who overwhelmingly hold rights to timber concessions and who are profiting from the activities of timber companies. Timber licenses are the currency with which politicians in Sarawak's parliamentary system lure those from other parties into their own party so that they may achieve a majority in the state assembly and thus continue to hold power. In Sarawak, it is difficult to be a successful politician without engaging in such practices.

11. For an account of factors that have contributed to this contrastive pattern of Eastern and Western Penan response to logging, see Brosius (1997b). In noting the contrast in Eastern and Western Penan responses to logging, it is important that this contrast not be overstated. Many Eastern Penan have recently

negotiated compensation packages with timber companies, and increasing numbers have begun to work with them. This has led to some tension between groups of Eastern Penan, particularly members of settled communities who are working for companies and nomadic groups on whose lands they are working. Likewise, there have been several incidents where Western Penan have resisted timber companies in various ways.

12. See Kumar (1986), Smythies (1963), Watson (1950), Wyatt-Smith and Vincent (1962). In West Malaysia the first forest officer was appointed in 1901, and the Sarawak Forest Department was established in 1919.

13. It must be noted that forestry in Malaysia is a state matter and is therefore not directly controlled by the federal government. Nevertheless, Malaysia's thirteen states all have detailed forest codes regulating the manner in which logging is to be carried out. Thus, for instance, in Sarawak timber concessionaires must file both a detailed Forest Management Plan and a Forest Engineering Plan, and they must comply with state laws regulating the harvest timber as to which species can be harvested, the number of trees that can be harvested per hectare, the minimum diameter of trees that can be extracted, and so forth. See Majid-Cooke (1995).

14. Left unspoken, of course, were details about the system of political patronage through which the granting of timber concessions was controlled in Sarawak, about ubiquitous violations of prescribed harvesting practices, and about the overall rate of logging in Sarawak, which was far in excess of what could be considered sustainable. On this latter point, see ITTO (1990) and World Bank (1991).

15. For instance, see Aplet et al. (1993), Cassells (1992), D'Silva and Appanah (1993), Grainger (1993), ITTO (1991, 1992), Johnson and Cabarle (1993), Kumari (1996), Panayotou and Ashton (1992), Poore (1989), Sandbukt (1995), Sharma (1992), and Vincent (1995).

16. For a comprehensive overview of timber certification, see Viana et al. (1996).

17. Against total timber revenues of US$5.1 billion (RM$13.5 billion) in 1994. The figure of RM$63 million is from a press release to the *New Straits Times*, while the figures of US$5.1 billion and US$4 million are from an official of the MTC, who asked to remain anonymous.

18. See *Encountering Development* for a similar point regarding what Escobar terms "the inscription of the economic onto the ecological" (1995:196–7).

REFERENCES

Apffel-Marglin, Frédérique, and Stephen Marglin, eds. (1990). Dominating Knowledge: Development, Culture, and Resistance. Oxford: Clarendon Press.

Aplet, Greg, Nels Johnson, Jeffrey Olson, and V. Alaric Sample, eds. (1993). Defining Sustainable Forestry. Washington, DC: Island Press.

Appadurai, Arjun. (1990). Disjuncture and Difference in the Global Cultural Economy. *Public Culture* 2(2):1–24.

——. (1991). Global Ethnoscapes: Notes and Queries for a Transnational Anthropology. *In* Recapturing Anthropology: Working in the Present. Richard Fox, ed. Pp. 191–210. Santa Fe, NM: School of American Research Press.

Arnold, Guy. (1958). Nomadic Penan of the Upper Rejang (Plieran), Sarawak. *Journal of the Malayan Branch of the Royal Asiatic Society* 31(181):40–82.

Bennett, Jane, and William Chaloupka, eds. (1993). In the Nature of Things: Language, Politics, and the Environment. Minneapolis: University of Minnesota Press.

Bevis, William. (1995). Borneo Log: The Struggle for Sarawak's Forests. Seattle: University of Washington Press.

Bonner, Raymond. (1993). At the Hand of Man: Peril and Hope for Africa's Wildlife. New York: Alfred A. Knopf.

Brenton, Tony. (1994). The Greening of Machiavelli: The Evolution of International Environmental Politics. London: Earthscan Publications.

Broad, Robin. (1994). The Poor and the Environment: Friends or Foes? *World Development* 22:811–22.

Brosius, J. Peter. (1986). River, Forest and Mountain: The Penan Gang Landscape. *Sarawak Museum Journal* 36(57, New Series): 73–84.

——. (1988). A Separate Reality: Comments on Hoffman's The Punan: Hunters and Gatherers of Borneo. *Borneo Research Bulletin* 20(2):81–106.

——. (1991). Foraging in Tropical Rainforests: The Case of the Penan of Sarawak, East Malaysia (Borneo). *Human Ecology* 19:123–50.

——. (1992). The Axiological Presence of Death: Penan Geng Death-Names. Unpublished Doctoral Dissertation, Department of Anthropology, University of Michigan.

——. (1993a). Contrasting Subsistence Ecologies of Eastern and Western Penan Foragers (Sarawak, East Malaysia). *In* Food and Nutrition in the Tropical Forest: Biocultural Interactions and Applications to Development. C. M. Hladik, et al., eds. Pp. 515–22. Paris: UNESCO – Parthenon Man and the Biosphere Series.

——. (1993b). Penan of Sarawak. *In* State of the Peoples: A Global Human Rights Report on Societies in Danger. Marc S. Miller, ed. Pp. 142–3. Boston: Beacon Press (for Cultural Survival, Inc.).

——. (1995) Signifying Bereavement: Form and Context in the Analysis of Penan Death-Names. *Oceania* 66:119–46.

——. (1995–6). Father Dead, Mother Dead: Bereavement and Fictive Death in Penan Geng Society. *Omega: Journal of Death and Dying* 32:197–226.

——. (1997a). Endangered Forest, Endangered People: Environmentalist Representations of Indigenous Knowledge. *Human Ecology* 25:47–69.

——. (1997b). Prior Transcripts, Divergent Paths: Resistance and Acquiescence to Logging in Sarawak, East Malaysia. *Comparative Studies in Society and History* 39:468–510.

——. (1999). Analyses and Interventions: Anthropological Engagements with Environmentalism. *Current Anthropology* 40(3).

Brosius, J. Peter, Anna L. Tsing, and Charles Zerner. (1998). Representing Communities: Histories and Politics of Community-Based Resource Management. *Society and Natural Resources* 11:157–68.

Brysk, Alison. (1994). Acting Globally: Indian Rights and International Politics in Latin America. *In* Indigenous Peoples and Democracy in Latin America. Donna Lee Van Cott, ed. Pp. 29–51. New York: St. Martins Press.

Caldwell, Lynton. (1996). International Environmental Policy: From the Twentieth to the Twenty-First Century. Durham, NC: Duke University Press.

Cassells, David. (1992). ITTO Develops Criteria for Measuring Sustainable Forest Management. *ITTO Tropical Forest Update* 2(1):2.

Clifford, James. (1988). The Predicament of Culture: Twentieth Century Ethnography, Literature, and Art. Cambridge, MA: Harvard University Press.

Colchester, Marcus. (1989). Pirates, Squatters and Poachers: The Political Ecology of Dispossession of the Native Peoples of Sarawak. London and Petaling Jaya (Malaysia): Survival International and INSAN (Institute of Social Analaysis).

——. (1990). The International Tropical Timber Organization: Kill or Cure for the Rainforests? *The Ecologist* 20:166–73.

Colchester, Marcus, and Larry Lohmann. (1990). The Tropical Forestry Action Plan: What Progress? Penang (Malaysia) and Sturminster Newton, Dorset (England): World Rainforest Movement and The Ecologist.

Conca, Ken, Michael Alberty, and Geoffrey Dabelko, eds. (1995). Green Planet Blues: Environmental Politics from Stockholm to Rio. Boulder: Westview Press.

Conklin, Beth, and Laura Graham. (1995). The Shifting Middle Ground: Amazonian Indians and Eco-Politics. *American Anthropologist* 97:695–710.

Cronon, William, ed. (1995). Uncommon Ground: Toward Reinventing Nature. New York: W.W. Norton.

Darier, Éric. (1996). Environmental Governmentality: The Case of Canada's Green Plan. *Environmental Politics* 5:585–606.

Deleuze, Gilles, and Félix Guattari. (1987). A Thousand Plateaus: Capitalism and Schizophrenia. Minneapolis: University of Minnesota Press.

Dizard, Jan. (1994). Going Wild: Hunting, Animal Rights, and the Contested Meaning of Nature. Amherst: University of Massachusetts Press.

D'Silva, Emmanuel, and S. Appanah. (1993). Forestry Management for Sustainable Development. EDI Policy Seminar Report no. 32. Washington, DC: The World Bank.

Dudley, Nigel. (1992). Forests in Trouble: A Review of the Status of Temperate Forests Worldwide. Gland, Switzerland: World Wide Fund for Nature.

DuPuis, E. Melanie, and Peter Vandergeest, eds. (1996). Creating the Countryside: The Politics of Rural and Environmental Discourse. Philadelphia: Temple University Press.

Elliott, Chris. (1995). Timber Certification and the Forest Stewardship Council. *In* Management of Tropical Forests: Towards an Integrated Perspective. Oyvind Sandbukt, ed. Pp. 319–39. Oslo: Centre for Environment and Development, University of Oslo.

Escobar, Arturo. (1995). Encountering Development: The Making and Unmaking of the Third World. Princeton, NJ: Princeton University Press.

——. (1996). Constructing Nature: Elements for a Poststructural Political Ecology. *In* Liberation Ecologies: Environment, Development, Social Movements. Richard Peet and Michael Watts, ed. Pp. 46–68. London: Routledge.

——. (1999). After Nature: Steps to an Antiessentialist Political Ecology. *Current Anthropology* 40(1):1–30.

Fairhead, James, and Melissa Leach. (1994). Contested Forests: Modern Conservation and Historical Land Use in Guinea's Ziama Reserve. *African Affairs* 93(373):481–512.

Featherstone, Mike, ed. (1990). Global Culture: Nationalism, Globalization and Modernity. London: Sage.

Ferguson, James. (1994). The Anti-Politics Machine: "Development," Depoliticization, and Bureaucratic Power in Lesotho. Minneapolis: University of Minnesota Press.

Fisher, William. (1997). Doing Good? The Politics and Antipolitics of NGO Practices. *Annual Review of Anthropology* 26:439–64.

Foucault, Michel. ([1978] 1991). Governmentality. *In* The Foucault Effect: Studies in Governmentality. Graham Burchell, Colin Gordon, and Peter Miller, eds. Pp. 87–104. Chicago: University of Chicago Press.

Fox, Richard, ed. (1991). Recapturing Anthropology: Working in the Present. Santa Fe, NM: School of American Research Press.

Friends of the Earth and World Rainforest Movement. (1992). The International Tropical Timber Agreement: Conserving the Forests or Chainsaw Charter? A Critical Review of the First Five Years' Operations of the International Tropical Timber Organization. London: Friends of the Earth.

Gadgil, Madhav, and Ramachandra Guha. (1993). This Fissured Land: An Ecological History of India. Berkeley: University of California Press.

Gale, Fred. (1996). The Mysterious Case of the Disappearing Environmentalists: The International Tropical Timber Organization. Capitalism, Nature, Socialism 7:103–17.

Gordon, Colin. (1991). Governmental Rationality: An Introduction. *In* The Foucault Effect: Studies in Governmentality. Graham Burchell, Colin Gordon, and Peter Miller, eds. Pp. 1–51. Chicago: University of Chicago Press.

Gore, Al. (1992). Earth in the Balance: Ecology and the Human Spirit. New York: Plume/Penguin.

Grainger, Alan. (1993). Controlling Tropical Deforestation. London: Earthscan Publications.

Gray, Andrew. (1991). The Impact of Biodiversity Conservation on Indigenous Peoples. *In* Biodiversity: Social and Ecological Perspectives. Vandana Shiva, Patrick Anderson, Heffa Schücking, Andrew Gray, Larry Lohmann, and David Cooper, eds. Pp. 59–76. Penang: World Rainforest Movement.

Guha, Ramachandra. (1989). The Unquiet Woods: Ecological Change and Peasant Resistance. Delhi: Oxford University Press.

Gupta, Akhil, and James Ferguson. (1992). Beyond "Culture": Space, Identity, and the Politics of Difference. *Cultural Anthropology* 7:6–23.

Gupta, Akhil, and James Ferguson, eds. (1997). Anthropological Locations: Boundaries and Grounds of a Field Science. Berkeley: University of California Press.

Haas, Peter. (1990). Saving the Mediterranean: The Politics of International Environmental Cooperation. New York: Columbia University Press.

Haas, Peter, Robert Keohane, and Marc Levy, eds. (1993). Institutions for the Earth: Sources of Effective International Environmental Protection. Cambridge, MA: MIT Press.

Harrisson, Tom. (1949). Notes on Some Nomadic Punans. *Sarawak Museum Journal* 5(1, New Series):130–46.

Hawkins, Ann. (1993). Contested Ground: International Environmentalism and Global Climate Change. *In* The State and Social Power in Global Environmental Politics. Ronnie Lipschutz and Ken Conca. eds. Pp. 221–45. New York: Columbia University Press.

Herndl, Carl, and Stuart Brown, eds. (1996). Green Culture: Environmental Rhetoric in Contemporary America. Madison: University of Wisconsin Press.

Hitchcock, Robert. (1995). Centralization, Resource Depletion, and Coercive Conservation among the Tyua of the Northeastern Kalahari. *Human Ecology* 23:169–98.

Hong, Evelyne. (1987). Natives of Sarawak: Survival in Borneo's Vanishing Forests. Penang (Malaysia): Institute Masyarakat.

Huehne, W. H. (1959). A Doctor among "Nomadic" Punans. *Sarawak Museum Journal* 9(13–14, New Series):195–202.

Humphreys, David. (1996). Forest Politics: The Evolution of International Cooperation. London: Earthscan Publications.

Hurrell, Andrew, and Benedict Kingsbury, eds. (1992). The International Politics of the Environment. Oxford: Clarendon Press.

Hurst, Philip. (1990). Rainforest Politics: Ecological Destruction in Southeast Asia. London: Zed Books.

INSAN (Institute of Social Analysis). (1989). Logging Against the Natives of Sarawak. Petaling Jaya (Malaysia): INSAN.

ITTO (International Tropical Timber Organization). (1990). The Promotion of Sustainable Forest Management: A Case Study in Sarawak, Malaysia. Yokohama: International Tropical Timber Organization.

——. (1991). ITTO Guidelines for the Sustainable Management of Natural Tropical Forests. ITTO Technical Series no. 5. Yokohama: International Tropical Timber Organization.

——. (1992). Draft Criteria for Sustainable Forest Management. ITTO Policy Development Series Publication no. 3. Yokohama: International Tropical Timber Organization.

Johnson, Nels, and Bruce Cabarle. (1993). Surviving the Cut: Natural Forest Management in the Humid Tropics. Washington, DC: World Resources Institute.

Kearney, Michael. (1995). The Local and the Global: The Anthropology of Globalization and Transnationalism. Annual Review of Anthropology 24:547–65.

Kedit, Peter M. (1982). An Ecological Survey of the Penan. Sarawak Museum Journal, Special Issue No. 2, 30(5l, New Series): 225–79.

Kemf, Elizabeth, ed. (1993). Indigenous Peoples and Protected Areas: The Law of Mother Earth. London: Earthscan Publications.

Khor Kok Peng, Martin. (1991). What UNCED Must Do to Resolve the Forest Crisis. Third World Resurgence 10:23–4.

King, Victor T. (1993). The Peoples of Borneo. Oxford: Blackwell.

Kothari, Smitu, and Pramod Parajuli. (1993). No Nature without Social Justice: A Plea for Cultural and Ecological Pluralism in India. In Global Ecology: A New Arena of Political Conflict. W. Sachs, ed. Pp. 224–41. London: Zed Books.

Kuehls, Thom. (1993). The Nature of the State: An Ecological (Re)reading of Sovereignty and Territory. In Reimagining the Nation. Marjorie Ringrose and Adam Lerner, eds. Pp. 139–55. Buckingham, England: Open University Press.

——. (1996). Beyond Sovereign Territory: The Space of Ecopolitics. Minneapolis: University of Minnesota Press.

Kumar, Raj. (1986). The Forest Resources of Malaysia: Their Economics and Development. Singapore: Oxford University Press.

Kumari, Kanta. (1996). Sustainable Forest Management: Myth or Reality? Exploring the Prospects for Malaysia. Ambio 25:459–67.

Langub, Jayl. (1972a). Adaptation to a Settled Life by the Punans of the Belaga Subdistrict. Sarawak Gazette 98(1371):83–6.

——. (1972b). Structure and Progress in the Punan Community of Belaga Subdistrict. Sarawak Gazette 98(1378):219–21.

——. (1974). Background Report on Potential for Agricultural and Social Extension Service in the Penan Community of Belaga District. Sarawak Gazette 100(1395):93–6.

——. (1975). Distribution of Penan and Punan in the Belaga District. Borneo Research Bulletin 7(2):45–8.

——. (1984). Tamu: Barter Trade between Penan and Their Neighbors. Sarawak Gazette 10(1485):11–15.

——. (1989). Some Aspects of Life of the Penan. Sarawak Museum Journal, Special Issue No. 4, Part III, 40(61, New Series): 169–84.

——. (1990). A Journey through the Nomadic Penan Country. Sarawak Gazette 117(1514): 5–27.

Lewis, Martin. (1992). Green Delusions: An Environmentalist Critique of Radical Environmentalism. Durham. NC: Duke University Press.

Lim Keng Yaik. (1993). Tropical Timber Trade Issues as Seen from the Perspective of the SE Asia Region Exporting Countries. Speech given at symposium on Forests and the Environment: A US Response to Rio, Fernbank Museum, Atlanta, Georgia, May 7, 1993.

Linden, Eugene. (1991). Lost Tribes, Lost Knowledge. Time. September 23:46–56.

Lipschutz, Ronnie, and Ken Conca, eds. (1993). The State and Social Power in Global Environmental Politics. New York: Columbia University Press.

Litfin, Karen. (1994). Ozone Discourses: Science and Politics in Global Environmental Cooperation. New York: Columbia University Press.

Luke, Timothy. (1995). On Environmentality: Geo-Power and Eco-Knowledge in the Discourses of Contemporary Environmentalism. Cultural Critique 31:57–81.

Mahatir bin Mohamed. (1992). Opening Speech at the Second Ministerial Conference of Developing Countries on Environment and Development, Kuala Lumpur, April 26–29, 1992. Reprinted in the New Straits Times, April 28, 1992.

Mahatir bin Mohamed and José Lutzenberger. (1992). Eco-Imperialism and Bio-Monopoly at the Earth Summit. New Perspectives Quarterly 9(3):56–8.

Majid-Cooke, Fadzilah. (1995). The Politics of Sustained Yield Forest Management in Malaysia: Constructing the Boundaries of Time, Control and Consent. Geoforum 26:445–58.

MTIDC (Malaysian Timber Industry Development Council). (1994). Malaysia Committed to a Green Vision. Scientific American 270(4):M56–M59.

Manser, Bruno. (1996). Voices from the Rainforest: Testimonies of a Threatened People. Basel and Petaling Jaya (Malaysia): Bruno Manser Foundation and INSAN (Institute of Social Analysis).

Marcus, George. (1995). Ethnography in/of the World System: The Emergence of Multi-Sited Ethnography. Annual Review of Anthropology 24:95–117.

Marcus, George, and Michael Fischer. (1986). Anthropology as Cultural Critique: An Experimental Moment in the Human Sciences. Chicago: University of Chicago Press.

Marshall, George. (1991). FAO and Tropical Forestry. The Ecologist 21:66–72.

Mason, Robert. (1992). Contested Lands: Conflict and Compromise in New Jersey's Pine Barrens. Philadelphia: Temple University Press.

McCormick, John. (1989). Reclaiming Paradise: The Global Environmental Movement. Bloomington: Indiana University Press.

McManus, Phil. (1996). Contested Terrains: Politics, Stories and Discourses of Sustainability. Environmental Politics 5:48–73.

Miller, Marian. (1995). The Third World in Global Environmental Politics. Boulder, CO: Lynne-Rienner.

Milton, Kay, ed. (1993). Environmentalism: The View from Anthropology. London: Routledge.

Milton, Kay. (1996). Environmentalism and Cultural Theory: Exploring the Role of Anthropology in Environmental Discourse. London: Routledge.

Ministry of Primary Industries (Malaysia). (1992). Forever Green: Malaysia and Sustainable Forest Management. Kuala Lumpur: Ministry of Primary Industries.

Moore, Donald. (1993). Contesting Terrain in Zimbabwe's Eastern Highlands: Political Ecology, Ethnography and Peasant Resource Struggles. Economic Geography 69:380–401.

Morehouse, Barbara. (1996). A Place Called Grand Canyon: Contested Geographies. Tucson: University of Arizona Press.

Needham, Rodney. (1954a). A Penan Mourning Usage. Bijdragen tot de Taal-, Land- en Volkenkunde 10:263–7.

——. (1954b). The System of Teknonyms and Death-Names of the Penan. Southwestern Journal of Anthropology 10:416–31.

——. (1965). Death-Names and Solidarity in Penan Society. Bijdragen tot de Taal-, Land- en Volkenkunde 121:58–76.

——. (1972). Punan-Penan. In Ethnic Groups of Insular Southeast Asia, vol. 1: Indonesia, Andaman Islands, and Madagascar. Frank M. Lebar, ed. Pp. 176–80. New Haven, CT: Human Relations Area Files Press.

Nicolaisen, Johannes. (1976a). The Penan of Sarawak: Further Notes on the Neo-Evolutionary Concept of Hunters. Folk 18:205–36.

——. (1976b). The Penan of the Seventh Division of Sarawak: Past, Present and Future. Sarawak Museum Journal 24(45, New Series):35–61.

——. (1978). Penan Death-Names. *Sarawak Museum Journal* 26(47, New Series):29–41.

Ngu, Lucas. (1988). Only Malaysians Could Aid Penans. *Borneo Post*, July 7.

Panayotou, Theodore, and Peter Ashton. (1992). Not by Timber Alone: Economics and Ecology for Sustaining Tropical Forests. Washington, DC: Island Press.

Peluso, Nancy. (1993). Coercing Conservation: The Politics of State Resource Control. *In* The State and Social Power in Global Environmental Politics. Ronnie Lipschutz and Ken Conca, eds. Pp. 46–70. New York: Columbia University Press.

Pigg, Stacey Leigh. (1992). Constructing Social Categories through Place: Social Representations and Development in Nepal. *Comparative Studies in Society and History* 34:491–513.

Poore, Duncan, ed. (1989). No Timber without Trees: Sustainability in the Tropical Forest. London: Earthscan Publications.

Porter, Gareth, and Janet Welsh Brown. (1991). Global Environmental Politics. Boulder, CO: West-view Press.

Princen, Thomas, and Matthais Finger, eds. (1994). Environmental NGOs in World Politics: Linking the Local and the Global. London: Routledge.

Proctor, James. (1995). Whose Nature?: The Contested Moral Terrain of Ancient Forests. *In* Uncommon Ground: Toward Reinventing Nature. William Cronon, ed. Pp. 269–97. New York: W. W. Norton and Co.

Rangan, Haripriya. (1995). Contested Boundaries: State Policies, Forest Classifications, and Deforestation in the Garhwal Himalayas. *Antipode* 27:343–62.

Rappaport, Roy A. (1993). Distinguished Lecture in General Anthropology: The Anthropology of Trouble. *American Anthropologist* 95:295–303.

Redclift, Michael. (1987). Sustainable Development: Exploring the Contradictions. London: Routledge.

Ritchie, James. (1994). Bruno Manser: The Inside Story. Singapore: Summer Times.

Rosaldo, Renato. (1989). Culture and Truth: The Remaking of Social Analysis. Boston: Beacon Press.

Rousseau, Jérôme. (1990). Central Borneo: Ethnic Identity and Social Life in a Stratified Society. Oxford: Clarendon Press.

Sachs, Wolfgang, ed. (1992). The Development Dictionary: A Guide to Knowledge as Power. London: Zed Books.

Sandbukt, Oyvind, ed. (1995). Management of Tropical Forests: Towards an Integrated Perspective. Oslo: Centre for Environment and Development, University of Oslo.

Schmink, Marianne, and Charles Wood. (1992). Contested Frontiers in Amazonia. New York: Columbia University Press.

Schoenberger, Karl. (1992). Malaysia's Trade Minister Exhibits a True Grit. *Los Angeles Times*, June 15.

Schwartzman, Stephan. (1991). Deforestation and Popular Resistance in Acre: From Local Social Movement to Global Network. *The Centennial Review* 35:397–422.

Scott, James C. (1998). Seeing Like a State: How Certain Schemes to Improve the Human Condition Have Failed. New Haven, CT: Yale University Press.

Sesser, Stan. (1991). Logging the Rain Forest. *The New Yorker*, May 17:42–67.

Sharma, N. (1992). Managing the World's Forests: Looking for Balance between Conservation and Development. Dubuque: Kendal/Hunt Publishing Company.

Shiva, Vandana. (1993). The Greening of the Global Reach. *In* Global Ecology: A New Arena of Political Conflict. Wolfgang Sachs, ed. Pp. 149–56. London: Zed Books.

Siva, Kumar G. (1991). Taib: A Vision for Sarawak. Kuching: Jacamar Sdn. Bhd.

Slater, Candace. (1995). Amazonia as Edenic Narrative. *In* Uncommon Ground: Toward Reinventing Nature. William Cronon, ed. Pp. 114–31. New York: W.W. Norton and Co.

Smythies, B. (1963). History of Forestry in Sarawak. *Malayan Forester* 26:232–52.

Soper, Kate. (1995). What is Nature?: Culture, Politics and the Non-Human. Oxford: Blackwell.

Sturgeon, Noël. (1997). Ecofeminist Natures: Race, Gender, Feminist Theory, and Political Action. New York: Routledge.

Takacs, David. (1996). The Idea of Biodiversity: Philosophies of Paradise. Baltimore: Johns Hopkins University Press.

Taylor, Bron, ed. (1995). Ecological Resistance Movements: The Global Emergence of Radical and Popular Environmentalism. Albany: State University of New York Press.

Thompson, M., and S. Rayner. (1998). Cultural Discourses. *In* Human Choice and Climate Change, vol. 1: The Societal Framework. S. Rayner and E. Malone, eds. Pp. 265–343. Columbus, Ohio: Battelle Press.

Turner, Terence. (1991). Representing, Resisting, Rethinking: Historical Transformations of Kayapo Culture and Anthropological Consciousness. *In* Colonial Situations: Essays on the Contextualization of Ethnographic Knowledge. George Stocking, ed. Pp. 285–313. Madison: University of Wisconsin Press.

Urquhart, Ian A. N. (1951). Some Notes on Jungle Punans in Kapit District. *Sarawak Museum Journal* 5(13, New Series):495–533.

Viana, Virgilio, Jamison Ervin, Richard Donovan, Chris Elliot, and Henry Gholz, eds. (1996). Certification of Forest Products: Issues and Perspectives. Washington, DC: Island Press.

Vincent, Jeffrey. (1995). Timber Trade, Economics, and Tropical Forest Management. *In* Ecology, Conservation, and Management of Southeast Asian Rain Forests. Richard Primack and Thomas Lovejoy, eds. Pp. 241–62. New Haven. CT: Yale University Press.

Visvanathan, Shiv. (1991). Mrs. Bruntland's Disenchanted Cosmos. *Alternatives* 16:377–84.

Wapner, Paul. (1996). Environmental Activism and World Civic Politics. Albany: State University of New York Press.

Watson, J. (1950). Some Materials for a Forest History of Malaya. *Malayan Forester* 13:63–72.

World Bank. (1991). Malaysia: Forestry Sub-Sector Study. Report No. 9775-MA. Washington, DC: The World Bank.

World Commission on Environment and Development. (1987). Our Common Future. New York: Oxford University Press.

World Rainforest Movement and *Sahabat Alam Malaysia*. (1990). The Battle for Sarawak's Forests. Penang: World Rainforest Movement and *Sahabat Alam Malaysia*.

Wyatt-Smith, J., and A. Vincent. (1962). Progressive Development in the Management of Tropical Lowland Evergreen Rain Forest and Mangrove Forest in Malaya. *Malayan Forester* 25:199–223.

Zerner, Charles. (1994). Through a Green Lens: The Construction of Customary Environmental Law and Community in Indonesia's Maluku Islands. *Law and Society Review* 28:1079–122.

——. (1996). Telling Stories about Biodiversity. *In* Valuing Local Knowledge: Indigenous People and Intellectual Property Rights. Stephen Brush and Doreen Stabinsky, eds. Pp. 68–101. Washington, DC: Island Press.

Zimmerman, Michael. (1994). Contesting Earth's Future: Radical Ecology and Postmodernity. Berkeley: University of California Press.

20

Becoming a Tribal Elder, and Other Green Development Fantasies

Anna Lowenhaupt Tsing

1999

How does a globally circulating social category come to mean something to people in a particular political context? Categories are dream machines as well as practical tools for seeing; the fantastic view we are offered and the familiar job at hand are inextricably related. This essay is a back-handed defense of environmentally-inflected rural policy, including that sometimes called "green" or sustainable development. I argue that at least in one village in the Meratus Mountains of Kalimantan, collaboration between urban environmentalists and village leaders offers promising possibilities for environmental and social justice, that is, for building a world in which we might want to live. Yet my argument is a planner's nightmare. The collaborations I describe are made possible only by clever engagements with green development fantasies of the rural, the backward, and the exotic. "Tribal elders" are made in the mobile spaces found within coercive international dreams of conservation and development, and these men and women – granted agency within the fantasies of their sponsors – are enabled to forge alliances that yet somehow present the hope of transforming top-down coercion into local empowerment. Categories often come to life in this round-about way. Yet we can only appreciate their creative intervention and their political charge if we move beyond a sociology of stable interest groups and hierarchies to investigate the social effects of shifting rhetorics and narratives and the reformulations of identity and community that they engender.

My argument is composed at a moment when many scholars have become critical of social movements committed to combining the protection of endangered environments and the empowerment of indigenous peoples (Brosius, Tsing, and Zerner 1998). Fearing simplistic representations of wild nature and tribal culture, scholars dismiss what in my opinion are some of the most promising social movements of our times. In contrast, my approach offers an alternative to the choice between unselfconscious stereotypes of nature and culture on the one hand, and ironic dismissals of environmental and indigenous politics on the other. I argue that our discussions might better begin with the circulation and use of "green development fantasies." My focus on collaboration – as opposed to contestation or misunderstanding – offers a methodological framework for facilitating this discussion. In the late 1990s, both scholars and activists know a lot about how to talk about contests; we have less precedence for discussing the awkward but necessary collaborations central to both intellectual and political work.

Several layers of context are necessary for my argument to emerge. I begin by locating my

essay within the concerns about upland transformations in Indonesia that form the subject
of this volume. I then turn to the Meratus
village of Mangkiling, which, already the
subject of many green development representations, seems well suited for a meditation on the
dynamics of representation. The fantastic
aspects of international thinking about exotic
and backward rural communities (for which I
deploy the term "tribe" as a kind of shorthand) are my guide to the field of attraction in
which Mangkiling representatives are able to
become potential collaborators and political
actors. Beginning conventionally enough in a
rural sociology, I draw my argument into the
unstable realm of pathos and love in which
things that did not exist before can emerge.
For it is in that realm that metropolitan fantasies *both* fulfil themselves *and* take the dreamers they construct by surprise.

Upland Transformations

The residents of uplands Indonesia have come
into a new visibility. For many decades,
lowland peasants were the only rural peoples
to figure in those great narratives of nationalism and development that plotted the country's
past and future. In recent years, however,
international concerns with the degradation of
fragile environments have focused attention on
rainforests and mountains – and their long-
time residents. Policy makers have been pressed
to rethink the uplands as key sites of environmental sustainability and to consider the role
of uplands communities within environmental
conservation as well as development programs.
Non-governmental organizations focusing on
issues of conservation and development have
joined state officials in negotiating the role of
uplands communities. Social scientists have
been drawn into practical discussion of upland
futures. Upland village farmers are aware of a
new sense of focus and urgency in their deal-
ings with state officials, NGOs, and social
scientists alike.

The new attention to upland communities
does not present itself in the form of a consensus. Discussion ignites fierce debates (Who
owns the forest?) as well as unstated disagree-

ments (What is a community?). Central to all
this are much disputed issues of representation. On one end of a continuum, upland communities are represented as closed and static
repositories of custom and tradition; on the
other end, uplanders are portrayed as hyper-
rational, individualistic entrepreneurs with no
commitments to local social life or culture.
Either side of the continuum can be presented
as politically promising or socially worthless:
uplanders as cultural communities may be
backward savages or guardians of the forest;
as individualistic entrepreneurs they may be
model citizens or undisciplined mobs. Both
ends of this continuum of representation draw
upon hoary historical roots as well as contemporary legitimacy. Terms are revitalized. International environmental and minority rights
movements work to transform the assumption
that "tribes" are backward remnants of archaic
humanity to argue instead that the world needs
tribal wisdom and tribal rights to preserve our
endangered biological and cultural diversity.
Other environmentalists celebrate the new
hegemony of free trade by portraying a post-
communal world of independent innovators
and entrepreneurs. In Indonesia, both ends of
the "individuals-or-communities" continuum,
as well as many compromises and middle
zones, engage some social scientists, some
community leaders and advocates, some village
farmers.

Given the variety of ways these dichoto-
mous strategies of representation have been
and are being used and abused, this does not
seem a moment to decide once-and-for-all
which one is really right. Instead, it seems an
important time to analyze the dynamics of representation itself, and particularly to look at
how representational categories come to mean
something to farmers, community leaders,
scholars, advocates, or development bureaucrats in a particular political moment. In this
spirit, this essay discusses representational
strategies, and the social categories on which
they rely, as dreams and fantasies that grab
people under certain circumstances. Preexisting complexities are of course important, but
by thinking of them as gates to, rather than
walls against the imagination, it is possible to
trace the emergence of unexpected ingenuities.

As we attend to both creativity and constraints in upland self-fashioning, a number of elements come into view.

First, a new role has become possible for rural minority leaders who convincingly "represent" the kind of community that environmentalists and green developers might choose for co-operation, learning, and alliance. These representatives take on the mediations that make collaborations between village people and advocates or policy makers possible. Their collaborations sustain and give life to concepts such as village development, tribal rights, sustainability, community-based conservation, or local culture. At the same time, these same concepts make political agency possible on both sides: they are the medium in which village leaders and those who study, supervise, and change them can imagine each other as strategic actors and thus can mold their own actions strategically. We might call these representatives "tribal elders" because it is they who, to hold the attention of potential rural-minority advocates, take responsibility for the fantasy of the tribe.

For tribal elders to flourish, it is not enough to posit the existence of "tribes"; a field of attraction must be created to nurture and maintain the relationship between the rural community and its experts. Without this field of attraction, the community will be abandoned to its own fate; neither mediation nor collaboration is possible. Thus the single most important sign of a community representative's success is his or her ability to conjure, and be conjured by, that emotionally-fraught space that keeps the experts coming back. In this space creative action is possible, and collaborations are forged.

Collaborations are the hopeful edge of a political project. To condemn a project, it is not enough to say that it engages in simplifications; all social categories simplify even as they bring us to appreciate new complexities. Instead, it seems more useful to judge the political valence of a project by the promise for remaking the world of the collaborations it has engendered. Thus "tribal" fantasies in South Kalimantan, combined in an ambivalent and ambiguous manner with rural development dreams and hierarchies, lead to collabo-

rations between urban activists and village leaders that offer possibilities for building environmental and social justice in the countryside as exciting as any I have heard of on the contemporary scene. At the end of this essay, I turn to two promising initiatives, collaborations between urban environmentalists and Mangkiling leaders that developed in the early 1990s. First, I show how "nature" is made into a utopian space of collaboration through the practice of naming trees. Second, I examine the mapping projects that, instead of clarifying land claims, amplify ambiguity in the system – and thus open the confusion in which village claims over forested land might hold their own.

It is not useful to be complacent about these collaborations. Tribal elders have no particularly striking powers; nor do they represent homogeneous or unified communities or grassroots movements. Their "community" representations are vulnerable and contested; even close kin and neighbors are not necessarily supporters. A few minutes' hike away, no one may know a thing about their projects. Furthermore, environmentalist and tribal collaborations with outside patrons are hardly the most powerful rural collaborations around. In Indonesia, development visions in which rapid environmental destruction is appreciated as progress or regulated as government-endorsed "sustainability" continue to be much more powerful than emergent "tribal" environmentalisms. Song-and-dance tourism predominates over ecotourism. The role of environmentally-friendly tribal elder deserves special attention because it is new and promising, but it does not speak for either long-standing culture or newly-made hegemony, whether locally, regionally, or nationally.

Then, too, there is nothing here to suggest the kinds of progressive politics we most easily imagine: coalitions of "interest groups"; workers and peasants and intellectuals in league. Instead, here are moments of creative intervention and the making of new identities. Ordinary villagers may or may not get involved; it is unclear how many will see their interests as being advanced. Yet the space is cleared for the tribal elder and for the field of attraction that makes his or her agency possible. The enactment of the tribe is, to use a term from the International Situationists (writing about the very different context of metropolitan spectacle), the making of a tribal "situation"; it is the recharging of political possibility through staging the fantastical realities of everyday life (Debord 1983).[1]

The Tribal Situation

Let me turn to a particular tribal "situation." Consider a fragment from a document written by Musa, a Meratus Dayak elder of the village of Pantai Mangkiling.

> [W]e, as Indigenous Original Peoples of the Local Area, for the sake of guarding our Livelihood Rights and Environmental Conservation, as well as from our Culture, state as follows:
>
> 1. Our livelihood is to work the soil by DIBBLE-STICK PLANTING, and our care for our local natural world's plants from generation to generation has been as a productive garden, thus THERE IS NO WILD FOREST in our area.
> 2. We will not condone it if there is a destruction of our local natural environment, because this interferes with OUR BASIC HUMAN RIGHTS.
> 3. If someone destroys our local natural environment, this means they destroy our Basic Human Rights, and thus the destroyer will be confirmed as Violator of the Law of the Indigenous Original Local People.

In the Meratus Mountains of South Kalimantan, shifting cultivators have created socially-marked forest territories in which planted, encouraged, named, and closely watched trees signal the economic claims and social affiliations of particular individuals and groups. As Musa states, "There is no wild forest" in this area. Yet since the late 1970s, timber companies, transmigration projects, plantations, and migrant pioneer farmers from the Banjar plains have made increasing claims on Meratus forests. None of these claimants recognize Meratus Dayak customary rights to the forests; instead, the forests are seen as uninhabited,

wild territories to be assigned to various users by the state.

Meratus Dayak responses have been various. Stories circulate about violence and the burning of timber company bridges. At the same time, people retreat farther into the hills, discouragement spreads, and young men sell trees to illegal loggers before the "legitimate" companies can take them without compensation. This has been a challenging time for community leaders, who maneuver within the government regulations and rhetorics that both disenfranchise their communities and provide the only legitimate channels for protest. Creative responses have been necessary to hold on to any community land and resources; the threat of involuntary resettlement in government camps for "isolated tribes" looms. It is in this context that Musa has composed this document.

The document is a land-rights claim of sorts. It makes its claim by overlapping three divergent streams of political culture that, outside of this text, have rather separate spheres of existence. First, regional administration: the typed document is an official statement (*surat keterangan*) signed by Musa "on behalf of the Committee of the Traditional Hall of the People of Pantai Mangkiling," as "acknowledged" by the village head and district military officer and "verified" by the district head. The stamps of various district officers occupy the bottom third of the page; the formality is recognizable and appropriate within the regional bureaucracy.

Second, international environmentalism: the document uses every globally circulating jargon word in the social ecologist's 1980s agenda. The author writes for indigenous people, original people, people who for generations have guarded and protected their natural environment. Their traditional conservation strategies are being threatened, and with them their human rights. To destroy the forest – as the unmentioned timber companies and plantations want to do – is against traditional law. Instead, as he explains later in the text, the forests must be used by village cooperatives. Where did Musa get this rhetoric? These are not terms that Meratus Dayaks ordinarily use; furthermore, neither district nor regency bureaucrats in South Kalimantan know much about this kind of talk. The Indonesian language of the text is official and elegant – much more so than either my translation or Musa's ordinary speech. Presumably there was collaboration here, and maybe collaboration with someone from outside South Kalimantan. However, this is not just a transplanted text, and there is a third stream evident: Meratus cultural ecology. For example, rather than engaging government problematics of shifting cultivation (*berladang berpindah-pindah*) or environmentalist endorsements of forest love and lore, the document goes straight to the cultural practice of dibble-stick planting (*menugal*), a much more locally relevant sign of social habitation.

Musa's tribal situation depends on his ability to evoke all three of these strands of political culture simultaneously. As a community representative, he can afford to show some agility with local knowledge. But he must articulate this knowledge within the discursive categories that make his community appear as an identifiable object to environmentalists, on the one hand, and government administrators and developers, on the other. His document is recognizable as a claim only to the extent that he evokes NGO and official ideas about rural minority communities. Thus my account detours momentarily from his text to introduce the community-like objects of environmentalism and development. I begin with the "tribe."

Until quite recently, tribes were supposed to represent our planet's past – the part of human evolution that city people were done with; tribal remnants were irrelevant to our times except as museum pieces. Suddenly, tribes have reentered stories of the future. The rainforests were shrinking; the ozone hole growing; the progress of *progress* looked terrifying. As the millennium drew to a close, the suggestion appeared that we had better pay attention to the wisdom of the tribes, since, after all, they are the ones who know how to maintain nature over the long haul. Attentive to the alternatives, a cosmopolitan audience looked up and listened. Tribes, it was argued, could be the guardians of the biological, pharmaceutical, cultural, and aesthetic-spiritual diversity that

would make our future on earth p[...] the most hard-headed of futuri[...] ment planners, were forced to pay [...] this refigured planetary trajectory [...] of the tribal elder became a small [...] presence in the emergent rhetoric [...] able – that is, environmentally [...] development.

Like any other political rhetoric, [...] development plans can be idealistic and utopian or cynical and practical; they can be a tool in the hands of national military forces and transnational corporations or a rallying cry for community rights and social justice. Tribal rights is only one thin strand in an emerging "sustainability" rhetoric that more commonly takes for granted transnational capitalism and neocolonial management as it counts board feet, parts per million, growth rates, and the bottom line. Sustainability means different things to different groups. In the Indonesian context, sustainability has been debated in Jakarta by government bureaus and non-governmental organizations: conservation areas, laws, and goals have been proposed and sometimes adopted; the question of tribal rights has even garnered some interest.[2] However, at least in rural areas, attempts to deepen national commitments to environmental conservation have been impeded by the presence of an enormously bureaucratized, subsidized, and militarized machinery of non-sustainable development. This is a machinery not easily converted to new purposes. It is not just that administration and planning occur through this machinery; the ruling concepts and institutions of government, economy, culture, and citizenship in rural areas have been tailored within its workings. Attempts to ignore or evade this machinery are quickly labeled subversive, a label made serious by the pervasive presence of arms. Any suggestions about forest conservation or tribal rights in South Kalimantan must somehow make their way around or through the national and regional development apparatus.

In South Kalimantan, the goal of rural development is understood to be the management of rural peoples and places for the advancement of national priorities. Development is a top-down project for expanding administration; development brings villages and forests into line with national standards.[3] As with all administrative projects, there is negotiation of just what will count as locally appropriate. Yet I heard little disagreement about the importance of externally imposed directives in the administration of regional minorities, who are completely missing within the ranks of provincial administrators – and who are sitting on the province's most valuable forest resources. Development for them involves independent plans for forests and for people; the goal of development is to make the people orderly while simultaneously redirecting their forest resources to national priorities such as patronage, profit, and export production. Villages are to be units of administration; forests are national resource domains; there is no legitimate connection between the two. Thus, most regional development administrators have never given consideration to concepts of tribal rights or community-based forest management, each of which – whatever their constituency in Jakarta – contradicts the hegemonic logics of provincial development.[4]

In this context, Musa's endorsement of indigenous peoples' conservation is not a mimicry of ruling ideas; within provincial political culture, it is an innovative challenge. Musa's text argues that the traditional values of his village are not in need of development; they are the basis of the people's own equitable and sustainable development plans. Furthermore, even if Musa learned or copied the terms of his text from a Jakarta or Geneva visitor, to merely restate them in South Kalimantan could mean little, unless he could create a "situation" – that is, a dramatic enactment of phantasmic realities – in which these terms could come to mean something to the regional officials who control whether or not the village continues to exist.

How this situation was created is the subject of the rest of this essay. In the next sections, I examine a series of documents about the village of Mangkiling to look at how Mangkiling representatives became positioned as spokespersons for community conservation and development, or, in the shorthand I have been using here, as "tribal elders." On the one hand, Mangkiling can be said to be gifted with

smart leaders who have been able to transform a regional development rhetoric of backward status and exotic culture into community entrepreneurship and self-representation. This requires that they engage the textual intricacies of the discourse of development administration to find what literary critic Ross Chambers (1991) might identify as its "room for maneuver." Their tricky transformations and revisions of regional development make local initiatives possible. But Mangkiling representatives cannot strategize as if they were generals on a battlefield in which opposing armies and objectives are clearly demarcated and unchanging. Instead, they are produced as representatives by outsiders' standards of representation. They enact a fantasy in which whether they play themselves or someone else's understanding of themselves is ambiguous; the community they can represent is produced in their development-directed performances of "community."[5]

To make sense of this double-sided agency, so much their own and so much not their own, I show the importance of what I have been calling "fields of attraction," for it is the longings, the broken promises, the erotic draw, and the magic of that Mangkiling enacted in the tribal situation that makes the tribal elder emerge as a politically active and creative figure. To the extent that conservation and development discourses can be engaged through these fields of attraction, local initiatives – whether for better or worse – become possible.

The Native in the Document

If Musa's testament was an isolated object, it would be inspired but socially insignificant. However, Musa and his associates in Pantai Mangkiling have done more than write this text, and their ingenuity and persistence and sheer luck have paid off in making the village of Mangkiling a place that cannot be rolled over and erased easily. Whether or not Musa is properly considered an elder of a "Committee of the Traditional Hall of Mangkiling," as he signs himself, he has effectively constituted the village as an object of attention and respect for those interested in the conjunction of forest protection, community resource management, and ethnic pride. Government officials, eco-tourists, naturalists, social science researchers, environmental activists, and journalists have been attracted there. In the process, a small mound of documents about Mangkiling has been generated.[6] Pantai Mangkiling may be the best documented village in the Meratus Mountains. Most of these documents are about Musa and his fellow villagers, not *by* them. The portraits of the village and the villagers found in these documents serve the purposes of others. Yet reading them with my questions in mind, it is possible to find traces of the encounters in which Mangkiling representatives, empowered to be more than passive objects of study and command, have renegotiated the very purposes that gave them agency; they have turned regional dogma to unexpected ends. These traces guide us to appreciate the formation and deployment of tribal sensibilities in Mangkiling.[7]

Through the documents, I can ask how Musa and his fellow village leaders managed to get so much respect as "community spokespeople" while operating within the discursive and institutional constraints of expected village status – that is, as those with nothing to say. I can trace the transformations through which these leaders made the village a formidable ethnic-environmental object with forests under noticeable, if perhaps unenforceable, traditional claim. The documents can tell us something about how Mangkiling leaders positioned themselves to make more documents about them happen, that is, to keep the village a possible subject of tribal rights.

The documents generalize about the villagers, but, sometimes, too, they name individuals. Three leaders stand out: Musa, his sister Sumiati, who is the village head, and their brother Yuni, the village secretary. These three are consulted, profiled, and quoted extensively. My interviews confirm that they are major architects of the Mangkiling project. Let me begin with a document that features Yuni.

In April 1989 a one-day seminar was held in the provincial capital of South Kalimantan on the dilemmas of Mangkiling as an upland, forest village in an era of national development

and change (Yayasan Kompas Borneo 1989). Organized by a provincial environmental group and sponsored by the Ford Foundation, the seminar was attended by regional officials, scholars, and environmentalists. As the Assistant Governor who introduced the proceedings pointed out, the seminar's focus on one village could be generalized to propose concepts for the development of interior populations throughout the nation. The seminar featured a series of papers on the social, ecological, and economic features and challenges of Mangkiling. The papers, which were distributed afterwards in bound form, present a variety of research methodologies and perspectives. Some are based on field research; others contextualize the Mangkiling situation or offer theoretical viewpoints. Many authors are careful to point out the preliminary nature of their assertions.

Yet, to some, the results of the seminar were definitive. One of the province's two daily newspapers published a report on the seminar under the title, "The Economic System of the People of Mangkiling is Extremely Simple" (*Dinamika Berita* 1989a). The article focuses on a paper presented by the head of the regional office of the Department of Social Welfare. The paragraph from the original paper that inspired the headline reads as follows:

The isolated population group in South Kalimantan still holds to a simple economic system, that is, it still employs a barter system with other families but still within the group. The products that they are able to gain from their efforts are only enough to fulfill their own needs, such that the fulfillment of life needs in a proper manner, as with other peoples, is still far from the reach of their thought. (Mooduto 1989: 3, my translation)

The most amazing thing about this paragraph is that it is utterly and entirely untrue. It is not even a plausible interpretation of the Mangkiling economy or that of any other Meratus Dayaks for the last four centuries, at least. While subsistence and inter-family networking is an important concern within Meratus Dayak communities, they have long been involved in production for distant markets. The conditions of marketing have shifted over time, and the key products have changed. However, the idea that Mangkiling people are unfamiliar with cash and markets is absurd. (Other seminar papers describe the importance in Mangkiling of banana and chili production for regional markets; in the early 1990s, Mangkiling also produced a variety of cash crops besides these, including peanuts, mung beans, coffee, bamboo and light wood construction poles.) The fact that an important regional office with jurisdiction over Meratus Dayaks would promote the idea of a barter-and-subsistence economy in Mangkiling, and that the provincial newspaper would choose this item to report, suggests the blinding relevance of stereotypes about the backward and the primitive in regional development affairs. Because the persistent conviction of Meratus Dayak traditionalism seems so necessary to the trajectory of regional development, planners and their publicity-makers let stereotypes about tradition overcome their other forms of knowledge about the area.

These stereotypes lead to discrimination and persecution. Yet they cannot completely close off Meratus Dayak agency. To the extent that they stimulate research and administrative contact between Meratus Dayaks and development planners, they can even present, ironically, new opportunities for creative community leadership. The seminar documents themselves demonstrate such an opening.

The last section of the volume distributed after the seminar is a photographic essay documenting the proceedings. The heads of speakers rise over the podium out of official uniform shirts; the microphone arches toward each serious face. The audience sits in straight parallel lines along long tables draped neatly with cloth; the exact line of tea glasses before them marks out the orderliness of the row. Some audience members lean forward, taking notes; others lean back, listening or bored. No one leans to the side. But one page of photographs is different; it offers the "profile of a Mangkiling village member who attended the one-day seminar, Mr. Yuni, the Secretary of Mangkiling village" (Yayasan Kompas Borneo 1989: Appendix I). Yuni is shown in three photographs. He is serious and neatly dressed

but awkward, innocently out of place, standing as if on display between the audience rows. In one picture, the seated audience appears to be teasing him, laughing at him. He leans precariously, off balance or in a gesture of undisciplined motion.

Through his profile, Yuni "represents" the village in a number of senses. His photographs legitimate the seminar proceedings, and their images of primitive Mangkiling, both through the truth value of his attendance and his inability to pass as just another seminar member. At the same time, his pose reveals traces of the kind of leadership he is able to forge from this position. That artless, off balance stance presents him as the open, desiring subject of an imagined modernity yet with the untutored simplicity of tradition in his background and breeding. He is a tribesman longing for change. Nor need he have been "plotting" to devise this pose; what alternatives are there for the bureaucratically-undisciplined body in the midst of lines of authority and order? Yet, ironically, his lack of bureaucratic experience opens the possibilities of a community leadership role that even development planners can begin to imagine. If the "tribal situation" is to be enacted on the regional development scene, it is the cosmopolitan tribesman, the representative of unfulfilled desire, who can enact it. This representative is created within the opportunity spaces of the development apparatus itself, as villagers are brought in to join its activities. It is negotiated within encounters such as that recorded in Yuni's photographic profile; it finds its subtle traces in the documents that propose and debate the categories of development. My next sections offer more of the context in which I interpret Yuni's pose.

Villages as Fantasies and Frameworks

In the 1970s and early 1980s, the resettlement and resocialization of "isolated populations" (*masyarakat terasing*), including Meratus Dayaks, became an important component of the regional development plan in South

Kalimantan. By working to assimilate these peoples into normative Indonesian standards and grouping them into discipline-oriented villages, the program provided a striking and inexpensive model of how development was expected to operate at a national scale. The process of development could be imagined within the diorama of village resettlement, in which tribes – that is those who did not have the know-how to live in proper villages – were to become modern citizens. Development was the elimination of tribes and the creation of villages. Furthermore, because official definitions of "isolated populations" stressed an imagined landless nomadism (i.e., as an interpretation of shifting cultivation), tribal groups targeted by the "isolated populations" program were defined out of any land rights recognized by the state.

In the 1980s and 1990s, a new regional administrative initiative overcame and indeed reversed some of the consequences of the "isolated populations" program by disciplining existing settlements rather than creating new model sites. The regional government redoubled its administrative efforts in all rural areas – "isolated" and otherwise – by dividing its administrative units into smaller and more closely regulated districts and villages. Where once there was one "village" unit, three or four were created. Villages were to be further naturalized and normalized in the process; while still development models, they were also somehow to correspond to on-the-ground communities. At the same time, district and regency officials refocused their attempts to find and train appropriate village leaders. Instead of allowing older men with existing community status to assume official village positions, they appointed younger men with formal education and the ability to articulate commitments to the goals of development and orderly state administration. These new leaders were offered travel opportunities, gifts, and ceremonies; village subsidies controlled by these new leaders increased rapidly. Furthermore, subsidies were offered differentially, depending on leadership performance. Village leaders were pressed into a competitive relation with each other, in which pleasing regional officials, rather than cooperating with

each other, paid off in personal and village benefits.

In contrast to the "isolated populations" program (which continues to operate simultaneously, with reduced resources, but remaining a significant threat), this administrative initiative has promised a new stability for Meratus Dayak groups, in relation to their lands and resources. However, the terms of this stability have been community leadership that articulates and demonstrates compliance with the goals of regional development. There is a contradiction here. "Communities" in the Meratus Mountains are contentious, unstable social groupings, forged through day-to-day local initiatives. Yet to the extent that communities reaffirm themselves as communities, with independent initiatives and resources to manage, they refuse the demands of development, which require that they give up their autonomy and their resources to national planning. However, to the extent that leaders merely confirm national planning by forming villages without locally autonomous communal concerns, their communities slip away and they find themselves treated as pompous ideologues.

This contradiction is rendered more intense by the competition among factions and leaders. Since most contemporary Meratus "villages" only gained their current status sometime in the last fifteen years, the possibility of rearranging administrative affiliations – and thus capturing regional development resource flows – is obvious. As in Eastern Europe after the collapse of the Soviet Union, the struggle to create new polities before the polity-making time is over is zealous. Furthermore, current village leaders create the impression that they are in competition with all others for the survival of their communities; one group's advancement could mean the dissolution of another group. By the early 1990s, it was clear that the most successful village leaders were becoming rich and powerful from development subsidies in ways never before possible in the Meratus Mountains; the closest constituents of these successful leaders were also gaining disproportional benefits. Village offices had never been so important. Family ties were rearticulated, as young men cajoled their elders, hoping to coalesce some community to lead, while old men flattered the young, desperately needing a channel to regional power. Around these rearticulated family ties, factions fight and reform, each trying to channel the differential flow of resources from regional centers. Village leaders sense that if they are not sufficiently creative and aggressive in holding on to their positions, they can be quickly displaced.

It is important to understand that the unit of the "village" has not always been the most relevant to Meratus Dayak sociality. Most all Meratus Dayaks are shifting cultivators who clear new fields every one to three years, while turning old fields into more or less managed garden and forest areas. Small family-like groups (*umbun*) make their own farms; these groups affiliate in clusters of some five to twenty-five umbun to form work groups, share meat, fruit, and fish, and hold festivals and healing rites together. Living arrangements vary across the mountains. In the area that includes Mangkiling, clusters construct a large multi-roomed *balai* hall as their central settlement; every umbun makes its own room around the central floor. Single-umbun houses are also built near the umbun's fields. Until recent development subsidies offered the possibility of making balai with long-lasting construction materials, the halls were repaired or rebuilt every few years. On these occasions, the hall might be relocated, and new umbun might join or split off to join other clusters. Decisions to affiliate into another balai hall generally took into account the location of an umbun's familiar forests, gardens, and fields; it was rare to relocate far from one's most well-managed livelihood resources. However, because in any balai, the territories with which each umbun was most associated radiated out in different directions, toward different balai, each umbun had a number of options of groups with which to live, without ever straying from its familiar territories.

The village (*desa*) is a government administrative unit that operates over, within, and around these shifting clusters. Until the 1980s, villages were huge, unwieldy units, and it was mainly their constituent neighborhoods (*RT*) that had much meaning for local clusters.

Some neighborhood and village leaders were more successful than others in gathering and holding communities (Tsing 1993). Since the administrative reapportioning and the subsequent increase in development subsidies for successful village leaders, villages have become more significant. Village leaders have more tools with which to convince their constituents to stay; at the same time, factions attempting to displace those leaders abound. In this context, village leaders and would-be leaders need to find aggressive ways to articulate regional development goals without losing all local support.

Pantai Mangkiling has been one of the most successful models of this new kind of village. Pantai Mangkiling is the name of a place – a flat spot (*pantai*) along the Kapiau River. There has not always been a balai there, although fields, houses, and planted, productive trees have marked the spot continuously; between the late 1960s and early 1980s, the central balai in the area was at a place called Apurung. Yet Musa, Sumiati, and Yuni – all of whom lived in Apurung – had their familiar territories around Pantai Mangkiling. Musa was already a political mover and shaker by the early 1980s when the reapportioning happened there (he had once been village head of the much larger territory), and so it is not completely surprising that, in the competition for new political focal places, his home grounds became a village center. Mangkiling became a village in 1982. Musa's family gained control of village politics when the district officer accepted his sister Sumiati as village head, and his youngest brother Yuni as secretary. By the mid 1980s, the location boasted a balai, a village office, and a cluster of houses. Several other current balai were included in the village territory; and while each grumbled about Mangkiling's new dominance, none was strong enough to change the situation.

In consolidating a central position in the village reapportionments, Musa, Sumiati, and Yuni acted similarly to many successful Meratus leadership factions. However, over the next few years, their leadership became exceptional in making Mangkiling a strong village, one that attracted the attention of environmentalists, scholars, officials, and tourists.

Between 1985 and 1990, Mangkiling's leaders consolidated a set of national and regional connections and ties that brought them out of mainstream Meratus invisibility to become a focus of regional attention. It was in this period that their leadership creatively engaged with metropolitan fantasies and created what I am calling a "tribal situation." The events that led to these regional connections are complicated, and I analyze them in detail elsewhere (Tsing n.d.). Suffice it to say here that they involved a set of disputes with a timber company over rights to forest land and trees. By chance, a provincial environmental group got involved with Mangkiling's cause and took it as a training exercise to a national environmental forum that was scheduled in the provincial capital. After that publicity, the regent refused to renew the timber company's concession; Mangkiling had won a very major (if, perhaps, tentative) victory for village land rights.

In the process, Mangkiling leaders met a variety of advocates and adversaries including environmentalists, forestry officials, foreign visitors, and timber company workers, as well as regional administrators. The provincial environmental group, *Kompas Borneo*, decided to pursue their relationship with Mangkiling and wrote a successful grant proposal to the Ford Foundation for a research project there that would last several years and involve a large, shifting group of researchers. The 1989 one-day seminar was the first major event in this research relationship; field research, mapping, and various kinds of reports followed. The relationship also attracted funding and support from regional government. In 1992, Kompas Borneo applied to US AID for further support, although their grant was not successful. Meanwhile, Mangkiling became the subject of several series of articles in the provincial newspapers. Ecotourists from Indonesian cities as well as from foreign countries began to make their way there. South Kalimantan was already organizing for ecotourism by the mid 1980s, although the focus of organized tours was the most "developed" and therefore presentable Meratus village of Loksado. Adventurous tours and individuals, however, found Mangkiling. In the early 1990s, a Chinese Indonesian entrepreneur

married a Mangkiling woman and set up a hostel for ecotourists. He electrified the balai, using generator power, and built a huge, rickety guest house out of bamboo. Meanwhile development agencies and groups began various small model projects, digging fish ponds and planting cacao, coffee, and other "development-positive" trees. District officials assigned special funds to allow the villagers to repair the balai, build a generator-operated rice mill, and improve their trails and bridges. Islamic groups and health agencies visited. Journalists from a national women's magazine made a trip. A conservation education tour, sponsored by environmentalists from several Kalimantan provinces, made a long stop there. Mangkiling became a bright spot on the regional map.

To tell Mangkiling's recent history in this fashion highlights the contributions of outsiders, which, indeed, have piggy-backed upon each other to make Mangkiling a place of note. However, from the perspective of Mangkiling villagers, these outside contributions have been sporadic, short-lived, and often more ceremonial than substantive. Even the infrastructural improvements cannot be counted on. Thus, for example, in 1994 when I visited, the ecotourism entrepreneur and his wife had moved down to town, taking their generator; their guest hostel had deteriorated beyond use. Mangkiling's status as a "good" village, that is, a village that has the privilege to hold on to current leadership and resources, cannot rest on its past achievements; it depends on keeping a stream of these visitors and benefits coming. This, in turn, depends on the village representatives' continued ability to present the village as needy, that is, backward and primitive enough to require special development attention. At the same time, they must present themselves as open to change, such that development attention will not be lost on them. Mangkiling has continued to be successful because its leaders have figured out how to present it as a community caught between tradition and modernity – needing help, and ready to change, at the same time as entangled in primordial cultural values.

This leadership stance is recognized in documents about Mangkiling that label it a "transitional" village. In the 1989 one-day seminar, for example, the head of the provincial directorate of village development concluded the presentations with an evaluation of the village as already on the move: due to the guidance of outsiders, the villagers were already more able to solve their problems and to escape the "influences of traditional custom that have a negative quality" (Soemarsono 1989: 1). Most importantly, he found "a change in attitudes and an open perspective along with the desire for progress" (1989: 2). Similarly, the 1990 research report of the provincial environmental organization found the village in a "transitional phase." "On the one hand, they want to carry out innovations; however, on the other hand, they are still tied to a traditional culture that does not support innovative efforts. This situation represents at the very least a potential for efforts at guidance and development" (Kompas Borneo 1990: ii). These evaluations assume that development, for villagers, is mainly a psychological process. They must rid themselves of adherence to static tradition and open themselves to change, that is, national directives; then outsiders will be freer to come in and tell them what to do. The challenge to maintain this transitional status – this openness in the midst of tradition – while courting a long string of advice and "guidance" from many visitors is formidable. Yet it must be maintained to keep the village's privileged status. This returns my analysis to the awkwardly off-balance pose of the village secretary, Yuni, surrounded by so many orderly-development experts. The always-unrealized yearning for change of this stance is perhaps even easier to see in the ways his older sister Sumiati, Mangkiling village head, negotiates her presentation in a series of newspaper articles about the village.

Broken Promises and Unfulfilled Desires

In October 1989, a series of six articles about the village of Mangkiling appeared in the provincial daily newspaper *Dinamika Berita* ("News Dynamics"). The articles, by woman reporter Irma Suryani, focus particularly on Sumiati and pay considerable attention to issues of concern to village women. Suryani is open-minded and sympathetic; her writing is warm, straight-forward, and sometimes poetic. She has clearly worked to build rapport with Mangkiling people. These are rare traits for any non-Dayak writer to bring to reports of Dayak communities. As a result, the self-presentations of village leaders come through with startling distinctiveness. It is not that villagers presented themselves to her with more authenticity or cultural autonomy than to other interlocutors; rather, because she listened to them, their distortions of regionally self-evident truths seem unusually clear in her portrayals.

Suryani's first two articles (1989a and b) revolve directly around her discussions with village head Sumiati. The reporter is sympathetic, and respectful of Sumiati's double burden as a woman village leader; she must carry responsibility for her family and overcome assumptions of women's political irrelevance at the same time as keeping up her leadership training and doing her job. (Indeed, Sumiati is one of two women village heads that anyone I spoke to could remember ever taking office in that entire regency.) Perhaps, the reporter seems to imply, Sumiati's unusual status as a woman village head makes her leadership dilemmas that much more striking: as a woman, no one would distinguish her from any ordinary traditional villager, but, as a leader, she has a dream of progress beyond tradition.

From the outset, Sumiati tells the reporter of her "hopes," "dreams," and "longings": she dreams that the village might have the conveniences of the cities; she longs for a road to be built to the village; she yearns for proper educational facilities. She hopes to be a "light" within her village. (The term the reporter uses for "light," *pelita*, is especially laden because it is the acronym for national five-year development plans.) Sumiati is especially clear about roads: "I wish so much that Mangkiling would have a road so that it would be easy for motor vehicles to come to the village," she tells the reporter "in her plain words." Her longing looks less plain-spoken if we look back a few years to 1986, when a road constructed by a timber company did come through the village territory. (By 1989, the road had eroded away, taking large pieces of hillside with it.) At that time, another newspaper article recorded the experiences of Mangkiling villagers, the reporter again taking his cue from village head Sumiati. "Other problems have been faced precisely because of the presence of a company that has made roads in the area of managed orchards. The fruit orchards of Mangkiling have been destroyed because they were hit by the road-building project of a company working there. Efforts to ask for help [compensation] have been made but have not received a response" (Ihsan 1986). As this quotation suggests, the issues that arise around road-building are complex. However, longing for roads is key to the "openness" that development thinkers demand. Mangkiling is "isolated," that is, primitive, as long as it is not on a motor road. Almost every report on the village begins with the difficult experience of the outside experts getting there; as long as they cannot travel easily to the village, there is no way that it can qualify as up to national standards. Sumiati is not faking her opinions: to speak within the lines of intelligibility, she glosses over her knowledge of the village's history with roads to show plain, innocent longing.[8]

Furthermore, Sumiati describes her longing for roads as just another example of an unfulfilled promise.

> She has often taken up this matter by approaching the qualified officials, but evidently of Sumiati's wish, only hope remains. "Several times already we have submitted proposals to the district to improve our settlement; our requests have even been approved. But in reality, it's not our village that receives the help, but another village, and we feel that we have been patient enough, even weary from waiting for the reality from these promises," she says, half moving me to pity.

"The People of Mangkiling Wait on a Promise," proclaims the headline of the second article (Suryani 1989b). By the time Sumiati has finished her explanation of the village's problems, it appears that the village has been offered nothing but empty promises. Even

when they are offered "help," it comes in pointless, ritualistic forms that may satisfy regional administrators but is of little use for the village. The village has school buildings but no regular teachers to staff them. They have been given a television but no electric generator to run it. They have been formally converted to Islam but offered no religious instruction to learn it. If it wasn't so sad, one might say, it would be funny.

Empty promises have some local uses. The conversion story can illustrate: in 1985, the Mangkiling villagers decided to convert en masse to Islam. Regionally, Islam is equated with civilization, and thus this was a major step toward their acceptance of development. Hundreds of people hiked up to a wide spot in the timber road to meet the Ulamas who (arriving by motor vehicle) staged an official ceremony and duly noted and photographed the event. Then everyone went home. Afterwards, Mangkiling people continued to practice shamanic ceremonies and raise pigs and dogs. With a few exceptions, such as village leaders during their sojourns in town, no one practiced any Islamic religious rites. But they were then able to benefit from their ambivalence. On the one hand, one of the major attractions of Meratus Dayak villages for outside visitors is their colorful festival life. (One of Suryani's articles, entitled "Dancing Until Dawn" (1989e), describes a festival she attended.) On the other hand, no one can accuse them of being closed to the more cosmopolitan religion, Islam. They are not stuck in tradition, but they do not lose their enticements for visitors – or their well-loved local events.

Sumiati builds her leadership stance on this ambivalence by placing the blame for failed development on the regional authorities. In another newspaper article, she explains the lack of Islamic practices in Mangkiling after their conversions as due to the sporadic attention of the provincial religious apparatus. She begins with her own conversion in 1982 when she was chosen as village head. "At that time, the proselytizers came to our place, but after that they have only come a few times, and as a result we don't know how to do the devotional activities," she explains. The prayer house built for them is falling down, she adds, because it is inconveniently located and no one came to care for it (*Dinamika Berita* 1989c). Surprisingly to me, this placement of the blame was readily endorsed by the authorities. Instead of blaming the villagers for their indolence or greed, provincial religious leaders, challenged by the newspaper articles, agreed that they had not properly instructed Mangkiling villagers, and that they must work harder in extending their missionary efforts (*Dinamika Berita* 1989d). Similarly, the Education and Culture Department took full responsibility for not sending teachers in a regular enough manner, when they, too, were challenged by the newspaper's reporting of Mangkiling complaints about the schools (*Dinamika Berita* 1989b and e). This occurred in a context in which regional authorities routinely blame villagers for their ignorance, bad habits, and lack of initiative. However, these latter traits are rooted in the "static thinking" of traditional culture, the bane of development. In contrast, no one can fault longing for change; this is what development is meant to instill. The trick for Sumiati, then, is to make visible a trail of broken promises that can be seen to generate ever more intense forms of longing.

The danger looms: because most development inputs are, indeed, gaudy handouts and cheerful rites with little long-term value, most will not have the kinds of transformative effects development planners fantasize. To the extent that regional administrators can interpret failed development in the village as a resurgence of tradition, that is, static thinking, Mangkiling will lose its privileged status as a "transitional" village, worthy of special development inputs. To renew these inputs, and with them village identity and leadership, Sumiati must continually produce an insatiable development longing. The traditional village woman must always have hope in her eyes for the lights of the city.

Tradition is that which developers most despise; yet it is also that to which they are most attracted. Ordinary poverty is uninteresting to those who imagine themselves civilizing the tribes. (Besides, tribal peoples are often well-endowed with land and resources until these are stolen from them; they don't necessarily need a better livelihood situation until after they are "developed.") Even as she honestly longs for change, Sumiati must know that no one would come to the village if it wasn't "backward." Backwardness is her commodity for negotiation. My next section explores the ways Mangkiling leaders are caught up in a discourse on tradition and exotic culture as they create, and are created by, the tribal situation.

Love Magic

Every village leader who wants access to development funds in South Kalimantan must cultivate a longing for development. Only Dayak minorities, however, must learn to work with the stigma of being considered not just technologically and economically backward but also primitive and exotic. The stigma is terrible, and it is created together with economic, political, and cultural discrimination. However, particularly in the last decade, there have been some ways to use it. The alliances Mangkiling leaders have built with environmental activists and their appeal to ecotourists are two clear examples of opportunities that would not have been available to South Kalimantan villagers not marked by the classification "primitive." With this support, based largely on their ability to identify as "indigenous people," Mangkiling villagers can at least *try* to create legitimate claims over their forests. Here lies the difference between those who can only work to create a "village situation" – a demand for rural citizenship – and those who can aim for a "tribal situation" – a staging of community identity and resource rights. To transform exotic stereotypes into community designs, however, is a work of magic – and a work of seduction.

One beginning move for outside advocates of the tribal situation has been to take the most positive stereotypes they know of the primitive to try to build an alliance with those whom they imagine as tribes. In this spirit, journalist Irma Suryani portrays Mangkiling villagers as experts in traditional herbal medicine, especially that used for contraception (1989c). International interest in indigenous knowledge of rainforest pharmaceuticals has come together with Indonesian population control priorities to make contraceptive herbal knowledge one of the few most positive "traditions" a minority ethnic group can have in Indonesia. Thus, Suryani portrays village head Sumiati expertly explaining the names and uses of herbs to regulate women's fertility. "Mangkiling people don't have to hassle with birth control pills because our natural world has already prepared birth control for us," Sumiati says "with pride." The journalist even permits a little criticism of development expertise: "We are afraid of the side effects," says Sumiati of birth control pills. With traditional contraception in hand, the ground is relatively safe.

Watching over the shoulders of the Kompas Borneo researchers, the journalist learns the names of a variety of traditional medicinal herbs explained by Mangkiling villagers: earth axis tree; King Kahayan vine; white medicine root; King Hanoman vine. Reading through the article, these names did not catch my eye; while none of them were herbs I remembered from the villages I know better in the Meratus Mountains, I expect variation in terminology, knowledge, and flora across the mountains. Then I encountered the list again in Kompas Borneo's report (Yayasan Kompas Borneo 1990: 24). After the list, the report continues, casually, "These medicines are also known to city people." Suddenly I remembered these herbs from urban and rural markets. They are not particularly Meratus herbs but rather commodified, cosmopolitan medicinal herbs used throughout the region. The self-positioning of Mangkiling informants became blindingly clear: to forge the best relationship, given the circumstances, tell the researchers the traditional medicines they already know.[9]

There is something here of flattery and of submission, but it is also an enormously complex skill to reproduce the dominant group's stereotypes so beautifully that they only see their imagined Other. Perhaps it is helpful to think of it in relation to the skill that women in so many places have used to make themselves attractive to men, that is, to make themselves "feminine" as men see it. This is one way to understand the erotic charge that this strategy of sympathetic acquiescence

appears to have for outsiders and experts. Suryani is an honest enough reporter to let the reader see the male research group's compulsion to draw the village girls into a web of flirtation: "Wah . . . even without being dressed up you are so beautiful, let alone if you were dressed up, the city girls would lose," the men tease; "This one's name is Lili Marlen but she is lost in the Mangkiling forest" (1989d). But she also sexualizes the girls, describing their imagined ethnic innocence as seductive. The girls are natural objects of enticement, with their lively smiles and "golden skins" (the description often used regionally for Dayak women). Their naive efforts to adorn themselves are "cute" or "amusing" (*lucu*): they wear lipstick and curl their hair without knowing how. They wear their shirts open, revealing black brassieres, which sparks jokes with the researchers about the popular song, "Under the Dark Glasses."

In the hands of village head Sumiati, the seductiveness of asymmetrical ethnic acquiescence is both useful and hard to control. The primitive summons outside expertise into the community, but it also hints at illicitness and disorder. In this context, Sumiati appears in the newspaper as an ordinary Dayak woman: like other Meratus Dayaks, we learn, she has been married too many times (Suryani 1989b). The woman journalist tells us that this is unfortunate; even naturally seductive women, she seems to imply, can be victims. But she cannot completely suppress the sense that this is uncivilized sexuality. Indeed, those town people who had heard of Sumiati, who after all is a Meratus Dayak leader of some repute, warned me with rolled eyes that she was married to four men, not sequentially, but simultaneously. Whatever Sumiati says about her life, they do not believe her. For them, the seductiveness of Dayak exoticism turns quickly into savagery. Mangkiling leaders must handle this with care – for the closer they get to claiming the autonomy of tribal distinctiveness, the more erotically dangerous their claims.

Thus, according to reporter Suryani, when the Kompas Borneo researchers pin down the site where eroticism is thickest, they find it precisely in the formative place of exoticism and ethnic difference: magic. Magic is key to regional images of Meratus Dayaks. According to the regional majority, Meratus are sorcerers and concocters of magic oils, and it is this power that makes Dayaks both primitive and frightening. In my research in the region, I found that sorcery and magic oils were most important to Meratus Dayaks precisely as part of a regional trade with those who named Dayaks as sorcerers (Tsing 1993). In villages such as Mangkiling, outsiders make demands for mystical expertise, and, indeed, this expertise is produced. The importance of magic in regional images of Dayak "difference" is so great that I was not surprised that Suryani chose to devote half of her final Mangkiling article to magic oils (1989f). The oils she describes are used for seduction and for healing the wounds of fighting. In learning about them, the journalist and the researchers she accompanied place themselves in the middle of an ethnic exchange in which the seductions and healed-over hostilities of both exoticization and self-representation become difficult to disentangle. To follow this process, the article is worth quoting at some length:

The issue that the writer will discuss here is the strength of belief of the Bukit [Meratus Dayak] people toward what one would call magic. They tie everything to the power of "dewa" spirits in which, until now, they believe.

This is also the case with sorcery, which they always connect to mystical power. For example, this writer and the research group had the opportunity to meet with a resident of Pantai Mangkiling village whose condition was rather alarming because other than suffering from deafness, he also had a deformed body. However, from him we obtained information as well as research materials that could be used for our analysis. Although to communicate with him, we had to use "Tarzan" language (signs).

From him this writer and colleagues from the Institute "Kompas Borneo" obtained an account of several kinds of oils with special qualities. For example, there is the oil that they call "Unchaste Adam" that they use to entice someone. Usually it is used by a woman to entice a man or, in reverse, for a man to entice a woman.

There are also oils that cause a person to be able to stand blows or gashes, and according to Pak Sani (a pseudonym), he has already proved it himself. Indeed, we could see his misshapen bones that looked like the result of a break but evidently had connected again (There is also an oil for this). Concerning the truth of these special characteristics, as presented by Pak Sani, this writer does not know but can only say that this is what they use up until now if they encounter the difficulties I have explained.

It is hard to fathom why the research group decided to use an interview with a deaf man as their decisive entrée into traditional knowledge. It is quite a scene to imagine: the deaf man and the researchers each pointing and gesturing and mimicking each other enough to develop some communication. The reference to Tarzan calls up the colonial situation, in which Europeans and "natives" faced each other across such gaps of communication, and in which at least the Europeans thought they were communicating with animals. Ganneth Obeyesekere has argued that European ideas of cannibalism in the Pacific were in part conjured up by scenes in which Europeans and Pacific Islanders, unable to speak with each other, each mimed a fantasy of cannibalistic consumption, biting arms and legs while the other party copied the mime (1992). In the Mangkiling exchange, too, language was omitted, and the researchers, through mime, learned exactly what they hoped and feared: Dayaks have the power to entice and to heal injury; their magic entraps expert attention and reconnects the shards of modern alienation. A fantasy of seduction and erased violence was woven around the deaf man's signs; the indeterminability of who exactly wove this fantasy is the underlying "magic" of the situation.

Through this love magic, Mangkiling villagers attract a stream of visitors, experts, and tourists. The motivations of visitors range from development assistance to nature appreciation to personal adventure; but all are drawn by the magic of exotic nature and culture. One record of these seductions is the visitors' log that is kept in the village office, where Yuni, the secretary, sometimes resides.

Besides their names and the dates of their visits, visitors are asked to enter their trip's purpose and their impressions. Many of those who wrote in the log that I copied in 1994 explained themselves in the language of development; they came, they said, to examine, criticize, and help the villagers. But others wrote love notes – to nature, to the people of Mangkiling, and even in reference to their private affairs. Nature hikers expressed a platonic attraction: "Beautiful nature, friendly people"; "*Refreshing* while enjoying the ambiance of nature in the mountains of Pantai Mangkiling"; or, fully in English, "We are remember to Mangkiling. We can't stop loving you to Mangkiling." More ambivalent, perhaps, were the lovers who came to the village after it became a weekend destination for town toughs to bring their girlfriends; they drew on the hint of promiscuity that always accompanies love magic. Yet when one of these casual guests wrote that s/he had come to Mangkiling "carrying a heart wounded by my angry, jealous lover," s/he hinted at the dialogue in which Mangkiling had become an appropriate site for erotic recharging. Another guest drew an outline of a heart in the log.

The Utopian Project: Nature

In the ways I have been describing, Mangkiling leaders make themselves available to work with agencies interested in community development, ecotourism, rainforest conservation, and tribal rights. It is not enough to live in the forest. One must have a stable village that can be identified and funded. One must have a distinctive culture worth studying and saving. And one must have a strong, visible leadership to articulate community concerns in ways that these agencies can understand. To craft each of these is a work of imagination and artistry. Only with these prerequisites can Mangkiling be part of the global "sustainability" question: how can we meet the needs of the present without jeopardizing the resources of future generations? In that question, "tribal" forest communities have a special niche. Everyone wants to know: do these communities protect and manage the forest or destroy it? When

agencies and experts flock to Mangkiling, it is in part because they are thinking about this question.

Yet, amazingly enough, this question is investigated directly nowhere in the documents I found about Mangkiling. Occasionally, an author makes a wild stab from his prejudices. Thus, although no research of which I am aware has examined Mangkiling forest, use, an economist interrupts his otherwise modest survey of Mangkiling incomes to rant about the huge amount of money lost every time a Mangkiling farmer clears a swidden.

2,400 cubic meters – 2,800 cubic meters [of timber wood] × Rp. 50,000 = Rp. 120,000,000 – Rp. 144,000,000. If the problem of shifting cultivation is allowed to continue in the next ten years, one could estimate that forest products, especially wood logs, worth 12 to 14.4 billion rupiah will be thrown away, not to count the environmental destruction that this causes. (Siddik 1989: 3)

This kind of thinking would be very easy to refute (e.g., by questioning the truth of the assumption here that Mangkiling farmers regularly cut down mature dipterocarps, by studying patterns of post-swidden forest regrowth and tree management, by examining forest destruction in commercial timbering, or by questioning who benefits from timber versus swidden incomes). Yet, for some reason, none of the many advocates who have conducted research in the village – and who clearly don't believe this economist – have bothered to address this question in their studies. Instead, they offer traditional beliefs in support of the spirit of forest conservation:

The view of the people of the village of Pantai Mangkiling toward the world around them, such as the forest, mountains, rivers, and animals, is that it is a materialization from themselves (as human beings), and because of this they treat it carefully. (Yayasan Kompas Borneo 1990:35–6)

In explaining advocates' turn to traditional beliefs rather than local resource management practices, one might posit that advocates can't imagine officials taking local practices seriously; perhaps the idea that tribal people conserve forests is just too far from regional development dogma to imbue its technical features with any legitimacy. Alternately, perhaps conventions of separating social science and natural science research have made it difficult for researchers to ask questions about the human management of the environment. Yet a third possibility presents itself along with these: advocates' focus on abstract beliefs rather than a history of forest management practices creates a connection between environmentalists and villagers. Many environmentalists base their own hopes for forest conservation on the ability of their abstract beliefs in conservation to prevail, rather than on particular management practices. If village conservation is also based on an ecological vision, then villagers and environmentalists are ideal working partners.

Whatever the cause, there has been a noticeable silence on questions of the construction of the Mangkiling forest. Although researchers are clearly interested in the trees, no one has examined tree management; although they are interested in wild animals, no research has asked about hunting or the making of food-rich forest niches. The cycle of shifting cultivation is discussed, but researchers do not continue their studies after the harvesting of rice to ask about long-term vegetables, shrubs, and tree crops. And while one might assume that I bring up this silence as a criticism, in fact I want to point first to its positive effects. By ignoring the specificity of Mangkiling nature-making practices, and thus the differences in how nature is appreciated that divide urban environmentalists and rural shifting cultivators, environmentalists are able to imagine a utopian space of overlap and collaboration in which they join Mangkiling villagers in cherishing the forest. In this imagined space, loving the forest – the business of urban nature appreciation – is conflated with living in the forest – the business of Mangkiling village existence. The project of protecting this space of "nature" is utopian in both the best and worst senses. It is idealistic, offering the hope for making a liveable world. It is single-minded, glossing over its own improbabilities.

Furthermore, it has developed around its own distinctive and collaborative practice of naming the elements of nature. Most Meratus Dayaks know a great deal about their natural environment, including many plant and animal names, and, in my experience, people enjoy explaining these names to curious outsiders. Similarly, environmentalists love to learn the names of the flora and fauna. From these mutual pleasures, a characteristic event of environmentalist visits to Mangkiling has developed: the shared experience of hiking around identifying natural organisms. Of course, there are great differences in the significance of these names as a component of forest-management practices. Indonesian environmentalists draw on the European natural history tradition in which to name nature is to know it in all its universal abstraction; they also practice a more recent kind of nature loving in which to identify a plant is to identify with it, that is, to feel a sense of communion and mutual belonging on earth. In contrast, Meratus Dayaks tend to be most interested in the specificity of plants and animals as they occur in particular landscape locations. To know a tree it is not enough to know its species name; one must be able to understand the complex of other plants as well as human claims and histories that put that tree into a socially meaningful landscape. Despite the need to ignore these differences, however, plant and animal identification is a truly collaborative practice. Both environmentalists and Mangkiling villagers with whom I spoke felt a sense of having shared important information with the other.

My interpretation of naming nature in Mangkiling as collaborative diverges from recent scholarship that identifies "botanizing" as among the most insidious of imperialist practices. Both Mary Pratt (1992) and Paul Carter (1989) argue that European colonization was brought to a new standard of control through natural history, which, they argue, taught Europeans to imagine Third World lands as entirely without inhabitants. By describing landscapes full of plants and animals, but without humans, eighteenth century natural historians created narratives that facilitated colonial control. Recent events in Mangkiling do not tell us anything about the eighteenth century texts these authors analyze; however, they do suggest that natural

Table 20.1 Excerpt from "Inventory list of flora," Yayasan Kompas Borneo 1990

NO.	AREA NAME	LATIN NAME	PLOTS					
			1	2	3	4	5	TOTAL
01	LANDUR	LOPHOPETALUM JAVVANICUM (ZOLL) TURZ	3	–	–	2	4	9
02	HAMAK		1	–	–	1	1	3
03	MAHANG	MACARANGA HYPOLEUCA MUELL. ARG	4	–	–	–	–	4
04	HUMBUT	XYLOPIA SP.	1	–	–	–	–	1
05	MINJURUNG		3	1	–	–	–	4
06	TIWADAK	ARTOCARPUS RIGIDUS BL	1	–	–	–	–	1
07	LURUS	PERONEMA CANESCENS JACK	2	–	–	–	–	2
08	RAMBUTAN	NEPHELIUM SP.	1	–	–	–	–	1

history investigations can be more politically open-ended and flexible than these scholars imply. Mangkiling "botanizing" texts also do not contain any writing about Mangkiling people. They tend to focus on lists of plants and animals with perhaps short descriptions or discussions of the landscape. However, a closer reading of these texts suggests the way utopian collaboration peers out even from a list of trees.

I believe the excerpt [in Table 20.1] can stand in not only for the rest of that tree list, which goes on for pages, but also for other tree lists I have encountered, published and unpublished. It follows the convention of supplying two items: "area name" and "Latin name." The latter is the scientific, Linnean term that unites genus and species; presumably the botanist supplies this information after s/he sees the tree. But the former term, the local term, suggests that the botanist does not find and identify the tree alone; s/he is brought to the tree by a villager who serves not only as guide but also as first botanical identifier.

The priority of the Mangkiling identification is suggested by the fact that in two cases (#02,#05), an "area name" is not followed by any scientific identification. The villager appears to have shown the botanist a tree s/he did not know. (This is consistent with the rest of the list, in which there are many blank spaces in the "Latin names" column, but no blank spaces under "area name.") Sometimes,

perhaps, the botanist asks for a name for a tree about which the villager is unsure. (I have my doubts about #04, *Humbut*, "palm heart," as the best possible Mangkiling name for this plant, which I assume to be a palm; Meratus palm classifications can be very detailed.) But the local name is never omitted; it forms the first line of knowledge about the tree.

Other minor collaborations are suggested. For example, slightly later in the list, there are fourteen trees identified as *Damar* (area name)/ *Shorea* sp. (Latin name), suggesting a joint decision not to be too picky about identifications. Dipterocarpaceae, the big emergents of the forest, are notoriously divergent as well as hard to sort out – from the perspective of botanists as well as Meratus Dayaks. Yet both do sort them out for appropriate occasions. These fourteen trees may not have sparked that sense of occasion for either party to the identification. For other dipterocarp entries on the list, smaller divisions *are* made.

The inventory offers the chance for another collaboration, however, that is not pursued. If read with the right questions, the list is a striking testament to the managed nature of the Mangkiling forest. *Landur* (#01), *Tiwadak* (#06), *Rambutan* (#08), and *Siwau* (#25) are highly valued fruit trees; they were probably planted, or, at the least, claimed and managed carefully. *Kahingai* (#20), *Kembayau* (#21), and *Tarap* (#22) are less valuable fruit trees; while they may not have been planted,

Mangkiling residents would certainly have their eye out for them. *Damar* (#16, #17, #18) and *Bangkiray* (#09) can become sites for honey bee nests, in which case, they become expensive and carefully guarded claimed trees. Even without bees' nests, the *damar* trees may have been saved in swidden-making, encouraged, or claimed for their bark, resin, or other uses. *Lurus* (#07) has become highly commercialized in this region, since its price for construction poles rose sharply in the 1980s; it is a quick-growing and easy-to-foster secondary forest species, claimed by those on whose old swiddens it is encouraged. One could continue. However, this is not the framework to which this inventory has so far been deployed. Off the track of the utopian project, forest management raises difficult questions about nature's purity and purposes. While one must praise the inventory project for allowing this unbidden text to be recorded, one could also criticize it for not, or not yet, making it possible to discuss these issues. As Musa stated in the document with which I began this essay, "there is no wild forest here." Yet environmentalists still need the image of the wild with which to build their most promising alliances.

Maps and Dreams

Instead of listening to Mangkiling villagers' histories of forest management and use, environmentalists build their practical project of advocacy on a different front: the mapping of village territory. Perhaps this is their most important work for Mangkiling villagers; at least potentially, it offers the possibility of making a case for village control of land and forest resources. It draws together all the imaginative frameworks for collaboration that I have been discussing to create what appears to be a singular joint project: the map. The lines of the map offer a "common sense" obviousness. Either this is your territory, or it is ours; any administrator should appreciate that. However, mapping a politically charged landscape is never so simple. Environmentalists and Mangkiling leaders work together, I will argue, to use the technology of precision to increase fertile ambiguity, multiplicity, and

confusion. From ambiguity, the possibility of tribal rights might emerge.

The potential of Mangkiling maps to build tribal rights is based on the viability of attempts around the world to reclaim resources through what Nancy Peluso has called "counter-mapping," that is, the use of maps to argue against state claims by spatially depicting the explicitness and historical priority of local resource control (1995). (Peluso's term acknowledges that mapping has generally been the tool of colonial or state expropriation of local lands; as she explains, however, mapping can also become a strategy of local resistance and struggle.) In places across the Americas, Australia, and Southeast Asia, including Indonesia, the issue of tribal rights has been argued through mapping. Thus, for example, the title I have given this section, "maps and dreams," invokes one of these projects: the customary-use mapping project of Northwest Canadian Native Americans, as described by Hugh Brody (1981). In this project, a key challenge was the forgetfulness of the white-settler majority that living communities of Native Americans continued to exist; thus, when Native Americans mapped the spots they had gone hunting, fishing, or berry picking, they reminded the white majority of their presence. The maps Brody records show entangled lines of personal and community use of land and forest resources. In contrast, the mapping challenges or "dreams" in Indonesia are different. Since colonial times, the geography of local Indonesian peoples has been imagined in generally non-overlapping, bounded territories; local groups have been identified in relation to such imagined territories, and "indigenous" advocacy has often begun with the notion of territory. These are the territories recognized as *adat* lands, that is, the lands acknowledged under customary law. Counter-mapping projects make these adat territories explicit; they generally do not, however, break with historically legitimate conventions for imagining space – for example, to show overlapping patches and entangled lines marking histories of individual and collective use, as in Brody's maps. To be effective, mapping for tribal rights must be convincing within regional and national histories of policy and politics.

This need to convince opens opportunities even as it imposes constraints. In their maps, environmentalists and Mangkiling leaders have adapted the colonial and national advocacy-through-adat tradition to make a joint statement about village lands and forests. Since adat is nationally understood as an indigenous conceptual system, to map adat lands is to articulate the inner logic of indigenous minds. Maps are not seen as analyses or even descriptions of tribal life; like folklore or cosmologies, they are supposed to be direct expressions of the native point of view. Collaboration between environmentalists and village leaders does not, then, produce "the native in the document" for which my earlier questions searched; instead, it aims for "the document in the native." Unlike lists of trees in which collaboration is made evident, the goal in making maps of adat lands is to create a single, seamless product in which the technological expertise of the map-maker seems only to enhance the traditional knowledge of village elders. To make this joint product, both environmentalists and village elders must imagine they are mapping the same thing: here the common space created by the utopian project of nature becomes crucial. The maps then superimpose and join the tactics of village leaders and environmentalists, as each aims to convince the authorities of the legitimacy of adat lands.

Making adat claims legitimate is no easy task, despite the long history of administrative discussion of adat lands in Indonesia. It is never enough merely to establish the status of a given plot as adat land in order to hold it; one must then argue against all the other classifications to which that same plot is assigned. First, adat land is an insecure classification. Since the colonial era, arguments for the recognition of adat lands have always been "counter-arguments" in a debate in which state domain over land and resources has been the opposing opinion.[10] In Indonesian national law, adat lands are sometimes recognized and sometimes not. In the Basic Agrarian Law, for example, adat is said to be the underlying law of the land. In the Basic Forestry Law, in contrast, all forests are said to be the domain of the state. The partial recognition of adat

creates the possibilities for local arguments over the status of particular territories.

Second, official mapping offers contradictory views about the status of any given plot – whether or not adat status is at issue. Territories officially classified as "forests," i.e., government-controlled land, may include entire districts and multiple towns and villages with their agricultural terrains. Government departments often map areas differently, such that potential transmigration sites, production forests, and nature reserves may be found, in different maps, on precisely the same site. The forest in Mangkiling is simultaneously classified as protection forest, production forest, a proposed nature reserve, and village territory.

How can village rights be established in this mess? The counter-mapping projects in Mangkiling do not clarify the situation; instead, advocates and village leaders add to the layers of ambiguity. Rather than making a single, clear-cut map, environmentalists and village leaders in Mangkiling have confused and layered conventions and land claims. First, they have conflated varied map-making standards to create complex products in which different kinds of land claims appear to garner the same legitimacy. Second, they have stacked overlapping, contradictory, and redundant maps. All the possible claims on the forest are shown, sometimes on top of each other, sometimes on separate pages. In the context of village powerlessness, clear and simple village claims would probably be officially dismissed, while adding layers to already recognized claims creates the potential for tentative local successes. By adding to the pool of overlaid possibilities, they make openings for local claims that cannot hold their own as singular logics.

The chain of village maps I have seen begins with two maps attributed to Musa and drawn sometime in the 1980s. I am unsure who else besides Musa worked on these maps; I assume they are the collaborative product of Musa and village advocates. I reproduce the first, the easier to read, as Figure 20.1. At first glance, this is a nicely drawn but ordinary enough sketch map of village territory, as marked by the locations of the various constituent balai

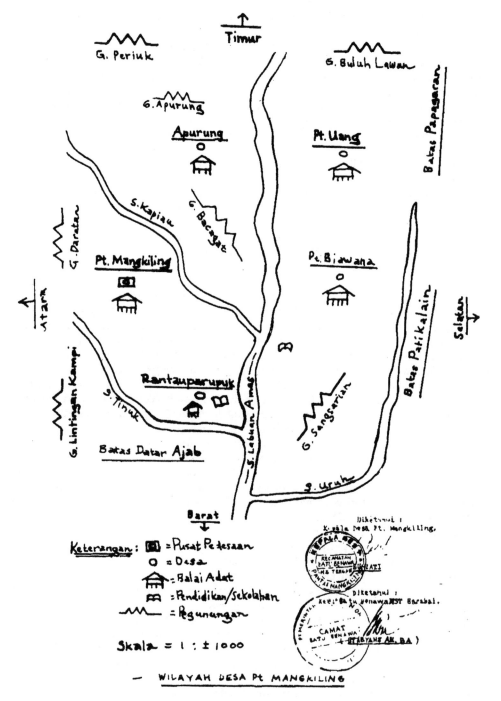

Figure 20.1 *Territory of Pt. Mangkiling village. Original map by Musa. Map redrawn by Brian Rounds.*
Legend: ▣ *village administrative center* ○ *village settlement* ⌂ *traditional hall* ⌷ *education/school*
〜 *mountain range*
Utara *"north"*: Selatan *"south"*: Timur *"east"*; Barat *"west"*; Pt. *[Pantai]. "flat"*; Batas *"boundary"*; S.
[Sungai] "river"; G. *[Gunung] "mountain"*

halls, as well as the village center and school buildings. Yet closer attention to the stylization of the map suggests that it offers more than the location of village settlement clusters; it creates the implication that these settlement clusters control territorial segments, which together constitute village land. In this sense, the map, like the written document to which it is attached, is a land rights claim. In order to achieve this effect, the map brings official mapping conventions to portray local conventions of land use and occupancy. However, neither mapping conventions nor local land-rights conventions go untransformed in the process. In order to make a hopeful village land claim, Figure 20.1 overlaps, combines, and deforms both local and official understandings of landscape.

The map presents the local river system as if it were a set of boundary lines both drawing together and dividing up the land; tree-like, there is a straight, upright trunk stream – which defines the unity of village settlement – with branching arms that mark off village subsections. (The stylization becomes evident when Figure 20.1 is compared to the more-standard geographic representation made by environmentalists in Figure 20.2.) The river system appears to divide village land into discrete and somewhat equivalent chunks. Each chunk has a traditional hall, the heart of a community, at its center. Mountains bound the territories where they are not marked by streams. In this representation, then, community centers appear to preside over segmented territories, whose unity makes up the village.

The map's success in drawing the village in this way draws on two key features of the Meratus Dayak social landscape: the association of particular kin and neighborhood groups with particular areas of the forest, on the one hand, and the focus of social ties around particular leaders, groups, and central sites, on the other. Areas of the forest are associated with groups of people who once created swiddens there, and who continue to plant, encourage, harvest, and manage the forest there. Old living sites as well as farm sites become orchards and foraging grounds for those who know them best. The managed and well-used

forest territories of different individuals overlap. However, group clustering around focal individuals, families, or sites creates the effect of center-controlled territories. When people live together in a balai hall, their familiar forest and swidden territories spread and radiate in each direction around the balai. It is these center-focused territories that are given the authority and permanence of graphic representation in this map. The mapped territories are not illusory; however, they stabilize and specify shifting aggregations.[11]

The map uses and confuses Mangkiling landscape conventions, but it does the same with official mapping conventions. Territorial domains claimed by settlements are never drawn in official maps in this region. Official maps offer a strict separation of settlement, on the one hand, and territorial divisions, on the other. They show settlement as a dot rather than a territory. Even huge villages with dozens of small, scattered settlements are depicted as a single dot. This dot represents the stability, and thus the administrative appropriateness, of settlement; no village can claim legitimacy without its dot. But a dot takes up no space. In contrast, territorial divisions are marked in official maps of land use, forest classification, concession areas, and the like. Settlements may be sketched in on these maps, but they are for place identification not territorial claims; these are maps of state and private domain. They offer villagers no rights. The Mangkiling map Musa sponsored conflates and combines these two bureaucratic conventions, to create an intelligibility that draws on and exceeds each. His map offers administerable centers yet implies territorial jurisdiction. It is a usefully confusing hybrid.

This kind of creative confusion was not the choice of the environmentalist mappers who followed Musa's lead to draw more maps of the village in the 1990s. These mappers show much more allegiance to official conventions; after all, they want their maps taken seriously in official circles. Thus, they reseparate out administrative and territorial maps. Their administrative map (Figure 20.2) shows the familiar dots, as these guarantee that Mangkiling will be administratively recognized. Like Figure 20.1, however, Figure 20.2 shows all

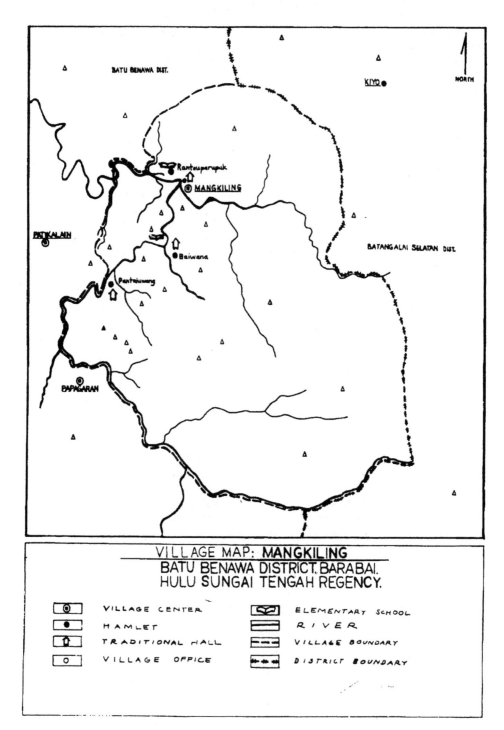

Figure 20.2 *Village map: Mangkiling*
Original map by Kompas Borneo Institute. Map redrawn by Brian Rounds
Original offers additional geographic detail and legend in Indonesian at a scale of 1:25,000

the constituent balai and settlement groupings of Mangkiling rather than just a single village center. It is a joint project of representation that employs local categories. It also includes village boundaries, but because of the irrelevance of their spatial relation to the settlements, it is hard to use this map to imagine that village people control all this territory.

The territorial maps produced in this project neatly depict village adat lands, including current and past swiddens and protected adat forest. Territorial maps insert Mangkiling claims into the realm of forestry department and land use planning representations; they argue for equal billing for village territories. The messiness and shifting status of forest territories thus must be eliminated; secondary forest and protected forest must be separated by neat lines. Here, too, village leaders and environmentalists must have worked together to form a joint product of hopefully-legitimate simplification.

The environmentalist maps, however, do not stop here; they proliferate in piles of overlapping territorial classifications. In showing all kinds of claims and classifications, these maps extend the concerns of village leaders into the agendas of environmentalists; they make it possible to imagine a democratic space of debate, that is, to make forest territories into a "public sphere" of pluralistic and open discussion. Kompas Borneo's Mangkiling project has produced not just maps of adat-protected forest and maps of village swidden areas, but also maps of production forest timber concessions and maps of nature reserve areas. And, most pointedly, there are maps in which many of these things are shown on top of each other. I reproduce one of the most intricate as Figure 20.3. This map shows the timber concession of the company that was logging Mangkiling trees in the 1980s. The concession neatly overlaps the zone of village territory, including both mature (*hutan*) and secondary (*belukar*) forest. The map, to me, is a *tour de force*. Village claims are given the same status as timber company claims – thus offering a sensitive official the chance to pick the villagers rather than the company as the appropriate local claimants, and all without

having to uphold a general principle of adat rights. By showing overlap and contest in forest classifications, environmentalists add – rather than subtract – layers of possibility in policy discussions. The precise technologies of mapping do not narrow down the truth but instead open territorial classifications as a matter of democratic public debate. Indeed, this proliferation of options makes the alternative conventions of the map attributed to Musa also come alive as the map that could be made by the tribal elder, the indigenous map. Its collaborative layers disappear as it too becomes one perspective in this debate, the village text in the technical dossier.

Reprise

What does it mean to speak of or for a "tribe" in the late twentieth century? The term has emerged in international movements for environmental conservation and minority rights to draw attention to the political and ecological importance of marginalized rural communities. At the same time, scholars have criticized the traditions of representation in which these communities have been understood to have backward customs and exotic cultures, that is, to be identified as tribes. The concept of the "tribe," recent scholars argue, calls up a history of metropolitan fantasies about the bizarre, the natural, or the originary lines of human evolution (e.g., Clifford 1988; Torgovnick 1990; Kuper 1988). It is never a simple descriptive term.

The political rehabilitation of the tribe and its scholarly rejection too often speak past each other. Instead, I have argued that we must begin both our political rapprochements and scholarly investigations with the question of how the concept of the tribe, with all its simplifications and codifications of metropolitan fantasy, comes to mean something to people caught in particular political dilemmas. The fantastic aspect of tribal identity does not make it irrelevant to marginalized people who pass as tribals; to the contrary, it is the fantasy of the tribe that becomes the source of engagement for both tribals and their metropolitan

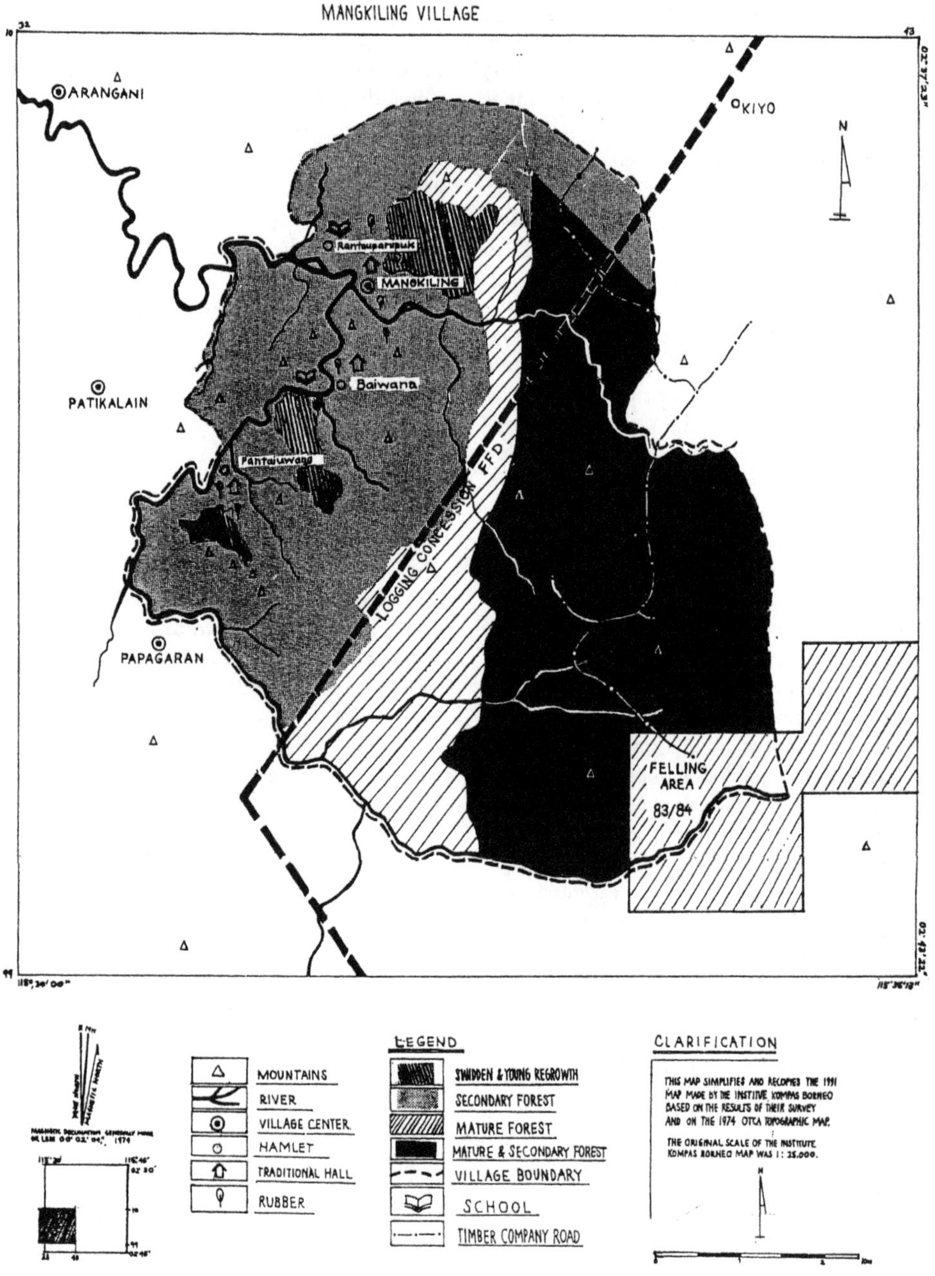

ARANGANI

KIYO

N

Rantauparvauk

MANGKILING

PATIKALAIN

Baiwana

Pantaiuwaaa

PAPAGARAN

LOGGING CONCESSION FFD

FELLING
AREA
83/84

LEGEND

△	MOUNTAINS
	RIVER
◉	VILLAGE CENTER
○	HAMLET
⌂	TRADITIONAL HALL
♀	RUBBER

	SWIDDEN & YOUNG REGROWTH
	SECONDARY FOREST
	MATURE FOREST
	MATURE & SECONDARY FOREST
---	VILLAGE BOUNDARY
	SCHOOL
	TIMBER COMPANY ROAD

CLARIFICATION

THIS MAP SIMPLIFIES AND RECOPIES THE 1991
MAP MADE BY THE INSTITVE KOMPAS BORNEO
BASED ON THE RESULTS OF THEIR SURVEY
AND ON THE 1974 OTCA TOPOGRAPHIC MAP.

THE ORIGINAL SCALE OF THE INSTITUTE
KOMPAS BORNEO MAP WAS 1:25.000.

Figure 20.3 *Mangkiling village*
Original map by Kompas Borneo Institute. Map redrawn by Brian Rounds
Original offers additional geographic detail and legend in Indonesian at a scale of 1:25,000

others. Both scholarship and advocacy deserve a closer look at such histories of engagement.

Recent cultural theorists have shown how cosmopolitan dreams and fantasies forge the categories and narratives through which central and peripheral social settings are segregated and aligned with each other. Emergent notions of polity and history – such as modernity (Foucault 1970), nationalism (Anderson 1983), colonial rule (Stoler 1991), or archaic folk traditions (Ivy 1995) – have rebuilt the framing architecture through which we organize and recognize the local, in city and countryside, lowlands and uplands. "Local" self-conceptions and notions of place, personhood, desire, marginalization, and resistance have changed to live within these emergent architectures. We assert ourselves as "rational men" as "citizens," as "natives," as "women," or as "community representatives" within the cosmopolitan dreams and schemes that make these self-imaginings possible. Yet these dreams and schemes never work out in the ways they are supposed to. Their formulations of difference get away from them, slipping into unexpected transformations and collaborations. No theory of resistance along the lines of already assumed, immutable material interests (workers on strike; peasants in community) can capture the nuances with which metropolitan desires fulfill themselves. What is needed is a theory of localization, in which attention can be focused on the ways categories become stretched beyond themselves in particular events and confrontations. Such a framework points us toward the situational deformation of globally circulating categories. In my examination of Mangkiling documents, I have focused on the staging of "situations" in which the categories of green development are creatively transformed to make Mangkiling a village, a tribal location, and a place on the map that cannot be erased.

The "tribal elder" is a position empowered by international concerns for environmental sustainability and community-based environmental justice. This is an agenda with powerful backers but also substantial enemies. Its local deployments, however, do not depend entirely on the international play of this agenda; instead, they involve attempts by would-be tribal leaders and their advocates to pick up on important local concerns, that is, to contextualize international agendas and shape them in new ways. Notions of community, territory, and culture are reconstructed around the new tribal discourse as it is interpolated with tribal deployments in government administration, commercial enterprise, regional religious doctrine, research, and tourism.

Local articulations of tribal autonomy and rights make use of "room for maneuver" within administrative categories for local people and activities. Even so, some creative transformations are needed to make the difference between resource loss and bureaucratic encompassment, on the one hand, and community initiative, on the other. In development programs that require local communities to function as docile administrative units, room for maneuver is particularly prominent in the community research components that readjust and align development initiatives at the regional level. Environmentalist concerns, which entered Indonesian regional development in the 1980s, increased this community research load and shifted some of it to nongovernmental organizations, some of which thought of themselves as community and environmental advocates. Through this trajectory, tribalism entered within the program of development.

In Mangkiling, then, tribal elders long for development at the same time as they hold on to markers of tradition. The appearance of tradition draws the guests who hope to change them and offers them legitimacy among these guests as authentic community spokespersons. With the right leadership stance, it becomes possible to enter into collaborative projects in which Mangkiling concerns assume the aura of urban professional environmentalism, and vice versa. The more layers of alternative interpretations collaborators are able to add, the better the chances, one might argue, of successful Mangkiling advocacy. These collaborative layers then form the space of local articulation for so-called global environmentalism. They also transform it, as it becomes a tool within local negotiations of related, but not synonymous, makings of Mangkiling.

NOTES

1. Nancy Peluso (personal communication) offers an important political contextualization: "These are clearly not inter-village movements because this would be politically impossible. Organizing across villages could raise various spectres; if not communist or "tribal" insurgency, any anti-government organization would be suspect. So the focussing of "development" on making documents happen, creating situations, etc., is of necessity focussed *on the village* and best served in the person of the village leaders."

2. Preliminary histories and analyses of the Indonesian environmental movement can be found in Belcher and Gennino 1993 and throughout the journal *Environesia*. For an account of environmentalists' attempts to use the concept of *adat* to build a national appreciation of tribal land and resource rights, see Tsing [2001].

3. Much of Escobar's (1995) analysis of development expertise is relevant to Indonesia.

4. There is a social forestry program with pilot projects in South Kalimantan, but the focus of this and other "participatory" efforts is to design model communities rather than to empower already existing community-based forest management.

5. If this seems odd, it may be useful to think of a woman's enactment of womanhood or an Asian country's enactment of the Orient; where are the lines between player and role? Self-making here brings to life the powerful desires that define one's Otherness; and only by inciting those powerful desires can one act "as a woman" or "as the Orient." Other kinds of agency are, of course, possible for these actors, but these do not lead to collaborations on these lines of difference, here manhood and womanhood, East and West.

6. To analyze documents written by and about relatively uninfluential people raises important questions about confidentiality and exposure. Once the analysis refers to a public document, it becomes impossible to change the names and places referred to; yet, it seems proper to protect the strategies and reputations of both writers and their objects from undue prying. In this essay, I have tried to keep my analysis to documents that have been distributed, registered, or published in public places. Furthermore, I have tried to avoid attention to idiosyncratic foibles and mistakes to focus instead on systematic meanings and asymmetries as well as acts of courage and imagination.

7. Mangkiling was never the center of my ethnographic research. I have stayed in the village and talked with Musa and other key figures, and my understandings of our conversations are guided by research in other Meratus areas (see Tsing 1993). Even without extensive participant-observation, the documents are revealing; they offer the kinds of historical materials so often unavailable to an ethnographer of rural areas.

8. Tsing [2003] offers a complementary but rather different analysis of Meratus road-longing.

9. It is unclear from the texts whether the researchers asked about medicinal herbs by name or solicited these names from Mangkiling informants. In either case, it appears that the villager did not challenge the researchers' ideas of what might constitute "traditional medicine." I imagine that the researchers were already so sure of the forms exoticism should take that a heroic effort to introduce new pharmaceutical models probably would still have been unsuccessful. Rather than intentional deceit, going along with researchers' preconceptions involved only villagers' willingness to avoid being annoying.

10. Potter (1988: 138–41) describes the debate among colonial officials over forest control in Borneo earlier this century; aspects of this debate are replicated in current controversies over Kalimantan forests.

11. Stabilization and specification began long before this map, and the map cites and rewrites other efforts. In particular, Musa's imaginative framework for the map appears to invoke an earlier document he helped design in 1967, when he was village head. This was a written text which put land rights on paper by assigning sectors of the village to particular neighborhood groups.

REFERENCES

Anderson, Benedict. (1983). *Imagined Communities: Reflections on the Origin and Spread of Nationalism*. London: Verso.

Belcher, Martha and Angela Gennino. (1993). *Southeast Asian Rainforests: A Resource Guide and Directory*. San Francisco: Rainforest Action Network.

Brody, Hugh. (1981). *Maps and Dreams*. New York: Pantheon Books.

Brosius, J. Peter, Anna Tsing and Charles Zerner. (1998). "Representing Communities: History and Politics of Community-Based Resource Management". *Society and Natural Resources*, 11, 157–68.

Carter, Paul. (1989). *The Road to Botany Bay*. Chicago: University of Chicago Press.

Chambers, Ross. (1991). *Room for Maneuver: Reading the Oppositional in Narrative*. Chicago: University of Chicago Press.

Clifford, James. (1988). *The Predicament of Culture*. Cambridge: Harvard University Press.

Debord, Guy. (1983). *Society of the Spectacle*. Toronto: Black and Red Books.

Dinamika Berita. (1989a). "Sistem Perekonomian Masyarakat Mangkiling Sangat Sederhana". April 13.

——. (1989b). "Hanyar Mangajar 2 Hari dalam Sebulan". October 16, 1+.

——. (1989c). "Warga Mangkiling Kembali Anut Kaharingan". October 17, 1+.

——. (1989d). "Perlu Keterlibatan Semua Pihak". October 18, 1+.

——. (1989e). "Dinas P & K akan Ambil Tindakan Kepegawaian". October 19, 1+.

Escobar, Arturo. (1995). *Encountering Development: The Making and Unmaking of the Third World*. Princeton: Princeton University Press.

Foucault, Michel. (1970). *The Order of Things*. New York: Vintage.

Ihsan, A. Muhaimin. (1986). "Pantai Mangkiling, Di Antara Benturan Tradisional Dan Modernisasi". *Banjarmasin Post*. December 21, 4+.

Ivy, Marilyn. (1995). *Discourses of the Vanishing: Modernity Phantasm, Japan*. Chicago: University of Chicago Press.

Kuper, Adam. (1988). *The Invention of Primitive Society: Transformations of an Illusion*. London: Routledge.

Mooduto, H.L.D. (1989). "Pokok-Pokok Pembinaan Masyarakat Terasing Daerah Kalimantan Selatan" in Yayasan Kompas Borneo 1989.

Obeyesekere, Ganneth. (1992). " 'British Cannibals': Contemplation of an Event in the Death and Resurrection of James Cook, Explorer". *Critical Inquiry*, 18(Summer), 630–54.

Peluso, Nancy. (1995). "Whose Woods Are These? Counter-Mapping Forest Territories in Kalimantan, Indonesia". *Antipode*, 274(4), 383–406.

Potter, Leslie. (1988). "Indigenes and Colonisers: Dutch Forest Policy in South and East Borneo (Kalimantan) 1900 to 1950" in *Changing Tropical Forests*, edited by John Dargavel, Kay Dixon and Noel Semple, pp. 127–53. Canberra: Centre for Resource and Environmental Studies, Australian National University.

Pratt, Mary. (1992). *Imperial Eyes*. New York: Routledge.

Siddik, Abdullah. (1989). "Makalah Mengenal Kehidupan Orang Bukit Di Pedalaman Mangkiling Ditinjau Dari Aspek Sosial Ekonomi" in Yayasan Kompas Borneo 1989.

Soemarsono. (1989). "Tanggapan Berupa Catatan Dan Masukan" in Yayasan Kompas Borneo 1989.

Stoler, Ann. (1991). "Carnal Knowledge and Imperial Power: Gender, Race and Mobility in Colonial Asia" in *Gender at the Crossroads of Knowledge*, edited by Micaela di Leonardo, pp. 51–101. Berkeley: University of California Press.

Suryani. (l989a). "Sumiati, Profil Wanita Desa Mangkiling". *Dinamika Berita*. October 7, 1+.

———. (1989b). "Masyarakat Mangkiling Menunggu Janji". *Dinamika Berita*. October 9, 1+.

———. (l989c). "'Akar Rapat' Populer Sebagai Alat KB". *Dinamika Berita*. October 15, 1+.

———. (1989d). "Keriting & Bibir Merah Jadi Model". *Dinamika Berita*. October 16, 1+.

———. (1989e). "'Batandik Sampai Pagi'". *Dinamika Berita*. October 17, 1+.

———. (1989f). "Minyak 'Sumbang Adam' Untuk Pemikat". *Dinamika Berita*. October 18, 1+.

Torgovnick, Marianna. (1990). *Gone Primitive: Savage Intellects, Modern Lives*. Chicago: University of Chicago Press.

Tsing, Anna. (1993). *In the Realm of the Diamond Queen: Marginality in an Out-of-the-Way Place*. Princeton: Princeton University Press.

———. (2001)."Land as Law: Negotiating the Meaning of Property in Indonesia" in *Land, Property, and the Environment*, edited by John F. Richards, pp. 94–137. Oakland, CA: Institute for Contemporary Studies Press.

———. (2003). "The News in the Provinces" in *Cultural Citizenship in Island Southeast Asia: Nation and Belonging in the Hinterlands,* edited by Renato Rosaldo, pp. 192–222. Berkeley: University of California Press.

———. (n.d.). "What Happened in Mangkiling: Localizing Global Environmentalism".

Yayasan Kompas Borneo. (1989). *Laporan Seminar Sehari: Kamis, 6 April 1989.* Banjarmasin, Indonesia: bound photocopy.

Yayasan Kompas Borneo. (1990). *Studi Diagnosa Tentang Komunitas Orang Bukit di Desa Pantai Mangkiling Kalimantan Selatan.* Banjarmasin, Indonesia: bound photocopy.

Part V

Knowing the Environment

21

People into Places: Zafimaniry Concepts of Clarity

Maurice Bloch

The Landscape

The Zafimaniry are a group of shifting cultivators living in eastern Madagascar who traditionally rely mainly on maize, beans, and taro. They number approximately 20,000. They are one of many such groups which are sometimes called Tanala and sometimes called Betsimisaraka but they differ from any of these because of the very specific environment in which they live. They inhabit a narrow band of montane forest found on a step of the sharp north–south escarpment which runs almost the whole length of Madagascar. This is an area at an altitude of approximately 1,400 m, which is very different in terms of climate and vegetation from almost anywhere else in Madagascar. To the west, lies the drier and treeless central plateau of Madagascar where the most important agricultural activity is irrigated rice cultivation. The neighbours of the Zafimaniry on this plateau are the Betsileo who are similar in many ways to the Merina who occupy the northern part.[1] To the east, at the foot of the escarpment, the forest is very different since the climate is much hotter. On that side the neighbours of the Zafimaniry are people usually referred to by the term Betsimisaraka who practise a different type of shifting cultivation and who mainly grow dry rice and sugar cane, two crops which the Zafimaniry cannot grow.[2]

Daniel Coulaud in his excellent geographical study of the Zafimaniry (1973) rightly characterizes their country as being cold, foggy, and damp. In the same book he also chooses to stress the fact that the Zafimaniry are running out of forest as a result of overswiddening which itself is caused by a rapid rise in population. As do many Europeans who have known Madagascar since the nineteenth century, he somewhat exaggerates the speed of deforestation and sees it in purely negative terms; nonetheless there is no doubt that this process is taking place. The deforestation, which is indeed due to overswiddening (itself in part due to the creation of nature reserves as well as to the growth in population), leads to people having to adopt a new kind of agriculture and so they turn to irrigated rice cultivation, which is possible in the valley areas of the deforested land. When I first studied the village – which I shall call Mamolena – in 1971, there were only two households out of a total of thirty-three which owned irrigated rice fields, but now, out of a total of fifty households only eight do not have such fields.

In fact most of these rice fields have only been created in the last three years, and this rapid change has been made possible by the irrigation work undertaken at the instigation of a local Catholic missionary and because of a general warming of the climate which enables the rice to ripen, and which the Zafimaniry, probably correctly, attribute to the retreat of the forest.

The Zafimaniry are therefore faced by two linked changes in the landscape as this would be understood by the outside observer. One is the gradual disappearance of the forest. This means that there are some areas where secondary forest has given way to steppe-like grassland, and that, more generally, primary forest is rarer and further away than it used to be. The second is that there are now wide, levelled valleys, terraced for irrigated rice fields, which in some cases are very extensive.

The Zafimaniry primarily interpret this process of change in ethnic terms. For them, people who live *an patrana* – that is, in the treeless land where irrigated rice cultivation is possible – are Betsileo; and, because their own land is becoming *an patrana,* they say that they too are becoming Betsileo. Similarly they will often say that the people who live to the west of them, in lands where the forest has practically completely disappeared, were once Zafimaniry, but that they have, by now, become fully Betsileo as a result of the environmental change. In some way this might seem strange to those unused to Malagasy notions of ethnicity but, as Astuti (1995) points out, Malagasy notions of ethnicity depend much more on the type of life one leads than on who one's parents were. Thus, in a case such as this, where the geographical change makes one adopt the way of life of another group, one becomes a member of that group.[3]

Rather surprisingly, the Zafimaniry do not seem to mind this de-ethnicization, though they find the process very interesting and are continually talking about it. They neither regret it or attempt to resist it.[4] This ethnic indifference is also reflected in the way they see the retreat of the forest and the growth of the steppe-like areas. When in the field, with my post-Rousseau, post-Sibelius sensitivities, strengthened every evening by the BBC World Service's lachrymose accounts of the disappearance of the world's rain forest, I tried as hard as I could to get my co-villagers to tell me how much they deplored the change in their environment and the extinction of all the biologi-

cal species which goes with it. I failed to get the slightest response, though people occasionally, and without much interest, noted a few minor inconveniences which deforestation causes.

One evening, sitting on a rock side-by-side with an older woman I knew well, indulging in the somewhat sentimental conversations which she much enjoyed, looking from the village to the forest lit up in the reds of the setting sun (one of the rare days when it was not raining), I thought the moment had come to make her say how much she liked the forest and regretted its passing, and so I asked her once more . . . After long reflection she said wistfully that, yes, she liked the forest. "Why?", I asked eagerly. "Because you can cut it down," she replied.

Ideas concerning the environment are thus in many ways the very opposite of those which characterize the recent "ecological panic" of the West. The Zafimaniry's concern with the environment is not with how not to damage it but with how to succeed with making a mark on it. This chapter is about what this means. My first reaction and interpretation of this total inversion of conventional modern European aesthetics was to assume that the landscape was apprehended by the Zafimaniry in a purely utilitarian manner. I soon became aware, however, that this was quite wrong. This realization was again and again forced on me by the one area of correspondence between my (modern, European) sensibilities and theirs. The Zafimaniry are as enthusiastic as are the *Guide Michelin* and municipal authorities about good views.

Good Views

On the path to the village where I lived there is a place where, before plunging into the valley which has to be crossed to reach it, one can view the houses and the hill on which the village is perched. Whenever people pass this spot, however foul the weather, and however much they are in a hurry to get back from a hard day's work, they will stop for a moment, or longer, and view the village from this vantage point. When the gangs of young men who have gone off for several months' waged work in other parts of Madagascar return home, they too will stop at this spot and sit there, singing songs for an hour or more, looking at the village, sometimes with tears in their eyes.

This almost institutionalized liking for good views and the places from which they can be seen is not exceptional. On expeditions to other villages with co-villagers, whenever we emerged from the forest on to a hilltop where one could see afar, we would also stop for a considerable time to enthuse about the clarity, to point out to each other this and that spot, to bask in the sunshine, to discuss the general topic of the beauty and value of good views and to feel sympathetically each other's euphoria at looking at such elating sights. This praise for good views emphasizes the "spaciousness" (*malalaka*) and, above all, the "clarity" (*mazava*), of the view: two words which seem to echo whenever people are commenting on viewed landscapes. This viewing takes on a very specific form. It consists in listing the hills and mountains in sight and the villages and towns which have been or still are on them. The further the mountains one can see, and some are very far, well beyond Zafimaniry country, the more the view is praised. Indeed my companions had much pleasure in demonstrating how many of these hills and villages they could name, in teaching and testing me, and occasionally showing me off to a friend who could not believe that a foreigner could know such things.

Above all it is the fact that one can see *clearly* that is endlessly stressed. The full impact of this evaluation can only be appreciated when one remembers two facts about the geographical environment of Zafimaniry country which explain how little clarity there normally is. First, the countryside is both mountainous and wooded so that it is usually very difficult to see far. The forest which has to be crossed to go from one village to another, or to go to a swidden, is often oppressively and menacingly enveloping, to the extent that Zafimaniry may easily become lost, something which often happens, occasionally with fatal consequences. Secondly the countryside is, for much of the time, shrouded in mists, rain, and clouds which cling to the forest most of the day and reduce the visibility to a few yards. Not surprisingly, the Zafimaniry much dislike and fear this cold lack of distance and are continually grumbling about it as they realize that they must go into the forest once again for their daily search for firewood or some other reason, shivering in their thin and permeable clothes.

Clarity is thus for the Zafimaniry a central value. It is both aesthetically valued and associated with pleasant living conditions. However, the notion of clarity is extended well beyond the visual in Zafimaniry culture. Thus, when one wants to show respect and admiration to a speaker who speaks in the authoritative ancestral code one should interject, every two sentences or so, the exclamation *Mazava!*, which means "Clear!" Yet another insight into the Zafimaniry valuation of clarity is that their most powerful medicine against most diseases is a wood called *fanazava*, a word which literally means "that which renders clear".

It is thus by understanding the central value of clarity and what lies behind the enthusiasm for viewing panoramas which display clarity that I feel we can share Zafimaniry ethical and aesthetic concepts about the landscape as well as understanding their equanimity towards the geographical changes occurring around them, whether these have been produced by them or not.

People into Places

The most commonly quoted Zafimaniry proverb is: *Ny tany tsy miova fa ny olombelona no miova.*[5] It is best translated as: "While the land[6] does not change the living people[7] change."

This proverb, and many others like it, can serve as a very useful introduction to Zafimaniry concepts of the relation of human beings and their environment. It reflects a constant awareness of the fragility and impermanence of human life in a world which is not concerned with their problems and which therefore affects them randomly. The way of talking about this uncaring environment – the forest, the sky, and the weather – is to refer to

Andriamanitra or *Zanahary,* words which the missionaries have chosen to translate as "God" but which for the Zafimaniry refer to a force somewhat different from the European version of the Christian God. This is because "God" is not associated with a moral purpose but manifests itself as a destiny which is neither reward nor punishment, simply a state of affairs which affects you and which you cannot resist.[8] "God", in this sense, is the external, unchangeable parameters of one's life, including the topography, which affect people in ways beyond explanation.

The countryside, a manifestation of God, is therefore a permanent but uncaring environment within which impermanent and weak human beings must live. However, things are not quite as bad as might appear because, although the land does not care and remains the same, human beings have the *potential* to transcend their impermanent nature and in this way become a part of the land.

Marriages into Houses

This potential becomes realized when human reproductive success comes close to immortalizing the producers. Every pregnancy brought to fruition, every child reaching adulthood, every adult producing living offspring, are outcomes of enterprises which one hardly dares to expect will succeed but which sometimes do.[9] However, when these uncertain projects succeed and cumulate in spite of the unconcern of the cosmic environment, then human life begins to take on an aspect which is not intrinsic to it, but which it can sometimes attain. It gains the potential for permanence, something which is characteristic of the unchangeability of land. Or rather, in these cases, through its reproductive success, which becomes a social success, human life becomes something lasting which can be *attached* to the land and thereby attempt to participate in its stasis.

This is because a successful growing family – or rather a successful "growing" marriage, since that is the true Zafimaniry focus – is realized in a material thing attached to the land: their house (see Bloch 1993 and 1995). Social achievement is to make a marriage a

lasting feature of society and to make the house, which is the material manifestation of this success, an enduring feature of the unchanging earth. This intimate association of marriage and houses exists because marriage is primarily thought of in terms of houses, thus the beginning of a marriage is referred to as "obtaining a house place for a hearth". Then, as a marriage stabilizes and produces children, grandchildren, etc., so the house of the couple becomes more permanent. This happens as the woven bamboo of which, at first, much of the house consists is gradually replaced by heavy hardwood beams which, ultimately, will be decorated with carvings which are said to "celebrate" the durability and hardness of the wood.[10] This transformation will all be due to the hard work of the couple, their relatives and descendants over many decades.

Even the death of the founding couple does not mark the end of this evolution. In a successful marriage, although the individuals die and disappear as flesh and bones, the couple survives in another form, as the material house itself. This continues to "harden" and beautify as children, grandchildren, great-grandchildren, and so on, contribute to the building by increasing the proportion of hard wood to soft material and continue to cover the surface of the wood with ever more decorative engravings. Such a "hardening, stabilizing, lasting"[11] house is what attaches itself to the land and gains permanence.

In fact, the continuing presence of the couple after their death in the house is, in some contexts, even more specific. Two parts of the house are more particularly seen as the material continuation of the original pair and these become the object of many cults to the ancestors (Bloch 1995). One is the carved central post of the house made of the hardest part of the hardest wood known to the Zafimaniry. This is associated with the man of the original marriage and remains the focus of all meetings of his descendants. The other focus is the three stones of the hearth which, together with a cooking pot (or in some cases a wooden plate) and a large wooden cooking spoon, are associated with the woman of the original marriage. It is really the conjunction of these artefacts which initially makes a marriage evident. And, after the death of the couple, it is the remaining linked presence of the central post and the hearth which represents the continuing productive existence of the couple. However this is only so because they are *conjoined* in a single enduring entity: the house as a whole which is their fertile union made manifest.

A house which is the material objectification of the continuing fecundity of a marriage which took place a long time in the past continues to become ever harder and more beautiful. This is because the descendants have an absolute duty to continue to look after it, to increase the proportion of its hardwood content and to magnify its growing durability by decorating its wood. The very appearance of such a house thus bears witness to the number of descendants that the original couple have produced and to their piety towards their ancestors. Such a house gradually becomes referred to as a "holy house": that is, a place where the descendants will obtain blessing from their ancestors. Significantly, there is a central rite that should occur at dawn when the rising sun makes the village "clear". At such times the descendants of the original couple congregate inside the holy house, they gather around the central post and eat food cooked on its hearth. Then they may address the central post and hearth as if they were the original man and woman respectively.

When, in this way, the house of the original couple has become a "holy house" it has usually also become the essential centre of a village. This is because the descendants of the original couple will gradually build less permanent houses around the holy house but in positions which mark their junior status, since these "children houses" will be to the south and lower from the summit than is the "holy house".[12]

The process of transformation from soft house to holy house, from single house to village, is always uncertain and takes a long time, but every existing village is evidence of the fact that it is possible. When the process has occurred it demonstrates not only that the original founders have had success as reproducers of impermanent human beings but that they have been able to transform this mutable living flow into a permanent, stable, material

feature of the land: a village, perched on a hill, firmly resting on the hard rock of which these hilltops consist. This is the successful attachment of active mobile living people on to the uncaring land to which the Zafimaniry dare to aspire.

In order fully to understand the visual impact of this success we must also take into account another Zafimaniry notion concerning the landscape: altitude. Every Zafimaniry village should be on the summit of a hill and one of the words for village also means hill.[13] Zafimaniry villages rise up out of the surrounding forest since they are placed on high rocky outcrops partly for defence but also so that they may be "in the clear". In the morning and sometimes during the day the villages are actually above the clouds which swirl past in dark greens and whites through the forest below, turning different villages into so many islands of clarity and definition above a chaotic and indistinct sea of vegetative growth and transformation. Clarity, altitude, and the pleasure of warm sunshine in a cold climate are thus inseparable in this region as this was continually pointed out to me.[14]

However, neither clarity nor altitude are absolutes; both are a matter of more or less since not all summits are equally high. In fact the difference in height and therefore clarity is of great importance in Zafimaniry thought because the differential altitude of villages is seen to illustrate differential seniority and legitimate political authority, two concepts which are inseparable throughout Madagascar. Thus, just as the houses within a village stand in a genealogical relationship to each other which can be seen at a glance in terms of which house is nearer the summit, so too with Zafimaniry villages. The village from which a couple set out to form a new one by establishing a house becomes the "parent" village which "gave birth" to the subsequent locality and should be higher than the "child" village. When this is so, this is pointed out as an illustration of the rule and, when it is not so, an *ad hoc* explanation is sought (Bloch 1975).[15]

The same principle is applied to explain the political order even beyond Zafimaniry country. Very high hills and mountains emerging from the mists of the lowlands, either within their boundaries or beyond, are always talked of admiringly as the past abodes of kings, even though the Zafimaniry never had their own kings, and have historically spent a great deal of their energies resisting the pretensions of various rulers. Similarly the Zafimaniry talk of Ambositra, the administrative centre of their region, as being above them and they will say they go "up" to Ambositra or to Antananarivo, the capital of Madagascar, in spite of the fact that both towns are far below them in altitude.

In fact, altitude, clarity, permanence, legitimate political power, and genealogical seniority are to them facets of the same thing, all different aspects of the successful couples, now ancestors, who, by transforming the uncertain turmoil of life and youth into houses and villages and making "places" which remain, have achieved a victory over time since, unlike living humans, "the land does not change".

Here, however, we must be aware of another aspect which makes this possible success of human beings much more ambiguous, almost ironic. An aspect of the transformation of a marriage into a house and then a village is that, as people become fixed to place, they are at the same time losing their much-valued "lively" and sensuous character as *olombelona*: living people, since they are becoming immobile "places".

The spatial aspect of people is apparent from the first. The Zafimaniry have a tendency to refer to anybody from outside their own village simply by the name of the locality. Thus, when I was confronted with a new face, which led me to ask who we had just crossed on our path, I would simply be told the name of a village. Similarly, as noted above, genealogy in terms of people is rapidly replaced by genealogies in terms of villages.[16]

The merging of people and places in this way is, however, little more than a celebration of the success of the ancestors who have *established* their marriage so that it has become a house, although a celebration already tinged with the sadness of the loss of the joy of being truly alive, since we must not forget that for the Zafimaniry, as for other Malagasy, youth, strength, and movement, although antithetical to the success of the establishment of the house, are nonetheless greatly but differently valued.[17]

But, in Zafimaniry culture, there exists a further stage in the process of the mutation of people into localized, permanent things, and then the loss implied in becoming an object and a place becomes much more apparent. In this other mode the very success of living beings transformed into permanent features of the land seems, ultimately, to undermine the point of the exercise.

Megalithic Monuments

A good while after death megalithic stone monuments to commemorate a parent[18] are sometimes built in prominent places. If the person commemorated is a woman, the monument takes the form of three stones, like a hearth, covered by a large flat stone by way of cooking pot. If the person commemorated is a man, the monument recalls the central post of the house and looks a little like a menhir.[19]

The differences in commemoration by means of a standing-stone as opposed to a holy house are revealing. First such commemoration by stone is an even greater success in inscribing the living person in the unchanging land since stone is, and is perceived to be, even more permanent than the hardest wood. However, commemorative stones, unlike holy houses, do not link the person with their descendants, while the house does so through the mechanism of blessing. First, this difference is reflected in the fact that such stones are erected *outside* the villages where their descendants live. Secondly, the stones commemorate individuals, not, like the houses, couples. This is true even if a number of standing-stones are, as is usual, all in one place. These groupings do not join couples or lines of parents and children in the way that houses do.

What unites the people who are commemorated together in a gathering of standing-stones is that they stand in a relationship of siblingship. Precisely for this reason, the stones represent the opposite to the married couples unified in houses. In Zafimaniry thought, sexual relations between brothers and sisters are highly incestuous and cannot produce normal offspring. Marriage and human reproduction necessarily require the spatial separation of cross-sex siblings as a necessary first step before the hearth and the central post can be united in a fruitful marriage and house. Thus, the postmortem rejoining of the central posts and the hearth of brothers and sisters implies the negation of growth through sexual reproduction and the destruction of the conjugal units to which the siblings belonged in life. The megalithic groupings of hearth and central post convey, above all, broken houses.

People, therefore, are made into places twice, as houses and as megaliths. These two ways celebrate, however, two completely different and opposed aspects of the social person. In one case, people are immortalized as successful and therefore lasting parts of the productive and reproductive side of life, as unified married couples. In the other case, they are immortalized as part of an unchanging unity which has refused the reproductive process in order to gain the permanence which comes from staying put as an undivided sibling group. The contradiction between these two states is particularly clear in the case of women, since it is they who normally move at marriage, and it is dramatically illustrated at their funerals. Then, a veritable tug-of-war occurs over the body, with the woman's natal family pulling at one end and her husband's family pulling at the other. The contradiction, however, also exists for men since they too are considered by the Zafimaniry to have become at marriage a part of their wife's family. All Zafimaniry are therefore pulled between the two poles of siblingship and marriage and when siblingship wins it is at the expense of the engagement in growth and reproduction which a successful house celebrates.

This means that the permanence gained by the construction of megalithic monuments is absolute but it is in opposition to the relative, but "growing", permanence of successful human life in houses and villages. Absolute stasis is thus gained at the expense of human reproduction.

Here the symbolic difference between wood and stone comes to the fore. What fascinates the Zafimaniry about wood is that it originates in a living thing which, nonetheless, ultimately gains far greater permanence than human beings. It is because of this fact that they use hard wood to make the houses and villages into which the living become transformed. Wood demonstrates a familial and metaphysical success in its passage from life to lasting object. It would seem however that, because it originates in a living thing, it is, although very hard and permanent, not eternal. Stone is seen as eternal but, on the other hand, it is not, nor has ever been, in any way alive. To become wood, as do the successful couple in the house, is therefore to succeed in transforming life as far as it will go towards stasis, but this cannot be all the way. To become stone, however, as do the groupings of siblings, is a way of becoming immortal but at the cost of the total abandonment of life and of marital reproduction and parent–child relationships.

Admittedly, the setting up of these standing-stones involves a great ritual organized principally by the descendants of the dead and therefore they might be thought to link the descendants to their parents in a permanent way. This is not so, however, since once set up, the stones do not remain the concern of any specific group and the name of the person for which they were set up is soon forgotten even by their direct descendants. Rather, the standing-stones are seen as places for offerings made by anyone who disturbs or profits from the land in which they are situated, irrespective of their connection to the dead. Thus the person who gathers honey from a nearby tree will leave a little on the stone, and so will the person who clears a swidden near one of these stones. In making these offerings the giver is usually totally ignorant of the one for whom the stone was raised. If, therefore, the stones are centres of cults, these are merely cults of placation of the environment or of God, since the environment is a manifestation of his power.

It is as if in achieving greatest permanence by attaching themselves most totally to the unchanging land by means of stone the living human has in fact become merely a feature of this land and not any more an ancestor of "living people". The extreme success of attaching people to places through standing-stones ironically renders its outcome pointless on a human scale. Perhaps nothing shows this better than the fact that people often say of the ancestors for whom these stones have been made, as they do of all very remote ancestors who have stopped being directly concerned with sanctioning the activities of their descendants according to moral rules, that they have become that uncaring power: *Zanahary*, that is, god/s.[20]

This assimilation of ancestors so commemorated and God can be seen in yet another way. When there is no such commemorative standing-stone nearby, the honey-gatherer or the maker of a new swidden will leave the offering he would have left on the artificially raised stone simply on a prominent natural rock in exactly the same way. They will do just as well. The Zafimaniry say of such prominent rocks that they are "standing-stones made by God" and the difference of authorship makes no difference to their function.

In making standing-stones people have been turned into places, but at the cost of losing all aspects of human vitality. The significance of houses and standing-stones, of God and of the ancestors as embodied in the central post and in the hearth, enable us to see a part of the meaning which the Zafimaniry attribute to the landscape when they look at it from a hill and praise the clarity of the view. They are looking at summits, many of which have villages on them and the others, it is presumed, once had such villages. These summits represent their history, the achievement of their ancestors who have inscribed themselves on to the unchanging land, especially on those points which rise out of the chaos of the forest and the mist and stand clear and certain in the sunshine. Their pleasure is a celebration of this achievement and they are quite explicit about this, but they are not so forthcoming in explaining the melancholy which is also palpably present and is so often expressed in the songs which are sung from places where there is a good view. What I felt this was about was that they also are aware that, seen from afar, this achievement is slight, many of the "villages" have returned to forest, the viewed landscape and especially its contours seem, in the end, unaffected by human activity, and the ultimate fruit of human efforts at immortality are nothing but rocks, largely indistinguishable from the many other rocks placed there by God, that power, which for the Zafimaniry, is the source of accidents beyond human control.

Clarity and the Two Kinds of Landscape

If I am right in interpreting Zafimaniry's emotions and understanding about the landscape in this way we can now understand the Zafimaniry's apparent indifference to the passing of the forest and the creation of the new irrigated rice terraces.

Apart from their practical evaluation of the process – which on the whole is more positive than negative – the Zafimaniry, to my surprise, often praised this new type of deforested land by using that same charged term *mazava* which they use for good views. On one level the reason is obvious. Cleared forests are indeed clearer, and so are terraced rice valleys. Not only do they enable you to see further, but they do not catch the mist and the clouds as the forest does. However, they also represent something else (though I must admit that I have never been told this in so many words). The cleared rice valleys are also a sign of living humans having finally successfully made their mark and attached themselves to the unchanging land. They represent an even greater success than villages in achieving what the ancestors sought to achieve, and they do this in a way which appears, at least viewed from the end of a newly made rice valley, as less pyrrhic than turning people into rocks.

NOTES

1. For accounts of the Betsileo in English see Kottak (1980). On the Merina see Bloch (1971) and (1986).
2. Recently new varieties of dry rice have been grown in Zafimaniry country on an experimental basis, but this is not yet significant economically.
3. This is made particularly easy by the fact that the Zafimaniry and the Betsileo speak an almost identical dialect of Malagasy.

4. They see the climate and the environment as directly affecting people. Thus they stress how hard they have to work and how this makes them strong. They say that if you live long in the hotter parts of Madagascar you become weak and that if you do not have to carry the heavy loads which they do, for example because you have carts like the Betsileo, you will also become weaker.

5. The proverb occurs in a number of variants but the meaning is constant. The version I have chosen is given because it is the simplest.

6. The Malagasy word *tany* has a very similar range of meanings to the English word "land".

7. The normal Malagasy word for people, *olombelona*, literally means "living people". I have kept the rather pedantic form in full as it seems to me most revealing. R. Dubois, partly rightly and partly wrongly, elaborates this point (Dubois 1978).

8. This notion is often referred to by the word *anjara* which is translated in the standard dictionary as part, lot, destiny, turn (Abinal and Malzac 1988: 49).

9. This statement is based on a wide range of ethnographic data which cannot be discussed here.

10. The part of the wood used for making such a house is the dark core of the tree which the Zafimaniry call *teza* which also means "lasting" (see Bloch 1993). The carvings on the house, which have often been described (e.g. Verin 1964), are seen by the Zafimaniry as a celebration of this "durability".

11. The words all attempt to translate the Malagasy verb *mateza* derived from *teza* (see n. 10).

12. These houses too may be referred to as "holy houses" but they are less "holy" than the houses of the founding couple. The holiness of a house is a matter of degree. Practical problems of topography mean that the rule which places houses in rank order is not always fully followed.

13. *Vohitra*: the word is also used in Merina and Betsileo in the same way.

14. Slaves in the past were obliged to build their villages on low ground and the first thing they did when they were freed, in the area where I worked, was to move their village to a summit.

15. For example, the explanation continually given for the fact that the very senior village of Ambohimanzaka was very low was that the inhabitants had been forced by the French to move its location. This had indeed been so.

16. There is an exception to this when people are actually in the presence of tombs, when they, or rather the senior people, do make an effort to remember individual names.

17. The conflict between the value of ancestralization and of vitality is extensively discussed for the Merina in Bloch 1986.

18. Because of the opposition of the Catholic church this has only rarely been done in the last few years though alternatives with similar meanings are being developed.

19. The monument for men was sometimes first of all of wood and identical in its carvings to the central post of a house. I believe the erection of such wooden posts was a first stage in the erection of a stone monument but I am not all that clear as these wooden posts have not been erected for a long time. Rather bewilderingly they are called "wooden male stones".

20. The ambiguity comes from the fact that the plural is not marked in Malagasy words.

REFERENCES

Abinal, R. P., and Malzac, R. P. (1988: 1st edn. 1888). *Dictionnaire Français-Malgache*. Paris: Éditions Maritimes et d'Outre-Mer.

Astuti, R. (1995). "The Vezo Are Not a Kind of People: Identity, Difference, and 'Ethnicity' among the Vezo of Western Madagascar", *American Ethnologist*, 22: 464–82.

Bloch, M. (1971). *Placing the Dead: Tombs, Ancestral Villages and Social Organisation among the Merina of Madagascar*. London: Seminar Press.

——. (1975). "Property and the End of Affinity", in M. Bloch (ed.), *Marxist Analyses and Social Anthropology*. London: Malaby Press.

——. (1986). *From Blessing to Violence: History and Ideology in the Circumcision Ritual of the Merina of Madagascar*. Cambridge: Cambridge University Press.

——. (1993). "What Goes Without Saying: The Conceptualisation of Zafimaniry Society", in A. Kuper (ed.), *Conceptualising Societies*. London: Routledge.

——. (1995). "The Resurrection of the House", in J. Carsten and S. Hugh-Jones (eds.), *About the House: Lévi-Strauss and Beyond*. Cambridge: Cambridge University Press.

Dubois, R. (1978). *Olombelona: Essai sur l'existence personnelle et collective à Madagascar*. Paris: L'Harmattan.

Coulaud, D. (1973). *Les Zafimaniry: Un groupe ethnique de Madagascar à la poursuite de la forêt*. Antananarivo: F.B.M.

Kottack, C. (1980). *The Past and the Present: History, Ecology, and Cultural Variation in Highland Madagascar*. Ann Arbor, Mich.: University of Michigan Press.

Verin, P. (1964). "Les Zafimaniry et leur art. Un groupe continuateur d'une tradition esthétique Malgache méconnue", *Revue de Madagascar*, 27: 1–76.

22

Pleasant Places, Past Times, and Sheltered Identity in Rural East Anglia

Charles O. Frake

East Anglia is the lost continent of Great Britain.
Len Deighton, XPD

How, and why, is a sense of remoteness – of a place lost – maintained with regard to a region that has not, in any obvious way, been marginal to much of anything since Roman times? I argue here that a search for answers to this question tells us something both about my natives, in this case the English, in particular and also about the issues of place and identity in general.

To begin the search, consider first one of the less momentous events that marked the end of the nineteenth century in England. At that time, along with *Country Life* magazine, the Ancient Monuments Act, the Society for the Protection of Ancient Buildings, the National Trust for Places of Historic Interest and Natural Beauty, the British Naturalists' Association, the Society for the Promotion of Nature Reserves, the Society for Checking the Abuses of Public Advertising, the Commons Preservation Society, the National Footpaths Preservation Society, and the Society for the Preservation of the Wild Fauna of the Empire, there appeared the organization whose name suggested the title for this chapter: the Selbourne Society for the Protection of Birds, Plants and Pleasant Places.[1]

It is not the task here to explain why such organizations appeared with curious near-simultaneity at that moment of history, nor is it to argue that their appearance had great impact on subsequent history. Their appearance, as I said, was not momentous. It was, however, symbolic. At least in retrospect, we can see something very "English" in this joint concern with such things as plants, animals, footpaths, natural beauty, ancient monuments, and old buildings – all to be protected and preserved, not so much "as they are" but rather "as they were" in an imagined past of pleasant places. It is the "Englishness" of all this that I propose to explore. The terrain of this exploration comprises the region of England known as East Anglia, specifically the County of Norfolk, which, although part of a "lost continent" to Len Deighton, is to James Wentworth Day, a popular journalist, "the most English corner of all England" (P. Wright 1985: 68). But first, in the tradition of "ethnographic background," something must be said of these "English" and of this corner of their homeland.[2]

The Natives and their Place

As subjects of anthropological investigation, the English are a rather troublesome tribe. They are easy enough to identify, and they know who they are. That's not the problem. The problem is that for anthropologists hungry for the taste of the exotic, the English seem to provide rather vapid fare (gastronomic metaphors somehow come to mind to an ethnographer in England). From the anthropologist's point of view, the English have no "culture," a failing that is very hard to explain to the English.[3] The English, an anthropologist might argue, have a restricted view of what "culture" really is. But so, in a complementary way, does the anthropologist. Anthropologists have long struggled to accord cultural dignity and intellectual interest to the strange practices of peoples of the world ignored by other disciplines. The struggle has been so successful, at least within anthropology, that culture, and therefore intellectual interest, has become tacitly identified with exotic practices. The height of culture for an anthropologist is not a Bach cantata; it is an asymmetrical circulating connubium. (It should be a well-executed conversational riposte in Toronto, Tulsa, or Tikopea.)

Every anthropologist would now deny this identification of "culture" with the exotic. But despite increasing interest in "the Western world," our practice still belies our denials.[4] Anthropologists now go to Europe in respectable numbers, but most head for the marginal, the rural, and the "ethnic" places. I decided to work in England, after long working with people as exotic as any anthropologist could desire, partly out of a perverse challenge. Could I make the English interesting? They are, after all, human in spite of their relatively central role in the world system. Still, I don't want to make them interesting by transforming them into some kind of exotic other. Much less do I want to make them interesting by transforming them into unwitting dupes of hegemonic oppression. I would like to make them interesting for the ways their lives inform what it is to be human in this world we all live in.

Yet despite these noble declarations, I seem to be sufficiently imbued with the anthropological habitus to have yearned for some bit of exotica. After all, I did pick a region of England that is rural, at least in local image. And that perhaps explains why, while reading a spy story to pass the time on a plane, I latched onto a characterization of my field site as a "lost continent." That, I must have subconsciously thought, might spark a bit of interest among my colleagues. The real reason this "lostness" is interesting, however, lies not in the factuality of it but in the image of it as both an outcome of and a contributor to local practices of constructing an identity for persons and their places.

East Anglia may be lost in the imagination of the English, but its inhabitants are, in everyone's mind, English to the core. They are not, in anyone's mind, "ethnic" or even "peculiar." They are sufficiently non-exotic to have never before, to my knowledge, attracted the attention of an ethnographer. The image of lostness may in fact be tied to the visible absence of ethnic minorities in rural East Anglia. My more cynical local friends tell me that this show of pure, white Englishness is, as much as the appeal of the countryside, what makes rural East Anglia such an attractive retirement area for British city dwellers. If one's place is "lost," perhaps all those foreigners and ethnics that one used to confront in London, Liverpool, and Manchester will not be able to find it. Of course one can be terrifyingly lost in a city or, outside England, in a wilderness. But romantic, poetic, pleasant lostness occurs in the rural English countryside, in a maze of narrow, hedged-lined roads obscured from but never too far from church, pub, or country house.

The image of ruralness associated with East Anglia has a firm historical foundation.[5] The water-powered industrial revolution of the eighteenth and early nineteenth centuries largely passed East Anglia by. This chalk and alluvial shelf jutting out into the North Sea was, the stock explanation goes, too flat and waterlogged for effective use of hydraulic power. But the absence of industry and its accompanying proletariat must also have been closely tied to the early capitalization of East

Anglian agriculture. That created a farming system dependent on the existence of a landless class of cheap farm labor. East Anglia led the way, not only in England but in the world, toward capitalized, commercial, mechanized agriculture, controlled by investors and landowners, operated by a managerial class of resident "farmers," and worked by landless farm laborers.[6] As long as this system was profitable for farmers and landowners, there was little incentive to attract alternate sources of employment for farm workers.

This history of a prosperous, rural, but commercial economy extends well back into the Middle Ages. East Anglia was then a major center of wool production and trade. Norwich, Norfolk's city, was second only to London in England. The profusion of medieval church towers that dot the skyline in any view over the landscape of Norfolk and Suffolk is testimony to the wealth possessed by landowners and merchants during that era.

After the postmedieval enclosure of farms and the capitalization of agriculture, the main source of wealth became the growing of grain, especially wheat. This rural economy has been an integral part of the world system since its beginnings. Prosperity was greatest at times of major European wars. The Napoleonic period, World War I, and World War II were the good times for farmers. In between, during most of the nineteenth century and the mid-twentieth, times were hard for farmers and farm workers. Since World War II, prosperity for farmers has been maintained by Common Market farm supports that encouraged a great expansion of grain and oil-seed fields, accomplished by the draining of wetlands and the appropriation of grazing land. These transformations of the real landscape have seriously threatened the image of the English countryside. Although farming is still by far the major source of wealth in East Anglia, the number of people engaged in farming is a very small percentage of the total population. For most of the rest, the land is not a source of wealth but a constituent of the ambience of their place, an ambience that contains their identities and inspires their lives.[7]

Talking about Place

"... I found myself in short in Thornton Lacey."

"It sounds like it," said Edmund.

"... you would never be able to prove that it was *not* Thornton Lacey – for such it certainly was."

"You inquired then?"

"No, I never inquire. But I *told* a man mending a hedge that it was Thornton Lacey, and he agreed to it."

Jane Austen, *Mansfield Park*

Not only are the English deficient as "natives" in the anthropological image but they also provide, in their talk, a special embarrassment to the ethnographer of place. One of the fundamental principles in the early days of cognitive anthropology was that if you wanted to know what was important to a people you had to find out what questions they asked of each other. "How're you two related?" "What's new?" "What do you do?" "What's happening?" As one of the alleged founders of this field once rashly advised ethnographers: "Look for query-rich settings" (Frake 1964). Unfortunately, English queries about place seem hardly more common now, at least in Norfolk, than in Jane Austen's time. True, one may sometimes hear inquiries about location from lost Londoners on holiday who have carelessly neglected to bring along their Ordnance Survey map or A–Z city plan. But the wait for a query about place of origin – the stock American get-acquainted ploy, "Where're yuh from?" – can be a long one. In marked contrast to American practice, one does not ask this of the English without seeming to cause a certain amount of understated discomfort.

There is, so far as I am aware, no real empirical evidence of the frequency of inquiries about place of origin in the discourse of the English, but the impression that one does not casually ask the provenance of someone one does not know well is certainly widespread. It is mentioned in humorous treatises on English-American differences: "Curiously, for people who identify so closely with region of origin, Brits refuse to tell outsiders where they're from.... [If you ask one] he freezes, tongue-tied. You have intruded somehow on private matters, and embarrassed him" (Walmsley 1987:82). An Englishman's place is sheltered, protected, secluded – a lost continent within which to hide the self. One does not intrude. We will return to this interactional peculiarity shortly.

The ethnographer's embarrassment is happily assuaged by the fact that the English do talk and write about place all the time and have been doing so for hundreds of years. It is, after all, their use of our language through all these years that has given the peculiarly English word "place" its rich semantic field, one that fills six three-column pages in the new edition of the *Oxford English Dictionary*. Its entry for "place" begins:

> Place has superseded OE. *stow* and (largely) *stede*; it answers to F. *lieu*, L. *locus*, as well as to F. *place*, and the senses are thus very numerous and difficult to arrange.

This characterization points up an etymological curiosity embedded in the English talk of place over the last nine hundred years since the conquest of England by French-speaking descendants of Norse-speaking Vikings. There are four sets of terms involved. First are the terms for the notion of "place:" "location," "position," "site," and so forth, which are all forms of Romance origin (although, as the OED definition notes, the meaning correspondences are not the same as in their French sources).[8] These Romance forms did not add to the English language; they replaced Anglo-Saxon forms that now survive only in placenames.

Second are terms for the description or study of places, words such as those defined for us by Thomas Fuller in 1642 (II, vii, 75):

> Acquainted with Cosmography, treating the world in whole joynts; with Chorography, shredding it into countries; and with Topography, mincing it into particular places.

These are learned adoptions from Greek, another language rich in worlds for "place." Today, "cosmography" and "chorography" are obscure, even though the latter term does appear in several old guidebooks and local histories such as John Norden's early-

seventeenth-century *Chorography of Norfolk* (Hood 1938). On the other hand, "topography," a nineteenth-century favorite, has survived as a well-known term today.[9] Almost every bookstore and library in East Anglia has shelves so labeled filled with guidebooks, travel descriptions, local histories, and racks of Ordnance Survey maps.

Third are terms that label kinds of "places," like "settlements," "villages," "hamlets," "lakes," "rivers," "streams," "creeks," "marshes," "fens," and so on, which present a mixed bag of Anglo-Saxon and Romance forms. Some are common throughout the English-speaking world, some, like "fen," "moor," and "mews," are peculiarly British (though well known everywhere to readers of British mystery novels), and some, like Norfolk's "broad," "carr," "staithe," and "loke," are associated with particular localities. Finally, there are names for individual places, names which in East Anglia and elsewhere in England are almost exclusively Anglo-Saxon (or in a few cases Saxonized Roman versions of earlier Celtic names). Neither Celtic precursors nor Anglo-Norman successors are recognized as having had a noticeable effect on the names that now fill the map of England, for the most part names already inscribed in the Domesday Book, William the Conqueror's inventory of the places and resources of his new land.[10]

Names for Places

> I grew up in a neighborhood right next to a Black . . . right next to Harlem. . . . We called our little neighborhood White Harlem – cuz it sounded bad.
> "Where're yuh from?"
> "White Harlem."
> "Heh!"
> The real name was Morningside Heights.
>   George Carlin, *Occupation: Foole*, 1973

Discussions over what constitutes "place" have, as Keith Basso (1988) pointed out in a classic contribution, often overlooked a simple but universal attribute of places: places, like persons, have individual names. In fact, unlike persons, whose creation precedes naming, places come into being out of spaces by being named. All cultures not only label kinds of places, such as "settlements," "streams," "lakes," and "mountains," but they also name individual places like "Paris," "Bull Run," "Tahoe," and "Pina-tubo." By finding what is named, one can quickly compile an inventory of local places with respect not only to their locations but also to their scope. For, unlike persons, whose phenomenal boundaries are (pace postmodern deconstructers of the self) relatively apparent, places can range from dimensionless points to infinite universes. The limits of a name serve, like a verbal fence, to enclose an individual place as a spatial self.

Peoples differ in how they mark off continuous spaces into bounded places. In Los Angeles, the same name attaches to a street for miles and miles regardless of interruptions by freeways, railroads, and airports. In London, each intersection and each bend seems to bring a new street name, a different place. Some Philippine peoples cut up rivers the way Londoners do streets. Americans, on the other hand, can get into political squabbles over which upstream branch continues the "same" river. Such a fight over the boundaries of a fluvial self occurred, I have been told by Rocky Mountain compatriots, in tracing the Colorado River (then the "Grand") to its "true" headwaters in the state of Colorado. The losing branch – the longer one, actually – became the Green, a river that arises in the rival state of Wyoming and joins the Colorado River in Utah, avoiding all but a tiny corner of Colorado. The state of Colorado, say its neighbors, stole a river and then renamed it for itself.

Names not only permit the demarcation of contiguous places but also reveal an organization of embedded places. This embedded structure, a universal feature of place naming, means that any given location can lay claim to a series of names. Where did I stay last summer? "Above Tom Plowman's shop," "on High Street," "in Stalham," "in North Norfolk," "in Norfolk," "in East Anglia," "in England," "in Britain," "in the UK," "in Europe," "overseas." Each of these answers truly names my location then. The answer I select says something about the degree of shared knowledge of

place, and hence of mutual experience and common identity, that I accord to my interrogator. The recognition that places have parts shows up not only in the naming of parts, as in "Norfolk" and "North Norfolk," but also in the talk of parts as such. If places are thought of as bounded spaces, then one can envision both the whole place and parts of the place. On many early maps of England, places that appear only partially on the sheet are identified as "parts," for example, "Parte of Suffolk" on Saxton's 1574 map of Norfolk. Maybe that is the source of expressions like "not much excitement in these parts."

This way of referring to place is of some antiquity in English. In a prefeminist backlash of 1558, titled *The First Blast of the Trumpet against the Monstrous Regiment of Women*, John Knox (1558) wrote of a place where "women in those partes, were not tamed nor embased by consideration of their own sex and kind." The practice, common to part-whole terminologies, of naming the whole for a part is shared by placenames. This usage reveals a presumption of prominence of place. The use of "England" is a notorious example, one that irritates non-English inhabitants of the United Kingdom. Those who, like myself, speak of England *sensu stricto* often feel obliged to note the restriction explicitly.[11] A parallel case is offered by the use of "Holland" for the "Netherlands" by English (and German) speakers. Large cities often toponymically annex their politically independent suburbs in this way. The city named New York thus appropriates its whole state.

Places are also related to each other in a network of distance and direction. I could have answered the inquiry about my summer whereabouts with "about twelve miles northeast of Norwich." Locating a place in relation to another place is another way of according that place a presumption of greater prominence. A guide to Norfolk and Suffolk placenames called *Where's That?* (Walker n.d.) locates place by distance to the nearest more prominent place, thus revealing a hierarchy of place prominence. How do I find Stockton? The guide informs me that it is five miles northeast of Bungay. Great, so where's Bungay? Well, the guide warns me that "strangers may have to turn first to another page." I, knowing now that I am a stranger, do so, and find that Bungay is five miles west of Beccles, which yet another page puts twelve miles southwest of Yarmouth. And Yarmouth? The last page tells me it is twenty miles east of Norwich. That actually puts Stockton closer to Norwich than Yarmouth!

The guide, like a human conversationalist, attributes to the person inquiring about place the greatest degree of familiarity with local places that is consistent with the person's original inquiry. If someone doesn't know the whereabouts of an obscure place like Stockton, then the guide first assumes he or she knows the nearest less obscure place, Bungay. It then abandons that assumption as, step by step, each answer is met with new inquiries. The procedure efficiently sorts out us strangers.

There is more to the use of placenames than the formulation and demarcation of place. Sorting out strangers is another kind of work – very important work in East Anglian social encounters – done by place names. Sounding "bad" in New York is another. In his landmark paper on the social entailments of using placenames, E. A. Schegloff (1972) explored various strategies exhibited in the selection and co-selection of alternative designations for the same location. George Carlin's "White Harlem" and "Morningside Heights" provide a choice example. Schegloff also pointed out, but did not fully explore, the use of placenames to formulate phenomena other than place. Occupation, for example:

A: You uh wha 'dijuh do, fer a living?
B: Ehm, I work inna driving school.
It turns out that B is, in fact, a messenger boy, not an instructor, in the school. (Schegloff 1972:98)

A critical formulation to be worked out in any English social interaction is social class. In most of England this work is accomplished primarily by one's voice, sometimes inadvertently, often in quite a studied way. In Norfolk and Suffolk, and doubtless elsewhere as well, the marking of one's speech by localisms, an advantage in some contexts and a disadvantage in others, greatly compounds the difficulty of this work. The range of accents displayed, both by the same individual in different situations and by different individuals in the same family, can be quite impressive.[12] Backing up the import of accent are dress and demeanor. Using placenames also supports this work. In situations where one endeavors to bestow as high a class as possible upon oneself – these are, of course, not all situations; sometimes it is better to be bad – it is important to reveal one's badges of identity as subtly and unobtrusively as possible. It is vulgar, a mark of low class, not to do so. Provenance, marked by the name of one's home place, is commonly one of these badges. Some places rank better than others. If one comes from a posh place, it is rather unsightly to proclaim it; if your conversational partner comes from a common place, it is unkind to ask about it. Better not to ask or be asked at all. One does not intrude.

Names are not simply markers and delimiters of place, verbal signposts and fences along a conceptual road. Nor are they simply tokens used to negotiate and mark positions in social interaction. True, as with personal names, their denotative use does not depend on any meaning that can be read into the name. If I tell you I stayed in Stalham last summer, what you need to know is not what "Stalham" means or once might have meant, but what place it names. If you do not know, you do not ask, "What does it mean?" but "Where is it?" Nevertheless, the use of placenames implicates much more than their denotation. In their phonological forms and their semantic suggestiveness, names often become remarkable – worthy of a story – in their own right. For Western Apaches, the mere mention of a placename can tell a story (Basso 1988). Not only are Apache placenames semantically transparent but their meanings also constitute topographic descriptions that are powerfully evocative of incidents in well-known stories. The English language does not seem to have the capacity to pack so much semantic content into a single name. Nevertheless, English placenames are no more mere signposts than are those of any other language. It just takes more work, or at least a different kind of work, to make the verbal signposts more than simple markers of place. The inhabitants of the language's homeland have a long history of crafting noteworthy names for places.

England is famous for its quaint placenames oddly pronounced. Although seldom displaying Cotswoldian excesses such as Stow-on-Wold and Shipton-under-Wychwood, East Anglia contributes its share of toponymic curiosities. Remarkability in an English placename is best achieved with a suggestive but somewhat opaque meaning requiring a bit of imagination to discern. One does not expect in England a "Salt Lake City" next to a big salty lake. The semantic opacity of a placename is much like the patina on a flint tool. It covers the past of the place, hiding a story and a history. The decypherment of an English placename is rather like an archaeological dig. One strips away the deceptive superficial layers to get at the original meaning. The more stripping required, the more ancient, and thus the more interesting, the past.

Consider the North Norfolk place called "Great Hautbois." Conforming to a great English tradition, "Hautbois" is pronounced in a way only a local could know: "Hobbus." This pronunciation, locals insist, demonstrates that the name is not, despite appearances, originally French at all, but real English. Written guides to English placenames support this assertion by giving a derivation from Old English *hobb* + *wisce*, "meadow by a hummock." Old books and maps reveal a long history of variant spellings. The eleventh-century Domesday Book has "Hobuisse" and "Hobuist," Saxton's map of 1574 has "Hobbes," and Faden's map of 1797 has "Hautboys Vulgo Hobbies," implying that the current pronunciation was then seen as a vulgar corruption.[13] What matters now is that the place can be seen as having an authentic English past more ancient than the Norman intrusion of 1066. That is not the end to the Hautbois story, however. It must also be noted that Great Hautbois is a very tiny place, not much more than a ruined church and a Girl Guides camp (Norfolk Federation of Women's Institutes 1990). It does not even show on the current Ordnance Survey 1:50,000 map. Nearby "Little Hautbois," which is on the map, is actually larger and more frequented – it is at the entrance to a major air base.

Such games with "great" and "little" occur elsewhere in North Norfolk. "Great Walsingham" is smaller than "Little Walsingham" (which has been a major pilgrimage destination since medieval times); "Great Snoring" is smaller than "Little Snoring" (and neither, locals delight in telling visitors, has anything to do with noises made while sleeping; the names, they say, are tributes to a distant Viking ancestor named Snorri).[14] "Great Yarmouth" on the other hand, has no "Little" partner. The attribute seems to be a modern addition to the name of this port city, yet citizens assiduously use it in even the most casual references to their place. The "great" and "little" attribution also has more pretentious versions. Some places are "Magna" and "Parva." Suffolk has a case of "Inferior" and "Superior" attached to a place called "Rickinghall."

Other attributes are also popular. Being near any kind of water frequently commands mention everywhere in England, and since being near, if not immersed in, water is not uncommon in that country, the command provides a challenge to toponymic ingenuity. As mentionable water, the sea is best: "Holme-next-Sea," "Wells-next-the-Sea," "Caistor-on-Sea," "Ogmore-by-Sea," "Sea Palling," and, resorting, perhaps in desperation, to Latin, "Weston-Super-Mare." In absence of a sea, however, soggy land will do: the Cotswold hills have their "Moreton-by-Marsh"; Norfolk has its less quaintly phrased "Marsham" and "Fenside."

English placenames may be oddly pronounced and quaint, but they must be *English*. They may never be "foreign." England is not a place for the likes of a "Palo Alto," a "Los Gatos," or a "Santa Cruz" – up-scale Anglo-American enclaves in northern California situated amid downscale, heavily Hispanic communities bearing names like "Mountain View," "Gilroy," and "Watsonville." Locals in Palo Alto not only acknowledge the Spanish origin of their placename but also know its meaning, and they can proudly show you a tall tree bearing a sign marking it as the authentic, original *palo alto* of Palo Alto. In Great Hautbois, on the other hand, not only is there no "high wood," there is also a denial of any French association whatsoever. Locals around (there are, actually, not many *in*) Great Hautbois take pains, in their pronunciation and their stories, to display the fundamental Englishness and (which is much the same thing) the deep antiquity of this Norfolk place.

East Anglia does have a number of placenames that locals consider to be "Danish" or "Viking." But the Norse invaders have, after a thousand years, been thoroughly acculturated as part of the "English Heritage."[15] The most noted heritage museum of England is devoted to glorifying the Viking period in York. In East Anglia, a placename ending in "-by," as opposed to the Anglo-Saxon "-ham," is proudly taken to indicate a Norse origin – for example, "Rollesby," "Clippesby," and "Filby," not far from "Ingham," "Stalham," and "Waxham."

On the other hand, the Norse who, as French-speaking Normans, conquered England several centuries later, had, in current views, little impact on placenames. In Norfolk, I have yet to hear any placename interpreted as being French in origin. The only example that the compiler of *A Popular Guide to Norfolk Place-Names* could come up with was a name that referred to the personal name of one of William the Conqueror's standard bearers. Even there, the spelling (Toney for "Toeni") does not make the reference completely transparent, and it is, after all, to a very old Frenchman (Rye 1991:8–9). Another case is instructive: it is said the second element of the South Norfolk village name "Kirby Cane" comes from another of William's knights who came from Caen in Normandy. To argue that an English form so seemingly transparent conceals a story in history is to make the name, albeit French in origin, very English indeed.[16]

In Norfolk, as everywhere else in the world, many kinds of spaces other than settlements become named as places. These names can, like village and town names, be used in ways that contribute to the construction and interpretation of ongoing social interaction. There is, of course, a rich coverage of topographic names for features such as rivers, lakes, marshes, woods, and dunes. Agricultural fields have a long history, diligently pursued locally, of individual names.[17] Residences, too, are commonly named – provided they are of the

proper type. To have a residence name rather than a street number in one's address adds both prestige and a presumption of country life-style. It implies that one lives in a "cottage" in a village and not in a house or flat in a town or city. In Norfolk, my address was "92 High Street"; my landlord's mail went to "Goose Marsh Cottage."

Even better than living in a named "cottage" is living in a "hall." A hall is the traditional residence of the lord of the manor. It is named for the place, which is often the name of the original lord. Lord Gresham lived in Gresham Hall near Gresham village. Nowadays, a hall is as likely to be occupied by a real estate agent as by a squire, but the name of the hall does not change. As with boats, there seems to be a sentiment that a residence name belongs inalienably to the building regardless of who lives there.

Placenames, semantically empty as proper nouns, when used in what Certeau calls "the practice of everyday life," become "names that have ceased precisely to be proper.... A rich indetermination gives them, by means of a semantic rarefaction, the function of articulating a second, poetic geography on top of the geography of the literal, forbidden or permitted meaning.... They seem to be carried as emblems by the travellers they direct and simultaneously decorate."[18]

The Inscription of Place

Baile Beag/Ballybeg, County Donegal, Ireland, 1833:

OWEN: The captain is the man who actually makes the new map. George's task is to see that the place-names on this map are ... correct. ...

MANUS: ... it's a bloody military operation, Owen. And what's Yolland's [George's] function? What's "incorrect" about the place-names we have here?

Brian Friel, *Translations*

A standard feature in any East Anglian village store is a rack of Ordnance Survey maps for the local area. Bookstores in larger towns have these maps for all of Britain. This cartographic

A New Topographical Map of the
COUNTY OF NORFOLK
surveyed and measured in the years
1790, 91, 92, 93 and 94
By Tho. Donald, Tho. Milne
AND ASSISTANTS].

Planned from a scale of one inch to a statute mile.
Executed and published at the expense of the proprietor,
William Faden, Geographer to his Majesty, and to H. R. H.
the Prince of Wales.

In the above map are described all the seats of the nobility
and gentry, woods, parks, heaths, commons, rivers, great
and cross roads, marsh and fen lands, market towns, parishes,
villages, farms etc. Also the remains of Roman roads, camps
and other antiquities; embellished with plans of the towns
of Great Yarmouth, Lynn and Swaftham. The map is printed
on six sheets of the largest atlas papers. Price to subscribers is
Two Guineas and a half, in sheets; to non-subscribers it
will be three guineas.

Figure 22.1 *Text from an advertisement in the* Norfolk Chronicle, *19 August 1797*

component of English culture has a long history, during which East Anglia was not slighted (Barringer 1989; Chubb 1928; Tyacke and Huddy 1980). Earlier mapping was sponsored by private investors, sometimes backed by the Royal Society. Notable county maps were Saxton's of 1571 and Faden's of 1797. Faden, who was the promoter, not the surveyor, sold his map by individual subscription and newspaper ads (Figure 22.1). The period of agricultural improvements and enclosures produced a large number of small mapping efforts covering individual estates. In 1791 the government set up an official mapping agency, the Ordnance Survey, headed by the Duke of Richmond in his role as Master of the King's Ordnance (he was perhaps motivated by a need to keep updating the surveys of his own estate, which increased from 1,100 acres to 17,000 acres during his tenure – this we learn from the current duke's foreword to the offi-

cial history of the Survey [Owen and Pilbeam 1992]).

The Survey was charged with the mission of covering the kingdom with maps. It has done a good job. Although it is a government agency with a military mission, the Survey has always been involved in the commercial aspects of map making; even before the Thatcher era, it was required to support itself by selling its maps to the public. Thus, what is on the maps depends much on public taste, public needs, and public political pressure. Cartographic power, as real as it is (Anderson 1991; Harley 1988), is not monolithic. The cartographic creation of place in Britain has been the outcome of the interplay of a complex of interests and pressures – one of which seems to have been a sincere concern "to get it right," a concern which reveals an underlying assumption that each place has a "correct" name to be discovered. In its history of inscribing placenames, the Ordnance Survey has gone to great lengths to demonstrate its commitment to toponymic, as well as topographic, accuracy. "Truth" in cartography, however, can be an illusive goal for all the familiar postmodern reasons.

Recording local names has caused difficulties for surveyors from the beginning. Regarding Faden's map, J. C. Barringer (1989:2) notes, "The Norfolk pronunciation clearly proved too much for the surveyor of the Aylsham area." But it was the colonial context of Celtic Ireland, where the Ordnance Survey began systematic mapping in the 1830s, that provided the greatest challenge to the aim of "correctly" recording placenames. The ensuing cultural and linguistic misunderstandings, as well as the political entailments of mapping, are wonderfully portrayed in Brian Friel's (1981) play *Translations*. In Ireland, the Survey developed a system of "Name Books" that was subsequently used by surveyors throughout Britain. In these books were listed the names for each place, the variant spellings, and the sources for each variant.

The spelling of each name was, wherever possible, endorsed by written evidence as "when taken down by word of mouth, errors are very liable to occur" and surveyors often pasted into the Name Books typed examples to support their recommendation. Almost anything seemed acceptable, from letter headings and local advertisements to extracts from Bradshaws' Railway Guides. . . . Names could be altered with the support of "at least two good authorities" but important names tended to remain, even if they dropped out of general use and the maps tended to preserve some that would otherwise have faded from existence. . . . In making their recommendations, the Committee always abided by the long-stated principle that Ordnance Survey names should follow those in common use by the residents of an area, even if these were etymologically incorrect or suspect. (Owen and Pilbeam 1992:75)[19]

Ordnance Survey maps not only inscribed the official name in its "correct" spelling but also revealed the importance and significance of the place.

The printing of names on the maps followed a careful hierarchy with the most important names written in the largest and boldest type. The typestyle used for each name gave further information. For example, if a Borough returned a member of Parliament, then its name was printed the same size as other Borough names but in bold type. Market towns were distinguished from ordinary towns in the same way. (Owen and Pilbeam 1992:75)

Antiquities, officially defined as features dating from before 1714 (the date of accession of George I), were marked as "Roman" by large Roman capitals (ROMAN ROAD) or as "Medieval" by Gothic lettering (𝔚𝔥𝔦𝔟𝔢𝔱𝔬𝔫 𝔅𝔯𝔦𝔡𝔤𝔢) (Owen and Pilbeam 1992:75, 152).

A glance at a Survey map, especially one in the small-scale 1:25,000 series, makes it appear that nothing is overlooked. Picking up at random from my desk sheet TG 22/32, Norfolk Broads (North), and beginning at the top righthand corner, I find a small triangle of blue for the sea, some pink for a sandy beach, a line marked MHW for Mean High Water, a seven-meter contour line (all that separates the rest of the map from the North Sea!), a gap through the dunes named "Cart Gap," and a road coded as "generally less than 4 meters wide" (generally much less!) that leads to "New Barn," "Green Farm," and "Whimpwell Green," with fourteen buildings including a "PO" (Post Office). Not far away is "Moat Farm" adjacent to a blue-bordered square labeled, in Gothic lettering to show its medieval antiquity, "𝔐𝔬𝔞𝔱." Convenient to the moat is perhaps the most sought-out symbol on Ordnance Survey maps, "PH" (Public House, i.e., a pub). It seems to be the only building at a place named "The Homestead." Then, isolated out in the middle of a field, is a church iconically coded to have a tower but no steeple. The isolation of churches and the nature of their towers, like the narrowness of roads, are critical constituents of the East Anglian countryside (Frake 1996). Then we come to "The Manor." We are now at the zero-meter contour line (we are heading inland from the coastal dunes, but we are going downhill) and not far from "Hempstead

Marshes," "Commissioner's Drain," and "Ingham Poor's Allotment."

Since we have yet to traverse a full mile, we might as well imagine ourselves walking. That way we can at times depart from the narrow road and take a footpath marked on our map by a dotted line. We must take care, however, to find a *green* dotted line. Green dotted lines mark "Public Rights of Way (Not applicable to Scotland)." Even though we are definitely not in Scotland, it is often impossible to see that green dotted line or anything else resembling a path on the ground. A locally published walking guide for North Norfolk explains how this can happen: "Regretfully, as is usually the case, this delightful lane ends suddenly in a ploughed field; it has so obviously been scrubbed out by some thoughtless landowner whose lust for profit has overridden any sense of duty or responsibility for the environment. Walk through the field . . ." (Birch 1988:49). The back of the map, in fact, warns us: "Public rights of way shown on this map may not be evident on the ground."

Apparent on the ground or not, those dotted green lines on Ordnance Survey maps are diligently defended by the English (except for the landowner whose field is traversed by a line). The nineteenth-century National Footpaths Preservation Society, whose founding was among those listed at the beginning of this essay, has flourished; its members are now "The Ramblers." They can be spotted almost any weekend in rural England trekking across farmers' fields to secure public rights thought to be guaranteed since antiquity by those dotted green lines on Ordnance Survey maps. Even though the Survey map assures us that "public rights of way indicated by these symbols have been derived from Definitive Maps as amended by later enactments or instruments," it goes on, in bold print, to protect itself: **"The representation on this map of any road, track or path is no evidence of the existence of a right of way."**

Deciding after all to stay on the road, we pass Ingham Corner and come to a junction where we find a "Pit (dis)," the "Remains of Priory [Gothic print again] (Trinitarian)," and a school (now a private residence). Very strangely, not marked here with a PH is one

of my favorite pubs in all of Norfolk. It is situated in a carefully restored building that goes back to Chaucer's time. The Ordnance Survey, whose maps miss not a single derelict windmill, ruined abbey, red telephone box, "tumulus," "moated site," or invisible footpath, does miss some things! Why it missed my pub I have no idea, but other omissions are interpretable. Their consideration leads into the realm of unofficial, everyday, practical knowledge tied to particular places.

Local Knowledge

. . . a vessel bound northward. . . . should proceed . . . until Blakeney church bears less than 238°.

. . . a vessel with local knowledge bound for The Wash, after passing Cromer (*Lat. 52° 56' N., Long. 1°18' E.*) may, if of light draught and if the tide suits, proceed along the coast inside of Pollard.

North Sea Pilot III

Maps and charts, by inscribing a place in official records, thereby open the place up. They make it accessible to all. They also improve the place to the official eye. They tidy it up, removing inconsistencies, fuzzy boundaries, and unimportant details. They make the place, all its parts and names, "correct." But the very nature of places, as known to locals in all their inconsistent, fuzzy, and trivial details, affords a built-in line of resistance to public inscription. We are talking naked reality here as well as veiled politics. It is the reality, for example, of that starkly real, unnegotiable world faced by a sailor offshore seeking shelter from a northwest gale. Frantically poring through the pilot book for this treacherous coastline, the sailor latches onto the entry for a nearby bay: "In N weather anchorage may be had in two coves on the N shore." After more instructions come the dreaded lines: "But local knowledge is necessary to avoid the dangers" (US Department of Commerce 1977).[20]

Details – rocks, sandy shoals, kelp beds – unmappable in their tininess, inconsistency, and fluidity, can, nevertheless, become matters of life and death. Such dramas are well known on the Norfolk coast. The pilot book for this coast is studded with references to local knowledge and with bearings to churches whose recognition requires local knowledge. The church at Blakeney, commended as a landmark to the navigator, has, unlike any of the many others visible from offshore in this area, two towers. But the pilot book does not tell us that. (I leave the foregoing sentence from an earlier version of this chapter to stand as a telling example of careless ethnography. My old Norfolk friend Norman Peake, after reading it, gently pointed out my error: "Well, Charles," he said, "actually the pilot book is quite right in not mentioning that second tower on the church at Blakeney – because, I must tell you, it is not, and never has been, visible from the sea. It is obscured by the church roof." Local knowledge is full of tricks for those who presume to report it.)

As one rounds the northeast corner of Norfolk after passing Cromer, heading south, the book reassures the navigator by noting as easily visible landmarks a good number of village churches – those at Trimingham, Bacton, Walcott, Knapton, and Trunch. Then the letdown: "As all these churches have similar square towers they are liable to be confused" (United Kingdom 1960:199.) At this point it is good to keep in mind the local knowledge of a range alignment encoded in a verse I learned over a pint of Suffolk ale at the Ten Bells in Norwich:[21]

Gillingham, Trimingham, and Trunch
Three churches all in a bunch.

Happily, the Happisburg church can be spotted standing out atop what passes for a hill in these parts. That is good news, for at this point the navigator must take great care to avoid the dreaded Haisborough sand, over which floats a buoy marked "N. Haisbro." All three placenames are pronounced the same way: another bit of local knowledge, not for navigating but for telling sea stories at the Ten Bells.

It is the nature of seafaring that some critical knowledge must remain local. One cannot blame the pilot books for that (unless one is John Steinbeck – see his complaints in *Log from the Sea of Cortez*).[22] Yet the necessity for local knowledge in navigation does not deprive

it of the possibility for strategic employment in other kinds of arenas, both economic and symbolic. Locals with this knowledge could sell it to others by piloting for them, or, in former, less upright times, they could withhold it from others, hoping to profit from the ensuing shipwrecks. Local knowledge also affords a symbolic protection from potential assailants. In past wars against the Dutch, French, and Germans there has been great fear of attacks along this exposed shore. In all these cases it is comforting to feel that one's local knowledge gives one some measure of control over outside forces.

The sea, in its navigation and its narratives, may provide prototypical exemplars of local knowledge, but everyday life on land also requires and exploits such knowledge in its maneuvering over both spatial and political terrains. This maneuvering, to use Clifford Geertz's (1983:167) characterization, is a craft of place, and like all such crafts it works "by the light of local knowledge." Just as nautical charts and pilot books contain many gaps, so do the detailed maps provided to the public by the Ordnance Survey. It is not simply a case of details too small to fit on the sheet (we have seen how even invisible footpaths are shown), or even a matter of occasional missing pubs. Early in my work, before I had acquired much local knowledge, I once thought I was lost – off the map – when, driving along a narrow, hedged-lined lane looking for a particular church, I suddenly found before me a cleared expanse surrounded by two rows of barbed wire, studded with machine-gun towers, filled with strange-looking space-age apparatuses, and marked with frightening warning signs. No mark of this on my map, no note of it in my guidebook. Could this be East Anglia? My "lost continent"?

Such military installations are common. Serving as a fixed aircraft carrier for the Royal Air Force and the United States Air Force has been a historic role of the East Anglian countryside since World War II. Some air bases are on the map, some are not. But the presence of all of them is locally obvious. Antennae intrude on the skyline, personnel become part of local life, and jets roar overhead. It is an unavoidable part of everyday life, but it has no place in the English image of the rural countryside as it is talked about, painted, or inscribed in books and on maps.[23]

Other intrusions on the image of the landscape are also missing from maps and guidebooks even when knowledge of them by anyone could in no way be considered a threat to anything except the image itself. There are, for example, mushroom-topped concrete towers periodically marring the otherwise bucolic landscape. The most radical of relativists would regard these silos as ugly. They provide, with local knowledge, great landmarks. But like ugly factories, waste dumps, junkyards, and the slaughterhouse in Stalham prominently signed "George Bush & Sons, Wholesale Butchers," they do not exist as places on the map.

Everyday knowledge of place is not just for filling in the gaps, the missing pubs, in official cartographic renditions of place. It fills a greater void in the renditions of space. It is, observes Michel de Certeau (1988:127), like the architect in a poem by Morgenstein who

Removed the spaces from the fence
and built of them a residence.

The architect is accomplishing "a transformation of the void into a plenitude, of the in-between into an established place." Local knowledge accomplishes such a transformation by telling stories. "What the map cuts up, the story cuts across" (Certeau 1988:127, 129). It creates places out of nothing. Margaret Rodman (1992:650), while mapping a Vanuatu village, experienced such a creation by a woman's stories about the birth sites of her children 'Although I put an X on my map in the locations she pointed out, they were marked by nothing I could see in the landscape. Yet for the old woman these memories were etched as clearly in the landscape as if they bore commemorative plaques."

There is power to this local knowledge that is part of everyday life. There is the counterpower of the everyday against the official, what Michael Herzfeld (1991), talking about time rather than place (which is much the same thing), calls the resistance of "social time" to official "monumental time." As in Herzfeld's Crete, a primary battlefield for the employ-

ment of this resistance in East Anglia is that surrounding government programs of preservation and restoration, especially as they conflict with the interests of local landowners and farmers. In East Anglia there are other battles, too. Outsiders, primarily tourists, often come into conflict with locals. The power of local knowledge helps both to identify the outsider and to give the local the advantage. Much of this conflict stems from the tourist invasion of the Broads, an arena for both terrestrial and nautical local knowledge.

There is yet another realm for the employment of everyday knowledge, one in which it is the everyday world, not the official one, that is an instrument of exploitation. Local knowledge not only can empower by creating places out of official cracks, it can also disempower by exploiting those who have fallen through the cracks – people who, in the view of others, have no place at all. They are known to locals, who have a place, as "travelers." Prototypically, "travelers" are Gypsies, but the term, in spite of its official recognition in the form of special school programs for them, is used very loosely. There are so-called "New-Age travelers." And there are people who are simply homeless. In rural Norfolk they fill the role of migrant workers for farmers needing cheap, temporary labor. A "traveler" is the ethnic identity assigned to someone who fills that role. A "traveler" has no place.

No place is where one finds the powerless. It is not to be confused with "nowhere," which, in East Anglia, is a place.

A Nowhere Place

But we lived in a fairy-tale place. In a lock-keeper's cottage, by a river, in the middle of the Fens. Far away from the wide world. . . . On those nights when my mother would be forced to tell me stories, it would seem that in our lock-keeper's cottage we were in the middle of nowhere. . . . A fairy-tale land, after all.
                                  Graham Swift, *Waterland*

Once, during a long chat about the meaning of life, the state of the world, and the depressing East Anglian weather, a Norfolk friend suggested that I read William Morris's utopian vision of 1890 called *News from Nowhere*.[24] The book itself is not especially relevant to this discussion, but the appeal to this Norfolk man, who lives in a place called "Fenside," of a utopia named "Nowhere" struck a resonant chord. "Nowhere" pops up regularly in East Anglian talk about place. It receives lyrical expression in Graham Swift's (1983) account in *Waterland* of a boyhood in the East Anglian fens. It occurs as a local name for various out-of-the-way places such as underneath an old medieval bridge near the two-towered church at Blakeney. Jane Hales (1969:25) reports: "Most people hereabouts should know that underneath Wiveton stone bridge is Nowhere.... 'Why that's called Nowhere, that's above my know,' said a man at Glandford Mill further upstream."

I have yet to encounter a field named "Nowhere" in Norfolk, but I would be surprised if there were not one somewhere in East Anglia. Agricultural fields have names, and remoteness, of which "nowhere" is the ultimate expression, is a common theme; witness the fields named for faraway places – China, Siberia, Babylon, End of the World (Field 1989). These field names, like Graham Swift's prose, suggest Nebraska or even Wyoming. But one is in East Anglia in a cozy cottage, under a medieval bridge, or within a securely hedged little field. Remoteness, Deighton's "lost continent," is difficult to construct in East Anglia, but people try.

There is said to be another Norfolk place called "Nowhere." It is a part of the estuarian wetlands of the parish of Acle (Walker n.d.). It also seems to be located only in local knowledge; I have not been able to find it inscribed on any map or in any guidebook. In recent decades, far from being nowhere, this area has been the battleground of a fight to preserve the traditional marshland grazing economy from conversion to drained grainfields, a more profitable alternative only because of European Community farm subsidies (Ewans 1992). The placename "Nowhere" conjures up an image of nonthreatening past, contained within local knowledge, as a battle flag in this conflict of local interests. How does one construe a populous, open, flat, accessible area as

Nowhere? By putting its buildings, its scenes, its stories into the past, a time now forever inaccessible except in nostalgic reconstructions. Like China, the past is a remote place.

An Improved Place

By such improvements as I have suggested ...you may give it a higher character. You may raise it into a place.

Jane Austen, *Mansfield Park*

In this passage Jane Austen is clearly poking fun at her character's improving talk. (The character is Henry Crawford, the same gentlemen who "never inquires.") There can be too much of a good thing. But that "improvement" is a good thing for the English, then and now, there can be no doubt. It is improvement that makes the place. Even "nature" needs improvement to become, or be restored to, a "natural" place. The alternative to improvement is to let it go, to invite decay, spoilage, unruly growth, untidiness. One's place can be "lost," but never should it be abandoned. "It is an English creed that all land requires human supervision. Far from knowing best, nature needs vigilant guidance.... The prospect of unmanaged wasteland is utterly repugnant" (Lowenthal 1991:218). No search here for the American dream of "unspoiled wilderness" – an oxymoron to the English.

These differences in the attitudes of the English and the Americans about nature are, of course, not unrelated to the kinds of nature each finds around them. The English do not have much in the way of untamed nature in their vicinity anyway. Not long ago it was thought that the Norfolk Broads of East Anglia were a rare example of pure nature in England. The Broads are lakelike widenings in the network of rivers and channels that thread through the marshes and wetland woods ("carr") of eastern Norfolk and northeastern Suffolk. They are billed as a natural wonderland, a boater's paradise, a bird watcher's dream. In the 1960s, a masterful piece of geographical, geological, pedological, hydrographical, botanical, and historical analysis demonstrated conclusively that the Broads, like the former inland lakes of Holland, were the product of peat digging on a massive scale in the late Middle Ages when Norfolk was heavily populated, poorly wooded, and fuel hungry. To find that one's natural paradise was manmade would be a disaster in the United States. Imagine the dismay of a backpacker in the Sierras upon discovering that the pristine lake before her was in fact a reservoir built by Pacific Gas and Electric. Not so in East Anglia. Even though they were published in a technical monograph of the Royal Society of Geography, the results of the Broads study became well known and accepted, so far as I can discern, without much comment almost immediately.[25]

The story of the origin of the Broads is now part of common knowledge. Most people I talk to express surprise that anyone could have thought differently. It is only natural that the Broads were the product of human activity. "The Broads are really very pleasant. Do you know how they originated?" The Broads, like the rest of the countryside, have become part of history. When one sails on them, one is sailing through very pleasant places, sheltered, like England, one's island, both by surrounding water and by stories that immerse one in a past of English accomplishments. It was improvement that raised the Broads, like an English garden, out of raw nature into a place. Of course, one cannot relax. As it does in a garden, it takes work, improving work, to keep the Broads from becoming overgrown. This has been the fate of many Broadland areas because of past neglect, pollution, and drainage. These areas must be restored to their prior, but not their original, state. They must be protected both from natural decay and from human despoilment (Ewans 1992).

Improvement, then, is a good thing. But the banner of "improvement" can fly over quite antithetical agendas for action. This has been true ever since the banner was first raised back in the times that informed John Clare's poetry, John Constable's paintings, and Jane Austen's novels. In that period a discourse emerged that has structured representations of place down to the present, accommodating within its dialectic the enormous changes in ways of life that have marked the emergence,

triumph, and crisis of modern society in its English version. This discourse was not, however, simply the product of imaginative novelists, inspired artists, and creative poets. Profound things were happening in the world of the English at that time, things that, strangely, do not at first sight appear very clearly in the novels, poems, and paintings of the time.

Artists remained indifferent to the spectacle of technical progress, environmental renewal and social unrest. . . . Landowners did not want pictures of new enclosures or new machines or new farmsteads and they certainly did not think of themselves as transforming the countryside. They were not in the business of revolutionizing rural society. On the contrary, they saw their role as pillars of stable communities and their efforts were devoted to securing and perpetuating their position at the top of the social hierarchy. . . . Arguably, agrarian improvements were regarded at the time as restoring the order and composure attained in a classical golden age, dispelling the ignorance and superstition that had supervened during the gothic middle ages. (Prince 1988:115–16)

Improvement could be interpreted not as leading to a new era, a new kind of society, but as an intervention that returned one to the more pleasant times of the past. Improvement reconstructed history.

The painters and poets of the seventeenth and eighteenth centuries were not hiding anything from the landowners or, most certainly, from the landless. The changes taking place were chronicled and praised by less literary observers. In 1804, for example, Arthur Young published his *General View of the Agriculture of the County of Norfolk* as a report to the "Board of Agriculture and Internal Improvement." It portrays, in the format of objective observation, improvement as innovation: new tools, new cropping methods, new field layouts. It also documents what is happening to the poor: sometimes they are better off, sometimes worse. Norfolk leads the country in agricultural improvement. No nostalgia here. No preservation of the past. The landowners may have wanted nostalgic pictures in their halls and romantic novels in their libraries, but they wanted profits in their fields.

There were objections to improvement, both in nostalgic portrayal and in brutal deed. A poet of the time, John Clare, composed pieces such as *The Shepherd's Calendar* (1827) that at first glance seem to be rather simple pastoral verses. On closer inspection, they reveal themselves to be subtle yet powerful protests against the agricultural transformations occurring in Clare's home place (Barrell 1972). Agricultural improvement was neither a return to the past golden age nor a step to a better future. It was a move toward exploitation that was producing hardship and deprivation among masses of people. This message was carried more forcibly, with no pretense at poetic subtlety, by William Cobbet (1967 [1830]), who rode around the countryside in the early nineteenth century writing reports of what he saw. The painters, too, took some poetic hits. Here is an obscure one penned by the Reverend John Eagles in 1826 – not commendable poetry perhaps, but the point is clear:

Learn this ye painters of dead stumps,
Old barges, and canals, and pumps,
Paint something fit to see, no view
Near Brentford, Islington, or Kew
Paint any thing, but what you do.

These lines appear as an epigraph in Francis Klingender's (1972) work on the industrial art of the nineteenth century – art depicting, sometimes as beautiful, sometimes as ugly, the changes in the real landscape. Such art did not have much of a future, at least locally in East Anglia.

Local paintings, local poetry, and books of local history continue to improve the visual reality of contemporary landscapes by ignoring the RAF installations, concrete silo towers, slaughterhouses, suburban housing tracts, and travelers' caravans. They attend only to old windmills, medieval churches, hedged roads, and gaff-rigged sailing barges (the famous Norfolk "wherry") – authentic constituents of the East Anglian countryside. I showed the Reverend Mr. Eagles's nineteenth-century verse to a Norfolk friend who was complaining about the plethora of unimaginative landscapes by local painters in an art show at the village church. He quickly composed a modern version:

Learn this you painters of Grebe and Heron,
Old windmills and wherrys, whereon the
    Broads they've long since gone.
Paint something fit to see,
That speaks of the 20th century,
Paint anything, a pylon, a parking lot, a dying
    tree.
Well maybe not – there's too much grief in
    everyday reality
And nostalgia is not the thing it used to be.

The notion of "improvement" as the restoring of a past that not only was more pleasant and more sheltered but also is a part of heritage, a component of identity, lives on today in opposition to the idea of "improvement" as progress, development, modernization, and urbanization. National commentators like Patrick Wright portray the institutions of preservation and reconstruction in British society, the flourishing successors to the nineteenth-century societies listed at the beginning of this chapter, as tools of the conservation establishment.[26] He cites, in horror, a rather comically extreme expression of the conservative view given by Arthur Bryant in 1929 (P. Wright 1985:53): "And the spirit of the past – that sweet and lovely breath of Conservatism – can scarcely touch him. It is for modern Toryism to create a world of genial social hours and loved places, upon which the conservative heart of Everyman can cast anchor." Echoing Wright's lament, Robert Hewison (1987), in his *The Heritage Industry: Britain in a Climate of Decline*, warns that "a creeping takeover by the past" is Britain's most dangerous enemy.

At the local level, at least in North Norfolk, the battle lines are drawn somewhat differently. It is difficult to discern a stable front line with the same troops always on one side. The preservation people are seen to be at odds with the bastions of local conservatism, the local farmers. The new outsiders, ex-urbanites and commuters, whether Conservative, Labor, or something else in politics, see themselves as progressive and forward-looking in the active defense of the countryside as "heritage." They see the farmers as the enemies of the countryside, with no concern to preserve anything. "They think the hedges, barns, and windmills belong to them!" The government, far from having the monolithic agenda ascribed to it, is caught in between. Various branches and levels of it find themselves at odds in particular conflicts, which are very local. They are fights over particular places: who owns them, who defines them, who uses them. Another place, another battle.

In North Norfolk, the bloodiest recent confrontation was the battle of Waxham Barn. This is an old barn even by local standards. It has been around, they say, in one form or another on this spot for some four hundred years. The farmer on whose land it was figured it had outlived its usefulness. He applied for a permit to demolish it so he could replace it with something more useful. The local agency, dominated by farmers, approved. Nonfarmers, nonlocals, and, especially, county preservation officials were appalled. "Why, that barn has got a hammer-beam roof! There's no other like it in all England." Before the farmer could lift a sledge hammer, the county had bought the barn out from under him and embarked on a several-million-pound restoration project.

Now local farmers were appalled. "Two million pounds for a barn! The country's full of old barns with any kind of roof you could want. If it were up to me, I'd blow 'er up." (I was told this by a farmer at the fourteenth-century pub not marked on the map. We were deep into local knowledge). Even local preservationists, eager to save their fifteenth-century church (and every locality has one), were disturbed. In discourse everyone wants "improvement"; in practice people fight wars over what it means to improve a barn. The arguments are old and the images much the same: "I have heard a defence of Covent Garden against plans for development, which repeated in almost every particular the defence of the commons in the period of parliamentary enclosures," reports Raymond Williams (1985 [1973]:291), who goes on to say of two persistent images of this discourse, "Clearly the ideas of the country and the city have specific contents and histories, but just as clearly, at times, they are forms of isolation and identification of more general processes."

What one cannot fail to learn when trying to do ethnography in England is the horrible complexity of it all. It is very difficult to sort out the oppressors from the oppressed, the colonialist from the colonized, the improver from the degrader, the good guys from the bad guys. In some respects, when standing in the middle of a Norfolk field I am in the center of a busy, active world; in other respects, standing there I am on the periphery, in a marginal, lost, nowhere world. More typically, ethnographic places somehow, perhaps because of their greater strangeness, seem simpler. Their people are the oppressed, the colonized, the marginal – the good guys. Working in those kinds of places, anthropologists have begun to seek out the salient issues of exploitation and power in discourse and practice. This search seems harder when the places are more familiar, more like our home place. Whether or not our kinds of places are "really" more complex than other places or just seem that way to us, we must entertain the possibility that there are overlooked complexities still to uncover back in our second homes, the ethnographic places of the anthropologist's world. Perhaps all places should be seen as equally ethnographic and, like human language, equally complex and equally rich.[27]

As an anthropologist I have learned to find the English interesting. Even more remarkable, as a reader of novels, I have learned to find Jane Austen interesting. Having begun with Len Deighton, let me give the final word back to her. Her character Emma, in the novel of the same name, upon seeing "Abbey-Mill Farm, with meadows in front, and the river making a close and handsome curve around it," construes a place, an English place:

It was a sweet view – sweet to the eye and the mind. English verdure, English culture, English comfort, seen under a sun bright, without being oppressive.

This construction remains firmly in English imagination and English discourse. It is a pleasant image, embedded in past times, of sheltered identity. It also mentions the weather.

NOTES

1. Selected from listings in Lowe (1989:114), Wright (1985:49–51), and Lowenthal (1985:104).
2. This study builds upon a previous exploration of these themes (Frake 1996). The references and acknowledgments listed there are relevant to this work as well.
3. "Within particular nations, those who most nearly resemble 'ourselves' appear to be 'people without culture'" (Rosaldo 1988:79).
4. For some recent complaints on this theme, see Rosaldo (1988), Keesing (1990), and Frake (1994).
5. The archaeologist Tom Williamson (1993:1) has claimed that "Norfolk is arguably the last truly rural county in south-eastern England."
6. Many "farmers," now and in the past, have owned the farms they operate, but precise statistics on landownership in England are difficult to come by. See Newby (1988), Barnes (1993), and Frake (1996).
7. The census for 1992 tells us that "East Anglia has the fastest growing population. . . . Despite this it remains the most thinly populated English region" (United Kingdom 1992:12). For more description and documentation of this economic and demographic history, see Riches (1967 [1937]), Newby (1978), Wade-Martins (1993), and Williamson (1993), as well as Frake (1996) and the references cited therein.
8. English translations of current French attempts to sort out place-related meanings are instructive in this regard; see, for example Certeau (1988:117–18) and Berdoulay (1989:124–5).
9. For Norfolk, see Blomefeld's (1805–9) ten-volume classic, *An Essay Toward a Topographical History of the County of Norfolk*, Cooke's (1822) *A Topographical and Statistical Description of the County of Norfolk*, and Woodward, Ewing, and Turner's (1842) *The Norfolk Topographer's Manual*.
10. The phrasing here is intended to make it clear that I make no claims about the "real" sources of English placenames; my claims refer to the contemporary English discourse about placenames. This discourse is well documented in the many books on placenames, all of which seek the true, original meaning and original language of each name; the classic reference for England is Ekwall (1960), now in its fourth edition. For Norfolk there is Rye (1991).
11. See Newby (1988:5) as well as the discussion by Lowenthal (1991:209–10) in a paper whose title, "British National Identity and the English Landscape," displays the contrast.
12. East Anglians feel strongly not only that their speech is still distinctive in England but also that specific regions within East Anglia can be distinguished: "When my wife and I moved from East Suffolk to North Norfolk I was immediately struck by the difference in the people. There were even facial differences to be noted and more especially a different approach to life. . . . I did once live south of the river Stour for a year. They laughed at me when I went home and said that I had an Essex accent" (Hill 1990:18). The archaeologist and historian of Norfolk, Tom Williamson (1993:184), has described the county as "a land apart, distinct in the appearance of its landscape, and in the speech of most of its inhabitants, from London and the South-East." Some sense of the linguistic realities behind these claims can be gained from Trudgill's professional studies (1974, 1990). Mardle's (1973) *Broad Norfolk* gives a unprofessional account of local speech forms and speech style. His pseudonym and title entail wordplays whose interpretation requires local knowledge. It is not only in rural pubs that one can witness multivocalic displays by the British – see the description in the *Economist* (1993) of Parliamentary sessions: "The hotchpotch of accent and language remains a fascinating testimony to the durability of the

British class and regional chasms. In no country in the world can the personae of parliament be so type-cast by the inflection of their voices." The phrase "in no [other] country" is a predictable introduction to English descriptions of themselves (Frake 1996). In this case the statement may well not be literally true – there are plenty of multivocal parliaments in the world – but it is a true reflection of English attitudes about their speech, their classes, and their localisms.

13. Morris and Brown (1984) give the original Latin text of the Domesday Book for Norfolk with an English translation. Barringer (1989) reprints Faden's map. The story of Saxton's map is told by Tyacke and Huddy (1980).

14. Snorri is a venerable Norse name. I learned that when I turned to Jorge Luis Borges as an escape from working on this chapter: "In the course of my reading," says Borges, "I discovered another historical date. It happened in Iceland, in the thirteenth century of our era: in 1225, let us say. The historian and polygraph Snorri Sturlason, at his country house in Borgarfjord, wrote down, for the enlightenment of future generations, the details of the last exploit of the famous king Hararld Sigurdarson, called the Implacable (Hardrada)." There is an English connection. Hararld the Implacable, Borges says Snorri wrote, fought against King Harold of England at York. He lost (Borges 1967:180). Harold went on to be conquered by William of Normandy. We can imagine that much earlier, in 943, let us say, two other Norse Snorris, one great, the other little, each founded a village among the Saxons in the land of the North folk.

15. The Englishness of the Norse heritage was certified by Winston Churchill (1963 [1956]:82) himself in his usual style: "The blood-stream of these vigorous individualists [the Vikings], proud and successful men of the sword, mingled henceforward in the Island race. A vivifying, potent, lasting, and resurgent quality was added to the breed. . . . All through English history this strain continues to play a gleaming part."

16. Some inhabitants of a village called Trunch, shortly to be commemorated in verse, feel their peculiarly abrupt, monosyllabic placename is the only "Celtic" one in Norfolk.

17. See Field (1989) for a guide to Norfolk field names.

18. Certeau (1988:104–5). I have here reversed the order of his sentences.

19. Unfortunately the original Name Books for Norfolk County were destroyed by enemy action in 1940 (United Kingdom n.d.).

20. Geertz's essay entitled "Local Knowledge" is about the law, whose practitioners do not, I believe, often use the phrase itself in their practice. Among seafarers, on the other hand, not only is local knowledge critical to the practice of their craft, but the phrase itself is an integral part of that practice. Its use at sea provides the prototypical meaning of "local knowledge." (During the seminar at which this paper was presented, Geertz informed us that he has since learned that lawyers who practice in the American South do, in fact, have a term for "local knowledge." They call it "home cookin'.")

21. Variants of this verse seem to have a long history. One, dating back to 1681, is cited by Hales and Bennett (1971:102).

22. Steinbeck and Rickets (1962 [1941]).

23. Harley (1988:289), in his discussion "Maps, Knowledge, and Power," notes that nuclear waste dumps are omitted from official USGS maps.

24. Morris's "Nowhere" is the name of Samuel Butler's earlier utopia, "Erewhon," spelled backward.

25. The report (Lambert et al. 1960) is one of those rare masterpieces of true science, both natural and human: it is clearly written and thoroughly documented with evidence gathered by painstaking research within a variety of disciplines. It adds a bit of solid truth to what we know of the world. I recommend reading it as an aspirin for postmodern headaches. Frake

(1996) has more on the symbolic and political significance of the Broads.

26. The National Trust now has 2 percent of the English population as registered members; the Royal Society for the Protection of Birds has some 400,000 members (Rogers 1989:100).

27. See the recent work of John and Jean Comaroff (1992:158), who compare Raymond Williams's analysis of discourse, history, and power in England with their own in tribal South Africa: "In his study of *The Country and the City* in modern English literature, he notes that the rural-urban opposition served as a very general model for interpreting a radically changing social order. Inasmuch as this opposition lent itself to the expression of differing visions of English life, it evoked a complex discourse about society, production, class, and gender – a discourse, that is, about history. . . . It is not only in Africa that those caught up in the processes of radical change come to terms with their history by means of a suggestive opposition."

REFERENCES

Anderson, Benedict. (1991). Imagined Communities: Reflections on the Origin and Spread of Nationalism. 2nd ed. London: Verso.

Barnes, Pam. (1993). Norfolk Landowners since 1880. Norwich: Centre of East Anglian Studies, University of East Anglia.

Barrell, John. (1972). The Idea of Landscape and the Sense of Place, 1730–1840: An Approach to the Poetry of John Clare. Cambridge: Cambridge University Press.

Barringer, J. C. (1989). Faden's Map of Norfolk. First printed 1797. Dereham, Norfolk: Larks Press.

Basso, Keith. (1988). "Speaking with Names": Language and Landscape among the Western Apache, *Cultural Anthropology* 3(2):99–130.

Berdoulay, Vincent. (1989). Place, Meaning, and Discourse in French Language Geography. *In* The Power of Place: Bringing Together Geographical and Sociological Imaginations, John A. Agnew and James S. Duncan, eds., pp. 124–39. London: Unwin Hyman.

Birch, Mel. (1988). Historic Walks in Norfolk. Woolpit, Suffolk: Images Publications.

Blomefeld, Francis. (1805–9). An Essay toward a Topographical History of the County of Norfolk. 10 vols. London: W. Bulmer.

Borges, Jorge Luis. (1967). A Personal Anthology. New York: Grove Press.

Carlin, George. (1973). Occupation: Foole. LP. New York: Dead Sea Music and Little David Records.

Certeau, Michel de. (1988). The Practice of Everyday Life. Berkeley: University of California Press.

Chubb, T. (1928). A Descriptive List of the Printed Maps of Norfolk, 1574–1916. Norwich, U.K.: Jarrold & Sons.

Churchill, Winston. (1963 [1956]). The Birth of Britain. New York: Bantam.

Clare, John. (1827). The Shepherd's Calendar. London: James Duncan.

Cobbet, William. (1967 [1830]). Rural Rides. Harmondsworth, U.K.: Penguin.

Comaroff, John, and Jean Comaroff. (1992). Ethnography and the Historical Imagination. Boulder, Colorado: Westview Press.

Cooke, G. A. (1822). A Topographical and Statistical Description of the County of Norfolk. London: Sherwood, Neely, and Jones.

Deighton, Len. (1982). XPD. New York: Ballantine.

Economist. (1993). Jolly Good Show. 326.7796, January 30, p. 55.

Ekwall, Eilert. (1960). The Concise Oxford Dictionary of English Place-Names. 4th ed. Oxford: Oxford University Press.

Ewans, E. (1992). The Battle for the Broads. Lavenham, Suffolk: Terence Dalton.

Field, John. (1989). English Field Names: A Dictionary. Gloucester, U.K.: Sutton.

Frake, Charles O. (1964). Notes on Queries in Ethnography. *American Anthropologist* 66:132–45.

——. (1994). Cognitive Anthropology: An Origin Story. *In* The Remaking of Psychological Anthropology, M. M Suárez-

Orozco, G. Spindler, and L. Spindler, eds., pp. 244–53. Fort Worth, Texas: Harcourt Brace.

——. (1996). A Church Too Far Near a Bridge Oddly Placed: The Cultural Construction of the Norfolk Countryside. *In* Redefining Nature: Ecology, Culture and Domestication, Roy Ellen and Katsuyoshi Fukui, eds., pp. 89–115. Oxford: Berg.

Friel, Brian. (1981). Translations. London: Faber.

Fuller, Thomas. (1642). The Holy State and the Profane State. London.

Geertz, Clifford. (1983). Local Knowledge: Further Essays in Interpretive Anthropology. New York: Basic Books.

Hales, Jane. (1969). The East Wind: An Unusual Guide to Norfolk. Hunstanton, U.K.: Anglia Publications.

Hales, Jane, and William Bennett. (1971). Looking at Norfolk. Wisbech, Cambridgeshire: Charles N. Veal.

Hallowell, A. Irving. (1965). The History of Anthropology as an Anthropological Problem. *Journal of the History of the Behavioral Sciences* 1:24–38.

Harley, J. B. (1988). Maps, Knowledge, and Power. *In* The Iconography of the Landscape, Denis Cosgrove and Stephen Daniels, eds., pp. 277–312. Cambridge: Cambridge University Press.

Herzfeld, Michael. (1991). A Place in History: Social and Monumental Time in a Cretan Town. Princeton, New Jersey: Princeton University Press.

Hewison, Robert. (1987). The Heritage Industry: Britian in a Climate of Decline. London: Methuen.

Hill, David. (1990). A Living in the Past: An East Anglian Venture in Antiques and Bygones. Woolpit, Suffolk: Images Publications.

Hood, Christobel M., ed. (1938). The Chorography of Norfolk: An Historicall and Chorographicall Description of Norffolck by John Norden (early 17th c.). Norwich: Jarrold & Sons.

Keesing, Roger. (1990). Theories of Culture Revisited. *Canberra Anthropology* 13:46–60.

Klingender, Francis D. (1972). Art and the Industrial Revolution. 2nd ed., edited and revised by Arthur Elton. London: Paladin.

Knox, John. (1558). The First Blast of the Trumpet against the Monstrous Regiment of Women. London.

Lambert, J. M., J. N. Jennings, C. T. Smith, Charles Green, and J. N. Hutchinson. (1960). The Making of the Broads: A Reconsideration of Their Origin in the Light of New Evidence. RGS Research Series, no. 3. London: Royal Geographical Society.

Lowe, Philip. (1989). The Rural Idyll Defended. *In* The Rural Idyll, G. E. Mingay, ed., pp. 113–31. London: Routledge.

Lowenthal, David. (1985). The Past Is a Foreign Country. Cambridge: Cambridge University Press.

——. (1991). British National Identity and the English Landscape. *Rural History* 2(2):205–30.

Mardle, Jonathan. (1973). Broad Norfolk. Norwich, U.K.: Wensum.

Morris, John, and Philippa Brown, eds. (1984). Domesday Book: Norfolk. 2 vols. Chicester, U.K: Phillimore.

Morris, William. (1933 [1890]). News from Nowhere, or, an Epoch of Rest, Being Some Chapters from a Utopian Romance. London: Longmans, Green and Company.

Newby, Howard. (1988). Country Life: A Social History of Rural England. London: Cardinal.

Newby, Howard, Collin Bell, David Rose, and Peter Saunders. (1978). Property, Paternalism and Power: Class and Control in Rural England. London: Hutchinson.

Norfolk Federation of Women's Institutes. (1990). The Norfolk Village Book. Newbury, U.K.: Countryside Books.

Owen, Tim, and Elaine Pilbeam. (1992). Ordnance Survey: Map Makers to Britain since 1791. London: Her Majesty's Stationery Office.

Prince, Hugh. (1988). Art and Agrarian Change. *In* The Iconography of the Landscape, Denis Cosgrove and Stephen Daniels, eds., pp. 98–118. Cambridge: Cambridge University Press.

Riches, Naomi. (1967 [1937]). The Agricultural Revolution in Norfolk. London: Frank Cass & Company.

Rodman, Margaret. (1992). Empowering Place: Multilocality and Multivocality. *American Anthropologist* 94(3):640–56.

Rogers, Alan. (1989). A Planned Countryside. *In* The Rural Idyll, G. E. Mingay, ed., pp. 92–102. London: Routledge.

Rosaldo, Renato. (1988). Ideology, Place, and People without Culture. *Cultural Anthropology* 3(1):77–87.

Rye, James. (1991). A Popular Guide to Norfolk Place-Names. Dereham, Norfolk: Larks Press.

Schegloff, E. A. (1972). Notes on Conversational Practice: Formulating Place. *In* Language and Social Context, P. P. Giglioli, ed., pp. 95–135. Middlesex, U.K.: Penguin.

Steinbeck, John, and E. F. Rickets. (1962 [1941]). Log from the Sea of Cortez. New York: Viking Press.

Swift, Graham. (1983). Waterland. London: Picador.

Trudgill, David. (1974). The Social Differentiation of English in Norwich. Cambridge: Cambridge University Press.

——. (1990). The Dialects of England. Oxford: Blackwell.

Tyacke, Sarah, and John Huddy. (1980). Christopher Saxton and Tudor Map-Making. London: British Library.

United Kingdom. (1992). Regional Trends 27. London: Central Statistics Office.

——. (n.d.). Records of Ordnance Survey held at the Public Record Office. London: Public Records Office.

US Department of Commerce. (1977). US Coast Pilot, vol. 7. Washington, D.C.: United States Department of Commerce.

Wade-Martins, Peter, ed. (1993). An Historical Atlas of Norfolk. Norwich, U.K.: Norfolk Museum Services.

Walker, Bob. (n.d.). Where's That? A Guide to Over 700 Norfolk Villages. Norwich, U.K.: Petersen Publicity.

Walmsley, Jane. (1987). Brit-Think, Ameri-Think: An Irreverent Guide to Understanding the Great Cultural Ocean that Divides Us. New York: Penguin.

Williams, Raymond. (1985 [1973]). The Country and the City. London: The Hogarth Press.

Williamson, Tom. (1993). The Origins of Norfolk. Manchester: Manchester University Press.

Woodward, Samuel, W. C. Ewing, and Dawson Turner. (1842). The Norfolk Topographer's Manual. London: Nichols and Son.

Wright, Patrick. (1985). On Living in an Old Country: The National Past in Contemporary Britain. London: Verso.

Young, Arthur. (1804). General View of the Agriculture of the Country of Norfolk Drawn Up for the Consideration of the Board of Agriculture and Internal Improvement. London: B. McMillan.

23

Effects of Conscious Purpose on Human Adaptation

Gregory Bateson

"Progress," "learning," "evolution," the similarities and differences between phylogenetic and cultural evolution, and so on, have been subjects for discussion for many years. These matters become newly investigable in the light of cybernetics and systems theory.

In this paper, a particular aspect of this wide subject matter will be examined, namely the role of *consciousness* in the ongoing process of human adaptation.

Three cybernetic or homeostatic systems will be considered: the individual human organism, the human society, and the larger ecosystem. Consciousness will be considered as an important component in the *coupling* of these systems.

A question of great scientific interest and perhaps grave importance is whether the information processed through consciousness is adequate and appropriate for the task of human adaptation. It may well be that consciousness contains systematic distortions of view which, when implemented by modern technology, become destructive of the balances between man, his society and his ecosystem.

To introduce this question the following considerations are offered:

(1) All biological and evolving systems (i.e., individual organisms, animal and human societies, ecosystems, and the like) consist of complex cybernetic networks, and all such systems share certain formal characteristics. Each system contains subsystems which are potentially regenerative, (i.e., which would go into exponential "runaway" if uncorrected. (Examples of such regenerative components are Malthusian characteristics of population, schismogenic changes of personal interaction, armaments races, etc.) The regenerative potentialities of such subsystems are typically kept in check by various sorts of governing loops to achieve "steady state." Such systems are "conservative" in the sense that they tend to conserve the truth of propositions about the values of their component variables – especially they conserve the values of those variables which otherwise would show exponential change. Such systems are homeostatic, (i.e., the effects of small changes of input will be negated and the steady state maintained by *reversible* adjustment.

(2) But "*plus c'est la même chose, plus ça change.*" This converse of the French aphorism seems to be the more exact description of biological and ecological systems. A constancy of some variable is maintained by changing other variables. This is characteristic of the engine with a governor: the constancy of rate of rotation is maintained by altering the fuel supply. *Mutatis mutandis*, the same logic

underlies evolutionary progress: those mutational changes will be perpetuated which contribute to the constancy of that complex variable which we call "survival." The same logic also applies to learning, social change, etc. The ongoing truth of certain descriptive propositions is maintained by altering other propositions.

(3)   In systems containing many interconnected homeostatic loops, the changes brought about by an external impact may slowly spread through the system. To maintain a given variable (V_1) at a given value, the values of V_2, V_3, etc., undergo change. But V_2 and V_3 may themselves be subject to homeostatic control or may be linked to variables (V_4, V_5, etc.) which are subject to control. This second-order homeostasis may lead to change in V_6, V_7, etc. And so on.

(4)   This phenomenon of spreading change is in the widest sense a sort of *learning*. Acclimation and addiction are special cases of this process. Over time, the system becomes dependent upon the continued presence of that original external impact whose immediate effects were neutralized by the first order homeostasis.

Example: under the impact of Prohibition, the American social system reacted homeostatically to maintain the constancy of the supply of alcohol. A new profession, the bootlegger, was generated. To control this profession, changes occurred in the police system. When the question of repeal was raised, it was expectable that certainly the bootleggers and possibly the police would be in favor of maintaining Prohibition.

(5)   In this ultimate sense, all biological change is conservative and all learning is aversive. The rat, who is "rewarded" with food, accepts that reward to neutralize the changes which hunger is beginning to induce; and the conventionally drawn distinction between "reward" and "punishment" depends upon a more or less arbitrary line which we draw to delimit that subsystem which we call the "individual." We call an external event "reward" if its occurrence corrects an "internal" change which would be punishing. And so on.

(6)   Consciousness and the "self" are closely related ideas, but the ideas (possibly related to genotypically determined premises of territory) are crystallized by that more or less arbitrary line which delimits the individual and defines a logical difference between "reward" and "punishment." When we view the individual as a servosystem coupled with its environment, or as a part of the larger system which is individual + environment, the whole appearance of adaptation and purpose changes.

(7)   In extreme cases, change will precipitate or permit some runaway or slippage along the potentially exponential curves of the underlying regenerative circuits. This may occur without total destruction of the system. The slippage along exponential curves will, of course, always be limited, in extreme cases, by breakdown of the system. Short of this disaster, other factors may limit the slippage. It is important, however, to note that there is a danger of reaching levels at which the limit is imposed by factors which are in themselves deleterious. Wynne-Edwards has pointed out – what every farmer knows – that a population of healthy individuals cannot be directly limited by the available food supply. If starvation is the method of getting rid of the excess population, then the survivors will suffer if not death at least severe dietary deficiency, while the food supply itself will be reduced, perhaps irreversibly, by overgrazing. In principle, the homeostatic controls of biological systems must be activated by variables which are not in themselves harmful. The reflexes of respiration are activated not by oxygen deficiency but by relatively harmless CO_2 excess. The diver who learns to ignore the signals of CO_2 excess and continues his dive to approach oxygen deficiency runs serious risks.

(8)   The problem of coupling self-corrective systems together is central in the adaptation of man to the societies and ecosystems in which he lives. Lewis Carroll long ago joked about the nature and order of *randomness* created by the inappropriate coupling of biological systems. The problem, we may say, was to create a "game" which should be random, not only in the restricted sense in which "matching pennies" is random, but meta-random. The randomness of the moves of the two players of "matching pennies" is restricted to a finite

set of known alternatives, namely "heads" or "tails" in any given play of the game. There is no possibility of going outside this set, no meta-random choice among a finite or infinite set of sets.

By imperfect coupling of biological systems in the famous game of croquet, however, Carroll creates a meta-random game. Alice is coupled with a flamingo, and the "ball" is a hedgehog.

The "purposes" (if we may use the term) of these contrasting biological systems are so discrepant that the randomness of play can no longer be delimited with finite sets of alternatives, known to the players.

Alice's difficulty arises from the fact that she does not "understand" the flamingo, i.e., she does not have systemic information about the "system" which confronts her. Similarly, the flamingo does not understand Alice. They are at "cross-purposes." The problem of coupling man through consciousness with his biological environment is comparable. If consciousness lacks information about the nature of man and the environment, or if the information is distorted and inappropriately selected, then the coupling is likely to generate meta-random sequence of events.

(9) We presume that consciousness is not entirely without effect – that it is not a mere collateral resonance without feedback into the system, an observer behind a one-way mirror, a TV monitor which does not itself affect the program. We believe that consciousness has feedback into the remainder of mind and so an effect upon action. But the effects of this feedback are almost unknown and urgently need investigation and validation.

(10) It is surely true that the content of consciousness is no random sample of reports on events occurring in the remainder of mind. Rather, the content of the screen of consciousness is systematically selected from the enormously great plethora of mental events. But of the rules and preferences of this selection, very little is known. The matter requires investigation. Similarly the limitations of verbal language require consideration.

(11) It appears, however, that the system of selection of information for the screen of consciousness is importantly related to "purpose," "attention," and similar phenomena which are also in need of definition, elucidation, etc.

(12) If consciousness has feedback upon the remainder of mind (9, above), and if consciousness deals only with a skewed sample of the events of the total mind, then there must exist a *systematic* (i.e., nonrandom) difference between the conscious views of self and the world, and the true nature of self and the world. Such a difference must distort the processes of adaptation.

(13) In this connection, there is a profound difference between the processes of cultural change and those of phylogenetic evolution. In the latter, the Weismannian barrier between soma and germ plasma is presumed to be totally opaque. There is no coupling from environment to genome. In cultural evolution and individual learning, the coupling through consciousness is present, incomplete and probably distortive.

(14) It is suggested that the specific nature of this distortion is such that *the cybernetic nature of self and the world tends to be imperceptible to consciousness,* insofar as the contents of the "screen" of consciousness are determined by considerations of purpose. The argument of purpose tends to take the form "*D* is desirable; *B* leads to *C*; *C* leads to *D*; so *D* can be achieved by way of *B* and *C*." But, if the total mind and the outer world do not, in general, have this lineal structure, then by forcing this structure upon them, we become blind to the cybernetic circularities of the self and the external world. Our conscious sampling of data will not disclose whole circuits but only arcs of circuits, cut off from their matrix by our selective attention. Specifically, the attempt to achieve a change in a given variable, located either in self or environment, is likely to be undertaken without comprehension of the homeostatic network surrounding that variable. The considerations outlined in paragraphs 1 to 7 of this essay will them be ignored. It may be essential for *wisdom* that the narrow purposive view be somehow corrected.

(15) The function of consciousness in the coupling between man and the homeostatic systems around him is, of course, no new phenomenon. Three circumstances, however, make the investigation of this phenomenon an urgent matter.

(16) First, there is man's habit of changing his environment rather than changing himself. Faced with a changing variable (e.g., temperature) within itself which it should control, the organism may make changes *either* within itself *or* in the external environment. It may adapt to the environment or adapt the environment to itself. In evolutionary history, the great majority of steps have been changes within the organism itself; some steps have been of an intermediate kind in which the organisms achieved change of environment by change of locale. In a few cases organisms other than man have achieved the creation of modified microenvironments around themselves, e.g., the nests of hymenopstera and birds, concentrated forests of conifers, fungal colonies, etc.

In all such cases, the logic of evolutionary progress is toward ecosystems which sustain *only* the dominant, environment-controlling species, and its symbionts and parasites.

Man, the outstanding modifier of environment, similarly achieves single-species ecosystems in his cities, but he goes one step further, establishing special environments for his symbionts. These, likewise, become single-species ecosystems: fields of corn, cultures of bacteria, batteries of fowls, colonies of laboratory rats, and the like.

(17) Secondly, the power ratio between purposive consciousness and the environment has changed rapidly in the last one hundred years, and the *rate* of change in this ratio is certainly rapidly increasing with technological advance. Conscious man, as a changer of his environment, is now fully able to wreck himself and that environment – with the very best of conscious intentions.

(18) Third, a peculiar sociological phenomenon has arisen in the last one hundred years which perhaps threatens to isolate conscious purpose from many corrective processes which might come out of less conscious parts of the mind. The social scene is nowadays characterized by the existence of a large number of self-maximizing entities which, in law, have something like the status of "persons" – trusts, companies, political parties, unions, commercial and financial agencies, nations, and the like. In biological fact, these entities are precisely *not* persons and are not even aggregates of whole persons. They are aggregates of *parts* of persons. When Mr Smith enters the board room of his company, he is expected to limit his thinking narrowly to the specific purposes of the company or to those of that part of the company which he "represents." Mercifully it is not entirely possible for him to do this and some company decisions are influenced by considerations which spring from wider and wiser parts of the mind. But ideally, Mr Smith is expected to act as a pure, uncorrected consciousness – a dehumanized creature.

(19) Finally, it is appropriate to mention some of the factors which may act as correctives – areas of human action which are not limited by the narrow distortions of coupling through conscious purpose and where wisdom can obtain.

(*a*) Of these, undoubtedly the most important is love. Martin Buber has classified interpersonal relationships in a relevant manner. He differentiates "I–Thou" relations from "I–It" relations, defining the latter as the normal pattern of interaction between man and inanimate objects. The "I–It" relationship he also regards as characteristic of human relations wherever purpose is more important than love. But if the complex cybernetic structure of societies and ecosystems is in some degree analogous to animation, then it would follow that an "I–Thou" relationship is conceivable between man and his society or ecosystem. In this connection, the formation of "sensitivity groups" in many depersonalized organizations is of special interest.

(*b*) The arts, poetry, music, and the humanities similarly are areas in which more of the mind is active than mere consciousness would admit. "*Le coeur a ses raisons que la raison ne connaît point.*"

(*c*) Contact between man and animals and between man and the natural world breeds, perhaps – sometimes – wisdom.

(*d*) There is religion.

(20)   To conclude, let us remember that Job's narrow piety, his purposiveness, his common sense, and his worldly success are finally stigmatized, in a marvelous totemic poem, by the Voice out of the Whirlwind:

> *Who is this that darkeneth counsel by words*
>   *without understanding . . .*
> *Dost thou know when the wild goats of the*
>   *rock bring forth?*
> *Or canst thou tell when the hinds do calve?*

24

Globes and Spheres:
The Topology of
Environmentalism

Tim Ingold

detachment ↑

Experimental

My purpose in this chapter is no more than to try out a rather embryonic idea. It concerns the significance of the image of the globe in the language of contemporary debate about the environment. Though the image has long been deployed in geopolitical contexts, and even longer in connection with navigation and astronomy, my impression is that its use as a characterization of the *environment* is rather recent. I have in mind such phrases, which slip so readily off the tongues of contemporary policy-markers, as "global environmental change". One is immediately struck by the paradoxical nature of this phrase. An environment, surely, is that which surrounds, and can exist, therefore, only in relation to what is surrounded (Ingold 1992: 40). I do not think that those who speak of the global environment mean by this the environment surrounding the globe. It is *our* environment they are talking about, the world as it presents itself to a universal humanity. Yet how can humans, or for that matter beings of any other kind, possibly be surrounded by a globe? Would it not be fairer to say that it is we who have surrounded it?

My idea is that what may be called the global outlook may tell us something important about the modern conception of the environment as a world which, far from being the ambience of our dwelling, is turned in upon itself, so that we who once stood at its centre become first circumferential and are finally expelled from it altogether (Figure 24.1). In other words, I am suggesting that the notion of the global environment, far from marking humanity's reintegration into the world, signals the culmination of a process of separation.

The image of the globe is familiar to all of us who have gone through a Western schooling and are used to studying models upon which are drawn, in outline, the continents and oceans, and the grid-lines of latitude and longitude. We are taught that this is what the earth looks like, although none of us, with a handful of significant exceptions, has ever seen it. By and large, life is lived at such close proximity to the earth's surface that a global perspective is unobtainable. The significant exceptions comprise, of course, that privileged band of astronauts who have viewed the earth from outer space. In a sense, the astronauts's relation to the real globe seen through the window of the spacecraft mirrors the schoolchild's relation to the model globe in the classroom: in both cases the world appears as an object of contemplation, detached from the domain of lived experience. For the child the world is separately encapsulated in the model; for the astronaut life is separately encapsulated, albeit temporarily, in the space module. My point with this comparison is a simple one:

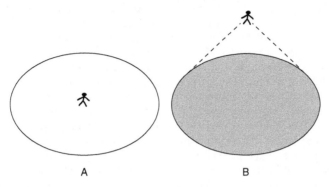

Figure 24.1 *Two views of the environment: (A) as a lifeworld; (B) as a globe*

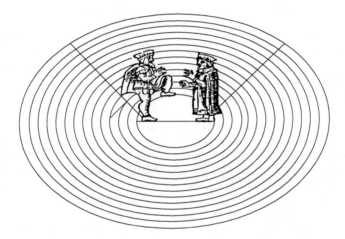

Figure 24.2 *The fourteen spheres of the world, as drawn by Giovanni Camillo Maffei of Solofra in his Scala Naturale (Venice, 1564). Giovanni's patron, the Count of Altavilla, is shown beginning his ascent through the spheres*

ultimate objectification?

with the world imaged as a globe, far from coming into being in and through a life process, it figures as an entity that is, as it were, presented to or confronted by life. The global environment is not a lifeworld, it is a world apart from life.

Before pursuing the implications of this view, I should like to introduce an alternative image of the world which, at least in European thought, is of far more ancient provenance. This is the image of the sphere. Something of the difference in connotation between "globe" and "sphere" is suggested in their very acoustic resonance: "globe" is hard and consonan-

tal; "sphere" soft and vocalic. A globe is solid and opaque, a sphere hollow and transparent. For the early astronomers, of course, the cosmos itself was seen to be comprised of a series of such spheres, at the common centre of which stood man himself. The idea was that as man's attention was drawn ever outward, so it would penetrate each sphere so as to reach the next. This is illustrated in Figure 24.2, taken from the *Scala Naturale* of Giovanni Camillo Maffei, published in Venice in 1564, and dedicated to the Count of Altavilla. Here there are fourteen concentric spheres which – Maffei tells us – may be envisaged to

always? How about orb?

form a giant stairway, the ascent of which affords, step by step, a comprehensive knowledge of the universe. In the picture, the Count is shown taking the first step, under Maffei's direction (see Adams 1938: 58–9).

Unlike the solid globe, which can only be perceived as such from without, spheres – as is clear from this figure – were to be perceived from within. The global view, we might say, is centripetal, the spherical view centrifugal. Nor is it any accident that the perception of the spheres was imaged in terms of listening rather than looking. Visual perception, depending as it does on the reflection of light from the outer surface of things, implies both the opacity and inertia of what is seen and the externality of the perceiver. The spheres, being transparent, could not be seen, but undergoing their own autonomous rotations about the common centre, they could be heard: thus the motion of the spheres was supposed to make a harmonious sound that could be registered by the sufficiently sensitive ear.

The idea of the spherical cosmos is by no means exclusive to the history of European thought. Let me present one further example, taken from Fienup-Riordan's (1990) account of the lifeworld of the Yup'ik Eskimos. Her cross-sectional depiction of the cosmos as perceived by the Yup'ik, bears an uncany resemblance to Maffei's diagram. At the centre is the dwelling, from which roads lead in various directions through the several surrounding spheres.

> A person journeying far enough in any direction would eventually arrive at a point where the earth folded back up into the skyland, the home of the spirits of the game . . . Not only was the earth encompassed by a canopy from above, but below its thin surface resided the spirits of the dead, both animal and human, each in separate villages. Four or five 'steps' separated these two distinct but related domains. (Fienup-Riordan 1990: 110)

Notice how in this image the surface of the earth, far from bounding the world externally, is but a thin and permeable membrane dividing the world internally, between upper and lower hemispheres.

What I hope to have established, at least in outline, is that the lifeworld, imaged from an experiential centre, is spherical in form, whereas a world divorced from life, that is yet complete in itself, is imaged in the form of a globe. Thus the movement from spherical to global imagery is also one in which "the world", as we are taught it exists, is drawn ever further from the matrix of our lived experience. It appears that the world as it really exists can only be witnessed by leaving it, and indeed much scientific energy and considerable resources have been devoted to turning such an imaginative flight into an achieved actuality. One consequence is the alleged discrepancy between what, in modern jargon, are called "local" and "global" perspectives. In so far as the latter, afforded to a being outside the world, is seen to be both real and total, the former, afforded to beings in the world (that is, ordinary people), is regarded as illusory and incomplete. Retrieving from my shelves a geology textbook published in 1964 – two years before the earth was first photographed from space – I read on the very first page that "races of men [whose] horizons are limited to a tribal territory, the confines of a mountain valley, a short stretch of the coast line, or the congested blocks of a large city" can have no conception of the true nature and extent of the world about them (Putnam 1967: 3). If true knowledge is to be had by looking *at* the world, this statement is self-evidently valid. My point, however, is that this visualist assumption is precisely what has given us the imagery of the world as a globe. And it is this assumption, too, that privileges the knowledge we get from school by looking at model globes over the knowledge we get from life by actively participating in our surroundings.

Do not misunderstand me. I am not some latter-day flat-earther or pre-Copernican. I do not mean to deny that the earth takes the form of a globe – something that has been known, if not universally accepted, at least from the time of Pythagoras – or that it is one of a number of planets revolving around a rather insignificant star. My question is how it came to pass that this globe, the planet we call earth, was taken to be an environment, or what my geology textbook called "the world about us".

We can take a cue from the writings of Kant who, in his *Critique of Pure Reason*, drew a sophisticated analogy between the topological form of the earth and that of the universe as a whole – that is, the "world" conceived as the domain of all possible objects of knowledge. Kant first places himself in the shoes of one ignorant of the fact that the earth is global in form:

> If I represent the earth as it appears to my senses, as a flat surface, with a circular horizon, I cannot know how far it extends. But experience teaches me that wherever I may go, I always see a space around me in which I could proceed further. (Kant 1933: 606)

One is thus in the hapless position of realizing that one's knowledge is limited, but of having no way of knowing just how limited it is. Once it is recognized, however, that the earth is a globe, and given a knowledge of its diameter, it is immediately possible to calculate, from first principles, its surface area. And so, even though – as we traverse the surface – new horizons are always opening up, not only can we work out, by subtraction, how much there remains to be discovered, but also every fresh observation can be slotted into position, in relation to each and every other, within a complete, unifying spatial framework. Thus, to obtain a comprehensive knowledge of the environment, we must already have in mind an image of the globe, or come pre-equipped with what Kant called 'an extended concept of the whole surface of the earth", on to which may be mapped the data of experience (see Richards 1974: 11). Moreover, the same applies to knowledge in general, which the mind sees as arrayed upon the surface of a sphere, at once continuous and limited in extent:

> Our reason is not like a plane indefinitely far extended, the limits of which we know in a general way only; but must rather be compared to a sphere, the radius of which can be determined from the curvature of the arc of its surface. (Kant 1933: 607)

In this analogy, the topology of the earth's surface comes to stand for the fundamental idea, which the mind is said to bring to experience, of the unity, completeness and continuity

of nature. Here, surely, is to be found the very essence of the global outlook.

Let us, then, compare an imaginary Kantian traveller, journeying across the globe in search of new experiences to fit into his overall conception, with the Yup'ik Eskimos, in whose cycles of everyday and seasonal movement the cosmos, as they see it, is continually being re-created (Fienup-Riordan 1990: 110–11). For both, the earth provides the ground on which they move, but whereas for the Yup'ik, this movement is conducted *within* the world, the Kantian traveller, for whom the world is a globe, journeys upon its *outer surface*. It is at this surface, the interface between world and mind, sensation and cognition, that all knowledge is constituted. Not only is the surface a continous one, it also lacks any centre. Anywhere upon it can serve, in principle, equally well as a point of origin or as a destination. Thus if the "world about us" is the globe, planet earth, it is not a world *within* which we dwell, as is the Yup'ik world depicted with the house at its centre, but one *on* which we dwell. The globe, of course, *does* have a centre, yet a journey to the centre of the earth, as immortalized in Jules Verne's celebrated novel, is a voyage into the unknown, a domain of strange and terrifying primordial forces.

In short, from a global perspective, it is on the surface of the world, not at its centre, that life is lived. As a foundational level of "physical reality", this surface is supposed already to have been in existence long before there was any life at all. Then somehow, through a series of events of near-miraculous improbability, there appeared on it first life and then, very much later, consciousness. These appearances are commonly pictured in terms of the addition of extra layers of being to that basic layer represented by the earth's surface: hence the tripartite division into lithosphere, biosphere and noosphere, corresponding respectively to the inorganic substance of rocks and minerals, the organic substance of living things and the superorganic substance of human culture and society.

Although spherical imagery is employed here, the spheres are defined as layered surfaces that successively *cover over* one another and the world, not as successive horizons

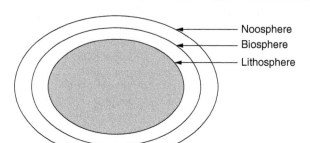

Figure 24.3 *Lithosphere, biosphere, and noosphere*

disclosed from a centre. And the outer wrapping is none other than the human mind and its products. This picture (see Figure 24.3) is the complete obverse of the medieval conception illustrated in Figure 24.2. The difference may be considered in relation to the genesis of meaning. The world which the Count of Altavilla is setting out to explore in Maffei's diagram is itself a world of meaning which, through a kind of sensory attunement, an education of attention, will be gradually revealed to him as he proceeds from one level of understanding to the next. This world has properties of both transparency and depth: transparency, because one can see into it; depth, because the more one looks the further one sees. By contrast, the world depicted in Figure 24.3, in so far as it corresponds to "planet earth", consists of pure substance, physical matter, presenting an opaque and impenetrable surface of literal reality *upon which* form and meaning is overlaid by the human mind. That is to say, meaning does not lie in the relational context of the perceiver's involvement in the world, but is rather inscribed upon the outer surface of the world by the mind of the perceiver. To know the world, then, is a matter not of sensory attunement but of cognitive reconstruction. And such knowledge is acquired not by engaging directly, in a practical way, with the objects in one's surroundings, but rather by learning to represent them, in the mind, in the form of a *map*. We discover, here, a direct connection between the notion of the world as a solid globe and the idea, commonly encountered even in anthropological literature, of

the environment as a *substrate* for the external imposition of arbitrary cultural form. The world becomes a *tabula rasa* for the inscription of human history.

The familiar globes of geography classrooms provide a vivid example of such inscription or covering over. Though the sea is painted blue, the continental landmasses are frequently painted in a mosaic of contrastive colours, representing the territories of nation states. Thus, we are led to think, has the order of human society wrapped itself around the face of the world. Yet that order, we know, has its roots in the history of colonialism, and the attendant voyages of (principally maritime) discovery and exploration. The image of the world as a globe is, I contend, a colonial one. It presents us with the idea of a preformed surface *waiting to be occupied,* to be colonized first by living things and later by human (usually meaning Western) civilization. Through travel and exploration, it is said, mankind has *conquered* the globe, everywhere – in Engels' (1934: 179) imperialistic phrase – impressing "the stamp of his will upon the earth". Having now filled it up, and still multiplying in numbers at an alarming pace, we are urgently searching around, not just in fantasy but also in fact, for new worlds to colonize. Not only, then, does it appear that the world existed prior to life; it also appears that life can hop from world to world and even – like a parasitic vector flying between successive hosts – exist temporarily in worldless suspension.

The idea that the world exists prior to the forms of life that come to occupy it, and hence that each of these life forms is itself separately encoded in a context-free vehicle, a kind of free-floating capsule that can carry form from one site of occupation to another, is deeply entrenched in both biological and anthropological thought. In biology it appears as the doctrine of genetic preformation, according to which every organism may be specified, independently of the environmental context of its development, as a unique configuration of self-replicating elements (genes). Through a process of variation under natural selection, organisms are supposed to evolve in ways that make them better adapted to the conditions of their environments, yet the very notion of adaptation implies that these conditions are given in advance as a set of exogenous specifications, quite distinct from the endogenous, genetic specifications of the adapting organisms. There is thus one set of specifications for life, and another set for the world (see Lewontin 1983). In anthropology, cultural information is made to play much the same role as is played by the genes in biology. Again, there is one set of specifications for the forms of life that are carried around – as it used to be said – "inside people's heads". And there is another set for the environment, often identified with 'nature' or 'the physical world', upon which these forms are inscribed. And if we ask "What kind of world is this, that is an environment for every form of life yet external to all of them?", the answer, as we have seen, is planet earth, the globe.

Moreover, once the world is conceived as a globe, it can become an object of appropriation for a collective humanity. In this discourse, we do not belong to the world, neither partaking of its essence nor resonating to its cycles and rhythms. Rather, since our very humanity is seen to consist, in essence, in the transcendence of physical nature, it is the world that belongs to us. Images of property abound. We have inherited the earth, it is said, and so are responsible for handing it on to our successors in reasonably good condition. But like the prodigal heir, we are inclined to squander this precious inheritance for the sake of immediate gratification. Much of the current concern with the global environment has to do with how we are to "manage" this planet of ours.

That it is ours to manage, however, remains more or less unquestioned. Such management is commonly described in the language of intervention. But to intervene in the world, as Raymond Williams (1972: 154) has pointed out, implies the possibility of our choosing not to do so. It implies that human beings can launch their interventions from a platform above the world, as though they could live *on* or *off* the environment, but are not destined to live *within* it. Indeed, this notion of action towards the environment as planned intervention in nature is fundamental to the Western notion of production. History itself comes to be seen as a process wherein human producers, through their transforming reaction on nature, have literally constructed an environment of their own making.

The idea is epitomized in the title of an influential volume, published in 1956, called *Man's Role in Changing the Face of the Earth* (Thomas *et al.* 1956). There are two points about this title to which I wish to draw attention. The first is that with the world envisaged as planet earth, it is its *face* that is presented to humanity as the substrate for the latter's transforming interventions. This recalls my earlier observation that in the global outlook, life appears to be lived upon the outer surface of the world rather than from an experiential centre within it. The world does not surround us, it lies beneath out feet. The second point concerns the notion of change. It is not of course the case, as was believed by some of the early advocates of uniformitarianism, that the earth has persisted since the beginning of time in homeostatic equilibrium, at least until humans came along to upset the balance. On the contrary, it has been – and continues to be – racked by geological forces acting on such a scale as to make the most impressive feats of human engineering seem puny by comparison. These earth-shaping processes, however, are considered to be immanent in the workings of nature. They are what the world *undergoes*. But in speaking of the role of humanity, the world appears as an *object* of transformation. Change figures as what is *done to* the planet by its present owner-occupiers, human beings. It is thus exogenous rather than endogenous, not nature transforming itself, but nature transformed through the imposition of non-natural, human design.

This is what is meant when, in "changing the face of the earth", the universal agent – man – is said to have replaced the natural environment with one which is, to an ever-greater extent, *artificial*. Thus the construction of the human order appears to entail the destruction of the natural one, as production entails consumption. We are, today, increasingly concerned to limit what are perceived to be the destructive consequences of human activity. My point, however, is that the very notions of destruction and damage limitation, like those of construction and control, are grounded in the discourse of intervention. That is to say, they presume a world already constituted, through the action of natural forces, which then becomes the *object* of human interest and concern. But it is not a world of which humans themselves are conceived to be a part. To them, it is rather presented as a spectacle. They may observe it, reconstruct it, protect it, tamper with it or destroy it, but they do not dwell in it. Indeed, what is perhaps most striking about the contemporary discourse of global environmental change is the immensity of the gulf that divides the world as it is lived and experienced by the practitioners of this discourse, and the world of which they speak under the rubric of "the globe". No one, of course, denies the seriousness of the problems they address; there is good reason to believe, however, that many of these problems have their source in that very alienation of humanity from the world of which the notion of the global environment is a conspicuous expression.

This point brings me back to the distinction, mentioned earlier, between "local" and "global" perspectives. The difference between them, I contend, is not one of hierarchical degree, in scale or comprehensiveness, but one of kind. In other words, the local is not a more limited or narrowly focused apprehension than the global, it is one that rests on an altogether different *mode* of apprehension – one based on an active, perceptual engagement with components of the dwelt-in world, in the practical business of life, rather than on the detached, disinterested observation of a world apart. In the local perspective the world is a sphere, or perhaps a nesting series of spheres as portrayed in Figure 24.2, centred on a particular place. From this experiential centre, the attention of those who live there is drawn ever deeper *into* the world, in the quest for knowledge and understanding. It is through such attentive engagement, entailed in the very process of dwelling, that the world is progressively revealed to the knowledge-seeker. Now different centres will, of course, afford different views, so that while there is only one global perspective, indifferent to place and context, the number of possible local perspectives is potentially infinite. This does not mean, however, that they are in any sense incomplete, or that they represent no more than fragments of a total picture. It is only when we come to represent local differences in terms of a globalizing discourse that the centre from which each perspective is taken is converted into a boundary *within* which every local view is seen to be contained. The idea that the "little community" remains confined within its limited horizons from which "we" – globally conscious Westerners – have escaped results from a privileging of the global ontology of detachment over the local ontology of engagement.

To the extent that it has been used to legitimate the disempowerment of local people in the management of their environments, this idea has had serious practical consequences for those among whom anthropologists have conducted their studies. To adopt a distinction from Niklas Luhmann (1979), it might be argued that the dominance of the global perspective marks the triumph of technology over cosmology. Traditional cosmology places the person at the centre of an ordered universe of meaningful relations, such as that depicted by Maffei (Figure 24.2), and enjoins an understanding of these relations as a foundation for proper conduct towards the environment. Modern technology, by contrast, places human society and its interests *outside* what is residually construed as the "physical world", and furnishes the means for the former's control over the latter. Cosmology provides the guiding principles for human action *within* the world, technology provides the principles for human action *upon* it. Thus, as cosmology gives way to technology, the relation between people and the world is turned inside out (Figure 24.1), so that what was a cosmos or lifeworld becomes a world – a solid globe – externally presented to life. In short, the movement from spherical to global imagery corresponds to the undermining of cosmological certainties and the growing belief in, and indeed dependence upon, the technological fix. It is a movement from revelation to control, and from partial knowledge to the calculated risk.

Let me add one further comment in conclusion. I have written throughout as though the characterizations of the environment, respectively, as globe and sphere were irrevocably opposed, and thus mutually exclusive. But this is not really so, since each view contains the seeds of the other. To regard the world as a sphere is at once to render conceivable the possibility of its logical inverse, the globe; and of course vice versa. We could say that both perspectives are caught up in the dialecti-

cal interplay between engagement and detachment, between human beings' involvement in the world and their separation from it, which has been a feature of the entire history of Western thought and no doubt of other traditions as well. Concretely, this is perhaps most clearly manifest in the architectural form of the dome (Smith 1950). A sphere on the inside, a globe on the outside, this form has a cosmic resonance of near-universal appeal. But for any society, at any period of its history, we may expect one perspective to be ascendant, and the other to be associated with its more or less muted undercurrent. And my sense of the contemporary discourse on the environment in the West is that it continues to be dominated by global imagery associated with the triumph of modern science and technology, but that it is under increasing threat from those – including many anthropologists – who would turn to local or indigenous cosmologies of engagement for sources of insight into our current predicament.

– Instinct ?

The   Globe   as   Ontology

REFERENCES

Adams, F. D. (1938). *The Birth and Death of the Geological Sciences,* London: Baillière, Tindall and Cox.

Engels, F. (1934). *Dialectics of Nature,* Moscow: Progress.

Fienup-Riordan, A. (1990). *Eskimo Essays: Yup'ik Lives and How We See Them,* New Brunswick: Rutgers University Press.

Ingold, T. (1992). "Culture and the perception of the environment", in E. Croll and D. Parkin (eds.) *Bush Base: Forest Farm – Culture, Environment and Development,* London: Routledge.

Kant, I. (1933). *Immanuel Kant's Critique of Pure Reason,* trans. N. K. Smith, London: Macmillan.

Lewontin, R. C. (1983). "Gene, organism and environment", in D. S. Bendall (ed.) *Evolu-*

tion from Molecules to Men, Cambridge: Cambridge University Press.

Luhmann, N. (1979). *Trust and Power,* Chilchester: Wiley.

Putnam, W. C. (1964). *Geology,* New York: Oxford University Press.

Richards, P. (1974). "Kant's geography and mental maps", *Transactions of the Institute of British Geographers (n.s.),* 11: 1–16.

Smith, E. Baldwin (1950). *The Dome: A Study in the History of Ideas,* Princeton, New Jersey: Princeton University Press.

Thomas, W. L., Sauer, C. O., Bates, M. and Mumford, L. (eds.) (1956). *Man's Role in Changing the Face of the Earth,* Chicago: University of Chicago Press.

Williams, R. (1972). "Ideas of nature", in J. Benthall (ed.) *Ecology, the Shaping Enquiry,* London: Longman.

Index of Subjects

adaptation
  general 16, 18, 37, 39, 57, 285, 457, 457–8
  cultural 10, 12–13, 19, 39, 169
  to disaster 19, 25
  of ecological systems 18, 57, 138, 458, 460
  Enga 22, 24, 25, 224–5, 227, 231, 233–5
  environmental 13–14, 17, 39, 168, 467
  and human consciousness 57, 457
  of humans to environment 13, 18, 23, 37, 39,
    460
  San 285
  strategies 22–4, 225, 316
adat 324, 344–6, 348–9, 352, 355, 412–13, 417
agency 3, 47–8, 51–2, 105, 325, 341, 344, 352,
    356, 366, 393, 395, 399–400
agricultural mounding
  general 24–5, 225–7
  distribution of 226, 228
agriculture
  general 3, 10, 16–18, 27, 109–10, 115, 142,
    148, 182–3, 186–7, 204–6, 210, 212,
    215–16, 219, 228, 234, 256, 267, 272,
    290–1, 311–12
  capitalization/commercialization of 55, 103, 437
  development/improvement 30–1, 107, 113,
    449–50
  enclosures 443
  fallow periods 105, 107–8, 112, 115, 182,
    215, 228
  farming 35, 37, 41, 104, 110, 113–14
  intensification 18, 28, 29, 42, 111–12, 141,
    215, 332
  irrigated 28–30, 54–5, 193–5, 290, 425
  and livestock 6–11, 17, 105

plow 183
  representation of 31
  traction by cattle 140–1
  transformation 55, 108, 425–6, 429, 432, 450
  upland/mountain 29, 106, 109, 311, 313
  see also swidden
agro-pastoralism 40, 42, 289–90, 294, 296–7,
    312–14
ahimsa 7, 138, 140–4, 147–50
alliances
  between ethnic groups 169, 254, 259, 261–2,
  between local and extra-local groups 329, 348,
    351–2, 355, 372, 393, 395, 406, 412
alpine environments 41, 309–10
anthropogeography 158–9
anthropology
  cognitive 53, 437
  cultural 30
  ecological/environmental 2–4, 9–10, 12, 16, 30,
    32, 37, 42–3, 47–8, 53, 61, 309, 312, 316
  economic 19
  ethnography 5, 7, 9–10, 12–13, 24, 31, 33, 37,
    39, 50, 53, 56, 60, 106, 297, 327,
    363–4, 106, 177, 241, 246, 267, 284, 286,
    297, 327, 342, 363–4, 420, 435–8, 451
  symbolic 16
apêtê
  general 90–3, 95, 98–100
  creation of 91, 100
  zones 99
articulation (following Stuart Hall)
  general 340–2, 344, 350, 352–3, 355–6
  of claims/rights 348–9
  of identity 46–7, 345–6, 348–4, 351–2, 354

Index of Names

CPSIA information can be obtained
at www.ICGtesting.com
Printed in the USA
LVHW020222040119
602695LV00006B/17/P

9 781405 111379